MODERN ARCHITECTURE IN LATIN AMERICA

MODERN ARCHITECTURE

ART, TECHNOLOGY, AND UTOPIA

Joe R. and Teresa Lozano Long Series in Latin American and Latino Art and Culture

IN LATIN AMERICA

LUIS E. CARRANZA *and* **FERNANDO LUIZ LARA**

Foreword by Jorge Francisco Liernur

UNIVERSITY OF TEXAS PRESS, AUSTIN

The University of Texas Press gratefully acknowledges the support of the Office of the President of the University of Texas at Austin, which provided funds toward the publication of this book.

LIBRARY OF CONGRESS CATALOGING-IN-PUBLICATION DATA

Carranza, Luis E., 1968–, author.
  Modern architecture in Latin America : art, technology, and utopia / Luis E. Carranza and Fernando Luiz Lara ; foreword by Jorge Francisco Liernur.
      pages   cm — (Joe R. and Teresa Lozano Long series in Latin American and Latino art and culture)
  Includes bibliographical references and index.
  ISBN 978-0-292-75865-0 (hardback) —
  ISBN 978-0-292-76297-8 (paper)
  1. Architecture—Latin America—History—20th century. I. Lara, Fernando Luiz, author. II. Liernur, Jorge Francisco, writer of supplementary textual content. III. Title.
  NA702.5.C37 2015
  720.98'0904—dc23   2014013883

doi:10.7560/758650

To our children:

Alison, Helena, Clemente, and Beatriz,

for representing the spirit of the diverse

and beautiful American continent.

To Denise and Leticia

for giving us all that

and more.

CONTENTS

FOREWORD

Jorge Francisco Liernur
(TRANSLATED BY LUIS E. CARRANZA)

PARADOXICALLY, thanks to this book, we can begin to think that discussions like the one included herein on architecture in Latin America will gradually cease to exist. I'm not suggesting with this statement that the book has reached a type of *summae scientiam* on the subject—something that the authors themselves have ruled out. What I mean is that a book like this brings us closer to the end of the narratives about "architecture in Latin America."

To begin, we must note that Carranza and Lara's text is entitled *Modern Architecture in Latin America*, and not *Latin American Modern Architecture*. In this way, it separates itself from the line that links Henry-Russell Hitchcock's book (*Latin American Architecture since 1945*) with Francisco Bullrich's (*New Directions in Latin American Architecture*) and with the more recent "Latin American Architecture Seminars." The difference is that Latin America is not presented here as an attribute but as a geographical support. The use of the word as an adjective assumes that the attribute is an essential category and that it is able to permeate the entire production that can be identified with it. In this sense, "Latin American" work is not just a building in that region of the world but rather a building that *expresses* this region.

By pointing out this difference, I am not asking the reader to get lost in the sophisticated subtleties of language that might be somewhat insignificant. Rather, the issue is of greater importance: "Latin Americanists" argue that the culture produced in the region is radically different from that which is generated in other parts of the world. They think that there is a constitutive, constant, and shared core that generates a dynamic sense of "ownership" or "critique" with regard to what happens outside the region. Moreover, in the last instance, they think that there is a sort of indivisible "I" that belongs to the region (perhaps a soul?) that expresses itself in clearly identifiable traits and that makes it react in unison against any external stimuli. I do not rule out that there might be those who think

this form of reasoning may seem anachronistic. The nation-state and, with it, the notion of "the people" that upholds and justifies it, has long been questioned, and a statement of its coherence is no longer part of any important intellectual discussion. There have even been proposals to replace the very idea of an essentialist notion of "the people" with a more contemporary notion of "the multitude" as an articulation of its changing uniquenesses.

The use of the term "Latin America" as a noun is crucial, and it is what determines the structure chosen for this book, which is clearly articulated in the introduction. The book is constructed as a quilt: composed of different parts, each joined together by a formal structure. The parallelogram that determines the shape of the quilt is itself constructed by the very book itself. Although different from each other, the parts that make up the book, like the individuals in a crowd or the pieces of a quilt, do not end up dispersed but rather are articulated together by a fortuitous purpose. The narrative does not lead to a conclusion with ideological claims but relies on a chronological structure. We should not be deceived, however, because devoid of any teleological impulse, the chronology employed has the same arbitrary unifying structure as does the rectangular shape of the quilt.

However, this is not the most important change in approach through which the book, I believe, enacts a paradigm shift or, if you will, announces the end of a process. I think its main contribution to the knowledge of modern architecture in Latin America lies in its character as a type of compendium. Its chronological structure serves as an arbitrary organizing system, given that its authors did not intend to put forth a *single* interpretative key to support *a conclusion* that, by definition, they do not believe in. The chronology also serves as an axis along which, as on a skewer, pieces with very different characteristics are inserted: buildings, artistic movements, events, biographies, social processes, institutions.

The book is a compendium of those pieces that, in turn, are the result of the steady growth in recent decades of the historiography of modern architecture in Latin America. In contrast to what has happened in previous decades, this field has only partially been organized around strong ideological assumptions (the "Latin Americanists"). For the most part, the studies on the subject have manifested themselves as the result of the increasing proliferation and expansion of scholarship on the subject, both within the region itself as well as in the United States and, to a much lesser extent, in Europe. Of course, this growth is an effect of its appealing issues but also, and perhaps more so, reflects the general growth of the knowledge industries that, in turn, have instituted new structures and demands in recent decades. Through them, the number of master's and doctoral programs has multiplied in an unprecedented way throughout the region, and, as a consequence, the means of disseminating, exchanging, and legitimating the scholarship in this area have also increased. Thus, as with other branches of academic knowledge, there has been a marked increase in the number of monographs, essays, theses, articles, magazines, and books destined to complete the processes of emergence and consecration of this field.

This is a very different scenario to that within which the pioneering narratives of Hitchcock or Bullrich were constructed. It is also as a part and a consequence of this new context that this book is meant to be read. Its invaluable character as a compendium gives us for the first time, presented in the arbitrary order of a chronology, the most relevant results of this new and vast universe of scholarship that has resulted from the growth to which I referred. To which we must add, and especially considering *where* this book is being published for the first time, the role of the development of these studies within the U.S. academy. We can also not help noting the fact that this first compendium is *not* written in Spanish or Portuguese, but in English. Of course, it needs to be highlighted that the use of this lingua franca is what will facilitate the wider dissemination of this knowledge to an international audience. But this is not enough. That this compendium of modern architecture in Latin America has not been written and published in Latin America can be understood as a result of two factors. On the one hand, it should be noted that this is a study of a grouping of twenty-seven countries and dependencies (including the Caribbean) with very

different economic and political conditions, covering a total area of 22,000,000 sq. km, with enormous geographical formations that separate them across equally vast distances extending some 14,000 km between the north and the south. It is a grouping that is not bound together through homogeneous or appropriate ground transportation systems, so the only way to cover the vast distances needed to understand it is via airplane. The scholars from this region who propose such a study must overcome these obstacles and with very limited resources, despite, in the best of cases, coming from "developing" countries; this explains the aforementioned conditions. But the obstacles do not end there. It is no accident that the first version of one of the primary studies of modern architecture in the region, Francisco Bullrich's *New Directions*, came from a U.S. publisher, or that another survey, *América Latina en su arquitectura*, edited by Roberto Segre, was sponsored by UNESCO. The diversity of the countries and their political regimes, the specificity of their economies, and the differences in the values of their currencies or import duties make the existence of regional publishing houses extremely difficult. Additionally, the linguistic differences that exist in the subcontinent between the languages of Hispanic or Lusitanian origin work against any sense of cultural unity.

On the other hand, the growing importance of "Latinos" in the United States has not only increased the presence of students and academics of Hispanic background throughout its academic institutions but has also increased their economic and political clout within the community. This condition is also tied to the major shifts in the approaches of these studies due to the work Edward Said introduced into the American academy, conceived through the adoption of post–Cold War postmodernist positions. The increased interest in the multiplicity of Latin America's voices is part of a phenomenon of questioning singular narratives and was made possible through the dissolution of the ghosts of communism that lurked behind any pretense of autonomy by Latin Americans of the south from their northern Anglo-Saxon cousins.

I think that these are the new conditions in which this book is written and published. But as I said at the beginning of this brief text, I also believe that as a development of these new conditions, its publication allows us to begin to imagine a near future when these kinds of approaches will no longer be fostered or necessary.

By their very definition, approaches such as this one cannot lose, despite all precautions, an adjectival condition. In other words, the canon of modern architecture is not constituted geographically. The emergence of geographic (or regional) constructions is contradictory to the very notion of modernity within which the idea of universality is implicit. It is, in any case, an oxymoron, a contradiction in terms: if an architecture is modern, it cannot be regional. Or if you prefer: the more regional something is, the less modern it is. Beyond the many attempts to contradict this principle, regional architecture cannot be modern because to be regional it must introduce elements (from the past, from the place, or from its traditions) that make it ineligible for the requirement of the tabula rasa, the imperative of the always-already new that is a fundamental attribute of modernity. In other words, the idea of a modern architecture *of a certain place* is theoretically inadmissible. A work, an idea, a design belongs or does not belong to the universe of modernity regardless of the place where or the circumstances under which it was conceived or created. Now, if this statement is correct, then it only makes sense to place that work, idea, or design, in terms of its intrinsic value as a modern work, idea, or design, within the vertical coordinate of time and the horizontal coordinate that entails values. Its location in the perpendicular coordinate of the place only makes sense in relation to events or to an axiology outside of architecture.

Having said that, my statement about the near and very plausible end to the narratives about "architecture in Latin America" can be understood. To write a book such as this, or like the others that, for a while, will probably still need to be produced, can only be understood because the works, ideas, or events described in it have not been integrated into the international canon. That lack of integration is pathetic when sections devoted to "Latin America" are added to the classical texts on the history of modern architecture as if the works, projects, or ideas generated in Latin America were not part of the general development of modern architecture. And if we accept this absurd distortion of the real and complex construction mechanisms of culture, it is because that historiographical fabrication has been imposed on us with the very strength that its ownership within the general dynamics of North Atlantic hegemony has given it over the global phenomenon of modernization. With the arrogance

that feeds on that ownership, the main perpetrators of these classic texts have been allowed to build their global stories with surprising (and extremely insulting) ignorance of the characteristics and stories that took place beyond their European or U.S. provinces. Only one or, in the best of cases, a couple of trips and interviews were needed so they could include in their books some chapter or mention of works or ideas originating in Latin America.

The presumption underlying this attitude was, needless to say, that Latin America was an area of pure derivation or perhaps of the bizarre—and certainly wrong—development of proposals that originated in those provinces of the world it calls its center. The idea of "influence" was based on that presumption. But after Mikhail Bakhtin, Julia Kristeva, Emmanuel Levinas, or Tzvetan Todorov, it is no longer possible to continue to emphasize the single directionality of the relationships of meaning. "Dialogic," "the other within us," "speech over listening," or "heteroglossia" are concepts that have dismantled this alleged unidirectionality and have taught us to conceive of culture as a construction of multiple agents and of crossed signals. In the following book, these agents and crossing planes are clearly present, and, no less clearly, one can see the power of the inner dynamics of cultural construction. And it is that same emergence of cultural construction that makes us expect that the works and ideas composing it can find their place in the future construction of a truly global history of modern architecture—a history that will not only include these examples and processes, but also one whose own canonical structure will be understood as a result of that multiplicity of actors and signals. To move toward this new history, the book that Carranza and Lara have so carefully constructed and so adequately articulated will no doubt be an excellent instrument. Henceforth, the excuse of an insufficient dissemination platform and of the difficulties in accessing information about the complex picture of modern architecture in Latin America will no longer be acceptable.

From now on, whoever intends to reorganize tout court the knowledge about the development and evolution of modern architecture can no longer use a few clichés about what has been produced in the region. The vastness, interest, diversity, ideological intensity, and originality of the enormous process of collective creation that modernization mobilized in the region will be here, from now on, for all to see.

ACKNOWLEDGMENTS

THIS BOOK would not be possible without the effort of hundreds of scholars who came before and alongside us. We would like to acknowledge the contribution of every single colleague mentioned in the bibliography. Moreover, the book would not be possible without a series of conferences and meetings that brought Carranza and Lara together since we first met in 1997. Architecture in Latin America, as Jorge Francisco Liernur explained so well in the foreword of this book, has always been perceived as a sideline in the major history of modern architecture. However, we did use every opportunity possible at meetings of the Association of Collegiate Schools of Architecture, Architecture and Urbanism in Las Americas, Latin American Studies Association, and Society of Architectural Historians, as well as the institutions where we have been teaching, to enhance those conversations. As a result, we are thankful for their support and, in particular, are grateful to Roger Williams University and the University of Texas at Austin.

To a smaller group of colleagues we are also indebted. First of all, to Jorge Francisco "Pancho" Liernur for his intellectual guidance since the beginning of this project. Much of the initial intellectual direction and structure began as an unsuccessful proposal for a show on Latin American architecture for the Guggenheim Museum in 2007. Fortunately, many of those ideas found a home within this book. Rafael Longoria and Patricia Morgado offered thoughtful suggestions and directions in their original review of the manuscript. Thank you also to Enrique Larrañaga, Stella Nair, Renato Anelli, Carlos Teixeira, Carlos Comas, Felipe Hernández, Ruth Verde Zein, Sylvio Podestá (and his beautiful drawings), Hugo Mondragón, Sonia Marques, Fernando Vasconcelos, Jose Castillo, Inés Zalduendo, Mónica Ramírez Montagut, Gloria B. de Carranza, Claudia Schmidt, Uri Drachman, Paco Rodríguez, Marisa Oliver, Sandra Vivanco, Robert González, Barry Bergdoll, and others for so many insightful conversations, assorted forms of support, and encouragement.

At UT Austin's School of Architecture, Dean Frederick Steiner, Christopher Long, Richard Cleary, Danilo Udovich-Selb, and Kevin Alter have provided invaluable support and good advice. Graduate students Jorge Villota, Doris Reina-Bravo, Mari Rodríguez, Christine Taylor, Amy Freedberg, José Carlos García, and María Raquel Basílico have also taught us a lot. And our thanks to the Teresa Lozano Long Institute of Latin American Studies for the research support and stimulating debates that could not be found anywhere else.

At Roger Williams University, Dean Stephen White, Sarah Butler, and Jeffrey Silverthorne offered support and encouragement. Research assistants Rachel Hampton, Molly Katchpole, and Caitlin Osepchuk provided invaluable help drawing, researching, and documenting works. Some of the research was funded with a grant from Roger Williams University's Foundation to Promote Scholarship and Teaching. This publication was also funded by a University of Texas Book Subvention Grant and a University of Texas School of Architecture Research Grant.

At the University of Texas Press, we would like to thank Jim Burr, who believed in and supported the project from the very beginning. Jim has been kind and patient with what was really a project that exceeded all possible complexities in everybody's expectations. Our thanks also go to Lynne Chapman, who helped us navigate those complexities, and Sarah Rosen. In addition, we are grateful to Teresa Wingfield for a design that elegantly and coherently organizes those same complexities. But our most sincere thanks go to Nancy Warrington, our copy editor, who helped us express a common voice within the text and who surveyed, edited, and corrected the text to its present form. We are extremely grateful for her work and her patience with us.

Finally, we would also like to thank all of the people who helped us with the daunting task of image and permission gathering as well as those kind friends who graciously let us include their photographs here.

These include José and Rafael Yee; Jessica Sánchez Lizárraga at Patronato Ruta de la Amistad; Arq. Miguel Braceli; James Oles; Federica Zanco and Martin Josephy at the Barragán Foundation; Inés Zalduendo at Harvard's Graduate School of Design; Paulina Villanueva and Cecilia Castrillo at the Fundación Villanueva; Enrique Norten and Ana Elena Torres at TEN Arquitectos; Fernando Vasconcelos and Blanca Cortes at Nuevo Espíritu; Gyula Kosice; Christian M. Korab; Christina Zappa at the Instituto Moreira Salles; Bettina Cetto; Ana María León; Montse Viu and Andreu Carrascal Simon at the Arxiu Històric del Col·legi d'Arquitectes de Catalunya; Claudia Garcés and Barbara and Tomás Gunz at the Fundación Gego; Fernando García-Huidobro; Diego Torres; Nicolas Tugas; Bruno Stagno and Jimena Ugarte de Stagno; Isabelle Godineau at the Fondation Le Corbusier; Nelson Kon; Tamera Reub and Carol Gross at the United States Olympic Committee; Carmen Ortega González and Francisco Manosalvas at Arquitexto; Margot Rumler at the Bauhaus Dessau; Arq. Facundo Savid; Wendy Hurlock Baker at the Smithsonian Institution; Robbi Siegel at Art Resource; Elizabeth Schaub at the University of Texas School of Architecture Visual Resource Collection; Alvaro Puntoni and Angelo Bucci; Mauricio Pezo and Sofia von Ellrichshausen; Ariane Figueiredo at Projeto Hélio Oiticica; Arq. Juan Fernando Yáñez; Rodrigo Baeta; Leonardo Finotti; Adriana León at Taller Arquitectura X; Sonia Reyes Moreno at Fundación ICA; Alison Carranza; Denise Dea; Paulo Mauro Meyer de Aquino at Arquivo Warchavchik; Donatella Calabi; Walter Salcedo; Farès el-Dahdah; Instituto Bardi; Ken Dineen; Jorge Villota; Casa de Lúcio Costa; Paulo Mendes da Rocha; Luis Manoel do Eirado Amorim; Prefeitura de Curitiba; Doris Reina Bravo; Gustavo Frittegotto; Kykah Bernardes and Thiago Manuel Bernardes at Projeto Memoria/ Acervo Sergio Bernardes; Bruno Santa Cecilia; Sylvio de Podestá; Gonzalo Núñez Melgar; Enrique Browne; Edward Rojas; Germán del Sol; Carlos Teixeira; Daniel Ducci; Al Borde; Mauricio Alfaro Moreno; Cristina Pujol; Ing. Daniel Goeritz Rodríguez; Carlos Sallaberry; Hugo Mondragón; and Sofía Gaytan and Mauricio Rocha at Taller de Arquitectura.

MODERN ARCHITECTURE IN LATIN AMERICA

(NOTES TOWARD AN) INTRODUCTION

1

When the Mexican writer Octavio Paz defined Mexican history in *The Labyrinth of Solitude* (1963) as "a search for our own selves, which have been deformed or disguised by alien institutions, and for a form that will express them," he might as well have defined the central character of Latin America as a whole.[1] This is especially true for the late nineteenth and twentieth centuries when Latin America, according to some, experienced an "incomplete modernization." What this means is that during the period of European and North American modernization, Latin America was setting up the political, economic, and material conditions and infrastructure for modernization as part of broader initiatives and aspirations. Many of the elements that allowed Latin American countries to compete with other more "advanced" ones were generally imported, including new means of transportation (railway), communication (telegraph, newspapers, etc.), production (factory machinery, etc.), and governmental ideals (i.e., positivism and neoliberalism). Latin America, in other words, became dependent on European (and, later, North American) capital and development as well as its political systems. In many cases, Latin American countries and cities, as a result, quickly modernized and acquired the effects and characteristics of that modernization. Modernism—or the effect of modernization on art, culture, or sensibilities—developed and took form in the many cultural movements and styles that proliferated throughout Latin America in the twentieth century. In the end, because of the unevenness and speed with which modernization and modernity were implemented or acquired, the result was an inchoate integration into the fabric of the everyday traditional, cultural, and physical environment.

Many of the architectural expressions that arose in the twentieth century reflect this paradoxical condition. They show an interest in local traditions, in the character of the people and their culture, and in the context, as well as in the legibility of these within the architectural form. At the same time, we find within them experimentations with new languages, forms, and materials of modernity. Among these was the consideration of Latin America as a tabula rasa within which European and North American modern architecture could develop unobstructed by the limitations of the "past" or, as some émigrés believed, couched within the idealized/imagined coming of a new—frequently socialist—society. In many cases, the conditions of the local and the abstract were mediated into innovative or challenging architectural productions.

One of the characteristics that exists in Latin America with regard to the development of art and architecture in the twentieth century is, in fact, the tension between a realist representational attitude and abstraction. The investigations into realist pictorial practices and their communicative abilities are emblematic of the first half of the twentieth century when political changes (especially those in Mexico following the Mexican Revolution) demanded new legible and understandable forms to enable race and class consciousness and to generate new subjectivities congruent with the desires of the state. In some cases, this literally meant architectural works that incorporated legible murals or sculpture, but in others, the exploration with architectural languages was intended both to address historical (pre-Hispanic or European) legacies and to reconfigure them for a new moment. The turn toward more universal and abstract principles in the second half of the last century was often defined in response to the earlier moment. In Venezuela, Brazil, and Argentina, for example, this meant a turn away from the pervasive Mexican paradigm and toward European practices of Concretism and abstraction. In other cases, the aim was either toward a more universal communicative medium, a formalism more attuned to the figurative and aesthetic requirements of the new (International style) architecture, or toward a system that challenged the ideological straightforwardness and passive reception of the earlier muralist model (through a turn to phenomenological reception, for example).

2

In setting about to write a history of the architectural developments of a region as vast as Latin America, one must begin, however, by acknowledging the limitations and problems inherent in the task as well as the impossibility of achieving a complete result. Instead of attempting to find ways of expressing some totality or coherence to the history we set about to present, we have developed an open-ended model that is based more on Michel Foucault's and Manfredo Tafuri's notion of genealogy than on the previous models that make up the discipline of Latin American architectural history.

After all, how does one set up an organizing structure to describe the indescribable? How does one write the history of a series of disciplines—architecture, plastic arts, landscape, urban design, etc.—that are separate but interrelated when they materialize in the lived world? Generally, we have attempted to address the ways that the built, the molded, the manipulated constructed environments in Latin America are effects of the practices of environmental planning, architecture, urbanism, and landscape architecture in very particular historical moments and cultures. Yet, what we have found is that, in many cases, these practices find themselves reproduced throughout Latin America. The result of travel, of emigration, of publications, of influences, and so on, the similarity of production in different places and times makes this history more complex as it acknowledges not singularities but rather something that might be characterized as a zeitgeist ("the intellectual, moral, and cultural climate of an era"—*Webster's Collegiate Dictionary*, 11th ed.) or a *Kunstwollen* (will to form)—both terms used by Latin American scholars throughout the century to describe their own production. Despite this, it is the uniqueness that comes from the material and contextual limitations and possibilities that gives individual valences to similar productions. In addition, we have also been interested in the way that architectures, spaces, and cities are historicized and theorized. This not only gives us a sense of how they have been valued in the past but what they seem to suggest for the future. But, beyond that, the analysis of the historiography also points to how the discursive practices of history and theory affect the way we understand the material production of

space or city, to name two, or the way that, as material practices in and of themselves, history and theory—as understood or employed by architects or cultural producers in general—affect that production as well.

In a way, the problem is further compounded when, moving away from a general historical project, the definition of the limits of our investigation is tied to a particular context that is itself ill defined—in our case, Latin America. After all, how do we define it? Is it everything south of the Rio Grande? Is it that which defines itself by the effects of colonial imposition (be it Portuguese, Spanish, or French) and which, as a result, has as its linguistic root Latin and/or Romance languages? Is it defined by religious preferences; development (or the lack thereof); income or productive standards; racial or class affiliations; historical connections to the land, culture, or other characteristics?

Inevitably, the first question we addressed when framing our work had to do with the very idea of Latin America and the artificiality of the concept. Proposed by French intellectuals in the nineteenth century with the aim of solidifying Paris's sphere of influence over parts of the New World, the idea of Latin America had an arbitrary and foreign point of departure. The main problem with this "idea" is the contradictions that appear when one tries to reduce it to simple definitions. Language is surely a major characteristic, since the majority of the region speaks Spanish or Portuguese, with a minority speaking French. However, French-speaking Quebec is not considered part of Latin America. Geography is no help either, since the majority of Mexico sits in North America, a fact that many people tend to overlook when they think of that continent. Religious differences between a Protestant north and a Catholic south might be another important characteristic, but that is also challenged by the growth of Pentecostalism in the south and the growth of Catholicism in the north. Even the twentieth-century division between a richer north and a poorer south is becoming irrelevant with the United States expected to become as unequal as Brazil in little more than a decade if the current trajectories continue.

Nevertheless, after being widely used for two centuries, the term "Latin America" has gained enough traction and does serve to define a multiplicity of layers (language, geography, religion, economy) that overlap in the American continent, south of what Guatemalan architect Teddy Cruz defines polemically as the Political Equator: the line approximately at the 30°N parallel separating the United States from Mexico. Any attempt to precisely define Latin America would fall short in light of those superimposed layers.

Our main point of departure here is the fact that the term "Latin America" does refer to a certain building culture, a series of technologies and practices that prevail throughout the region, stitching together works that span one century and 6,000 miles (ca. 9,660 km). Moreover, there is indeed a common history that reaches back five hundred years to the encounter with Spanish and Portuguese navigators and, in many cases, the transformation of existing urban and architectural cultures to make them fall in line with European ideals and serve European ambitions and goals.

The particular historical legacy of preexisting cultures (be it formal or ideal(ized)/imagined) is one of the characteristics that affects the development of architecture within a particular zone; this is especially true in areas—such as the Andean region or the Yucatán Peninsula, to name two—where there was a strong pre-Hispanic culture and where its remains were still visible by the twentieth century. In other places without those deep or visible roots, the interest in syncretism between the original architectures and the Spanish or Portuguese colonial traditions would be explored. Besides this, as with any other architecture, the specificity of modern architecture in Latin America will also result from the material conditions that affect its production and the necessities to which architecture must respond to (i.e., climate, location, available materials for construction, programmatic needs and concerns, ideological implications and directives, etc.).

Another consideration for the development of architecture in the twentieth century is the representation of the nation-state. Originally, the importation of styles and forms was part of a desire by the ruling class to link itself to North American or European expressions of culture, democracy, or modernity. This is particularly obvious in the late nineteenth century and beginning of the twentieth century as many of the Latin American capitals looked up to Paris as the quintessential capital of modern culture. Later, as part of the structures of modern capital, modern architecture progressively moved into more standardized forms and materials that became part of broader cycles of transforming the production of architecture through the homogenization of needs and consumption patterns. Many of the formal similarities of modern architecture throughout Latin America (characteristic of functionalism and, later, the International style) can be ascribed to an evolutionary process in which cultural bonds and traditions were replaced by common traits. While many architects in Latin America reproduced this process within the logic of their works, others, in response, sought to imbue their work with characteristics (formal, material, historical, etc.) that might relate it to the place of its production and to the character of its designer. Although, as the twentieth century advanced, many places and their architectures were transformed into what the anthropologist Marc Augé defines as "non-places," characterized by the transmutation of anthropological referents to locale and culture to more abstract and universal ones. In the end, these have created compelling architectures and urban environments where the focus is no longer tied to identifiable, historical, or cultural traditions and forms.

3

The movement and circulation of ideas, forms, and traditions between Latin America and the rest of the world has been a constant since Columbus first arrived on the continent. In the early twentieth century, these movements would be codified in the development of modern architecture and culture in Latin America by exiles; émigrés; students; visitors to and from Europe and North America; and, to a certain extent, the exchanges between Latin American countries themselves. However, in the later part of the twentieth century, new forms of economic integration—Mercosur, for instance, in South America—have created economic and intellectual exchanges between neighboring countries while at the same time facilitating travel. Travel between São Paulo and Buenos Aires, for instance, increased from six flights per day in 1990 to over fifty per day in 2010. A series of meetings, academic conferences, and exhibitions (architectural biennials would be the best example) brought together Latin American architects as never before. Architects from Brazil and Argentina were traveling to Quito and Bogotá; the centers of culture and work were no longer limited to New York and Paris. And, as had happened at the turn of the century, the growth of magazines ensured that information was shared directly between Latin American practitioners and not only through the traditional transatlantic channels. As a result, the parameters that define and represent modernity and the conditions that define identity—either localized or one that, as an effect of globalization, becomes deterritorialized—have been transformed and made more complex than what was, at first, understood as a simple North–South (or Europe–Latin America) relationship.

Characteristic of the changes is the way they have occurred. The term "transculturation," developed by the literary critic Ángel Rama, helps theorize the active transformations that have occurred. Widely used to define the strategies and effects of modern development, it specifically addresses the systems through which modernity is altered by the judicious reliance on or incorporation of local, traditional, or historic traditions, forms, and cultural critiques. After all, in many cases, architects and artists critically and selectively appropriated elements and structures from "modern" cultures and contexts in order to combine them with (similarly selected) elements or structures from their "existing" cultures—many times not always as expected or as proposed by the "originating" cultures. This is what the Brazilian *antropofagia* movement of the late 1920s radicalized by linking the act of appropriating both local and foreign culture to cannibalism, devouring, and regurgitation. The effects of transculturation have been to highlight the artificial nature and construction of culture—reminiscent of the characterization of the birth and development of the historical avant-garde by the cultural critic Raymond Williams—and to suggest that the maker has control over how forms are created (rather than being a mere passive operator who is forced to accept forms or traditions that are "imposed").

4

In that Empire, the Art of Cartography attained such Perfection that the map of a single Province occupied the entirety of a City, and the map of the Empire, the entirety of a Province. In time, those Unconscionable Maps no longer satisfied, and the Cartographers Guilds struck a Map of the Empire whose size was that of the Empire, and which coincided point for point with it. The following Generations, who were not so fond of the Study of Cartography as their Forebears had been, saw that that vast Map was Useless, and not without some Pitilessness was it, that they delivered it up to the Inclemencies of Sun and Winters. In the Deserts of the West, still today, there are Tattered Ruins of that Map, inhabited by Animals and Beggars; in all the Land there is no other Relic of the Disciplines of Geography.

JORGE LUIS BORGES,
"ON EXACTITUDE IN SCIENCE" (1946)

In addressing the effects of these historiographic and geographic complexities on spatial production and practices, the biggest trap one must avoid in writing a history of modern architecture in Latin America is to suggest completeness. To write a history of anything is, from the outset, ideologically suspect, as it advocates the canonization of certain lines and ideas, traditions and forms, and ways of reading the world that, in reality, are only based on a limited number of available facts, observations, and knowledge. Yet, as part of an attempt to propose coherence, one must acknowledge previous historiography and reinforce, in some way, the already established canon of works, architects, and ideas that have been deemed to be important contributions to the development of architecture because of a pivotal role they might have played—as unique or as originary structures—or because they were influential to their own and later generations.

We learned very early from Jorge Luis Borges that one should not pretend to describe or encapsulate in a totalizing way the history of any discipline, the limits of any territory, the character of any production. In setting out to write a history of modern architecture in Latin America, one must be mindful of this. After all, not only are the terms contested (What is "Latin America"?), but the important or necessary conditions used in describing this history might be the product of one's limited (and, worse, ideologically constructed) worldview. We must remember that one cannot pretend to encompass a vast region (if we may define it, provisionally, in this way) where every place has different historical, social, and cultural conditions that affect the way the material character that exists is converted into the cultural fabric that we can define as architecture, landscape, or urbanity. To write of twentieth-century modern architecture in Latin America in a complete and totalizing way would be to write and present the information, as those mapmakers that Borges describes did, that encompasses the scale of the region and the time of the investigation. And that is impossible.

This presents a double problem: on the one hand, we have had to choose things that are "canonical" for the reasons described above—examples of what Friedrich Nietzsche defined as monumental history. This, of course, leads to the traditional problem of exclusion that is characteristic of history that avoids "deviances" that go against the rationality or smoothness of the arguments. In this way, as Tafuri argues in "The Historical Project," "history is . . . determined by its own traditions, by the objects that it analyzes, by the methods it adopts."[2] On the other hand, we have made subjective choices of examples and cases that might have fallen outside the list of what is considered "monumental," which, in turn, threatens to make them canonical in the views of some.

5

The three characteristics of minor literature are the deterritorialization of language, the connection of the individual to a political immediacy, and the collective assemblage of enunciation. . . . There is nothing that is major or revolutionary except the minor.

G. DELEUZE AND F. GUATTARI,
KAFKA: TOWARD A MINOR LITERATURE

In acknowledging the limitations and ideological problems of any canonical historiography, we propose other works that might be considered "minor" in the Deleuzian and Guattarian sense, that is, works that despite their seeming insignificance or unimportance cause an effect on traditional practice/production or its understanding and theorization. In a way, we can say that because of the so-called incomplete modernization (i.e., García Canclini in *Hybrid Cultures*), modern architecture in Latin America is, in fact, an effect of a deterritorialization of a language (of forms, references, etc., from the "outside") of modern architecture. This has many reasons: the importation of ideas, forms, materials, people (exiles, émigrés, travelers), as well as the incorporation or reappropriation of historical models and traditions (that are taken from other/earlier contexts) within new works or ideas. "Minor" architectures work in a similar way by taking the existing/incorporated and reconstituting, reinventing, or radicalizing it, and, in doing so, they begin to place the structure of the existing in question. Through this, the "minor" highlights the political and collective nature of architectural production. However, in many of the examples that we address herein, the political comes not only from an attempt to define a place/location through which to assert oneself that stands in contrast to what is established elsewhere (i.e., Europe, North America, etc.) but also from an attempt to investigate places of action that are outside the established practices or actions. In other cases, the architecture becomes political by being didactic: it tries to teach traditions, the values of function over ornament, the possibilities of a new world (i.e., utopia), the ideological conditions that are pervasive within the existing

context. Finally, minor architecture is collective in that it is the expression of the will of a group (who may be subaltern vis-à-vis normative practices) that materializes itself through the voices, instruments, and methods of the architects. The architecture then occupies collective space and allows that collectivity to express itself through it. Interpolating Deleuze and Guattari's concepts, these examples are of a "revolutionary condition [of any literature/architecture/etc.] within what we call the great (or established)."[3] It is because of this that we might be tempted to call much of the production of modern architecture in Latin America "minor" in this revolutionary sense.

6

To address the complexity of writing a survey that adequately covers the myriad countries; the historical, social, and political conditions; and the scales of productions from small houses to urban plans while keeping in mind the aforementioned set of concerns, the basic premise behind this book is to construct a chronological history of modern architecture in Latin America by focusing on key examples/paradigms. What makes this survey different, as attested by the table of contents, is its ability to articulate the multitude of architectural productions that occurred throughout Latin America, including their similarities, cross influences, and other features. The selected cases studies range from specific buildings or designs and important publications or events to artistic examples related to the production or advancement of architectural or urban ideas. In some instances, these paradigms are more generally defined as movements or expressions that span Latin America. In addition, we have tried to make many of the definitions of architecture, art, urbanism, or landscape broad, transient, and flexible to acknowledge that they are in a constant state of mutation. In fact, the overlap of these terms and definitions in many cases aids in the transformation of their meaning (this is particularly true, for instance, in the development of plastic integration—the introduction of art into architecture—throughout the twentieth century and in the different countries that explored it).

All of the examples presented include an analysis of the particular context within which they developed, as well as their historical evolution and, where appropriate, similar examples in different countries. The book also provides a critical evaluation of the movements presented in relation to their overall goals and architectural transformations. Drawings, photographs (historical and contemporary), and diagrams are included to aid the reader in comprehending the project's material expressions. And while the sum of the entries aims toward a degree of comprehensiveness, we have found instances where it was appropriate to expand upon and explain certain examples or buildings centrally or tangentially related to the information addressed within a main entry. In those cases, we have included "boxes" within the narratives that reinforce and extend the information provided by addressing related movements, personalities, ideas, or other elements. Finally, as part of the organization of the book, we have devised a navigational system to connect the different ideas of the book by further subcategorizing the entries according to how they relate to or address, broadly or specifically, issues of art, utopia, or technology.

These three themes and the way they are articulated are intended to define the particularities and character of the examples while being flexible. As should be expected, the three themes are present simultaneously in many (if not all) entries and examples analyzed (albeit with different intensities). By grouping the works under a certain theme, we mean to emphasize some particular condition that we feel strongly defines them (because of historiographical, theoretical, formal, or material reasons). We have considered the themes in this way:

ART: These examples address works that directly include works by artists; that manifest explicit connections with them or with concepts, concerns, or operations explored by them; and/or that express the association, dialogue, and mutual interrelation between artists and architects. In many of these cases, the work of artists is intrinsic to the architectural design or buildings. These examples represent an attempt to simultaneously show important architectural and artistic work.

TECHNOLOGY: The works within this theme emphasize the use of different building technologies: brick, reinforced concrete, "regionalist," and highly industrialized structural systems. In it, the means of production, the development of industries to support them, and localized productive practices are addressed. As a whole, the examples chosen contribute to the historiography of modern architecture that results from novel constructive techniques, from the introduction of sophisticated materials and forms, from handcrafted or artisanal techniques, or from construction by untrained and inexpensive labor.

UTOPIA: Because of the relative degrees of "development" throughout Latin America, the examples under this theme present attempts to improve the living and working conditions of the region's citizens. The most sensible architects have attempted to resolve these by focusing either on the possibilities of the future and the modern or on a nostalgic reconsideration of a harmonious, idyllic, and premodern (and thus unproblematized) past. In addition, these examples may address the possible transformation of society through a change in the role of art/architecture that leads to a new life praxis. This theme also focuses on urban contexts and sociopolitical expectations.

All in all, through the development of these "short" narratives and the "navigational system" outlined, the reader will be able to access the information in the book in different ways: by reading it chronologically, the reader can follow a historical narrative that could be made more pointed by selecting country- or area-specific entries (to focus, for instance, on the development of modern architecture in Brazil or in countries of the Caribbean); by focusing on thematically specific entries (i.e., those that discuss the relationship between art and architecture), the reader can pursue particular interests; and so on. It is through these possibilities, through the multiple points of entry that a book composed of a number of entries allows, and through a book partly embedded within the logic of Julio Cortázar's *Rayuela* that the book becomes more "genealogical" and dismantles traditional devices that construct a comprehensive, linear, and coherent view of history. Instead, in the organization of major and minor works, in the character of the entries and the relationship to the "boxes" and to the "navigational systems," we have acknowledged and accepted the condition of discontinuity of history as a central part of our proposal because, as Foucault notes, "The forces operating in history are not controlled by destiny or regulative mechanisms, but respond to haphazard conflicts. They do not manifest the successive forms of a primordial intention and their attraction is not that of a conclusion, for they always appear through the singular randomness of events."[4] So, by operating more "genealogically," the book allows the reader to simultaneously see the development of multiple and parallel historical strands and, at times, their interconnections and overlaps—to see, in short, the existing pluralities and that the history being presented within is provisional and interminable.

1903

FRANCISCO PEREIRA PASSOS BEGINS A PROJECT TO "CIVILIZE" RIO DE JANEIRO BY APPLYING BARON HAUSSMANN'S IDEAS AS AN ANSWER TO THE TROPICAL (LACK OF) URBANISM.

BRAZIL

DEMOLITION IS THE EXACT OPPOSITE of building, but, generally speaking, much of the American experience has always been about starting again, about experimentation, about the productive potential of the tabula rasa. Central to the condition of modernity is, paradoxically, that progress is based on destruction. This is precisely what needed to happen in Brazil's capital, Rio de Janeiro, in order to turn it into a modern city.

When he was named mayor of Rio de Janeiro in December of 1902, the engineer Francisco Pereira Passos was an experienced public official. He had served the Brazilian Empire since the 1860s, primarily in building railroads. The republic he was serving, however, was not as seasoned. The end of the empire in 1889 brought years of political and economic turmoil that lasted until the turn of the century. By 1902, almost one hundred years after the country's de facto independence from colonial rule, the political alliance between the state of São Paulo and the state of Minas Gerais was cemented. With the consequent political stability, the national treasury was able to finance much-needed improvements in the country's infrastructure.[1] Pereira Passos was the man appointed to make them happen. As early as January of 1903, a few weeks into his term, Pereira Passos began to limit the powers of Rio de Janeiro's city council and the National Congress in order to implement his plans for the city based on the triad of sanitation, circulation, and beautification.

Pereira Passos was a graduate of Rio de Janeiro's Military Engineering Institute (1852–1856) and the École Nationale des Ponts et Chaussées in Paris (1858–1860). At the Brazilian military academy, he and his classmates were strongly influenced by Auguste Comte's positivism. Many of his classmates, involved in the movement behind the proclamation of the republic in 1889, went so far as to inscribe the positivist motto "Order and Progress" on the Brazilian flag. In Paris, Pereira Passos took classes in railroad construction but witnessed firsthand the urban transformations being carried out under Baron Haussmann. Upon returning to Brazil in 1860, Pereira Passos began to work on the railroads throughout the country. In 1875, he was part of a team charged with the design of a plan to improve the central areas of Rio de Janeiro. The proposal considered opening large boulevards, draining swamps, reclaiming land from areas filled with mangroves, and demolishing existing hills to solve the problems of congestion and epidemics that were seen to be holding back the development of Brazil's capital. Positivism was the philosophy of choice as the team tried to organize the apparent (or real) chaos of the city. Nature had to be tamed and controlled; hills and mangroves were viewed as impediments to an ordered and progressive city. In contrast to this was engineer André Rebouças's proposed integration of forests and waterways into the city fabric, an idea very different from Pereira Passos's plan to impose his ideal geometry over the old town. Nevertheless, the political crisis of the last decades of the empire, the economic crisis of the 1890s, and the first decade of the republic all colluded to postpone the implementation of the 1875 plan. But in 1903, with Pereira Passos in power, the old plan was brought back to life.

Contrary to the Portuguese empirical approach to urban planning that is pragmatic and piecemeal, addressing each problem as it appears, Pereira Passos's plan was grandiose, idealistic, and highly symbolic—in short, extremely modern. By 1903, however, the plan was already thirty years old.

The most visible facet of Pereira Passos's plan consisted of opening a large boulevard, Avenida Central, to connect the old center of town with the newly developed areas of Botafogo, Gloria, and Flamengo (to the south). To do so, 1,225 buildings were demolished in 1904 alone. In addition, several other streets were enlarged and the port was moved to the north of the city and improved. Two other important avenues were built: The one following the coastline to the southwest

consolidated the expansion of bourgeois residential areas to the south. The other avenue, northbound, helped connect the expanded port to the nascent industrial area located farther north by Guanabara Bay. For these streets, asphalt was used as pavement in Brazil for the first time. The new avenues, like their Parisian counterparts, were for more than just circulation. They included gardens and public squares, the spaces par excellence for Rio de Janeiro's new republican elite. The occupation of the southern beachfronts was facilitated by the new avenues being built. Copacabana, for example, which had been considered too far from the city center, started to become settled as a result. Architecturally, Pereira Passos began the construction of the Theatro Municipal. Designed by his son, the theater is an eclectic composition inspired by Charles Garnier's Opera House (Paris, 1861–1874). This would certainly be the last important neoclassical building constructed in Rio de Janeiro (see 1904 entry).

If the new boulevards improved circulation and changed Rio de Janeiro's center of gravity, the sanitation component was addressed mostly by the choice of what to demolish. Similar to the Parisian precedent, the bulk of the demolitions was endured by low-income Brazilians who lived in extremely high-density housing blocks known as *cortiços*. While middle- and upper-income *cariocas* (as the residents of Rio de Janeiro are called) had started moving southwest toward

the ocean (Flamengo, Gloria, and Botafogo were populated by 1904, with Copacabana following soon after), population growth led to densification of the city, with the poor finding shelter in rooms-for-rent in the backyards of old colonial buildings. Because the traditional Portuguese way of selling lots by *testada*—based on their width at the street front—resulted in narrow properties going deep into the hilly terrain of its cities (as seen in Lisbon, Salvador de Bahia, Rio de Janeiro, Goa, or Macau), the deep and narrow backyards were built up and divided into dozens of rooms, each of which could be rented to whole families. With favelas still in their infancy (see 1994 entry), the *cortiços*, often with a single latrine and water source for all of its inhabitants, were blamed at the time for the city's constant disease epidemics. In addition, the living conditions of the poor were also blamed for their low (or lack of) moral values. The positivist response to those troubles was to eradicate them; metaphorically, the tumor on the city fabric needed to be extirpated in order to heal the body of the city.

In hindsight, it seems absurd that Pereira Passos's grandiose plan for downtown Rio de Janeiro had no provision to house the people displaced by the demolitions. Since most *cortiço* inhabitants were renters, they received no compensation and were told to find housing elsewhere. The growth of self-built houses on steep hillsides, now commonly known as favelas, was certainly fueled by the large-scale demolitions in 1904–1906 that displaced an estimated four thousand people.

In conjunction with the urban surgery, the epidemiologist Oswaldo Cruz was named director of public health in 1903 and started working with city and federal authorities to eradicate mosquito-borne illnesses such as malaria and yellow fever. Federal agents were hired to fumigate the entire city, and they had the authority to enter any property. The population, terrified by the demolitions and aware of the authoritarian ways of both Pereira Passos and Cruz, revolted against the idea of mandatory smallpox vaccinations put into law on November 5, 1904. Five days later, the city witnessed widespread chaos. Central Rio de Janeiro came to a halt with the erection of barricades, the stoning of storefronts, the destruction of urban rail lines, and general attacks against the police. By the time the government declared a state of emergency on November 16, fifty people had died and the event had been dubbed the Revolta da Vacina (Vaccine Revolt).

The label, however, is misleading. The vaccination campaign was the last straw on a long list of conservative transformations that were being imposed on the population of the Brazilian capital. The positivist ideas behind sanitation, circulation, and beautification were part of a larger project of Europeanizing, or "whitening," Brazilian society. Rio de Janeiro, the capital and the most important city of the nation (later to be replaced by Brasília and surpassed by São Paulo, respectively), was to be seen as a tropical offspring of European modernity. For this, Brazil had been under pressure to abolish slavery since the 1850s, something it did in 1888. By the turn of the century, the economic goal was to attract foreign investment and a foreign labor force to the country. Pereira Passos's urban transformations addressed both by creating a European façade and modern infrastructure while at the same time tackling the epidemics that tainted the image of the city. The old Rio de Janeiro had to be obliterated, and the poor, seen as a large part of the problem, were pushed to the northern suburbs or to the hillsides.

Pereira Passos's urban transformations were the first in a long series of spatial interventions aimed at "modernizing" (understood here as a synonym of Europeanizing or Westernizing) the tropics. The second large boulevard planned by Pereira Passos (now Avenida Presidente Vargas) was only opened in the early 1940s. The plan carried on for decades with the removal of two historical hills at the center of town: Morro do Castelo, demolished in the 1920s, and Morro de Santo Antônio, removed in the 1950s, whose dirt was used as fill to create the now famous Aterro do Flamengo (see 1965 entry).

The racial undertones of Pereira Passos's ideas—he often equated poverty and blackness with vice—would soon be transformed by José Vasconcelos's celebration of an American *raza cósmica* (cosmic race) in his 1925 book by the same name or Mário de Andrade's exaltation of Brazilian mulatto identity in *Macunaíma* (1928; see 1922 and 1925 entries, respectively). But from Buenos Aires's Avenida 9 de Julio (1912–1930) through Brasília's monumental axis, Curitiba's radial growth plan, and all the way to Bogotá's TransMilenio (bus rapid transit system, 2000), the twentieth century had more than its fair share of dramatic urban transformations in search of an evanescent utopia.

FURTHER READING

Abreu, *Evolução urbana do Rio de Janeiro*.
Chaloub, *Cidade febril*.
Costa, *Ordem médica e norma familiar*.
Pereira, S. G., "A reforma urbana de Pereira Passos."
Ribeiro and Pechman, *Cidade, povo e nação*.

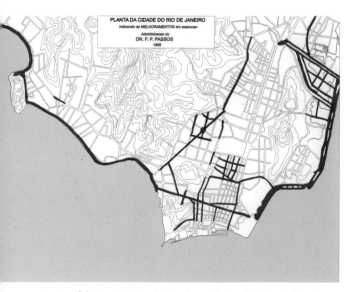

Map of downtown Rio de Janeiro with Pereira Passos's interventions highlighted.

1904

VÍCTOR MEANO, FRANCISCO DE OLIVEIRA PASSOS, AND EMILE JÉQUIER BUILD A LATIN AMERICAN CHARACTER WITH A CLASSICAL VOCABULARY.

ARGENTINA • BRAZIL • CHILE

The Theater is still today the great hall of the city, its social forum, the elegant arena where tournaments of fashion, grace, conversation, and courtesy are waged.

OLAVO BILAC ON THE INAUGURATION
OF THE THEATRO MUNICIPAL IN RIO DE JANEIRO
(*DIÁRIO DE NOTÍCIAS*, RIO DE JANEIRO, JULY 14, 1909)

NORTH AMERICAN AUDIENCES know well the "murder of the century": the assassination of architect Stanford White by the jealous husband of his lover in 1906. The fact that the architect Víctor Meano suffered the same exact fate two years earlier in Argentina is an interesting coincidence, especially in light of how similarly their architecture was being used at the time to define a place's character, identity, and national politics.

Víctor (Vittorio) Meano was born in Italy in 1860 and studied architecture at the Accademia Albertina in Turin, from which he graduated in 1880. In 1884, Meano traveled to Buenos Aires to join the studio of his compatriot Francesco Tamburini, who was, at the time, the Argentine Inspector General of National Architecture. Meano's first job in Buenos Aires was to assist in the renovation and expansion of the Casa Rosada, the offices of the Argentine presidency.

In 1888, Tamburini was commissioned to build the Teatro Colón, to this day the most traditional theater in Argentina and the South American rival to Milan's La Scala or Paris's Opera House. Founded in 1857, the Teatro Colón already had an established opera troupe when the municipality of Buenos Aires decided to build the largest theater south of the equator in 1888. The new Teatro Colón was designed to have an Italian proscenium and a horseshoe-shaped hall, rising to six stories of balconies, that was capable of accommodating 2,500 people or 4,000 standing. With Tamburini's death in 1891, Víctor Meano inherited the job and worked on it until he was assassinated in 1904. The original design team included the French architect Victor Dubugras, who moved to São Paulo after Meano

took over the project and whose practice was centered on designing Art Nouveau structures (see 1910 entry). The Teatro Colón, with its Italian form decorated with French elements, was ultimately finished by the Belgian architect Jules Dormal and inaugurated in 1908. In the end, the building is a characteristically European-styled and French-inspired building in South America, built by Italian immigrants speaking Spanish and financed by English investors. Architectural design could not be more eclectic than that.

A thousand miles (1,610 km) north and a decade later, Rio de Janeiro would build a similar theater. The campaign started in 1894 when the writer Arthur Azevedo called for the formation of a municipal acting troupe modeled after the Comédie-Française. As a result, a municipal law was passed to create the troupe and a tax to support it.[1] In 1903, with Mayor Pereira Passos dismantling hills and cutting avenues throughout downtown Rio de Janeiro, the opportunity to build a theater appeared on a new boulevard where the Morro do Castelo once stood. A competition was held for its design and was won by the mayor's son, Francisco de Oliveira Passos, working in collaboration with French architect Albert Guilbert. Cries of nepotism were heard everywhere but were soon dismissed, as the mayor had a special legal provision giving him full authority to demolish and build anything that reinforced his plans for beautifying downtown Rio de Janeiro and turning it into "the Paris of the tropics" (see 1903 entry).

The winning entry is a miniature copy of Charles Garnier's Paris Opera House. To decorate it, the best Brazilian painters and sculptors were called in, resulting in an early version of plastic integration that would become a mainstream staple of many Latin American debates decades later. Rodolfo Amoedo decorated the ceilings, the Bernadelli brothers Rodolfo and Henrique painted wall panels, and a young Eliseu Visconti painted the stage curtains. The stained glass was brought from England, ironworks from Belgium, and fabrics from France.

Inaugurated in 1909, the 1,800-seat theater was an icon of the Brazilian belle époque. If the architecture of the turn of the century was all about character, in this case it was understood as capable of expressing a new identity. The Theatro Municipal speaks about the strength of French culture and its influence among the Brazilian elite. Not coincidentally, its inauguration took place on July 14, France's National Day (Bastille Day).[2]

In Santiago, Chile, Emile Jéquier built the Museo Nacional de Bellas Artes in 1905 based on many of the same ideas. Born in Chile and educated in Paris at the École Spéciale d'Architecture and at the École des Beaux-Arts, Jéquier was inspired by the Parisian Petit Palais (Charles Girault, 1900), which was built for the Universal Exposition of 1900 and turned into a museum in 1902. Following a classical vocabulary, the Chilean Museo Nacional de Bellas Artes has its character embedded in the form, not so much in the decoration. Its curved frontispiece was labeled baroque, but its large glass greenhouse-like vaults covering the atrium signal a change in public buildings toward a more elaborated treatment of light that would soon be radicalized by Adolf Loos's "Ornament and Crime" (1908) and Ludwig Mies van der Rohe's dictum of "less is more." Nevertheless, the Museo Nacional de Bellas Artes still uses ornamentation to deliver its messages: its façade, for example, is lined with dozens of medallions that depict Phidias, Praxiteles, Donato Bramante, Eugène Viollet-le-Duc, and Rembrandt, among other Beaux-Arts heroes. Given that the museum was inaugurated during the centennial celebrations of Chilean independence in 1910, the architectural language was part of a system that sought to express the "European" nature of the national character and the elites in power. As noted by architectural historian Jorge Francisco Liernur, the focus on character was a strategy to stitch a universal classical vocabulary to the construction of local identity.[3]

If French culture was celebrated by South American cultural elites, the issue of finding the right character for local architecture became more complex in governmental buildings. National identities were being transformed by the modernizing aspirations of South American nations split between

Francisco de Oliveira Passos and Albert Guilbert, Theatro Municipal, Rio de Janeiro, 1909.

Víctor Meano, Congreso Nacional, Buenos Aires, 1906.

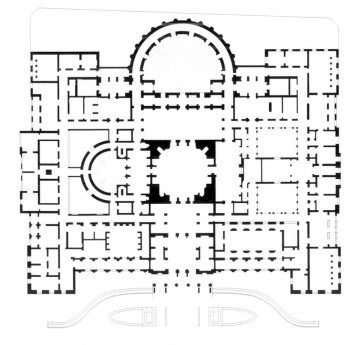

Plan of Congreso Nacional, Buenos Aires.

honoring their past histories and celebrating their new roles in the global arena. In Brazil and Argentina, immigration policies aimed at Europeanizing, or "whitening," society. The same policies that facilitated the emigration of Italian, French, Belgian, and German artists also supported the pedagogic message of a "European" architecture that would create a scenario of development for the local elites. In the case of Argentina and Uruguay, their economies were enjoying such unprecedented growth by the turn of the century that several new buildings were needed to materialize their successes in stone. For those young democracies flooded with cash, there was nothing more important than the theater of public life.

In 1894, the Argentine government held a competition for a building to house the nation's Congress. The site offered was located at the opposite end of Avenida de Mayo from the Casa Rosada. Twenty-eight designs were submitted, and Víctor Meano won the competition. Construction started in 1897 and dragged on for decades. With Víctor Meano's murder on June 1, 1904, Jules Dormal became responsible for finishing this structure, too. The Argentine Congress building was partially inaugurated in 1906, but the cupola remained unfinished until 1930. The building was fully completed in 1946.[4]

The organization of the Congress building shows a classical rectangular plan with the corners highlighted and a cupola in the center of the composition. Repetitive series of smaller rooms are carefully arranged to create separate circulation routes for the public and the representatives (*diputados*). At the back, a larger auditorium was built as the meeting room for the representatives, its cylindrical form protruding onto the street. The Senate meets in a much smaller room asymmetrically placed in one of the patios. Here, the search for an Argentine character with classical vocabulary is rendered through the use of more austere forms. The building's main façade resembles the German Reichstag in Berlin, designed in the 1870s and inaugurated the same year that the competition for Argentina's Congress building was held, with its central pedimented portico and structures on the side; the Argentine dome, however, is taller and more ovoid that its German counterpart.

In Uruguay, a competition was held in 1904 to build a Legislative Palace in Montevideo. When the commission finished its deliberations and opened the envelopes that guaranteed the anonymity of the process, it was discovered that Víctor Meano's project had also won that competition, thus inscribing him in the history of legislative architecture on both sides of the Río de la Plata. However, his death a few days before the deliberations, as well as the change in site where the building was to be located, forced the Uruguayan government to modify Meano's design and hire the Swiss-Italian architect Cayetano Moretti in 1914. Though the building is similar in appearance to its Argentine counterpart, one marked difference is that it has no central dome.

Surely, one of the main concerns of this generation of architects in Latin America was how to better "transplant" elements that would aid in the construction and definition of a European culture in South America. In this way, architecture was to become an agent intended to "civilize" or provide a "Europeanized" expression to a society that was not "cultured enough." The model for this was not any generic European architecture or civilization, but rather, specifically the Parisian culture of the nineteenth century, with Italian, German, and British culture having a secondary role and Spanish and Portuguese traditions being completely ignored and brushed aside as second class. The local designers, even when educated abroad, were not good enough to build the main theaters of this new public life. Although many provincial governmental buildings were commissioned from local architects such as Domingo Selva in Tucumán, Argentina (1908); Francisco Ferrari in Santa Fe, Argentina (1911); Juan Coll in Corrientes, Argentina (1886); José de Magalhães in Belo Horizonte, Brazil (1895); or Francisco Ramos de Azevedo in São Paulo, Brazil (1901), the national monuments of Rio de Janeiro, Buenos Aires, and other South American cities were being designed by Europeans. Most emblematic of the latter were the buildings designed in Mexico City during the presidency of Porfirio Díaz that similarly tried to portray a Europeanizing image to itself and the exterior. These include the Legislative Palace (1904) by the French architect Émile Bénard; the Palace of Fine Arts (1904) and the Post Office Building (1907) by the Italian architect Adamo Boari; and the neoclassical Communications Building (1911) by the Italian Silvio Contri.

A case like the Capitolio building in Havana, Cuba, is emblematic of a focus on North American architecture, as its architects, Raúl Otero and Eugenio Rayneri Piedra, worked with U.S. construction firms and imported much of its material to create something modeled on the U.S. Capitol building in Washington, DC.

With the rising interest in indigenous or neocolonial traditions and forms (see 1910 and 1915 entries) coming from within the most conservative architectural circles, critiques of European neocolonialism, and the perceived decadence of the European cities in the face of a new and growing culture, the focus on Europe and commissions to Europeans would soon change, paving the way for a process of identity construction that would become one of the pillars of modernism throughout Latin American architecture.

FURTHER READING

Braun and Cacciatore, *Arquitectos europeos y Buenos Aires*. Gutiérrez, *Arquitectura y urbanismo en Iberoamérica*.

1906

JULIÁN GARCÍA NÚÑEZ'S HOSPITAL ESPAÑOL DEFINES A CHARACTERISTIC SEARCH FOR A NEW LANGUAGE: SECESSION/ART NOUVEAU.

ARGENTINA • BRAZIL • MEXICO

SOME OF THE EARLIEST experiments with architectural form and language in Latin America result from the search for and development of architectures to represent a particular nation. In this way, the various experiments throughout the continent with Belgian or French Art Nouveau, Austrian Secessionism, or Catalan Modernisme are, as with their European counterparts, characteristic of a renewal of architecture. This was to be achieved, in the words of the architectural historian Henry-Russell Hitchcock, through a "total rejection of historicism."[1] In the first decades of the twentieth century, the turn away from classical European architecture in Latin American architecture signified a search for new styles as well as a desire to develop a new architecture for a "new place"—an attempt, in other words, to leave the European past behind, in the old continent, and to start afresh. This desire was either led or strongly influenced by the very immigration that helped to accelerate the cosmopolitanism and modernization of Latin American cities, not to mention the radical transformation of the local culture. By 1914, for example, 966,780 foreigners (primarily Italian and Spanish) lived in Buenos Aires.[2]

The development of a new style grew out of the investigations by a new generation of architects—either immigrants trained abroad (primarily in Europe) or those aware of new architectural developments through the emergent mass media—wanting to create new forms that questioned architectural traditions. In Argentina, we find examples of this in the Confitería El Molino (1916) by Francisco Gianotti—a native of Turin who emigrated to Buenos Aires in 1909—whose main decorative feature plays off the dome of the National Congress building (see 1904 entry); in the Argentine Yacht Club (1915) by French-trained Édouard Le Monnier, whose lighthouse dome references Joseph Olbrich's Secession Building (Vienna, 1898); or in the Palacio Barolo (1919–1923) by Milanese architect Mario Palanti (see 1923 box).

The search for a national architecture also involved the incorporation of local elements or traditions—seen as antithetical to European architectural forms—into the vocabulary being developed; this was primarily the case where a strong pre-Hispanic tradition already existed. In Mexico, the 1904 National Auditorium (now known as the Palacio de Bellas Artes), designed by the Italian Adamo Boari, included a stylized sculptural program that blends classical forms with pre-Hispanic motifs.

Julián García Núñez's Hospital Español (Spanish Hospital; 1906) can be categorized within these conditions and investigations. García Núñez was an Argentine architect who studied architecture and began his professional career in Barcelona under Lluís Domènech i Montaner, the Catalan modernista architect who, like Antoni Gaudí, was searching for a unique form to represent Catalan identity. Upon his return from Spain in 1903, García Núñez began a construction practice with his father. The Hospital Español commission resulted from a competition by an Argentine society of Spanish immigrants and descendants whose goal was to aid fellow Spaniards. The existing hospital, located in an area with a high number of migrants, had been built in the 1870s and was in need of expansion. García Núñez's strategy consisted of placing an additional floor on the original building. However, it is in the redesign of the façade where a new formal language is developed through the use of towerlike pavilions that emphasize the building's central axis and edges, as well as through the use of a new formal decorative language. The verticality of the composition is highlighted through the towers, the pilasters framing them, and the use of abstracted vertical lines (reminiscent of fluting) that covers some of the upper windows (which, in turn, are quite tall in comparison to those on the ground floor, where the horizontality of the rustication is most prominent). In addition, the upper windows are emphasized through the use of an upside-down U frame that is connected to other windows via a decorative frieze of flowers (a

AR

BR

MX

Julián García Núñez, Hospital Español, Buenos Aires, 1906

organizational elements as the Hospital Español. However, given García Núñez's ability to design the totality of the project, rather than working with or renovating an existing building, a stronger formal continuity exists between the ground floor and the upper level. The verticals are emphasized by means of pilasters that extend past the roof plane of the building. The central tower that marks the entrance also emphasizes its verticality through its mass and the vertical fluting placed over the large window. Like the earlier project, this pavilion is also topped by a shallow dome covered in mosaics. Overall, this building demonstrates a marked restraint in the decorative work made up primarily of the stylized garlands and wreaths atop the pilasters, the simple checkered ironwork and abstract patterning on the central tower (reminiscent of the work of the Viennese Josef Hoffmann), and a marquee on the front that utilizes a font reminiscent of Secessionist typographical design. One can see that the various material and formal choices made by García Núñez—such as the use of shiny colored tile to dissolve the mass of the wall or the elimination of horizontal elements—radically changed the perception of the architecture and traditional or classical notions of monumentality.[3]

Clearly, new materials such as cement and iron also played an important part in the new forms. In many cases, the linear decorative motifs of European Art Nouveau (characterized, for example, by the work

similar motif is found in the stained glass in the higher portion of the windows). Although the two edge towers are topped with small ogival domes, stylized garlands, and wreaths, the dome of the central pavilion is really the focus of the composition because of the larger scale of the bay, the more rounded nature of the dome, and its cladding with colored mosaics.

The Temperley Hospital, begun in 1907 and inaugurated in 1913, uses similar decorative motifs. Intended as a recovery annex to the Hospital Español, the buildings consist primarily of pavilions organized diagonally to the square shape of the site. This planning was derived from Domènech i Montaner's own design for the Hospital de Santa Creu i Sant Pau in Barcelona (begun in 1902). The admissions pavilion of the Argentine example follows some of the same formal and of the Belgian architect Victor Horta and the French architect Hector Guimard) were imitated in much of the ironwork of some of the buildings. In addition, the use of structural glass helped express the lightness of this new architecture, as it contrasted the heaviness of past or European styles. This is clear in García Núñez's 1911 office building on Chacabuco Street, where the walkways surrounding an interior four-story atrium are of cast glass, allowing the zenithal light to penetrate to the bottom of the space.

In Brazil, the work of the French-born architect Victor Dubugras is characteristic of both the investigations with new materials as well as the desire for renovation. Dubugras had relocated to South America to work and train under Francesco Tamburini during the construction of the Teatro Colón in Buenos Aires (see 1904 entry). After Tamburini's death, Dubugras moved to São Paulo, where he established an architectural practice. His early work there shows characteristics of nineteenth-century eclecticism: combinations of Spanish or Portuguese colonial styles interspersed with gothic motifs and forms. His work for the Mayrink train station (1906), however, represents a dramatic shift that, according to Nestor Goulart Reis, is the result of a competition project that did not need to fulfill the

desired stylistic nuances of his bourgeois clientele and became instead an important protomodernist building. The station is composed of a central waiting and ticket space with two symmetrically placed wings for waiting and concessions. Surrounding the structure are the railroad platforms covered with a cantilevered awning. The interiors of the lower portions are characterized by the expression of the reinforced concrete beams. The building's simplicity results from its restrained ornamentation and the volumetric use of the reinforced concrete for its construction. The ornamental program is limited to four light towers that frame the central section of the building, the use of scallop-shaped glass placed on a slight incline to allow light and natural ventilation into the waiting area, the simple expression of industrial elements such as the structure supporting the canopy around the building or the clocks on the main façades, and the Art Nouveau–inspired typography of the station's name that hangs from the four towers.

In addition to the formal and material characteristics of the new buildings, we also find that the use of these types of idiosyncratic forms and handcrafted ornamentation—as with the English arts and crafts movement—stood throughout Latin America as a

Victor Dubugras, Mayrink Train Station, Mairinque, Brazil, 1906

rejection of industrialization and of the internationalization of architecture. In Mexico, for example, the poet José Juan Tablada advocated the handicrafts. In a 1914 review of fine arts and handicrafts, he called for a return of craft production as a means to make art democratic and intellectually accessible to all and as a way to vindicate manual labor.[4] His concern for crafts also carried over to the traditional arts (based on the colonial past) that others, such as the architect Federico Mariscal (see 1914 entry), saw as a means to produce a work that was unique to its context. However, given the dictatorship of Porfirio Díaz (known as the Porfiriato) and the stronghold of the Fine Arts Academy in Mexico during the first part of the century, the early development of new architectural languages was not as pervasive in Mexico as we find elsewhere.

While the developments of new architectural languages continued throughout the century, the direct lineage of the Art Nouveau or Secessionist styles discussed here continued in many countries with the influence of the Art Deco style. A result of the 1925 International Exhibition of Modern Industrial and Decorative Arts in Paris, this new style incorporated and subdued some of the earlier formal investigations into a new architecture. However, as was the intention of the 1925 exhibition, the goal was now primarily commercial and the new style was intended to return a type of luxury lost with modernization.

Architects searching for new forms—seen, for example, in Juan Segura's Edificio Ermita (Mexico City, 1930–1931) or Tomás Gore y José A. Cuevas's YWCA Building (Mexico City, 1933)—experimented with reinforced concrete to generate a stylized Art Deco characterized by the buildings' streamlined forms and decorative lines as well as through the abstraction of traditional architectural motifs (in the case of Mexico, the preference was for pre-Hispanic motifs). In addition, the conclusion of the Mexican Revolution allowed architects to produce work that questioned

the expectations regarding what a Mexican architecture should look like. Segura's speculative apartment or mixed-use buildings (such as the Edificio Ermita, which contained a movie theater, retail space, and housing) utilize this new commercial architectural language. Similarly, Mario Palanti's Palacio Barolo in Buenos Aires and Palacio Salvo in Montevideo can be read in this light because of their ornate forms and intended use (see 1923 box).

The radical difference between the earlier architectural experiments and the use of Art Deco can be seen, then, in the patrons that commissioned them. The new Art Deco style is not subaltern, relegated to the marginal, or a site for investigation, but rather, it is a style adopted by business, elites, and governments alike. In this way, we find highly visible Art Deco expressions in Ángel Guido and Alejandro Bustillo's Monument to the Flag (Rosario, 1939–1957), a simple tower with a boat-like prow and a colonnade structure; or in the Cristo Redentor statue (Rio de Janeiro, 1931), described as the largest Art Deco sculpture in the world. The same is true for the monumental yet idiosyncratic work of Francisco Salamone for government buildings and cemeteries in the Buenos Aires provinces (see 1937 box).

In the end, the search for new forms and innovative use of materials that began at the start of the new century had become, by the end of the twenties, an established style. All linguistic transgressions of traditional architectural form had been co-opted and homogenized as new formal expressions of architectural nationalism.

FURTHER READING

García Núñez, *Julián García Núñez.*
Goulart Reis, *Racionalismo e proto-modernismo.*
Liernur, *Arquitectura en la Argentina del siglo XX.*
Toca Fernández, "Juan Segura."

1914

JESÚS T. ACEVEDO AND FEDERICO MARISCAL LECTURE IN MEXICO ON THE CHARACTER, IMPORTANCE, AND ROLE OF THE SPANISH COLONIAL LEGACY.

MEXICO

BY THE TIME Jesús T. Acevedo died in 1918, the polemics regarding the importance of the colonial legacy in Mexico were well established. Along with architect Federico E. Mariscal, Acevedo lectured publicly on architecture and the vindication of colonial architecture for modern Mexico at the Sociedad de Conferencias (Society of Conferences).[1] The valorization of the colonial legacy was nothing new. This could be seen, for instance, in the 1893 publication by Manuel G. Revilla, *El arte en México en la época antigua y durante el gobierno virreinal*. In 1904, Guillermo Kahlo, father of the noted painter Frida Kahlo, was hired by Mexico's Treasury Department to record colonial churches throughout Mexico (these would eventually be published in 1923 by the Ministry of Education under José Vasconcelos). In 1915, the Inspección General de Monumentos Artísticos (Department of Artistic Monuments) was founded to protect and document works from the period of the conquest that were neglected or in the process of decay.[2]

Acevedo, one of the most prominent members of the Ateneo de la Juventud (Athenaeum of Youth)—a gathering of young thinkers interested in discussing social, political, and intellectual issues and whose members would become the principal intellectual, political, and artistic leaders at the conclusion of the Mexican Revolution—delivered a series of lectures revolving around three recurring themes in Mexican architecture. The first was "the relationship . . . between the structure of human life and the style of its architecture."[3] Architecture, in other words, always represented the people and the race that built it. Second, colonial architecture in Mexico was paradigmatically Mexican because

at the moment of translating, with admirable dedication, the foreign designs that served as models for them, something of the native and inaccessible hid within their work; something unknown in the depths that, without mistaking the dimensions or varying the design guidelines, would create a new gesture, unforeseen nuance, or

special color. It was, in the end, our Mexico that began to show its idiosyncrasy. . . . Nothing more natural, in the meanwhile, than when the colonizers implanted any style and architectural tendency, these would be modified by that dark current, always latent in the native.[4]

According to Acevedo, this form of Mexican architecture was not continued because it did not adapt to the necessities of "constant progress"[5] characterized by the expression of modernization through the use of imported or foreign architectural styles. For him, the immediacy between architecture and the people who created it was lost. Acevedo's third theme was centered on the need for and the importance of a guiding architecture (*arquitectura directriz*). This guiding architecture was to link contemporary architecture with the past by formally basing it on colonial architecture. In this way, architecture would reflect the experiential richness of its predecessor, it would fit into the climate and region from which it developed (unlike the unmediated importations typical of the Porfirio Díaz regime), and it would also be recognizable by the population. Ultimately, the colonial style not only re-created a monumental architecture—and a desired return to the monumentality of the past it expressed—but also instituted different means of production. In this way, the style could be understood as a variant of William Morris and John Ruskin's valuation of craft production in contrast to the current industrialized means of production. For Acevedo, "the worker, invariably destined to machine labor as a consequence of our sad social regime, must occupy his/her new position as teacher, as creator, as artist!"[6] In the end, these products would also be accessible to and comprehensible by the population at large. This would be a way that architects could respond to the aims and needs of the revolution itself.

Acevedo's requirements for this guiding architecture also included the necessity, as with its historical counterpart, that it be created by Mexican architects. However, in order to make it current, these architects would rely on modern construction materials and techniques. In this way, both the historical roots and the modern period would be addressed.

Acevedo's lectures were published posthumously in 1922 as *Disertaciones de un arquitecto*. In the introduction, Federico Mariscal noted Acevedo's practical architectural training within the atelier of Émile Bénard, who, at the time, was working on the neoclassical design of the Palacio Legislativo (Legislative Palace) for Mexico City. In doing so, Mariscal inadvertently pointed out Acevedo's ability to work in the very Beaux-Arts design systems that he saw as corrupting, making Acevedo, in other words, a critic who knew and had been engaged directly in that practice rather than someone who criticized from a distance.

Mariscal, like Acevedo, also advocated for the contemporary valuation of colonial architecture. His lectures, published in 1915 as *La patria y la arquitectura nacional*, similarly noted the relationships that existed between the "social organism and the different types of architectural works." For him, the geographical, natural, and material conditions of the land, in conjunction with the society that inhabited them, became expressed in the national architectural works of art (*obras de arte arquitectónico nacional*).[7] The colonial legacy was part of that society and, as a result, it was indelibly linked to Mexican architecture, as it represented

the life and more general customs characteristic of the whole life of Mexico as a nation. The current Mexican citizen, who forms the majority of the population, is a result of the material, moral, and intellectual mixture of the Spanish and aboriginal races that populated the Mexican land. As such, Mexican architecture emerged and developed during the three viceroyal centuries which constituted *"the Mexican"* and that has been developing independently ever since.[8]

For Mariscal, as for Acevedo, the evolutionary end of colonial architecture resulted from the importation of foreign styles—"exotic" and antithetical to Mexican life—and by the pervasive modification and destruction of colonial buildings. The past, however, offered clues for the present state of architecture and could, if followed carefully, re-create a monumental legacy and bring about a rebirth of the Mexican architectural art. Like Acevedo, Mariscal argued for the importance of mixture; for him, this was also to be understood in racial terms rather than simply stylistic or material ones. Ultimately, the colonial architecture was one of the "constitutive elements that made up the Nation."[9]

It should be noted that for many Mexican and other Latin American architects and thinkers, theorizing the importance of the colonial legacy for the production of a modern architecture meant two things: first, it was an affront to the nineteenth-century importation of French Beaux-Arts neoclassical models that were prominently and predominantly used to signify Latin America's entry into a European-style modernity (characterized by Paris as the capital of the nineteenth century; see 1904 entry); and second, it made reference to an idealized historical period when architecture, society, and culture were unified. In both cases, the interest in the colonial architecture (and the neocolonial style it engendered) reflected a search for a characteristically local and representative style—in many cases, described as "nationalist"—which, in addition, fulfilled the requirements for a sought-after monumentality that made few allusions to current European architecture.[10]

While these searches in Mexico were articulated by Acevedo and Mariscal (and materialized shortly thereafter by Vasconcelos's building program for the Department of Education in the early 1920s [see 1922 entry]; Carlos Obregón Santacilia, for example, built the Centro Educativo Benito Juárez [Mexico City, 1925] in a modernized colonial style), similar reevaluations were also undertaken throughout Latin America. In Brazil, Lúcio Costa's service for the SPHAN (Serviço do Patrimônio Histórico e Artístico Nacional [Department for the Conservation of Historic Monuments],

MX

formed in 1937) forged the connection of modern architecture in Brazil with the baroque architecture of the colonial period and, through this, implied continuity with a local expression that ignored nineteenth-century French academicism. Through this, modernist production could be understood as inherently autochthonous through the historical erasure of European Beaux-Arts influences (see 1943 entry).[11] Costa found in the eighteenth-century baroque a "myth of origins" that responded both to the need for local roots and as a justification for a more free-formed modernism going against the orthodoxy of an older generation that was heavily influenced by French eclecticism or a younger one by strict functionalism. In Argentina, it was Martín Noel and Ángel Guido who promoted it most prominently. Noel had traveled through Spain and Peru after his studies at the École des Beaux-Arts. Upon his return to Buenos Aires, he became interested in promoting colonial architecture. In a 1914 lecture at the Museo de Bellas Artes

Carlos Obregón Santacilia, Centro Educativo Benito Juárez, Mexico City, 1925

entitled "Arquitectura Colonial," he focused on the colonial architecture of Peru and defined it as a contemporary model that reflected the "canon of our artistic inheritance."[12] As with his Mexican counterparts, a uniquely American architecture resulted from the fusion between the Spanish and indigenous peoples that was materially expressed within the architecture. Noel believed that this idea of fusion could be used in the formation of a new modern national(ist) architecture; examples of this would be the Escuela San Marón (San Marón School; Buenos Aires, 1920) or his own house (1922; now the Museo Fernández Blanco). Like Noel, Guido's publication of *Fusión hispano-indígena en la arquitectura colonial* (1925), also a result of his travels to Peru, formally outlined the characteristic syncretism of Latin American colonial architecture by referencing elements from Inca architecture on that built by the Spaniards. The book's prologue, entitled "Towards Our Own Architecture," on the other hand, suggested a direction that could be undertaken based on this architecture and, obliquely, served as a critique of European architecture.

FURTHER READING

Acevedo, *Disertaciones de un arquitecto.*
Amaral, *Arquitectura neocolonial.*
Mariscal, *La patria y la arquitectura nacional.*
Noel, *Fundamentos para una estética nacional.*

Martín Noel, Escuela San Marón, Buenos Aires, 1920.

1915

ANTONIN NECHODOMA INTRODUCES THE PRAIRIE STYLE TO PUERTO RICO.

FRANK LLOYD WRIGHT'S early impact in Latin America is extremely limited despite the international prominence he received after the 1910 publication of his *Wasmuth Portfolio*. One of the early adopters of Wright's Prairie style outside of the United States is Antonin Nechodoma, who began to use it in Puerto Rico in 1915.

Born in Czechoslovakia in 1877, Nechodoma and his family emigrated to Chicago in 1887. As noted by historian Thomas S. Marvel, little is known about Nechodoma's youth and training: his father was a carpenter, and his earliest architectural work was done as a contractor for fellow immigrants, as he never trained officially as an architect. Nechodoma's skills and interest in architecture and decorative arts developed from being in one of the richest and most fertile environments for architectural innovation and experimentation at the time—which included not only the 1893 World's Columbian Exposition but also the development of the skyscraper typology and the work of notables such as Louis Sullivan and Frank Lloyd Wright—from working with his father, from possible apprenticeship with architects, and from opportunities to listen to debates regarding the Arts and Crafts movement at Chicago's Hull House. At the end of 1904, he abruptly left Chicago to practice in Florida, Puerto Rico, and the Dominican Republic. His work from this period is stylistically eclectic, as can be seen in two Methodist churches in Puerto Rico of 1907–1908: one is neo-Gothic while the other is neocolonial. In 1912, he settled in Puerto Rico and, until about 1915, his practice is distinguished by Arts and Crafts bungalow–inspired residences that demonstrate an awareness of the island's climatic and material conditions. His own house of 1913, for example, uses an asymmetrical hip roof covered with tile, a porch and passageways that link the main body of the house to the open studio and bedrooms, and Arts and Crafts ornamentation and decorative elements in the interiors.

The 1915 Luchetti House is emblematic of a radical change in Nechodoma's design process: the form of the residence refers directly to work published in Wright's *Wasmuth Portfolio* (in particular the design for the 1904 Ullman House). Marvel and other historians speculate that Nechodoma obtained a copy of Wright's publication around 1914 and, at the same time, his designs begin to mimic Wright's. The Luchetti house follows the form of Wright's design in the use of cantilevered low hip roofs, massive piers that encase the ground floor, and low boundary walls. The plan is almost identical to Wright's with some important modifications: Nechodoma eliminates the hearth from the center of the composition; adds an entry and service wing; and compartmentalizes the main rooms through the

Antonin Nechodoma, Luchetti House, San Juan, 1915

Antonin Nechodoma, perspective of Korber House, San Juan, 1917

use of built-in shelves, a linen closet, and stairs. Through these, he contradicts some of the central tenets of Wright's notions of domesticity as well as his reconceptualization of the modern house and its interconnected spatial character. To adapt the Midwestern design to Puerto Rico, Nechodoma used local materials and building traditions such as tile roofs and white stucco walls. He also modified the design so that the second floor is taller than its northern counterpart to allow for natural cooling.

That Nechodoma was reworking Wright's original designs and adapting them to Puerto Rico can be seen by comparing the exterior perspective of the Korber House (1917) to Wright's published perspective of the Dana House (1902). Compositionally, the two drawings are identical. It appears that the primary formal elements of Nechodoma's design, which vary slightly from Wright's, are directly traced. The most substantial difference in the drawings is how Nechodoma framed the house within

a lush tropical landscape that includes palm trees and makes the house appear to recede from the street. In addition to its new siting, Nechodoma's redesign of Wright's building incorporates a terrace surrounding most of the house. In contrast to the pinwheel quality of Wright's plan, Nechodoma also centralized the reception and library and, through that, the composition of the plan.

While European architects were eager to translate the spatial and formal conditions of the Prairie style, it is clear that for Nechodoma, Wright's architecture was more of a stylistic alternative that could be adapted to the Caribbean. Yet, despite his extensive residential production and its notoriety (much of his work was published in contemporary journals on the island and in the U.S.), the Prairie style wasn't continued in Puerto Rico after Nechodoma's accidental death in 1928.

1922

IN AN ATTEMPT TO CREATE A BUILDING EXPRESSIVE OF THE "COSMIC RACE," JOSÉ VASCONCELOS INAUGURATES IN MEXICO CITY THE HEADQUARTERS OF THE SECRETARÍA DE EDUCACIÓN PÚBLICA AND FORMALIZES THE MURALIST PROJECT

MEXICO

I tried, some years ago, when they were not yet well defined, to [give shape to the ideas of the cosmic race] in the new Palace of Public Education in Mexico. Lacking sufficient elements to do exactly what I wished, I had to be satisfied with a Spanish renaissance building, with two courtyards, archways, and passages that give somewhat the impression of a bird's wing. On the panels at the four corners of the first patio, I had them carve allegories representing Spain, Mexico, Greece, and India, the four particular civilizations that have most to contribute to the formation of Latin America. Immediately below these four allegories, four stone statues should have been raised, representing the four great contemporary races: The white, the red, the black, and the yellow, to indicate that America is home to all and needs all of them. Finally, in the center, a monument should have been raised that in some way would symbolize the law of the three states: The material, the intellectual, and the aesthetic. All this was to indicate that through the exercise of the triple law, we in America shall arrive, before any other part of the world, at the creation of a new race fashioned out of the treasures of all the previous ones: The final race, the cosmic race.

JOSÉ VASCONCELOS, *LA RAZA CÓSMICA* (1925)

Secretaría de Educación Pública, Mexico City, 1922.

MX

THUS CONCLUDES the theoretical portion of José Vasconcelos's *La raza cósmica* (*The Cosmic Race*) and establishes the work for the headquarters of the Secretaría de Educación Pública (SEP; Department of Public Education) as part of a broader search to express the ideas on art, race, and culture that he started developing before the Mexican Revolution. In this building, Vasconcelos would attempt to unify art and architecture to create a complete work of art intended to transform society. The building for the SEP would be the earliest and most coherent example of plastic integration—the use of murals and sculpture to define and express a political, social, or cultural message—in Mexico. After all, if the revolution was characterized by the conclusion of Porfirio Díaz's regime, it was clear to most artists and architects that the political and social changes should be met with cultural ones reflecting the new ideals. For many, this meant a rejection of the architectural styles associated with the old regime (mainly neoclassicism and imported styles from Europe) and a search for a

23

new art and architecture that was legible by the population at large and that represented its values and history. Despite these ambitions, the integration of art into architecture would become a highly contested yet distinguishing characteristic of much of modern architecture in Mexico and, later, of twentieth-century architecture in Latin America as well.

Hired as minister of education by President Álvaro Obregón at the conclusion of the Mexican Revolution, José Vasconcelos set out to develop a comprehensive educational system based on his own philosophical ideas. As a young intellectual, he had been critical of Díaz's regime and its reliance on French positivism (and its social counterpart, social Darwinism). Vasconcelos, in various philosophical texts, responded to Auguste Comte's "law of the three stages" by proposing his own "law of the three states," which placed the aesthetic state, the "third period," at the highest plane of the development and interest of humanity (akin to Comte's scientific or positive stage). This would play a central role in his understanding of art's vocation in the educative environment and in the transformation of society. As Vasconcelos's philosophical ideas became clearer (and as he became more influential), he began manifesting them in projects that were under his responsibility and sphere of influence.

As minister of education, Vasconcelos hired artists to decorate many of the public educational buildings. He was responsible, for example, for hiring Diego Rivera and José Clemente Orozco to paint murals (alongside other artists) in the Escuela Nacional Preparatoria. There, Rivera painted *La Creación* (*The Creation*, 1922–1923), a work that expressed, among other things, Vasconcelos's philosophical interests in Pythagoras's sense of order. Orozco's murals primarily depicted scenes from the Mexican Revolution superimposed with Christian iconography intended to render them more legible to the largely Catholic and illiterate population.

For the headquarters of the Secretaría de Educación Pública, Vasconcelos wanted to represent the centrality of miscegenation to Latin American culture, an idea that he had been developing and that would eventually find its form in the 1925 publication of *La raza cósmica*. At the center of this was Vasconcelos's notion that, historically, all great works of art and periods of culture resulted from the mixture of various races. Latin America stood to benefit from the miscegenation effected by the Spanish Conquest and subsequent colonization and was poised to be at the center of a new "cosmic race"

derived from the mixture of all of the attributes of the great human races. The architecture of the SEP building represented this, in the first instance, through the combination of the pieces that made it up. The SEP headquarters occupied a structure that was originally a colonial courtyard building built in 1639 that had been used as a convent until the nineteenth century. Under Vasconcelos, it was modified and adapted to its new needs by the addition of a neoclassical façade designed by the engineer Federico Méndez Rivas and his team. The building also included murals, reliefs, and an extensive sculptural program to represent the foundational races for the cosmic race as well as a sculpture to express Vasconcelos's "law of the three states."

The use of a colonial building had inherent conditions that Vasconcelos valued. First of all, it was an expression of architectural syncretism, given that the Spanish architecture of the colonizer was transformed by the introduction of pre-Hispanic forms, references, and characteristics by the largely indigenous population that built it. This was something that the architects Federico Mariscal and Jesús Acevedo, Vasconcelos's contemporaries, had established as being quintessential to the formation of a unique and telluric Mexican architecture (see 1914 entry). Second, colonial architecture stood as an excellent model for an educational architecture, as it had been created to fulfill the needs of ideological dissemination required for colonization. Writing in 1926, Vasconcelos noted the relationship between this architecture and its pedagogic intentions, which emphasized the centrality of the arts, in both their production and their integration into the architectural environment:

The hours of the day . . . were used for work in the fields and in the construction of powerful works . . . In the evening or as of nightfall, the mission, which had been a beehive of manual labor during the day, would transform into a school: a school of religion, a school of language, a school of art—since drawing, music, and singing were taught. We can only imagine what those schools of labor and art were like.[1]

Third, the fact that colonial architecture was common throughout Mexico also made it recognizable by the population at large despite any programmatic adaptations (such as the integration of modern and secular educational functions) and material changes (including the use of reinforced concrete for its construction).

Reflecting this, the construction campaign undertaken by the SEP produced buildings that relied on the neocolonial style. Examples include Carlos Obregón Santacilia's Centro Educativo Benito Juárez (Mexico City, 1923–1925) and José Villagrán García's Estadio Nacional (1924). As part of Vasconcelos's international campaign to promote his ideas and the importance of the colonial style as expressive of Mexico, his building campaign also included the construction of the Mexican Pavilion for the 1922 International Exposition in Rio de Janeiro (designed by Obregón Santacilia and Carlos Tarditti), an event he attended as Mexico's emissary.[2]

In most cases, the neocolonial buildings commissioned for the SEP were built with reinforced concrete; used traditional local materials—such as the igneous *tezontle* stone—for many of the architectural details; had a strong decorative program that included murals, sculptures, or both; and offered large collective gathering spaces (similar to the courtyards of the SEP headquarters) that were used for public festivals and performances.

Perhaps the most enduring and prominent characteristic of the SEP headquarters, however, was the decorative program that included the painting of murals throughout the walls surrounding the courtyards, the stairway, and the minister's offices as well as sculptural reliefs in the corners of the courtyards and free-standing sculptures throughout the building (many of which were never realized as Vasconcelos had planned). For Vasconcelos, the task of the building's art was to educate as well as to engender in the user of the building an aesthetic experience characteristic of the "third state" of human development. The radicality of the use of public art (and, in particular, murals that realistically depicted the history, society, and characteristics of the Mexican people) lay in its ability to democratize the experience of art, to communicate to a larger audience (through its collective perception as well as in its accessibility by virtue of being in public buildings), and to educate (as the information is absorbed or perceived not through contemplation alone but through apperception, as the critic Walter Benjamin argued).[3]

Additionally, for the artists engaged in its production, art had an ideological function. In the *Manifesto of the Union of Mexican Workers, Technicians, Painters and Sculptors*, published in 1923, its signatories—David Alfaro Siqueiros, Diego Rivera, Xavier Guerrero, José Clemente Orozco, Germán Cueto, Carlos Mérida, and

others—highlighted the importance of art to the revolutionary project and the necessity of politicizing art. Like Vasconcelos, their call was for a monumental art that was "useful" by serving as "ideological propaganda for the people . . . something of beauty, education, and purpose for everyone."[4] The scale and public nature of muralism provided them with new models of artistic distribution and of collective reception. This emphasized art's pedagogical potential and, ultimately, its value as a tool for political change. In addition, by being placed within the public realm, this art became an affront to private art—works such as easel paintings that are individually produced, collected, and experienced—and could also transform the perception and understanding of the spaces in which they were located.

The subjects of some of the murals for the SEP expressed Vasconcelos's early philosophical concerns as well as his interest in Eastern philosophies and in the mixtures of races and traditions. Characteristic of these were the murals painted by Roberto Montenegro for the offices of the minister, assistant minister, and their waiting rooms. In other cases, the murals had direct educational intentions. The Guatemalan painter Carlos Mérida, for instance, painted *Caperucita Roja*, a mural in the children's library depicting the story of Little Red Riding Hood. While its nature was didactic (using both text and the images to convey the story), the paintings maintained an avant-gardist formal complexity as they compressed the space and time characteristics of the narrative into the two-dimensional plane.

The majority of the murals, however, were produced by Diego Rivera. Born in Guadalajara, Jalisco, in 1886, Rivera studied at the Academia de San Carlos in Mexico City before traveling to Europe and settling in Paris, where he became a prominent member of the European avant-garde. Although strongly influenced by and adept at cubism, Rivera became more influenced by the work of Paul Cézanne, which produced a shift in his work toward a more realist and legible pictorial tradition—a result also of his travels through Italy in 1920. Upon his return to Mexico, Rivera traveled throughout Mexico with Vasconcelos during his campaigns to promote the new federal education department. In bringing painters along, Vasconcelos hoped that they would not only document regional artisanal techniques that were disappearing because of modernization but also record Mexico's varying landscapes, types of labor, and peoples in order to later reproduce them within their works.

Interior courtyard of the Secretaría de Educación Pública, Mexico City, 1922.

In a speech inaugurating the SEP building, Vasconcelos's vision for Rivera's murals was limited to paintings of the regional dresses of every Mexican state and a mural decorating the staircase that represented the geographical characteristics of Mexico from the sea to the central region where Mexico City was located. Rivera's early production for the SEP, however, did not follow those ideas precisely but more broadly expressed the races, traditions, and labor characteristic of Mexico. In addition, as called for by the union's manifesto, he represented social injustices of the past and present. Although other painters were also part of Vasconcelos's vision and were hired by him, Rivera ultimately became responsible for the majority of the buildings' murals, in some cases, incorporating the work done by others into his own compositions, and in others, repainting them or erasing them completely.[5]

In addition to mural paintings, sculpture was used to depict Vasconcelos's ideas of racial miscegenation. In the "Court of the Races," Manuel Centurión sculpted for each corner allegorical reliefs of the four civilizations that have "most to contribute to the formation of Latin America": Quetzalcoatl, representing the Mexican culture; Plato, representing the culture of Greece; Buddha, representing Indian culture; and, Las Casas, representing Spain at the height of its

colonial power and as the initiator of a new culture.[6] Under these reliefs, the sculptor Ignacio Asúnsolo was to carve "four stone statues . . . representing the four great contemporary races . . . to indicate that America is home to all and needs all of them."[7] In the second courtyard, Centurión carved reliefs for the corners representing the branches of the plastic arts: sculpture, painting, music, and architecture.

Clearly, the first patio represented the primary racial and cultural components of the "cosmic race," and the second patio contained the aesthetic components of Vasconcelos's theories. The exaltation of these ideas through their architectural placement also suggests the importance they maintained, symbolically, in the formation of the cosmic race.

Finally, the synthesis of race, philosophy, and art was to be represented in two other sculptures for the building. The first was a sculpture, commissioned for Asúnsolo but unbuilt, to represent Vasconcelos's third state of humanity, based on his "law of the three states," and the developmental process for the cosmic race. The second was a triad of Apollo and Dionysius flanking Minerva that Vasconcelos considered

Mural by Cândido Portinari, Ministry of Education and Public Health (MESP) building, Rio de Janeiro, 1945.

symbolic of Mexican culture. Carved by Asúnsolo, it stands atop the main façade of the building. The central figure of Minerva allegorically represents ancient wisdom, the Hegelian will to Spirit, and Mexican culture itself. Apollo and Dionysius characterize, respectively, educational and artistic proposals.[8]

While debates ensued during the building's construction and following its completion about its exorbitant cost and its formal similarities to the works done under the Díaz dictatorship prior to the revolution, the SEP building and its art became paradigmatic of a new relationship and codependence between architecture and the plastic arts. While Vasconcelos's philosophies regarding art and its effects were esoteric, idealistic, and romantic, the aim of the SEP building to be legible by the masses reflected a more accessible educational and consciousness-raising campaign. The public and monumental character of the work and its didactic potential became of interest and extremely valued by artists and architectural patrons throughout Latin America, and, in a way, plastic integration became— and some argue, it still is—a de facto characteristic of its architecture. Examples include the murals by the

Brazilian artist Cândido Portinari for the interiors of the Ministry of Education and Public Health (MESP; Rio de Janeiro, 1936; see 1936 entry); *Ejercicio plástico* (1933), a work by David Alfaro Siqueiros, Antonio Berni, and others in Argentina; the National University in Mexico City (UNAM; see 1952 entry); and Mario Roberto Álvarez's Teatro San Martín (Buenos Aires, 1953–1961; see 1953 box), to name a few. While the politics of those associated with the muralist movement became a central concern in the discussions of plastic integration throughout the first half of the twentieth century, others argued for a more direct relationship between art and architecture. This was especially true as architectural forms became more abstracted and internationalized and used a more limited material and formal palette, as we see, for instance, in the work of Mario Pani and Carlos Mérida for the Multifamiliar Benito Juárez (Mexico City, 1947; see 1947 box) or the Ciudad Universitaria in Caracas, Venezuela (see 1952 entry).

FURTHER READING

Carranza, "If Walls Could Talk: José Vasconcelos' *Raza Cós-mica* and the Building for the Secretaría de Educación Pública," in *Architecture as Revolution.*
Vasconcelos, *The Cosmic Race/La raza cósmica.*

1923

MARIO PALANTI: PALACIO BAROLO AND PALACIO SALVO

MARIO PALANTI'S PALACIO BAROLO (1923) and Palacio Salvo (1928) are two of the earliest and most emblematic skyscrapers in South America. The first is located on the prominent Avenida de Mayo in Buenos Aires and in close proximity to the National Congress (Víctor Meano, 1914). The Palacio Salvo is also prominently located, on a corner of Montevideo's Plaza Independencia and the principal Avenida 19 de Julio. Both buildings are part of Palanti's larger interest in developing a new skyscraper variant for Latin America, a mystical scheme for uniting the Old and New World and creating "pillars of Hercules" for the South American continent.

Born in 1885, Palanti studied architecture at the Polytechnic of Milan. He moved to Argentina in 1909 to design and build the Italian Pavilion for the 1910 Exposición Internacional del Centenario, commemorating the independence of Argentina. During World War I, he returned to Italy in 1916 to serve as a volunteer in the armed forces. When he returned to Argentina in 1919, he developed an extensive practice working primarily for Italian immigrants,

Mario Palanti, Palacio Barolo, Buenos Aires, 1923.

Mario Palanti, Palacio Salvo, Montevideo, 1928.

such as Luis Barolo and the Salvo brothers, who had made their fortunes in South America. He remained in Argentina until 1929 when he permanently relocated to Italy.

The Palacio Barolo, begun in 1919, is the first of the two commissions. The building's structure is divided into three programmatic parts: a commercial passage on the ground level, offices in the building's lower volume, and the tower—also intended as offices—culminating in a lighthouse. Given existing height restrictions, a special variance was granted that allowed the building to be 100 m (328 ft.) tall, making it almost four times higher than allowable and taller than the existing urban fabric with the intention that it would frame and emphasize the dome of the Congress building. While the building's structure is modern through its construction with reinforced concrete, the decorative character can be described as a variant of Art Deco or late-nineteenth-century eclecticism: the passage uses Gothic-like vaults and ornamentation; the exterior façades and the dome of the tower have been attributed to Palanti's interest in Indian architecture such as the Palace of the Winds in Jaipur and the Raja-rani Temple in Orissa; the building's mass

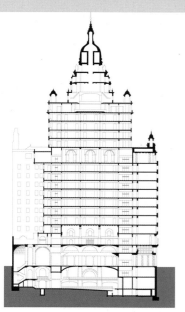

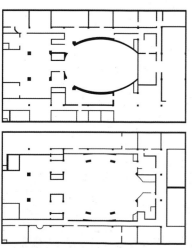

Section and plans of Palacio Salvo, Montevideo, 1928.

culminates in a mansard-like roof; and many of the decorative details are classical in nature.

The Palacio Barolo also had the mythical intention of becoming a modern-day temple to Dante and serving as the final resting place of Dante's remains. For this, the building is constructed in alignment with the Southern Cross constellation, referred to by Dante in the *Divine Comedy*, and based on the very structure of Dante's text itself. This includes its use of the golden section both in plan and elevation; its height of 100 m to relate it to the text's one hundred cantos; the subdivision of the building into fourteen floors in the base, seven floors for the tower, and one floor for the lighthouse that correspond to the twenty-two verses of each stanza; and the façade of each floor made up of eleven bays, corresponding to the number of stanzas in each canto. In addition, through its tripartite division, the basement and ground floor symbolize Hell—where the nine levels of Hell are represented not only in the nine vaults that make up the passage but also by texts from Dante's work inscribed on them; the building's lower section corresponds to Purgatory; and the upper portion, tower, and lighthouse stand for Heaven, whose light was represented by the beacon with 300,000 candelas of brightness that could be seen all the way over in Montevideo.

Like its Argentine counterpart, the Palacio Salvo was designed as an urban skyscraper. Originally intended to house commercial spaces, a hotel, and residential apartments, the building has a similar formal organization to the Palacio Barolo. Given its location, the ground level is composed of a commercial portico, which opens onto the plaza, and a lower mass from which a tower rises, marking the corner. Like the Palacio Barolo, this latter element brings the height of the Palacio Salvo to 100 m, making it the tallest structure in the Uruguayan capital. Instead of a lighted beacon, however, the Palacio Salvo culminates in a series of domes. The prominence and exceptionality of the Palacio Salvo can be seen in Le Corbusier's urban proposal for Montevideo (1929), where the profile of the urban fabric is suggested by Palanti's building at the end of the avenue that becomes the roadway leading to his "seascraper" (see 1929 entry).

1924

MARTÍN FIERRO PRESENTS ALBERTO PREBISCH AND ERNESTO
VAUTIER'S CIUDAD AZUCARERA EN TUCUMÁN AND FORMALIZES

ARGENTINA • BRAZIL • MEXICO

PUBLISHED IN 1925 in *Martín Fierro*, one of the most important avant-gardist journals of the period, "Cuidado con la arquitectura" (Careful with Architecture) was Oliverio Girondo's praise for the modern architecture of Alberto Prebisch and Ernesto Vautier.[1] As one of the journal's founders, the poet Girondo was an active participant—along with writers Jorge Luis Borges and Macedonio Fernández, painters Xul Solar and Norah Borges, the sculptor Emilio Pettoruti, and others—in the introduction to Buenos Aires of a new sensibility centered on modern aesthetics and formal innovations. In the 1924 *Martín Fierro* manifesto, they called for a culture rooted in Latin America (as

suggested by their journal's name) that integrated cultural and aesthetic developments from abroad.[2] And while the *Martín Fierro* group didn't engage in political issues as many contemporary avant-gardist groups did, its central aspirations had to do with a comprehensive renovation of culture that included architecture as part of that mission.

As a whole, *Martín Fierro* limited its architectural focus to the work, writings, and influences of Prebisch and Vautier. One year before Girondo's praise, images of their utopian proposal for a Ciudad Azucarera

Alberto Prebisch and Ernesto Vautier, Ciudad Azucarera Project, Tucumán, 1924.

THE CONNECTIONS AND INTERESTS IN ARCHITECTURE AMONG THE LITERARY AND ARTISTIC AVANT-GARDES.

(Sugar-Refining City) for Tucumán (1924) were published as an example of work shown at that year's Fine Arts Exhibition.[3] The design stands as an example of the authors' interests in the ideas of the modern movement (such as the development of urban theories to combat the chaos of the metropolis as well as investigations into the design of industrial cities) and in the valorization of technology and aesthetics (over social issues) to solve local problems. These fit precisely into *Martín Fierro*'s conception of culture. In addition, the Ciudad Azucarera followed and adapted contemporary European precedents that the two architects knew from their 1922–1924 trip to Europe.[4] Specifically, the strongest reference was to Tony Garnier's utopian *Cité Industrielle* (Industrial City), published in 1917. As Girondo noted in 1925, Prebisch and Vautier's architecture used new techniques and materials to find new solutions to contemporary architectural problems in contrast to an architecture that had become purely ornamental and out of touch with the times. In his typically hyperbolic style, and similar to Adolf Loos's "Ornament and Crime" (1908), Girondo condemned the architecture profession: "Prison or firing squad? In any case, aesthetics has little to do with either. In fact, architects fall into either the penal code or psychiatry." The solutions employed by Prebisch and Vautier, on the other hand, were derived from the experiences of the European masters (who, according to Girondo, are Adolf Loos, Auguste Perret, and Le Corbusier), followed a new organizational logic (the plan—and program—as the definer of the form), and had exterior façades that were like the "smooth and naked skin of a healthy and well proportioned skeleton."[5]

Martín Fierro's other publications on architecture were limited to projects and theoretical writings by Prebisch and Vautier—as members of the editorial staff—on the character and qualities of the new (modern) architecture. Besides the perspective and plan for the Ciudad Azucarera project, *Martín Fierro* published images of their proposal for a housing complex in Belgrano (these illustrate Girondo's essay) and their entry for a fine arts museum for La Plata.[6] Close to the theories of Le Corbusier, their writings emphasized the centrality of rationality, mathematics, and calculation to the aesthetic experience. They also underscored the importance of utility, economy, and natural (or mechanical) selection.[7] Many of their essays were illustrated with images of Le Corbusier's projects or taken from his books, which, in addition to the ideas expounded, served to criticize some contemporary Argentine architecture (such as Mario Palanti's Palacio Barolo [see 1923 box]). In keeping with these theories, the journal also published Le Corbusier's "The Aesthetic of the Engineer" chapter from *Vers une architecture* in May 1927.

Emblematic of the cultural avant-garde's interest and relationship with modern architecture, *Martín Fierro* published works by a limited group of architects and also helped disseminate important ideas and works of some European architects to a broader public. Prebisch's work continued to be marked by the influences of Le Corbusier, which can be seen, for instance, in his own house in Buenos Aires (1930) and his development of a rational expression of architecture at a grander scale that characterizes the Cine Gran Rex on Avenida Corrientes (1937; see 1937 box).

Victoria Ocampo is another emblematic figure of the Argentine cultural avant-garde who played a large role in the dissemination of modern architecture. Ocampo's interest in modern architecture can be seen in her own design for a summer house in Mar del Plata (1927), which followed modernist principles of volumetric simplicity and lack of ornamentation. She was also one of the first Argentines to commission Le Corbusier to design a house for her—a design (ca. 1927) that Le Corbusier adapted from his villa for Madame Meyer (1925)—and was central in inviting him to speak in Buenos Aires (see 1937 entry). Ocampo was, in fact, one of the people who greeted Le Corbusier upon his arrival in Argentina. In the end, her

AR

BR

MX

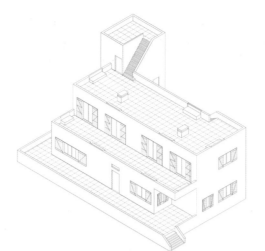

Victoria Ocampo, axonometric drawing of Villa Ocampo, Mar del Plata, 1927.

Alejandro Bustillo, interior of Villa Ocampo, Buenos Aires, 1928.

house in Buenos Aires—a more somber and classically inspired structure—was instead designed and built by Alejandro Bustillo in 1928. Ocampo's interest in architecture can be seen throughout *Sur*, the journal that she founded in 1931, which, like *Martín Fierro*, emphasized the importance of European and North American culture to Argentina.[8] In its first issue, for example, *Sur* (1931) published Walter Gropius's Total Theater project (1927).

In Mexico, the incorporation of architectural discussions into avant-gardist journals can also be found. This is the case, for instance, of David Alfaro Siqueiros's polemics regarding the new architecture being produced for José Vasconcelos's Secretaría de Educación Pública (see 1922 entry). Writing "En el orden burgués reinante, hay que buscar la causa de la decadencia arquitectónica contemporánea" (In the Ruling Bourgeois Order, We Must Find the Cause of Contemporary Architecture's Decadence) for *El Machete*, the publication of the Union of Revolutionary Painters and Artists, Siqueiros attacked architecture produced under the bourgeoisie as being not only ideologically suspect (i.e., reproducing class values) but also economically problematic (produced cheaply and quickly to increase profits). Like Girondo, Siqueiros denounced the simplistic copying from history and the reproduction of historical forms with new materials, both of which were characteristic of the new architecture. Siqueiros argued that instead of building solid and lasting architecture based on logic, solidity, and balance, architects were building an "arbitrary architecture" based on the ideology of the bourgeoisie. What was needed, instead, was to

demolish the ruling bourgeois order and the mercantilism that corrodes everything[. These have] made out of architecture the most ignoble means of exploitation . . . [By eliminating] that which is superfluous, improvised, hollow, and every piece of junk that has been invented by the rich to exploit the poor, [architecture] *will introduce the solid, the transcendental, the definitive, pure science, and the perfect manual labor.*[9]

In this way, architecture would serve the social goals of the Mexican Revolution. Siqueiros's call for architects and their state patrons to rely on the collaboration with technical specialists and on a rejection of the superficial qualities of building would become one of the earliest pronouncements regarding functionalist architecture in Mexico (see 1933 entry). Similar polemics regarding the new rationalist architecture can be found in other Mexican avant-gardist journals. *Horizonte* and *¡30-30!*, both led by members of the Estridentista avant-garde (see 1925-a box), not only addressed poetry, literature, and the plastic arts but also praised the new architecture. This is clear, for instance, in their support for the new reinforced concrete stadium in Jalapa, Veracruz (designed by Modesto Rolland in 1925). In both publications, the stadium was emblematic of a logical and modern architecture for the postrevolutionary society that contrasted with the stylistic decorative architecture of the past.[10]

A very different case and relationship with architecture is established in *Noigandres*, the journal of the Brazilian concrete poetry group of the same name founded in 1952. The journal, as the principal outlet for its members' poetic experimentations, published their manifesto "Plano piloto para poesía concreta" (Pilot Plan for Concrete Poetry) in issue number 4 (1958). For its authors, Augusto de Campos, Décio Pignatari, and Haroldo de Campos, the leading figures of the movement, the new (concrete) poetry stood in direct relationship to Lúcio Costa's Plano Piloto (Master Plan) for Brasília and the development of the new capital (see 1956 entry), which Haroldo de Campos called "an epistemological metaphor for the capacity for innovation of the Brazilian artist."[11] In their manifesto, the poets not only defined the character and quality of their poems (i.e., the directness of language and its visuality) but also, in a quasi-architectural or functionalist manner, the poems' necessity and use-value: "Concrete Poetry . . . To create precise problems and to solve them in terms of sensible language . . . The poem-product: useful object."[12] Later, its authors would crystallize the link between poetry and the architectural developments occurring in Brazil with regard to the new capital: ". . . our country, which has just given the world a highly significant example of construction, . . . more perhaps than any other, offers the conditions for the production and consumption of art that is truly contemporary, because, as aesthetic information, it is commensurate with today's man."[13] For Pignatari, in "Construir e expressar" (Building and Expressing; 1959), this had political implications, since the modern worker who deals with machines is taught by them a new sense of order and rationality that underscores the irrationality of capitalist relations of production: the worker "constructs buildings out of *rayban* glass and knows that he will never be able to fly in them."[14] Poetry, in the end, needed to teach the reader to act and think in the same rational way modern architecture, urbanism, and machines were structured.

The Argentine *Perceptismo: Teórico y Polémico* magazine, through its discussions on painting, also addressed the importance of architecture. Perceptism, a movement developed in the early 1950s by Raúl Lozza (an artist originally associated with the Argentine Arte Concreto-Invención group), was extremely interested in the architectural surface as a color field or plane onto which paintings were placed. The wall, in other words, was to be considered part of the painting and the perception of the painting itself. Abraham Haber, an art critic who supported the group, characterized this role in his "Pintura y arquitectura" (Painting and Architecture). In discussing the work of the Dutch painter Piet Mondrian, Haber addresses Mondrian's interest in plastic integration, the universalist aspiration of the work of art, and the eventual elimination of the distinction between architecture and art in favor of their dematerialization into a "new unity." Haber is critical of this and, through his criticism, enunciates the principal tenets of perceptism and architecture's role within it: "The synthesis between architecture and painting takes place in perceptism through the consideration of the wall, as the determining limit of the architectural space, which does not disappear nor which is incompatible with the pictorial plane but rather it serves as its background."[15] As with other avant-gardist journals, *Perceptismo: Teórico y Polémico* considered the role of architecture in the transformation of the understanding of culture. By using architecture's public condition, these avant-gardist groups challenged the autonomy of art within the praxis of everyday life and, thus, instituted a newer, broader vocation for their aesthetic and cultural experimentations.

FURTHER READING

Alberto Prebisch: Una vanguardia con tradición.
Perrone, *Seven Faces.*
Ramírez and Olea, *Inverted Utopias.*
Solt, *Concrete Poetry.*

1925

MODERN ARCHITECTURE BEGINS WITH GREGORI WARCHAVCHIK AND RINO LEVI PUBLISHING MANIFESTOS ON THE NEW ARCHITECTURE; CATCHING UP TO THE 1922 SEMANA DE ARTE MODERNA.

BRAZIL

Tupi or not Tupi: that is the question.

OSWALD DE ANDRADE (1928)

OSWALD DE ANDRADE's seminal question from his 1928 *Manifesto Antropófago* (Cannibal Manifesto) summarizes the Brazilian intellectual moment of the 1920s: simultaneously embracing local traditions (the Tupi being the indigenous group of southeastern Brazil) and international culture in a critical manner that questioned both in a format that was shockingly new.

Coincidentally organized around the centennial of Brazilian independence, the Semana de Arte Moderna (February 11–18, 1922) was a type of manifesto exhibition that brought together cubists, fauvists, and futurists and gave Brazilian avant-gardists their first widespread publicity in newspapers and radio. It consisted of one week of lectures; poetry readings; musical recitals; and painting, sculpture, and drawing exhibitions. Architecture was represented by drawings of Antonio García Moya (Spanish) and Georg Przyrembel (Polish). Both showed sketches of neocolonial or indigenous motifs in tune with the overall theme of rediscovering Brazilian identities, but these were completely out of tune with international currents. These two architects and their works were so forgotten that most texts on early Brazilian modernism state that architecture was "absent" from this paradigmatic event—a construction that reveals how much Brazilian modernists would later be successful in writing their own history.

Although the traditional historiography portrays the Semana as the mythical beginning of modernism in Brazil, the gears had already been set in motion. Since the second decade of the 1900s, the work of young writers Paulo Menotti del Picchia and Oswald de Andrade started to generate interest in São Paulo. Andrade published a tabloid called *O Pirralho* (1911–1917), a literary review with a strong satirical tone. Del Picchia's early works such as *Juca Mulato* (1917) are not so vanguardist in form but already Brazilian in content. These authors were basically using nineteenth-century frameworks such as expressionism and naturalism to explore Brazilian identity in their characters and landscape descriptions. Explorations on Brazilianism were being pursued since the turn of the century and are present in Euclides da Cunha's *Os sertões* and Graça Aranha's *Canaã*, both from 1902, and Monteiro Lobato's *Urupês* from 1918. The radical novelty of the Semana de Arte Moderna was in the formal, linguistic, compositional, and artistic experimentations it showcased, an issue that would place Graça Aranha and Monteiro Lobato in opposing camps of the intellectual debate despite their agreement on the need to focus on Brazilian issues.

The spark that ignited this debate and, as a result, the Semana de Arte Moderna, was Lobato's reaction to Anita Malfatti's 1917 painting exhibition in São Paulo. The twenty-eight-year-old Malfatti had returned from New York in 1915 and was exhibiting for the first time in her native Brazil. Paintings such as *A boba* (1915–1916) were radical in content (portraying a mentally ill woman) and form (wide brushstrokes of primary colors, angular distortions). They were also expressive of her contact with German expressionism and French fauvism. Already an established cultural critic and journalist, Lobato wrote an aggressive newspaper review calling her canvases "a mystification of paranoia." Enraged by such reactionary comments, many young intellectuals—Oswald de Andrade, Menotti del Picchia, Graça Aranha, and Mário de Andrade among them—came to the defense of Malfatti. The arguments, in print or in cafés, that followed would bring them together in planning the Semana four years later. Polemics apart, Brazilian avant-gardist artists gradually turned to the issue of adapting the avant-garde to Brazilian reality and to Brazilianness.

Furthermore, the experience of such "modernisms" in Brazil was restricted to a very small part of the population, and the modernization that should have preceded it was clearly deficient. Such modern and at the same time premodern society provided the paradoxical framework within which European avant-gardist currents arrived in the first decades of the twentieth century. Nestor García Canclini reminds us that "the elite cultivates vanguard poetry and art, while most of the population is illiterate. Modernity, then, is seen as a mask. A simulacrum conjured up by the elite and the state apparatuses, above all those concerned with art and culture, but which for that very reason makes them unrepresentative and unrealistic."[1] Although we do not completely agree with García Canclini because he implies that there is only one path for (European) modernization, the paradox he describes is fundamental for us to understand Latin American modernism more generally and Brazilian modernism specifically. The first phase of Latin American modernism was promoted by artists and writers, primarily from the elite, who were returning to their countries after living, studying, and working in Europe for some time. It was not so much the directly transplanted influence of the European that gave rise to the modernizing vein in the visual arts on the continent, but rather the questions that Latin Americans posed to themselves on how to make their international experience compatible with the tasks presented to them by their own (developing) societies. Here, the search for (or construction of) Brazilianness was already going on, but the attitude of bold experimentation and formal exploration was radically new.

The paintings of Tarsila do Amaral are characteristic of those issues. In her early works, the influence of her studies with Fernand Léger in Paris between 1922 and 1923 is unquestionable. By the early 1920s, she was painting the Brazilian context: *A negra* (The Negress; 1923), *São Paulo* (1924), and *Morro da favela* (Hill of the Favela; 1924). The search for (or construction of) a Brazilianness continued to evolve in the late 1920s as she moved further toward abstractionism. Both *Abaporu* (1928) and *Antropofagia* (1929) attempt to resolve the apparently opposing forces of abstract internationalism and the representation of local identities and cultures within the works of art. Influenced by Andrade's manifesto's idea of cultural cannibalism, Amaral was free to depict Brazilianness in the form of a human being with large hands and feet, under a scalding sun, and in front of a cactus. The word *abaporu* comes from the Tupi language and means "men who eat men," a metaphor for cannibalism. At the same time, the bodies are represented as flat and abstract; in some cases, the forms and modeling are geometric and mechanistic (in a manner derived from Léger) and the color palette is simplified and limited (similar to that of Purist paintings).

It is worth noting that in the search for Brazilianness, the avant-gardists of the Semana discarded forms of modernism that were not aligned with their ideas. Instead, as they wrote then or decades later, they constructed their own continuities, their own roots. At that time, many different projects came to coexist simultaneously as different groups promoted different ideas of modernism. Monteiro Lobato and Plínio Salgado, for instance, led other modern movements: the former identified with nationalism, and the latter closely associated with Italian fascism. In the 1920s, there were many competing modernisms in Brazil. By the end of the 1930s, however, one would prevail over all others.

This plurality was still very much present in 1925 when architecture caught up with the artistic avant-garde. Two articles appeared in São Paulo's newspapers in November of that year that mark the starting point of modernism's debate in architecture: Rino Levi's "A arquitetura e a estética das cidades" (Architecture and the Aesthetics of the City) and Gregori Warchavchik's "Acerca da arquitetura moderna" (About Modern Architecture).

Warchavchik deserves the credit for being the first to write about modern architecture in Brazil because his article was first published on June 14 in *Il Piccolo*, a weekly news bulletin of the immigrant Italian population in São Paulo. Later translated to Portuguese, it was published in Rio de Janeiro's *Correio da Manhã* on November 1. Born and trained in Odessa and later studying in Rome, Warchavchik worked for Marcello Piacentini for two years before moving to Brazil in 1923. Titled "Futurismo," the Italian version of his article aspired to have a clear connection to Filippo Marinetti's and Antonio Sant'Elia's manifestos, surely known to the Italo-Brazilian community. For Warchavchik, "Our architecture must only be rational . . . based only on logic . . . [it must be] comfortable and cheap as possible . . . the beauty . . . must come from rationality . . . [it must be built] using as the basis the building material that is available."[2] The article, however, does not carry the radical futurist stance against the past and, instead, is much more aligned with Le Corbusier's machine aesthetic. The beauty of a façade, according to Warchavchik, should result from its function, just as the form of the machine is determined by its mechanism. Ultimately, he argued, architects should not think about style but be "slaves to the spirit of their times."

Son of Italian immigrants, Rino Levi was born in São Paulo in 1901. Levi had been living in Rome since December 1921 and was attending the Scuola Superiore di Architettura when he sent an editorial letter to the *Estado de São Paulo* newspaper. Published on October 15, 1925, his text defines the main concern of modern architecture to be aesthetic with little space given for technical matters. Levi defends "simple lines with

few sincere decorative elements with enough significance but not in a way that overwhelms the structure." Ultimately, the focus of the article is on the morphology of the city, on the relationships with the surrounding context, and on lines of vision. The influence of the ideas of the Viennese architect Camillo Sitte is clear. Levi, however, mentions Piacentini as the main authority of this nascent discipline of "city aesthetics." More important for the local scene is Levi's last paragraph. Here, he argues that due to Brazil's climate and traditions, Brazilian cities should be different from European ones: "[The Brazilian] flora, light and color could give their cities a unique vivacity and grace." This is a remarkable coincidence with the ideas expressed at the Semana de Arte Moderna despite the fact that Levi did not attend, as he had left for Rome two months before the event.

Levi and Warchavchik's paths would soon cross in an interesting set of encounters and divergences. Levi came back to São Paulo in 1926, and his first job, coincidentally, was to replace Warchavchik at Santos Building Company, since the Russian-born architect had left to build the iconic Casas Modernistas at Rua Santa Cruz (1927) and Rua Itápolis (1929). The house at Rua Santa Cruz was designed for himself and his wife, Mina Klabin. The house is a cubic volume with a symmetrical, white, plain façade reminiscent of the work of Adolf Loos. The plan, however, speaks of the paradoxical character of the place, as it erodes in the rear to create an open loggia that is covered with clay

Gregori Warchavchik, House at Rua Santa Cruz, São Paulo, 1927.

roof tiles and, in this way, responds to local climatic and material conditions. Two years later, Warchavchik built the house at Rua Itápolis and opened it up with an exhibition in March/April 1930. At Rua Itápolis, the plan is more compact, but unlike Rua Santa Cruz, the fenestration and passages are treated as cuts in the volume, and two main open slabs articulate interior and exterior spaces. The gardens of both houses were designed by Klabin (see 1965 entry) and use native vegetation in what might be described as the beginning of the Brazilian tropical garden movement, where she used cactus several years before Juan O'Gorman did at the Diego Rivera and Frida Kahlo house and studio (see 1931 box) and before Burle Marx did in Recife.

In the 1930s, Warchavchik played an important yet brief role as Lúcio Costa's partner. He also served as the first Latin American delegate to the Congrès International d'Architecture Moderne (CIAM; International Congress of Modern Architecture), having been invited by Le Corbusier himself during his first visit to Brazil in 1929 (see 1929 entry).[3]

Warchavchik's career would fade from the spotlight in the 1940s, at the same time that Rino Levi was becoming the leading modernist architect in São Paulo by designing important buildings like the headquarters of the Brazilian Institute of Architects (IAB, 1947) and the Olivio Gomes residence (1949/1951). Interestingly enough, Levi, whose text of 1925 was not so concerned with structural or technical aspects, is now recognized for his elegant balance of modern spatiality and savvy tectonics. Warchavchik, at that time so concerned with functionality and machine efficiency, molded doorknobs in cast iron to "look like" folded tubes of the Bauhaus designs. All of it is very much part of the spirit of those Brazilian times. Or as de Andrade wrote in the opening lines of his 1928 manifesto: "Only anthropophagy unites us. Socially. Economically. Philosophically . . . I am only interested in what is not mine."[4]

As pioneers of modern architecture in Brazil, both Levi and Warchavchik were struggling to materialize in São Paulo an architecture inspired by the European avant-garde and at the same time adapted to the local building culture. The concept of cultural cannibalism as articulated by Andrade gave them the liberty to choose which elements to challenge and which elements to rescue from local traditions. Theory here was used to support what they already wanted to build (and many times did not have the means or materials to do so), not so much to guide spatial explorations. The

Rino Levi and team, IAB building, São Paulo, 1947.

Plan of House at Rua Santa Cruz.

same might hold true for Lúcio Costa, Oscar Niemeyer, Affonso Reidy, and others ten years later (see 1930 and 1936 entries). Undoubtedly, intellectuals gathered around and, in response to the Semana de Arte Moderna, did manage to dislocate the conversation by proposing a new way to look at what is Brazilian.

FURTHER READING

Amaral, *Artes plásticas na Semana de 22.*
Anelli, Guerra, and Kon, *Rino Levi.*
Lira, *Warchavchik: Fraturas da vanguarda.*
Schwartz, *Brasil 1920–1950.*

1925-A

ESTRIDENTÓPOLIS EN 1975: LITERARY ARCHITECTURE AND THE AVANT-GARDE

IN 1925, THE MEXICAN ARTIST Germán Cueto created Estridentópolis, an image of a city fifty years in the future, and the locus of the Estridentistas (literally translated as the Stridentists), the Mexican avant-gardist group that inspired it. The 1975 city that Cueto depicts is an expression of the preoccupations actively promoted by the group: the transformation of European avant-gardist ideas as they affected and inspired the Mexican context. For the Estridentistas, this translated into falsifying (a term they preferred over *inventing*) a new reality—the modern city—and generating a perceptual mechanism through which one could

Germán Cueto, *Estridentópolis en 1975*, 1925.

read the existing conditions and enact social change. The need to relate art to the praxis of life, characteristic of the historical avant-garde, was part of that mission; after all, the Estridentistas were primarily a literary group that emerged after the Mexican Revolution, and they were intent on using plastic and literary art to continue the social revolution inaugurated by it. One of the group's goals was, therefore, to defamiliarize or denaturalize the world through artistic production in order to allow people to look at both critically.

Estridentópolis en 1975 (*Estridentópolis in 1975*) responds to the main principles articulated by Manuel Maples Arce, the founder and leader of the group, in *Actual #1* (1921), the group's first manifesto. First, as an image of the modern city, it expressed an interest in technology and speed that was central to the Italian Futurists, whom Maples Arce acknowledged as an important reference. It also addressed the need to create anew, which was characteristic of the poetic principles of Creacionismo, a literary movement developed by the Chilean poet Vicente Huidobro. Maples Arce referenced it because it promoted not only the role of poetic metaphors in combining disparate linguistic elements to create new ideas but also the role of rational and constructive principles of modern technology to develop the new without copying from nature or the past. Although part of Maples Arce's manifesto integrated different perspectives of various avant-gardist groups, Estridentismo ultimately promoted itself as outside of those official movements by self-marginalizing itself through the unconventional use of the other groups' ideas and by choosing their ideas and combining them with Estridentista principles while taking into account the Mexican

cultural environment. So, while the image presented by Cueto is of a modern city as he imagined it in fifty years, it presents the city as something that might already exist. After all, the Estridentistas called for an art that was of the present while simultaneously rejecting both the past—through attacks on tradition and on conservative and reactionary critics—and an idealized future. *Estridentópolis in 1975*'s peculiarity lies in the fact that Cueto, a nonarchitect, accurately predicts the morphological development of cities in the second half of the twentieth century. Yet, despite his lack of architectural training, its form never materialized into the romantic utopias of European or North American architects. Cueto's image of that modern city in the future is more representative of the group's cosmopolitanism and, as such, dismisses utopian and unrealistic aspirations without basis in the present, such as those of futurist architect Antonio Sant'Elia. *Estridentópolis in 1975* ultimately reflects Maples Arce's manifesto and other Estridentista texts, as it accentuated and articulated the present through the glorification of the effects of modernity, metropolitan life, and technology.

In the context of a burgeoning postrevolutionary Mexican avant-garde, the ideas of Estridentismo ultimately served in the reconceptualization of visuality wherein the traditional object of contemplation is placed under a modern/metropolitan lens and thus radicalized. Traditions would mix with technology to create the new. In this way, Estridentista art could address the Estridentistas present reality, context, and audience and propose the transformation of society. Estridentópolis, with its mixture of artistic and literary ideas, responded to the Estridentistas' vision of modern life and social change.

1928

THE COLUMBUS MEMORIAL LIGHTHOUSE COMPETITION SPARKS AN INVESTIGATION INTO WHAT ARCHITECTURE FOR LATIN AMERICA SHOULD BE LIKE.

CARIBBEAN: DOMINICAN REPUBLIC

DESPITE ITS MANY IRONIES and its ultimate failure, the Columbus Lighthouse project is a very good metaphor for the challenges and (missed) opportunities of Pan-Americanism, or the search for common denominators between North and South American societies.

The idea of Pan-America is not new. It started in the early 1800s when liberators Simón Bolívar and José de San Martín attempted to create a union of newly independent Latin American nations. Soon after that, the economic rise of the United States established the opportunity for the development of a protectionist sensibility, the Monroe Doctrine, through which the United States pledged to keep the Americas free of colonialism, which also meant under its own (exclusive) influence. In 1889, the First International Congress of American States meeting took place in Washington, DC, with eighteen members founding the International Union of American Republics. This institution would change its name to Pan-American Union in 1910 and to the Organization of American States (OAS) in 1948.

The first two decades of the twentieth century saw plenty of activity around the idea of Pan-Americanism, which resulted in the creation of two important structures. The first was the Pan-American Union building in Washington, DC (1908–1910), designed by the American architect Albert Kelsey and the French-born architect Paul Philippe Cret. Resulting from a U.S.-only competition in 1907 and built by U.S. architects, the international institution elicited protests from its Latin American delegates; it showed how much the Pan-American Union was the result of regional asymmetry as the United States placed itself as the leading nation with all Latin American nations following it. John Barrett, director at the time of the Pan-American Union, described the building as a "monument with the intention to give visible expression to the ideas of unity, of solidarity, of amity that found realization in the Union of American Republics . . . This is not only a palace, but the spiritual home of the citizens

of the twenty-one American republics."[1] However, the combination of Spanish colonial architecture punctuated with carvings of exotic plants and animals does speak to a patronizing view of Latin America. All that is modern in the building is associated with the United States, while all that is not modern is associated with its southern neighbors.

To counterbalance this stormy beginning (and to make financial contributions from the Latin American members more palatable), the Pan-American Union decided to hold a more international competition for a monument and lighthouse dedicated to Christopher Columbus in the Dominican Republic, the site of his first arrival in the Americas according to some.

Organized by Albert Kelsey, who was then serving as the main advisor to the Pan-American Union, a competition was held for a design to occupy an empty site selected by Kelsey in East Santo Domingo, an area across from Río de la Ozama. The idea of a lighthouse as a monument to Columbus was not new. It had been proposed earlier by Antonio del Monte y Tejada, a Dominican historian, in his *Historia de Santo Domingo* (1852). Kelsey was so influenced by del Monte's narrative that he reprinted long excerpts of it in the competition brief. For Kelsey, the lighthouse referred to navigation and sailors but also stood as a metaphor for knowledge and enlightenment. To make it more contemporary, an airstrip was added to the program, an idea endorsed by the Dominican government in hopes that it could become an aviation hub connecting the Americas as well as boost the prospects of international tourism to the island.

Launched on January 1, 1928, with a worldwide distribution of five thousand brochures in English, Spanish, and French, the brief called for a two-stage competition: the first part focused more on the ideas. From this stage, several projects were to be selected for further development before being presented, as the second stage of the competition, to another jury. Responding to critics of the Pan-American Union building, Kelsey worked assiduously to emphasize that the Latin American character of the Columbus lighthouse should be expressed in the submitted designs. In the brief, he included his personal impressions of Santo Domingo, describing local behaviors while at the same time trying to sell the city as a modern and evolving society. Kelsey even went on tour throughout Latin America that year in an attempt to boost the participation of local architects as both competitors and jurors. Latin American architects, however, were so unknown in the United States that he had trouble selecting a single one to sit on the jury. In addition, many of the leading architects at the time complained that the two-stage process did nothing to protect their authorship—competitors were encouraged to modify their designs between the two stages, opening the potential for their ideas to be incorporated—and decided not to participate. Nevertheless, the competition was a success with 1,970 registrations and 455 submissions, a world record at the time and almost twice as many as for the iconic Chicago Tribune competition of 1922. Despite Kelsey's efforts, however, only 39 of the submissions were from Latin America.

The judging of the first stage took place in Madrid in March 1929, just weeks before the opening in May of the Ibero-American Exposition in Seville (see 1929-a entry) and the Barcelona International Exhibition. Three architects were selected for the jury: Raymond Hood (representing the United States), Eliel Saarinen (representing Europe, prompting some protests because he had been living in the United States for five years), and Horacio Acosta y Lara from Uruguay (representing Latin America). According to historian Robert González, Kelsey's diary entries describe the meetings as a diplomatic exercise as much as a jury session.[2] Hundreds of entries were discarded in the first two days, and Kelsey noted that Acosta y Lara was very quiet, leaving Saarinen and Hood free to exercise their preferences. Almost all modern entries were discarded, among them many

Columbus Lighthouse Competition entry by Konstantin Melnikov, 1928

from celebrated architects such as Alvar Aalto, Tony Garnier, and Konstantin Melnikov. Melnikov's entry had a double-helix intended to interact with the elements, rotating with the wind and with the pressure of accumulated rainwater. Aalto also used a helix, but in his design, it elegantly spiraled around a simple cylinder. Tony Garnier's reinforced concrete tower held a spiral ramp moving upward and was formally and structurally reminiscent of the central clock tower of

seen from a distance of 160 m, from a height
of 2 m. above the black disc level, and making
an angle of 57° with the front face of the monument

1:20

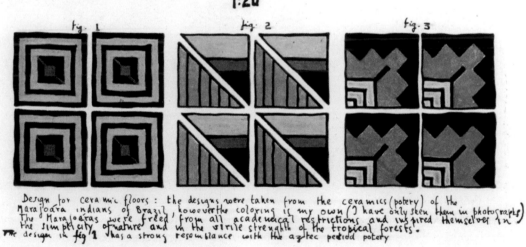

fig. 1   fig. 2   fig. 3

Design for ceramic floors: the designs were taken from the ceramics (potery) of the
Marajoara indians of Brazil, however the coloring is my own (I have only seen them in photographs)
The Marajoáras were freed from all academical restrictions and inspired themselves in
the simplicity of nature and in the virile strength of the tropical forests.
The design in fig 1 has a strong resemblance with the aztec period potery

Columbus Lighthouse Competition entry by
Flávio de Carvalho, 1928

his *Cité Industrielle* (1917). Among the Latin American entries, important ones included the Brazilian Flávio de Carvalho's entry (see 1930 box), which fused a Futurist-inspired lighthouse tower with a massive base reminiscent of pre-Hispanic forms and surrounded by neocolonial arcades. The interior, which caught Kelsey's attention, was to be decorated with Carvalho's abstract interpretation of Marajoara Indian motifs (much like Kelsey's own work at the Pan-American Union building in Washington). Also important was the entry of the Mexican architect Carlos Obregón Santacilia, whose streamlined modernist tower had a sculptural relief decoration at its base depicting ships.

Ten entries were selected to move on to the second phase: six European and four from the United States. The absence of any Latin American entries worried Kelsey, but that would shortly be the least of his worries.

In February 1930, a rebellion broke out in the Dominican Republic, and army chief Rafael Trujillo, instead of fighting to defend the elected government, supported the rebellion. In exchange for his support, Trujillo was elected president three months later with 95 percent of the vote, a number only achievable through massive fraud. Trujillo decided to continue with the Columbus lighthouse project, but the corruption within his government made it harder for the United States and other Latin American nations to continue supporting and funding the endeavor.

Despite the political troubles, the competition continued its course, and the ten selected entries were shipped to Rio de Janeiro in 1931 for the final jury deliberations. This time, Raymond Hood declined to participate as a juror, and as a result, Frank Lloyd Wright was called in to substitute for him. Wright's participation brought significant change to the jury dynamics. He made it very clear that he favored a more modernist scheme, making that point in public several times. In addition to this, Wright lectured at the School of Architecture of the Escola Nacional de Belas Artes in support of modernism and of Lúcio Costa's curricular reform (see 1930-a entry). This was a big boost to architecture students in Rio de Janeiro who were on strike protesting the removal of Lúcio Costa from the school's deanship. Because of Wright's prominence and support of the student movement and of Costa, Brazilian newspapers reported the local debate and quoted Wright extensively.

In the jury room, Joseph Lea Gleave's entry was crowned the winner. Gleave, a student in Great Britain when he was selected in the first stage in 1929, reworked his cross-shaped monument to become a more modernist and streamlined composition. The overall volume is an extruded cross, its arms reaching out to the airstrip on one side, the city on another, and the ocean in front. Light sources shooting up from the monument project another cross on the sky, visible from miles away. At ground level, one can enter the monument from all four arms of the cross into canyon-like spaces. If the cross shape of the building was not enough of a metaphor for Christianity, the tall and narrow interior spaces illuminated from above make it resemble a cathedral, giving the interior of the monument a mystical ambience. In Gleave's initial design, the extent to which any Latin American "features" can be perceived is questionable. The jury, in both phases, did not seem too inclined to follow Kelsey's personal readings of Latin America. The final entry, however, does resemble a pre-Columbian temple with its stepped walls and base, neo-Maya abstracted decorative motifs, and altar (light source) at its top. Because of the literalness of its shape as a cross and its canyon-like interior as expressions of Pan-Americanism, the metaphoric qualities about enlightenment that Kelsey expected were not there.

Interestingly enough, although the official Pan-American project was on the side of Christianization, local inhabitants of Hispaniola have always talked about a Columbus curse, or *fucu*. Trujillo's excesses prompted the U.S. government to keep its distance from his initiatives. And while the Dominican dictator

Columbus Lighthouse Competition entry by Donald Nelson and Edgar Lynch, 1928

Joseph Lea Gleave, Columbus Lighthouse,
Santo Domingo, 1992

laid the cornerstone of the monument in 1944, nothing else was done for decades: Kelsey died in 1950, Trujillo was assassinated in 1961, and Gleave died in 1965. The idea of Pan-Americanism faded during the Cold War as a result of both U.S. interventionism and Latin American governments fearing annexation every time there were talks of integration.

The story of the monument continues, however. In the late 1980s, the Dominican government under Joaquín Belaguer revived the project in preparation for a five-hundred-year celebration of Columbus's arrival, and the monument was finally inaugurated on October 6, 1992, mostly as designed by Gleave. Its initial meaning and intention, however, had been lost forever. All invited chiefs of state declined to attend the ceremony, and the whole idea of celebrating Pan-Americanism focused around Columbus was now seen as part of a long

history of oppression. Furthermore, the monument's "Wall of Fame" was now labeled the "Wall of Shame" by indigenous communities and Afro-descendants.

Despite all its potential and all the effort to build it, the Columbus Lighthouse became not much more than a sad footnote in the history of twentieth-century architecture in Latin America.

FURTHER READING

"El Concurso del Faro de Colón."
González, *Designing Pan-America*.
Irigoyen, "Frank Lloyd Wright in Brazil."
"The Pan-American Union Monument Competition."

THE IBERO-AMERICAN EXHIBITION OPENS IN SEVILLE,
REVEALING THE COMPLEX AND CONTRADICTORY RELATIONS
BETWEEN SPAIN AND ITS FORMER AMERICAN COLONIES.

MEXICO

THE 1929 IBERO-AMERICAN Exposition in Seville, along with the International Exposition in Barcelona, was intended to highlight Spain's international importance. The Seville exposition, more particularly, was organized to create stronger ties between Spain and its former colonies on the American continent. In the exhibition's official brochure, Spain's colonizing role was emphasized:

Seville, center of centuries of Spanish culture, has invited Portugal and the countries of North and South America, which owe their birth to the intrepid spirit of Spain's early maritime adventurers, to come and congratulate with the *Mother of Nations* the progress made in their history, their art, and their cultural advancement.[1]

While this suggested that the invited American countries were subject to the politics of cultural debt for Spain's discovery and colonizing mission, it also insinuated the lack of culture before the conquest. Thus, the exhibition and the planning of the fairgrounds reflected these characteristics and political prejudices.

The layout of the Parque de María Luisa, begun initially in 1914 by the French landscape architect Jean-Claude Nicolas Forestier, followed traditional exhibition design conventions. In Seville, the principal area was reserved for the hosting country: the Plaza de España. In contrast, the Plaza de América, placed at the edge of the fairground and on a secondary axis blocked by the Spanish Palace of Antique Art, was given lesser stature. Although the exposition's name suggested an egalitarian, or at least proportional, relation between Spain and the American countries that participated, this was not formally expressed.

Architecturally, the Plaza de América—which did not contain any pavilions from the American countries—was flanked by the Royal Pavilion (built in the Gothic style), the Palace of Antique Art (built in the Mudéjar style), and the Renaissance Palace (built in the Plateresque style); none of these represented the continent stylistically, programmatically, or architecturally. Instead, the American pavilions were relegated to the edges of the Parque de María Luisa. The designs of most of these were based on or influenced by Spanish colonial architecture. The United States pavilion by the San Diego architect William Templeton Johnson, for example, was designed in the California Mission style; the Cuban pavilion was a replica of a colonial house in Havana; the pavilion of Uruguay, designed by Mauricio Cravotto, was based on the nationalist aesthetic theories of Alberto Zum Felde; the Argentine pavilion by Martín Noel was based on his personal observations of the syncretic nature of South American colonial architecture and showed characteristics of the colonial architecture of Peru (see 1914 entry). As part of the colonial style, we can also include a number of hybrid buildings that, to a more attenuated extent than Noel's design, showed the fusion of the Spanish and pre-Hispanic cultures: the pavilion of Peru, designed by the Peruvian architect Manuel Piqueras, used sculptural

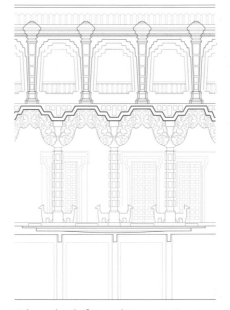

Column detail of Manuel Piqueras's Peruvian pavilion, Seville, 1929.

MX

and structural elements that evoked Incan architecture (this is most evident in the interior courtyard), as did the Chilean pavilion by Juan Martínez Gutiérrez. Likewise, the pavilion of Colombia, although designed in the colonial style by the Seville architect José Granados de la Vega, had a sculptural program by the Colombian artist Rómulo Rozo that evoked pre-Hispanic culture. Out of the twelve American pavilions at the exposition, only two were designed using pre-Hispanic forms or motifs: the pavilion of Guatemala, designed by the Spanish architect José Granados de la Vega, whose tile exteriors by the Sevillian artist Ramos Rejano depicted quetzales and Maya stelae, and the Mexican pavilion by Manuel Amábilis, a Mexican architect from Yucatán.

Historically, pre-Hispanic architecture was used to represent Mexico (and, to a certain extent, Latin America in general) in international expositions. For the Exposition Universelle in Paris of 1867, the French archaeologist Désiré Charnay designed the Mexican pavilion as an eclectic and inaccurate replica of the Temple of Quetzalcóatl at Xochicalco.[2] A similar archaeological representation of Mexico, including exhibits and plaster-cast reconstructions of Maya structures, was manufactured for Chicago's World's Columbian Exposition of 1893. For the Parisian Exposition Universelle of 1889, the Mexican architect Antonio M. Anza and archaeologist Antonio Peñafiel designed an eclectically and controversially derived pre-Hispanic style for the exterior façade of the Mexican pavilion. Its interior, however, reflected a more modern expression of Mexico through the use of iron staircases and interior columns, glass skylights, and marble ornaments typical of the time.[3]

Throughout Latin America, the use of pre-Hispanic architecture for the creation of a national architecture at the beginning of the twentieth century was highly debated. In Mexico, however, the pre-Hispanic architecture and culture were seen as important vehicles for the transformation of society as a result of the Mexican Revolution and the exalted nationalist fervor it generated. For some, the importance of the pre-Hispanic architecture rested on its being recognizable and understood by the majority of the population (in contrast to imported European architecture) and, as such, made it essential for achieving race and class consciousness.

Clearly, the inclusion of a pre-Hispanic pavilion in a world's exhibition was not new. What was radically different, however, was the ideological charge that Manuel Amábilis placed on the Mexican pavilion for Seville

Manuel Amábilis, Mexican pavilion, Seville, 1929.

that responded to these nationalist ideas as well as concerns for legibility. Characteristic of the Mexican pavilion for Seville was the use of pre-Hispanic forms and compositional systems that refer specifically to the Maya architecture in Yucatán. Amábilis was well versed in this, as he had researched and published *La arquitectura precolombina de México* (1928) before the construction of the pavilion. Throughout the building, a number of details and sculptures are replicated from different Maya sites, such as the *chac-mools* and feathered-serpent columns that appear on the front façade. The use of more subtle proportional systems and organizational strategies, such as the diagonal symmetry of the plan, is also drawn from Maya architecture. Despite its historical exterior forms, the central interior space can be understood as a modern Maya expression through its use of tall, double-height spaces created with corbel-shaped reinforced concrete vaults. The central space, filled with furniture designed in the neo-Maya style, led to the exposition rooms that axially radiated out in a cruciform manner, creating a dynamic spatial experience. Its interior decorative program was also modern, as it was based primarily on the experiments of plastic integration that characterized Mexican architecture after the revolution and on the muralist works of artists like Diego Rivera. For the pavilion, the sculptor Leopoldo Tommasi López and the painter Víctor M. Reyes created large-scale works, including mural reliefs, sculptures, frescoes, and stained-glass windows to be perceived by a large audience and with legible images that alluded to all aspects of Mexican culture and that, at times, relied on socialist iconography.

In addition to the formal pre-Hispanic references throughout the building, Amábilis's research showed the relationship between architecture, people, culture, and the place where it was created and raised three important points about the development and character of pre-Hispanic architecture. The first was centered on the Maya's ability to abstract nature into architectural forms without literally copying it. In this way, pre-Hispanic cultures and their cultural manifestations could be seen as stylistic alternatives to the abstract and functionalist forms of modernity and the metropolis. While they reflected the perceptual transformations inherent within the metropolitan condition and modernity

Manuel Amábilis, interior of Mexican pavilion, Seville, 1929.

itself, pre-Hispanic architecture and decorative forms could be understood as paralleling modern forms of abstraction. In addition, the turn to abstract "primitive" or premodern forms could be found in the European avant-garde's interest in and imitation of foreign cultures (exemplified in the cubists' interest in African crafts) that signified a transhistorical and universal impetus toward abstraction.

The second was Amábilis's construction of a mythical history and theory of pre-Hispanic Maya architecture. Basing his research on contemporary theorizations and scholarship, Amábilis deduced that American civilizations were descendants of the mythical peoples of Atlantis. In this way, he was able to articulate that Maya forms and designs paralleled those developed in classical Greek architecture, since, according to the myth, both cultures shared a similar ancestry. Through this argument, Maya architecture could be seen as purer and less contaminated than the colonial architecture of Spain.

The third point Amábilis made in his study concerned the importance of the pre-Hispanic architecture to the sociopolitical project begun by the Mexican Revolution. Amábilis's *Arquitectura precolombina de México* established that a renaissance of pre-Hispanic architecture was linked not only to contemporary nationalistic intentions of creating a legible and known architectural language for the indigenous population but also to an opposition and critique of the elitist academic establishment. The Mexican Revolution, in other words, had transformed the meaning and role of art to not only empower the population but also reinforce social traditions inherent within it, such as, in particular, the then-believed socialist qualities of the Maya culture.

In the end, two things are important to note about Amábilis's theorizations regarding pre-Hispanic architecture, its role in the present, and the material impact of these ideas on the pavilion itself. First of all, the use of a pre-Hispanic architectural language was centered on the pavilion's social vocation. At the center of this was the socialist nature of Yucatán, the state where Amábilis was from and the center of many of the important Maya cities. The Maya were, as noted earlier, considered socialist in contemporary scholarship, but, at the same time, Yucatán itself was led by the socialist governor Felipe Carrillo Puerto. Carrillo Puerto not only called for the use of Maya forms for nationalist and populist aims; he also spoke to the people in Mayan and reinforced the value of the past Maya culture. Through this, the people would not only identify with the greatness of the past but also reestablish a group identity in order to regain race and class consciousness. Second, the use of pre-Hispanic forms also reestablished its importance as one of the highest forms of culture, parallel to that of the Greeks because of the same historical lineage via the myth of Atlantis. This implied that Maya culture was more advanced, higher and purer than the Spanish.

The construction of the Mexico pavilion in Spain, then, was a colonizing gesture: it imposed a culture and values onto Spain to advance its own aims—populist and socialist—using local workforce and materials. In addition, through its theorizations and style, the pavilion was modern. For Amábilis, the European avant-garde search for modernity in the foreign did not have to be copied in Mexico, since it possessed the formally advanced visual culture that Europeans were seeking elsewhere. Making the pavilion and its forms using pre-Hispanic architecture was not only an affront to the Spanish but also an intervention that operated within the principles of the most progressive traditions of universal abstraction.

FURTHER READING

Amábilis, *La arquitectura precolombina de México*.
——, *El pabellón de México*.
Carranza, "Colonizing the Colonizer," in *Architecture as Revolution*.
Tenorio-Trillo, *Mexico at the World's Fairs*.

1929-B

LE CORBUSIER'S FIRST ENCOUNTERS WITH SOUTH AMERICA: LECTURES AND EARLY PROJECTS FOR ARGENTINA, BRAZIL, AND URUGUAY

ARGENTINA • BRAZIL • URUGUAY

LE CORBUSIER first embarked for Latin America on September 14, 1929, aboard the transatlantic ocean liner *Massilia*. His first physical contact with Latin America after two weeks at sea was with Guanabara Bay and the city of Rio de Janeiro, where he would exclaim: "To plan here, as well waste my time! Everything would be absorbed by this violent and sublime landscape."[1] After passing through Montevideo, he finally arrived in Buenos Aires at night, which he described as "the simple meeting of the pampa and the ocean, in one line, lit up at night from one end to the other."[2] His trip to South America, primarily to lecture and to develop work opportunities, reflected his interest in establishing himself as an important figure in the development of its architecture but also served as the western analogue to his earlier "Journey to the East" to find the expressions of the Latin/Mediterranean culture that had been brought to the continent by colonization. In France, Le Corbusier had also established a number of friendships and associations with Latin Americans, including Paulo Prado (a wealthy and important cultural promoter from São Paulo) and his Mexican client, Carlos de Beistegui. Adding to this, in 1927 he had been commissioned by Victoria Ocampo, a wealthy patron of the arts and avid supporter of modernism, to build a house for her, for which he prepared a variant of the 1925 design for the Villa Meyer he was working on at the time. Her house, however, was ultimately designed by the Argentine architect Alejandro Bustillo (see 1924 entry).

During his stay, from October 1929 to January 1930, he would travel throughout Argentina as well as to Paraguay, Uruguay, and Brazil. Many of the long-distance travels were primarily done by airplane in what was, at the time, a nascent industry. One of these trips even included the pilot and author Antoine de Saint-Exupéry. Le Corbusier's experiences of flying over the territory became influential to his understanding of the landscape and would transform his ideas

of planning. Specifically, on his first trip from Buenos Aires to Asunción, he recognized what he defined as the "law of the meander" as well as the importance of new ways of seeing the world from above. He used this opportunity to develop new urban theories, many of which emanated from his early sketches on the airplane, such as his proposals for Rio de Janeiro, São Paulo, and Montevideo.

Le Corbusier's first extended stay took place in Buenos Aires, where he had been invited to give a number of lectures by various groups: the Friends of Art Association, the Friends of the City Association, and the Department of Exact Sciences of the University (which included the School of Architecture). These lectures, which were revised on his return trip to France, were later published as *Precisions* in 1930.

The primary results of his stay in the Argentine capital didn't amount to any built work but to a series of proposals that Le Corbusier would continue to develop in later years. These include a proposal for Victoria Ocampo of adapting seventeen Villa Savoyes in a field, which he used to test the possibility of the city as a continuous green field, the *ville verte*, and the potential reproducibility of objects of quality. He also designed a summerhouse for Matías Errázuriz, the wealthy Chilean ambassador to Argentina, in a Chilean seaside town facing the Pacific Ocean. For this, Le Corbusier would attempt to generate a modern vernacular form through the use of local materials (wood and stone) as well as the butterfly roof that alluded to modern farm buildings he'd seen during his travels. His most important project—one that he would work on for most of his life—was the master plan for Buenos Aires, a design that was based primarily on his maritime and nighttime approach to the city. Again in Rio in 1936 (see 1936 entry), Le Corbusier seemed more comfortable designing works for a European audience. For Buenos Aires, Le Corbusier's initial idea was to create a new business center of tall skyscrapers and an airport

AR

BR

UY

51

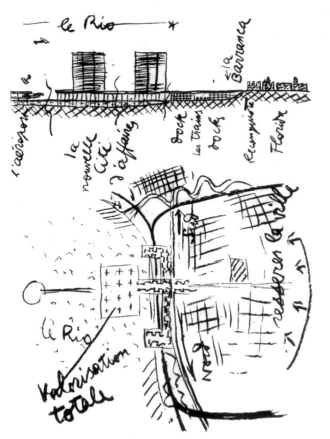

Le Corbusier, proposal for Buenos Aires, 1929.

The ten lectures that he presented dealt primarily with general theoretical concerns, housing, larger structures, and urban issues. In some, he addressed specifically his views on Buenos Aires's urban conditions and presented his general ideas; in others, he spoke about some of his current work (such as the League of Nations project). Besides these Argentina lectures, he also spoke in October in Montevideo, in November in São Paulo, and in December in Rio de Janeiro. In many of these, his presentations included initial ideas about these cities' reurbanization.

Le Corbusier arrived in Montevideo by hydroplane in October 1929 as a guest of the School of Architecture. His initial arrival there, as noted earlier, had

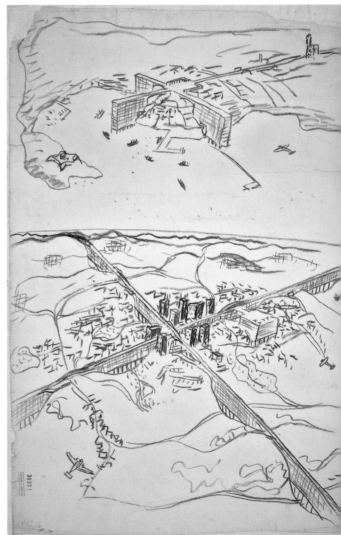

Le Corbusier, proposals for Montevideo and São Paulo, 1929.

in front of the existing city and on the Río de la Plata. It also included developing the coastline and locating strategic program pieces throughout the city linked by new circulation elements. By placing the major intervention on the river, he would avoid the problems caused by the city's grid and the complex debates about the fate of the city at the time. In addition, in contrast to his earlier, speculative urban proposals (such as his 1922 Contemporary City for Three Million or the 1925 Plan Voisin), which were predicated either on an open site or on the (unrealizable) erasure of parts of the city, the plan for Buenos Aires didn't radically disrupt the existing city structure, making the proposal more practical and realizable. What is clear, however, is that the proposal for Buenos Aires consisted of the central part of the 1922 Contemporary City plan and its circulation. In addition to the design, Le Corbusier would establish a number of personal connections with Argentine architects, politicians, and urban planners in order to continue to develop and materialize his proposals for the city (see 1949 box).

Le Corbusier, proposal for Rio de Janeiro, 1929.

been a stopover on his way to Buenos Aires aboard the *Massilia*. His proposal for Montevideo shows a change in attitude of his urbanistic approach, turning toward the creation of a business district formed by a single structure that would link the bay with the higher elevations of the city. Restricted to a few sketches, the structure—which he would later call a "seascraper"—is in a cruciform shape that appears to be an extension of 18 de Julio Avenue (where Mario Palanti's Palacio Salvo stands and which can be seen in the sketch [see 1923 box]) and is intended to address the city's congestion: "Suppose we start by raising the problem of future

circulation? From above on the plateau . . . I continue towards the sea, to the south, at the same level . . . the main street of the city coming from the north, coming from the country."[3] In this way, the structure can be seen as part building and part viaduct, something that he would continue to explore in the proposals for the other Latin American cities.

The proposal for São Paulo was similar: the creation of 45 km long viaducts that crossed at right angles over the central business area of the existing city. These would allow automobile transportation to pass through it unobstructed and serve to link its suburbs together. For this proposal, the structures of reinforced concrete "will make up offices in the center of the city and homes in the outskirts" and will "overcome the curves of the hilly plateau of São Paulo."[4] By playing with or contrasting against the topographical character of the city, these "earthscrapers" would further allow the bottom of the valleys to be open, green, and continuous spaces made possible by being raised on reinforced concrete *pilotis*. The form of the structures, as seen in some of the sketches, would also serve as a windbreak protecting those parks from breezes.

Rio de Janeiro, as we have seen from his reaction upon his arrival from Europe, provided the greatest challenge but, as a result, also the most complex of the preliminary schemes. Instead of approaching the design as he first experienced it from the ocean (as he had done with Buenos Aires), he created the design for Rio de Janeiro from an airplane and, thus, considered it on a scale that would respond to its strong geography. For this, he again created a viaduct-based scheme that connects the city and becomes a horizontal datum to the existing "violent and sublime" geography. In this case, however, the expressway was placed on *pilotis* 330 feet (101 m) over the city—high above the existing urban fabric—and connected the different sections, landmarks, and beaches of the city and led out toward São Paulo: it would encompass an area from Niterói on the northeast, through Copacabana, and past Ipanema. The structure, like the designs for Montevideo and São Paulo, could also be occupied. In this case, however, Le Corbusier proposed that the housing units be made up of *immeuble-villa*-type apartments, similar to those he had designed for the Contemporary City of 1922, with gardens and large windows overlooking the sublime landscape and coastal features of the city. In response to the other view, from approaching boats, he imagined how these horizontal superstructures would link the different plateaus and geographical features of the city with the Pão de Açúcar, Corcovado, Gávea, and so on, the built structure again serving as a reference point to the natural conditions of the site that would be "much improved by that faultless horizontal."[5]

In effect, the presentations in these cities opened up possibilities, contacts, and reference points that Le Corbusier would actively pursue beyond this trip. In addition, the formal expressions of his investigations would find materialization in the work of those architects who were influenced by him: Affonso Reidy and Oscar Niemeyer in Brazil and Jorge Ferrari Hardoy in Argentina, to name a few (see 1936 and 1938 entries; 1946 and 1949 boxes).

FURTHER READING

Benton, *The Rhetoric of Modernism.*
Liernur and Pschepiurca, *La red austral.*
Pérez Oyarzún, "Le Corbusier: Studies for South American Cities."
———, *Le Corbusier y Sudamérica.*

1929-C

WITH THE *HISTORY OF THE SKYSCRAPER*, FRANCISCO MUJICA
ARTICULATES THE SKYSCRAPER'S LATIN AMERICAN
DIMENSION.

ARGENTINA • CARIBBEAN: CUBA • MEXICO

WHEN SKYSCRAPERS began to emerge in Latin America at the beginning of the twentieth century, little attention was paid to theorizing and historicizing the reasons for their character and form. This lacuna might be due, in part, to the fact that the skyscraper was, relatively speaking, a new North American typology that originated in the final decades of the nineteenth century as a result of structural and mechanical advances. In some cases, Latin American skyscrapers reflect the application of styles explored by North American or European skyscraper designers. Characteristic of this is Mario Palanti's stylized and eclectic Palacio Barolo (see 1923 box), which, because of its 328-foot (100 m) height, was, for a time, the tallest building not only in Buenos Aires but also in South America. This honor passed on to Sánchez, Lagos, and de la Torre's 1936 Art Deco Edificio Kavanagh in Buenos Aires (see 1936-a box). Some of the skyscrapers expressed the use of new materials and emerging structural systems; this is the case of Manuel Ortiz Monasterio's thirteen-story La Nacional (Mexico City, 1930–1932), considered the first skyscraper in Mexico City, whose character is the result of steel and reinforced concrete. The material and tectonic expression in skyscrapers, which continues today, is clearly expressed in Amancio Williams's 1946 Suspended Office Building project, whose exterior rigid frame and truss-structured cap allow the floors to hang, providing open and free floor plans throughout the building.

Emerging in the late 1920s is a body of writing that attempts to define the skyscraper as a truly North and South American phenomenon. The "Americanness" of the skyscraper was determined, in part, by the application of pre-Hispanic forms to contemporary production. Seen as a search for an appropriate expressive language based on the past as well as a reaction to or critique of the modern American city (specifically, to the formal incoherence resulting from unrestrained urbanism and the materialization of a laissez-faire ethic), the references to pre-Hispanic forms were part

of a broader quest for an uncontaminated language. According to the historian Manfredo Tafuri, this was "a search for the roots of a 'pure' Americanism, liberated from the mortgages fixed by European culture and founded on a neo-Rousseauean [sic] naturalism of the 'noble savage.'"[1] This exploration is reflected in the analysis and use of pre-Hispanic forms by modern architects and historians. Examples include Esther Born's reading of Le Corbusier's housing development for Oued Ouchaia in Algeria (1933–1934) in relation to Mexican pyramids in her 1937 book, *The New Architecture in Mexico*;[2] the ornamental program of Ely Jacques Kahn's Two Park Avenue Building; the pyramid-like forms of the New York Zoning Ordinance of 1916, which required the stepping back of tall buildings to allow light into the street; or the pyramidal forms used by European architects such as Jean Dupré, Henri Sauvage, or Adolf Loos.[3] One stunning example of the reliance on pre-Hispanic forms is found in the work of the British architect Alfred Bossom, whose "35 Storey Building of To-day" (1925) project literally uses forms from the Temple II Pyramid at Tikal, archaeologically reconstructed and imagined by him as the "original American skyscraper."[4] Bossom's design methodology is explicitly shown in an image of him studying alternative crests, derived from the Maya Castillo of Chichén Itzá, for different skyscrapers.

Within the theoretical and critical work of the Argentine critic and architect Ángel Guido, the Cuban architect Joaquín Weiss, and the Mexican architect Francisco Mujica, we find not only the theorization of the skyscraper but also a glimpse of how modernization and its effects on the metropolis were understood by Latin American critics. These investigations and search for roots would ultimately lead Francisco Mujica to propose a highly idealized and personalized version of the pre-Hispanic culture, an architecture based on it, and, ultimately, a utopian neo-American city that responded, theoretically, to the problems of the metropolis.

Born in Mexico in 1899, Francisco Mujica studied architecture and archaeology in Mexico and Chile, urbanism in Paris, and sociology at the university in Chile. He taught at universities in Mexico City and Buenos Aires. In Mexico, Mujica undertook archaeological investigations and prepared reconstructions of pre-Hispanic ruins. For these and for his proposals for a neo-American architecture derived from them, Mujica received numerous prizes in the various international meetings of the Pan-American Congress of Architects, which focused on developing a continental American architecture and encouraged the teaching of the history of the architecture of the American continent (see 1928 entry).[5] Ultimately, all of these investigations, theories, and proposals became rearticulated and disseminated in his introduction to the *History of the Skyscraper* (published in Paris in 1929 and in New York in 1930).

The History of the Skyscraper analyzed the skyscraper and its relationship to the contemporary city within the context of a broader historiographical work. Here, he reevaluated and vindicated the indigenous architectures of America—specifically the pre-Hispanic architecture of Mexico—as appropriate precedents for the skyscraper. Mujica's formulation was centered on a belief that the skyscraper is the principal manifestation of a truly American architectural typology as well as on the argument that pre-Hispanic forms were essential to represent its American character.[6] His analyses and proposals, consequently, emphasized not only the expression of "place" (i.e., America) but also their relationship with past "native" architectures. He also explored how common architectural threads developed and looked at the resulting effects of the European colonization.[7] First, he described preconquest architecture as an expression of its people. He was also interested in its formal similarities with Egyptian and Assyrian architecture, leading him to propose the possibility of a relation between the Mediterranean architectures and those of pre-Columbian America via the mythical continent of Atlantis (Mexican minister of education José Vasconcelos had argued something similar in relation to the formation of the "cosmic race" [see 1922 entry]).[8] Through this, he could suggest that skyscrapers using European forms ultimately had a filial relation to those inspired by pre-Hispanic architecture.[9] Second, Mujica described how the Spanish conquerors zealously destroyed any preexisting architecture that could have been adapted to new uses. The very force used

Francisco Mujica, neo-American skyscraper project, 1929.

to destroy the natives' architecture was also used to impose a foreign architecture in America. Yet, given that there were few trained people qualified to guide its development, colonial architecture exhibited a tremendous amount of syncretism as it integrated the pre-Columbian spirit, techniques, and formal interests of its builders; for Mujica, this had prevented the outright annihilation of pre-Hispanic cultures and traditions. It was only after their independence from Spain that the colonies became interested again in pre-Hispanic architecture. Mujica, following his own schematic history, believed that the only way to recover the evolutionary thread of American architecture (which he saw occurring in his present) was to knowingly incorporate the pre-Hispanic forms into modern types. The stepback forms that resulted from the implementation of the New York Zoning Code of 1916 prompted a

Francisco Mujica, neo-American City of the Future, 1929.

search for architectural precedents that could be used or applied to them to validate these forms as part of an architectural legacy. For Mujica, the new buildings derived from them inadvertently recalled the forms and qualities of pre-Hispanic architectures. His study led him to conclude that "architects are seeking inspiration in alien styles of architecture closely resembling our primitive style . . . [the forms of modernity appeared to] unconsciously recall the forms peculiar to our continent."[10]

To prove his theories, Mujica's own work shows the application of pre-Hispanic forms and structures at the level of ornamentation, the skyscraper type, and the city. His earlier work shows an unmediated transposition of pre-Hispanic ornamentation and forms onto contemporary designs and programs; this is the case with his design for the temple to the glory of American

art or the school for 360 pupils, which are highly reminiscent of Mujica's archaeological reconstructions.[11] For his "Thirty-Four-Story Skyscraper" project, Mujica simply echoed his own reconstructed drawing of a pyramid in Huatusco.

Mujica's later work, included in *History of the Skyscraper*, moved beyond this servile imitation of ornament and form to become more abstract, simplified, and modern—expressions appropriate for the twentieth century.[12] This shift is attributed in part to the study that Mujica himself conducted about contemporary skyscraper designs, which gave him a keen awareness of the economic and speculative needs of the skyscraper, the problems of contemporary cities, and proposals for their improvement and modernization. Formally, Mujica's "Sixty-Eight-Story Office Building" followed the guidelines set by New York's 1916 zoning ordinance and, in particular, its form derived from Hugh Ferriss's illustrative rendering of the fourth stage of the zoning law. Secondarily, Mujica's proposed skyscraper abstracts into outlines the columns of the Temple of the Warriors in Chichén Itzá. In addition, instead of using the columns to span the whole height of the façade—as the Gothic-influenced builders had done to maintain a vertical unity—Mujica remained true to the original by proposing their use only at the ground-level arcade. The design also clearly availed itself of its reproducibility: every element was modularized and reproduced throughout the scheme. The abstracted decorative elements were thus chosen for their mass reproducibility. Mujica described this proposed skyscraper in the following manner: "The results obtained in the last and most perfect skyscrapers of the modern school have been embodied in this building on American lines. Is it more than a slight step which separates modern skyscraper architecture from the architecture of primitive America?"[13] The logic of mass reproduction is maintained in Mujica's design for a City of the Future, where the basic neo-American skyscraper type is placed on a base and reproduced endlessly at regular intervals (see 1971 entry).

Like Mujica's writings, those of Joaquín Weiss and Ángel Guido also recognized that the American skyscraper was undergoing a crisis of meaning and form because of its reliance on European precedents, its relation to the metropolis and other buildings, and its need to represent its time and location within the American continent. In *El rascacielos: Su génesis, evolución y significación en la arquitectura contemporánea* (The skyscraper: its beginning, evolution, and meaning in contemporary architecture; 1934), Weiss, a Cuban architect and historian, defined the skyscraper as being in a dialectical struggle between the desire for American verticality and European horizontality. For architecture to truly be a product of modern times, he believed that a synthesis needed to be reached between these two dominant aspirations. For him, this union would create a truly extraordinary architecture unseen since the days when, at the end of the Middle Ages, "the book killed the building."[14]

Weiss's reference to the lost communicative ability of the Gothic cathedral, articulated in "This Will Kill That" by Victor Hugo in *Notre-Dame of Paris* (1831), was similar to the central argument made by the Argentine architectural historian Ángel Guido (see 1914 entry). In studying the qualities of the skyscraper type, Guido believed that to restore its status as more than a mere effect of economic and real estate necessities, the analogies with the Gothic cathedral needed to be articulated, as the title of his 1936 book, *Catedrales y rascacielos* (Cathedrals and skyscrapers), suggests. Guido also considered the skyscraper to be a uniquely American product of synthesis between utilitarian functionalism and machine aesthetics. The skyscraper as "cathedral," he argued, exemplified the constructive coordination of tremendous human force and spirit. As such, the skyscraper represented a synthesis of man in a particular time and a particular place.[15] In the end, Guido and Weiss both maintained a similar sense of optimism regarding the skyscraper: its reinvigoration would represent the collective thoughts and abilities of a tumultuous and complicated era.[16]

For both writers, the Gothic cathedral also reflected a utopian period of harmony between builder and community, making architecture into a symbol of communal experience and ideals. For Weiss, then, skyscrapers reflected only the interests and needs of a small elite who used them to increase their profits and reproduce their power. Skyscrapers had the potential to organize and improve the city and to become representatives of the height of contemporary civilization. For Guido, likewise, the Gothic cathedral, which represented the adventure of the human spirit, stood in contrast to the skyscraper, the expression of the adventure of the machine. This, he concluded, could not be trusted to orient humanity.[17] For both authors, a crisis ensued when the skyscraper lost its collective sense and meaning by an exaggerated veneration of the machine (Guido) and by an exacerbated individuality engendered and represented through the pathetic rivalries of builders, speculators, and businessmen (Weiss). In the end, Guido and Weiss intended to find a way to redeem the skyscraper by highlighting the legibility, community, and collectivity associated with Gothic cathedrals.

FURTHER READING

Bossom, *Building to the Skies.*
Guido, *Catedrales y rascacielos.*
Mujica, *History of the Skyscraper.*
Tafuri, "The New Babylon."
Weiss, *El rascacielos.*

1929

SERGIO LARRAÍN AND JORGE ARTEAGA'S OBERPAUER BUILDING INITIATES A NEW DIRECTION IN CHILEAN ARCHITECTURE.

CHILEAN ARCHITECTURE has always had a strong relation to its geography. A country that has 3,100 miles (4,989 km) of ocean shore and a width of no more than 155 miles (250 km) from the Pacific to the Argentine border has to feel the strong presence of the sea. Like a character from Italo Calvino's *Invisible Cities*, Chileans see ships everywhere; their retinas are impregnated with ocean views. The landscape is absorbed by the architecture that, in turn, seems to celebrate its surroundings. As noted by historian Horacio Torrent ("Abstraction and Tectonics," 101), "The development of works of architecture in areas strongly influenced by geographic conditions" would become the trademark of Chilean modernism in the twentieth century (see 1966 and 1997 entries). This is made even more evident by the fact that two of its first modern structures were compared to boats: the Santa Lucía Building (1934) and the Cap Ducal hotel and restaurant (1936).

The Santa Lucía is an apartment building in Santiago built for wealthy patrons. When Sergio Larraín and Jorge

Arteaga designed it in 1932, its curved façade with small round windows on the side was immediately associated with a ship. As a result, the Santa Lucía has been called Edificio Barco (Boat Building) ever since.

Before designing the Santa Lucía, Larraín and Arteaga had already shocked the Chilean elite with the Oberpauer Building (1929), also located in Santiago. People were outraged that both architects, who came from wealthy conservative families, had inscribed such a radical structure in explicit contrast to the provincial architecture of 1920s Santiago. However, Larraín had studied architecture in Chile and traveled to Europe in 1928, where he came in contact with Le Corbusier and with ideas from the Bauhaus. Jorge Arteaga had studied in France. The Oberpauer Building represented the influences of these trips through its use of horizontal windows on a rounded corner and reinforced concrete construction as a solution to the program of a department store, both of which are characteristic of Erich Mendelsohn's work for the Schöcken department store in Stuttgart, Germany (1926–1928), that Larraín might have seen on his trip to Europe. The Oberpauer's six-story height and streamlined corner stood in contrast to the Beaux-Arts-inspired downtown of Santiago.

Another important boat-shaped building in Chile is Roberto Dávila Carson's Cap Ducal hotel and restaurant in Viña del Mar. Dávila had worked with Le Corbusier in the early 1930s and would later try to bring him to Chile to design a master plan for Santiago after the 1939 earthquake. A professor for most of his life, Dávila centered his scholarship on Chilean colonial architecture.

For the Cap Ducal, he designed a restaurant that would be part of

Sergio Larraín and Jorge Arteaga, Santa Lucía Building (aka Edificio Barco), Santiago, 1934.

a much larger tourism infrastructure for Viña del Mar. The restaurant is located atop some rocks at the edge of a beautiful beach and was built with a triangular plan: a hard edge faces the city, and the terraces, like ship decks, open to the ocean. The city side hides the kitchen and service areas, allowing for generous verandas and glazed areas for tables to be right over the sea. The horizontality of the building is also emphasized, making its five-story-tall profile not so massive in relation to the beach.

An architecture more acceptable to the general public was being developed by Juan Martínez Gutiérrez in buildings such as the School of Law of the University of Chile (1938), a monumental Art Deco building with a visible structure that protrudes onto the façade. Martínez had designed the Chilean pavilion for the 1929 Ibero-American Exhibition in Seville (see 1929-a entry), and his search for a modernism with local expression led him to develop a more restrained and localized form of Art Deco (as seen, for instance, in the Maipú Votive Temple, 1943) that would eventually be more akin to the fascist Italian and Spanish monuments of Benito Mussolini and Francisco Franco. This restraint and monumental character can also be seen in the Estadio Nacional (1938), designed by Ricardo Müller, which served as the site of the 1962 Soccer World Cup (where the Brazilian "Garrincha" [Manuel Francisco dos Santos] mesmerized all) and of the torture and executions in the weeks following the military coup d'état that overthrew President Salvador Allende on September 11, 1973.

LEFT: Sergio Larraín and Jorge Arteaga, Oberpauer Building, Santiago, 1929.
BELOW: Roberto Dávila, Cap Ducal, Viña del Mar, 1936.

1930-A

GETÚLIO VARGAS TAKES POWER IN BRAZIL AND APPOINTS TWENTY-EIGHT-YEAR-OLD LÚCIO COSTA AS DIRECTOR OF THE ESCOLA NACIONAL DE BELAS ARTES (ENBA).

BRAZIL

IN 1930, BRAZIL was engulfed in a political and economic crisis. The so-called República Velha (Old Republic), 1889–1930, mirrored the U.S. model in which individual states have a relatively high degree of autonomy from the federal government. From 1904 to 1926, São Paulo and Minas Gerais, the two most populated states, took turns providing the candidate for the presidency. Order and Progress, the positivist motto inscribed on the Brazilian flag, was still valid. People questioned, however, how much progress was being sacrificed for order to be sustained. The political crisis arose in August 1929 when São Paulo's elite, emboldened by unprecedented economic growth fueled by coffee exports, decided to move alone in the nomination process and forced a candidate without negotiating with the other seventeen states. Two months later, the whole coffee economy would collapse with the stock market crash. In March 1930, the Paulista Júlio Prestes was elected president, but a coup d'état in October (sparked by the discontent of the states of Minas Gerais, Rio Grande do Sul, and Paraíba) prevented him from taking office and effectively placed Getúlio Vargas in charge. The new government led by Vargas centralized power around the federal government (transforming forever the federative balance) while pushing for industrialization (import substitution) as well as the modernization and expansion of the public educational system.

Among many changes in that tumultuous 1930 is one that concerns Brazilian architecture the most. On December 8, 1930, Lúcio Costa, a twenty-eight-year-old architect, was named director of the Escola Nacional de Belas Artes (ENBA; National School of Fine Arts). Costa graduated from the ENBA in 1924 and despite his Beaux-Arts training, he identified with the mainstream neocolonial movement of the school. Having worked at the studio of Heitor de Melo (designer of neoclassical structures) and as a close friend of the neocolonial ideologue José Mariano Filho, Costa seemed to be the perfect political choice to lead the ENBA in the coming years.

Created by João VI, king of the United Kingdom of Portugal, Brazil, and the Algarves in 1816, the Imperial Academy of Beaux-Arts brought to Brazil a number of French artists, mostly those identified with the ancien régime, who were running away from Napoleon. Throughout the nineteenth century, with Brazil being an empire (1822–1889), the Beaux-Arts Academy served as the official art school of the regime, following its French monarchical roots. In the 1920s, thirty years after Brazil's change to a representative republic, the ENBA, as it had been renamed, still maintained nineteenth-century methods in its curriculum and also in its yearly exhibitions, the Salões Nacionais de Belas Artes.

Costa, however, had a mandate from Francisco Campos, then minister of education, to change the direction of the school to reflect curricular changes taking place at the University of Rio de Janeiro. Created in 1920, this institution included the schools of law, medicine and pharmacy, and the polytechnic institute. The ENBA, however, remained outside of the university structure and was, as such, unchanged. On December 29, only seventeen days into his tenure, Costa stated in an interview to the newspaper *O Globo* that

the architecture program needs a radical transformation. Not only is it necessary to change the overall curriculum but the syllabus of each discipline and the general pedagogic orientation. The current [direction] is an absolute failure.[1]

Such emphasis might have been a surprise for leading academics such as Arquimedes Memória (director of the ENBA following Costa from 1931 to 1934 and 1938 to 1941) and Mariano Filho but not for the students who were already discussing modern avant-gardist ideas published in *L'Esprit Nouveau* and *Modern Bauformen* and who were taking parallel courses to those offered by the school with a younger generation of professors. The change turned out to be very popular with students but not part of the main curriculum.

The historiography on Brazilian modernism places a strong emphasis on the reformation of the ENBA as a fundamental event that changed the course of

Lúcio Costa, Frank Lloyd Wright, and Gregori Warchavchik at Casa da Rua Toneleros, Rio de Janeiro, 1931.

the country's architecture. Costa's tenure as director supposedly marks the "official" beginning of modern architecture in Brazil. But the extent of the change really deserves more careful consideration. Costa did invite young instructors such as Gregori Warchavchik (fourth-year architectural composition; see 1925 entry), Alexander Buddeus (fifth-year architectural composition), and Leo Putz (painting) to teach at the school. Buddeus is said to have introduced the magazines *Form* and *Modern Bauformen* to an environment influenced by the French Beaux-Arts Concours d'École and the Grand Prix de Rome.

Costa was not able to fire the existing and more academically focused faculty, and whether he ever intended to do so remains unclear. His hiring of new professors was enough to prompt a strong reaction. In

addition, in 1931, when he changed the rules for the yearly student exhibition, the Salão de Artes Plásticas, to accommodate modernist works previously censored, Mariano Filho took Costa's action as a personal betrayal; in response, he wrote a series of newspaper articles denouncing the "Bolshevik" and "un-Brazilian" changes taking place at the school.

When Costa tried to change the curriculum by decree in April 1931, the reaction was fierce and culminated with his demotion in September 1931, after only ten months as director. Students went on strike in support of Costa and sought to reverse the action. Meanwhile, Frank Lloyd Wright—who, along with Eliel Saarinen, was in Rio de Janeiro as a juror for the Columbus Memorial Lighthouse Competition (see 1928 entry)—took full advantage of the situation and lectured to the turbulent ENBA in favor of modernism and the proposed reforms.[2]

Following the events of 1931 at the ENBA, the academically conservative faculty regained control of the school and Costa never returned. The main impact, however, was a strong generational bond among the students who had supported him. Although the 1931 curricular changes introduced new technical disciplines, those were to be taught primarily by engineers. The young architects he had brought in to teach, who would have had an impact on the curriculum eventually, left one by one in the following years while the older and more traditionalist faculty maintained control over the school pedagogy.

Five years later, an event would make the gap between the academics and the modernists unbridgeable: the design competition for the new Ministério da Educação e Saúde Pública (MESP; Ministry of Education and Public Health) building. Arquimedes Memória's winning entry was a classically and Art Deco–inspired design. Minister Gustavo Capanema, however, decided not to build it and, instead, hired Lúcio Costa to lead a team of young architects (including Le Corbusier as a consultant) to design a new building (see 1936 entry). Because of this, the MESP building is now part of the mythological rise of modernism in Brazil as well as of the design team composed of Costa (coordinator), Carlos Leão, Jorge Moreira, Roberto Burle Marx (gardens), and Affonso Eduardo Reidy, all students in 1930–1931, in addition to an intern called Oscar Ribeiro de Almeida Niemeyer Soares Filho, who later would go on to become one of the most important figures in the development of modern architecture in Brazil. Costa repeated many times that what he was not able to achieve at the ENBA in 1931 he accomplished five years later with the MESP building: "It is all there," he would say.[3]

The ENBA reaction against modernism would continue as late as 1944 through its yearly art show, the Salão de Artes Plásticas, which continued to forbid the exhibition of modern work. It seemed extremely out of touch with the times that modern architecture would still encounter such resistance at the main school of architecture in Rio de Janeiro two years after the Pampulha buildings were inaugurated (see 1941 entry) and one year after the *Brazil Builds* exhibition at the Museum of Modern Art (MoMA) in New York (see 1943-a entry).

The ENBA, however, would pay a price for its fierce opposition to modernism. In 1945, the city of Rio de Janeiro assisted in the creation of another school of architecture, the Faculdade Nacional de Arquitetura. With support from the Brazilian Institute of Architects, this school instituted Lúcio Costa's 1931 curricular proposal. At this point, the separation between modern architecture and the Beaux-Arts teachings was already going full force in Brazil: in 1930, a school of architecture was founded in Belo Horizonte, Minas Gerais, independent from either a Beaux-Arts or a polytechnic institution; in São Paulo, an architecture program was started at Mackenzie University in 1947 and at the University of São Paulo the following year. By 1948, not only were there other schools of architecture much more allied with modernist ideas, but there was also the international appraisal of Brazilian modernism. Most major architecture magazines dedicated full issues to Brazilian architecture after World War II, and the modern architect Oscar Niemeyer proved his rise to fame and notoriety by the fact that he had been invited to participate in the design of the United Nations headquarters, allegedly one of the most important commissions of those years (see 1947-a box).

The most unfortunate result of this fifteen-year struggle between modern and academic architecture resulted in the brightest and most talented Brazilian architects of the twentieth century being alienated from participating in teaching. Lúcio Costa, for example, never returned to the ENBA after his brief ten-month tenure as director. Instead, he became one of the founders of the Serviço do Patrimônio Histórico e Artístico Nacional (SPHAN; National Conservation Service) in 1937—which eventually became the Instituto do Patrimônio Histórico e Artístico Nacional (IPHAN)—and later the designer of the urban plan for Brasília, the new capital of Brazil (see 1956 entry). Oscar Niemeyer only taught for about three years at the University of Brasília, as he was forced out after the military coup of 1964. Affonso Eduardo Reidy was appointed assistant professor at ENBA in 1931 and remained there until 1933, when he resigned to work for Rio de Janeiro's municipal administration (see 1946 box). Architects like Niemeyer and Reidy instead influenced a large generation of students through their own separate practices, as they received hundreds of interns searching for contemporary architectural training.

While Lúcio Costa seems to be the most rational in characterizing his ten-month tenure at ENBA as "a failed intervention on education—failed because it resulted in demolishing what, for better or for worse, existed without leaving anything in its place," others continue to fuel the legend of the disturbances at the ENBA as being the pivotal event that changed everything.[4]

Nobody embodies this latter attitude better than Oscar Niemeyer. Countless times he said that he didn't learn much at school, insisting instead that he learned "everything" from a few weeks he spent as Le Corbusier's assistant in 1936. Moreover, when asked in 1993 about how architecture should be taught, he stated that students should "give more emphasis to matters of the plastic arts, insisting on the practice of figurative drawing that allows the architect more malleability when designing spaces. And, thus, they would have the necessary intimacy with the problems of painting and sculpture with which architecture should be integrated whenever possible."[5]

Ironically, this was precisely what Lúcio Costa was fighting against when he tried to change the ENBA curriculum. This seeming contradiction is what makes that generation of architects so great, as they had the rigorous classical Beaux-Arts training and the modernist freedom of composition. Costa's 1930 reform failed, but in failing, it offered Oscar Niemeyer, Affonso Reidy, Roberto Burle Marx, and Carlos Leão a unique set of training and other opportunities that turned them into the Brazilian golden generation.

FURTHER READING

Cavalcanti. *As preocupações do belo.*
Costa, *Lúcio Costa: Registro de uma vivência.*
Xavier, *Arquitetura moderna brasileira.*

1930-B

COMMEMORATING THE CENTENARY OF ITS INDEPENDENCE,
URUGUAY TAKES THE FIRST SOCCER WORLD CUP AT HOME, AND
MONTEVIDEO IS AT THE CENTER OF ITS MODERN AMBITIONS.

URUGUAY

"AMONGST ALL unimportant subjects, soccer is by far the most important."[1]

The quotation above could have been written by a devoted Uruguayan soccer fan, such as writer Eduardo Galeano, summarizing the mood in the country after winning the first FIFA World Cup at home in 1930. With the North Atlantic depressed by the 1929 economic crash, Uruguay volunteered to host the first World Cup tournament. The final game, between Argentina and Uruguay, ended up as a rematch of the 1928 Olympic Games final. Uruguay, again, came out victorious.[2] The noble sport developed in England a few decades earlier was now dominated by South American teams. By 2002, Brazil, Argentina, and Uruguay had won nine tournaments while all European countries together had won eight, all of them in Europe.

In architecture, a similar movement was happening by 1930. Modernism, once the "intellectual property of Western Europe and the U.S.," as the architectural historian William J. R. Curtis defined it as late as 1982,[3] was taking root and flourishing in South America. And as happened with soccer, Uruguay sprinted ahead of its neighbors, aided by strong economic development and relative financial stability that allowed it to be defined as the "Latin American Switzerland" in the 1920s. Such economic success attracted European talents such as Mario Palanti (see 1923 box) and allowed the Uruguayans to actively develop their architectural culture through the reorganization of the city but also through the expansion of the built work. These opportunities brought prominence to the architectural establishment developing in Montevideo.

In 1920, Montevideo was the location of the First Pan-American Congress of Architects. As the decade concluded, the dean of the architecture school in Montevideo, Horacio Acosta y Lara, was judging the Columbus Memorial Lighthouse Competition (see 1928 entry) as the only Latin American juror, a testament to the excellence of Uruguayan architecture. Montevideo was also the place where Le Corbusier had stopped in 1929 to deliver a lecture and, at the same time, propose the reorganization of the city based on a new urban paradigm, the "seascraper" (see 1929-b entry). So, when the celebrated Uruguayan painter Joaquín Torres-García returned to Montevideo in 1934, the avant-garde ideas that he proposed on canvases were already being built on the streets.

The result of the reorganization of the city begun in the late nineteenth century, Montevideo's modernization was centered on the development of new urban parks and tree-lined axes as well as, in 1928, the expansion and widening of streets throughout the Uruguayan capital. However, this would be the preface to the 1930 Regulating Plan (commissioned to Mauricio Cravotto) that would modernize the city by recentering it away from its colonial past, by reorganizing the city's circulation (giving more prominence to a new central avenue), and by increasing the city's density. Additionally, the architecture being developed coincided with this renovation and search for a new, more modern identity. This could be seen through the very stadium built to host the World Cup, the Estadio Centenario (1929–1930), designed by Juan Scasso and built in Parque Batlle, the central park of Montevideo, with its modern Art Deco–inspired tower at one side (see 1968 entry). It is also expressed in the Edificio Centenario, designed by Octavio de los Campos, Milton Puente, and Hipólito Tournier, a twelve-story commercial tower with clean, streamlined lines that is influenced by both the Dutch expressionism of Michel de Klerk in the tower as well as Dutch functionalism in the expression of the services on the façade. To this, of course, we must add the work of Julio Vilamajó, such as the mixed-use building Almaceneros Minoristas (1929), which combined offices, apartments, and a movie theater.

Julio Agustín Vilamajó, born in Montevideo in 1894, graduated from the Universidad de la República in 1915. Trained in a rigorously academic system focused on problems of composition and expression—typical of Beaux-Arts-inspired architectural education

64

De los Campos, Puente, and Tournier, Edificio Centenario, Montevideo, 1930.

at the time—he was also well versed in construction technology, since the School of Architecture was part of the Faculty of Mathematics and Exact Sciences. In 1920, he won the school's Gran Premio (Grand Prize), allowing him to travel to Europe and North Africa. Once abroad, he became more interested in urbanism and sent home essays arguing against the monotony of Montevideo's Spanish grid along with proposals to make the capital city more grandiose and monumental. Upon his return from Europe in 1924, Vilamajó designed three major structures for Montevideo, but none of them were built. The National Library and the Central Market were "commissioned" as studies by the municipality. As part of these projects, Vilamajó included a structure for the fishermen's pier by the river. In those projects, we can see a clear classical inspiration—detailed in diverse stylistic combinations such as the Spanish colonial colonnades of the market and the Roman loggias stacked in four stories of the library—while striving for a more functional expression.

UY

The residences he designed in his early years show the same talent for diverse styles enclosing very functional plans, characteristic of a type of eclectic modernism. In these houses, some of the internal walls are gradually carved out and new spatial relationships emerge (similar to the plans in Adolf Loos's work) while emphasizing the circulation promenade (like Le Corbusier had done). Historian Mariano Arana calls those early works "avant-garde without utopia" due to their emphasis on gradual progress rather than rupture.

Those spatial investigations would culminate in the 1930 design of his own house in Montevideo. In a small 36-by-48-foot (11 x 15 m) corner lot, Vilamajó organized the five-story-high tower-house in the inner portion of the site. At the ground level, a little more than half the lot was excavated and leveled with the street, forming a small garden at the entrance. Judging from photographs and construction drawings, we can infer that the dirt removed by excavating this level was placed at the corner, creating an elevated garden

Julio Vilamajó, Vilamajó House, Montevideo, 1930.

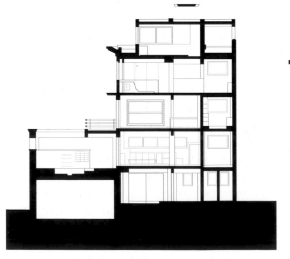
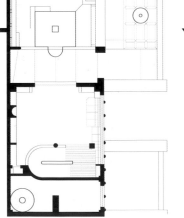
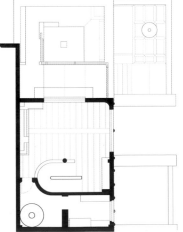

Section and plans of Vilamajó House.

Julio Vilamajó, garden of Vilamajó House, Montevideo, 1930.

and terrace 10 feet (3 m) above the street. Alongside the entrance, the garage "cave" is placed, and this is connected to the house through a stairway that runs all the way through the volume and up to the terrace. In the lower floors and behind the stairs are the utilities and a second and much smaller helicoid service stairway. The garden is accessible from the second floor, where the living room occupies most of the area, with a servant bedroom hidden, again, behind the stairs. On the third floor are the dining room and an adjacent balcony (with more stairs connecting to the garden below); the functional space, the kitchen, is again tucked behind the stairs. The master bedroom and bathroom, with two adjacent rooms for dressing and a small guest room, make up the fourth floor. Above it is the architect's studio, surrounded by a terrace on three sides. With little vertical integration besides the stairs, each floor of the Vilamajó house has its own character and its own scripted domesticity organizing the different functions that take place in the floor plan in addition to the tension that exists between the more formalized architectural forms and the more expressive architectural functions (seen, for instance, in the radiators). The main stairs work to connect it all together while segregating the served from the service spaces. The house's spatial disposition places a strong focus on circulation, being closer to Le Corbusier's houses of the same time but without the clean lines; its decorated walls are reminiscent of Loos's earlier work through the use of rich materials and, sometimes, historical forms. On the exterior, the volume is expressive of its functions through the apertures. Vilamajó also integrated historical decorative motifs such as the interspersed glazed shell-like tiles (inspired by the House of Shells in Salamanca, Spain) and the round relief of Medusa on the façades, as well as in his use of mutules and guttae underneath the roof's cornice.

Vilamajó's spatial, tectonic, and plastic investigations would converge in the building for the School of Engineering (Montevideo, 1936), undoubtedly his masterwork. For the school, Vilamajó created an emblematic building whose central characteristics are the expression of the classical and, as such, honorific character of its reinforced concrete structure while developing, at the same time, complex interior sectional spatial relationships (see 1936-c box).

Also prominent in the development of modern architecture in Uruguay was Mauricio Cravotto. Son of Italian immigrants, Cravotto was born in Uruguay in 1893. Like Vilamajó, Cravotto won the Gran Premio in 1917 after graduating. This prize allowed him to travel to Europe through South America (visiting Valparaíso, Chile; Buenos Aires; and the Caribbean) and the United States, where he visited New Orleans and traveled back and forth by car between New York and San Francisco. In Europe, he traveled through Great Britain and Italy before settling in Paris. Here, he attended lectures by the French urbanist Léon Jaussely. Upon his return in 1921, he taught at the School of Architecture until he left again for Europe in 1925 and visited Spain,

Mauricio Cravotto, Cravotto House, Montevideo, 1932.

Italy, and Paris, where he attended the 1925 Decorative Arts Exhibition. His early work is characterized by various stylistic experimentations such as the simple volumetric forms of the Álvarez Cortés House (Montevideo, 1926) or the 1929 neocolonial Uruguayan pavilion for the Ibero-American Exhibition in Seville (see 1929-a entry). In 1929, following a national competition, he was awarded the commission for Montevideo's Municipal Palace, a symmetrically organized building with a low mass and tower. The building's façade expresses its civic character through an open columnar loggia. The corner openings and other decorative details allude to Frank Lloyd Wright's California work as well as to Willem M. Dudok's in Hilversum. The construction began in 1936, but for financial and other reasons was not completed until 1962 and then with the height of the tower lowered by 130 feet (40 m).

Cravotto's own 1932 house sits across a wide street from Vilamajó's house and shares many formal similarities with it. Its entry, limited to the garage and a door, is closed to the exterior context, giving the appearance of a base onto which the rest of the house sits but which contains the architect's studio. Like its counterpart, Cravotto's house is also located on a corner lot and, consequently, the architect chose to place the primary mass toward the rear of the site, allowing for a terrace level at the front of the site on the second floor, above the studio. Cravotto placed the service elements on the rear corner and, with the central stair, separated them from the public and served spaces of the house. The stair also serves as the main connector through the house. The building is topped with a roof garden that is enclosed with a horizontal fin. Characteristic of the compositional strategy is the use of horizontal elements that protrude from the volume of the house while, at the same time, the mass itself is carved away. These reflect the influences of neoplasticism and the work of Dudok.

The military coup d'état in 1933 would alter the intensity of investigations into modern architecture for Uruguay. Vilamajó's long-standing prominence, however, would lead him to be chosen as one of eleven distinguished architects brought together by the nascent United Nations to design its headquarters in 1947 (see 1947-a box). In April 1947, he traveled to New York to take part in the design workshop but could not stay until the end of the work; his fragile health forced him to return to Uruguay in June of the same year. Vilamajó died in Montevideo in April 1948 before Oscar Niemeyer's design was chosen at the UN workshop and before Uruguay would win the second of two World Cup participations in 1950, beating favorite Brazil at home.

FURTHER READING

Arana and Garabelli, *Arquitectura renovadora en Montevideo, 1915–1940*.
"Julio Vilamajó: Guía de obras."
Luchini, *Julio Vilamajó: Su arquitectura*.
Mauricio Cravotto, 1893–1962.
Silvestri, "Julio Vilamajó."

1930

FLÁVIO DE CARVALHO, "CITY OF THE NAKED MAN"

PRESENTED ON JUNE 28, 1930, at the Fourth Congress of Pan-American Architects held in Rio de Janeiro, Flávio de Carvalho's "City of the Naked Man" incorporates some of the tenets of the Brazilian anthropophagist avant-garde into an architectural and urban proposal. The central metaphor of *antropofagia* is a desire to cannibalize culture: a consuming of both local and foreign civilization, values, and forms to arrive at a new form of culture (something akin to the contemporary idea of "transculturation"; see 1925 entry). In Oswald de Andrade's founding *Manifesto Antropófago* (May 1928), culture is to be formed through the rejection of the "sacred" or inherited aspects of culture, the interest in the telluric and instinctual

characteristics of Brazilian culture (something heavily influenced by surrealism), and the critical assimilation of the "foreign" elements of culture.

Carvalho, a civil engineer by training, began his architectural investigations in 1927 with a proposal for the palace for the governor of São Paulo, self-described as the "first piece of modern architecture in Brazil." This design and others he produced—including his submission for the Columbus Memorial Lighthouse Competition (1928; see 1928 entry), his house in Valinhos (1933), and the Alameda Lorena housing complex (1936–1938)—are distinguished by the combination of diverse formal characteristics and traditions that include pre-Hispanic forms

Flávio de Carvalho, Palace for the Governor of São Paulo competition entry, São Paulo, 1927.

and motifs, elements reminiscent of the Futurist designs of Antonio Sant'Elia, and references to functionalist architecture.

The central proposal of the "City of the Naked Man" is to provide an environment for the "man of the future, without God, without property" ("A Curious Thesis," 341). It is also "a home for thought; men produce ideas that are guided towards and used for the betterment of the whole human race and the attainment of progress" (ibid., 343). In a time of machine production and mechanical selection, the application and use of ideals from the past in the present, as he saw it, only harmed humanity. The "naked man," in the tradition of Karl Marx, is one who is stripped of the outdated lineaments that hold him/her back, who seeks collective and spontaneous organization, who is guided by natural desires: "The anthropophagic man, stripped of his taboos, is like a naked man. The city of naked men will certainly be a proper dwelling for the anthropophagic man" (ibid., 342).

The characteristics of Carvalho's utopian city are based on the new American cities: related to their geographical conditions; collective; appropriate for rational thinking; and, like the machine, organized, productive, and efficient (see 1971 entry). The design of the city as a "single uniform monolith" was to be based not only on addressing the functionalist necessities of humans but also their intellect through its mathematical organization.

Since Carvalho believed that human needs were to be "concentric," the city would also take the same shape in order to be available to all as well as to lead to an efficient organization of the various zones that would make it up. The most important zone was to be the ring-shaped Research Center at the outermost edge of the city. This Research Center would house the hospital and would be linked to the Center for Teaching and Guidance. The Management Center, where "life is studied and catalogued," would be separated from the Research Center by a park. The Sex Zone is the second major zone in the proposal. It is a "vast laboratory where a wide range of desires are indulged in . . . without repression . . . [in order to] shape [the inhabitant's] new ego, guide his libido[,] and destroy the illogical . . ." (ibid., 343). Religion and food would be located within this zone. At the center of the whole complex would be the Government Administration (with housing nearby) and Transportation Hub, from which its different transit lines would radiate outward.

The "City of the Naked Man," like many of Carvalho's other writings based on the anthropophagist ideas, reflects an assimilation of some Corbusian ideas of rationality and purism, of Frank Lloyd Wright's exaltation of the machine and its liberating possibilities (as articulated in his 1901 "The Art and Craft of the Machine"), and of Ebenezer Howard's ideas and diagrams for his *Garden Cities of Tomorrow* (1902).

1931

JUAN O'GORMAN, DIEGO RIVERA AND FRIDA KAHLO HOUSES AND STUDIOS

IN 1929, JUAN O'GORMAN designed a house for his father, the Cecil O'Gorman House, on a parcel that had initially been a tennis court he bought when the Altavista Tennis Club decided to sell some of its land for a housing subdivision. This house, which O'Gorman touted as the first functionalist house in Mexico, responded to his desire to create a building "whose form was derived completely from its utilitarian function." Its simple form built of reinforced concrete featured a studio space with an operable window that spanned the full length of the façade, as well as a concrete helicoidal stair connecting the ground floor to the studio on the upper level. Impressed by the building upon seeing it, the muralist Diego Rivera commissioned O'Gorman to build him a house using the same functionalist principles. Despite O'Gorman's polemics regarding

functionalism's rejection of aesthetic considerations, Rivera argued that the house's efficiency and minimalist cost could aid in the country's reconstruction and thus could also be deemed aesthetically beautiful.

For the houses/studios that he built between 1931 and 1932 for Rivera and his wife, Frida Kahlo, O'Gorman utilized an architectural vocabulary that was not only indebted to other modern examples but that also sought to be efficiently organized, to be inexpensive, and to express the functional aspects of the building. On the lot immediately next to the Cecil O'Gorman House, also a repurposed tennis court that O'Gorman sold to Rivera, he built two houses that are unique examples of the functionalist

Juan O'Gorman, Cecil O'Gorman House, Frida Kahlo House and Studio, and Diego Rivera House and Studio (from left to right), Mexico City, 1929–1932.

architectural language he was developing at the time. As its model, Rivera's house and studio refers to Le Corbusier's studio for the painter Amédée Ozenfant (Paris, 1922) that O'Gorman knew of through its publication in Le Corbusier's *Vers une architecture* (1923). The Rivera House and Studio reproduces the spiral stair (here as a helicoidal one similar to that of his father's house) and sawtooth skylight roof of the Parisian example. The organization of the plan and volume of the house are also indebted to Le Corbusier's Maison Citrohan project (1920). Like Le Corbusier, O'Gorman raised the main volume of the house on *pilotis* (allowing the house to be lifted off

Juan O'Gorman, Frida Kahlo House and Studio, Mexico City, 1932.

the ground), designed a double-height studio space, and sectionally separated the private space of the bedroom above from the more public space of the studio below. As in the Corbusian precedent, O'Gorman also organized the services toward the rear of the house and enclosed the home primarily with solid sidewalls. For the front, the double-height space of the studio space is covered with a floor-to-ceiling operable industrial sash window that mimicked, albeit on a larger scale, the fenestration for the Cecil O'Gorman studio; in the rear, facing the street, the fenestration is made up primarily of horizontal windows.

The Frida Kahlo House and Studio is perhaps more original. The three-story structure is composed of a filled-in reinforced concrete frame with openings that respond to the programmatic necessities of the interior, such as the larger windows for the third-floor studio. On the exterior, O'Gorman not only expressed the circulation via a cylindrical volume that unifies the first and second floor but also through a stair of cantilevered treads that connects the studio to the roof. Both houses were connected via a small bridge that linked the roof terrace of Kahlo's building to the office, bedroom, and small terrace of Rivera's building.

For O'Gorman, these two buildings were intended not only to express the functional aspects that made up the buildings but also to reconceptualize architecture itself. The clear expression on the exterior of the structure, circulation, and function (as manifested through openings and forms); the outright rejection of ornamentation; and the fetishization of the industrial elements that made up the houses (i.e., the water tanks, the steel tubing used as railings, the exposed wiring, and even the cactus fence that surrounds the property, which is more object-like than natural)—all indicate a new value for these secondary and, usually, unartistic elements of architecture. In addition, the use of the skylights on the roof of the Rivera House and Studio express the nature of the artist himself as a factory worker and member of an industrial working class. Finally, the use of bright, strident colors (such as the apache red of the Rivera House and electric blue for Kahlo's) defamiliarizes the already radical forms from their more traditional context for unaccustomed passersby.

1933

IN HIS *PLÁTICAS SOBRE ARQUITECTURA* LECTURE, JUAN O'GORMAN HIGHLIGHTS THE EXISTING POLEMICS BETWEEN FUNCTIONALISM AND ACADEMIC ARCHITECTURE.

MEXICO

ONE OF THE ISSUES that emerged in architectural debates in 1920s Mexico after the Mexican Revolution was the role that architecture would play in solving the lack of hygienic housing and schools for the majority of the population. In a way, like many socially minded architects throughout Latin America and Europe, Juan O'Gorman publicly called for a strictly rationalist and functional architecture as a means to address the pressing needs made apparent by the revolution. Through the use of new technologies, modern materials, and the rationalization of architectural problems, the architect could solve the needs of the population in a direct, efficient, economic, and unmystifying way. This type of radical functionalism, however, meant that all aesthetic qualities of architecture as well as any references to past forms and traditional elements would be rejected as unnecessary expenditures and anathema to the spirit of rationalization. Instead of architecture—that was, according to the Swiss architect Hannes Meyer, anachronistic—O'Gorman developed a radical functionalism that was more akin to pure building.

In 1933, to explain his positions, O'Gorman made his clearest pronouncements on functionalism at a conference organized by the Sociedad de Arquitectos Mexicanos (SAM; Society of Mexican Architects). Intending to address the future of architecture in Mexico, the conference was the most prominent reaction from the SAM to the Mexican government's overt interest in functionalist architecture—manifested in both the construction of functionalist public schools for the Secretaría de Educación Pública (SEP; Department of Public Education) and the establishment of the School for Construction Technicians to teach the design and building of this new type of architecture. The conference, however, highlighted the two architectural directions being practiced in Mexico at the time: the "functionalist" line and the "academic" line.

Juan O'Gorman began his architectural studies at the National University in 1921. During this time, he worked in the offices of Carlos Obregón Santacilia and José Villagrán García (see 1925-b box). Both architects were responding in their own way to the architectural and social problems raised by the revolution by exploring the possibilities of reinforced concrete construction, the appropriate styles for building (such as the neocolonial style requested by the minister of education, José Vasconcelos; see 1922 entry), and the application of functionalist organizational and design strategies. As an architecture student, O'Gorman found in Le Corbusier's *Vers une architecture* (1923) and in the experiments of the international avant-garde

Juan O'Gorman, Tres Guerras Technical School, Mexico City, 1932.

MX

the impetus and precedents for solving the most pressing architectural problems with the most minimal economic outlay and waste. O'Gorman read Le Corbusier's book as a manifesto calling for a rationalist functionalism and for a self-referential, autonomous architectural modernism whose pure formal language was devoid of tradition and, therefore, class values. For him, the rational logic of mass production and engineered works that Le Corbusier advocated could be used to solve the urgent architectural needs of the revolution-torn country in an efficient and economic way. Demonstrating these ideas and concerns are the Houses-Studios for the painters Diego Rivera and Frida Kahlo (1931–1932; see 1931 box) as well as his 1932 work for the SEP, which came about as a result of Rivera suggesting to Secretary of Education Narciso Bassols that he hire O'Gorman to design and build functionalist schools.

Juan O'Gorman, Public Elementary School, Mexico City, 1932.

In 1932, O'Gorman, with a budget of $1 million pesos, built or renovated fifty-three public schools in Mexico City for 30,000 children who lacked adequate schooling facilities. Of the twenty-five schools built, O'Gorman and his small team relied solely on the functionalist dictum of "logic and economy" that reflected Bassols's desire for an architecture "where not one meter of land, nor the value of one peso, nor one ray of sun is wasted"[1] and for an education guided by a "truly scientific basis, by the modernization of its methods, and by a new social direction, a new human sense, a new concrete and transcendental plan in the transformation of the national reality and of Mexican consciousness."[2] To reflect these demands, the schools, therefore, were built out of concrete (in many cases by the very families that were to use them), efficiently planned on a 10-foot (3 m) grid, and had fixtures and architectural elements that were not only standardized and mass-produced but placed at the scale of the would-be users. Many of these schools could serve as community centers when not in use during the day. In addition, architectural ornamentation was abolished. The schools were painted, however, in what O'Gorman referred to as "strident" colors with the unifying sign

of "Escuela Primaria," and, in some cases, murals were painted with the theme left to the discretion of the muralist. Another result of his work for the SEP was the organization of the School for Construction Technicians (1932), which taught its students how to build rational buildings (what he termed as "engineering of buildings") while avoiding the problems of aesthetics and composition inherent in traditional bourgeois architectural education.

A direct affront to traditional architectural culture, the emerging functionalist movement clearly defined architecture as a solution to purely utilitarian and constructional requirements and was, by implication, uninterested in any transcendental goals associated with artistic production and beauty. The SAM, in contrast, began to designate as nonprofessional any architect or builder who was not capable of manufacturing architecture that moved beyond the purely utilitarian in order to reproduce the historical tradition and legacy of architecture. As a result of this impasse, the 1933 conference "Pláticas sobre Arquitectura" (Talks on Architecture) was organized by the SAM to clarify a limited number of questions about the definition and role of architecture in Mexico and, subsequently, the role of functionalism within that definition, especially given

from the SAM by defining his ideas of functionalism and its theories as they related to an international framework of rationalist architecture. In it, he emphasized three major points: a critical look at the artistic, spiritual, or transcendental notions within architecture; the importance of rational architecture; and the role of the architect within modern society.[3]

First of all, O'Gorman determined that the artistic vocation of architecture (what he called the "spiritual necessities") imposed and demanded by academic architects for Mexican architecture to be "correct" was simply a pretext by those architects to maintain the status quo. O'Gorman criticized this position as an attempt to make subjective needs appear objective; in short, of making artistic, spiritual, and transcendental qualities primary human necessities to be addressed by architecture. By claiming the first-order importance of the aesthetic and the transcendental in architecture and by placing the task of aesthetic awareness on the user, those architects took advantage of and imposed their beliefs on an unknowing and trusting public while propagating a messianic self-image whose role was to impart some secret knowledge or quality to the work: "The architect who does not use reason is a mystic who takes advantage of the lack of knowledge of the humbly accepting public, which has no opinions, and which, with empty words, fills other voids."[4] Instead, O'Gorman argued that reason was to become the central characteristic of architecture to address the needs of hygienic housing and work places for the proletariat.[5] O'Gorman defined it in the following terms: "Life imposes its economic, social, and material conditions. The technical, with its means, is given the task of solving them in the best possible way, through the best avenue for the maximum of efficiency with the minimum of effort."[6] Needed were the solutions to real, material necessities through architecture rather than maintaining the aesthetic as the end-in-itself of architecture. By suggesting this, O'Gorman rejected the traditional bourgeois notion of sublimation through artistic experience as holding a utopian possibility of a future transcendence in favor

the polemical positions that architecture had struggled with after the Mexican Revolution.

The presentations began in October of 1933 and represented the positions of the aforementioned two camps: the radical functionalists and the "traditional," or "academic," architects. The radical functionalist group—composed of O'Gorman, Álvaro Aburto, and Juan Legarreta—rejected the aesthetic importance of architecture in favor of functional and rational architecture for the Mexican population. The other group—consisting of Manuel Amábilis (see 1929-a entry), Mauricio M. Campos, Juan Galindo, Federico E. Mariscal (see 1914 entry), Manuel Ortiz Monasterio, Silvano Palafox, Salvador Roncal, and José Villagrán García (see 1925-b box)—stressed the aesthetic character of architecture despite its functional aspects. The opinions of the second group, however, were more diverse, ranging from the wholehearted and virulent rejection of functionalist architecture to the acceptance of functionalism with the caveat that it needed to also respond to aesthetic necessities. Despite their differences and in agreement with the radical functionalists, most of the members of this group advocated that architecture needed to address social issues in order to improve the architectural conditions of the Mexican people.

The speech that Juan O'Gorman delivered for the "Pláticas" in October 1933 responded to the critiques of the more immediate and pragmatic solution to the material needs of the population.

By expressing a functional and material honesty, O'Gorman argued, architecture expressed the beauty and harmony of the scientific world itself and would also be, therefore, an expression of its present. However, in a dialectical moment of his discussion, O'Gorman described the possible problems of functionalism: becoming too dogmatic or becoming the banner of fashion. His implication was that functionalist architecture could become aestheticized and then, ideologically, propose to solve new spiritual necessities.[7] It was, ultimately, that very "stylization" of functionalism in Mexico and its use for speculative housing that would lead O'Gorman to abandon architecture in 1936.

Over aesthetic requirements, architecture had to respond directly to the objective necessities of the time. In other words, it had to apply the present technical and rational structures to solve the given problems of the present. What was important for O'Gorman was to seek efficient and inexpensive architectural solutions that represented the current conditions and materials of production and expressed the drive toward rationalization and internationalization. O'Gorman's positions were summed up in the following way:

The architecture that some call functional or rational and others German, Swedish, International, or Modern—creating confusion with so many names—we will call technical architecture with the goal of clearly defining it in order to understand that its aim is to be useful for mankind in a straightforward and precise manner. The difference between a technical architect and an academic or artistic architect will be perfectly clear. The technical architect is useful to the majority, and the academic is useful to a minority. The first to serve the majority of needy individuals who only have material needs and to whom spiritual necessities are not essential. The second to serve a minority of people who enjoy the profits of the land and industry. Architecture that serves mankind or architecture that serves money.[8]

Within the parameters of economy, construction, and labor investment, O'Gorman saw functional architecture as responding to the interests and needs of the masses, since its very efficiency allowed for a greater number of buildings to be built for the same amount of money, materials, and work needed to build more ornate and artistic ones.

FURTHER READING

Carranza, "Against a New Architecture: Juan O'Gorman and the Disillusionment of Modernism," in *Architecture as Revolution*.

O'Gorman, *Juan O'Gorman*.

Rodríguez Prampolini, *Juan O'Gorman: Arquitecto y pintor*.

LE CORBUSIER IS BACK IN RIO DE JANEIRO.

BRAZIL

IN 1929, LE CORBUSIER traveled to Argentina, Brazil, Uruguay, and Paraguay in search of opportunities (see 1929-b entry). The boldness of the Americas seemed much more open to his ideas. Despite his best efforts, years passed and nothing materialized. The much-awaited opportunity came seven years later when the Brazilian government, by means of its Ministério da Educação e Saúde Pública (MESP; Ministry of Education and Public Health) invited him to return as a consultant on two projects: a campus for the University of Brazil and a new building for the ministry.

Created in 1931, the MESP was part of Getúlio Vargas's strategy to modernize Brazil but also to centralize in Rio de Janeiro the decision-making process that had previously been under the purview of each state.[1] With the appointment of Gustavo Capanema to lead the ministry in 1934, a group of intellectuals connected to the modernist avant-garde were hired to assist him. Carlos Drummond de Andrade—Capanema's chief-of-staff—and Rodrigo Melo Franco were there from the beginning. Other prominent individuals who surrounded him included Mário de Andrade, Cândido Portinari, Manuel Bandeira, Heitor Villa-Lobos, Cecília Meireles, and Vinícius de Moraes. Lúcio Costa would soon join them in 1937 when the Serviço do Patrimônio Histórico e Artístico Nacional (SPHAN; Brazilian Conservation Service, now known as IPHAN) was created.

In 1935, the MESP held a competition for its new headquarters. The neocolonial Marajoara-style design by Arquimedes Memória was chosen as the winner.[2] Minister Capanema and his close collaborators, Drummond and Melo Franco, in particular, were not happy with the choice of a traditional-looking building. In contrast to José Vasconcelos in Mexico a decade earlier (see 1922 entry), Capanema believed that modern architecture perfectly embodied the task of modernizing the Brazilian educational system. More to the point, since his own defense of universal public education was tepid, at best, his decision was based more on the influence of his close collaborators, who were all enthusiastic defenders of modernism. Whether or not Capanema was sold on modern architecture, it is clear that he wanted the MESP to convey an image of the future and not of the past. With the results of the competition voided by the government, the commission for the design of the new building was awarded to Lúcio Costa.

To face the fierce criticism that would ensue (echoing the ENBA debacle of five years earlier; see 1930-a entry), Costa brought together a team of the best young modernist designers in Rio de Janeiro to work on the MESP building: Affonso Eduardo Reidy, Carlos Leão, Jorge Moreira, and Ernâni Vasconcellos. Sensing the opportunity and seeking further support, Costa suggested that the Brazilian government invite Le Corbusier to join the team. Since Brazilian legislation did not (and still does not) allow foreigners to be responsible for architectural projects without a lengthy process of diploma registration (which, by the way, Le Corbusier did not have), the Swiss-French master was hired to give six lectures and to work as a "consultant" for the MESP building as well as for the new campus of the University of Brazil, with the understanding that he would be the lead designer.[3]

During the five weeks he stayed in Rio de Janeiro, Le Corbusier worked on both projects but seemed more enthusiastic about the university campus, probably thinking that it would give him more visibility. Le Corbusier's lesser involvement with the design of the MESP building was also based on his dislike for its proposed location, an urban block behind the church of Santa Luzia at Esplanada do Castelo, a new area left open by the removal of the hill of the same name (see 1903 entry). Le Corbusier lobbied strongly for a site at the seashore, close to the airport, and next to where Affonso Reidy's Museum of Modern Art would eventually be built in 1953. The "consultant" insisted on designing for this alternative site, and his sketches show a low horizontal building facing Guanabara Bay and Sugarloaf Mountain while turning its back to the city. The glass façade and the *pilotis* are there, but Le Corbusier's proposal is very much disconnected from the city fabric, and it appears to be more of a showcase building to be seen from the airport and the ocean liners—in other words, to be seen from abroad.

Soon after Le Corbusier departed for France, Capanema ordered the team of Brazilian architects to forget about a seashore site and resume the design of the MESP building on its original, intended site while deliberations on the university campus project took place. Not surprisingly, the committee composed of the academic faculty rejected Le Corbusier's plan in favor of that by Marcello Piacentini. The Italian architect delivered his design in 1938, but it, too, was ultimately rejected. By then, the battle between modernists and academics was being decided in favor of the former, and Le Corbusier was indirectly responsible. His five weeks in Rio de Janeiro were enough to transform the local team.

As the 1930s progressed, the "modernistas" were able to get more commissions and to align themselves with a government that needed a modern façade to showcase its achievements. Costa and his team were part of this equation. The most important piece of this team, however, was just about to be discovered.

Although Costa might have been a last-minute modernist, Reidy, Leão, Moreira, and Vasconcellos had all been followers of Le Corbusier since they were students. The great transformation on the team was the rise of an unpaid intern called Oscar Ribeiro de Almeida Niemeyer Soares, who, despite being the same age as the others, had entered the ENBA later (1929–1934). In 1936, sensing the opportunity, he begged Costa for an internship in the MESP and university campus projects.

As a result, Niemeyer and Le Corbusier would start a relationship that would continue until the latter's death in 1965. The myth is that Le Corbusier was enchanted by Niemeyer's free-hand drawings and asked him to assist in all presentations. This tale is corroborated by a letter from Le Corbusier to Costa dated November 21, 1936, in which he asks "How are the valuable Oscar and his beautiful perspectives doing?" Costa's December 31, 1936, reply states that "Oscar was moved" by the reference to his drawings and, according to Costa, "was doing several beautiful things." Six months had passed between Niemeyer being an unpaid intern to being the subject of praise by Le Corbusier and Costa.

Less explored by the historiography is the question of why Le Corbusier relied on Niemeyer and not on others. Is it possible that Oscar Niemeyer was already

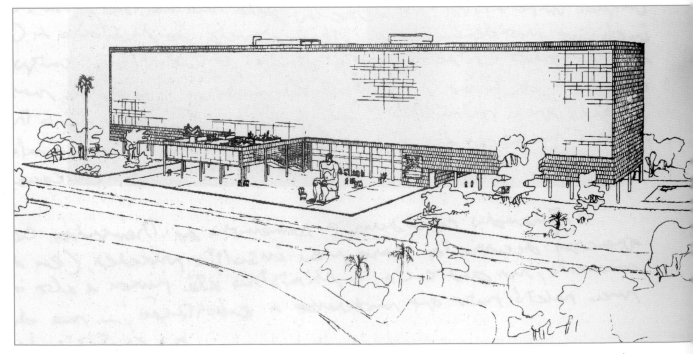

Le Corbusier's proposal for the Ministry of Education and Public Health, Rio de Janeiro, 1936.

Lúcio Costa et al., north façade of the Ministry of Education
and Public Health, Rio de Janeiro, 1945.

an outstanding designer at that time? If that is the case, why did he not win any honors at ENBA or garner anyone's attention before his five weeks with Le Corbusier? More plausible is that Niemeyer, having entered the ENBA in 1929 and without much exposure to art and architecture, never actually learned academic drawing. His "loose" sketches would surely not have attracted the attention of the conservative faculty that took over after Costa's removal in 1931. His drawings

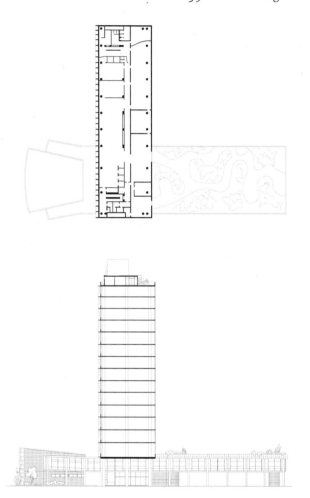

Plan and longitudinal section of the Ministry of Education and Public Health.

were being valued for the very first time and being valued by one of the most important contemporary architects: Le Corbusier.

In an attempt to brush aside the grandiose narrative of Niemeyer's discovery as written by himself and Costa, what is clear is that Le Corbusier's compliments gave Niemeyer the confidence to be much more

aggressive and forceful in his designs, something that he continued to exercise until his death in 2012.[4]

With Le Corbusier gone and with Capanema's orders to work on the first site, Niemeyer rose to the forefront of the team—at first timidly, as when he showed some sketches to Carlos Leão but threw them away before Costa arrived. As the design work progressed, the horizontal volume originally proposed by Le Corbusier became a tall vertical slab in the final design. The slab, in turn, subdivides the urban block while a lower interlocking mass perpendicularly spans the width of the site along its eastern edge. The tower houses the offices of the ministry, while the lower volume is composed of an auditorium and an open gallery. In the tower, the ground-floor *pilotis* proposed by the European visitor for his scheme would be elongated to 33 feet (10 m), making for a much more elegant and "light" composition (and seemingly allowing the lower mass to slide under it). The columns, however, are clearly bigger than structurally required for the building but, in a more classical and traditional way (as part of Costa's Beaux-Arts training), are compositionally proportional to the space that they open up and the overall height and proportions of the building. These overscaled *pilotis* make the entrance hall much more monumental while allowing for the interconnection between the exterior plazas and the whole composition to be more permeable.

The MESP, as one of the first modernist high-rise buildings ever built, incorporates Le Corbusier's five-points system for a new architecture: free façade, free plan, horizontal windows, *pilotis*, and roof garden. In addition, the two fully glazed façades are treated differently to accommodate the tropical climate: the southern one, with an oblique view of the ocean, is transparent, while the northern one is protected by horizontal movable *brise-soleil* (sunscreens) that pivot on fixed concrete panels. The use of this system was later described by Le Corbusier as an additional point of his architectural system. The *brise-soleil*, it should be noted, had already been used by Luis Nunes in Recife (1934) and by the Roberto brothers (Maurício, Milton, and Marcelo; aka MMM Roberto) at the ABI Building (1936–1938) a few blocks away.[5] As movable parts, however, they gave the MESP building a dynamic quality, as the fins were adjusted according to the desired views and seasons (lower or higher sun angle), while the vertical panels that hold them protected from the afternoon glare.

Roberto Burle Marx, terrace garden at the Ministry of Education and Public Health, Rio de Janeiro, 1945.

Following Le Corbusier's advice, the Brazilian team incorporated *azulejo* (traditional Portuguese tile) murals as protection and decoration for the major external walls. Cândido Portinari was hired to design those as well as other interior murals. In addition, sculptures are scattered throughout, as the building aspired to become a total work of art and an open lesson on modernism. This ambition for totality is further enhanced by the gardens designed by Roberto Burle Marx (see 1961 entry) that include those on the ground-level plazas, on the terrace over the exhibition hall, and on the roof of the building where the minister's offices would be located. At ground level, the vegetation beds break up the two plazas and penetrate under the *pilotis*, in dialogue with the columns that rise like artificial trunks from the ground. At the terrace garden of the lower mass, Burle Marx created one of his most important early designs. Here, the beds of different flower species and their colorations are shaped into various curvilinear forms and patterns that have the advantage of being visible from all south-facing offices, turning it into a living canvas—a concept that Burle Marx would develop throughout his life with undisputed mastery. At the roof level of the tower, for the more sculptural forms of the minister's offices, Burle Marx would create a more subdued and controlled garden space.

Ultimately, it was the gardens, as large setbacks, that linked the building to the modern urban fabric by providing a type of respite from the dense urban grid and traditional walls immediately adjacent to the property. The modern composition with large setbacks and permeable ground floor under the elegant *pilotis* highlights the insertion of a modernist building and its qualities within the traditional urban fabric of Rio de Janeiro.

Given the changes that the Brazilian team enacted, the relationship with Le Corbusier became somewhat turbulent. In 1937, when Costa sent him the final drawings, he received compliments in response. It wasn't until 1945, after the end of World War II, that Le Corbusier saw pictures of the completed building. He replied bitterly that he wasn't adequately paid and that his authorship was not properly acknowledged. Le Corbusier was most likely reacting to the international success of Brazilian architecture and the members of the MESP design team (such as Costa and Niemeyer), who, for instance, were featured in the Museum of Modern Art's *Brazil Builds* exhibition (1943; see 1943-a entry) as well as throughout European magazines. Costa replied stating that Le Corbusier's participation had been acknowledged as a building "inspired by Le Corbusier's initial sketches." Costa was appalled later to find that Le Corbusier published new sketches, drawn over photographs of the building, as if they were process studies.[6]

Despite the later turbulence, Niemeyer would continue to be Le Corbusier's devoted disciple—at times emphasizing his deviations from the master's orthodoxy (as in Pampulha; see 1941 entry), other times accommodating his demands (as in the United Nations building; see 1947-a box). Niemeyer always stated, however, that he learned "everything" from Le Corbusier in 1936. Le Corbusier's influence on Brazil's architectural modernism would be further inflated by Brazilian historiography at the expense of many other actors or events. Mostly based on Costa's arguments and publications like *Brazil Builds* (1943), Henrique Mindlin's *Modern Architecture in Brazil* (1956), and Yves Bruand's *Arquitetura contemporânea no Brasil* (1981), the foundational myth of Brazil's modern architecture was established on the ENBA's frustrated reformation and the consequent contact with Le Corbusier at the MESP building. This happened, of course, at the expense of the pioneering contributions of Gregori Warchavchik, Rino Levi, and Flávio de Carvalho in São Paulo, to name a few.

The reality is much more complex. The works by Luiz Nunes in Recife and Warchavchik in São Paulo are important precedents to the MESP building, as is the influence of others like Frank Lloyd Wright, who visited Rio de Janeiro in 1931. Even the struggle with more traditional or academic architects (as defined by Costa) was far from being over after Le Corbusier's second visit, as seen by the results for the 1936 competition for the headquarters of the Finance Ministry to be built a few blocks away from the MESP in Rio de Janeiro. The winning entry was a modernist design by Wladimir Alves de Souza and Enéas Silva (Oscar Niemeyer and Jorge Leão won the second prize). Minister Artur de Souza Costa, however, was not happy with the design because, according to him, bankers and financiers would prefer the solidity of heavy walls over the transparency and lightness of large glass panels. The competition was cancelled, and a team led by engineer Ary Fontoura de Azambuja designed a neoclassical structure supported by a series of Doric columns.

The battle would not end until the early 1940s when Niemeyer designed the Grande Hotel in Ouro Preto and the Pampulha buildings in Belo Horizonte (see 1941 entry). By then, his designs deviated widely from Le Corbusier by incorporating historical references (Grande Hotel) and putting into question the centrality of the *angle droit* (right angle; Pampulha).

FURTHER READING

Andreoli and Forty, *Brazil's Modern Architecture.*
Cavalcanti, *When Brazil Was Modern.*
Cavalcanti and Caldeira, "The Role of Modernists in the Establishment of Brazilian Cultural Heritage."
Guillén, "Modernism without Modernity."
Lara, "One Step Back, Two Steps Forward."

1936-A

THE KAVANAGH BUILDING IS FINISHED, BECOMING THE TALLEST SKYSCRAPER IN LATIN AMERICA.

BEFORE AIRPLANES became ubiquitous, no matter how one arrived in Buenos Aires, the Kavanagh Building was there to greet you. Coming by train, the Kavanagh would be right in front as you left Retiro Station. Arriving by sea, the 390-foot-high (119 m) structure was visible from every dock of the new Puerto Madero. For many years it was the tallest building in South America and tallest reinforced concrete structure in the world.

Built in only fourteen months for Corina Kavanagh, a wealthy Argentine widow who sold two (of her many) country estates to build a luxury residence in downtown Buenos Aires, the Kavanagh is home to 105 no-expense-spared rental units designed for the wealthiest *estancieros*, or Argentine landowners. The apartments utilized the latest in technological advances such as central air conditioning and modern plumbing. The spacious bathrooms were all completely finished in marble. Hardware details were cast in white steel to avoid interfering with the hand-crafted looks of the interiors. Those with apartments on the upper floors have exquisite terrace gardens with views of the river, parks, and the city.

Designed by the firm of the Uruguayan engineer Gregorio Sánchez and the Argentine architects Ernesto Lagos and Luis María de la Torre, the Kavanagh is the most "modern" of all buildings designed by the group. Before the Kavanagh, they designed a similar Art Deco structure at the corner of Córdoba and Libertad (1931) and were already experimenting with modernism as seen by the *pilotis* proposed for the building at Libertador 3080 to be sold as commercial space. For Corina Kavanagh, they designed an elegant thirty-story structure that takes full advantage of its angular corner position and location on a small hill across from the Plaza San Martín to further emphasize its verticality.

As it rises, the building volume steps back like the early skyscrapers in New York, emphasizing its character and sculptural forms rather than the maximization of floor-area ratio, as was the case in Chicago. By stepping the volume, the architects developed opportunities for several gardens and balconies. Thirty percent of the units have some type of balcony or open area that affords them beautiful views of the city, Puerto Madero, and the elegant neighborhoods of Retiro and Barrio Norte.

At the base, the building's triangular plan is completely occupied by an elaborate lobby. As this is a residential skyscraper (in contrast to the large majority of its North American counterparts of the time), the architects' main concern was not maximizing daylight nor developing flexible and adaptable plans but, rather, the individualization of the access points to the apartments. Thus, twelve elevators are placed throughout the mass and create separate routes to the different floors, minimizing the interactions between the tenants as well as the common spaces where these could occur. For herself, Corina Kavanagh reserved the fourteenth floor—the only apartment to occupy a full floor and have an area close to 7,000 square feet (650 sq. m).

Sánchez, Lagos, and de la Torre, Kavanagh Building, Buenos Aires, 1936.

According to historian Jorge Francisco Liernur, the Kavanagh is the best example of a "reactionary modernism": a modern program of a residential high-rise that is symmetrically arranged and organized in a classical manner. As if representing the paradox of the Argentine society of the 1930s, the Kavanagh was built by and for the only sector that could prosper from the economic depression: wealthy landowners who needed new forms of investment for their capital in times of reduced demand for their agricultural production.

83

1936-B

FRANCISCO SALAMONE: FASCISM AND MONUMENTAL ARCHITECTURE IN THE PAMPA

THE BUILDING PROGRAM supported by Manuel Fresco, the governor of the province of Buenos Aires, during his tenure in office between 1936 and 1940 presents one of the most particular uses of a new form of public and political architecture. Fresco, a radical right-wing nationalist and open supporter of Benito Mussolini, actively exalted militarization, Catholic education, and the use of public funds and government bonds to provide public services and develop public works and infrastructures within the vast outskirts of the province. Many of the towns affected were far from Buenos Aires, having initially been settled as military outposts to protect against the natives. The work was intended to be part of an antiurban response to the growth of city centers by providing work, culture, and other amenities to the outlying areas to limit the emigration out of these communities. These towns were also part of a larger system that provided food and other resources not only to the capital but also for export. Fresco, who eventually would be dismissed because of electoral fraud, used his position to commission his friend, the architect Francisco Salamone, to design a number of representative buildings that would communicate his political ideals of a strong state while pacifying the growing radicalism within the working class by providing them with employment.

Francisco Salamone was born in Italy in 1897 and immigrated to Argentina in 1903. He attended the National University in Córdoba, where he graduated with an engineering degree in construction. His early work was both within the family construction and paving business and as an architect working primarily in Córdoba producing unexceptional work in the neocolonial style. Because of his association with Fresco, Salamone became an important participant in the works

for the small provincial towns and communities, which included not only paving but also the design and construction of emblematic structures for each. Between 1936 and 1940, he designed and built town halls, municipal offices, and public squares; slaughterhouses; and cemetery portals.

Representative of the works are the town hall for Rauch, the model slaughterhouse at Coronel Pringles, and the cemetery portals at Azul and Laprida. The town halls have in common the use of symmetry as an organizational system for the façades, a tall clock tower at the center (which, in many, is decorated with elements that evoke the Christian cross), decorative elements that give the buildings a crenellated character, and their placement as urban landmarks on the town square. Typologically, Salamone's town halls have a strong affinity with medieval Italian town halls, a common referent for Italian fascist architects. The slaughterhouses, usually located in the outskirts of the town, were emblematic buildings that used signage (such as "Matadero Modelo" [Model Slaughterhouse]) on towers or marquees to evoke the goings-on within these functionally efficient yet typologically nondescript buildings. Salamone's most dramatic works are those for the cemetery portals. In

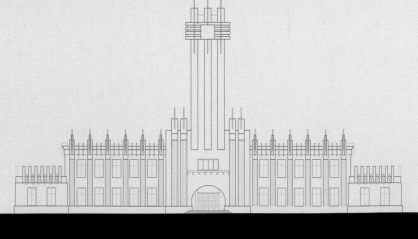

Elevation of Francisco Salamone's Rauch town hall, 1937.

Francisco Salamone, cemetery portal, Laprida, 1936.

Azul, the monumentally scaled letters RIP (*requiescat in pace*) adorn the front of the chapel and administrative building, while a stylized winged angel with a sword stands at attention on the front. On the sides, stylized eternal flames are built over small rooms that look like pedestals for the fire basins. For Laprida, Salamone built a monumental cross with a figure of Christ over the main functional spaces (some of which are located in conical forms).

For many of the works, Salamone's task included the design of interiors, furniture, urban equipment, fountains, lighting, and other elements, which helps them to be read as total works of art. Ultimately, however, the characteristic attributes of Salamone's buildings are monumentality, severity, and reliance on a modernized classical vocabulary that, together, give them an impersonal and paternalistic quality. In addition, their simplified decorative vocabulary alludes to characteristic Art Deco buildings (such as Robert Mallet-Stevens's 1925 Tourism pavilion for the Decorative Arts Exposition) or Futurist designs (such as Nikolay Diulgheroff's 1930 Tower Dedicated to the Victory of the Machine) that, as is well known, were exalted by the fascists. According to historian Jorge Ramos, Salamone's works were to be urban condensers, not intended for social purposes or gathering but rather as propagandistic and expressive of strong government as well as reducible symbols of work, order, and rest, values that matched Mussolini's ideals of *lavoro, ordine, eternità*.

1936-c

JULIO VILAMAJÓ, SCHOOL OF ENGINEERING

IN 1933, A COMPETITION was called for a new build-ing to house the Facultad de Ingeniería y Ramas Anexas (School of Engineering and Related Disciplines) for the Universidad de la República in Montevideo, Uruguay. The site was a triangular peninsula that projected onto the Río de la Plata on the southernmost point of Montevideo. Ar-chitect Julio Vilamajó knew the site very well, since he had designed, four years earlier, a stadium for Club Atlético Peñarol, the most traditional soccer club of Uruguay. Exca-vations had begun, but the project was abandoned in the early 1930s. Since the municipality still owned the land, a competition was held in 1933 for a new building for the School of Engineering. However, disputes over the owner-ship of the land (which might have also impacted the sta-dium project) resulted in the canceling of the competition. Vilamajó, according to a 1970 publication from the School of Architecture, submitted a competition entry in 1933. In it, a symmetrical arrangement of buildings is organized along a central axis bisecting the diamond-shaped lot at the western edge of the peninsula.

A second proposal is dated 1936 and coincided with a legislative decree transferring the property to the univer-sity and authorizing it to spend a certain amount on the construction of the building and appointing Vilamajó chief architect of the project. This proposal shows the curving of the main axis of circulation (instead of following the

earlier central axis) to adapt it better to the existing topog-raphy that was excavated for the unbuilt stadium.

The first two proposals sketched by Vilamajó obses-sively pursue an efficient circulation that is characterized by blocks of classrooms and laboratories intersecting a major corridor at different levels. Vilamajó is praised in documents of the time for displaying great flexibility in adapting his scheme to all kinds of obstacles that occurred during the design process, including the continuation of the land ownership disputes and the reduction of the avail-able buildable area for the project. Budgetary constraints also haunted the project, as the program kept growing as one would expect of a large educational project.

The final design occupies only the front part of what was once the stadium site. The main blocks are disposed on a north–south orientation, and the main volumes are raised in order to open views to the Río de la Plata on the west. In addition, the volumes are slightly dislocated from each other and, thus, create a series of semi-enclosed patios. The symmetry of the early proposals was discarded in favor of a slightly asymmetrical composition; the main axis is broken as one walks under the *pilotis* of the dif-ferent volumes, but the organization still presents direct views at ground level. The use of the ground floor under

Julio Vilamajó, School of Engineering, Montevideo, 1936.

pilotis allowed Vilamajó to cut a significant portion of the area previously devoted to circulation. On writing about the project, he emphasized the importance of the circulation not only for the efficiency of accessing the building's sections but also as a social space and a place of interaction. Vilamajó had tamed the circulation to work with the overall composition and, in the process, created a much more fluid and permeable complex where the ground floor can be traversed in multiple directions, increasing exponentially the possibility of chance encounters.

The character of these spaces is suggested in Vilamajó's highly evocative and quasi-Piranesian charcoal sketches. These focus not only on the permeability of the ground level but also on the spatial layering resulting through the expression of the structural frame. Above the ground floor, bridges are used to connect adjacent volumes when necessary—a complicated system of circulation that has a strong presence but doesn't impose itself on the composition. In addition, many of the large public spaces are characterized by complex sectional relationships that allow for dynamic spatial experiences. These changes are significant, as they summarize in a single project decades of evolution from French academicism, through Adolf Loos's Raumplan (spatial plan) and Bauhaus functionalism, to Le Corbusier's *promenade architecturale*.

With the composition freed from the dictates of the circulation, Vilamajó could focus on the tectonic expression of every block. The use of a 24-foot (7 m) reinforced concrete module gives the interior spaces a high degree of flexibility. The main classroom volume (six stories plus *pilotis*) is connected to other, lower volumes that house laboratories, the library, and the offices of each engineering specialization. The fenestration varies according to the program of each block: full glazed panels for some laboratories, large windows for classrooms, smaller openings for the administrative rooms, and so on. The exterior treatment also varies from rough concrete, to void cement blocks, to polished cement. At the School of Engineering, the structure—with very little added to it—becomes the architecture. As Vilamajó's sketches suggest, the

Julio Vilamajó, interior of School of Engineering, Montevideo, 1936. BELOW: Plan of School of Engineering.

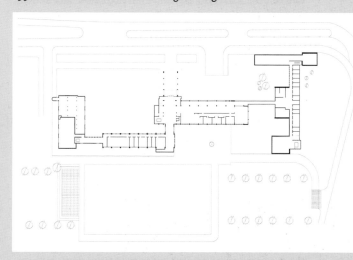

structural order was to give the building its classical yet modern character and, as for the French architect Auguste Perret, to define the interior space itself by delineating its limits. The sketches also suggest the integration of decorative panels into the surfaces of the building as well as protruding concrete elements (that evoke the shell tiles of his house) that, although limited in the final construction to a cast-in-place relief mural, speak to a desire for a broader plastic integration.

Wladimiro Acosta, Helios House project (Casa del Dr. J. B.),
Buenos Aires, 1934–1935.

gymnasium. The Casa en La Falda (Córdoba, Argentina, 1940) is notable not only for Acosta's use of the Helios to shield the northern sun but also for its use of local materials; in this case, stone is used to construct the house (with the exception of the Helios system, which is constructed with reinforced concrete) and passively cool or heat it. The Helios system covers a terrace on the ground floor that results from the living room being partially placed behind the Helios. On the second floor, where the bedrooms are located, the Helios creates a semicovered terrace over the living room of the house. In the Avenida Figueroa Alcorta Apartment Building (Buenos Aires, 1942), Acosta is forced to adapt his systems to the laws of the market that require that he maximize the use of the site. Given his desire to include a garden, Acosta builds a small tower, as allowed by the zoning code, with eight single-story units and a double penthouse unit at the top. Because of the morphology of the tower, the Helios does not

have the same visibility and presence as in the houses or other low-rise apartment buildings he designed. Here, the Helios frames the living rooms and creates the balconies for each apartment. To really protect the main spaces from the sun, Acosta designs the plan in a T shape, placing the bedrooms and services to block the northeastern sun.

Although the Figueroa Alcorta Building includes elements of the Helios system and Acosta's ideas of modern living, the building should be understood as a built prototype of the urban ideas and proposals that he also addressed in *Vivienda y ciudad*. In response to the breakdown of order of the modern city (and, specifically, that of Buenos Aires) and the lack of fresh air, nature, and sunlight, Acosta developed a City-Block project for Buenos Aires (see 1971 entry). Following Ludwig Hilberseimer's design from *Groszstadt-architektur* (1927) and Le Corbusier's Contemporary City for Three Million (1922), Acosta proposed the transformation of the typical, existing Buenos Aires city block; a radical rethinking of the city of Buenos Aires would also be undertaken by Le Corbusier beginning with his 1929 trip to South America (see 1929-b entry). Acosta proposed two schemes: the first, City-Block (1927–1932), used cruciform towers that covered the metropolitan grid (reminiscent of Le Corbusier's towers), and the second, City-Block Integral (1933–1935), employed a series of linear buildings with service braces that were separated by open garden spaces. While the second scheme was reminiscent of Hilberseimer's 1927 designs for the city, Acosta's introduction of nature into the city and a clear separation of traffic from the ground tied his project to current ideas of the city articulated by the Congrès International d'Architecture Moderne (CIAM; International Congress of Modern Architecture) in its 1933 "Athens Charter" as well as by Le Corbusier's Ville Radieuse project (1935). Like Acosta's earlier works, the City-Block Integral project responded to the specificity of the place through its north-facing orientation and with the ground between the buildings left open for the "spectacle of nature" to provide relaxation and enjoyment. In the later version of the project, in particular, Acosta stated that "city and nature will no longer be antagonistic terms. Being placed again on the earth, the inhabitant's fragmentary existence regains its lost integrity."[10]

While Acosta maintained a presence in the international circuits as the Argentine delegate to the CIAM, the impact of his work was limited primarily to his publications and, even then, specifically to his *Vivienda y clima*, which had wider distribution in Latin America than his earlier book. What is important to highlight, however, is his transformation of the formal characteristics of European modernism to adapt specifically to the South American context—through the separation of the sun-shading device from the volume of the house and through the emphasis on the exterior spaces—and to the character of Buenos Aires, particularly through his investigations about transforming the city to address the natural realm.

TOP: Wladimiro Acosta, Helios House, Córdoba, 1940.
ABOVE: Wladimiro Acosta, City-Block Integral project, 1933–1935.

FURTHER READING

Carranza, "Transgressing Function."
Gaite, *Wladimiro Acosta*.
Katzenstein, "Argentine Architecture of the Thirties."
Molina y Vedia, "Lo moderno y lo nacional en nuestra arquitectura": Wladimiro Acosta."

1937

CINE GRAN REX AND ARGENTINE CLASSICIST MODERNISM

EMBLEMATIC OF A VARIANT of modern architecture in Buenos Aires is Alberto Prebisch's Cine Gran Rex, located on Avenida Corrientes, which, at the time of its inauguration, was the largest movie theater in South America. To respond to its context, the building maintains the continuity of height and edge of the neighboring façades, yet its large sign cantilevers out and becomes a visible icon in the already busy street. From the exterior, one can peer in through a large window that, in turn, is indicative of the radical structural developments that occur immediately inside. The structure, however, is uncelebrated. As a result, one walks from the street into a large multistory lobby space that allows for the spectacle of the theatergoers themselves, who can be seen circulating on the multiple levels. Supporting all of this is a reinforced concrete beam that spans the façade (making the large window possible) and that, in turn, supports a series of beams from which the upper-level lobby space hangs. Both the

Alberto Prebisch, Obelisk, Buenos Aires, 1936.

Alberto Prebisch, interior of Cine Gran Rex, Buenos Aires, 1937.

interior and the exterior exhibit an undecorated and restrained expression of materials (unpolished travertine on the façade; marble, bronze, and whitewashed reinforced concrete in the interior).

Similar in character is the Obelisk (1936), located a few hundred feet away at the intersection of Avenida Corrientes and Avenida 9 de Julio, Buenos Aires's largest avenue, on its own plaza called the Plaza de la República. Intended to celebrate the four hundredth anniversary of the founding of the city, the Obelisk, like the Cine Gran Rex, hides the complex structural elements needed for its construction: principally, that it is located over a series of underground subway tunnels that intersect nearby. The structure's modernity is highlighted by its abstract plain character and reinterpretation of the proportions of traditional obelisks.

In a way, these two structures by one of the members of the Argentine avant-garde (see 1924 entry) are indicative of a restrained and classically inspired notion of modern architecture that developed in Argentina in the 1930s. Here, generally speaking, modern architecture was based on logic and reason, as advocated by Le Corbusier, but also on a search for restraint.

This same attitude can also be seen in the work of Antonio Vilar. An engineer by training, Vilar designed his own house (San Isidro, 1935–1937) using elements of Corbusian modernism—whitewashed reinforced concrete, *pilotis*, horizontal windows, open glass façade expanses, etc.—while responding to its site near the Río de la Plata through a gentle curve of its façade and the use of nautical references. Vilar would be instrumental in introducing modern architecture into the provinces by means of the buildings that he designed in 1939 for the Automobile Club of Argentina, an association promoting automobile driving throughout the country and offering rest stops, gasoline stations, and restaurants at its locations. The structures that Vilar produced show different solutions for the interface between the automobile and the architecture—sometimes as bridges, other times as covered spaces—and used traditional modern structures and

forms in very restrained ways. Because of their locations, many of these buildings also incorporate local materials (such as brick or local stone) in their construction. Most emblematic, however, is the main building for the association (Buenos Aires, 1943). Located on the important Avenida Libertador, its front is a simple volume whose façade is classical in nature through the use of large pilasters and classically inspired decorative elements (such as sculptural reliefs). At the ground level, the edges of this structure become the passages where vehicular entry occurs for the gasoline and service stations and for the garage, which are located on the rear part of the site. The back of the building, semicircular in form, responds to the mechanical character of the automobile by having a more industrial expression with exposed brick and industrial sash windows.

Antonio Vilar, Automobile Club of Argentina, Buenos Aires, 1943.

1938

CHARACTERISTIC OF THE GROWING REACH OF SURREALISM INTO ARCHITECTURE AND LATIN AMERICA, THE CHILEAN

ARGENTINA • CHILE • MEXICO

SINCE THE BEGINNING of the surrealist movement, its members have been strongly attracted to Latin America because of its historical development, the coexistence between "primitive" and "modern" cultures, and the possibility that it was a place uncluttered by Western civilization. This is evident in Antonin Artaud's travel to Mexico in 1936 and André Breton's in 1938. In addition, because of generous immigration laws, the growth of Nazism, and the Spanish Civil War, a number of important surrealists exiled themselves to Mexico and other parts of Latin America (see 1939 entry).

The case of the Chilean artist Roberto Matta Echaurren (known simply as MATTA) is particular. Matta

had trained as an architect at the Catholic University in Santiago, Chile. His thesis project for a League of Religions, based on the concept of the League of Nations, drew upon organic biomorphic forms to shape its interior spaces. In 1934, following his graduation, he moved to Paris, where he began working for Le Corbusier. There he made important connections not only with some of the central surrealist figures of the time, such as Salvador Dalí and Breton, but also with other architects working in Le Corbusier's office, such as the Catalan Antoni Bonet, who began working there in 1937 and emigrated to Argentina in 1938. Characteristic of MATTA's personal explorations on space is *Wet Sheets* (1936), which combines perspectival spaces,

Roberto Matta Echaurren, image from *Sensitive Mathematics—Architecture of Time*, 1938.

ARCHITECT-TRAINED ARTIST MATTA PUBLISHES "SENSITIVE MATHEMATICS—ARCHITECTURE OF TIME" IN *MINOTAURE*.

biomorphic forms, and collage to create, as historian Anthony Vidler describes, an "inner, non-Euclidian space . . . a multiple space of the imaginary."[1] *Architectural Study* (1936) similarly collages figures and landscape onto a perspectival architectural space whose walls are curvilinear, fluid, and inhabited by curvilinear sculptural objects or furniture. In 1938, MATTA formalized his ideas of architecture and space in "Mathématique sensible—Architecture du temps" (Sensitive Mathematics—Architecture of Time), published in the surrealist journal *Minotaure*. In it, he advocated for an organic, womb-like architecture centered on the experiencing subject and stood in contrast to rational or

stylized form: "We need walls like damp sheets which lose their shapes and wed our psychological fears . . . furniture which rolls out from unexpected spaces, receding, folding up, filling out like a walk in the water . . . an unformulizable course designing a new architectural, livable space. . . . To find for each person those umbilical cords that put us in communication with other suns, objects of total freedom that would be like psychoanalytic mirrors. . . . We need a cry against the digestions of right angles in the midst of which one allows oneself to be brutalized."[2] Similar to the two works mentioned above, the illustration accompanying the essay depicted an apartment that emphasized human verticality and had differing plans, psychological

Antoni Bonet, Suipacha and Paraguay Artists Ateliers, Buenos Aires, 1938.

ionic columns, and inflatable furniture. Its materiality included plaster, concrete, rubber, and "the framework of rational architecture."

Although Antoni Bonet's interest in surrealism predated his partnership with MATTA in Le Corbusier's office, we find the presence of characteristics similar to those ascribed to and presented as the new architecture by MATTA in an early variant of the design of Le Corbusier's Maisons Jaoul (1938) that Bonet and MATTA worked on. Here, they introduced curvilinear forms and the use of collage into the design. In Bonet's words, the experience in Le Corbusier's office would galvanize his interest in how to apply surrealist variants to architecture: "[When I created this work,] I incorporated surrealist ideas into the current functionalist architecture; it was a freedom from the excessive subjection demanded by rationalism."[3]

As a result of the Civil War in Spain, Bonet decided to emigrate to Argentina in 1938 at the insistence of Jorge Ferrari Hardoy and Juan Kurchan, who, at the time, were working in Paris on Le Corbusier's Plan for Buenos Aires. Emblematic of Bonet's attempts to incorporate surrealism into architecture would be the Suipacha and Paraguay Artists Ateliers (with Horacio Vera Barros and Abel López Chas, 1938). A corner building, it integrates retail spaces on the ground level, two-story apartments above, and atelier units on the roof. Through the juxtaposition of different materials and forms, the building is intended to create a "surrealist" shock by the contrasts it presents: between steel and glass, with the traditional Buenos Aires urban fabric, between orthogonality and curvilinear forms, between modernist construction techniques and the traditional Catalan vaults used as the roofs of the ateliers. The curvilinear forms of the ground-floor shops are also emblematic of the rejection of rationalist orthogonal design and, through their "automatic" design, expressive of creative liberation and the potentials of the unconscious.

In this way, the emblematic furniture piece designed for the Artists Ateliers, the 1938 BKF Chair (an acronym of its designers' names—Bonet, Kurchan, and Ferrari Hardoy—and most commonly known as the Butterfly Chair), is also expressive of the same operations. Designed in an improvised and automatic way, the chair's curvilinear forms and hanging leather operate similarly to the Artists Ateliers in creating strong juxtapositions: traditional (of the Argentine leather crafts) and modern (of the, initially, bentwood frame),

physical stability in contrast to the "unstable" organic form, and irregular yet controlled form. In addition to these characteristics, the chair—albeit part of a broader search for new forms of furniture at the time—also introduced new forms of spatial and physical occupation and seating that were radically different and more physical than its rationalist counterparts.[4]

The contact between Bonet and the Argentines led to the formation of the Austral Group in 1939 with a manifesto, "Voluntad y Acción" (Will and Action), touting the importance of the individual, the artistic, and surrealism—which "denounces established truths and addresses psychological issues"—as an antidote to the "intellectual and dehumanizing" solutions of functionalism. The Austral Group is perhaps the most avant-garde group that emerged in Latin America at the time: it was indebted to Le Corbusier, but at the same time it reshaped and evolved his ideas into new directions and forms. This influence and transformation can be seen in the Virrey del Pino Apartment (Buenos Aires, 1940). Designed by Jorge Ferrari Hardoy and Juan Kurchan in the Belgrano neighborhood of Buenos Aires, the ten-story apartment building with a penthouse was placed on the rear of its lot. This freed the front for an open garden and a single-story restaurant building, allowing it to follow Le Corbusier's ideas about architectural form and the need for the city to have more green spaces (which both architects had witnessed firsthand working on Le Corbusier's Plan for Buenos Aires). Like the Artists Ateliers, the Virrey del Pino Apartments made use of contrasts: curvilinear forms in the ground floor and penthouse roof in contrast to the orthogonal structure, as well as the reinforced concrete and modern forms of the tower in contrast to the more autochthonous brick and pitched-roof forms of the restaurant. But perhaps its strongest element was the introduction of a eucalyptus tree into the building's structural frame. For historian Jorge Francisco Liernur, this amounts to a typical surrealist operation of "placing objects in unusual or even impossible contexts [in order to] generate new meanings." For Ferrari Hardoy, the tree in contrast to the other elements of the façade would give the building an uncommon, "poetic" quality.[5]

In Mexico, a similar surrealist architecture of contrasts developed at the hands of the German émigré Max Cetto (see 1939 entry). Cetto had studied architecture in Germany under the expressionist architect Hans Poelzig and had served in building administration in Frankfurt under Ernst May in the 1920s and

Max Cetto, Max Cetto House, El Pedregal, Mexico City, 1948.

1930s. After a brief pass through the United States to work with Frank Lloyd Wright and Richard Neutra, Cetto established himself in Mexico. Emblematic of a new form of architecture is his vacation house in Tequesquitengo, Morelos (1940), that employs irrational curvilinear forms that contrast with the rationality and efficiency of the programmatic organization of the plan. In addition, Cetto uses river rocks for some of the structural elements, sharply contrasting them to the reinforced concrete of the roofs, which also gives the house a treelike characteristic.

Cetto's work in El Pedregal subdivision is perhaps the most well known and recognized. Not only did he design the model homes for its developer, Luis Barragán, which evoke a sharp contrast between the lava rock terrain and the cubic modernist forms, but he also built a home for himself that expresses similar contrasts (see 1947-a entry). The Max Cetto House (1948) accentuates the tension between materials and forms (such as the house's orthogonal volumes constructed with the local rock, glass, and reinforced concrete forms), the lava-formed landscape, and the edge of the site as they contrast with the formal geometries of the building. On the interior, despite its cubic qualities, Cetto used organic curvilinear forms for the fireplace

as well as stone mosaic with abstract yet historical symbols depicting fire and other elements on the ceiling in the architect's workspace.

Perhaps the most dramatic expression of a surrealist architecture in Mexico can be attributed to Juan O'Gorman. At the end of the 1920s and beginning of the 1930s, O'Gorman had championed functionalist architecture as part of a solution to fulfill the lack of shelter and hygienic structures for the majority of the population (see 1933 entry and 1931 box). In 1936, however, he became disillusioned with and ultimately rejected the functionalist architecture he had advocated because it had become a style that was used by developers and speculators to sell more buildings. O'Gorman's rejection was also based on that architecture's inability to communicate directly and clearly to the masses about their class interests and the fact that it reinforced the tendencies of capitalism to reproduce profits and class distinctions. His turn toward muralist and realist painting should be seen as part of his critique of the failure of modernist forms to communicate. With the design of his own house (Mexico City, 1948) and the library for the UNAM (Mexico City, 1950–1951; see 1952 entry), O'Gorman began to work again on architecture. This return to architecture was centered primarily on his desire to create a "realistic" architecture—similar in values to muralist

Juan O'Gorman, view of garden entrance of Juan O'Gorman House, Mexico City, 1948.

painting—which, at the same time, was collective, was expressive of the social condition of the people, and emanated from the soil as a telluric expression. To communicate his social message and to highlight the importance of the consciousness of it by the viewer/user, O'Gorman added didactic messages via mosaic murals (as in the case of the exterior decoration of the library at the UNAM) or sculptural forms (throughout his house).[6] His house at the edge of El Pedregal subdivision attests to his attempt to make architecture more visceral in its experience and irrational in its design (through the use of the natural qualities of the site and the construction of a "grotto" or "cave-like" interior space). The house was also to be "organic." In other words, it was based on O'Gorman's readings of Frank Lloyd Wright's ideas on organic architecture—an architecture whose forms and character were derived from the place where it was built. However, true to his functionalist background, O'Gorman coupled those ideas with functionalist details (e.g.,

the expression of the stair on the façade of the house, as he had done with the studio for Frida Kahlo), the expression of the materials (in this case, the lava rock and mosaics), and the expression of the elements that made up the site (the rocky terrain and its vegetation). O'Gorman's paintings of the same period similarly reflect a rejection of rational or discursive thinking by depicting landscapes whose forms evoke other images and other paintings (such as, through references, the work of Hieronymus Bosch) and could be said to be dreamlike in character and composition.

FURTHER READING

Arenós, *A.B.C.: Casa de Estudios para Artistas, Canòdrom.*
Katzenstein, Natanson, and Schvartzman, *Antonio Bonet.*
Liernur, "The Tree in the Box."
Pschepiurca, "BKF: Annuncio di una Modernita."
"Tate," http://tate.org.uk/magazine/issue4/matta.htm.
Vidler, "'Architecture-to-Be.'"

1938

JOAQUÍN TORRES-GARCÍA, *MONUMENTO CÓSMICO*, MONTEVIDEO, URUGUAY

Any primitive culture progresses along [that line where the sign is part of tradition]. Its art, always geometric in expression, is a ritual, something sacred. . . . The sign is something natural [so that one] can grasp the essence of this point of incidence between the living and the abstract.

JOAQUÍN TORRES-GARCÍA,
LA TRADICIÓN DEL HOMBRE ABSTRACTO (1938)

Joaquín Torres-García, *Monumento cósmico*, Montevideo, 1938

THE TRADITION OF ABSTRACT MAN articulates Joaquín Torres-García's interest in the geometric and abstract characteristics of pre-Hispanic and primitive cultures, something that he represented within his work and advocated for in his writings and teachings.

Despite being born in Uruguay in 1874, Torres-García was educated in Europe, where his family moved when he was seventeen. His 1906 murals for the Palau de la Generalitat in Barcelona attest to his skill, reputation, and ability to integrate historical and nationalist concerns. The influence of the avant-garde in the 1920s can be seen in his interest in abstraction and geometry as well as his early adoption of primitive forms; all of these seemed to suggest to him the notion of universal truths that could be found in both ancient and modern art. In the late 1920s, Torres-García met Theo van Doesburg and Piet Mondrian, whose rationalist conception of the world he began to incorporate into his work as well as to criticize. In his work from the late 1920s and early 1930s we can note his interest in pre-Hispanic cultures (through the incorporation of archetypal images) as well as the use of neoplastic orthogonal grids to organize his compositions. By the time he returned to Uruguay in 1934, Torres-García had already become an established artist, theorist of constructivist art, and advocate for the development of a "universal" constructive art rooted in the Americas. Through the Escuela del Sur (School of the South), Torres-García sought to develop an avant-gardist artistic production centered in Montevideo. Its sign, the *Inverted Map of South America*, an upside-down map of South America, reflected this new vision: "Our North is the South. For us there must not be a North, except in opposition to our South."

Torres-García's interest in pre-Columbian symbols and his search for a universal synthesis can be seen in his design and construction of *Monumento cósmico* (*Cosmic Monument*) in Montevideo's Parque Rodó (1937–1938). The monument is a two-dimensional grid built of granite blocks that has signs and symbols carved in relief on it. Some of these refer to pre-Hispanic cultures such as those found in Nazca pottery. In addition, the Gateway of the Sun, built by the pre-Inca civilization of Tihuanaco and known to Torres-García through a plaster cast at the Trocadero Museum, becomes a direct precedent for the monument. This is clear not only through the form of the monument itself but also through the reference to the monument as an astronomical piece (similar to the function the ancient example had served) where the figure of the sun is located in the center of the monument's composition (next to the monument is also a stele dedicated to the sun). The sculpture is topped with a cube, a sphere, and a pyramid, the three primary volumes suggesting the universality and timelessness of geometry.

Ultimately, the *Monumento cósmico* would serve as one example of a series of planned constructions that were intended to "teach the public that a new art is here, to familiarize people with geometry, and through geometry, with universal art." In addition to the public dissemination of his ideas, Torres-García's influence in Latin America's burgeoning abstract art scene would be profound. Through his Escuela del Sur, a number of Uruguayan artists continued exploring the architectural scale of such proposals. This can be seen, for example, in Edwin Studer's mural for the Columbarium in Montevideo's Northern Cemetery (see 1962 box) or in Gonzalo Fonseca's Tower of the Winds, a reinforced concrete structure for the 1968 Mexican Olympics (see 1968 entry).

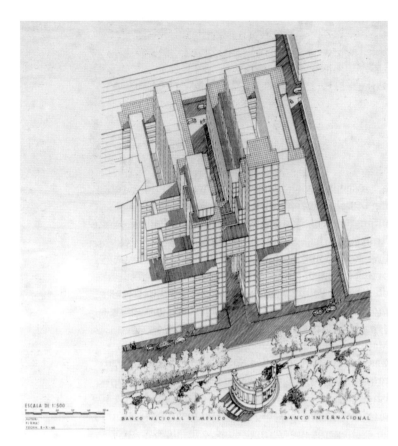

Hannes Meyer, Manzana de Corpus Christi project, Mexico City, 1946–1947.

manifestos—such as *Building* (1929)—argued for the need of building (against an outmoded sense of architecture rooted in the past and ornamentation) structures intended to fulfill social needs while addressing functional necessities in an economic way. For Meyer, building had nothing do with aesthetics but, instead, was about the organization of the program, materials, and social elements to solve the functional and biological needs of its user and nothing else. His interest in Mexico (and the interest of Mexico in him) resulted from his participation in the 1938 International Congress of Planning and Housing (organized by the Mexican architect Carlos Contreras), where he was warmly received by the Unión de Arquitectos Socialistas (Union of Socialist Architects; see 1971 entry). As a result, Meyer was invited to head the Instituto de Urbanismo y Planificación (Institute of Urbanism and Planning) by the Lázaro Cárdenas government, one of the most progressive governments after the Mexican Revolution. Meyer's influence on architecture and planning was short lived, however, since his arrival

coincided with the political change from the Cárdenas regime, which sponsored him, to the more conservative government of President Manuel Ávila Camacho. Subsequently, Meyer was not very well accepted by the architecture community and, because of his time in the Soviet Union, was considered a Soviet agent. He was implicated (but never charged) in the death of Leon Trotsky (assassinated in 1940) and, again, in the death of Italian photographer Tina Modotti in 1942. Furthermore, in his ten years in Mexico, Meyer explored regionalist architecture in an attempt to find appropriate forms and particular expressions of "place" within modern architecture (something that he had begun to explore with his Children's Home [Mümliswil, Switzerland, 1938]) rather than the strict functionalism and International-style architecture that people expected from him. The majority of his designs for Mexico of this period, although expressive of functionalist principles, dealt with regionalist forms and attempted to reintroduce classical principles. The bulk of his architectural or planning work was produced for Swiss or German émigrés, such as the Centro Deportivo Cultural Suiso (1940), or for capitalist concerns, like the Manzana de Corpus Christi (1946–1947) for the National Bank of Mexico. Despite this, Meyer, along with his wife Lena, became associated with the important Taller de Gráfica Popular (Popular Graphics Workshop) and its antifascist efforts. With the growing frustration of being unable to build anything in Mexico, Meyer returned to Switzerland in 1949.

Although he was involved with political issues, it is clear that Meyer didn't maintain the socialist and critical position that he had held in the past. In a way, this is emblematic of the effects of the transfer to a new place. The speed with which it occurs usually translates into a lack of or limited interest in the mundane—as outsiders who think their time in the country is limited—as well as avoidance of becoming overtly compromised with political or problematic issues of or within the new country. The latter is typically a carryover from the precarious situation the immigrant may have experienced before moving.

For our purposes, however, the most important characteristics of the émigré or exile are centered on the effects of being nomadic and the qualities that it engenders. Particularly, immigrants' nonattachment to the new place is important because it means that they can operate without the weight of local traditions, debates, or formal expectations. In addition, without a full awareness of the material limitations or their common usage within their new home, they are able to explore materials in new ways. Félix Candela's structural innovations in Mexico can be seen in both of these lights: in Mexico, he was able to explore and develop his reinforced concrete constructive and structural shells autonomous, as he claimed, of program or context.

Memory (of the previous existence, architecture, etc.), then, becomes productive during exile. In other words, émigrés bring a vast amount of knowledge from their previous existence to bear within the new context. In many cases, the architecture that they designed resulted from a negotiation of the work and ideas from the past context with the new environment and situation; in this way, new correspondences, relations, parallels, and comparisons are made by the exiled architect in the development of a new architecture.

This can be seen in the aforementioned work of Daniele Calabi and the German émigré Max Cetto. In São Paulo, Calabi, who worked in the Veneto region in the early 1930s exploring the classical roots of modern architecture, merged traditional and modern architecture at the Edifício Autogeral (1940), in partnership with Henrique Mindlin. A few years later his Medici

Pavilion (1945) would use high walls and opaque façades to create a series of private patios, a predecessor of the Paulista school of the 1950s. These types of patios were, for him, part of the legacy of Mediterranean architecture and became the driving force of his own 1945–1946 house. Thought of as an abstracted classical or Roman house, Calabi's design not only uses honorific materials (like travertine) but contrasts them with more traditional local materials (e.g., tile roof). In addition, to address the locale, Calabi includes on the front façade a *brise-soleil*.

Cetto, who arrived in Mexico in 1939 after a brief stay in the United States, likewise brings his background to the fore in the work that he would produce with Luis Barragán. Here, Cetto's experience in the European modernist milieu would become apparent through his simple volumetric cubic compositions (most clearly noted in contrast to Barragán's earlier work). But it is perhaps in his own work, such as his house for Tequesquitengo (1940), where the influence of his old mentor, Hans Poelzig, is most clearly seen (see 1938 entry).

For Cetto, Candela, and Bonet, we can say that their foreign gaze, along with a sensibility for valuing

Daniele Calabi, Villa Daniele Calabi, São Paulo, 1946.

Max Cetto, Weekend House in Tequesquitengo, Morelos, Mexico, 1940.

certain local conditions, was fundamental to their successful careers. The same is also valid for Lina Bo Bardi (see 1985 entry; 1951-c and 1957-b boxes), who emigrated with her husband, Pietro Maria Bardi, in 1946. But the same São Paulo that gave Bo Bardi a new life and a new career (along with Lucjan Korngold, Giancarlo Palanti, and so many others) was also a frustrating place for Bernard Rudofsky, who moved to the United States in 1942, and Daniele Calabi, who returned to Italy in 1949. Hannes Meyer was the most significant example of incompatibility, having managed to build nothing in Mexico City while his colleagues and previous Bauhaus directors Walter Gropius and Mies van der Rohe were leading architectural conversations in the United States. In the end,

architects forced to emigrate for one reason or another showed a tremendous resilience to the situation they were forced into by adapting their ideas and architecture to the new circumstances but also by introducing something foreign into an existing environment. Without a doubt, these architects contributed tremendously to the development of modern architecture in Latin America.

FURTHER READING

Daniele Calabi: Architetture e progetti, 1932–1964.
del Cueto Ruiz-Funes, "Cien años de Félix Candela."
Gorelik and Liernur, *La sombra de la vanguardia.*
Heredia, "The Work of Max Cetto."
Sánchez-Albornoz, *The Population of Latin America.*
Vicente, *Arquitecturas desplazadas.*

1939

THE BRAZILIAN PAVILION AT NEW YORK WORLD'S FAIR

BRAZILIAN MODERN ARCHITECTURE had its international debut in the architectural media with the 1939 pavilion for the New York World's Fair. Besides being the first
Brazilian success abroad, the pavilion is a perfect example
of a partnership that would dominate the country's architectural scene: Lúcio Costa's ideas materialized by Oscar
Niemeyer's talents.

The pavilion was the result of a competition held in 1938
by the Brazilian government to represent the nation at the
New York World's Fair. Costa was awarded first place with
Niemeyer coming in as runner-up. The winning entry had a
central patio surrounded by a symmetrical gallery raised on
pilotis and, at the rear, an attached auditorium. Niemeyer's
entry was a combination of three volumes: a meandering
exhibition hall following the form of the site, an independent auditorium at the front, and an open foyer/main entrance mass connecting the other two volumes.

Playing the role of mentor to the fullest, Costa brought
Niemeyer with him to New York, and together they worked

Brazilian pavilion under construction, New York, 1939.

Lúcio Costa and Oscar Niemeyer, Brazilian pavilion, New York, 1939.

Interior of the Brazilian pavilion, New York, 1939.

Plans of the Brazilian pavilion, New York, 1939.

on a third proposal that joined the best of both and garnered the effusive approval of the fair's organizers.

The final design used the asymmetrical and curved composition of Niemeyer's plan with the auditorium incorporated inside the main entrance volume. Based on Costa's original design, the whole building was elevated on *pilotis*. The entrance is a clear mix of both previous designs. Enclosed by *brise-soleil* on one half (from Costa's scheme) and fully opened on the other half (from Niemeyer's), it was now complemented by an elegant free-form ramp that in Costa's previous design only existed at the rear of the composition. To avoid a halfway landing that would have forced the ramp to be longer and to curve a bit more (to fit the site), Costa and Niemeyer got a special variance from New York's building code. The exhibition hall was a double-height space accessed on the second level from the ramp, and it contained an organically shaped mezzanine that expressed the rigidity of the structure in contrast to the playfulness of the plan. The curved form for the exhibition hall also gave the pavilion some distance from the massive neighboring French pavilion while at the same time creating a space for the "tropical" garden on the ground floor, which was accessed from the restaurant and cafeteria located under the exhibition space. The *New York Times* (May 5, 1939), in reviewing the pavilions of the fair, noted that "most structures were cast in quaint, traditional styles: a Japanese tea garden, a Chinese pagoda, a rustic Finnish village. Brazil, however, built a huge modern edifice in keeping with the International Style."

In the 1939 pavilion, the influence of Le Corbusier was very visible in the massing of the programmatic pieces and the use of *pilotis* that dominated the composition. However, the combination of meandering ramps, *brise-soleil* panels, *pilotis*, and curvilinear plans would become the formal characteristics of the early phases of Brazilian modernism and, more specifically, of the so-called Carioca school of Rio de Janeiro. So, while the curves are still a bit unassertive as compared with Pampulha (see 1941 entry), Niemeyer's House in Canoas (Rio de Janeiro, 1954; see 1953-c entry), or the Ibirapuera pavilion (São Paulo, 1951), the 1939 pavilion would serve as a testing ground for some of Niemeyer's later experiments.

It is also important to note the choice of content for the exhibition. Photographs of Ouro Preto were displayed alongside photos of the not-yet-completed MESP building. At the same time, the courtyard garden (designed by Roberto Burle Marx) was made as tropical as possible through the inclusion of Brazilian flora and fauna. The "modern-baroque connection in the tropics" was being enthusiastically pushed by Costa: an intellectual articulation that would become hegemonic after the 1943 Museum of Modern Art *Brazil Builds* exhibition (see 1943-a entry).

The 1939 pavilion had all the seeds that would soon flourish as the exuberant Brazilian modernism. This exuberance, however, was very different from that of the Brazilian singer Carmen Miranda whose show was Broadway's main attraction that same year. Trying to avoid the caricatured image of the tutti-frutti hat, Brazilian architects embraced a more international architecture in their desire to express a modern sensibility about themselves. Celebrated abroad as a step ahead of functionalist and rationalist theories, the new Brazilian architecture acquired at home the status of a paradigm. Abroad, however, the image of exoticism and eroticism that the Brazilians were trying to avoid still prevailed.

1941

PAMPULHA REPRESENTS AN ENCOUNTER THAT WOULD CHANGE THE FUTURE OF BRAZIL.

THE FIRST WEEKS OF 1941 seem very far away from today's perspective. Stalin and Hitler still had their nonaggression treaty, and the United States would not endure the attack on Pearl Harbor and enter World War II until the end of the year. In Brazil, the thirty-three-year-old Oscar Niemeyer was overseeing the construction of a hotel in the historic city of Ouro Preto. The Ouro Preto Hotel was the result of a frustrated competition that left the client, the Brazilian Office of Conservation (SPHAN, later renamed IPHAN), unhappy with all the entries. Niemeyer had proposed a very modern structure, and Lúcio Costa convinced him to make a few changes to his design: to use a ceramic tile roof, wooden trellises, and squared-section columns instead of a flat roof, *brise-soleil*, and *pilotis*. The result was a modern hotel that fit quite well in the eighteenth-century urban fabric of Ouro Preto. This would be one of the first moments when the narrative of stitching the modern with the baroque, hegemonic a decade later, would be used.[1]

In Belo Horizonte, the new capital of Minas Gerais (inaugurated in 1897), Mayor Juscelino Kubitschek was troubled by a suburban development north of the city that was not selling very well. The city had drained a swamp to build a new airport in the flatlands and formed the artificial lake of Pampulha upstream to control the flow. Around the lake, the area was subdivided into thousands of large lots (10,000 to 50,000 sq. ft./930 to 4,645 sq. m) intended to attract the city's upper classes. Sales and construction, however, had been slow. In order to boost development, the municipality decided to invest in "public" infrastructures for the area. As a result, Kubitschek traveled 60 miles (97 km) to Ouro Preto to meet Oscar Niemeyer and make him an offer he couldn't refuse.[2]

As Kubitschek toured Oscar Niemeyer around, he talked about building a chapel, a casino, a dance hall, a yacht club, and a hotel. If modern architecture was about new programs and new clients, Pampulha was a contradiction from the beginning, given its traditional and bourgeois programs. Kubitschek, however, wanted these buildings as soon as possible and asked Niemeyer if he could come back to Belo Horizonte the following week. Eager to go back to Rio de Janeiro, Niemeyer spent the night sketching and by the next morning had his hotel room full of drawings to show the mayor.

Scattered around the artificial lake, the four buildings designed by Oscar Niemeyer and completed in 1942 would become the landmarks of modern Brazilian architecture. The Capela da Pampulha, Casino, Iate Clube, and Casa do Baile quickly became the paradigm for Brazilian architectural modernism for decades as well as international icons for a new type of modern architecture.[3]

The Capela da Pampulha, or the Saint Francis of Assisi Chapel, is a little church built on a small peninsula in a curved piece of land between the lake and a surrounding road. The building's form results from the creation of four parabolic vaults that are united

Cândido Portinari, ceramic tile mural, Capela da Pampulha, Belo Horizonte, 1942.

Oscar Niemeyer, Capela da Pampulha, Belo Horizonte, 1942.

together, with only the two ends touching the ground, and with a taller one emphasizing the main space of the chapel. With its back facing the street, the first view the visitor encounters is Cândido Portinari's mural of azulejos, traditional Portuguese painted ceramic tiles, that covers the wall. The use of azulejos is a Portuguese tradition used in Brazilian modernist buildings since they were first applied to the MESP building (whose azulejo murals were also done by Portinari; see 1936

entry). The landscape designed by Roberto Burle Marx, another alumnus of the MESP, guides the visitors around the structure and toward the *adro* (open area in front of the church used as transition space) that lies between the entrance and the edge of the lake. The *adro*'s floor has an amoeboid pattern in white marble and black granite that penetrates the church and unites the inside and outside in an unconventional manner. From this vantage point, one can see the whole form: the parabolic vaults covered by *pastilhas* (small ceramic tiles) and their intersection by a taller vault that extends toward the lake, the fenestration and *brise-soleil* of the façade, and the inverted bell tower and its inclined canopy uniting the tower to the main door, marking and defining the entrance. Inside the chapel, defined by the larger parabolic vault, the ceiling is covered in wood, and an azulejo-covered free-standing curvilinear wall defines the baptistery on the left side. On the wall behind the altar is a fresco by Portinari depicting the life of St. Francis that is naturally illuminated through a gap between the larger of the four vaults facing the street and the taller vault of the chapel. The remaining smaller vaults house the sacristy and the offices of the parish. Celebrated by the architectural community, the Capela da Pampulha, however, was viewed by the church as inappropriate for Catholic rituals and, as a result, remained unconsecrated for many years.

The Casino was also built on a peninsula between the lake and the road. For this building, however, Niemeyer placed the main entrance to the cubic volume on the driveway and garden side, facing the street. The garden was also designed by Burle Marx. The

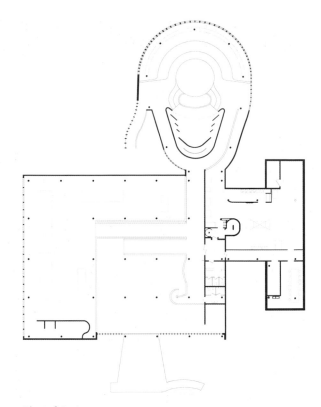

Plan of Casino.

Oscar Niemeyer, interior of Casino da Pampulha, Belo Horizonte, 1942.

Oscar Niemeyer, Casa do Baile, Belo Horizonte, 1942.

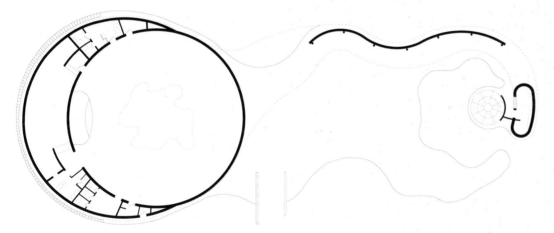

Plan of Casa do Baile.

entrance's free-form canopy is supported by thin steel columns and is connected to the continuous glass wall on the façade. Inside the main cubic volume, a ramp dominates the space, and the round concrete columns covered in stainless steel accentuate the rhythm of the interior space. In addition, the Casino's interior space appears larger and more open through the use of a mirrored wall on the side (covering the service spaces). At the back of the building, closer to the lake, an elliptical dance hall is integrated with the main volume by another ramp, and its continuous glass wall brings the lake's landscape inside. With the pink-tinted mirrors, the light onyx of the ramp and handrails, the stainless steel, and the openness created by the enclosing glass walls, Niemeyer created something that though in principle formally follows the canons of Corbusian architecture, is, materially, exuberant and even baroque in its character. According to historian Kenneth Frampton, the Casino represented the height of Niemeyer's genius as he "reinterpreted the Corbusian notion of *promenade architecturale* in a spatial composition of remarkable balance and vivacity."[4]

At the Iate Clube (Yacht Club), Niemeyer experimented with the butterfly roof to maximize the view of the lake for those using the main upper hall for dining during the day or for balls at night. That roof form would also become a trademark of Brazilian modernism. This structure is the only one of the Pampulha buildings designed by Niemeyer that is now privately owned, privatized in the 1960s.

The Casa do Baile (Dance Hall) is an island pavilion composed of a cylindrical building defined primarily by a crescent shape that houses the bar, stage, and restaurant as well as by a meandering canopy supported by rounded columns that connects the main structure to a second cylindrical volume, at the end of the composition, where the dressing rooms are located. All of the volumes and walls are covered with painted ceramic azulejos. The canopy, however, is the highlight of the composition, following the curves of the lake, providing shelter, defining the external space for those seated under it, and framing the view for those who pass by on the road.

In Pampulha, Niemeyer produced an architecture that finally broke away from the Corbusian syntax and was more mature and personal than the design for the 1939 Brazilian pavilion for the New York World's Fair (see 1939 box) or his hotel in Ouro Preto (1940). So, while Niemeyer was applying Le Corbusier's ideas of the promenade, he was also challenging the Corbusian five points of a new architecture through the form of the Capela. In this way, the Pampulha buildings begin to address and solve the conflict between local and international references, representation and abstraction, and industrialization and artisanal construction.

The relevance and originality of the Pampulha buildings resonated in Brazil and abroad even before the buildings were completed. The still unfinished buildings were prominently displayed in the Museum of Modern Art's 1943 *Brazil Builds* exhibition (see

1943-a entry). In it, the relationship between modern and baroque architecture was framed to help explain the success of Pampulha at home and abroad. Initially articulated by Lúcio Costa (see 1943-a entry), the idea would become the dominant historiographical paradigm after Pampulha, establishing a link between the Brazilian past and the formal experiments of the young designers. It was, more specifically, an important tool to justify Niemeyer's formal liberties and digressions from the Corbusian syntax. So, when he was questioned about the meandering canopy of the Casa do Baile, Niemeyer replied that he was just following the contours of the lake, never mentioning that the building's site was a small artificial island also designed with his favorite curves. The baroque connection would serve, then, a double function: to avoid the critique of eclecticism or willfulness, so scorned by modern architecture, while justifying Niemeyer's formal vocabulary.

The impact of the Pampulha buildings was considerable, first in Brazil and then abroad. At home, Niemeyer would quickly become the favorite not only of Kubitschek but also of almost every government following him. Abroad, Pampulha would play an important part in the architectural debates of the following decade: Nikolaus Pevsner labeling it as subversive work, Reyner Banham defining it as the first national style in modern architecture, and Gillo Dorfles characterizing it as neobaroque.

Presented as modern buildings strongly rooted in past traditions, the structures in Pampulha solidified, as early as 1941, the conceptual foundation that Brazilian architecture would follow and react to for the rest of the twentieth century. In one way or another, the meeting between Niemeyer and Kubitschek would change the image of Brazil, produce some of the most influential Latin American buildings in the twentieth century, and culminate in the construction of Brasília fifteen years later.

FURTHER READING

Bruand, *Arquitetura contemporânea no Brasil.*
Comas, "Pampulha y la arquitectura moderna brasileña."
Frampton, *Modern Architecture: A Critical History.*
Lara, "One Step Back, Two Steps Forward."
Underwood, *Oscar Niemeyer and the Architecture of Brazil.*

1942

AMANCIO WILLIAMS, CASA SOBRE EL ARROYO

THE CASA SOBRE EL ARROYO (House over the Brook, aka Bridge House) designed by Amancio Williams in Mar del Plata, Argentina, is often compared to or described as a simplified version of Frank Lloyd Wright's Fallingwater (Bear Run, PA, 1938–1939). It is highly probable that Williams knew about Fallingwater, since it graced the cover of *Time* magazine in 1938 in addition to being widely published in architectural magazines. Wright's house might have influenced Williams's decision to locate the house above the creek. The idea of simplification does not hold any water, for lack of a better metaphor. Williams's Casa sobre el Arroyo is indeed much more radical than Wright's famous precedent.

Amancio Williams was born in 1913 and graduated from architecture school in 1941 after trying other trades such as aviation and mechanical engineering. Soon after graduation, the twenty-eight-year-old Williams was

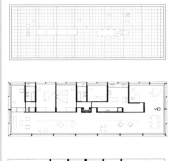

Section and plans of House over the Brook.

Amancio Williams, House over the Brook, Mar del Plata, 1942.

commissioned by his father, Alberto Williams, a well-known Argentine composer of modernist classical music, to design a house for him on a 5-acre lot in the suburbs of Mar del Plata. Although Williams would later serve as the local architect for Le Corbusier's Curutchet House in La Plata (see 1954 box), the house for his father was his only fully realized structure despite his prolific architectural vision (see 1971 entry).

The house is located on a property divided by a creek, so, in response, Williams designed the house as a bridge to span it and connect the two sides of the property. The bridge-like structure is made up of an arched slab of reinforced concrete that mirrors the creek's natural depression. Two massive columns at the ends serve as anchors, absorbing the lateral force of the arched slab. The columns, in turn, serve as entrance halls on both sides of the bridge, besides housing a restroom on one side and a utility room on the other, characteristic of Argentine creole entrance galleries. From those columns/vestibules, the visitor climbs upward via stairways built on the arched slab. The stairs provide the visitors with views of the creek and the landscape as they enter the house from its underside. From here, the visitors arrive at a landing in the middle of the bar that houses the living quarters. All of the elevations are identical and are made up of strip windows resting on a 3-foot-tall (91 cm) reinforced concrete beam folding inward. This creates the windowsill and encloses the main volume. The roof slab, in turn, is totally independent from the external envelope, as it is supported by a series of walls that wrap around an inner core of *pochè* spaces: fireplaces, closets, and service spaces.

The main floor of the house (90 x 30 ft./27 x 9 m) is divided longitudinally. On one side, facing the northwest—considered the front in all the photographs—are the stairs and a long strip of living spaces that wrap around the western edge to house the dining room and music room. In the other half are the kitchen, three bedrooms, and two bathrooms. Many of the interior partitions as well as the built-in furniture were built out of wood in a workshop and later disassembled and transported to the site. This resulted in an austere but carefully detailed interior. Skylights above the closets capture a bit of northern sun for the bedrooms, which otherwise would not get much light in the subtropical winters. The height of the house over the brook creates a sense of openness and allows the inhabitants unobstructed views toward the site at the level of the tree canopy.

At the Casa sobre el Arroyo, Williams was searching for a light and airy structure achieved by taking advantage of his engineering background. The resulting bridge house is both structurally simple and functional. For Williams, the house was "a form in space that does not deny nature. The form is at the same time, in its wholeness, structure shown naked in its authentic quality: the concrete—its material—is exposed, textured by mechanical and chemical procedures. Form, structure, and quality are thus here the same thing" (quoted in Silvetti, *Amancio Williams*, 28).

The synthesis between house and landscape is achieved here in harmony with the very idea of modernism. The Casa sobre el Arroyo is not a simplified version but a rationalist variant of the organic architecture characteristic of Wright's Fallingwater.

1943-A

THE *BRAZIL BUILDS* EXHIBITION AT THE MUSEUM OF MODERN
ART IN NEW YORK HIGHLIGHTS THE ARCHITECTURAL AND
POLITICAL INTERESTS OF U.S. RELATIONS WITH BRAZIL.

BRAZIL

ON JANUARY 28, 1943, U.S. president Franklin D. Roosevelt met Brazilian president Getúlio Vargas in the northeastern Brazilian city of Natal. That meeting, like so many others between heads of state, was arranged as a photo opportunity to sign a deal negotiated many months before. The United States had entered the Second World War in December of 1941, and Brazil followed in August of 1942. The Roosevelt-Vargas summit of 1943 was a showcase of U.S-Brazil relations to signify to the world that Brazilian troops would join the allies in Europe and that U.S. armed forces would use Brazilian bases such as the airfield in Natal.

Indeed, the negotiations between the two countries date to 1940 with the United States financing the first Brazilian steel mill in Volta Redonda in exchange for contracts supplying minerals and rubber. A fascinating facet of these talks was the role played by cultural organizations in that effort, including, interestingly enough, architecture (see 1943-b entry).

In the late 1930s, with Europe on the verge of World War II, a series of cultural initiatives aimed at Latin America were devised in New York and Washington under the name of the Good Neighbor Policy. As Nelson Rockefeller and others anticipated, internal forces in Brazil (and in other Latin American countries) were uncertain if the new center of the Western Hemisphere was going to be Washington or Berlin. With the Axis advancing in Europe, Northern Africa, and East Asia, Latin America became decisively strategic. The Good Neighbor Policy was designed to reinforce American influence in the region and prevent the expansion of pro-Germanic ideas. As a result, Nelson Rockefeller was named the Coordinator of Inter-American Affairs in 1940 and charged with establishing cooperation and stronger ties between the United States and Latin American countries. The most well known of the initiatives to introduce Latin American culture into the United States to make it more widely acceptable include Walt Disney's movies about Brazil and Mexico (such as the 1942 animated film *Saludos Amigos*); exhibits such as the Museum of Modern Art's (MoMA's) *Twenty Centuries of Mexican Art* (1940) or the one-man show dedicated to the work of Cândido Portinari (1940); and the boost of Carmen Miranda's career on Broadway and, later, in Hollywood. Architecture played a part as well with MoMA's exhibition *Brazil Builds*, produced after Rockefeller's tenure as president of the museum, and resulting from both the Good Neighbor Policy and the success of the Brazilian pavilion at the 1939 New York World's Fair.

The pavilion, the result of the partnership between Lúcio Costa and Oscar Niemeyer, was a curvilinear, elegant, and graceful modern building (see 1939 box). The combination of Corbusian volumes with sensual curves caught the attention of the New York architectural métier, and with support from the Good Neighbor Policy, a special exhibition was organized in 1942 at MoMA highlighting the pavilion. At that time, Nelson Rockefeller was the president of the museum's board of trustees while working as Roosevelt's Coordinator for Inter-American affairs.

In 1942, MoMA sent its chief architect, Philip Goodwin—who had just finished the museum's building at West 53rd Street under Rockefeller's leadership—and architect and photographer G. E. Kidder Smith on a tour of Brazil. Armed for the first time with 4 x 6 inch (10 x 15 cm) Kodachrome film, a recent introduction, the *Brazil Builds* exhibition would be the first full-color architecture exhibit at MoMA. In Brazil, they traveled widely, hosted by local government officials and architects. As revealed by the acknowledgments section of the catalogue, Goodwin and Kidder Smith relied heavily on Lúcio Costa's connections, not only with architects but also with scholars linked to the Brazilian Office of Preservation (IPHAN), whose department of architecture Costa had led since its founding in 1936. "Architecture New and Old," the subtitle of the exhibition and its main curatorial argument, fit precisely with Costa's discourse at the time, which linked modern buildings to Brazil's eighteenth-century colonial architecture. The exhibition, depicting eighty-five buildings (new and old) opened on January 13, 1943. After closing on February 28, 1943, it traveled to Boston, Mexico City, London, and Rio de Janeiro. While it is clear that the forty-five winter days of exhibition at the height of the war effort did not attract the largest crowds, the accompanying publication would indeed become paradigmatic.

Published in 1943, *Brazil Builds*, the catalogue of the show, included Goodwin's text and Kidder Smith's photographs (in black and white with the exception of a photograph of Niemeyer's Casino at Pampulha opposite the book's title page) and became the first book on modern architecture in Brazil to be published in English. In the book, Goodwin addressed the blending of modernity and heritage as a theoretical support for the early modernist buildings. For the first time, the articulation of the baroque effect and modern forms was published abroad, reinforcing the position of Costa and the young group of architects who were fighting for commissions in Brazil.

The catalogue's text started describing Belo Horizonte as the first city visible after flying over the Amazon (not geographically correct) and situates Brazilian independence in 1807 (when the king moved there), not 1822 as most history books do. This small diversion hints at the influence of the *modernistas* and, in particular, of Lúcio Costa. When presenting Jesuit architecture, the catalogue highlights the mission of São Miguel,

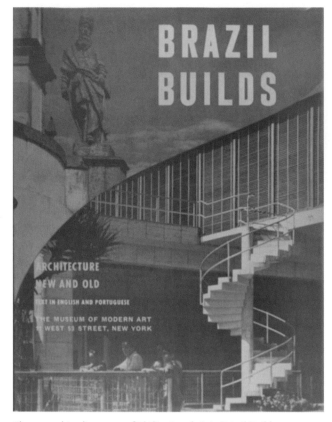

Photographic slip cover of Philip Goodwin's *Brazil Builds*, 1943.

Frontispiece to *Brazil Builds*, showing the recently completed Casino da Pampulha by Oscar Niemeyer, 1943.

where Costa had just finished building a museum, instead of the more exuberant cathedrals of Salvador da Bahia or Olinda. Late in the text, Goodwin briefly mentions the French artistic mission of 1816 and devotes a few lines to nineteenth-century architecture, which is described as sterile, dreary, and pretentious warmed-over Palladio where "perhaps the less said about them the better." The creation of the IPHAN in 1936 also plays a prominent place in Goodwin's narrative. Its story concludes with a happy ending: "Almost overnight the lovely capital city was cured of its disease and began to reconsider its architectural possibilities in terms of modern life and modern building technique."[1]

Goodwin's line of argumentation could not have been more like Costa's. This stitching of modernism to eighteenth-century baroque is traceable to the path taken earlier by Brazilian modern architecture: from an international and Corbusian starting point to a more nationalistic one while, at the same time, achieving worldwide recognition. At first articulated by Costa in response to local disputes (see 1930-a entry), this rhetorical turn toward the baroque proved to be a very fruitful discourse, allowing the *modernistas* to become the ultimate authority for both the past and the future. For the traditional modernist avant-garde, the past is used as an alterity, as something to be opposed to. In contrast, the Brazilian case is singular for the use of historical memory in the construction of a modern identity. It should be noted that it is not every "past," but rather a carefully designed and chosen myth of origin.

Many examples of Brazilian architecture, old and new, were not presented at the MoMA exhibition or in its famous catalogue. However, the references to the past allowed the Brazilian modern project to solve the conflict between nationalism and universalism characteristic of the first decades of the twentieth century. Historical and modern were put together, suggesting a continuation with an older baroque past while successfully criticizing and denying the importance of the eclecticism of nineteenth-century Beaux-Arts ideals. This articulation also joins the international and the local in the argument for modernist architecture. In this case, memory was designed and used to anchor the modernist project both in the useful past and the prospective future. In the careful choreography strategized by Lúcio Costa, Brazilian avant-garde took one step back in order to advance two steps forward.[2]

The *Brazil Builds* catalogue also addresses the theories behind Brazilian modern architecture: while the intellectual affiliation is French (stretching the Corbusian connection), many practical applications came from the United States: bathroom plumbing, elevators, lighting devices. Indeed, the U.S. cultural policies of the 1940s played a major role in publicizing Brazilian modernism abroad, and its success certainly influenced the United States during the following decade. In addition, the desire evident in Goodwin's text is toward the development of an American modern architecture to contrast its German counterpart and the "Prussian spirit of the drillyard."[3] For Goodwin, this is made more clear when direct connections are made between the United States and Brazil, such as when he describes the mayor of São Paulo as a combination of Robert Moses and Mayor Fiorello La Guardia, or when he notes that "Manhattan and Rio have very much in common."[4] Meanwhile, Brazilian architects paid close attention to North American trends and debates, while the tremendous penetration of North American cultural innovations affected the built environment as well. All this would change following the war as the U.S. government became more consumed by the Cold War and leading Brazilian architects (Oscar Niemeyer in Rio de Janeiro and João Vilanova Artigas in São Paulo, to name two) steered the conversation to the left, weary of growing inequalities at home and U.S. interventionism all over the Americas.

In 1955, MoMA would mount another exhibition on Latin American modern architecture, *Latin American Architecture since 1945*, under the leadership of Henry-Russell Hitchcock and Philip Johnson. The bridges built by the Good Neighbor Policy, however, had not been maintained, and relations degraded fast. The United States had just invaded Guatemala that same year and would, eventually, support military coups or dictatorships in Brazil (1964), Chile (1973), and Argentina (1976). Ironically, those same twenty-two years would go by before architecture in Latin American returned to MoMA in 1976, when the Argentine curator Emilio Ambasz organized an exhibition on the Mexican architect Luis Barragán (see 1980 entry). In it, MoMA and its New York vantage point would, once again, redefine the relationship between modernity and tradition in Latin America.

FURTHER READING

Goodwin, *Brazil Builds*.
Liernur, "'The South American Way.'"
Quezado Deckker, *Brazil Built*.

1943-B

TOWN PLANNING ASSOCIATES (TPA) IS COMMISSIONED TO DESIGN
A NEW BRAZILIAN TOWN AROUND AN AIRPLANE FACTORY,
CIDADE DOS MOTORES. THIS WILL BE THE BEGINNING OF TPA'S

BRAZIL • CARIBBEAN: CUBA • COLOMBIA • PERU

THE LATIN AMERICAN CITIES designed by Town Planning Associates (TPA), a New York–based design firm headed by Josep Lluís Sert, Paul Lester Wiener, and Paul Schulz, can be considered urban case studies that attempted to mediate the theories and forms developed in Europe by the Congrès International d'Architecture Moderne (CIAM; International Congress of Modern Architecture) within the context of preexisting Latin American historical traditions and urban forms. In particular, the cities become, once again, expressions of broader Corbusian principles with regard to the organization of the city as well as emblematic of the debates that will lead to the dissolution of the CIAM in 1959.

The TPA was formed in 1942 as a result of the contact between Sert and Weiner, a German-born architect; Schulz was added shortly thereafter. Sert, a Catalan architect and active participant in CIAM meetings since 1929, emigrated to New York in 1939 as a result of the Spanish Civil War. By the time he arrived in the United States, Sert was completing *Can Our Cities Survive?* (1942), a book promoting the principles of the CIAM's functionalist city as spelled out in the 1933 "Athens Charter." As historians note, however, Sert had begun to change his point of view regarding the issues that contemporary cities needed to address. These, of course, would be reflected in the call for the integration of culture and history into a new form of monumentality that Sert, with Fernand Léger and Siegfried Giedion, developed as the "Nine Points on Monumentality" (1943).

Initially, the interventions of the TPA in Latin America were part of a broader cultural outreach—a type of Good Neighbor Policy—by the U.S. Department of State (see 1943-a entry). Weiner, the son-in-law of the secretary of the treasury of the Roosevelt administration, was asked to participate in advisory and educational initiatives in South America with the intention of securing U.S. support during the Second World War and of thwarting any attempts by the Axis powers to gain influence in the American continent. Shortly after the TPA was established, both Sert and Weiner became deeply enmeshed in lecturing and

Town Planning Associates, Cidade dos Motores aerial perspective, 1943–1947.

INVOLVEMENT WITH LATIN AMERICA THAT WILL INCLUDE NOT ONLY PLANS FOR CHIMBOTE, PERU, BUT ALSO MASTER PLANS FOR MEDELLÍN AND BOGOTÁ, COLOMBIA, AND HAVANA, CUBA.

touring throughout Brazil, where their first commission would be located.

According to its designers, Cidade dos Motores, Brazil, was a model city "conceived for its inhabitants . . . to fully satisfy the physical and moral needs of the population."[1] It was also the beginning of a series of explorations to develop urban ideas for the Latin American context that were based on rearticulations of those developed by the CIAM. Designed between 1943 and 1947 as part of President Getúlio Vargas's strategy of modernization of the country, Cidade dos Motores (Motor City) was to be a company town centered on the production of military equipment and machines. The factory's construction was backed by the United States—because of its interest in the region—which provided economic as well as intellectual and advisory support.

The city, which was to be built on an undeveloped site near Rio de Janeiro, was to house 25,000 inhabitants. Its initial design was based on earlier studies and schemes by the Brazilian architect Attilio Corrêa Lima. His death in 1943 led to the TPA being brought in to work on the project. The development of the master plan took "The Athens Charter's" four functions—housing, recreation, work, and transportation—as guidelines for the organization of the city. The design of the city included the subdivision of the territory into four discrete neighborhoods composed of zones of housing blocks integrated into large open garden spaces and supported by various programs such as retail, schools, etc. The housing blocks were, in turn, both separated and connected via peripheral roadways and internal pedestrian walkways. The housing units developed into low- to mid-rise structures that were designed to accommodate the life cycles of their inhabitants.[2] Their façades were designed with enough variability to address climatic concerns but also to overcome the perceived monotony of modernist architecture.

As the "heart of the city" and, in later designs, treated as the equivalent of the "fifth function," the civic center was based primarily on Spanish-influenced

Latin American urban planning traditions and, as such, revolved around a public square considered the social nucleus of the community. The center also included a public promenade and public areas spatially defined by cultural buildings (theater, café, museum, etc.) and administrative spaces.

In the end, the privatization of the factory led to the dismissal of the backers of the project and to the eventual incompletion of Sert and Wiener's proposal. Despite this, however, the key elements for the development of modern urban ideals for Latin America were in place.

This is clear in the design for the industrial port of Chimbote, Peru (1947–1948). Commissioned by a government organization, the town was to be located on the edge of the Pacific Ocean and serve as an industrial town housing warehouses; factories to process raw materials such as coal, ferrous, and other chemical products; a fishing industry; and power plants. Chimbote's location also meant that the town and its industries could benefit from it as a port. The plan called for the housing of 12,000 inhabitants and the transformation of an old slum area and its population into a productive part of the city. Like Cidade dos Motores, Chimbote relied on the division of the city into its four functions—with the industrial area located to the north of the living and recreation zones—with a particular focus on the city's housing with internal or edge courtyards and, again, on the addition of the civic center.

As the models and perspectives attest, the civic center was designed to a higher degree of completion than the previous project. In it we can see that, as for the housing, many of the public buildings also included courtyards. The formal character of the public spaces within the civic center was formed by the juxtaposition and adjacencies of the different buildings. As many of these structures were lifted on *pilotis*, their edges and undersides became covered shaded areas that could protect the inhabitants from the sun, much like the colonnades surrounding public spaces in many

BR

C: CU

CO

PE

Another important element of the design was, of course, the city center. Programmatically made up of both administrative and cultural functions, the open spaces were defined, as in the earlier projects, through the spatial and architectural relationships between the elements. The central square, to be located on the site of Plaza Bolívar, was to be a two-level plaza that tied together the religious and civic programs surrounding it while, at the same time, expanding the space through the demolition of blocks adjacent to the square.

TPA's last large master plan would be for the city of Havana, Cuba. Prepared for the government of the U.S.-backed dictatorship of Fulgencio Batista, the plan was to reflect the Cuban government's interest in developing a modern image of the country in order to attract foreign investment and tourism. In this way, TPA's early planning considerations included not only the organization of the city based on the four functions but a broader network that would connect national and regional resources together; linking the city and the surrounds through Le Corbusier's "Theory of the 7 V."[8]

TPA also designed the Presidential Palace (with Cuban architects Mario Romañach and Gabriela Menéndez; Félix Candela served as structural engineer) to be located in front of the historic city and across the entry channel into the Bay of Havana. Like some of the earlier designs for the churches, the new palace was to mitigate the effects of the weather through an immense concrete canopy that covered and shaded the bulk of the program. Also important for the design were the spaces around the structure, designed by Hideo Sasaki, which integrated fountains, terraced gardens, and vegetation into larger squares and public spaces.

The Cuban Revolution of 1959 and the end of the Batista regime once again brought an abrupt end to the project.[9] The damage, however, was done. In Roberto Segre's words, the ideas for Havana had been compromised from the onset: "[In the plan], the precepts that Sert declared in *The Heart of the City* [1952], those of respecting 'the customs of a people and their lifestyle' and the pre-existing dwelling typologies that conform to the historical memory of society, have been forgotten . . ."[10] Instead of the naïve idealism of the earlier projects—which had more amenities for the working class than those sought by the commissioning bodies (such as proximity to work, expanded leisure opportunities, conveniences for their families, etc.)—the conception of the city under Batista was centered on its economic and touristic optimization. Nevertheless, in many ways, it can be seen as the obvious conclusion that stemmed from a search that had originated in Brazil in 1943. The plan for Havana was the sum of many urban design ideas and architectural forms that emanated from Europe, were tested throughout various Latin American environments, and were proposed for specific locations and cultural milieus. But, perhaps it was this lack of clarity that reflected the very place that the CIAM found itself in in 1959 shortly before its eventual dissolution.

FURTHER READING

Mumford, "CIAM and Latin America."
Mumford and Sarkis, *Josep Lluís Sert*.
Rovira, *José Luis Sert*.
———, *Sert, 1928–1979: Half A Century of Architecture*.

1944

HENRY KLUMB MOVES TO PUERTO RICO AND FORMALIZES INVESTIGATIONS OF MODERN ARCHITECTURE IN THE TROPICS.

CARIBBEAN: PUERTO RICO

The architect must use the benefits of our industrial, technical, and scientific advances not only for materially determined ends but also for man's social and spiritual development to improve the quality of life.

HENRY KLUMB, 1947

GOTTFRIED SEMPER's theorization of the Caribbean hut shown at London's Great Exhibition of 1851 can be defined as one of the foundational strands of modern architecture. For him, the small tropical building unmistakably emphasized the primary elements of architecture and, in particular, its tectonic character. The structural frame not only enclosed and protected the interior (hearth) but also provided the support to nonstructural elements such as lattices or screens that helped shield the interior. In this way, a theory of modern architecture developed from this "primitive hut" that emphasized the importance of the tectonic frame while acknowledging the transformation of the elements that created it (Joseph Paxton's own Crystal Palace, which housed the exhibition and contained the hut itself, stood as a paradigmatic early example).

That Semper's theory of modern architecture was based on an example of tropical architecture is interesting because of the way modern architecture in the tropics has developed in relation to the simple elements contained within the earlier case.[1] In the first instance, the vernacular architecture described by Semper is characteristic of a flexible architecture that allows surfaces to be changed based on necessities for protection (from predators, sun, etc.) but also for opening the structure to natural ventilation.

The success of the example was tied to its ability to be adapted to a myriad of conditions and, especially, to the complex environmental ones of the tropics. An area defined geographically by its location between the Tropics of Cancer and Capricorn, the tropics are composed of a wide variety of locales, each one constituting particular climatic and material conditions. This range includes the hot and humid areas of the rain forests to dry savannahs of the desert. In Latin America, the tropics primarily include areas of high heat and humidity.

In response, tropical architecture, as Liane Lefaivre and Alexander Tzonis argue, developed to meet these characteristics and adapted to the specific climate, locale, material availability, and cultural traditions. For them, modern architecture in the tropics has had to respond not only to the legacy of colonialism but also to the effects of modernization and globalization. Using Lewis Mumford's ideas on regionalism, Lefaivre and Tzonis develop a more inclusive sense of what tropical architecture might be: one that "compliments rather than contradicts higher technology and a more global economy and culture. [It is an architecture that demands] respect for individual contexts within a framework of . . . interconnectedness."[2]

While climatic concerns have been central to many modern architects building in Latin America (as can be seen, for instance, in the work of Wladimiro Acosta and others; see 1937 entry), the question of designing for the tropics has most prominently been posed in the elaboration of a modern architectural language and strategy that can adapt to the island of Puerto Rico. In this case, it is particularly interesting to see how both locals and outsiders shaped the early discourse of what modern architecture should be like in this locale.

One of the early and prominent promoters of a new architecture for Puerto Rico was the Viennese architect Richard Neutra. In his book *An Architecture of Social Concern in Regions of Mild Climate* (1948), he describes his work and ideas for Puerto Rico between 1943 and 1945 when he was the planning and architectural consultant to the U.S.-appointed governor of Puerto Rico, Rexford G. Tugwell. Neutra, who had initially moved to the United States to work with Frank Lloyd Wright, had been developing a modern architecture that responded to the climatic conditions of Los Angeles, California, where he had established himself after leaving Wright's office. Tasked to primarily

C: PR

Henry Klumb, San Martín de Porres Church, interior, 1950.

Plan of San Martín de Porres Church.

Nothing is more evocative of these ideas than the two churches that Klumb built in Cataño, near San Juan: the San Martín de Porres Church (1950) and Nuestra Señora del Carmen Church (1960). The simplicity of the square plan in the first is countered by the use of unglazed openings that, according to Hitchcock's simplistic reading, addressed the problem of ventilation and controlled lighting. The success of the scheme rests on the orientation of the central axis, across the diagonal, and the way the diagonal piers along the side focus the viewer's vision toward the altar where Father Marcolino Maas's crucifix is located. As one exits the church (under the mural by Narciso Dobal), the same piers allow one a view outward toward an open-air shrine and the baptistery. Finally, it is the delamination of walls in the plan that allows indirect light to enter through multiple apertures, including those that frame the altar on both sides of the central axis as well as the openings behind the wall that holds the crucifix and altar. While the first church is more representative of Klumb's International-style aesthetics, the second church is more structurally and materially expressive; the exterior surfaces are left unadorned and rough. Located on a site with irregular boundaries, the building's hexagonal shape helps mediate the context with the church's programmatic and spatial requirements. The interior, as in its predecessor, is oriented toward the altar. Because of the placement of the columns on the exterior periphery, the mass of the building appears to

float above the ground (a screen of terra-cotta blocks allows light and air to penetrate into the bottom part), and higher up, through openings at the base of the dome, the dome itself likewise appears to float. This openness allows for cross ventilation and natural light; the dome, in contrast to the earlier church, allows the hot air to escape through the central vent at the top. In both, although more expressively in the second, Klumb was able to synthesize Wright's articulation of light and shadow as shown in the so-called Princeton Lecture drawings that Klumb prepared for Wright in late 1929. Through the light contrasts in the churches (as with the drawings) he was able to respond to "the intellectual rationalization . . . [of] two-dimensional architecture" of the International style by emphasizing "the poetic depth and power of the third dimension."[10] The specificity of the lighting and ventilation forced a reconsideration of simplistic and abstracted forms to become receptive to "the moods of nature" and their influence on the user.

The impact of modern architecture and its adaptation within the context of the island is nowhere more visible than in José Fernández's *Architecture in Puerto Rico* (1965). Not only is the prominent work of Klumb present but also the work of a myriad of other architects who were developing new architectural forms and expressions for different programmatic types that either accepted the challenges of intelligently using design to take advantage of the natural conditions or, in some instances, relied on the integration of modern technology to counteract climatic issues. It is a question of balance rather than a complete acceptance or rejection based on principle that characterizes the architecture of Osvaldo Toro and Miguel Ferrer, the other architects prominently presented in Fernández's book. Both architects had finished their studies abroad (Toro at Columbia University in 1937 and Ferrer at Cornell in 1938). Their most paradigmatic work is the Caribe Hilton (done with Luis Torregrosa) located in the so-called Golden Strip in San Juan, which resulted from a competition in 1945 to promote the economy of the island via tourism. The desired form was to be both modern and efficient and should take advantage of the climate and history. The resulting ten-story slab building was described as paradigmatic of a "Tropical modern" style for its open-ground-plan lobby floor, the ambiguity between interior and exterior spaces, the use of transparency, and the expression of the structural logic behind the building and its new materials. For the architects, tradition consisted in referencing the openness of the building to the colonial legacy of the courtyard. While the building's façade relied on deep balconies for the rooms to minimize the solar heat, there was an acknowledged necessity to use air conditioning within the building (something that Klumb had criticized the building for). It is not until their later La Concha Hotel (1958) where layers of patterned *brise-soleil* and balconies facing the swimming pool are used to control the light. The expression of the rigid structure and open floor plan is counteracted by the curvilinear roof of the cabana and ballroom buildings in the rear and by the shell-like form of the restaurant facing the beach.

In the end, the simple formal characteristics of the modern architecture developed for Puerto Rico

Toro, Ferrer, and Torregrosa, Caribe Hilton, San Juan, 1945–1949.

responded to the basic elements of the vernacular model described by Semper as emblematic of architecture. The success of the system depended precisely on the flexibility of the surfaces that could be changed based on necessities for the definition of the social space and its protection but also on their possibilities for modification to mitigate the sunlight while allowing for natural ventilation. The experiments in Puerto Rico show the development of these systems as they adapted to the climate, to the programmatic necessities, and to the people who used them.

FURTHER READING

Fernández, *Architecture in Puerto Rico*.

Klumb, *Klumb: Una arquitectura de impronta social/An Architecture of Social Concern*.

Neutra, *An Architecture of Social Concern in Regions of Mild Climate*.

Tzonis, Lefaivre, and Stagno, *Tropical Architecture: Critical Regionalism in the Age of Globalization*.

Toro and Ferrer (with Mario Salvadori), La Concha Hotel, Puerto Rico, 1958.

1945

ANTONI BONET, PUNTA BALLENA, URUGUAY

WATER WAS ALWAYS PART of Antoni Bonet's life and oeuvre. Born in the port city of Barcelona in 1913, Bonet had settled and established a practice in Buenos Aires, Argentina, as a result of the Spanish Civil War (see 1938 and 1939 entries). Bonet flourished as a practitioner as well as an intellectual while mentoring several young Argentine designers. In addition, as a member of the Austral Group, he reworked and reconsidered many of Le Corbusier's ideas. However, like the other members and according to historian Francisco Bullrich, Bonet was "not obsessed with national tradition. . . . [Austral's members] understood regionalism or national architecture in terms of social, economic, technical, and climatic problems" (Bullrich, *New Directions*, 31). This position can clearly be seen in Bonet's 1945–1947 designs for a resort in Punta Ballena, Uruguay.

Named after a hill formation shaped like a whale, Punta Ballena is located on an isolated triangular peninsula near the famous beach town of Punta del Este and where the Río de la Plata is so wide that it is indistinguishable from the Atlantic Ocean. Punta Ballena's relative isolation kept the peninsula almost untouched for centuries. The contrast between the water and the hills, however, helped sell the area as a beautiful and exclusive resort. Bonet was commissioned to design the urban plan for a subdivision as well as several buildings. In one of the few buildings executed, the Berlingieri House (1947), he collaborated with the young Uruguayan engineer Eladio Dieste (see 1955 entry), who convinced him that Catalan brick vaults could be made light and elegant.

The 3,700-acre triangular site was mostly occupied by a forest of eucalyptus and pine trees bordered by a lake, the ocean, and a small mountain range. Bonet's design called for an organically shaped urbanization composed of vehicular streets and separate pedestrian paths. The latter linked all of the houses with the sea, and any pedestrian conflict with the streets was resolved via elevated passageways made up of tree-trunk bridges; in this way, the urbanization of the forest followed some of the urban principles set up by the Congrès International

d'Architecture Moderne (CIAM; International Congress of Modern Architecture).

One building deserves careful attention, the Hostería Solana del Mar (1945). Built between the sand dunes and the beach, the hotel is organized around a horizontal structure that penetrates into an existing dune and generates three distinct levels. At the beach level, a double-height space containing a bar connects to the restaurant above, in the second, or middle, level. Inside, the horizontality of the structure parallels the water to one side, but the verticality of the glass mullions reinforce the verticality of tall pines and eucalyptus trees that surround it. A sculptural chimney resembling Le Corbusier's later work creates a dynamic atmosphere that seems to spin the whole space around it. On the middle level, accessible via a staircase from the beach or from the gently sloping dunes,

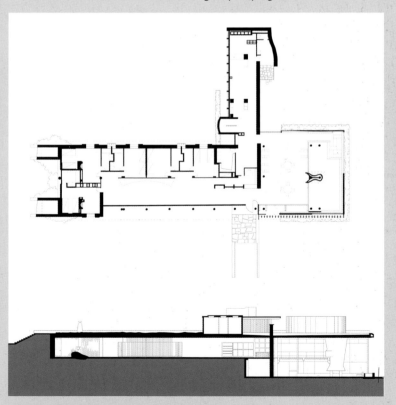

Plan and section of Hostería Solana del Mar.

1947-A

LUIS BARRAGÁN AND MAX CETTO, THE ÉMIGRÉ GERMAN ARCHITECT, BEGIN WORKING ON THE DESIGN OF THE FIRST HOUSES IN MEXICO CITY'S JARDINES DEL PEDREGAL SUBDIVISION.

MEXICO

IN 1945, LUIS BARRAGÁN, along with José Alberto Bustamante, purchased 865 acres of rocky and uninhabitable badlands in the southern part of Mexico City to be urbanized as a residential subdivision. The harsh rock terrain, known as El Pedregal, was the result of eruptions of the nearby Xitle Volcano and, because of it, the area had been considered unlivable since pre-Hispanic times and therefore available and inexpensive to purchase—something that would also be important for the southern relocation of the National Autonomous University (Universidad Nacional Autónoma de México; UNAM) to an area at the edge of El Pedregal (see 1952 entry). The area's harsh terrain yet pristine and surreal character attracted not only Barragán but artists such as Diego Rivera and Dr. Atl (Gerardo Murillo), who saw it as a uniquely Mexican landscape. Barragán, however, developed it by subdividing the territory and building a number of modernist demonstration homes and exhibition gardens to show prospective buyers the aesthetic possibilities of their contrast with the rocky terrain.

The work of Jardines del Pedregal de San Ángel, as the subdivision would be called, coincides with the beginning of what might be defined as the third phase of Barragán's work. Born in Guadalajara in 1902, Barragán studied civil engineering before embarking on what would be a life-changing trip to Europe in 1924. His formative years included not only these travels but also a keen awareness of the landscape and vernacular architecture of his family's ranch. In Paris, because of the 1925 Decorative Arts Exposition, he was exposed to some of the most progressive architectural work being produced—such as Le Corbusier's L'Esprit Nouveau Pavilion and Konstantin Melnikov's USSR Pavilion—yet he was mostly drawn to the work of Ferdinand Bac, a landscape architect and writer (whom he would meet in 1931), whose work was also exhibited at the Exposition. During this trip, he also traveled through Spain (including visits to the Alhambra and the Generalife in Granada) and North Africa, which would also have a strong impact on his ideas and designs of gardens and buildings. In his 1980 acceptance speech for the Pritzker Architecture Prize, Barragán notes Bac's influence by restating that "I have done nothing else but joined the millenary solidarity to which we are all subject," but also in establishing for him the historical links of Mexican architecture to Mediterranean architecture, including that of North Africa and Morocco (see 1980 entry).[1]

Upon his return to Guadalajara in 1926, Barragán began the first phase of his architectural production, which takes place from about 1927 to 1936. This phase is centered on a search for the Mediterranean roots of Mexican architecture as attested by references to the simple volumetric forms of Spanish colonial architecture and references to the Alhambra's gardens. The 1934 Orozco and De Garibi Houses in Guadalajara are characteristic examples of this period. These houses also project the influence his meeting in New York with José Clemente Orozco had on his production. In particular, works such as the lithograph *Pueblo mexicano* (1930)—which Barragán owned—attest to an interest in a cubic, simple, and unadorned vernacular architecture that sits in, and sometimes strongly contrasts with, the Mexican landscape.

Barragán's appreciation for the simple Mediterranean architectural forms helped usher in the second phase of his production (1936–1940), which also coincided with his relocation to Mexico City. This phase is characterized by his adoption of a rationalist or functionalist style for a number of speculative houses and apartment buildings he designed and built there. While this type of architecture had been promoted by socially minded architects as a solution to the shortage of housing and educational facilities after the Mexican Revolution, its lower cost and modernist appeal made it a desirable building style for speculators. The Duplex in the Colonia Hipódromo (1936) and the Four Painters' Studios on Plaza Melchor Ocampo (1939) are characteristic examples of this period. Both structures clearly express the houses' functions on their façades

Luis Barragán Studio with aerial view and plan of El Pedregal development.

Luis Barragán, Luis Barragán House, interior, Mexico City, 1947–1948.

the private garden in the rear and toward the sky in the roof terrace. The house is primarily made up of plain, unornamented walls. In some cases, color is used—such as the bright Mexican pink that will become emblematic of Barragán's work—but despite this, the walls remain plain in their composition. As one enters the house, the central hall, a small space with doors, leads the user to the various rooms of the house. The living room is a large space that connects a sitting area and the library with views toward the garden. Characteristic of this space are the heavy walls and large openings with reinforced concrete beams that allow for the continuity of space. Paradoxically and emblematically, however, Barragán employs traditional exposed wooden rafters on the ceiling. The library contains his famous staircase, a complete abstraction and reduction of a stair to its treads and risers, which leads to a sitting space on the second floor. From the entry hall, one also has access to the upper floors through a stair that, on its first landing, exhibits a large gold-leaf *Monochrome* (1960) by the artist Mathias Goeritz, a frequent collaborator with Barragán, that both reflects light into the space and begins to dematerialize the corner of the staircase (see 1953 entry). The bedrooms and private spaces are located on the second floor. The third floor, or roof terrace, is, perhaps, the most private area of the house. Through the use of tall walls, its outdoor rooms are stark open spaces that serve to isolate the inhabitant from the surrounding metropolitan environment.

The explorations inherent in Barragán's house coincide with the time when his work on El Pedregal would take place.

Influential in the transformation and development of the site of El Pedregal was a text that the painter Diego Rivera had written regarding its possible development. In this text, Rivera called for the preservation and protection of the character of the area through the subdivision of the property into large lots and the articulation of circulation and infrastructure to follow the natural topography. He also advocated the placement of amenities within the site and a modern architecture that, following predetermined aesthetic principles, would not only be regularized throughout the project but would also serve as a backdrop to the severe landscape.[4] These principles were ultimately advertised as characteristic of the subdivision and were reflected formally in its architecture and organization—at least in its earliest moments.

As part of the marketing of the subdivision,

and also include Corbusian elements such as the white walls and roof gardens.

The last and more well-known phase of Barragán's production begins in 1940 and ends with his death in 1988. It is in this phase where his wholehearted interest in and work on landscapes begins (his first gardens of this period were built between 1940 and 1945 on the site where he would eventually build his house).[2]

Luis Barragán's house (Mexico City, 1947–1948) is emblematic of what will become Barragán's recognizable style as well as of his ideas regarding tradition, modernity, and the poetics of architecture, something that would find expression in his desire to "find a formula so man could be calm in his home, so that he could recover from the aggressions of the city."[3] The house's front façade is imposing, austere, and with few openings. Instead, Barragán chose to open the house toward

Luis Barragán and Max Cetto, demonstration house, El Pedregal, Mexico City, 1950.

Barragán built a number of modernist exhibition gardens and demonstration homes to show prospective buyers the aesthetic appeal caused by their contrast to the rocky terrain. For him, the relationship posited between house and garden reflected a broader interest in the development of the traditional Mexican private realm that also responded typologically and contextually to Bac's call for tradition. "Mexicans prefer to face away from the street and to direct their eyes to the interior of a private garden," Barragán would state, and thus he would transform El Pedregal's unique terrain into primarily individual private gardens.[5]

In tune with Rivera's statements, Barragán advocated the use of simple or modern elements—that is, architectural structures, walls, water pools and fountains, grass lawns or clay surfaces—to contrast with the jagged and baroque forms of the lava and characteristic vegetation of the area. This unique type of architectural and landscape response would be codified by Barragán

and Bustamante as a set of strict guidelines to prevent that "this jewel in our valley be converted, due to an aesthetic misunderstanding or to the ignorance of the settlers, into a showcase emporium of houses or palaces. . . . A carefully created set of rules, with legal force and backed by a Presidential decree, will guarantee that a clean modern architecture emerge from El Pedregal in harmony with the landscape and with the natural conditions of the site."[6]

The response that this elicited, similar to that depicted by Orozco of traditional Mexican dwellings and landscapes, was an architecture of pure forms, lines, and flat surfaces that would not detract from the natural beauty of the site.

The original buildings of El Pedregal reflected this. For their design, Barragán collaborated with Max Cetto, a German émigré who had studied with Hans

Luis Barragán, demonstration garden, El Pedregal,
Mexico City, 1950.

Poelzig, had worked under Ernst May, and had collaborated with Barragán before (see 1939 entry). Initially, Cetto's work in El Pedregal began as he assisted Barragán in the design of the Prieto López House (1947–1951). This first house established some of the characteristic conditions to be used in the organization of lots, the placement of the houses within them, and the forms of the houses themselves. The Prieto López House was placed on the corner of the 161,500 sq. ft. site. Because of its topographic conditions, the entry level would be located on grade with the street, whereas the bedroom level, because of the site's slope, would be one story below. In addition, for privacy, the public face of the house was composed of closed architectural volumes, whereas the private side, facing the garden and swimming pool, was provided with large openings that frame the landscape. The most important integration of the local lava rock in the design was the use of a rock outcropping that serves as one of the edges of the swimming pool.

In 1948, Cetto also built his own modern house in El Pedregal that, more than the Prieto López House, tried to incorporate the terrain's form and highlight its character. In this case, the architecture was composed of a simple horizontal volume of glass and reinforced concrete and a simple tower made with the lava rock that contrasted sharply with the site's rocky terrain. The side edge wall of the house extends toward the front and follows the organic form of the lot; this curvilinear edge will be a motif carried into the interior of house, as seen, for example, in the subtle curve of the hearth. In addition, this building's edge as well as the rear façade of the house were also built with lava rock walls. In contrast to the Prieto López House, Cetto sited the house close to the center of the narrow lot, allowing him to juxtapose the rockier character of the backyard to the simpler and flatter one of the front.

For the two demonstration houses built in 1950, Barragán and Cetto designed white cubic volumes that contrasted sharply with the lava terrain within which they were set. In some cases, the lava rock seems to emerge from the architecture; in others, the lava rock terrain and vegetation contrasted with the gridded paving stones that surrounded the houses' first floors. In both cases, the houses' locations on the corner of their large lots helped to free up and organize the remaining part of the landscape, which, in turn, was framed by large windows that looked onto it.

In addition to the houses, Barragán also designed three demonstration gardens that sought a similar timeless or traditional character through the combination and juxtaposition of modern forms—grass lawns, plazas, pools, modern iron work, and rock-carved pathways—with the jagged lava rocks and plants characteristic to El Pedregal. The Plaza de las Fuentes, one of the entrances to the subdivision, shows this juxtaposition most strongly. The ground is organized by an orthogonal gridded plaza that contrasts against the edges of the rocky terrain, the railings and hardware of the fountain and gate, and the vegetation preserved on the site. The water-jet fountain is framed by volcanic rock walls that—in a simple, abstract, and almost Miesian way—organize the space. These walls also stand in stark contrast to the gnarly landscape within which they sit. Finally, the plaza featured *El animal del Pedregal* (1951), a sculpture by Goeritz. The other gardens included simple meandering walkways and stairs that had been carved into the stone; grass lawns with crystalline water pools and cement platforms; fountains and ponds (such as the Fuente de los Patos); staggered walls that, like the earlier 1934 Orozco House, reinforced the form of the immediate landscape and that of the mountains beyond it while simultaneously juxtaposing them.

The final design piece of El Pedregal consisted of its public presentation. Asked to frame the spaces "abstractly" in order to preserve the ideal character of the landscape, Armando Salas Portugal photographed the homes and gardens to be used for the marketing campaign of the subdivision. In the photographs, El Pedregal was touted as the "ideal place to live," and the unique character and serenity of the newly modified landscape and its architecture was emphasized. And, while much of the initial work of El Pedregal has been radically altered or destroyed, it is these compelling yet elusive photographs that provide clues as to the original character and sensibilities of the place (see 1980 entry).

FURTHER READING

Ambasz, *The Architecture of Luis Barragán.*
Eggener, *Luis Barragán's Gardens of El Pedregal.*
Pérez-Méndez and Aptilon, *Las casas del Pedregal, 1947–1968.*
Rispa, *Luis Barragán: The Complete Works.*
Zanco, *Luis Barragán: The Quiet Revolution.*

1947-B

SEEKING TO SYMBOLIZE POSTWAR EFFICIENCY AND ORGANIZATION, LATIN AMERICAN CITIES EMBRACE THE NORTH AMERICAN "ARCHITECTURE OF BUREAUCRACY."

ARGENTINA • COLOMBIA • MEXICO • VENEZUELA

THERE IS A SCENE in Jacques Tati's *Playtime* (1967) in which a bewildered North American tourist passing through a Parisian travel agency gazes at images advertising Stockholm, Hawaii, other places in the United States, and Mexico. In one of Tati's typical gags and jabs at modern architecture, the posters depict identical white modern skyscrapers for each destination and present them as virtually identical. It is only through the text and, in the case of Mexico, a small fragment of the Aztec calendar in the background and a small image of a mission colonial bell tower at the margin that we might deduce any difference between them. In this way, Tati shows the extent of the homogeneity of postwar modern architecture and its impact on the world's architecture, legitimizing it as the new standard while at the same time criticizing it as absolute.

Emblematic of the postwar boom in North America, this new international architecture was characterized by generic corporate buildings designed by a reorganized architectural profession composed of larger and more integrated design studios (such as the office of Skidmore, Owings & Merrill; SOM). These buildings mimicked both the earlier typological experiments in skyscraper design as well as contemporary investigations, such as those embodied in Mies van der Rohe's Seagrams Building (New York, 1958), that redefined some of the parameters of the earlier International style. The result of typological standardization, the new International-style buildings had simple curtain wall–covered volumes, regularized interiors, and flexible open plans as a consequence of their constructive systems. Additionally, modular and uniform details—both in the interior spaces and exterior systems—reflected the advances in the construction industry. Writing in 1947, Henry-Russell Hitchcock explained how these new buildings were based on technological and technocratic efficiency and commercial profitability. What is more, they were emblematic of what he defined as the new "architecture of bureaucracy": "all building that is the product of large-scale architectural organizations from which personal expression is absent."[1]

Contrasting this "architecture of bureaucracy" was the "architecture of genius," which Hitchcock used to allude to the continuous and singular experimentations of architects like Mies van der Rohe and Le Corbusier, whose work was an important reference for the emergence of the new International style. For Gwendolyn Wright, a historian of American architecture, the characteristics of this new architecture also reflected the incorporation of military strategies into business—such as centralized management and decentralized organization that Peter Drucker outlined in *Concept of the Corporation* (1946)—and a desire for efficiency, organization, cleanliness, and transparency that could literally be seen through their glass façades.[2] Not only was this new architecture indicative of changes in the architectural profession and the corporate world, its aggregation within the metropolis created cities without qualities that would transform the appearance of all urban centers. Tati's gag in *Playtime*, in other words, simply describes the dystopian image that had indeed become a reality.

For Latin America, to look at and reproduce the aesthetics and formal characteristics of this new model of architecture was an attempt to express its emergent modernization by, once again, mimicking the new capitals of the twentieth century. With the United States controlling one-half of the world's manufacturing following World War II and bankrolling much of the postwar reconstruction, North American culture became the new model to emulate. Traditional historiography would say that Latin America was mimicking the image of the United States to signify their capabilities for industrial production and efficiency and, as a result, increase investment opportunities.[3] Through the creation of technologically neutral and dignified spaces based on both a common and an assimilable architectural language, they were able to represent new models of economic and political stability that followed the war—and the economic boom that resulted because of it—as part of what the historian Manfredo Tafuri would describe as their collective destiny.

efficient, corporatist expression for the new government of Brazil.

Although Mies van der Rohe would be considered an important reference point for this new architecture and an emblematic actor to aid any Latin American country in the construction of this representation, his production in Latin America is limited to the design of the headquarters for Bacardí rum in Havana, Cuba (1957–1960), a project that was abandoned and never built after the Cuban Revolution, and a built office building for Bacardí in the outskirts of Mexico City (1958–1961; see 1957-a box).[4] Instead, as in most countries around the globe, Latin American corporations adopted the model exemplified by SOM's Lever House (New York, 1950–1952), a building that, according to Alison and Peter Smithson, "was not frightening, [as] it made no demands." Its applicability to any situation was based on the fact that "there was nothing in it which could not be copied by an average team of average architects with a fair amount of money and fairly developed industry . . . [It gave] the illusion to a foreign city that it had a genuine technological culture: the glamour without the two centuries of effort."[5]

So, not only was this a new architectural reference point, the United States was also the source to enlist for expertise in development itself, such as the work done by Josep Lluís Sert and Town Planning Associates (see 1943-b entry). The Bank of Bogotá (1956–1960) represents the use of both the North American architectural model and experience. To develop a variant of the Lever House for the Colombian city, architects Pablo Lanzetta and Reinaldo Valencia worked with SOM. The lower five-story platform defines the boundaries of the site onto which a seventeen-story curtain wall glass tower sits similarly to its New York counterpart.

The new architecture was also used to control the urban environment—or, at least, give the appearance of that. Nowhere is this clearer than in Caracas. In the 1940s, the transformation of the urban core led to the development of Carlos Raúl Villanueva's El Silencio district (1942–1945; see 1950 entry) on the

Mario Pani, Edificio Reforma 76, Mexico City, 1946.

Characteristic of a developmentalist mentality—placing economic development at the center of political, cultural, and social activities in an attempt to legitimize Latin America in the eyes of the United States and Europe—the acceptance of this new architecture signified the acceptance of the new postwar economy and stabilized development. The apotheosis of this developmentalist aesthetic is, of course, Niemeyer's design for the ministry buildings in Brasília flanking the monumental axis (see 1956 entry). Here, Niemeyer succeeded all too well in developing a systematic, northeastern side of the city, adjacent to El Calvario Park, and to the desire to modernize the urban fabric through the creation of a monumental avenue that would link El Silencio with Caobos Park and the Botanical Garden on the southeastern side of the city. Avenida Bolívar, as it would be known, became further defined through the development of the Centro Simón Bolívar (Cipriano Domínguez, Tony Manrique de Lara, and José Joaquín Álvarez, 1949–1957). Composed of two thirty-two-story modernist towers and a large multilayered urban plaza that serves as the towers' base, the complex and skyscrapers stand at the northeastern edge of the avenue and flank its axis. The whole structure is lifted from the ground on reinforced concrete *pilotis*, allowing the avenue to pass under it. Despite the buildings' strict academic symmetry, the intricate separation of vehicular and pedestrian circulation; the use of modern Corbusian-inspired forms; and the expression of the structural system, *brise-soleil*, and thin glass membranes help define this complex as a constructed version of contemporary utopian ideals being developed in Europe at the time.

Equally emblematic in the construction of a modern international aesthetic in Caracas is the Torre Polar (Polar Tower, Martín Vegas and José Miguel Galia, 1951–1954). That this would be the first glass curtain-wall building in Venezuela should come as no surprise; after all, Vegas had studied architecture with Mies van der Rohe at the Illinois Institute of Technology (IIT). The Torre Polar is a complex that includes not only an office tower but also an auditorium, restaurants, and retail and public spaces. Each of these programs is formally and functionally articulated on the exterior or given different expression through the buildings' curtain wall. In addition, the use of a reinforced concrete structural system allows the edges of the floor slabs of the tower and the three-story plinth on which it sits to cantilever out, further emphasizing the autonomy of the four curtain-wall façades. On the ground, a large winding staircase at the front serves to separate the tower and plinth from the functionally and materially expressive auditorium building. Also built with reinforced concrete, the auditorium outwardly expresses the structural ribs that make up its structure in contrast to the adjacent tower that hides it all beneath its exterior sheathing.

Although not as ambitious as the Caracas examples, the glass-clad box—generally built in reinforced concrete—had become the new norm throughout Latin

Cipriano Domínguez, Tony Manrique de Lara, and José Joaquín Álvarez, Centro Simón Bolívar, Caracas, 1949–1957.

America. In Mexico, the principal proponents of this new style were using the curtain wall, according to Francisco Bullrich, as an "antidote" against contemporary nationalist revivals.[6] On a large scale, Mario Pani's Edificio Reforma 76 (Mexico City, 1946), Abraham Zabludovsky's Apartment Building (Mexico City, 1958), and Vladimir Kaspé's Laboratorios del Grupo Roussel (Mexico City, 1962) are emblematic of this style and approach with their simple volumes and articulated glass curtain walls. On a domestic scale, Francisco Artigas's House on Calle Risco (Mexico City, 1952) and Del Olmo House (Mexico City, 1953) show an exploration of the emblematic Miesian glass box, in the first, or courtyard house, in the second, both autonomous from their contexts. While many of these developed uncritically the stylistic language of the new

International style, a few emblematic buildings sought to explore new tectonic or stylistic lines. These include, for example, Enrique de la Mora and Fernando González Pozo's Compañía de Seguros Monterrey (Mexico City, 1960) and Ricardo Legorreta's Edificio Celanese (1966–1968), which minimize the internal structure to a few cores and armatures in order to have the buildings literally "hang" from them and thus allow for the most flexible, open floor plates.

In Argentina, Mario Roberto Álvarez became the most prominent representative of the new International style. Beginning with the tall structure on Corrientes Street for the Teatro General San Martín (Buenos Aires, 1953–1961; see 1953-b box) and the Centro Cultural Ciudad de Buenos Aires (1960–1970) behind it, Álvarez's trajectory goes from the pristinely glass-clad and autonomous reinforced concrete box to the later buildings that respond to their context by articulating the party walls as solid while maintaining the other façades as open grids infilled with glass or other materials. The Paraguay Housing Block (1964–1965) with its gasoline

station on the ground floor expresses the structural frame as a singular unit that unifies the elevations in contrast to the lightness of the glass, screens, and balconies. The Stock Exchange (Buenos Aires, 1972–1977) surely is emblematic of an autonomous and indifferent modernism. Placed between the Beaux-Arts-inspired early Stock Exchange (Alejandro Christophersen, 1913–1916) and the Comega Building (Enrique Douillet and Alfredo Joselevich, 1931–1933)—a building emblematic of Argentina's investigations of the skyscraper typology—Álvarez's building articulates the interior programmatic conditions through its curtain wall: a larger, more open section of glass denotes the trading floor, while the standardized and repetitive section of the tower serves as an index to the office spaces.

In his 1955 *Latin American Architecture since 1945*, Henry-Russell Hitchcock notes that the contemporary quality of Latin American cities reflects the "presence of great numbers of new office buildings, and in some cases, apartment blocks, rising above the generally low urban structures of earlier periods."[7] Despite his earlier ambivalence about the "architecture of bureaucracy," Hitchcock's catalogue concludes by showing the new urban façades in terms of an evolutionary movement to distance architecture from tradition (i.e., baroque curves) and local specificity (i.e., use of *brise-soleil*) and move toward pure and simple buildings sheathed in "various combinations of glass and opaque panels mounted in continuous metal chassis-frames" more akin to those in the United States.[8] Emblematic of this trend are the aforementioned Torre Polar; Rino Levi's Banco Paulista do Comercio (São Paulo, 1947–1948); Juan Sordo Madaleno's Office Building (Mexico City, 1952–1953); Luis Miró's Edificio Radio El Sol (Lima, 1953–1954); and Cuéllar, Serrano, Gómez y Cía.'s Sudamericana de Seguros Building (Bogotá, 1954). Despite rising above the rich historical fabrics within which they are located, these buildings reflect instead the anonymity characteristic of postwar corporate U.S. architecture. In form, they materialize the impersonal and illusionless velleities of modernity.

Martín Vegas and José Miguel Galia, Torre Polar, Caracas, 1951–1954.

FURTHER READING

Adrià, *Mario Pani: La construcción de la modernidad.*
1950: El espíritu moderno.
Piñón, *Mario Roberto Álvarez.*
Tafuri, "The International Panorama in the Fifties and Sixties."

assembly hall toward the center, diminishing the size and the prominence of the plaza.

The fact is that Oscar Niemeyer's proposal was the one chosen by the group (albeit later modified by Le Corbusier), yet he was not credited for this. The Brazilian architect recounted the story in several books, never blaming Le Corbusier but nevertheless confirming the intellectual ownership of the building scheme.

Niemeyer's accounts are corroborated by many of the architects present. Max Abramovitz, for instance, stated that "there was a period of kicking ideas around, and slowly we caught ourselves using more of the input of Niemeyer than almost anybody else. It was all around that kernel of Niemeyer's idea—the positioning of things. We were slowly heading in the direction of Niemeyer's Scheme 32. I was in the drafting room, where we had all the sketches on the wall and the models on the tables. Corbu came into the room and took down something like this (pointing to a photo of Niemeyer's Scheme 32), disappeared somewhere, then came back in, made his sketch, which he called 32A, and signed his name to it. He just couldn't stand it" (Underwood, "Interview with Max Abramovitz," 155).

Beyond the credits and the merits of each scheme (after all, it was a workshop in which ideas were supposed to bounce back and forth among the participants), one must ask why Niemeyer's important collaboration disappeared from architectural history. What prompted experienced architects and historians to overlook the account of those meetings, seeing only a Harrison-Corbusier struggle while leaving Niemeyer and the others presented as peripheral figures?

1947-B

MARIO PANI—*MULTIFAMILIARES*

RESPONDING TO THE exponential growth of Mexico City, Mario Pani developed an architectural and urban system of buildings intended to shelter and provide for the needs of its population. Despite Pani's classical architecture education in Paris at the École des Beaux-Arts (graduating in 1933), it was Le Corbusier's work on housing and, specifically, his Ville Radieuse (Radiant City, 1935) that would formally and organizationally impact Pani's designs for mass housing. Called *multifamiliares*, these are, as the name suggests, housing complexes for multiple families. These government-financed low-rent complexes increase the city's population density by housing more people in a smaller area through the construction of higher and more efficient buildings that, at the same time, provide amenities such as commerce, education, sports, recreation, and, most importantly, green space for the occupants.

The Multifamiliar Miguel Alemán (1947–1950) was Pani's first housing complex. The proposal was the result of an ideas competition for two hundred houses for government employees of the federal pension system (Dirección de Pensiones Civiles y de Retiro). Placed within a singular superblock in the Colonia del Valle neighborhood of Mexico City, Pani's design consists of six three-story buildings and nine thirteen-story buildings in a zigzag pattern—modeled on Le Corbusier's housing block for the Ville Radieuse yet completed before the Unité d'Habitation at Marseilles (1952). These structures contain 1,080 units (which translates to 1,000 inhabitants per hectare) and, because they are lifted off the ground on columns, occupy only 20 percent of the site. Besides green areas reserved for recreation and circulation, the site is filled in with offices; a school for six hundred students; commercial spaces; and sporting, childcare, and gathering facilities. There are four different types of units that are accessed from exterior corridors that, in the towers, occur every three floors. While the units are accessed from these levels, their program is split over two levels and accessed via internal stairs to "avoid spatial monotony," according to Pani. The visual complexity and character of the buildings result from the variation of the units as well as from the use of exposed reinforced concrete and brick. Furnishings for the units consisted of mass-produced designs by Cuban-born Clara Porset.

Following the success of his first *multifamiliar*, Pani (with Salvador Ortega) designed and built the Multifamiliar Benito Juárez (1952), which, like its predecessor, included nineteen buildings in a 25-hectare parklike setting, with a main circulation road that partially passed under a portion of the complex. The heights of the structures vary from four to thirteen stories and include twelve types of units intended to house 1,060 families. In addition to the housing and green space (only 1.3 of the 25 hectares were occupied by buildings), the design accommodated a school, offices, retail spaces, and sports facilities. To provide a more varied character for the complex, Pani's design integrated inset or cantilevered balconies and closets that protruded from the elevation, decorated by the Guatemalan-born painter Carlos Mérida. In addition to those mural-reliefs, Mérida provided similar decorations based on pre-Hispanic motifs for the stair towers as well as for the nursery school. All of the art was done in a more abstract painterly language that reflected the character of this new modern architecture. Unfortunately, the complex suffered extensive damage in the 1985 Mexico City earthquake, and many of its buildings have been torn down.

Because of its sheer size (built on 80 hectares for 70,000 people in 11,916 apartments) and highest density (almost 1,000 people per hectare), the 1964 Multifamiliar Nonoalco-Tlatelolco is the most impressive. Like its predecessors, the complex had different housing morphologies and a limited occupation of the ground area (25 percent) to allow for uninterrupted pedestrian movement. The lowest blocks are four stories tall with two-bedroom, one-bathroom units. These have no elevators but rely on stairs as social spaces and provide access to the units at the half level. Perpendicular to these blocks are the medium blocks of eight stories with three-bedroom, 1½-bathroom apartments. Interspersed throughout the complex are fourteen-story blocks and twenty-four-story towers. Commercial spaces and services such as sports facilities,

Mario Pani, aerial view of Multifamiliar Miguel Alemán, Mexico City, 1950.

thirteen schools, a cinema, etc., were found at the ground level. The sheer size of the complex also led to the use of standardized mass-produced panels, resulting in a more gridded, repetitive, and homogeneous treatment of the buildings' façades, which gave them an anonymous and impersonal character. On the southwestern corner of the site is the Plaza of the Three Cultures where one can simultaneously see pre-Hispanic (the Pirámide de Tlatelolco), colonial (Iglesia de Santiago), and modern architecture (the Secretaría de Relaciones Exteriores [Pedro Ramírez Vázquez, 1966]). This was the location where scores of student demonstrators were killed by government forces on October 2, 1968, ten days before the beginning of the 1968 Mexico Olympic Games (see 1968 entry).

Mario Pani, Multifamiliar Benito Juárez, Mexico City, 1952.

1947-C

AGRUPACIÓN ESPACIO

IN 1945, TWO IMPORTANT events marked the rise of modern architecture in Peru: Fernando Belaúnde Terry was elected to the National Congress, and Luis Miró Quesada published his book *Espacio en el tiempo: La arquitectura moderna como fenómeno cultural* (Space in Time: Modern Architecture as a Cultural Phenomenon). Both would be crucial for the development of modern architecture in Peru.

Belaúnde was the main political force behind modern architecture in Peru. A graduate of the University of Texas in 1935, he founded the first Peruvian architectural magazine two years later. The success of *El Arquitecto Peruano* took him to congress and to the deanship of the School of Architecture in 1955. In 1963, Belaúnde was elected president on a platform of modernization that, of course, included architecture and urbanism as one of its main tenets. During his presidency, Belaúnde initiated the world-famous PREVI project (see 1969-b entry). Deposed in 1968, he was reelected in 1980.

Luis Miró Quesada, on the other hand, was the main intellectual force behind modern architecture in Peru. Son of the mayor of Lima, Miró Quesada decided not to go into politics but was no less argumentative or polemical. His *Espacio en el tiempo* (Space in time) contained the seeds of the 1947 manifesto of the Agrupación Espacio (Space Group), of which he was the main leader and articulator.

The book starts with discussions on Immanuel Kant and Arthur Schopenhauer—very sophisticated arguments for any architect at that time and half a century before the rise of critical thinking took over schools of architecture. We should note that he titled the book "Space *in* Time," meaning that space is subdued by time, a typical avant-garde argument. According to Miró Quesada, architects should build for the present. His argument rejected the need for continuity despite the fact that Peru is home to one of the most remarkable pre-Columbian cultures, the Inca. Ironically, however, the book mentions every important Indo-European architectural example from ancient times.

Miró Quesada's ideas galvanized a group of students and young architects into forming a group they called Agrupación Espacio. By 1947, they were actively pursuing membership in the Congrès International d'Architecture Moderne (CIAM; International Congress of Modern Architecture), encouraged by Josep Lluís Sert and Richard Neutra, but they never received any response (positive or otherwise) from their European colleagues.

For the 1947 Pan American Congress of Architecture in Lima, Agrupación Espacio issued a manifesto. "Man is a product of its time," states the first sentence of the text, reinforcing Miró Quesada's argument that place is not as important as time. Yet, the manifesto points out, architecture in Peru was severely anachronistic. Instead of responding to present needs for clarity and sense that can be verified in the spatiality of the interior, the architecture that had developed was most concerned with exterior appearances and the continuation of traditional academic lines. It is not enough, the manifesto continues, that a few architects "use new materials according to a 'new style.'" What is needed is a large contingent of artists and architects with like-minded ideas interested in working in the present, rejecting the past, and forming "an architecto-social conscience, aimed toward the needs of the new inhabitant of what is human" ("Expresión de principios"). Based on functionalism, this architecture would be free from historical attributes and, instead, would stand as an index of its time. Emblematic of their rejection of historical roots, the manifesto defines Le Corbusier, Mies van der Rohe, and Frank Lloyd Wright as important points of reference. In their manifesto, they also called for a series of conferences to address present themes affecting architectural production, including art, philosophy, regionalism, and structures.

Such a radical ahistorical approach seems a bit out of place in a Peru where a strong socially conscious interest in history, modernity, and the indigenous population had been forged by José Carlos Mariátegui in the 1920s or in a Latin America that was more and more looking at its own roots (Lúcio Costa in Brazil, Juan O'Gorman in Mexico, Joaquín Torres-García in Uruguay), yet these ideas became the seeds of Peruvian modern architecture and helped define what was built (and not built) in the decades that followed. So, while Miró Quesada and Agrupación Espacio defined the discourse and theory of modern architecture, Belaúnde opened up the space for modern architecture to develop and be disseminated through government initiatives.

1949

LA CIUDAD FRENTE AL RÍO IS RELEASED, SHOWING THE TRANSFORMATIONS OF LE CORBUSIER'S PLAN FOR BUENOS AIRES.

LA CIUDAD FRENTE AL RÍO is a short film produced in 1948 describing the needed changes to the city of Buenos Aires. This film and the entity that commissioned it, the Estudio del Plan de Buenos Aires (EPBA; Committee to Study the Plan for Buenos Aires), was one of the results of Le Corbusier's association with a group of young Argentine architects who would become prominent advocates for urban renewal in the city. Developed in 1948, the EPBA was founded to study the possible implementation of Le Corbusier's plan for Buenos Aires (see 1929-b entry). Under the direction of Jorge Ferrari Hardoy, who had worked with Le Corbusier in the original development of the plan between 1937 and 1938, the EPBA also included Antoni Bonet and Juan Kurchan, who, along with Ferrari Hardoy, developed the BKF chair (see 1938 entry).

Photo collage of Le Corbusier's Plan of Buenos Aires.

What the film presents is a general overview of the urban problems of Buenos Aires and a call for its transformation loosely based on Le Corbusier's plan. While the film makes use of traditional documentary techniques to show the problems of the modern city, its congestion, and the effect of its unchecked growth, Enrico Gras, a progressive Italian film director hired for the project, utilized various techniques of montage and collage to present the analysis of the existing city and the proposed solutions being developed by the EPBA. One such solution was a prototype piece of the plan for the area of Belgrano, on the southern edge of Buenos Aires, that becomes, ultimately, the focus of the film. As historian Anahí Ballent explains in *Las huellas de la política*, however, the project for Bajo Belgrano didn't fully incorporate Le Corbusier's proposal but rather tried to contextualize it within the particular necessities and characteristics of the Argentine culture, such as the development of housing suited for the climate and people as well as the importance placed on the plaza as a locus for civic activity in Latin America (see 1943-b entry). As a result, the film presents a more general outlook on the urban problems and their solutions.

The film is organized around three main parts. The first defines the city and its problems as a result of its evolution from colonial times: "[Buenos Aires] suffers from the consequences of one hundred years of urbanism errors." Machine technology and modern construction are also blamed, as they cover the green pampa that exists beneath the city. Contributing obstructions to a better way of life, industry creates pollution, traffic creates dangerous living conditions for the pedestrian, and urban congestion blocks the rays of the sun and impedes breezes and air from entering the city: "The city, which was built by man, is now fighting against him."

The second part of the film begins to define the solution to these problems by proposing the need to "conquer the pampa that lies under the city itself by lifting the blocks vertically." Here, an architectural model of city blocks is manipulated by turning and reorienting these blocks vertically, revealing an underlying photograph depicting a more open and park-filled urban environment.

Enrico Gras (director), still,
La ciudad frente al río, 1949.

The blocks are then compacted together to create greater open green space and what the narrator defines as a "more humane city at the edge of its historical river . . . in this way, the green city, the parklike city, is born."

The final segment shows the plan for Bajo Belgrano as a solution to the city's problems. In this section, the model of the proposal is superimposed on aerial views of the site. Models and drawings of its architecture are also collaged onto film footage of green spaces to show how the city will look and operate. These manufactured images show an idyllic environment where traffic and pedestrians are separated (as advocated by tenets of the International Congress of Modern Architecture [CIAM]), where greenery and open space for outdoor activities dominate, and where housing blocks—each composed of five hundred units—will stand separate from each other and thus away from traffic and noise and therefore will be filled with light and fresh air. In this section, images of Bonet's Punta Ballena urbanization (see 1945 box) and Ferrari Hardoy and Kurchan's 1940 Virrey del Pino apartment building (see 1938 entry) are collaged into the film, allowing the film to provide views of what the new city would look like, expand on its qualities, and, in the latter, show interiors of the new housing types proposed. The film concludes with the urban model of the plan for Bajo Belgrano superimposed on its existing site in Buenos Aires and with the motto: "To regain the river; to conquer the sun, space, and nature."

Enrico Gras (director), still, *La ciudad frente al río*, 1949.

1950

PUBLIC HOUSING REACHES A MONUMENTAL SCALE: MARIO PANI, CARLOS RAÚL VILLANUEVA, AFFONSO REIDY, OSCAR NIEMEYER.

BRAZIL • MEXICO • VENEZUELA

THE YEARS AFTER WORLD WAR II were all about housing in the Western world. The United States was going full force on the suburbanization process, Europe was committed to reconstruction, and Latin American urbanization rates were demanding millions of housing units. In different ways, all those processes proposed opportunities and challenges to previous theories of modern architecture. While in North America suburbanization was putting to the test modern ideals of urbanism, in South America the challenge was to optimize the infrastructure. For this, verticality was the answer.

In the whole region, a combination of industrialization, intense migration, and high fertility rates brought unprecedented growth to the main cities. Caracas grew from 100,000 in 1900 to 650,000 in 1950. Mexico City grew ninefold in the same first half of the twentieth century, from 345,000 to 3.1 million. In Brazil, Rio de Janeiro grew from 650,000 to 2 million, while São

Paulo had the most extreme expansion, from 230,000 at the beginning of the century to 2.2 million by 1950. All this growth left Latin American cities with huge deficits in infrastructure and housing. The private sector did respond with apartments for the middle and upper classes, but it was the public sector that built the most radical experiments for the working classes.

Mexico, the leader in public works following the revolution that began in 1910, started earlier than anybody else. Actually, despite the fact that all vertical housing complexes were very much inspired by Le Corbusier's ideas (published since the 1920s), Mexico's "El Multi," as the residents call the Multifamiliar Miguel Alemán (1947–1950), was designed about the same time—yet finished earlier—than the famous Unité d'Habitation at Marseille (1947–1952). "El Multi," designed in 1947 by Mario Pani, is a complex of 1,080 apartments and

Carlos Raúl Villanueva, El Silencio, Caracas, 1941.

Carlos Raúl Villanueva, El Paraíso housing development, Caracas, 1952–1954.

support service structures that occupy only 20 percent of its site (see 1947-b box).

Another notable example of working-class housing is the Pedregulho complex designed by Affonso Eduardo Reidy for the city of Rio de Janeiro in 1946. Getúlio Vargas's administration (1930–1945) had built thousands of units distributed on the fringes of the main cities, but it was not enough.[1] The city of Rio de Janeiro then took the lead on building a housing complex much like Pani's in terms of service but unlike any other in terms of its architecture. On dealing with a hilly site in what was then the outskirts of Rio de Janeiro, Affonso Reidy designed a curvy bar that would become a landmark of Brazilian modernism (see 1946 box).

In Caracas, Carlos Raúl Villanueva had already built large housing complexes beginning in the 1940s. El Silencio, for instance, was built between 1941 and 1945 but used a neocolonial style for its architecture.

Composed of blocks that abut the sidewalk, El Silencio has austere façades that resemble simplified versions of Art Deco buildings with small windows for bedrooms and balconies for the living rooms. At ground level, arched colonnades create sheltered circulation for its commercial spaces. Paradoxically, as much as the main façade uses classical composition, the back elevation resembles a Russian constructivist project with the stairway volumes protruding to hide the laundry and service spaces that are as open as balconies. The site planning was also premodern: the apartment volumes line the edges of the blocks and generate large internal patios. With a total of 7,797 apartments, El Silencio is one of the largest housing complexes ever built. Had it used *pilotis* to free the ground as well as modern windows, it would have been the first modernist housing complex in the world. It should be noted, however, that El Silencio is a redevelopment that relocated an existing informal settlement into these new apartments. As much as the practice is now unanimously condemned, El Silencio seems to be a success in terms of keeping the quality of the spaces thus far.

Ten years later, Villanueva and Carlos Celis Ceparo fully adopted Corbusian modernism in El Paraíso

(Caracas, 1952) by introducing two small towers and a larger one with seventeen floors and perpendicular wings resting on a two-story service base. The high-rise is characterized by an independent and exposed structure. To avoid the monotony of the repetitive structural frame, the architects created a modulating façade paneling system that is further articulated through the variation of split-level apartments as well as by the polychrome design on the façade by Venezuelan artist Alejandro Otero. As large as the "superblock" of El Paraíso seems, it pales in comparison to 2 de Diciembre (now known as 23 de Enero; 1956). December 2 was the day that General Marcos Pérez Jiménez came to power in 1952. When he commissioned Villanueva, already the most established architect in Venezuela, the idea was to celebrate the "advances" of his government with another successful relocation: building fifty high-rise blocks of fifteen floors each where slums previously existed. Like El Paraíso, this was the result of a National Housing Plan funded primarily by the Banco Obrero (Worker's Bank) and intended to transform the character of the city by funding large-scale public works and by eradicating informal settlements throughout the city. Also like its predecessor, the 2 de Diciembre development took rationalism to its limits: exposed structure, simple windows, large green areas, and parking spaces between the buildings. A bare-bones approach to housing on a massive scale, the complex includes nine thousand simple but comfortable, well-lit, and well-ventilated apartments. In addition to housing, the architects organized the site to take full advantage of the views to the city as well as the topography to locate amenities for the inhabitants such as playing fields, social centers, schools, and commercial buildings.

TOP: Carlos Raúl Villanueva, 2 de Diciembre (now 23 de Enero), Caracas, 1955–1957. ABOVE: Carlos Raúl Villanueva, aerial view of 2 de Diciembre (now 23 de Enero), Caracas, 1955–1957.

However, before the buildings were completed, another coup ousted Marcos Pérez Jiménez. The unfinished apartments were occupied by the rioting crowd. In response to the forced relocations, the site became the epicenter of the

Oscar Niemeyer, Edifício Copan, São Paulo, 1951.

revolt. People also occupied the open spaces between
the buildings, the informal settlements blanketing the
ground area. The complex was renamed to celebrate
the date of the end of the Pérez Jiménez era: January
23, 1958. Today, the colorful high rises are witness to
this history, each occupant painting his or her own
façade with a different color while the ground level is
dominated by the reds of exposed bricks and the grays
of asbestos roof tiles.[2]

Back in Brazil, Oscar Niemeyer would build on the
experience accumulated by Reidy and make the curves
even more prominent. The Edifício Copan (Copan

Building) in downtown São Paulo (1957) was not, however, built around a hill. Instead, the curved slab was
made to become a reference in the vertical landscape
of the Brazilian city, now the largest in the country. In
1951, Niemeyer was hired by a subsidiary of PanAm to
build a complex of hotel rooms and apartments for the
downtown as the city prepared to celebrate its quadricentennial (1554–1954). The Companhia Panamerica
de Hoteis (Co-Pan) commissioned two blocks: one for
a hotel and another for apartments. Disagreements

between PanAm and the Brazilian partners interrupted the construction several times between 1952 and 1957 until it was finally purchased by Bradesco Bank, which, in turn, only built the apartment tower. Enlarged from 900 to 1,160 units, its thirty-eight floors (three commercial, thirty-five residential) follow a subtle S shape on a very prominent triangular corner of downtown São Paulo. The horizontal concrete slabs spaced at 3-foot intervals (three per floor) cover the entire north façade and characterize the building. Less known but no less important is the ground-level articulation of the building. Niemeyer designed an internal street that connects both sides of the property and makes for a lively connection with the city, accentuating the commercial viability of its seventy-three stores.

Niemeyer also designed the JK complex in Belo Horizonte (1951). Two slabs on two adjacent urban blocks were to be united by a (unbuilt) catwalk and would provide the provincial capital with 1,100 units. That proved too much for a city of 350,000 people (70,000 households). The developer's money was exhausted before the building was completed in the

late 1950s. As a result, the state government bought a large share of the enterprise in deference to the then-current president, Juscelino Kubitschek, for whom the building was named, and with the intention of selling it fast. Construction moved slowly until 1964 when the military coup d'état changed the political landscape drastically. Since Kubitschek was now persona non grata to the new government, the state pulled the plug on the project. As a result, the building was never properly finished, and individual owners moved in after years of desperately waiting for completion. Living in a large building with unfinished common areas and none of the promised services working made the small apartments worthless, attracting a marginal crowd that made the condominium even less manageable and gave the complex a terrible reputation as a haven for marginality. The Copan had a similar "bad rep" in São Paulo in the 1970s and 1980s. It has since become a fashionable address for urban professionals. The JK complex has slowly improved, but its apartments are still underpriced.

In a certain way, many Latin American housing projects suffered the same fate as their northern counterparts. It is true that modern architecture promised too much and that changing a society takes much more than large windows and permeable grounds. However, it is also true that the worst cases are those in which the funding came up short or the arbitrariness of relocations and social control made the conditions worse than before. The young hip professionals who now live at Copan in São Paulo and the love that many residents show for "El Multi" in Mexico City are important counterexamples. Along with El Silencio, these complexes have a much better relationship with the surrounding city, while Pedregulho, 2 de Diciembre/23 de Enero, and the JK Building are urban islands that remain isolated from their cities by design or by prejudice. In this way, the monumental housing complexes in Latin America are not at all different from their counterparts in North America or Europe.

Oscar Niemeyer, JK Complex, Belo Horizonte, 1951.

FURTHER READING

Bonduki, "Habitação social na vanguarda do movimento moderno no Brasil."
Garay Arellano, *Modernidad habitada.*
Lara, "Incomplete Utopias."
Villanueva and Pintó, *Carlos Raúl Villanueva.*
Williams, *Brazil: Modern Architectures in History.*

1951-A

CARLOS RAÚL VILLANUEVA, VILLANUEVA RESIDENCE

LIKE MOST ARCHITECTS, Carlos Raúl Villanueva used his own house as a means through which to express and explore his most intimate architectural concerns. Built in the La Florida neighborhood of Caracas, this reinforced concrete dwelling is, first of all, an attempt at mediating the interior with the exterior. This is reflected in the nuanced and ambiguous interior-exterior spaces that would become prevalent in the Universidad Central (see 1952 entry).

Given the site's compact width, the ground plan is divided into three strips, with both party walls and the front closed off (with the exception of a volumetric opening for the garage). Moving from the front of the house to the back, one experiences the dematerialization of enclosure as the walls become columns and, thus, allow for an interconnected living and dining room in the rear, which can also be opened completely to the garden on the west, creating an ambiguity between inside and outside. To alleviate the solar issues associated with the orientation of the most open part of the house, the garden and plants shield the interior and let a naturally filtered light into it. In contrast to the open ground floor, the upper floor is more traditionally organized. The majority of the bedrooms face the garden, while the front is reserved for the master bedroom and a laundry area located in the volume above the front garage.

Following vernacular traditions, Villanueva locates an internal courtyard on the central axis in the house. Adjacent to the entry, this small covered patio mediates the user's transition between the exterior and interior and provides for light and cross breezes through the house despite the front's closed character. The courtyard also demarcates the boundary between the served and service spaces, with the northern band (on the party-wall side) housing the garage, kitchen, and maids' quarters. The formal character of the house's simple, continuous, and unornamented exterior (like that found at the 1941 El Silencio complex [see 1950 entry]) also indicates Villanueva's adherence to colonial traditions, as does the use of clay tiles in its interior.

The house, finally, is a repository for Villanueva's artwork. Again, as in the university design, the simple modern volumes become the foil for work by many of the artists that he commissioned for the university: from the garage to the garden are works by Alexander Calder, Jean Arp, László Moholy-Nagy, Jesús Soto, and others—all accessible to the inhabitants of the house. Placed at the top of the stairs, Soto's *Cajita Villanueva* (1955), a three-dimensional optico-kinetic piece, becomes the transition between the house's public and private realms.

LEFT: Ground-floor plan of Villanueva Residence.
BELOW: Carlos Raúl Villanueva, Villanueva Residence, interior, Caracas, 1951.

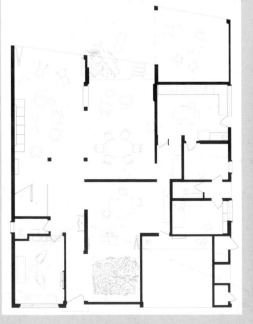

1951-B

FOUNDED BY CARLOS MARTÍNEZ in 1946, *PROA* was (and still is) the most influential Colombian magazine on architecture and urbanism. As the name indicates, *PROA* refers to the prow of a boat, the most forward and active part of the vessel. Five years later, the magazine published the book *Arquitectura en Colombia*, edited by Martínez and Jorge Arango, which reviewed the five years of Colombian architecture since *PROA* had been in existence. In the book, Martínez's text claims that there was no worthy architecture in Colombia since the country's independence in the early 1800s. Very much like *Brazil Builds* (see 1943 entry), *Arquitectura en Colombia* articulates a relationship between contemporary (modernist) architecture and its colonial precedent.

The book starts with a description of Colombia's geography and a historical overview of the region's development, emphasizing the isolation of each province/city during the three centuries of Spanish rule. In a sentence full of Corbusian rhetoric, Martínez claims that Colombia was a constellation of isolated provinces united only by the arrival of the first airplanes in 1919.

A significant portion of the text is then dedicated to the analysis of Colombian colonial architecture. Here, the author extracts a series of characteristics that would later overlap with modernism: functionality, austerity, logic, sobriety, and economy of means. In Martínez's own words, "Our architecture, in relation to others in the Americas, is more disconnected from symbolism, it is less eclectic, more *criolla*, it is the least imported and, because of all this, the most functional" (*Arquitectura en Colombia*, 18).

That said, Martínez also acknowledged that the very same Spanish house built for the coast was also, despite climatic variations, built for the mountains. Colombian architecture, according to him, had never been as exuberant as Brazil's or as monumental as Mexico's. Starkness and temperance defined the character of Colombia's colonial architecture, making it more in tune with the modernist avant-garde.

The basis upon which the modern movement is established in Colombia is reviewed in five pages. Continuing his stitching of the modern and the colonial together, Martínez notes that Colombian architecture was built primarily by the population at large with very little input from the government. To make the connection stronger, the fact that both government buildings and churches had been built with imported plans and imported architects is presented by Martínez as supporting his thesis that this important continuity was built by the people. By the end of the text, contemporary architecture in Colombia is clearly defined as a popular movement.

The book concludes with documentation of fifty-five projects, mostly single-family houses with a few office buildings and high-rise apartments. In tune with Martínez's claim that Colombian modernism was not a state-sponsored endeavor (like that of Mexico or Brazil), only three works that might have been state commissions are shown: two public housing projects and one baseball stadium, although very few details are given about them.

The important point to consider is that despite differences in scale and sponsorship, the way the relationship between modernism and local traditions became articulated here was characteristic of Colombia's central architectural discourse until the end of the twentieth century. Was Martínez operating like Lúcio Costa and trying to make an international trend more palatable to his provincial public? Or was he more of a nationalist trying to "Colombianize" the modern movement? If we think that by the 1950s modernism was already well established throughout the Americas, then there was not much of a battle left to fight. Martínez indeed created a "Colombianized" version of modern architecture that survived for more than half a century. This vision has been challenged only since a new generation of Colombian architects, supported by state-sponsored competitions, took the world stage at the beginning of the twenty-first century (see 2000 entry).

Aerial view of Universidad Nacional Autónoma de México (UNAM). RIGHT: Mario Pani and Enrique del Moral, Rectoría building, UNAM, Mexico City, 1952.

serves as the reading rooms and some administrative offices. What make this building so unique are the stone-mosaic murals by Juan O'Gorman covering the surface and representing the history of Mexico (see 1933 entry). The murals negate the tectonic logic and construction of the building and have been criticized as turning the building into a "decorated shed." At the base of this building, we also find large walls surrounding an exterior reading room built using the local stone and covered in pre-Hispanic-inspired motifs.

Adjacent to this administration area is the large-scale quad that has been likened (because of its size and proportions) to pre-Hispanic quadrangles as well as to the Zócalo, or central plaza, in the historic center of Mexico City. Surrounding this open space and the buildings that enclose it is a vehicular circulation system that is sectionally separated from the ground, allowing uninterrupted passage for pedestrians that

connects them to the city and the rest of the university. The main quadrangle is bordered on the long northern side by a 985-foot (300-meter)-long Humanities building (Vladimir Kaspé) that serves as a strong link between the eastern and western parts of the campus. On the southern side is the School of Engineering (Francisco Serrano), and the Science building (Raúl Cacho) lies on the central axis on the eastern side of the quadrangle. While the modern character of the School of Engineering is tempered by domes on one of its masses that echo the domes of the Capilla Real in Cholula, Puebla, the Humanities building strongly emphasizes its horizontal floor plates held up by *pilotis* and its very limited artistic program, making it one of the purest expressions of the International style. The Science building is, likewise, very international in nature and expresses many of the principles found in Le Corbusier's buildings. On both its east and west façades, the architect employed a glass curtain wall despite the strong solar orientation, representative of how the new technologies (made possible by science) are to ameliorate the impact of nature. Science serves as the geographic center of the university and, more specifically, it is the area where the Institute for Nuclear Physics (and the first Van der Graaf nuclear fission machine to be installed in Latin America) would be located.[3] The *Conquest of Fire* mural by José Chávez Morado on the façade of the small auditorium building in front of the Sciences tower represents the paradoxical condition

TOP: Plan of UNAM, Mexico City, 1952.
LEFT: Gustavo Saavedra, Juan Martínez de Velasco, and Juan O'Gorman, UNAM library (mosaic mural by Juan O'Gorman), Mexico City, 1952.

of atomic energy following the Second World War. Farther east is the science quadrangle, including the Schools of Chemistry, Medicine, Veterinary Science, and Dentistry. The School of Medicine (Roberto Álvarez Espinoza, Pedro Ramírez Vázquez, and Ramón Torres) reflects influences of Dutch functionalists like Jan Duiker with its expression of the structure and how the programmatic volumes hang from it, its circulation ramps linking the classroom block with the administrative and library volume, and its thin *brise-soleil* fins on its façade. Covering the auditorium-shaped classroom mass and serving as a visual connector to the humanities section of the campus is Francisco Eppens's *Fire, Earth, Air and Water: Life and Death*, a glass mosaic mural of pre-Hispanic motifs and symbolism.

Outside the central quadrangle, on the southern edge and at an angle, sports facilities, fields, and other recreational spaces are located, similarly surrounded by a circulation system. All in all, the whole complex emphasizes the autonomy of each individual building through its placement on an open field that itself references its utopian garden-city precedents. In addition, the organization of the whole campus reflected the desire to balance science and technology with classical humanist culture. The design of the buildings was the work of a number of teams consisting of architects working with artists, the intended users of the buildings, and students from the School of Architecture.

CU, CARACAS

The authorship of the Venezuelan example, in contrast to the Mexican one, can be assigned to one person: Carlos Raúl Villanueva. Beaux-Arts trained, Villanueva had worked primarily in the neocolonial style (see, for example, his El Silencio redevelopment project in Caracas, 1941–1945 [see 1950 entry]) until the beginning of the Universidad Central de Venezuela (UCV; Central University of Venezuela) project. However, as the single author of the immense complex that characterizes the university and because of the project's longevity, one can see the different stylistic explorations that he undertook in the CU's organization and architecture from its inception.

The initial organization of the campus—on an acquired hacienda—was symmetrical and arranged on a central axis whose northern side is defined by the city's botanical gardens and, on the south, by the Paseo Los Ilustres avenue. The two terminuses are marked by a

medical building on one end and the sports facilities at the other. The final design of the campus loses that initial east-west axial symmetry, and the primary axis shifts to a north-south orientation that begins with the Plaza del Rectorado (bordered on three sides by the Communications, Museum, and Administration buildings) and ends with the library. Despite this, the organization of the buildings is no longer formalized by the axis, as it had been before, but rather by the circulation. The trajectory that Villanueva had developed for pedestrians not only serves to connect the buildings to each other but also frames views of the campus and its art that, like the Mexican example, can be found throughout the complex. As noted earlier, the art in the Caracas campus, however, does not operate within the same canons of legibility, realism, or nationalism. Instead, the artists that Villanueva commissioned were primarily European or Venezuelans who had studied in Europe—such as Alejandro Otero and Mateo Manaure, who formed part of the group Los Disidentes (The Dissidents), since they had moved away from Latin America to break away from the still-present legacy of the Mexican muralist tradition.

The path that Villanueva organized through the complex is based on a choreography of five movements (akin to musical scores) designed to create a synthesis between art and architecture: "to corroborate, to accentuate, and to enhance the form-space reality of architectural design; or, in a reverse process, to disperse, transform into pure space relationships the solids of architecture."[4] The first movement, which takes place at the entry court of the Plaza del Rectorado, aims at dematerializing the structure and form of the Museum building, which is a characteristically functional building with an expressed structural grid.

The second movement is part of the threshold between the entry plaza and the cultural center beyond it; the murals by Oswaldo Vigas are intended to give an impression of lightening the feeling of the Administration building and to highlight the dynamic form of the Communications building.

The third movement is the most complex not only in its integration of the art to the environment but also in its architectural and spatial qualities. Characterized by an amorphously shaped covered plaza, this is an intermediary space that lies between the administration building and the Aula Magna (the main lecture hall for the university). The architectural covering articulates the relationship between inside and outside,

Aerial view of Universidad Central de Venezuela, Caracas, 1948.

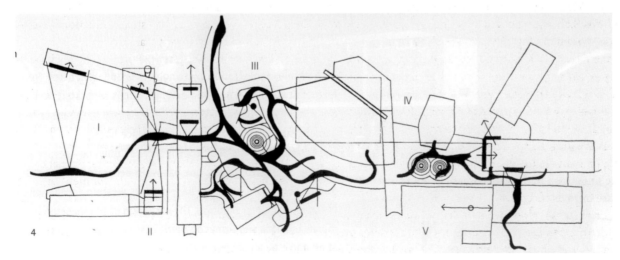

Carlos Raúl Villanueva, organization of movement through the main campus, Caracas, 1948.

between covered and uncovered spaces (some of which have tropical vegetation), and creates a continuously changing play of light and shadows. The art pieces in this area include free-standing murals (some double sided) by Fernand Léger, Mateo Manaure, and Pascual Navarro as well as sculptures such as Jean Arp's *Cloud Shepherd* (1953). The importance of the pedestrians' movement through this space and around the art pieces is central to their understanding, as they materialize Villanueva's desire for the "contemporary concept of Time-Space."[5] The covered plaza, connected to a perforated-brick enclosed foyer, also serves as a transition to the Aula Magna. The interior of the hall is covered with Alexander Calder's *Flying Saucers* (1953), resulting from the collaboration between the North American artist, the architect, and acoustical engineers, as they were also intended to mitigate the echoes in the hall. These colorful and organic shapes playfully hang from the ceiling and, in some instances, are attached to the side walls. With the artificial lighting systems, they create a dynamic spatial environment that is, dialectically, both decorative and functional.

RIGHT: Carlos Raúl Villanueva, circulation ramps at Aula Magna, Universidad Central de Venezuela, Caracas, 1948.
BELOW: Carlos Raúl Villanueva, interior of Aula Magna (with Alexander Calder's *Flying Saucers*), 1953.

The fourth movement, which takes place between the Aula Magna, the library, and the concert hall, is perhaps the most visually dynamic. Transitioning from the Plaza Cubierta, the pedestrian passes a circular shape decorated by Manaure and is confronted by two bold mural forms. The first is a zigzagging triptych by Pascual Navarro that serves as the entry to the concert hall. In front of it and at the edge of an open courtyard is an aluminum louvered screen by Victor Vasarely that provides a constantly changing visual and architectonic experience that changes according

to the viewer's movement and position as well as that of the sun.

The fifth and final movement takes place outside the concert hall, whose rear exterior has been covered in a mosaic mural, an abstraction of music by Manaure; beyond it is *Maternity* by Baltasar Lobo. Across from the entry to the concert hall is a mural on the cooling tower by Vasarely and, immediately in front of that, a bronze sculpture by Antoine Pevsner. These works become transitional to the final building in the choreography of pedestrian movement: the twelve-story central library building with its exposed structural grid. The library is closed off, as in the Mexican example, to respond to the need to protect the books from the sun and other climatic conditions. In this case, however, the last three stories are open and enclosed with recessed windows. On the side facing the rear of the concert hall is the library's reading room. Like the other buildings already discussed, the library incorporates art as part of its overall design: a stained glass by Léger, murals by Navarro, and other works. Other notable buildings in the university include the nine-story School of Architecture with its polychrome tile façade by Alejandro Otero, who, through his choice of blues to match the Venezuelan sky, attempted to dematerialize the mass of the building and the School of Humanities that stands behind the Aula Magna. Separated from the central complex by a reinforced concrete covered walkway (these walkways are found as links throughout the campus and are expressive of the articulation of circulation in this "urban" form), the School of Humanities is composed of a series of smaller block buildings for the individual departments and discreet structures to house libraries or auditoriums placed around courtyards or patios.

Despite both campuses' formal similarities (highlighted in comparing the two libraries), their utopian aspirations to redefine cities, their use of art, and the desire to integrate plastic arts into their architecture are radically different. The UNAM campus is, in effect, the result of a multiplicity of languages and styles working in close proximity with one another. While some attempts were made to create focal points and spatial continuities through the art that reinforced some of the large-scale planning techniques used, the fact that each building was designed by different groups of architects working with artists led to unique architectural and artistic expressions that, in many cases, do not create a coherent whole or dialogue. The CU in Caracas, in contrast, is the vision of a single individual with a clear goal of placing contemporary art at the service of the architectural and urban environment. The turn toward abstraction, both as a rejection of "traditional" narrative art of Latin America and as a way to express modernity, allowed Villanueva to create a campus that favored the experiential and reinforced the formal aspects that he intended. Here, the scale—both of the art and the complex—is personal and intimate, whereas in Mexico it is monumental. This last distinction is crucial to the understanding of their uniqueness. The role of art in Mexico was still believed to be political and, thus, still bound by the requirements for legibility and communicability. At the Caracas campus, the responsibility lies more on the experiencing subjects moving through the structures and forms and understanding their place within the construction of the modern nation.

FURTHER READING

Carranza, "Horror Vitreo: Ciudad Universitaria and the New Humanism."

Larrañaga, "Toward the Visibility of the Invisible: Notes on Caracas, Modernity, and the University City of Caracas by Carlos Raúl Villanueva."

Moholy-Nagy, *Carlos Raúl Villanueva and the Architecture of Venezuela*.

———, "Mexican Critique."

1952

ELADIO DIESTE, IGLESIA DE CRISTO OBRERO, ATLÁNTIDA, URUGUAY

EDUCATED AS AN ENGINEER, Eladio Dieste spent the first forty years of his life calculating and building large warehouses with long-spanning brick vaults. The now-celebrated Uruguayan architect didn't see himself as a designer until much later in life. In 1952, a wealthy donor approached Dieste with the idea of building a church in a poor community populated by manual and domestic workers employed by the nearby resort town of Atlántida, 25 miles from Montevideo. Aware that a church is a much more complex commission than a warehouse, Dieste suggested they hire an architect. To this, the donor responded that an architect was not needed, since all he wanted was an inexpensive building for a community that had no aesthetic taste or sensibility. Instead of building a simple warehouse to be used as a church, Dieste decided to prove his client wrong about the working class's hunger for beauty. He accepted the commission with the caveat of having total freedom of design and with the promise that his church would not cost more than a *galpón* (warehouse). With that in mind, he set to work for almost a decade on the Iglesia de Cristo Obrero (Church of Christ the Worker), built between 1958 and 1960.

The church is a single brick-built volume of 52 x 98 ft. (16 x 30 m) and 23 ft. (7 m) tall that could easily be described as a warehouse in its simplicity. The plan at ground level is a rectangle with a curving wall framing the altar and separating it from the sacristy. A few inches above the ground, however, the enclosing side walls begin to change into a wavy form that encloses the space and holds the structure together. The maximum curvature of the wave is reached at the height of the building's eaves. Intended to control lateral forces, the curves give stability to the brick-only walls and transfer all vertical and horizontal loads

efficiently to the foundations while simultaneously giving the structure an appearance of lightness. Following the same principle, the roof is also an undulating membrane that rests neatly on the wavy walls. For Dieste, the biggest problems were how to connect the roof and walls and how to bring light into the volume through the shape of the walls. Here, he created small and irregularly sized rectangular openings enclosed with colored glass and onyx to filter the incoming light at the very upper parts of the meandering walls.

The wall that makes up the entry is a recessed semi-curvilinear wall that penetrates into the church's volume, folded to create an entrance at ground level that also supports the choir. The upper portion of this wall, in plan, is orthogonal and composed of brick louver planes filled between them with operable onyx panels to allow light and ventilation into the structure. Opposite it is the church's rear wall that is flush with the boundary of the volume. This has a small reveal that makes it seem as if its edges do not touch the side or the roof, referencing a similar gap on the front that is covered in onyx to illuminate the interior space.

Eladio Dieste, Iglesia de Cristo Obrero, Atlántida, Uruguay, 1958.

170

Beyond the structural wonders of the project, the function of the church was no less advanced for those times. By solving the church in a single volume, without niches, without columns, and without transepts, Dieste created a nonhierarchical space that brings the priest closer to the people. Remarkably enough, Dieste anticipated the changes that Pope John XXIII would endorse at the Second Vatican Council of 1963 by reorganizing the performance of the Mass to be directed toward the congregation rather than toward the altar. At the same time, through the undulating forms, the colored openings on the walls, and the character of the space, Dieste references and reworks Le Corbusier's Notre Dame du Haut at Ronchamp (1950–1954), which was a highly emblematic model for anyone building churches at the time.

The worker that the church's name alludes to is omnipresent in its very construction. For Dieste, the bricks are expressive of the humble nature of "the faithful for whom the church is built." What is more, the church in Atlántida purposefully uses the best available technology (brick construction) to achieve an economy of materials that can be assembled by a poorly educated labor force specialized in artisanal construction techniques (see 1955 entry). What differentiates this church from his previous buildings is the intensive search for a poetic effect as well as a desire to develop a humble but worthy art for the working class.

In Atlántida, Dieste materialized the best of his moral commitment to an honest and economic use of resources made into an intelligent use of form for the common good.

Interior view of Iglesia de Cristo Obrero, Atlántida, Uruguay, 1958.

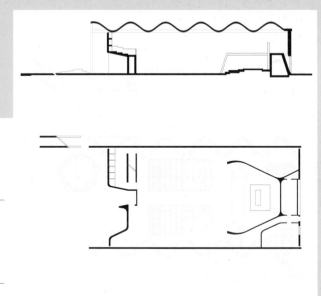

Sections, elevation, and plan of Iglesia de Cristo Obrero.

1953-A

AFFONSO REIDY: HALFWAY BETWEEN THE CARIOCA SCHOOL AND THE PAULISTA SCHOOL

IF MOST OF THE HISTORY of twentieth-century Brazilian architecture is written in two distinct moments—the Carioca school of 1930–1950 and the Paulista school of 1950–1970, Affonso Eduardo Reidy can be considered the missing link between them.[1] Born in 1909, Reidy was sixteen years old when he entered the Escola Nacional de Belas Artes (ENBA; National School of Fine Arts) in 1926, graduating in 1930, shortly before Lúcio Costa's brief tenure as director (see 1930 entry). At that time, Reidy was working for the office of the French urban planner Alfred Agache on elaborating a master plan for Rio de Janeiro. From Agache, Reidy acquired a sensibility for urbanism, sociology, and public architecture that would be one of the pillars of his career.

With the end of Agache's work in 1932, Reidy went to work for the city of Rio de Janeiro, a job he would hold for the next thirty years. In the city's Department of Public Works, he met engineer Carmen Portinho, who was in charge of the department and who would become his life partner. Portinho played a fundamental role in Reidy's architecture, and he designed some of his best buildings for her department. Had they been in private practice, their collaboration would have been akin to that of Charles and Ray Eames and Peter and Alison Smithson; in other words, they would probably have been known as one of the greatest design couples of the century.[2] As the first woman to graduate as an engineer in Brazil in 1926, Portinho was deeply committed to the public recognition of women as professionals and was a leader in the Brazilian suffragist movement.

Under Portinho's leadership, Rio de Janeiros's Department of Public Works launched a magazine called *Revista de Engenharia da Prefeitura do Distrito Federal* (known as *PDF* for short; Magazine of the Prefecture of the Federal District). Published from 1932 to 1969, *PDF* was instrumental in establishing and guiding discussions about architecture and urbanism in Brazil as well as being the first magazine to publish many European avant-garde projects of the 1930s. Dedicated to the debate on housing, public space, and infrastructure, *PDF* played an important role in promoting modernism at a time when more conservative designers were fighting hard to keep their commissions and the government was still undecided on which architecture would better represent its ideas about the country. The fact that Rio de Janeiro's Department of Public Works strongly supported modernism played a role as important as Costa's curricular reformation or of Le Corbusier's visit, if not more.

Instrumentally, Reidy had been present at all three of those important events: first, after graduating, Reidy taught for a year during Costa's tenure (1931); second, Reidy was part of the team that designed the Ministry of Education and Public Health (MESP) building in 1936; and third, he had direct contact with Le Corbusier, who served as the consultant on the project (see 1936 entry). When Reidy returned to his job at the municipality the next year, he used the opportunity to perfect his abilities to work with rigid compositional systems—a skill that fit well with his search for efficiency and economy in public buildings—instead of following Niemeyer's exuberant ways. His designs, in this way, closely followed the critical characteristics of

Affonso Eduardo Reidy, detail of Colegio Experimental Paraguay-Brasil showing hanging rooms, Asunción, 1952.

Affonso Eduardo Reidy, Colegio Experimental Paraguay-Brasil, Asunción, 1952.

his formation: Working for the city, for example, Reidy designed the award-winning Pedregulho housing complex in 1947 and Gávea the following year in reference to some of Le Corbusier's investigations for the city (see 1946 box).

In 1952, the Brazilian government decided to donate a school to neighboring Paraguay, a soft-power diplomatic strategy that would lead to the binational Itaipu hydroelectric dam (the largest in the world before China's Three Gorges Dam). Reidy was

commissioned to design the Colegio Experimental Paraguay-Brasil on the periphery of Asunción, on a peninsula called Yta-Pyta-Punta (Guaraní for "red stone edge"). The composition of the Colegio Experimental Paraguay-Brasil resembles the school he designed for the Pedregulho housing development, with the main linear block for the classrooms and the gymnasium and auditorium structures on separate but adjacent volumes. The gymnasium is very similar to the one in Pedregulho with its parabolic concrete arches supporting the fiber-cement roof. The main school building, however, shows a different kind of investigation that would push Reidy's architecture away from his Carioca roots, more in tune with the architecture that would soon develop in São Paulo. A trapezoidal-shaped external structure elevates the building and doubles as a sun breaker on the northern side. In this way, the classroom block is placed atop an elevated platform. This creates a flat, shaded area under the volume and also provides for uninterrupted views of the Paraguay River (aka the Río de la Plata) at the ground level. The trapezoidal angled columns give the building a sense of lightness—also being explored by Niemeyer in schools in Cataguases (1948) and Diamantina (1951)—while the roughness of the exposed concrete makes the Colegio Experimental Paraguay-Brasil more in tune with the emerging brutalist movement of the

time. With the design for the Museu de Arte Moderna (MAM; Museum of Modern Art), this new direction in Brazilian architecture would be fully established.

In 1953, the City of Rio de Janeiro decided to build a permanent home for the MAM on the northern edge of Flamengo Park (composed primarily of reclaimed land from the bay), with magnificent views of Guanabara Bay and the city waterfront buildings at Flamengo and Gloria (see 1965-a entry). When state politicians suggested that Niemeyer be hired to design the building, the mayor of Rio de Janeiro intervened, stating that there was no need to spend a fortune on a design that could be done in-house by its Department of Public Works. As a result, Reidy would work on the building until his death in 1964; the museum

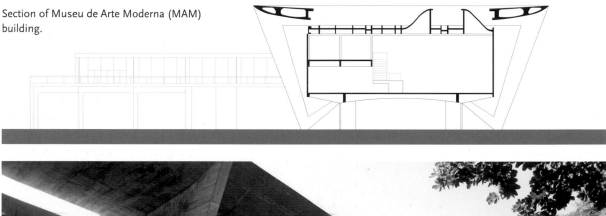

Section of Museu de Arte Moderna (MAM) building.

Affonso Eduardo Reidy, MAM, Rio de Janeiro, 1953.

was inaugurated (partially finished) in 1967. With the airport, the MAM anchors the northern edge of Flamengo Park and is located near the downtown office buildings, the Theatro Municipal (see 1904 entry), and the MESP.

A massive building designed not to interfere with the landscape and to allow uninterrupted views of the bay at the ground level, the MAM moves much further than the Colegio Experimental Paraguay-Brasil in the direction of rigorous but expressive structure. Again, the composition is made of three different volumes: the exhibition hall, a school, and an auditorium (the latter was never built).

An external skeleton is used here to allow maximum flexibility in the interior exhibition halls by creating free and unobstructed spaces. The trapezoidal structure holds a concrete slab that serves as the main floor of the museum. In this way, three-fourths of the ground is left open. The slab, in turn, serves as a brace for the angled columns that also provide some flexibility to the beams for openings of indirect lighting. Inside the main volume, a mezzanine hangs from the upper beams. The rigorous exposed concrete structure dominates the spatial arrangement, allowing an interior flexibility that is highlighted by changing horizontal planes. Finally, the gardens by Roberto Burle Marx complete the project, seeming to be paintings blanketed onto a landscape already made exuberant by the views of Guanabara Bay and the Pão de Açúcar (Sugarloaf Mountain).

While *pilotis* were a trademark element of the Carioca school since the MESP, Niemeyer's Ouro Preto hotel (1940), and numerous other projects, in Reidy's later work, the building is engulfed by an external skeleton that elevates and wraps around it at the same time instead of simply resting on *pilotis*. At the MAM, as in Pedregulho, it is the section that is the generator of form, giving the building order, rhythm, and enough variations to give the spaces experiential depth. In the end, both buildings anticipate many of the defining characteristics of the Paulista school that would materialize years later: free ground plan, generous internal social spaces, and opaque envelopes (see 1961-b entry).

The same year that the MAM was begun, Reidy's Pedregulho won the first prize at the São Paulo Biennial and was praised by the Swiss architect and critic Max Bill (while others were criticized; see 1953 entry). The connection with the Ulm School brought Tomás Maldonado and Otto Aicher to teach at the MAM's design school, later directed by Carmen Portinho. In 1957, a comprehensive book on Reidy's work was published in Germany, which included a preface by Sigfried Giedion. At that point, Reidy could have gone into a profitable private practice. However, he continued working for the city until he retired at the age of fifty-one in 1961. Reidy left a public job, but public works never left him: the following year he was invited (convinced actually) by Lota de Macedo Soares (who happened to be the partner of poet Elizabeth Bishop) to go back to public service, joining Roberto Burle Marx on the team that designed the Flamengo landfill park, reassessing a plan he had drawn for the city five years earlier.

Reidy died of cancer in 1964, at the age of fifty-five, interrupting a remarkable life dedicated to public architecture and defining a Brazilian architectural evolution that had begun Carioca and slowly but surely became Paulista. Carmen Portinho lived to be ninety-eight, working the rest of her life caring for Reidy's architectural legacy.

FURTHER READING

Conduru, "Razão em forma: Affonso Eduardo Reidy e o espaço arquitetônico moderno."

Guerra, *Affonso Eduardo Reidy*.

Nobre, *Carmen Portinho: O moderno em construção*.

The Works of Affonso Eduardo Reidy.

Xavier and Nobre, *Arquitetura moderna no Rio de Janeiro*.

Mathias Goeritz, *La serpiente*, courtyard of El Eco Experimental Museum, Mexico City, 1953.

exception of the freestanding wall in the courtyard, which was painted yellow and served as "a ray of sunlight"); and by integrating *La serpiente* (*The Serpent*; 1953), a "functional" sculpture intended to serve as a backdrop and set for dance performances.[9] Because of their character and scale, many of these devices denied references to human scale, prevented the logical understanding of their forms and structure, diminished the centrality of their visual appropriation in favor of their phenomenological experience. Ultimately, they served to challenge the perception and function of art as one of mere passive reception and cathartic contemplation. According to the art critic Anita Brenner, the effect of the building was "achieved primarily with space and light, so photographs don't convey it very well. One has to be in it."[10] Even its architectural representations fall outside the logic of the commonplace, functional, and architectural. The plans, for instance, are too general to serve as working drawings (yet, because of this, they emphasize the importance of the artist who worked in situ in its design and construction). The ideographic drawing, which is the closest to a perspective rendering of the building, presents a more synthetic experience rather than a visually perceived one, as attested, for example, by the transparency of the courtyard tower that, in the building, is built as solid.

Much of Goeritz's later work is based on the experiments of El Eco. As morphological reinvestigations of El Eco's tower, for example, we can find the Torres de Satélite (Satélite Towers, with Luis Barragán, 1957). Intended as markers for a new subdivision, Ciudad Satélite, in the northern part of Mexico City, these five reinforced concrete triangular towers range from 121 to 187 ft. (37–57 m) in height and, from a distance, appear to be the center of a high-rise metropolis. Goeritz wanted them to be, simultaneously, "painting, sculpture, and emotional architecture." Like the earlier precedent, Goeritz focused on the monochromatic quality of their walls. Their acute triangular form accentuates this, making the surfaces appear as simple color planes without material support. In addition, their form also makes their comprehension difficult, as it changes depending on the viewer's position relative to them and, like El Eco, creates exaggerated perspectival views through them and around them. Their height is intended to overwhelm the passerby, as they have no comprehensible reference to human scale. And, while the intended viewer of these was the high-speed passerby framed through the automobile windshield, Goeritz wanted to attach small flutes on them so that they would also produce an auditory experience, but this was not done.

While El Eco becomes a frame of reference or point of departure for Goeritz, we can also find similar or parallel interests in the work of Luis Barragán. The two men met in Guadalajara, Jalisco, where Goeritz had emigrated to teach "visual studies" at the University of Guadalajara at the request of architect Ignacio Díaz Morales, and where Barragán had started his architectural practice. As the two established a friendship and relocated to Mexico City, Barragán commissioned Goeritz to produce a number of pieces for works he was designing (such as, for instance, *El animal del Pedregal* (1951) for the El Pedregal subdivision that he had designed [see 1947-a entry] or the stained-glass window and *Monochrome Triptych* for the Convent of the Capuchin

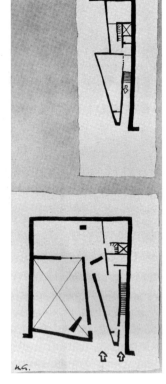

FAR LEFT: Mathias Goeritz, ideographic drawing of El Eco Experimental Museum, 1953. LEFT: Mathias Goeritz, Plans of El Eco Experimental Museum, 1953.

Nuns, Tlalpan, 1953–1960). They also worked together on a number of commissions, like the Satélite Towers (whose authorship would, ultimately, lead to a dispute that would end their collaboration). In the 1953 "Manifesto," however, Goeritz acknowledges Barragán's help with the design of El Eco, and in it, we can find formal qualities similar to the work that Barragán was producing in Mexico City at the time, such as massive simple walls and the introduction of bright colors.

Likewise, we can see the influence of Goeritz on Barragán, as we find similar references in the theorization of his work. When Barragán, in his "Acceptance Speech" for the Pritzker Architecture Prize, notes that "it is essential to an architect to know how to see: I mean, to see in such a way that the vision is not overpowered by rational analysis," we must understand that "vision" as a Goeritz-like way of "seeing" that was set against the "rationality" of functionalism and in favor of the "emotive." More specifically, in the 1976 catalogue for the Museum of Modern Art's show on his work (see 1980 entry), Barragán specifically defines his house as "an emotional piece of architecture" and restates Goeritz's positions: "I believe in an 'emotional architecture.' It is very important for humankind that architecture should move by its beauty; if there are many equally valid technical solutions to a problem, the one which offers the user a message of beauty and emotion, that one is architecture."[11]

Although their friendship was destroyed over the authorship of the Satélite Towers, Goeritz continued exploring some of their shared architectural ideas with other Mexican architects, most notably, Barragán's most important protégé: Ricardo Legorreta (see 1976 entry). Not only are there direct collaborations between Goeritz and Legorreta, such as the Automex Factory (with Goeritz's two smokestack-like towers, 1963–1964) or El Camino Real Hotel (with Goeritz's entry fountain and screen, 1968), there is also Goeritz's formal influence, such as the tower at the Tremec Factory in Querétaro, which shares its lineage with the tower in El Eco. In addition to his work with Legorreta, Goeritz's influence can be seen in the work of architect Pedro Friedeberg and those artists and architects associated with the design of the Route of Friendship for the 1968 Olympic Games in Mexico City (see 1968 entry).

FURTHER READING

Carranza, "Mathias Goeritz: Architecture, Monochrome and Revolution."
Kassner, *Mathias Goeritz: Una biografía, 1915–1990*.
Rodríguez Prampolini and Asta, *Los ecos de Mathias Goeritz: Ensayos y testimonios*.
Zúñiga, *Mathias Goeritz*.

Bernardes would again use light steel trusses in a pavilion for the principal Brazilian steel company of the time, Companhia Siderúrgica Nacional (CSN), at the Ibirapuera Park in São Paulo (1954). For it, he designed a box suspended by catenary cables and steel arches—an extremely airy structure combining the formal elegance of Niemeyer with Mies van der Rohe's focus on details, Bernardes's two main influences.

The structural research would lead Bernardes to his very best building in 1958, a year that was simply magical for Brazil. While the new capital was being built and still being celebrated by the international press (see 1956 entry), Cinema Novo and the bossa nova were taking the world cultural stage by surprise. On top of all that, the Seleção (Brazilian national soccer team) won the FIFA World Cup in Sweden for the first time, with the seventeen-year-old Pelé scoring a hat-trick in the semifinal game. And, while Le Corbusier was building a pavilion for Philips at the Brussels World Fair, Sérgio Bernardes was building the Brazilian pavilion. Located in a valley, his pavilion's slow ramp guided the visitors down to a tropical garden designed by Roberto Burle Marx that was covered by a thin concrete membrane (130 x 196 ft./40 x 60 m) supported by four metallic columns. The theme of the pavilion was "a new Western civilization in the tropics": Burle Marx's garden took over the internal space—the tropics—while Bernardes's

sophisticated roof framed the new civilization from above. In the middle of the roof membrane was a circular opening (the *pluvium*) and a large air balloon. On sunny days, the balloon was left to rise above the pavilion. On rainy days, the balloon would be pulled down to fill the opening, the water falling on its surface to a water table that was part of the garden below.

Bernardes would continue his explorations with cable-stretched structures for the São Cristóvão Fair (Rio de Janeiro, 1958–1960) and the Brasília Convention Center (1972). Unfortunately, none of those elegant buildings survived. The pavilions were dismounted, São Cristóvão was destroyed by fire in 1980, and the Brasília Convention Center was the victim of a mediocre renovation in 2005.

For Bernardes, it did not matter because he believed that architecture should only move forward. In the 1980s, he founded Laboratório de Investigações Conceituais (LIC; Laboratory for Conceptual Investigations), making research part of his architectural practice. His experimental approach was similar to the investigations of the French architect Yona Friedman or the visionary North American thinker Buckminster Fuller, whom he met in the early 1960s. Bernardes's proposal for the entire Brazilian territory would create large zones of occupation separated by rings (124 miles [200 km] wide) of preserved natural areas (see 1971 entry). His work also included furniture, such as a sofa that helps senior citizens stand up, and the redesign of the bicycle, his *biocleta*, to be propelled by legs and

Sérgio Bernardes, Casa Lota de Macedo Soares, Petrópolis, Brazil, 1951.

arms. In the end, the press called him the Brazilian Leonardo da Vinci.

João da Gama Filgueiras Lima, known as "Lelé," is another architect whose work responded generally to Max Bill's critique by always being framed in terms of social demands and labor-intensive techniques. In 1957, after graduating from the School of Architecture in Rio de Janeiro, he began working in Brasília. At first, he was building temporary workers' housing out of wood. This induced him to create a "factory" to expedite construction. This early experience with prefabrication allowed him to teach in the early 1960s at the University of Brasília, where he had the chance to build Colina Velha (1962), a faculty apartment complex constructed with prestressed slabs, prefabricated columns, and light paneling for internal partitions. At that time, Lelé traveled to Eastern Europe with the university president, Darcy Ribeiro, to study Soviet prefabrication (see 1983 entry). With the 1964 Brazilian military coup, Filgueiras Lima went to work in Salvador de Bahia, where he designed a whole complex of administrative buildings for the Centro Administrativo da Bahia, or the state government of Bahia, in the early 1970s (see 1975 box). Responding also to the immense demand for improving low-income neighborhoods in Salvador, Filgueiras Lima developed a whole set of reinforced masonry components. The most ingenious of all is a set of boxes and slabs that can drain wastewater underneath and work as stairs above, improving accessibility up the hills of the shantytown. However, the demand for such work was too dependent on politicians: increasing when they needed fast construction, decreasing when somebody else got elected. Despite this, Lelé was never able to see his prefabrication factory take off as a viable alternative to traditional construction. Political winds would bring him to Rio de Janeiro in 1983 (see 1983 entry) and back to Bahia four years later. Around that time, the industrial genius of Lelé found its perfect client: the Rede Sarah, a nonprofit hospital group specializing in the locomotor system. After designing the first Sarah Hospital in Brasília in 1980, Lelé established a working relationship with them that included also designing hospital beds and various structures to help the patients in their physical rehabilitation. As the Sarah hospitals grew to eight units (Brasília, Belo Horizonte, Salvador, Rio de Janeiro, Fortaleza, São Luís, Belém, and Macapá), Lelé continued developing their design by exploring strategies for passive cooling (ventilation

João Filgueiras Lima (Lelé), Colina Velha building, Brasília, 1961.

and humidification) and the incorporation of nature as part of the therapeutic process.

Clearly, both Bernardes and Lelé responded to a certain anxiety that became apparent in the 1950s, one that seemed to result from the quickly achieved but perhaps not completely warranted fame of modern architecture in Brazil. As a consequence of so much success, the Brazilian architects had to face a triple responsibility: first, to solve the urban and housing problems of the country; second, to push the envelope on technological improvement; and, finally, to keep up the pace of international recognition by creating exuberant buildings. While many architects in Brazil would say that they were working toward all three goals, it is clear that they were being forced to choose which expectations they would or could fulfill. Unfortunately, only a few of the most talented chose technological explorations like Sérgio Bernardes or socially oriented programs like João Filgueiras Lima.

FURTHER READING

Cavalcanti, *Sérgio Bernardes: Herói de uma tragédia moderna.*
Figuerola, "Razão, sensibilidade e maestria."
Lima, *Jornal do arquiteto.*
Valporto Leal, "Técnica e arte a serviço da cura."

1953-A

FÉLIX CANDELA, CHURCH OF OUR LADY OF THE MIRACULOUS MEDAL, MEXICO CITY

The design of a religious building might be somewhat irrational, governed more by emotional feelings than by strict, conventional logic.

FÉLIX CANDELA

THE OPENING SEQUENCE of Benito Alazraki's 1962 film noir, *Espiritismo*, takes place in the recently completed Church of Our Lady of the Miraculous Medal (1953–1955). By invoking the angular distortions and deep shadows of early German expressionist films, Alazraki was able to capture the spatial character and quality that the church's architect, the Spanish émigré Félix Candela, wanted to express in it. The Gothic-like properties that were sought by the client and created by Candela were, in the architect's own words, intended to capture "something transcendent": "Religious architecture is generally about buildings of only one floor and great height . . . about attaining an expressive interior space, a surrounding structure that one admires from the inside" (quoted in Thrall, Moreyra, and Billington, "Church of Our Lady of the Miraculous Medal," 116).

Born in Madrid, Spain, in 1910, Candela studied architecture and became primarily interested in the development of new structural forms. With the Spanish Civil War exploding shortly after his graduation in 1935, Candela joined the Republican Army in its fight against the Francoist regime. Forced to retreat into France in 1939, he was given political asylum in Mexico the same year (see 1939 entry). After a few years practicing as an architect and construction supervisor, Candela was joined in Mexico by his brother, and they established a design and construction company. Through it, Candela was able to continue developing his knowledge of and skills with structures, in particular thin-shell structural forms. His first major official commission to design these came in 1951 for the Universidad Nacional Autónoma de México (UNAM; Mexican National Autonomous University), which was being completed at the time (see 1952 entry). For the UNAM, he designed and built a structure intended to measure cosmic rays whose exterior shell had to be about ⁵⁄₈ inch (1.5 cm) thick in order for the recording equipment within to be able to work.

As Candela's national and international prominence grew, so did his commissions. With this came the opportunities to develop and, more importantly, to try out new forms and constructive systems. The 1953 commission of

the Church of Our Lady of the Miraculous Medal is one example. For it, Candela had already devised the structural design; all he needed was the opportunity to try it out. The forms for the structure's nave are hyperbolic paraboloids derived from asymmetrical umbrella forms that were tilted, pleated to create triangular openings, and then rested opposite each other. By using these forms, Candela could relate the constructive and engineering problem to the architectural and spiritual: "[I had the idea that] with the paraboloids I could make these forms of an 'ascending tendency,' which is in reality Gothic, and it is what is esteemed as Western religious architecture" (ibid.). The concrete shell that makes up the ceiling is a mere 1 5/8 in. (4 cm) thick. To counter any upward thrust, Candela designed a thickened and scallop-shaped ridge at the top of the structure. In addition, the nave increases in height as it approaches the crossing over the altar that is itself composed of larger hyperbolic paraboloids. In the interior, the columns supporting the roof planes, derived from the umbrellas, dynamically express the angularity and forms that they support.

The orthogonal floor plan belies the complex formal articulation of the building and its ceiling shell. The plan

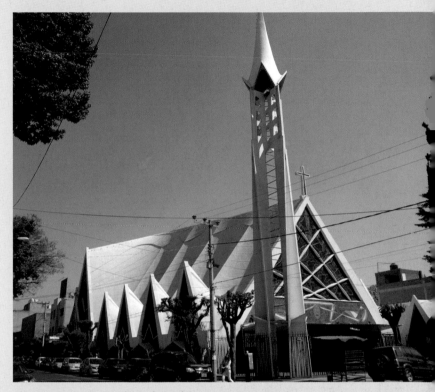

Félix Candela, Church of Our Lady of the Miraculous Medal, Mexico City, 1955.

is traditional in its organization, composed of a main aisle and side aisles. On the side of the main structure, Candela designed an accompanying hall formed by eight smaller hyperbolic paraboloids and a smaller chapel covered with folded concrete planes that is illuminated with stained-glass clearstory windows. The church's freestanding reinforced-concrete steeple is also topped with a hyperbolic paraboloid. In addition to this, light fixtures, sconces, and ironwork follow the dynamic and angular shapes of the building itself, creating, despite the engineered rationality of the structure, an expressionistic total work of art.

Félix Candela, interior view of the Church of Our Lady of the Miraculous Medal, Mexico City, 1955.

1953-B

MARIO ROBERTO ÁLVAREZ, TEATRO GENERAL SAN MARTÍN, BUENOS AIRES

ONE OF THE MOST comprehensive accounts of the spatial, material, and organizational complexity of the Teatro General San Martín is Lisando Alonso's film *Fantasma* (2006). The film follows Argentino Vargas, one of the stars of Alonso's earlier film *Los Muertos* (2004), who is searching for the premier of *Los Muertos* itself. Unfolding through the interior spaces of the building, *Fantasma* shows the sprawling complex that was intended to be a cultural center that would include all aspects of theatrical production.

Designed by Mario Roberto Álvarez, a graduate of the University of Buenos Aires, and Macedonio Oscar Ruiz, the Teatro General San Martín was the result of a competition conducted by the city of Buenos Aires. The building complex, which spans a city block, is divided into three main masses, each housing different programs. The taller

Mario Roberto Álvarez, Teatro General San Martín, Buenos Aires, 1961.

mass, which serves as the primary entrance on Corrientes Street—part of the city's theater district—programmatically houses two large performance theaters and a space for expositions on its lower levels. The theaters include contemporary theatrical devices such as vertical or rotating moving stages, modern lighting, adaptable orchestra pits, and extending stage platforms. On its upper levels, this block of the complex contains administrative offices and a movie theater that tops it on the tenth floor. A curtain wall composed of modular steel and glass panels with horizontal steel *brise-soleil*, the façade facing Corrientes Street is characteristic of Álvarez's interest in new materials and technology and in reducing the building to a more corporate and anonymous architecture (see 1947 entry). The complex's middle mass serves primarily as a support space for the theaters, including the fly space for the larger theater and other productive spaces. The last mass, which is on Sarmiento Street (on the other side of the block), was built later and was intended to house a school of dramatic arts. However, as of 2013, it houses offices and meeting spaces. In addition to this last change, a hard plaza was also added as a rear access to the building.

One of the characteristics that makes this building so unique is the integration of the different programmatic pieces within a single block (reminiscent of Dankmar Adler and Louis Sullivan's Auditorium Building [Chicago, 1886–1889]). By placing the theaters at different levels and in sectional relationship to each other, Álvarez is able to fit the large program into the site. In this way, the entrance lobby on Avenida Corrientes is a multilayered space that leads both to the entry level of the large auditorium upstairs and to a subbasement-level theater and exhibition space. At the entry level, the lobby space is terminated by the underside of a theater supported on piers (similar to Hans Scharoun's Philharmonie [Berlin, 1956–1963]). The complex connections between these spaces, on both the public and support sides of the building, are shown through Alonso's film as we follow the main protagonist through them.

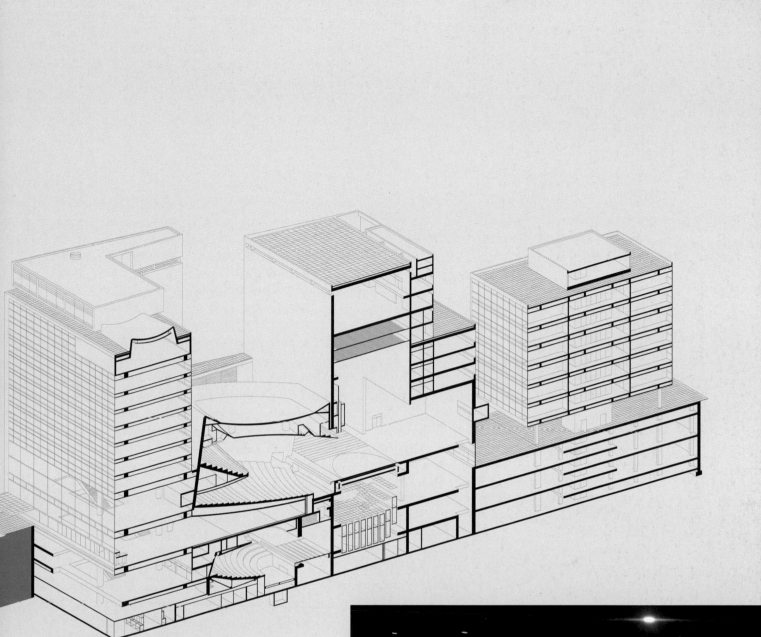

Axonometric section of Teatro General San Martín.

It should be noted that the Teatro General San Martín is also important because it is one of the few examples of modern plastic art integration in Argentina. Scattered throughout the public spaces are large-scale murals and sculptures, such as Luis Seoane's *Birth of Argentine Theater* (1960) in the lobby of the lower theater, Juan Batlle Planas's ceramic mural at the rear of the entrance floor lobby, José Fioravanti's relief mural, and Enio Iommi's stainless-steel sculpture in the first-floor lobby of the upstairs auditorium. There are also sculptures by Pablo Curatella Manes on the wall of the fly tower.

Mario Roberto Álvarez, lobby of Teatro General San Martín, Buenos Aires, 1961.

1954

LE CORBUSIER, CURUTCHET HOUSE, LA PLATA, ARGENTINA

ONE OF THE RESULTING COMMISSIONS from Le Corbusier's interest and involvement in Argentina since 1929 was the house for Dr. Pedro Curutchet. This house would be his only realized commission in South America and, along with the Carpenter Center at Harvard University (Cambridge, MA, 1963), one of two buildings built by him in the American continent. However, despite its modest size, the Curutchet House stands as a synthesis not only of Le Corbusier's general architectural principles but also of many of his ideas for Latin America.

This small house was intended as a home and office for Dr. Curutchet, an outsider to medicine due to his training in a university environment that highly valued arts and to his development of new surgical techniques and tools.

Le Corbusier, Curutchet House, La Plata, Argentina, 1954.

According to Jorge Francisco Liernur, for Curutchet, "art was not a complementary activity of a profession buried by technology. On the contrary, art and technology were fused together in his life and practice in an organic and integral way" (Liernur and Pschepiurca, "La red austral," 382). As a result, the medical technologies that he developed were steeped in, influenced by, and presented along with his interest in the arts.

Having worked primarily as a rural surgeon in the town of Lobería since the 1930s, Curutchet was intent on moving to La Plata, where he could not only reside but also continue his surgical work. For the house, Curutchet purchased a small, narrow lot in front of La Plata's large park and botanical gardens and in September of 1948 requested that Le Corbusier consider designing a house for him. Le Corbusier accepted the commission, stating that his interest in this project was related to his broader ideas for the Plan for Buenos Aires. The design of the house was finalized in 1949. Curutchet chose Amancio Williams (see 1942 box) to oversee the house's construction from a list of possible collaborators sent by Le Corbusier. Williams, in turn, not only executed its construction but, along the way, made interpretations and modifications to the design.

The house is divided into two parts that are connected via a ramp. The front of the house, facing the park through a *brise-soleil*, is composed of Curutchet's office, waiting room, and surgical space. Lifted on *pilotis*, this volume is located one story above the street and is accessed via the ramp. The ground floor was reserved for a one-car garage and services and mechanical systems located at the rear of the lot. Placed above these, also in the rear portion of the site, is a two-story structure that contains the living quarters. On the first floor, connected to the ramp via a stair, are the living and dining room as well as the kitchen and services. The living room, a double-height space reminiscent of Le Corbusier's Maison Citrohan project (1920), opens up to a roof garden that extends above the office to the front of the site. The second floor houses three bedrooms and curvilinear-shaped bathrooms. The house is built with reinforced concrete and uses a grid of *pilotis* as the primary structural support that also serves to unify the two distinct volumes of the project. Despite the placement of the living quarters at the rear of the house, the sectional quality of the design—with the taller volume at the rear and its double-height living room—allows for views to the park as well as for light penetrating into the family's spaces. To unify the house with the existing context (a higher building on its right and a lower one on the left), the façade uses *brise-soleil* and a high reinforced concrete baldachin covering part of the roof garden. The architectural vocabulary of *pilotis* and central ramp as well as the use of Le Corbusier's Modulor proportional system and elements of his "five points for a new architecture" testify to his continuing commitment to these architectural explorations. In addition, to unify the house not only in plan and in section and to bring nature into it, Le Corbusier's design relies on the placement of a tree at the center of the composition. The introduction of landscape into the city and, in this case, into the architecture itself was one of Le Corbusier's central tenets for his Plan for Buenos Aires. In addition, as part of Le Corbusier's interest in plastic integration, the sculpture *Continual Forms* (1953) by Enio Iommi, a sculptor associated with the Argentine Concretist movement, is placed on the ground level.

Given the constant attention by students and onlookers and the lack of privacy entailed by that and the design itself, the family only resided in the house until 1965, when Curutchet decided to move his practice back to Lobería.

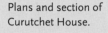
Plans and section of Curutchet House.

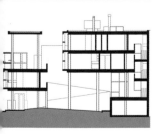

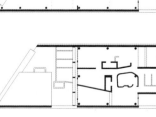

Le Corbusier, view of the roof garden, tree, and interior at Curutchet House, La Plata, Argentina, 1954.

1955

ELADIO DIESTE—TECTONICS DRIVING THE ACCIDENTAL ARCHITECT

URUGUAY

Development. What is development? Development, desired development, is that which makes mankind happier and able to fully develop.

ELADIO DIESTE

IT IS HARD TO RECONCILE the statement above with the Gaussian vaults that cover the latest fashions at the Montevideo Shopping Center (1984–1985), but both statement and building reveal different facets of a unique engineering genius turned architect. Eladio Dieste never thought of himself as an architect until much later in his professional life. His buildings were conceived as economical structures despite their ability to achieve intense poetical dimensions.

Born in the northern Uruguayan town of Artigas, near the Brazilian border, Dieste studied engineering in Montevideo in the 1930s. Growing up in a family of intellectuals, Dieste developed a passion for mathematics and physics that was complemented by a strong anchor in the humanities. His father was a historian, an uncle was a poet, and the artist Joaquín Torres-García was a friend of the family (see 1938 box). Dieste arrived in Montevideo the same year that Julio Vilamajó started the design of the School of Engineering building for the Universidad de la República in Montevideo (see 1936-b box), a structure widely discussed at the time of Dieste's training.

As a young engineer trying to push the limits of structure, Dieste worked with Antoni Bonet in 1947 (see 1945 box). At the Berlingieri House in Punta Ballena, Dieste is credited with convincing Bonet that cylindrical shells made of brick could be light and elegant.

In 1955, Dieste joined forces with Eugenio Montañez to create a construction firm specializing in brick vaults. Together, they successfully built over 15 million sq. ft. of large structures in Uruguay, Argentina, and Brazil. The extent of their achievement can be seen, for example, in the produce exchange pavilions in Porto Alegre, Brazil (1969–1972), whose vaults are 130 ft. (40 m) wide and 850 ft. (259 m) long.

At the same time that he was calculating and building large structures, Dieste was also teaching at Uruguay's Universidad de la República and writing specifically about his work or construction in general. The intellectual side of his practice allowed him to refine his thoughts into a dense and elegant defense of form as the origin of architecture. In his words, "The resistant virtues of the structures that we make depend on their form; it is through their form that they are stable and not because of an awkward accumulation of materials. There is nothing more noble and elegant from an intellectual viewpoint than this, resistance through form."[1] Dieste also wrote extensively on the relationship between technology and human needs. A devoted Catholic, Dieste professed a faith that was not at all dogmatic and orthodox but in fact critical and liberating. Living in South America in the 1950s and 1960s, he came in contact with liberation theology and the idea that the church has a duty to improve the living conditions of the poorest members of society.[2] Aligned with his morals was his search for a technology that would meet the different spatial needs through an economical use of materials and that could be assembled by poorly educated construction workers.

The chance to combine his faith and his expertise came in 1952 with the commission for a church in the community of Atlántida, 25 miles (40 km) from Montevideo (see 1952 box). The church is a single volume built of brick with undulating side walls and roof. In this way, Dieste created a nonhierarchical space bringing the priest and the worshipers together and one whose plastic form and light treatment create a truly magical space.

After Atlántida, Dieste would assume more and more the role of an architect. In 1962, he designed and built his own house in Montevideo. Organized around a courtyard, the social quarters in the front and the private ones in the back occupy the entire width

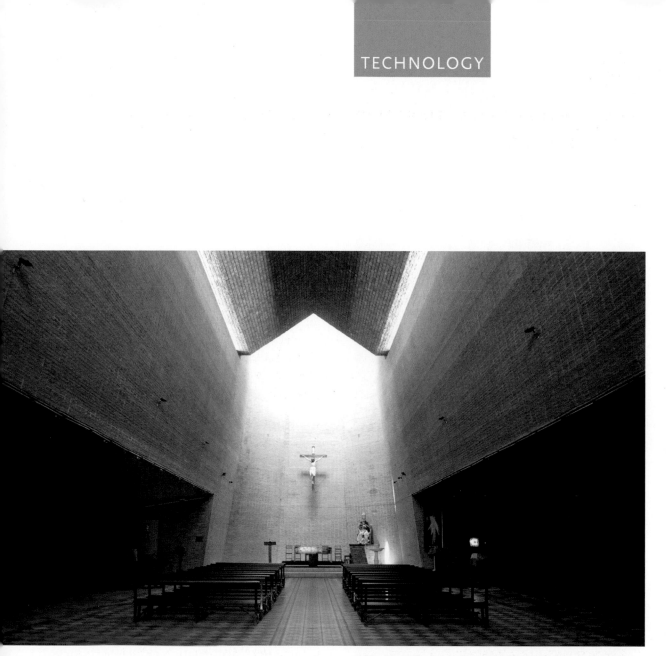

Eladio Dieste, interior of San Pedro Church, Durazno, Uruguay, 1967.

UY

of the narrow lot, sheltered by three long vaults that extend the whole length of the site. The height of the vaults varies according to the program as do the floor levels, creating a rich variety of ambiance despite the uniformity of the natural colors of the brick used for the vaults and the white-washed walls. In his own house, Dieste's stoicism is evident, as there were to be absolutely no decorations and, according to his son Antonio, no television until 1982—all of which, for Dieste, "became obstacles to our understanding of the essential."[3] Through this prohibition, one can also see how devoted he was to surfaces. Being the main generators of his forms, bent and folded to become structurally sound, surfaces were Dieste's primary tool. It is only natural that he rejected any form of decoration

that would interfere with the viewer's understanding of how these surfaces became structures and spaces.

In 1967, Dieste built a second church in the small town of Durazno, located in the prairies in the center of Uruguay. A fire had destroyed the local church of San Pedro, with the roof and many walls collapsing. Dieste proposed maintaining the original façade, to be repaired, and he created a whole new envelope following the layout of the original church. The planar brick walls that Dieste designed for this church are not as breathtaking as those in Atlántida, but the details are. A small gap between walls and roof, for instance, makes the latter appear to float when flooded by light. If brick

Eladio Dieste, detail of San Pedro Church, Durazno, Uruguay, 1967.

Eladio Dieste, exterior view of shopping center, Montevideo, 1985.

construction was defended by Dieste as an economical technique for developing countries, the reality is that his team was capable of such precise craftsmanship that only a very sophisticated designer could achieve it. At the back of the church, a presbytery tower 60 ft. (18 m) high is illuminated by a hidden window reminiscent of Le Corbusier's towers at Ronchamp (1950–1954). But the best of San Pedro is saved for the very last. As one exits the building, a large rose window built with brick occupies the whole wall and negotiates the transition between the old façade and the new building. Here, once again, plates of brick are made to appear as weightless thin surfaces against backlight.

In the 1980s, Dieste and Montañez applied their tectonic knowledge to a series of new programs that speak about the deep economic transformations taking place in Uruguay. Gone were the days of large infrastructure projects such as produce distribution centers and port warehouses. Gone also was the promise of a less unequal society as articulated by liberation theology or by dependency theory (see 1966 entry). Dieste's elegant shells were now sheltering shopping centers. In the city of Salto, a conic roof, also made of brick, placed on steel columns is a restaurant (Parador Ayuí, 1976–1977). Meandering walls protect the rowing club (Club Remeros, 1978). What started as an investigation into industrial economical structures was now turned fashionable by the growth of the service sector.

In the 1990s, his experience would take him to Spain, land of his grandfather, to design a church in Alcalá de Henares (1998). Here we see echoes of Atlántida everywhere, from the façade to the walls that now have a double curvature. In Mejorada del Campo, the church of Nuestra Madre del Rosario (1993–1997) very much resembles the San Pedro Church of Durazno. The Sagrada Familia in Torrejón de Ardoz (1997–1998) is another generic iteration of Atlántida.

Inverting the old path of architectural dissemination, Dieste had developed a successful investigation in South America and was now exporting his technology to Spain.

FURTHER READING

Anderson, *Eladio Dieste: Innovation in Structural Art*.
Dieste, *Eladio Dieste: La estructura cerámica*.
Eladio Dieste, 1917–2000.
Pedreschi, *Eladio Dieste: The Engineer's Contribution to Contemporary Architecture*.

1955-A

FRUTO VIVAS, CLUB TÁCHIRA

JOSÉ FRUCTOSO VIVAS VIVAS (known simply as "Fruto Vivas"), born in Venezuela in 1928, is among the most interesting Latin American architects unknown outside his own country. Immediately after graduating from the Universidad Central in 1956, Fruto Vivas worked for Oscar Niemeyer on his project for the Caracas Art Museum. It is hard to know if Vivas was influenced by Niemeyer's leftist ideas or if he got the job because of this ideological alignment. In the 1960s, for instance, Vivas would be very active in the Venezuelan Communist Party to the point

of building an explosives device plant and houses for the Fuerzas Armadas de Liberación Nacional (FALN; National Liberation Armed Forces), a local guerrilla group.

Paradoxically, like Niemeyer, Vivas was also building exceptional structures for the Venezuelan elite. His Club Táchira (1955) uses a thin concrete hyperbolic-parabola membrane to shelter the social quarters of a private club. Built on the slopes of one of Caracas's beautiful mountains, the curvy roof seems to land delicately on the site while providing the club members with a breathtaking

View of Caracas from Club Táchira.

view of the city below. The inclined hyperbolic parabola is related to the work of Oscar Niemeyer or Félix Candela, but the social club program allows it to be open at the front where the arch is at the highest, making for an airy and permeable space in contrast to the enclosed nature of the churches built by the aforementioned two.

One year later, Vivas would then experiment with the church program at the Iglesia del Divino Redentor de la Concordia with a single self-supporting curving wall of interlocking ceramic bricks with variable spacing between them. An S shape in plan, the wall divides the sacristy and offices from the nave. As the wall continues past the nave, it rolls into a cylinder that rises to become the church's campanile. The light modulation provided by the gaps between the bricks creates an ethereal atmosphere inside the nave as well as in the offices and sacristy. The roof is structured by tensile inverted trusses and does not touch the wall above the altar, providing zenithal light into the nave. The exposed roof structure combined with the exposed brick gives a certain roughness to the space and is similar to the contemporary work of Eladio Dieste in Uruguay (see 1952 box) or Rogelio Salmona in Colombia (see 1963 box).

In the 1980s, Fruto Vivas adopted an ecological discourse that used mimeticism as a strategy for form generation. His housing project El Árbol para Vivir (The Tree for Living) at Lecherías (designed 1990, built 1994) consists of four large apartment bars elevated off the ground around a patio. While one of the bars is only slightly above the earth, the other three are dramatically elevated with columns, much like Niemeyer's Alvorada Palace in Brasília (1957–1958), that hold the apartments 60 ft. (18 m) up in the air. The reinforced concrete structure of the majestic pillars (mostly in compression) hold a steel modulated truss (mostly in tension) that supports the apartment bars. Functionally expressive, all the plumbing and electrical cables run outside the units, coming down at the edge of the pillars.

By the turn of the twenty-first century, with President Hugo Chávez, Fruto Vivas became one of the favorite

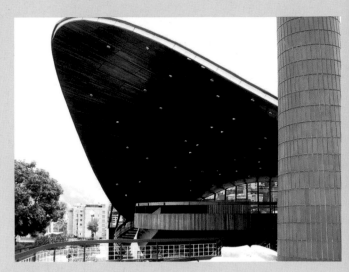

Fruto Vivas, Club Táchira, Caracas, 1955.

architects of the new government due to his (and his whole family's) long association with the Venezuelan left. In 2000, Vivas was hired to design the Venezuelan pavilion at Expo Hannover. Designed in the literal form of a flower, the pavilion is cylindrical with a small dome at the top. Covering the dome are twelve large moving petals. The petals are made of stretched canvas and structured in steel tubes. Articulated through the upper ring of the dome, they move vertically and independently, creating a variety of positions from "open flower" to closed and covered. To make it feasible, given the short time for its design, Vivas invited German architect Frei Otto to collaborate on the design. Once it opened, the pavilion was a big success, becoming the second most visited pavilion at the fair (behind only the German one).

Ironically, much like his comrade Niemeyer and despite his proximity with the populist Hugo Chávez government, Fruto Vivas has yet to build anything for the dispossessed masses of Venezuela. The commitment to a better life for all remains metaphorical, much like the "ecology" of suspended apartments for the upper middle classes or a flower-shaped Expo pavilion.

1955-B

THE HELICOIDE IN CARACAS: THE ULTIMATE PARKING AND SHOPPING CENTER

FRANK LLOYD WRIGHT'S influence and legacy in Latin America has always been unclear. Surely, during his time in Rio de Janeiro as a judge for the Columbus Lighthouse Competition in 1931, he was present and supportive of the changes in the curriculum of the School of Architecture (at the ENBA) under Lúcio Costa (see 1930-a entry). In addition, the Mexican architect Juan O'Gorman directly acknowledged Wright's influence in his own work after abandoning functionalism in 1936 (see 1933 and 1938 entries). With the construction of his own house in El Pedregal (1949), O'Gorman became one of the strongest proponents in Mexico of Wright's organic architecture—an architecture, he argued, that was rooted in its site, locale, and historical traditions. And though Wright designed a number of projects for Latin America (such as the Raúl Bailleres House for Acapulco, 1952), none of them were built. The Helicoide de la Roca Tarpeya in Venezuela is an

odd exception to this because of its inadvertent relationship to one of Wright's foundational projects: the Gordon Strong Planetarium and Automobile Objective (1924–1925) for Maryland, an essential precedent for Wright's Solomon R. Guggenheim Museum (New York, 1943–1959).

Designed by architects Jorge Romero, Dirk Bornhorst, and Pedro Neuberger to be a shopping center with spaces for the exhibition of industrial products, the Helicoide, like Wright's project for Gordon Strong, relies on the integration of the automobile into the architecture. The building is, in essence, a triangular-shaped spiral ramp placed on a massively excavated and graded hill (the Roca Tarpeya) that allows for the linear movement of the car up and down the hill. Along the gentle slope of the spiral ramp (intended to be 2.5%), cars can park and access

View of the Helicoide under construction, Caracas, 1955.

the businesses located on it and, at the top, reverse their path; in other words, the circulation plan is a double helix. The complex's goal was to achieve maximum retail efficiency by requiring all cars to drive past all of the shops without any intermediate turnaround. By incorporating the automobile as the principal motif of its design, the building facilitates the experience of shopping and access to other programs, materializing a condition of utopia: the simultaneous experience of "pleasure, efficiency, and complexity" (1950: El espíritu moderno, 67).

The importance of the automobile is most notable in the descriptions of the project as the necessary and obvious intervention within the regulating plan for Caracas. As noted in one of the most comprehensive accounts of the building, in the journal Integral 5 (1956), the building is placed on an area zoned for "special studies." It is also linked to major avenues, highway off-ramps, and public transportation that responded to the integration of the automobile within the urban fabric. And, despite the centrality of the automobile experience for the building (the design even boasted an auto center in a lower section of

the building and tangential to the ramps), the steeper part of the hill had a four-car inclined elevator to move pedestrians who arrived via public transportation.

Besides the commercial establishments and their parking located along the ramp, the building was intended to house offices, a private kindergarten, a small television station, a hotel, and a "palace of spectacles" where expositions as well as sporting and other events could take place. The spectacular nature of the new shopping center and exhibition space can be seen in the intention of broadcasting live not only the activities taking place in the "palace of spectacles" throughout the building (by means of a closed-circuit TV system) but also advertisements of products for sale throughout the complex. These events and commercials were also to be broadcast to the neighboring areas of the city.

Although the construction of the Helicoide was stopped in 1961, the project was featured in Roads, an exhibition that same year curated by Bernard Rudofsky for the Museum of Modern Art in New York, as an example of the integration of roads and architecture.

1955-C

GIO PONTI, VILLA PLANCHART

THE VILLA PLANCHART in Caracas, Venezuela—perhaps Gio Ponti's greatest work—is an exercise in all types of complexities.

First of all, it is a long-distance-designed house. Although Ponti, an Italian architect centered in Milan, Italy, had traveled to Latin America between 1952 and 1953, the design and discussions that led to the construction of the house took place via an elaborate epistolary correspondence between himself and the two patrons, Armando and Anala Planchart. These are curious letters and artistic objects in and of themselves: oscillating between different languages (French, Italian, and Spanish), they contain drawings and diagrams; collages and modified photographs of the construction process; and notes, questions, and indications of how things could, should, or must be done. Despite the distance and the necessity of translating and interpreting the wishes of his clients, Ponti managed to design all aspects of the house, from its overall organization to the furniture, porcelain dining service, and cutlery itself. Given full freedom of design, Ponti created a total work of art for Latin America. Everything he designed has some reference to the clients and their interests: for the Superleggera chair, he incorporated Venezuelan newspaper clippings sent by Planchart; for the plates, he had their initials printed upon them; the stucco sun and moon decorations on the roof of the hall reference his two clients. In some cases, such as for the placement of the hunting trophies in Armando Planchart's office, the architect disagreed with his clients (he tried to convince them that they were incongruous with their taste). Ponti's compromise to include them in the design, however, consisted of inventing a motorized cabinet system that rotates them into view when needed.

Second, it was a house that, despite being completely decorated, furnished, and filled with tropical plants, Venezuelan and international modern art, Italian design, and, of course, the Planchart's prized possessions, seemed to float in the landscape like "a butterfly sitting on a hill" (Irace, "Caracas Villa Planchart," 88). The exterior walls,

Gio Ponti, Villa Planchart, Caracas, 1955.

despite their massiveness, appear to be nonsupporting and as if they are levitating above the landscape. This is most clear at night when they are illuminated along their seams in what Ponti described as "nocturnal self-illumination." Ponti had been interested in making architecture appear lighter since the 1930s.

In his *La casa all'italiana* (1933), Ponti argued for the eradication of the wall as an enclosing and dividing element. For the Villa Planchart, the interior walls organize and limit the interplay between open spaces. Yet, it is that spatial interplay that characterizes the house's modernity. Despite its seemingly compact exterior form, Ponti described the house, in a Corbusian sense, as a "machine" of sorts to be experienced visually and, most importantly, kinetically. The experience of the building, through the floor plans, is organized by means of visual paths and views that the building sets up and controls as the inhabitants move through it. Privacy and, more importantly,

Gio Ponti, Interior View of Villa Planchart, 1955.

control through vision is still maintained where needed. The second floor of the house, the living quarters, is less open and, in the view lines that Ponti drew into the plan, clearly allows the Plancharts to have visual access to all aspects of their house while remaining unseen within their private quarters. Outside of this system of vision are the support spaces—servants' quarters, kitchen and pantry, etc.—located along the rear of the house, which are indicated on the plan by the absence of lines of vision that emanate from them (Anala Planchart, however, can see into them from her rooms) as well as by the human figures drawn in the plans. In contrast to the Plancharts and their guests, who are shown engaged in static leisurely activities, the servants are always indicated through lines of motion and as devoid of vision.

Finally, to locate the experience of the house in the landscape, Ponti organized and focused many of the views from the house toward the outside and created an ambiguity between inside and outside. The integration into the house of a courtyard filled with plants and zenithal light, a reference Ponti wanted to make to traditional Latin American courtyard house typologies, aids in the dissolution of the spatial boundaries of the house and reinforces the ambiguity between inside and outside. This is particularly clear at the entrance, where the views are focused across the courtyard and end in one of the dining rooms, the Comedor Tropical (Tropical Dining Room), which opens up into the house's central court.

1956

BRASÍLIA: A MODERNIST UTOPIA?

BRAZIL

Brasília, capital aérea e rodoviária; cidade parque. Sonho arqui-secular do Patriarca.

LÚCIO COSTA, *PLANO PILOTO DE BRASÍLIA*

DESPITE HAVING WON his bid for the presidency, Brazil's president-elect Juscelino Kubitschek was not enjoying the summer of 1956 in Rio de Janeiro. A group of conservative politicians had actually plotted an unsuccessful coup in November of 1955. In addition, the new year's conversations were dark with all kinds of rumors about maneuvers designed to prevent him from taking office. The fact that he was elected with only 35 percent of the vote meant that he had to walk a fine line to keep the fragile alliance between his centrist Partido Social Democrático (PSD; Social Democratic Party) and Vice President João Goulart's leftist Partido Trabalhista Brasileiro (PTB; Brazilian Labor Party). This unstable political arrangement would prevail throughout his five years in office. However, when he stepped into the presidency on January 31, 1956, he already had the answer to his troubles: a series of thirty-one developmental goals under the overall theme of advancing "fifty years in five." The crowning achievement of these goals would be the transfer of Brazil's capital to a new city to be built in the central highlands. Since Kubitschek lacked congressional support, Brasília would be the means to galvanize public support behind him. In this way, Brasília was, from day one, the *meta síntese* (main goal) of the Kubitschek presidency.

With a central capital somewhat equidistant from the outlying states and areas of Brazil, new relationships between these states, the central government, and foreign governments could be established. Since colonial times, the Brazilian capital had been located along the coast because of the ease of maritime access. However, this privileged coastal cities and limited interchanges with other countries to those on the coast while ignoring, with the possible threat of separation or annexation by other countries, the fringes of the country. The idea of a central capital was not new; it had been considered since 1789. It was inscribed in the Brazilian Constitution in 1823, only one year after formal independence from Portugal. The first Republican Constitution of 1891 ratified the idea and indicated an area of 5,560 sq. miles (14,400 sq. km) in the *planalto central* (central highlands) to be demarcated later. An exploratory team was sent the next year, and the 1894 Cruls Report (named after its head engineer, Luís Cruls) defined the boundaries and location of the future federal district. In addition to these rational approaches, there was a utopian prefiguration of Brasília by the Italian priest Don Bosco, founder of the Salesian Order, who dreamed in 1883 of a plentiful and just city located between the fifteenth and sixteenth parallels in South America, where Brasília would eventually be located.

Oscar Niemeyer, National Congress, Brasília, 1960.

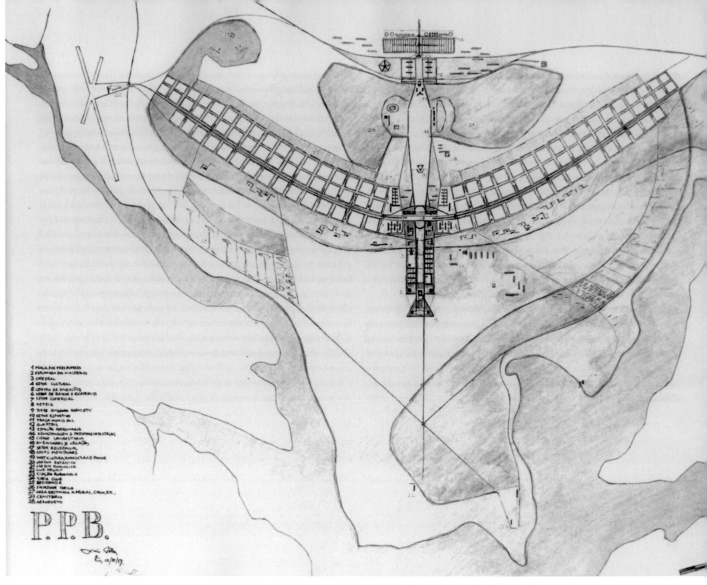

P.P.B.

Lúcio Costa, Master Plan for Brasília, 1956.

In 1922, as part of the development of a new capital, a foundational stone was placed outside Planaltina that lay within the zone demarcated by Cruls. In 1946, another surveying team was sent to the area, now expanded to 29,730 sq. miles (77,000 sq. km). The idea of moving the capital was discussed more and more in the early 1950s, becoming a reality when Juscelino Kubitschek decided to use it as the central objective of his presidential term.

For Kubitschek, Brasília would stand as an image of modernization and development that could stabilize a postwar Brazil and his administration. His policies of *"desenvolvimentismo"* (developmentalism) placed emphasis on the development of the economy to further strengthen the country's economic well-being and the political outlook. In other words, if politics were to be dictated by the economy, developmentalism would place the economy at the center of politics. In this way, the making of Brasília itself was a paradigm for

activating Kubitschek's policies to strengthen the economy and industry, as the project was dependent, first of all, on new and expanded modes of transportation for its construction (in this case, the development of highway and aerial transportation) and, secondarily, on the efficient and rapid adaptation of technologies (for the organization and construction of the territory, which, for the president, had to be completed before his term in office was over).

In September of 1956, nine months after Kubitschek's inauguration as president, the agency Urbanizadora do Nova Capital (Novacap; Urbanization Company of the New Capital) was formed to oversee the construction of the new capital. Oscar Niemeyer was appointed as lead designer and main advisor to its director, Israel Pinheiro. Learning about Kubitschek's plans for Brasília, Le Corbusier wrote a letter offering his services. Under pressure from the Brazilian

Institute of Architects, Kubitschek's government, however, called for an urban design competition open only to Brazilian professionals. The competition was announced that same September, with the proposals to be due in early March 1957. Le Corbusier was invited to be part of the jury but declined.[1]

On March 16, 1957, twenty-one proposals were submitted. The top prizes were awarded to Milton Ghiraldini, João Batista Vilanova Artigas, Henrique Mindlin and Giancarlo Palanti, MMM Roberto, Rino Levi, and Boruch Milman. Their entries generally show a rational subdivision of the territory and the impact of late Corbusian planning techniques (such as those characteristic of Chandigarh [India, 1951–1965]), with blocks subdivided by connected strips of green parkways. Rino Levi's entry was unique, as it proposed high-density skyscraper linear blocks over the largely unoccupied territory. In all cases, the proposals referenced contemporary ideas of modern planning advocated by the Congrès International d'Architecture Moderne (CIAM; International Congress of Modern Architecture), such as the separation of pedestrian and vehicular transportation, subdivision of the city into key functional spaces, and so on. In the end, however, Lúcio Costa's entry was declared a winner by the jury of Israel Pinheiro (Novacap president), Sir William Holford (England), André Sive (France), Stamo Papadaki (United States), Oscar Niemeyer (Novacap),

Luiz Hildebrando Horta Barbosa (Engineering Club), and Paulo Antunes Ribeiro (Brazilian Institute of Architects). While some architects complained that Niemeyer wanted Costa to design the city from the beginning and therefore influenced the competition, the exhibition and the publication of the proposals in April 1957 cemented the idea that Costa's *Plano Piloto*, or Master Plan, was—as described by the jury—the only one that balanced the functional aspects of a twentieth-century city with the symbolic demands of a new national capital. This was clear from the very conclusion of Costa's proposal, which encapsulated all of its aspirations and formal characteristics: "Brasília, capital aérea e rodoviária; cidade parque. Sonho arqui-secular do Patriarca" (Brasília, aerial and highway capital; garden city. Archi-secular dream of the Patriarch).[2]

Costa's proposal, famously submitted at the eleventh hour, consists of a series of hand drawings: one full plan, several sketches, and a twenty-four-page letter that starts with an apology for deciding to enter the competition at the last minute. The second paragraph reads: "I did not intend to compete and, in fact, I still don't—instead I am throwing out a possible solution that was not sought but that arrived, so to speak, ready."[3]

In Costa's winning entry, emphasis was placed on a cruciform shape: two axes crossing in the act of marking, defining, and taking ownership of a place. The east-west axis houses the most important

Oscar Niemeyer and Lúcio Costa, Esplanada dos Ministérios, Brasília, 1960.

Oscar Niemeyer, Alvorada Palace, Brasília, 1960.

governmental buildings, transportation, and businesses and is named the "Monumental Axis." On the east, a triangular plaza—the "Three-Powers Plaza," as Costa would describe it—defines the space of the three federal powers: the Presidential Palace, the Supreme Court, and the National Congress Building. From here toward the west, the axis was defined along the edge of a large open longitudinal space by the various governmental ministry buildings. With the exception of the Ministry of Justice and the Ministry of Foreign Affairs, both located nearest to the Congress Building, all of the other ministries are evenly spaced, repetitive modern buildings whose character is best reflected in Marcel Gautherot's photographs of their construction.

To better comply with the site's topography and the shape of the lake, the north-south axis was curvilinear. Along its 9.95 miles (16 km) are the famous *superquadras*, or housing blocks: 128 of them, in rows of four, serving as the residential areas of the *Plano Piloto*. The

composition and character of the *superquadras* are carefully described in the proposal; they have a row of trees in the outer perimeter and elevated six-story blocks organized inside. The bus station at the center of the city and the place where both axes meet is also described in detail in Costa's proposal, whereas other parts of the city are only briefly touched upon.

The form of the city, therefore, reflected not only contemporary urban planning ideas and positions but also an aspiration to create something completely new. The modern order of the world, in other words, could only be materialized through new forms and aesthetics. In this way, the first metaphor of progress is the form of the city itself as either a bird or an airplane—something that is only perceptible from the air, one of the new transportation methods necessary to access the city. Second, the city would be of a useful and utilitarian character, something that could be seen not only in the organization but also in the architecture. Niemeyer, in 1958, would characterize it as "compact, simple, geometric solutions . . . the advantages of unity and harmony between buildings and, moreover, the idea that they should no longer be expressed in terms of their secondary elements but through their actual structure, duly integrated into the original plastic conception."[4]

As Novacap's lead designer and advisor, Niemeyer had reserved the design of the main buildings for himself; he had actually published his drawings for the Alvorada Palace, or Presidential Residence, in February 1957, one month before the competition was judged. This fact alone forces us to question if Niemeyer devised his blending of classicism and modernism to fit Costa's vision of monumentality, or if Costa proposed an urban design into which Niemeyer's architecture would fit.

For the Three-Powers Plaza, Niemeyer developed a new form of architecture unlike anything that he had built in the past. Urbanistically, the different masses within the plan organized by Costa generated the spatial character of the area. The fact that there was nothing architectural to respond to forced Niemeyer to create an instantaneous city-like experience: something completely new and, thus, a city without history. The

Oscar Niemeyer, Itamaraty Palace, Brasília, 1960.

buildings themselves demonstrate that Niemeyer's new design principles—which aim toward a simplification and sobriety of the forms—were not only based on functional and programmatic needs but also on the investigation of structure and structural expression.

Niemeyer's shift toward monumentality and platonic forms actually happened before Brasília and can be seen, for instance, at the Ibirapuera pavilions in São Paulo (1953–1954) or in his 1955 unbuilt design for the Caracas Art Museum. Throughout the 1940s and 1950s, as Kubitschek moved from mayor of Belo Horizonte (1940–1945; see 1941 entry), to governor of Minas Gerais (1950–1955), to president (1956–1960), Niemeyer's commissions grew in size: schools, hospitals, exhibition pavilions—programs with thousands of square meters—and his architecture undoubtedly became more classical in nature.

Niemeyer achieved the highest degree of classicism and monumentality in Brasília, with the apex of this being the Brazilian National Congress. In it, a horizontal slab houses lobbies and support spaces for the two semispherical chambers: the smaller concave shape for the Senate and the larger convex one for the House of Representatives. These, in turn, are divided in the composition by a tower of two vertical slabs that houses the offices of the elected officials. Through the use of simple geometries (the concave and convex semispheres), Niemeyer's building creates the play of light and shadow that Le Corbusier had called for in architecture but also a geometric harmony within the architecture that is based on simple platonic forms. In this way, the building appears to be completely unprecedented, although, through the forms, it still makes reference to traditional domed congress buildings. The lower section of the building is more classical in nature, as it is lifted from the ground and has a repetitive columnar structure of more traditional white Corbusian *pilotis*. These create a separation between the edge of the building and the enclosed space but also reference classical buildings from antiquity.

The Presidential Palace and the Supreme Court are similar in their classical disposition. For them, however, Niemeyer developed a new structural and tectonic system based on tapering forms that spread out to form curves and are separate from the glass boxes that enclose their respective programs. These new elements were intended to lighten the visual aspects of the buildings and to give them an "appearance of unattachment."[5] In the end, the buildings have a character

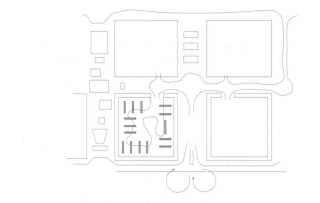

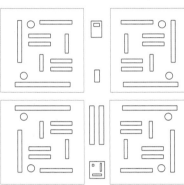

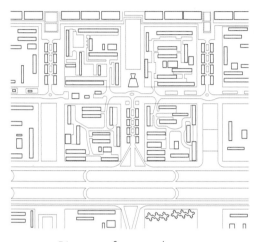

Diagrams of *superquadras*.

Aerial view of *superquadra*, Brasília.

that recalls classical temples, Corbusian modernism, and Miesian formalism while, in relationship to the mythology already established with the Brazilian baroque past, "expressing the same plastic intention, the same love of curves and richly refined forms that is so telling a characteristic of the colonial style."[6] In this way, the lyricism of his earlier works (see 1941 entry) was constrained to these type of details in addition to the elegant inverted columns of the Alvorada Palace, the majestic play of water at the entrance of Itamaraty Palace (Foreign Relations Ministry), or the concrete gargoyles of the Ministry of Justice (designed in 1962, modified in 1986). The latter are in tune with Roberto Burle Marx's gardens, his first creations for Brasília (see 1965-a entry).

While the explorations of the monumental and autonomous buildings for the government were going on, the other important developments of Brasília were centered on the *superquadras* (*superquadras* are city blocks approximately 300 m [ca. 1,000 ft.] square—whereas traditional blocks in Brazil are 100 m [328 ft.] square)—with residential buildings interspersed within a garden space). The *superquadras* are

then organized in groups of four that are accessed, primarily, from the highway that moves in the north-south axis. One arrives at an intermediary space between the blocks that acts as a communal street composed of public programs such as cinemas, retail, churches, etc. These can also be accessed from the residential blocks that lie behind them; in other words, all of the stores or businesses have two fronts, one to the vehicular public and the other to the pedestrian, residential public. In the blocks, housing is interspersed with garden spaces. In the earliest built *superquadras*, the ideal condition was to lift the six-story buildings off the ground on *pilotis* to allow for uninterrupted movement of the pedestrians through the garden, as it had been defined by CIAM principles and in keeping with ideas about garden cities. In addition to housing, within these blocks there are semipublic functions like schools and kindergartens. Finally, in between one quadrant of *superquadra* and the next *superquadra* were more public amenities such as sports fields, swimming pools, etc. Ideally, the inhabitants of the *superquadra* had all their needs taken care of within the surrounding few blocks.

Intended to have an air of classlessness and egalitarianism, Costa's description of the *superquadras* addressed how social gradation would be resolved by their being designed for mixed-income families and individuals. Costa's ideal placed Novacap as responsible for providing decent housing for the totality of the population. In this way, Niemeyer, as he worked for the left-leaning government of João Goulart in 1963, would publish designs for buildings that, according to him, could be inhabited by anybody: from a cabinet minister to a janitor, not according to income but according to family needs. One year later, a military coup ended any plans for Brasília to work as a socially distributive urban place and, instead, embraced and encouraged market forces (albeit controlled) as the main energy driving the development of the city. The result was that the working class of Brasília could not afford to live within its boundaries but was forced to live outside of the city. Because of the cordon sanitaire proposed from the very beginning to maintain Brasília's autonomy, this meant that many live in satellite towns.[7]

The result of such effects has heightened opinions on Brasília and its success. Yet, this is not new because, since its beginning, Brasília has been criticized both as too utopian and as not utopian enough. Angel Rama in his classic *Ciudad letrada* (1984) called Brasília "the most fabulous dream . . . in the new continent," while

Marshall Berman, in the preface to the second edition of *All That Is Solid Melts into Air* (1981), described it as "one of the most dismal cities in the world."

Immediately after its inauguration, Brasília was critiqued for being a desolate dystopia: a classic example of the failures of modern urbanism and the separation between housing, work, leisure, and transportation. Federal employees forced to move to the new capital from around the country had little or no empathy with the wide-open spaces and the absence of street life to which they were accustomed. The city was praised as the embodiment of hope and criticized as the materialization of despair. However, one of the major criticisms of the young city was the antiseptic quality of the *superquadras*, the neighborhoods for private life. Yet, today, they are thriving, with busy restaurants and bars every few blocks and noisy with children playing on the interstitial green spaces. What caused the change? The main factor is time. The small young trees planted at the city's inception have grown into large shady canopies. Stores that address the specific needs of the local inhabitants have thrived and multiplied.

Niemeyer buildings have been discussed in derogatory terms in every survey of twentieth-century architecture, often very superficially.[8] Most architectural critiques on Brasília do not engage with the complexity of the social, economic, and political contexts, focusing instead on the architects' discourse and on what is materially visible. The result of this gap is that Brasília's literature epitomizes both the achievements and the failures of twentieth-century modernization.

Brasília was designed to lead the country in a new direction: it certainly did when we look at what Brazil was in the 1950s and how it is now an emerging global power for the twenty-first century. Fifty years after inauguration, it is very hard to imagine Brazil without Costa's bold experiment.

FURTHER READING

Del Rio and Siembieda, *Contemporary Urbanism in Brazil: Beyond Brasília.*
El-Dahdah, *CASE: Lucio Costa, Brasília's Superquadra.*
Evenson, *Two Brazilian Capitals: Architecture and Urbanism in Rio de Janeiro and Brasília.*
Holanda, *Brasília: Cidade moderna, cidade eterna.*
Holston, *The Modernist City: An Anthropological Critique of Brasília.*
Williams, "Brasília after Brasília."

1957-A

MIES VAN DER ROHE, BACARDÍ BUILDINGS FOR HAVANA, CUBA, AND MEXICO CITY

IN DECEMBER 1956, Ludwig Mies van der Rohe was asked by José M. Bosch, president of Ron Bacardí y Compañía, to design the headquarters of the Cuban rum manufacturing company as an office without partitions "where everybody, both officers and employees, are seeing each other" (Lambert, "Mies Immersion," 475–480). Working in Havana in the summer of 1957, Mies and his assistant, Gene Summers, realized that both the sun and the humidity would have a tremendous impact on the character of the building and that its material realities would need to vary significantly from Bosch's expectations that the design be something akin to Crown Hall (Chicago, 1950–1956). The result of these reflections was a large clear-span, gridded roof that extended beyond the perimeter of the glass enclosure in order to provide shade to the interior. The reinforced concrete structure would be composed of a pair of cruciform columns placed at quarter points along each side of the roof's perimeter, allowing the corners to cantilever. The interior space was to be defined by two freestanding walls, a service core, and a stair leading to the lower level. The whole project was to be placed on a plinth and accessed, as with most Miesian projects, asymmetrically. As should be clear, this unbuilt project for Havana became a dress rehearsal for Mies's New National Gallery in Berlin (1962–1968).

Following the Cuban Revolution, Bacardí sought to establish headquarters and production facilities outside of Cuba, and as a result, Mies was again asked to design an office for the company, this time in Tultitlán, on the outskirts of Mexico City. Historian Salvador Lizárraga Sánchez points to the paradoxical absence of this building from the historical canon of modern architecture, especially given Sigfried Giedion's effusive praise for it in his 1962 edition of *Space, Time and Architecture*. The design of the Mexican building (1957–1962), unlike its Cuban counterpart, is composed of a stark rectangular block lifted above a travertine pad and supported by an exterior colonnade, travertine-covered mechanical cores, and a glass-enclosed circulation lobby. The glass entry affords views to the gardens that surround the structure but also, sectionally, links the upper story with the lower. Seen from the exterior, the upper block has been aptly described as a "slice" of any of Mies's skyscraper projects with its 13-inch (33 cm) black steel columns, 8-inch (20 cm) black steel mullions, and gray glass curtain wall. Its interior is characterized by a symmetrical open plan around the opening

Mies van der Rohe, photo collage of interior, Bacardí Building project, Havana, Cuba, 1956.

Mies van der Rohe, Bacardí Building, Mexico City, 1957–1962.

to the lobby (here one can appreciate the 26-foot (8 m) double-height space of the lobby) and has freestanding yet asymmetrical mahogany-covered service cores on the edges that define the conference rooms at each end of the building. While *Architectural Forum* in 1962 described it as a "monument to serenity and order" that is characteristic of Mies's later work, it is also easy to see how its symmetry, the transparency/reflectivity/opacity of the glass, and the formal and material similarities between the spaces create a disorienting environment. In this way, the building continues his earlier explorations of placelessness within the metropolitan environment.

Despite Mies's international reputation, this would be his only built commission in Latin America.

Mies van der Rohe, interior of Bacardí Building, Mexico City, 1957–1962.

1959

THE APPEAL OF CORBUSIAN MONUMENTALITY AND *BÉTON BRUT*: CLORINDO TESTA'S GOVERNMENT BUILDING

ARGENTINA

WITH THE END OF THE Second World War, architects, along with other cultural producers, became disillusioned with rationality and the rationalization of the world: many saw its outcomes in the more destructive weapons of war (culminating, of course, in the development and deployment of the atomic bomb over Nagasaki and Hiroshima). Philosophers, such as Theodor Adorno and Max Horkheimer, theorized that the war and the events leading to it were the effect of an instrumental reason and a project of enlightenment zealously promoted to the detriment of all things that

didn't follow their logic and that stood in their way. As a result, Le Corbusier, as well as other architects who had initially argued for a conception of the world based on logic, order, and control, would rethink this position and redirect their work's basis in a different way; after all, what the war had proved was the existence of uncertainties and discontinuities within logic and reason themselves. Like the Dadaists or surrealists after the First World War, Le Corbusier's reaction—in what many historians define as his postwar crisis—was manifested not only in his discovery of the obsoles-

Clorindo Testa, Government Building, Santa Rosa, La Pampa, Argentina, 1956.

cence of rationality but in a growing interest in the power of the imagination and the irrational. This change of direction can be seen in his later works, such as the Unité d'Habitation (Marseilles, 1947–1952), the Monastery of La Tourette (near Lyons, 1953–1957), or the Chapel of Notre Dame at Ronchamp (1950–1954). One of the more salient characteristics of this work is its use of *béton brut*, or rough, exposed concrete, and the continuing expression of functional programmatic pieces now used/perceived as assemblages in contrast to one another to evoke different qualities in a quasi-surrealist way (in many cases by using the *boîte à miracles* strategy of combining them within a single container, much in the way that the American sculptor Joseph Cornell would). This change in work, form, and expression would ultimately have repercussions throughout Latin America, where Le Corbusier's work was highly regarded and influential.

IN LA PAMPA AND, WITH SEPRA, THE BANK OF LONDON AND SOUTH AMERICA IN BUENOS AIRES

The work of the Argentine architect Clorindo Testa would fall under that spell, although it is necessary to be aware of noticeable differences. Testa, born in Italy in 1923, studied civil engineering for a year at the University of La Plata but graduated from the School of Architecture of the University of Buenos Aires in 1947. Shortly after graduating, he worked with Jorge Ferrari Hardoy, Juan Kurchan, and Antoni Bonet in the offices for the Plan for Buenos Aires; all three had worked with Le Corbusier in Paris and continued working with him to institute his urban ideas in Buenos Aires (see 1949 box). Testa's designs for the Government Building for Santa Rosa, La Pampa, are characteristic of his early work and of the influence of Le Corbusier's work in Chandigarh, India, such as the Secretariat and Palace of Justice (both 1952–1956).

For the Government Building, the commission for which resulted from a competition in 1956, Testa (with Boris Dabinovic, Augusto Gaido, and Francisco Rossi) designed a linear structure (590 ft. [180 m] long and 75 ft. [23 m] wide) that is placed on a slight depression within the site. A covering structure of reinforced concrete hyperbolic paraboloids in front of it is placed perpendicular to it to create a covered plaza. The building, which has been described as a docked steamship of sorts, has three main sections/levels: the lowest contains the ministers' offices, the middle is made up of a double-height public level accessed via ramps, and the higher two-story section contains the administrative offices. The use of exposed reinforced concrete construction along with its *pilotis*, an open floor plan, and reinforced concrete *brise-soleil* reflects the primary characteristics of Le Corbusier's contemporary formal expressions. In addition, because of the building's sectional openness and thinness, the programmatic or functional elements appear to float within the space of the reinforced concrete structural frame and, in particular, in the double-height spaces when they recede from the building's edge; this strategy will be expanded upon in the Banco de Londres y América

del Sud (Bank of London and South America, Buenos Aires, 1959–1966). The façades on the short sides of the building are clad with brick that, in most cases, is treated in very traditional ways: with lintels to create window-like openings or in alternating patterns to create screens, for instance.

The importance in Argentina of Le Corbusier's designs for Chandigarh can also be seen in the Manuel Belgrano School at the University of Córdoba (O. Bidinost, J. Chute, J. M. Gassó, M. Lapacó, and M. Meyer, 1960–1971), which not only contains elements such as the *béton brut* construction, sunshades, *pilotis*, etc., but also uses a large sunshade over the front façade, an interior access ramp, and an organization of the ground-floor plan that, with its circular auditorium, formalizes all of the echoes of Le Corbusier's Palace of Justice and Assembly Hall in Chandigarh.

Testa's and SEPRA's (Santiago Sánchez Elía, Federico Peralta Ramos, and Alfredo Agostini) Bank of London and South America is, however, the unqualified masterpiece of Le Corbusier's influence. Unqualified in the sense that it is difficult to ascribe to it a style or direct influence but also in the sense of its incredible success in solving a number of structural, urban, and architectonic problems.[1] The project brief stipulated the necessity of "expressing integrity, efficiency, and trust by means of a clear and concise architectural expression that does not rely on forms of the past nor on contemporary clichés that will later become antiquated."[2] As a result, Testa, in association with SEPRA, produced a complex building that responds contextually to the street and its architectural neighbors by means of scale, rhythm, and formal continuities, and that creates a rich interior open space where a multiplicity of programs overlap spatially. On the exterior, linear and perforated piers provide a sense of scale to the passerby. These same elements are used structurally to support the roof plane that, in turn, supports some of the interior floor planes that hang from it. Because of the separation between these and the

Clorindo Testa and SEPRA, Banco de Londres, Buenos Aires, 1966.

glass façade that encloses the interior, these structural piers not only provide shading and privacy but, despite their massive size, allow the occupant visual connection to the urban fabric. By organizing the structure in this way, the interior space achieves a degree of openness in both plan and in section; and in this space, a number of programmatic and formal elements are introduced, creating a sort of *boîte à miracles*. At the ground level, the entry to the building is on the corner and up a set of stairs that place the visitor at the center of the open hall (which has been described by various historians as "Piranesian"). Three floors acting as trays, supported on central columnar piers, rise from this level. These are connected to each other by a central bank of escalators as well as by stair and elevator towers that also access the upper levels. The three upper levels have more regular floor-to-ceiling heights, are more enclosed, and follow the sectional profile of the building (which, in the rear, steps back from the party wall of the adjacent building). In the initial diagram, this upper area and basement areas were defined as the private portions of the bank, whereas the open void is characterized as the public space.

Besides the rough exposed reinforced concrete that makes up the façades and is expressed in many of the interior forms, the materials employed also include wood, marble, stainless steel, and glass. It should be noted, however, that despite its expressive and "rough" quality, the concrete work and the expression of its making is of the highest quality, as the formwork itself was crafted by carpenters off-site rather than assembled by the builders on-site. In addition, the mechanical systems are seamlessly integrated into the structure (under the floor plates, for example), and, in many cases, its ducts and lighting banks are expressed or highlighted within the interior space (many times using bright colors), giving the building a high-tech quality characteristic of later buildings such as the Pompidou Center in Paris (Renzo Piano and Richard Rogers, 1977).

As a result of its structural and mechanical expression as well as that of the exposed reinforced concrete, the building has been paradoxically understood and promoted as either high-tech or brutalist. An appropriate middle ground would be to associate it with the new brutalist movement that, in its initial moment, defined the characteristics of Alison and Peter Smithson's Secondary School (Hunstanton, England, 1949–1954). For the critic Reyner Banham, the exposure of the structure, the architects' insistence on highlighting the inherent beauty and value of the materials, and the expression of the technical elements were the salient characteristics of this building and of the new brutalism.[3] By being both artisanal in its craft and hypermodern in its organization, its expression of the systems, and its aesthetic implications, the Bank of London and South America not only does this but also responds to the Smithsons' own call for the new brutalism to "drag a rough poetry out of the confused and powerful forces which are at work."[4] If technology stood as metonym for rationalization, then, as we have seen, its rejection was part of a broader historical critique. In the case of the Bank of London and South America, there is no outright rejection of technology—in fact, it is celebrated—just as there is no full acceptance of it—as proved by the handcrafted and expressive potential of the concrete used to build it. Instead, the building "did not constitute an escape of the increasingly dominant technological world (as proposed by Le Corbusier in Ronchamp or India), but [it represents] an attempt of a complete immersion in that world, basing its control on an exercise of sensitivity."[5]

The apparent monumentality of structures like the Bank of London and South America or the Government Building for La Pampa can also be understood in more traditional terms. Sigfried Giedion, Josep Lluís Sert, and Fernand Léger's "Nine Points on Monumentality" (1949) called for the importance of integrating tradition as well as historical and cultural references into architecture and urban designs that, in a way, were part of a broader reaction to the effects of the war but also of a "return to order" intended to combat the loss of center initially proposed by avant-gardist practices. In Latin America, the turn to monumentality, as we can see, is also a call for exceptionality: of the creation of architectural examples that are unique, fall outside the logic of (mass) reproducibility, and are different from the quotidian due to their particular attributes and character yet, because of their scale and program, are made for everyday use.

Symptomatic of this and yet expressive of the critiques and forms derived from the disillusionment with modernity are works such as Vilanova Artigas's School of Architecture (São Paulo, 1961; see 1961 box) or Nelson Bayardo's columbarium (Montevideo, 1962; see 1962 box). Both public buildings maintain a contradictory or ambiguous monumentality through the juxtaposition of the material expression (both are composed

Clorindo Testa and SEPRA, interior of Banco de Londres, Buenos Aires, 1966.

of massive exposed reinforced concrete forms) and their atectonic quality (both have delicate structural elements that allow for the ground to be open under the massive forms) while responding to the typological and characteristic notions of "courtyard buildings." In Mexico, the work of Abraham Zabludovsky, Teodoro González de León, and Agustín Hernández took a different direction in referencing pre-Hispanic forms and urban spatial practices while creating a more stereotomic architecture of solid volumes in rough-chiseled reinforced concrete (see 1976 entry). In many ways, all of these examples strive to achieve timelessness by not relying on traditional styles or forms but by seeking a character that transcends its time and place while being deeply rooted in it.

FURTHER READING

Bullrich, "Monumental Architecture," in *New Directions in Latin American Architecture.*

Cuadra with Corona Martínez, *Clorindo Testa, Architect.*

Cuadra and Wang, *O'Neil Ford Monograph 4: Banco de Londres y América del Sud—SEPRA and Clorindo Testa.*

1961-A

FIDEL CASTRO, IN CONVERSATION WITH ERNESTO "CHE" GUEVARA, DECIDES TO CONVERT A GOLF COURSE INTO ART SCHOOLS IN CUBA.

CARIBBEAN: CUBA

THE FOUNDATIONAL MYTH of the Escuelas Nacionales de Arte (National Art Schools; Havana, 1961–1965) is that they were conceived over a game of golf following the success of the Cuban Revolution in 1959—a game played by none other than Fidel Castro and Ernesto "Che" Guevara in one of Havana's premier country clubs in the posh area of Cubanacán. The myth goes on to suggest that the development of a new system of art schools and of architecture itself resulted from the discussions that the two men had on the type of culture the revolution would engender: one that opposed the decadent styles present in the country club and that sought a new architecture for a new society. It was a culture that would become materialized in the five buildings for the school: The School of Plastic Arts and School of Modern Dance by Ricardo Porro, the School of Dramatic Arts by Roberto Gottardi, and the School of Music and School of Ballet by Vittorio Garatti.

The requirements for the five schools were that they respond to the character of the site and that they be built using traditional and artisanal materials and construction methods. The latter requirements resulted from the 1960 Cuban embargo. After all, the limited availability of certain materials and technology forced

a reconceptualization of what this architecture should be like and how it should be built. The limitations imposed by the embargo further resulted in the material palette becoming one primarily of terracotta bricks and tiles and that the constructive system be based on the Catalan vaulting system. This latter, although labor intensive, was affordable and allowed for great spans without the use of much cement and steel rebar, both in limited supply at the time. However, the forms of the vaults responded more organically to the site and to the need to create a new and different architecture.

In a way, the desire to develop a new architectural language or direction after a revolution was not new to Latin America. It might be expected that Castro encountered some examples of this attitude in Mexico, where he was exiled in 1955. After all, it was Mexico, the country with a successfully realized revolution that had overthrown from power a longtime dictator, Porfirio Díaz, where the revolution's end in 1920 engendered the active exploration of architectural alternatives to best respond to its perceived aims and direction. Characteristic of these investigations were the multiple

Ricardo Porro, central court of School of Plastic Arts, Havana, 1961.

Ricardo Porro, interior view of School of Plastic Arts, Havana, 1961.

(to communicate new postrevolutionary values and to raise class and race consciousness; see 1922 entry). We can ascribe a similar goal to the work done by Luiz Nunes in Recife between 1934 and 1937. Although not the result of a national political and social revolution, as in the case of Cuba or Mexico, Nunes's work for the government of the state of Pernambuco to develop a new architecture intended to transform society and be directed toward the new inhabitant of that society did respond to much of the energy behind the Brazilian Communist Revolt of 1935. Nunes's work consisted of creating a number of buildings that would improve the life of the inhabitants (such as schools, hospitals, and infrastructural works like the 1937 Water Tower in Olinda) based on a rationalized organization of architecture and construction ("disconcertingly radical," in the words of historian Lauro Cavalcanti) yet through the introduction of new ideas of spatial inhabitation (such as, for example, the dissolution of boundaries between inside and outside seen at the Escola de Anormais [School of Gifted Children], Recife, 1943).[1]

The Cuban example is interesting because of the pervasiveness in Havana of an already established modernist architectural tradition. Scholars such as Eduardo Luis Rodríguez have argued this, and a simple visit through Havana will prove it. Modern architecture had become established since the 1920s and had an explosion of stylistic and formal investigations in the late 1940s and 1950s. During this time, we find work for Cuba by recognized foreign architects such as Richard Neutra's Alfred de Schulthess House (1956) with gardens by Roberto Burle Marx or Mies van der Rohe's Bacardí Office Building project (1957; see 1957-a box). High-quality work was also produced by a generation of foreign-trained Cuban architects like Max Borges and Mario Romañach, who had studied at Harvard University under Walter Gropius and who, in the case of Romañach, worked with Josep Lluís Sert (see 1943 entry). Romañach's 1949 José Noval Cueto House blends Miesian spatial strategies in its floor

formal and linguistic searches: from rational functionalism (to be devoid of class allegiances because of its scientific and, thus, non-ideological nature; see 1933 entry), to pre-Hispanic influenced modernism (as an architecture that could communicate to the vast majority of the population who shared that heritage; see 1929-a entry), to the use of pictorial art in public places

Ricardo Porro, aerial view of the School of Modern Dance, Havana, 1961.

plans with a Corbusian sense of materiality and aesthetics to develop a variant of an architecture that will respond to the climate by being open (and openable) yet with elements that provide generous shading, such as a cantilevered concrete roof. Borges's Tropicana Club (1951–1956) and Nautical Club (1953) developed a new architectural vocabulary that appears more organic through the use of reinforced concrete shells. And, while the success of the revolution inspired momentous changes in all aspects of life, in architecture it "did not provoke a sudden and complete break in the evolution of modern architecture." As Rodríguez notes, "Interesting works continued to appear that were faithful to the programmatic and conceptual principles of earlier years, even if their social and philosophical criteria were radically different."[2] The exception to this was the National Art Schools, which, based on the initial interest of its instigators, Castro and Guevara, aspired for something new. That desire for newness, however, would eventually dissipate with Cuba's stronger alliance with the Soviet Union and its advocacy of strict rationalist functionalism.

In charge of the overall art schools project was Ricardo Porro. Born in Cuba in 1926 and trained in the School of Architecture at the University of Havana, Porro continued his studies at the Sorbonne in Paris. In his "Architectural Autobiography," Porro claims as influences Mies van der Rohe's spatial organization and

proportions, Le Corbusier's later work (such as Ronchamp), Antoni Gaudí's interiors, and the articulation of interior and exterior spaces in Frank Lloyd Wright's work.[3] Porro's earlier work, Miesian in character in the disposition of organically formed walls as organizers of space in contrast to a rigid structure (seen, for instance, in his design for the 1957 Cao House), contained aspects not only of Cuban traditional architecture (e.g., courtyards and elements that responded to the climate) but also of forms laden with symbolic and spiritual characteristics derived from the African traditions and religions that were present on the island. These forms and ideas would be concerns that would carry over into his designs for the art schools. To aid in the design and construction, Porro invited Vittorio Garatti and Roberto Gottardi, both Italian architects, to participate.

For his design for the School of Plastic Arts, Porro organized clusters of elliptical domed studio spaces that are linked together and to the entry by linear curving pathways. The sprawling tendril-like shapes of the complex extend into the site yet do so after enclosing a tiled courtyard whose center is marked by an abstract curvilinear sculpture of a papaya covered in trencadis, or broken-tile mosaics. One of the edges of this courtyard is bounded by a more linear and orthogonal structure roofed by vaults that houses the administrative spaces and classrooms. For Porro, the overall curvilinear quality of the work was a result of his interest in an expressive sensuality intended to be "a conscious symbol of life and fertility, of the creative impulse as opposed to the forces of destruction."[4] This attitude and the forms that engendered it he attributed to the unique Afro-Cuban culture that he used to represent the structures' uniqueness and Cuban roots and is similar in nature to the references of the Cuban painter Wilfredo Lam.

All of the school buildings of the complex aspire to express an urban character and experience. In this aspect, the School of Modern Dance is no different. In it, Porro uses octagonal vaulted structures with an open lower section that, for him, metaphorically express the explosive passion of the revolution. Forming a V shape in the overall plan, these structures are placed at one side of a colonnade-surrounded central plaza and juxtaposed by a linear bar that houses more traditional classrooms. In contrast to those spaces, the large dance rooms are open double-height spaces topped, under the domes, with clerestory windows that are layered with open clay tiles to provide interior shading.

Gottardi's School of Dramatic Arts has the most urban character of the complex. The form is reminiscent of a walled Italian town in which its programmatic forms create interstitial circulation spaces that meet in a larger open square. In some of these spaces, stairs mediate the different topographic changes in the site. In addition, the more orthogonal forms are built with exposed clay brick, again, reminiscent of Italian towns.

The most ambitious and radical of the schools are those designed by Garatti: the School of Music and the School of Ballet. The first is composed of a series of linear ribbons with a total width of 50 ft. (15 m) that are embedded into the site. Because of the topographic change of the site between one side and the other in the width of the building, the band itself sectionally cascades toward a river existing on the site. Placed in a ravine, the School of Ballet is formed by larger vaulted spaces whose interstices are connected by lower vaulted forms that, in plan, open toward the landscape and enclose it with its curvilinear forms. These create, in short, an exterior spatial equivalent to that of the interior space. Although largely unfinished, some of the vaults dramatically rest on pendentives, expressing the structural and formal character of the vaults.

Despite their formal innovativeness and radicalism, the schools were declared finished in 1965 and their construction stopped and left in various stages of completion, which, in the case of Garatti's buildings, meant unfinished. Porro and Gottardi's schools, which were the most advanced in their construction, were actually used, although they were never properly maintained and eventually fell into disrepair. Garatti's buildings were left to crumble. With the turn toward Soviet-backed construction technology that relied on prefabrication, rationalization, and a rejection of individualist expression, the schools and their architects were criticized.

Disillusioned, Porro and Garatti left for Paris and Milan, respectively, while Gottardi remained in Cuba. Despite many attempts to restore and increase awareness of the schools in Cuba, it was the publication *Revolution of Forms: Cuba's Forgotten Art Schools* (1999) by the architect and historian John Loomis that brought these schools and the story of their makers into the international limelight.

Site plan of National Art Schools (from the top, clockwise: School of Plastic Arts, School of Dramatic Arts, School of Modern Dance, School of Ballet, and School of Music).

FURTHER READING

Loomis, *Revolution of Forms: Cuba's Forgotten Art Schools.*

Rodríguez, *The Havana Guide: Modern Architecture, 1925–1965.*

1961-B

JOÃO BATISTA VILANOVA ARTIGAS AND PAULO MENDES DA ROCHA ARTICULATE THE PAULISTA SCHOOL: FREE GROUND PLAN, GENEROUS SOCIAL SPACES, AND OPAQUE ENVELOPES.

BRAZIL

FOR DECADES, São Paulo had to conform to being runner-up in the area of Brazilian cultural production. That seemed natural in the beginning of the twentieth century, since Rio de Janeiro, as the federal capital since colonial times, was much bigger: half a million inhabitants in 1900 while São Paulo had only 64,000. But, as a result of capitalist development surrounding the coffee industry, São Paulo began experiencing an accelerated growth as well as many early cultural initiatives, like the 1922 Semana de Arte Moderna (see 1925 entry) that attracted young progressive architects like Gregori Warchavchik and Rino Levi (see 1925 entry). By 1922, São Paulo, with 500,000 inhabitants, was already half the size of Rio de Janeiro. That would be partially reversed in the 1930s when Getúlio Vargas's government imposed a more centralized decision-making process, prompting the growth of the arts, publishing, radio, and, later, television in Rio de Janeiro. In architecture, it was not much different: Lúcio Costa, Oscar Niemeyer, and the so-called Carioca school would be hegemonic until the 1960s.

A similar Paulista variant would have to wait. By 1950, both cities had almost the same population (2.3 million), and São Paulo was growing at a faster rate. Governmental commissions nationwide, however, were still dominated by Carioca modernists. Even for the quadricentennial of the city, the government of São Paulo commissioned Oscar Niemeyer to design the Ibirapuera pavilions (1954). Architects from São Paulo had to rely on private patrons—who were not always very keen on modernism—for commissions. Nevertheless, the growth of the construction industry induced the creation of two schools of architecture in São Paulo—one at Mackenzie University started in 1947 and another at the University of São Paulo (USP) the following year— which, in turn, galvanized a group of young architects around the idea of creating a curriculum centered on design instead of the old antagonism between polytechnic versus Beaux-Arts schools of thought.

João Batista Vilanova Artigas was one of these architects. Having graduated from the São Paulo Polytechnic in 1937, he was already an experienced builder when he joined the Faculdade de Arquitetura e Urbanismo, Universidade de São Paulo (FAU-USP; School of Architecture and Urbanism, University of São Paulo) at its foundation in 1948. In the early 1950s, his political views to the left would distance him from Frank Lloyd Wright's influence of his earlier years. Soon after, Vilanova Artigas would go as far as writing a text denouncing "Le Corbusier and Imperialism" (1951). Nevertheless, a visit to the Soviet Union in 1953 left him deeply depressed with the "old-fashioned and ugly" architecture that he saw there. His response would be a devotion to the development of a Brazilian way of building, committed to social-oriented programs that also aspired to beauty.

In a speech to the graduates of 1955, Vilanova Artigas stated:

We see that the new architectural expressions of Brazil are being accepted by the masses, even when they are presented in their most audacious forms. We may even say that Brazilian people open a trust credit to architects . . . and in the very vulgarization of certain achievements of Brazilian modern architecture we shall see a reflex of a general sympathy toward our renovation efforts and the solutions they propose. There are those who see the rapid acceptance and reproduction of certain building forms without sufficient critical assimilation as a symptom of decay. The democratization of architecture's achievements must be seen as a burning desire, from the masses, to acquire a new architectural language.[1]

The pursuit of this new architectural language would be the central theme of his works in the decades ahead. Sensing the exhaustion of the Carioca vocabulary, Vilanova Artigas pushed for a new spatiality and a new materiality as an opportunity to create a new architecture further adapted to the Brazilian conditions. Instead of trying to resolve the conflicts inherent in the Brazilian context, Vilanova Artigas wanted to have them all exposed. So, while Niemeyer and Costa tried to adapt European modernism to Brazilian conditions (as if to promote development), Vilanova Artigas wanted to create architecture from those harsh conditions. Ethics and aesthetics would be stitched together, each exposing the flaws and the incompleteness of the other. We are reminded by historian Ruth Verde Zein that the Paulista school was being formed at the exact moment that members of Team X were developing a similar articulation between ethics and aesthetics that Reyner Banham would baptize as "the new brutalism."[2]

Traditional European historiography rarely mentions Brazil when discussing brutalism, but the reality is that the *béton brut* was still fresh in Le Corbusier's Unité d'Habitation in Marseille (1947–1952) when Vilanova Artigas started working on the Morumbi Stadium (São Paulo, 1952–1960). In 1953, the following year, Affonso Eduardo Reidy, an exponent of the Carioca school, would be extremely influential in the development of a new Brazilian way of building with his design for the Museum of Modern Art in Rio de Janeiro (see 1953-a entry). Reidy's external skeleton of sequential pillars—thinner when meeting the ground, thicker above—supporting large slabs for maximum flexibility would later be used in Vilanova Artigas's paradigmatic 1961 building for the FAU-USP (see 1961 box). In 1956, Joaquim Guedes built the Vila Madalena church, and the following year Lina Bo Bardi started working on the MASP building (see 1957-b box). Also influential was the work of Rino Levi, who, by the mid-1950s, was already thirty years into a very successful career. In buildings such as the Sedes Sapientiae Educational Institute (São Paulo, 1940–1942) and the Cultura Artística Theater (São Paulo, 1942–1943), Levi was working with a rigorous tectonic approach using reinforced concrete combined with a sophisticated preoccupation with the urban context as attested through the screening of the façade on the first, and through a generous and open entry level with an enclosed mass for the auditorium above it on

the second. These were all pioneering works that used elements that would become trademarks of the Paulista school: exposed reinforced concrete and simple envelopes with flexible floor plans.

In 1958, a thirty-year-old Paulo Mendes da Rocha built in São Paulo the Paulistano Stadium, a 2,000-seat sports arena. Winner of a competition, Mendes da Rocha's design sinks the sports court below ground and elevates the surrounding platform to maximize the interior-exterior relationship. The roof is a flat concrete ring, 115 feet (35 m) in diameter, covered with translucent plates on stretched cables attached to only six triangular columns. The shape of the columns is perfect for transferring the tensile forces to the foundations, stabilizing the roof, touching the ground minimally, and dramatizing all gravitational efforts. Mendes da Rocha would later become one of the most active participants of the Paulista school (see 1988 box).

It is important to remember that all of this was happening while Brasília was being built (see 1956 entry). The international attention (and to a much higher degree the Brazilian attention) was focused on the construction of the new capital and would not recognize the outstanding architecture being built in São Paulo until much later. What is interesting to note is how Brasília would indirectly influence the rise of the Paulista school. After the transfer of government to the new capital on April 21, 1960, São Paulo was, in a way, free to exclaim its own centrality. Rio de Janeiro would still be a strong cultural center for decades, but it is symptomatic that the transfer from an interest in Carioca modernism to a Paulista one happened around the same time that the national government moved to the Planalto Central, first explored not by the Portuguese but by the seventeenth-century *bandeirantes paulistas*.[3]

The exceptionalism of São Paulo induced the creation of a state university system that is the wealthiest in Brazil, while all other research universities are federally funded. In 1961, the School of Architecture needed a new home, and Vilanova Artigas was commissioned

BR

Paulo Mendes da Rocha, Paulistano Stadium, São Paulo, 1958.

with the task. He had been very active in the 1940s, although not as much in the 1950s—a decade in which he worked on political organization, on writing, and on reforming the FAU-USP curriculum. For him, a new type of architect was needed—one that would be able to work with the masses in creating a socialist society—and Vilanova Artigas had the chance to build the curriculum and the building that would make it happen: a large raised reinforced concrete box with an open interior where all of its members could participate collectively.

During the 1960s, the tectonics and spatiality of the Paulista school would be further developed by Joaquim Guedes, Carlos Milan, Fabio Penteado, João Walter Toscano, and, as noted already, Paulo Mendes da Rocha. As classic characteristics of the Paulista school, the emphasis is on the full exposure of its materiality, on single volumes with generous entries, and on open plans that allow for visual connections in the interior. Paulista organization is more visible through the sections, which very often dictate the external appearance of the building. The ground floor is generally very permeable, and the roof, with plenty of openings for sunlight, is treated as a fifth façade. The resulting structures have hard envelopes that focus the attention onto large and autonomous internal spaces that stand in opposition to the urban context.

Unfortunately, at the height of his creative and intellectual capabilities, Vilanova Artigas's career was

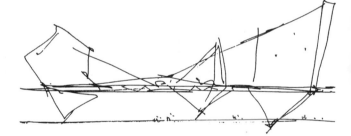

Paulo Mendes da Rocha, sketch of Paulistano Stadium, 1958.

interrupted by the 1964 military coup. Arrested shortly thereafter, he went into exile, returning in 1967 only to be summarily dismissed from the university the following year. During that short interregnum, Vilanova Artigas delivered the inaugural lecture of 1968, not on politics but on "drawing" as the transformative tool of the architect. The 1979 Amnesty Law allowed Vilanova Artigas to resume his teaching, holding his post until his death in 1985. His legacy (and that of all other *brutalistas paulistas*) survived all that and is clearly visible in the best contemporary architecture of São Paulo (see 1991 entry).

FURTHER READING

Carvalho Ferraz, *Vilanova Artigas*.
João Vilanova Artigas.

1961

JOÃO BATISTA VILANOVA ARTIGAS, SCHOOL OF ARCHITECTURE AND PLANNING, UNIVERSITY OF SÃO PAULO

CHARACTERIZED BY THE USE of bold and unornamented yet compact forms, exposed concrete construction expressive of its making, and interior spatial complexities, the building designed by João Batista Vilanova Artigas to house the Faculdade de Arquitetura e Urbanismo da Universidade de São Paulo (FAU-USP; School of Architecture and Planning of the University of São Paulo) is the most emblematic of the Paulista, or São Paulo, school (see 1961 entry). The design of the school shows not only his architectural and structural interests—Vilanova Artigas was trained as both an engineer and an architect at the Polytechnic of São Paulo, from which he graduated in 1937—but also his personal ideas regarding the role of modern architecture for society. In this way, the FAU-USP building is representative of the third stage of Vilanova Artigas's production. The work he produced at the beginning of his career is primarily domestic and formally inspired by Frank Lloyd Wright. The second stage (from the 1940s through the mid-1950s) continues some of his earlier concerns with housing (although, at this time, he was designing not only individual residences but also apartment houses) where he began developing an architectural language that would be characteristic of

the Paulista school. The third stage, which begins in the late 1950s, is defined by an interest in large-scale public buildings that are semiautonomous from the city. Many of these buildings can be described as Wrightian, given their internal sense of spatial continuity and expansiveness as well as their rejection of the metropolitan environment.

The exterior of the FAU-USP is composed of a large reinforced concrete box supported by fourteen tapering columns. In contrast to the plain and heavy volume, the lower floors of the building are open and made up of transparent glass-clad volumes. In the interior, the ground level is where the great open hall is located—a space surrounded by the administration offices, cafeteria, museum, and main circulation ramp. This open and top-lit space is the center of the building and is the architectural manifestation of Vilanova Artigas's sustained interest in political issues and continuous space. Like Wright's Guggenheim Museum (New York, 1943–1959), where the spatial continuity is achieved via the architectural form, the FAU-USP is defined to follow a thesis of "spatial continuity." For Vilanova Artigas, the "floors are connected by wide, gentle

João Batista Vilanova Artigas, FAU-USP, São Paulo, 1967.

João Batista Vilanova Artigas, FAU-USP, view of the interior spaces, São Paulo, 1967.

access ramps at levels that tend to give the feeling of one single plane. There is a continuous physical interconnection throughout the building" (quoted in Wisnik, "Faculty of Architecture and Planning," 72). The interconnected design of the school also reflects a commitment to the reevaluation of its curriculum to integrate architecture, urbanism, industrial design, and visual communication within a single structure.

If the school is a place to educate the citizenry, its central space is the area within which political and social relations are carried out: the openness of the space "increases the degree of conviviality, of meetings, of communications. . . . There the individual learns, becomes urbanized and gains a spirit of team work" (ibid.). Beyond this, its intention is to be a "spatialization of democracy, in dignified spaces, without front doors . . . where all activities are valid" (ibid.). The second floor of the FAU-USP—with the offices, studio spaces, and the volume of the library that overhangs into the central space—and its upper floors—composed of intermediary levels of open studios—reinforce that continuity by wrapping around the central space. Even the basement level, with the auditorium and workshops, is sectionally connected to the space via an opening on the ground and the access ramps that, as noted, connect the different levels of the building. The building's spatiality, however, is internal and controlled. The FAU-USP is introverted and separates itself from the context; it avoids contact with and contamination from the city.

Although the references to curvilinear shapes in the building are minimal (in comparison to contemporary projects by Oscar Niemeyer), the space is predominantly open, ambiguously defined, and dramatic through the use of zenithal light. The exterior columns, like other contemporary explorations, read both as tectonic and atectonic by means of a tapering profile that changes from a square base on the ground to a flat surface on the reinforced concrete box. In this way, besides the formal elements that determine it as an example of Paulista architecture, the building can be linked to other, broader concerns of contemporary Brazilian architecture such as the recuperation of baroque forms or interior spaces and the development of an atectonic structural system.

1962

NELSON BAYARDO, COLUMBARIUM, MONTEVIDEO

CONTEMPORARY TO Vilanova Artigas's School of Architecture and Planning of the University of São Paulo, the columbarium designed by Nelson Bayardo is a work that by all indications could be described as emblematic of the São Paulo school (see 1961-b entry and 1961 box). Built in Montevideo's Northern Cemetery between 1960 and 1962, the columbarium suggests, in its form and material expression, the influence of Le Corbusier's postwar monumental work and his use of *betón brut* rather than an adaptation of the Brazilian example to Uruguay. The structure is composed of a simple, unornamented and unfenestrated reinforced concrete volume raised on a series of triangular supports. The seemingly floating box creates an open lower level accessible from all sides that appears, on first impression, as a dark and somber loggia-like space while allowing for the landscape to pass uninterrupted underneath it. For Bayardo, the goal was to create a "shamelessly naked" and simple structure

Nelson Bayardo, columbarium, Montevideo, 1962.

that didn't detract from its intended use and that didn't rely on traditional funerary materials and ornamental excesses. At its center, a sunken courtyard filled with vegetation contains a ramp/stair leading upward into what seemed like an impenetrable volume from the exterior. The courtyard also serves as a transition between the darkened space and the upper area: the final resting place of the small stacked boxes, eighteen thousand in total, that contain the skeletal remains. On the ramp side of the courtyard, there is a constructivist mural cast into the concrete by Edwin Studer, a disciple of Joaquín Torres-García (see 1938 box), that is expressive of the material character of the concrete, the formwork, and the effects of light and shadow on it. The mural also shows the tectonic order of the building and articulates the play between the scale of the interior space of the columbarium and that of the visitor. Despite the powerful experiential character of this monumental funerary structure, Bayardo's work was primarily limited to teaching at Montevideo's School of Architecture and serving as the city's architectural director. His lasting legacy, however, is the scholarship he undertook to prove the Uruguayan provenance of the famous tango singer Carlos Gardel.

Nelson Bayardo, columbarium, courtyard view, Montevideo, 1962.

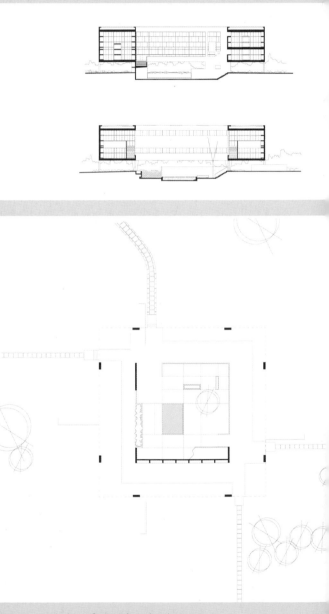

Sections and plan of Bayardo columbarium.

1963

IN BOGOTÁ, ROGELIO SALMONA TAKES OLD BRICKS TO A NEW DIMENSION IN THE TORRES DEL PARQUE.

BORN IN PARIS IN 1929 of Spanish parents, Rogelio Salmona moved to Bogotá when he was only two years old. His childhood in Bogotá took place between the Tudor homes of the Teusaquillo neighborhood and his French lessons at the Lycée Française. Having entered the School of Architecture at Universidad Nacional in 1947, Salmona would soon meet Le Corbusier in his own house when the Swiss-French architect visited Bogotá in June of 1947 in search of new opportunities, which led to the production of a master plan for Bogotá (see 1943-b entry). Invited by Le Corbusier to work in his Paris office, Salmona abandoned his studies one year later (political disturbances in Colombia adding an extra incentive) to work at the Rue de Sèvres office from 1948 to 1955. During this time, he worked on paradigmatic projects such as the Unité d'Habitation (Marseilles, 1947–1952), Notre Dame du Haut (Ronchamp, 1950–1954), and Chandigarh (1951–1956), in addition to the master plan for his own city of Bogotá. Salmona also attended sociology seminars at the Sorbonne and became a follower of Pierre Francastel and his criticism of modern urbanism. Growing more and more critical of Le Corbusier's ideas and unhappy about his treatment at the master's office, Salmona returned to Colombia in 1957, and he was able to get his degree and license in 1962. At that time, he worked with Fernando Martínez Sanabria and Guillermo Bermúdez and designed a few residences on his own such as the Casa Latorre (Bogotá, 1959–1968) and Casa Cajial (Bogotá, 1961–1962).

In 1963, he was commissioned to design the Torres del Parque complex on a site with commanding views of Bogotá's center and surrounding mountains and located next to Parque Independencia and the Santamaría Bullring. The commission of apartment towers with 294 units was a breakthrough in Salmona's career. A design of such scale was everything Salmona needed to materialize his thoughts about an organic architecture made with the bricks that were, at the time, becoming a trademark of Colombian architecture.

In response to the challenges of the site—a sloped terrain adjacent to the bullring and at the foot of Monserrate

mountain (9,940 ft./3,030 m)—Salmona divided the apartments into three towers, each with a unique morphology. As if embracing and mimicking the bullring and the public space below, the Northern and Southern Towers have a higher vertical core attached to a curved wing that scales back as it rises, creating terraces on every other floor. While the inner core of the curve is continuous, the external surface is faceted as if rectangles were arranged around a circle. The Central Tower is higher and more compact, its façade also broken in pieces as if rectangles

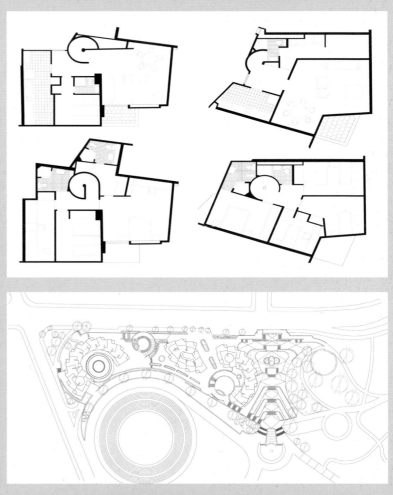

Unit plans and site plan of Torres del Parque.

were overlapped around a central axis. The movement of those stepping façades is reinforced by the balconies at alternating floors made up of small solid volumes protruding from the gap between each one of the collapsed vertical bars (which are themselves formed by the aforementioned extruding rectangles). The result is a very dynamic geometry that captures the eye with an ascending movement as if mimicking the neighboring mountain.

If from a distance the geometry of the towers is captivating, the detailed craftsmanship at close range calls our attention. Salmona always valued craftsmanship, and his devotion to brick was no doubt a decision based on a search for the best quality possible in the Colombian context. Even after forty years, the Torres del Parque look impressively new, helped of course by their prime real estate value. When compared to recent apartment construction in similar wealthy neighborhoods, however, the Torres del Parque are quite monastic. The apartments are not ostentatious and are reduced to housing what is absolutely necessary: compact service spaces are located toward the rear (or core) of the building and large open spaces toward the front. The excess, as seen from our consumerist society, lies in the generous public ground-level spaces that meander up and down the slope. For these, Salmona designed and built terraces with planters and integrated urban furniture also made with the same brick as the towers.

A decade after their inauguration in 1970 when Salmona helped organize meetings of Latin American architects in Cali (1980) and Manizales (1987), the Torres del Parque became paradigmatic of Latin American modern architecture: contextual, highly urban, and sensible to public needs.

As Rogelio Salmona would become more recognized in the late twentieth century, he stood as the very embodiment of modern Colombian architecture while at the same time being a rebellious disciple of Le Corbusier. The rebel had found (and built) his cause.

Rogelio Salmona, Torres del Parque, Bogotá, 1970.

1964-A

THE MILITARY DICTATORSHIP ENDS DELFIM AMORIM AND ACÁCIO GIL BORSOI'S INVESTIGATIONS INTO AN ARCHITECTURE FOR THE BRAZILIAN NORTHEAST.

IN 1931, THE ARTIST CÍCERO DIAS shocked Rio de Janeiro's Beaux-Arts community with a 48 ft. (15 m) long panel called *Eu vi o mundo . . . Ele começava no Recife* (I saw the world . . . It started in Recife). The Salão de Arte Aberta (Open Art Exhibition) was organized by Lúcio Costa, who, at the time, was encountering enormous obstacles to displaying modern art at the Escola Nacional de Belas Artes (ENBA; National School of Fine Arts) that he directed (see 1930 entry). Dias's panel was a free and quite abstract interpretation of the geography and history of Recife, a very important part of Brazilian culture often overlooked by the overwhelming omnipresence of São Paulo and Rio de Janeiro. Conservative critics pointed to naked figures as the issue that galvanized public reaction (the panel was vandalized during the exhibition), but the ambitiousness of the title surely enraged the Rio-centric art world of the time.

Located on the easternmost shore of the Americas, Recife was the place chosen by the Dutch in 1630 to be the capital of their Brazilian endeavors: Mauritsstad. Built around a two-river delta with plenty of islands and coral reefs (*recifes* in Portuguese), the city to this day still resembles the geography of the Netherlands, 350 years after their expulsion in 1654. The prosperity of the sugar plantation economy, the legacy of religious tolerance implemented by the Dutch, and the proximity to Europe turned Recife into the cultural capital of the Brazilian northeast. Several of the most distinguished Brazilian intellectuals came from the region, among them sociologist Gilberto Freyre, writer Manuel Bandeira, and educator Paulo Freire.

In architecture, Recife's eclectic townhouses (*sobrados*) contrasted with the colonial Portuguese houses of Olinda, a city 30 miles (48 km) north, built on a hill much like Lisbon and Salvador. Throughout the nineteenth century, the prosperity of Recife was inscribed in its beautiful eclectic architecture. Modernism would arrive with the works of Luiz Nunes. Born in Minas Gerais and a graduate of the National School of Fine Arts (ENBA), Nunes was a student leader of the strike

Delfim Amorim, Casa Lisanel, Recife, 1953.

Delfim Amorim, shading intervention at Luciano Costa building, Recife, 1959.

227

Pedro Ramírez Vázquez, interior with sun calendar of Museo Nacional de Antropología, Mexico City, 1964.

also continues historic ornamental and material traditions through its façades of lava rock, its abstracted geometric grill in the form of an abstract serpent that recalls Maya ornamentation, and its integration of murals and other arts characteristic of post-Revolution Mexican architecture (such as the mural by Rufino Tamayo at the entrance to the auditorium, the abstract stained-glass mural *Los adoratorios* (1964) by Carlos Mérida, or the Huichol Indian–inspired tapestry mural by Mathias Goeritz). Also important to the project was its museographic organization to facilitate the understanding and appreciation of the works presented and the cultures behind them. For this, Ramírez Vázquez hired a team of historians, museum curators, designers, and artists—many of whom had worked with him on the Mexican pavilions—to design the twenty-six rooms of the museum. With the courtyard at the center of the project, visitors can move in and out between exhibition rooms at their leisure or follow the linear chronology set up by the organizers; the flexibility was intended to avoid museum fatigue. On the ground level are located the archaeological exhibits, and on the second floor, immediately above each archaeological display, are the social, anthropological, and ethnographic exhibits as well as the educational and research facilities. Each of the spaces was precisely organized and designed yet had a built-in flexibility and adaptability that could allow for changes or respond to new requirements.

Despite the museum's immense scale, the desire was to ultimately "provide an atmosphere in which the visitor, in spite of crowds, would be able to enjoy a suitable degree of privacy and repose for contemplating the museum displays in a leisurely and rewarding way" (ibid., 29). This includes not only the ability to move in and out into the courtyard, as noted above, but also to move to exterior exhibits on the building's periphery (many of these being reconstructions of historical structures). The spatial character of the exhibition rooms, which ranges from lower-height spaces to larger open spaces, similarly creates varying experiences from focused concentration to dramatic exhibition.

The museum's modernity, according to Ramírez Vázquez, rested on its ability to "provide a scientifically exact presentation which at the same time would be visually so effective that a museum visit might constitute a true dramatic spectacle and experience. . . . [In order] to awaken and enhance the observers' interest and enjoyment and to elicit some emotional response before the relic or work of art . . . this building required the utmost in technical resources and innovation" (ibid.).

1964-C

MARTÍN CORREA AND GABRIEL GUARDA, LAS CONDES BENEDICTINE MONASTERY CHAPEL

MARTÍN CORREA and Gabriel Guarda's chapel for Las Condes Benedictine Monastery near Santiago, Chile, is a work whose complexity derives precisely from its very lack of complexity. It is the work of two young architects, freshly graduated from the School of Architecture at the Catholic University in Chile, who had left architecture to dedicate themselves to monastic life. It was a commission they received after the order had rejected two previous proposals for it; the last one had been deemed too excessive and expensive. Located on a hill, the chapel serves, first of all, to contrast the human-made and geometrically ordered building with the beauty and sublimity of the Andes mountain range that lies, on approach, behind it.

Secondarily, it reorganizes the experience of the visitors through a series of geometrical shifts so that they may focus on the religious experience rather than on the architectural one. To meet this goal, the chapel is composed of two cubes (46 ft. and 49 ft. [14 m and 15 m]) that intersect diagonally at the corners. The semicircular entry is connected to a path leading upward and along the side of the shorter cube and toward a statue of the Virgin Mary that is also the terminus of the axis, or nave, composed of the diagonal connection between the two cubes. The two cubes,

Martín Correa and Gabriel Guarda, Las Condes Benedictine Monastery Chapel, near Santiago, 1964.

Aerial view of Aterro do Flamengo, Rio de Janeiro, 1967.

temperate, with pine trees and grasses, while the other was tropical, lush, and colorful.

It should be noted, however, that predating Burle Marx's use of native plants within the modernist architectural environment is the work of Mina Klabin. Klabin, from a wealthy industrialist family from São Paulo, had married Gregori Warchavchik. His earliest designs for houses, such as his own house in São Paulo (1925–1927), the modernist demonstration house he designed in Rua Itápolis (1930), or the Silva Prado Residence (1930), all featured gardens designed by Klabin where native plants were used to accent the simple modern forms or used in traditional modernist ways (such as organized in patterns or grids; see 1925 entry).

In 1937, Roberto Burle Marx would be back in Rio de Janeiro and, again invited by Lúcio Costa, he would work on the gardens for the Ministry of Education and Public Health (MESP) building (see 1936 entry). If the Recife gardens show his early experimentation with plants (and with the metaphorical meaning behind their use), the MESP gardens demonstrate his early experimentation with form. Different iterations of the design for the MESP terrace gardens show Burle Marx starting from a more orthogonal parti and slowly moving to the curvy tempera drawings that would be materialized with colorful Brazilian species. The particular condition of the garden is that it is to be experienced primarily as a visual artifact from the offices of the building's tower. In addition to this, Burle Marx also designed the roof garden of the tower itself for the minister's offices.

Following the gardens for the MESP building, Burle Marx was invited by Oscar Niemeyer to design the gardens for his paradigmatic buildings at Pampulha (see 1941 entry). That collaboration would lead to some of the most poetic and serene creations by Burle Marx around the lake in Pampulha. At Pampulha, Burle Marx met the botanist Henrique Lahmeyer de Mello Barreto, whom he credits with teaching him about "ecology" by looking at the relationships between plants. In this way, Brazilian species and bold curvilinear forms come together in a way that allowed Burle Marx to treat the landscape as an unstable canvas, with colors changing every season, and incorporating growth (but also maintenance and control) as part of the design. In addition to landscapes, Burle Marx's interventions into buildings also included murals, such as those he did for Affonso Reidy's Pedregulho complex (see 1946 box), which contain many of the same formal and pictorial characteristics as the gardens.

Because of the commission for Pampulha, Burle Marx and Juscelino Kubitschek (then mayor of Belo Horizonte) would have a strained relationship for the rest of their lives. Burle Marx, for instance, did not work in Brasília until after Kubitschek stepped down from office. His antipathy toward Kubitschek helped Burle Marx concentrate on his highest achievement: a series of gardens in Rio de Janeiro stretching from the Santos Dumont Airport (designed by the Roberto

brothers in 1937, gardens from 1952), past Reidy's Museum of Modern Art (1954; see 1953-a entry), through the Flamengo Park (1961–1967), and ending in the Copacabana sidewalks (1970). Burle Marx designed a total of 6.2 miles (10 km) that are an important part of the already spectacular city of Rio de Janeiro. So, while Niemeyer and Costa were busy building the new capital from 1957 to the late 1960s, Burle Marx was busy redesigning the old capital.

Built on land reclaimed from the ocean, the Parque do Flamengo is the result of the demolition of a set of hills that separated old downtown Rio de Janeiro from the wealthy southern zone (see 1903 entry). By the mid-1950s, the Santo Antonio hill was being excavated and work had begun on the western edge of the Flamengo area, closer to the Santos Dumont Airport (also built on reclaimed land). A set of expressways would connect Cinelândia (the entertainment area by the airport and next to the MESP building) to Copacabana. A public park would negotiate the large area (300 acres/121 ha) between the auto lanes and the beach.

The governor of Rio de Janeiro at the time, Carlos Lacerda, named his friend Lota de Macedo Soares as director of the Flamengo project and Burle Marx as its lead designer. Since the 1950s, Lacerda, a conservative journalist, was an important figure in the opposition, first to Getúlio Vargas and later to Juscelino Kubitschek. His 1955 speeches became famous for stating that "Kubitschek cannot be elected, if elected he cannot take office, if he takes office he cannot govern." Ironically, it was only after Kubitschek transferred the capital to Brasília (see 1956 entry) that Lacerda was elected governor of Rio de Janeiro and started transforming his city. Flamengo Park was the most visible of his initiatives that also included the demolition of many favelas that were relocated to the now infamous Cidade de Deus (City of God) on the western periphery of the city.

View of Aterro do Flamengo, Rio de Janeiro, 1967.

At Flamengo, Burle Marx was able to create a landscape that works on many different scales. The park is experienced by the pedestrians through the relationship between the shade, paths, and plantings that work together to create a rich experience of walking along Rio de Janeiro's beachfront. For those who drive by the park, the sequence of trees and shrubs frames the view of the ocean with a sense of rhythm and movement that is unique at 50 miles (80 km) per hour. And yet there is a third scale. As with other Burle Marx landscapes, the ground works as a canvas painted by vegetal species that can be experienced from the neighboring buildings of the Flamengo and Gloria neighborhoods.

In Copacabana, the same happens again but this time with less vegetation and therefore less of an impact on those driving by. It is by walking on the ground that one experiences the changes in color and texture of different stones used by Burle Marx on the sidewalk. Even more impressive is the view from the adjacent buildings' balconies: a 3 mi. (5 km) long drawing in the pavement that is strong enough to capture your eye in competition with the astonishing views of the Copacabana beach and the ocean in front.

The possibility of those multiple points of view makes the Flamengo Park and Copacabana Beach the most successful projects by Burle Marx. While many of his gardens in private homes or secluded farms are better maintained, the intense public use of Rio de Janeiro's beachfront in its three scales (walking, driving, and viewed from above) allow one to claim them as his true legacy. By using plants as his color palette and carefully combining the artificial with the natural, Burle Marx might be the only designer who managed to improve Rio de Janeiro's exuberant landscape.

While Burle Marx became an ardent advocate of the environment later in life, his landscape works are never the expression of a pristine natural condition but rather of a carefully chosen set of species that are placed together and organized for maximum visual effect. In this way, there is a high degree of artificiality in Burle Marx's work. Such artificiality, or craft (*artifici* in Latin), is fundamental to understanding Burle Marx's extensive and exquisite work.

FURTHER READING

Cavalcanti and El-Dahdah, *Roberto Burle Marx: A permanência do instável—100 anos.*
Cavalcanti, El-Dahdah, and Ramber, *Roberto Burle Marx: The Modernity of Landscape.*
Dal Co and Trombetti, "Statica, Struttura, Natura: Oscar Niemeyer e Roberto Burle Marx."
Fraser, "Cannibalizing Le Corbusier: The MES Gardens of Roberto Burle Marx."
Giedion, "Burle Marx et le jardin contemporain."

1965-B

THE (RE)INVENTION OF CURITIBA: FROM THE PLAN OF JORGE WILHEIM TO THE IMPLEMENTATION BY JAIME LERNER

BRAZIL

MILITARY DICTATORSHIP and open planning competitions don't usually come together, but that is exactly what happened in Curitiba, Brazil, in 1965. At the time, the city had a little fewer than 500,000 inhabitants but was growing at a rate of 5 percent a year, and Nei Braga, the governor of the state of Paraná, called for a competition for a new *plano diretor*, or master plan, for the state capital. Brasília was still a proud achievement for the country as a whole—something that the military never challenged—and this fact might have helped to prompt such a call.

Also important is the long history of planning already established in Curitiba. Alfred Agache, the French urbanist who worked on so many Brazilian cities, designed Curitiba's master plan in 1943. Agache's plan was actually implemented—a rare occurrence in midcentury Brazil—and was based on concentric circles (much like Ebenezer Howard's 1902 Garden City) with generous public spaces allocated throughout and a Civic Center proposed for its core. The Civic Center, built between 1952 and 1953, contains most of the buildings that house the local and state governments. In addition, Curitiba's first zoning law was signed into

law in 1953, and its first mass-transit plans date to 1955—all of which helped establish Curitiba as a city in the forefront of planning in Brazil. By the early 1960s, however, Agache's rings were not able to accommodate the fast growth of Curitiba, and therefore a new master plan was needed.

A competition was held in 1965 and won by Jorge Wilheim from São Paulo. It was further developed in conjunction with city officials and local business leaders and approved by City Hall the following year. The main idea behind Wilheim's master plan was the proposal for radial axes of growth combining mass-transit corridors with a variation in density and uses along them. Despite sharply departing from Agache's original plan, it had the advantage of bringing together transportation, housing, density, and zoning under one proposal. The core of the idea can be explained by looking at a simple section. Along the radial corridors, a mass-transit system of buses would run on dedicated lines. The blocks immediately adjacent to these corridors would have higher densities (induced through

Aerial view of Curitiba, 1970s.

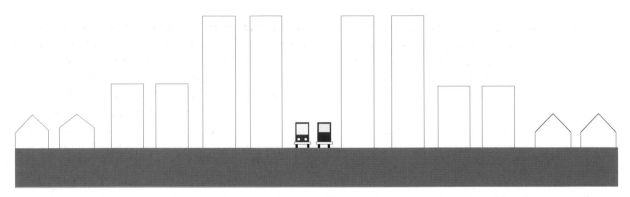

Diagram showing how the zoning of Curitiba works, with higher densities adjacent to the bus corridors.

higher Floor Area Ratios [FARs]), which targeted a lower middle class that was more prone to use public transportation. As one moves away from the corridors, the densities (FARs and height limits) decrease, which make it more attractive to the upper middle class, who, in turn, use public transit less and private automobiles more. As one approaches the next radial corridor, the densities grow again.

In the corridors, a more efficient bus system was implemented. The main goal was to decrease the overall time spent on the bus. This was achieved through the use of dedicated bus lanes and boarding platforms already level with the bus floor, whose tubular design would become an icon of Curitiba's innovative transportation. By paying the fare before entering the platform, there would be no lost time in boarding the bus. What seems like a minute or so saved per stop adds up to significant amount of time, considering that the buses stop every few blocks. The dedicated lanes also increase the efficiency of the system, especially in peak hours, as they avoid the vehicular congestion of the streets. In addition, the high-density housing built near the radial corridors is less expensive and, therefore, prone to being inhabited by the working class. Higher density allows for more buses (less time between them) running faster, thus making the whole system more efficient, attracting more passengers, and, in the end, making it more profitable (or with less need for subsidies). Given the fact that developers appreciated the higher FARs of the radial corridors, the master plan became successful by stitching together private and public interests.

But as the old saying goes, "the road to hell is paved with good intentions" or, in the case of city management, good master plans. Hundreds of cities at the time tried similar strategies, but only Curitiba became a success story. The achievements of Curitiba are strongly related to a successful implementation of the master plan, and that is precisely where the role of the military dictatorship enters the picture. The centralized autocratic model of Curitiba was developed during the military dictatorship (1964–1985) and had little concern for inviting or even consulting with the population as part of the planning process.

The original plan called for the creation of Instituto de Pesquisa e Planejamento Urbano de Curitiba (IPPUC), Curitiba's planning and research institute, also developed in 1965. The IPPUC would be responsible for more than just managing Curitiba's master plan. Given enough authority to bypass any other municipal offices and working directly under the mayor, the IPPUC was free to impose its planning ideas in a process that would only be possible under a military dictatorship. This is clear in the actions of Jaime Lerner, IPPUC director from 1968 to 1970 and mayor of Curitiba from 1971 to 1974 and again from 1979 to 1983 (all three terms appointed by the military). In order to create the first pedestrian-only street that was facing opposition from suspicious shop owners, Lerner just ordered the street closed one Sunday and proceeded with sidewalk renovation during the week. It is very difficult to envision such procedures occurring under normal democratic conditions.[1]

What is remarkable in Curitiba's case, however, is how planners have been able to successfully influence the municipal government since at least the 1960s. That strong planning tradition would open innumerable opportunities for creative public policies, the kind that architects are known to be great generators of but not so good as executors. The preservation of Curitiba's downtown, for instance, started in the 1970s under Lerner's leadership. In it, several abandoned or underutilized buildings were refurbished to house orchestras, workshops, theaters, museums; old buses were turned into mobile libraries and job-training workshops. Another famous municipal program was the exchange of food vouchers for recycled garbage in the peripheral areas. In 1975, a new zoning law passed that strongly encouraged environmental preservation, and, in 1982, the city started allowing for the transfer of building rights, opening up opportunities for the preservation of historical structures or natural areas without fighting property rights or developers' demands.

It's interesting to note that all this creativity applied to urban planning and management did not exactly translate into a remarkable architecture. While Belo Horizonte was booming with postmodernist creations in the 1980s (see 1979 entry) and São Paulo was nurturing the revival of its best modernist traditions (see 1991 entry), Curitiba's achievements in terms of individual buildings pale in comparison to Salvador, Recife, or Porto Alegre, not to mention Rio de Janeiro and São Paulo, both of which would be *hors concours* in such a contest. Curitiba's Ópera de Arame's tubular arches (1992) and the Universidade do Meio Ambiente's wooden structure (1993), both designed by Domingos Bongestabs, are pedagogical examples of reuse and house very interesting programs but are not exactly elegant buildings. The most prominent building built in Curitiba in the last decades is Oscar Niemeyer's "eye" museum (2002). Two curved slabs are elevated

from the ground (in the shape of an eye) and work as an entry hall to a building that he designed back in the 1960s, now refurbished into a museum whose main collection is a set of Niemeyer's drawings and models.

Despite being architecturally unexceptional, Curitiba is present in every book on urban policy as a successful case of planning and urban design in the developing world because of the innovative, efficient, and cost-effective way it has addressed transportation, land use, and sustainability. In this context, Curitiba has been celebrated in North America and Europe because its basic principles of urban intervention reinforce the twentieth-century paradigm of planning when a group of well-trained specialists control the process of land use and transportation in tune with developers' needs in order to provide a "comfortable" environment for a population that, in exchange, has no reason to challenge the political status quo. That critique of the process and result, absent from most of the earlier literature, is supported by a more inquisitive analysis focused on the planning processes or its environmental results.[2] At the core of the problem lies the issue of representation and participation. But there is also no doubt that Curitiba's planners were extremely successful in generating and implementing simple ideas that had a significant and positive impact on people's lives. The extent to which such innovative policies could be applied under normal democratic processes has been the subject of heated and heavily politicized debates after the redemocratization of Brazil in 1985. Meanwhile, Bogotá, Colombia, 2,600 miles (4,185 km) to the north and thirty years later, has shown that it is indeed possible to continue Curitiba's investigations (see 2000 entry).

Curitiba bus stop, 1970s.

FURTHER READING

Abrahams, "Interview: Jaime Lerner."
Del Rio, "Urban Design and Conflicting City Images of Brazil: Rio de Janeiro and Curitiba."
Kroll, "Creative Curitiba."
Macedo, "City Profile: Curitiba."
Wilheim and Richards, "Jorge Wilheim: Desiring Global Change."

Emilio Duhart, CEPAL Building, Santiago, 1966.

intended to be here as well but was never built), which are placed as autonomous freestanding objects. The assembly's *caracol* (spiral) form rises above the complex and breaks its horizontality. The structure of the external ring is part of the building's expression: its twenty-eight concrete columns have a pyramidal shape and exposed metal connections in response to Chile's history of earthquakes. Throughout the building, the connections between beams and columns are highlighted and used as plastic motifs to enhance the tectonic character of the reinforced concrete. According to Rodrigo Pérez de Arce, this element is based on Chile's seismic risk, which does not allow the architecture to be as light as its Brazilian counterpart and must resort to artifice to be elegant.[2] In the end, in Duhart's own words, "The United Nations building for Santiago is set up as a house and a monument. The House for nations in community. The Monument, a visible expression of its spiritual and social aspirations. House and Monument rise in a plastic and functional unity understood by all."[3]

It was this desire for legibility that led to many of its design choices and intentions. In front of the building, for instance, an oval-shaped fountain references the Mapucho River that runs alongside the site and, in this way, highlights the lacustrine character of the site and its architecture—something that would have been further emphasized through the riverbed park called

for in the original plans, to be designed by Roberto Burle Marx (see 1965-a entry). A reinforced concrete curving canopy shelters the entrance and makes a direct reference to Le Corbusier's Legislative Assembly in Chandigarh (1961), an allusion highlighted by the orthogonal arrangement of offices around a free-form auditorium. Duhart, it should be noted, had worked with Le Corbusier on the project for Chandigarh, India, in 1952. The formal organization of CEPAL also owes a debt to Le Corbusier's La Tourette (near Lyon, 1957), whose open courtyard is inhabited by semiautonomous freestanding structures and circulation. As was the case with the Latin American architects associated with Le Corbusier, the dependence on his work was sought by both the master, who was always happy to showcase his influence, and by the disciples, who were always happy to foster it. An article in *Progressive Architecture* from 1966 is quite ironic about this, however, calling some elements of the CEPAL building "undigested Chandigardisms."[4] References to Le Corbusier's postwar work must be seen as part of a larger zeitgeist associated with the Latin American brutalist movement (see 1959 entry). Duhart's elevated platforms on rough stones also reference the stadium at the National Autonomous University in Mexico City (see 1952 entry), and the structural solution of an external skeleton also used as shade control parallels the investigations of João Batista Vilanova Artigas and Paolo Mendes da Rocha in São Paulo (see 1961-b entry). Duhart even employed Vilanova Artigas's same language when describing the building's terraces as a fifth façade, visible from the hills nearby or from planes landing at Santiago's airport. Looking farther into the structure, we find that the offices actually hang from the upper beams, a solution not particular to Le Corbusier's vocabulary but more akin to Lina Bo Bardi's São Paulo Art Museum (MASP, 1957; see 1957-b box), Clorindo Testa's Bank of London and South America (1959; see 1959 entry), or Amancio Williams's early skyscraper project of 1946 (see 1929-c entry). In the *caracol*, the building's cross influences are made even more explicit. Several icons of Latin American history are imprinted into its concrete. These range from references to pre-Hispanic cultures all the way to Lúcio Costa's plan of Brasília, inaugurated the same year of the competition. In addition, the building's very forms, such as the *caracol* and

courtyard, refer to many Latin American traditions, from the astronomical observatories of the Maya to the early housing typologies of the colonies.

After its completion, the CEPAL kept growing; enclosures were added to the terraces above and the platforms below. In 2010, an earthquake damaged part of the structure and another competition was called by Docomomo Chile for its restoration and expansion. The CEPAL building was paradigmatic when it was built and has the chance to be significant again as a case study of how to intervene on a modern jewel.

FURTHER READING

Bruna, "Restauro e ampliação no edifício da Cepal em Santiago do Chile: Uma intervenção controvertida."
Montealegre Klenner, *Emilio Duhart, arquitecto.*
Quantrill, *Chilean Modern Architecture since 1950.*
"Santiago Caracol," *Progressive Architecture* 47 (December 1966).
"United Nations Building, Santiago, Chile."

View of courtyard, CEPAL Building, Santiago, 1966.

1967

HÉLIO OITICICA BUILDS *TROPICÁLIA*, CHALLENGING THE TRADITIONAL BOUNDARIES BETWEEN ART, POPULAR CULTURE, CONSTRUCTION, AND ARCHITECTURE.

BRAZIL • VENEZUELA

"THE THEORETICIANS AND promoters of Concretism ignore a basic fact: there is no perfect cultural equivalence between developed and underdeveloped countries," wrote Ferreira Gullar, author of the 1959 "Neo-Concrete Manifesto," in response to the excessive rationality and objectivity of the São Paulo Concretists.[1] Initially, the Concretists had formed in reaction to the 1951 São Paulo Biennial, which they found to be too expressive, individualistic, and hedonistic. Instead, they proposed to create a purely constructive art based on universal and intellectual principles that was, at its core, not representational or a mediation of reality. The emphasis on the fundamental elements of visual art—space-time, movement, and matter; geometric forms and organization; and production likened to that of mechanical drawings—generated autonomous works of art whose concern was their own manufacture and creating a vehicle that would visibly express ideas.

In reaction, the Rio de Janeiro–based Neo-Concrete artists—composed of Lygia Clark, Hélio Oiticica, Lygia Pape, Ferreira Gullar, and others—believed that in an underdeveloped country, the real avant-garde is one that, "in seeking the new, secures liberation of the human being, starting from his own concrete national and international situation."[2] As a result, their work would highlight subjectivity and expression, the sensorial over the rational. Similar to the work of Mathias Goeritz (see 1953-b entry), Neo-Concrete work "could only be understood phenomenologically . . . a work of art represents more than the material from which it is made . . . because it transcends mechanical relationships and generates a tacit signification. . . . Neo-Concrete art lays the foundation for a new expressive space."[3]

While the earliest work of the Neo-Concrete artists wrestled with the shift from abstraction to art intended to draw the spectator into the work, the later work is much more dependent on the active participation of the spectator as well as his/her presence, tactility, and body. This change can be seen, for instance, in the shift in Lygia Clark's early paintings, such as *Egg* (1959), to the transformable *Bichos* or, later, her *Relational Objects* series (1966–1968).

Hélio Oiticica, a central figure of the Neo-Concrete movement, similarly follows a path set up by Clark, his closest colleague: the shift from the geometrical and formal *Metaesquemas* (which transform the constructivist palette into an animated surface through the distortion of the grids) to the three-dimensional hanging picture plane *Relevos* and ending in the *Bolides*, boxes with multiple compartments that demand the active manipulation of the spectator. With his 1964 move into the Mangueira favela in Rio de Janeiro, the work that Oiticica developed became centered on participation: either the works (the *Parangolés*) were to be worn and required the "direct corporal participation" of the user, according to Oiticica, or they were to be experienced by the spectator moving through them (the *Penetrables*).

Tropicália (1967) reflects these environment-defining developments in Oiticica's work. Prepared for the 1967 *Nova Objetividade Brasileira* (New Brazilian Objectivity) show for the Museu de Arte Moderna of Rio de Janeiro, Oiticica created a favela-like inhabitable setting that refers to the characteristic conditions of many Brazilians' daily life. In the descriptions, he refers to it as an "objectification of a total 'Brazilian' image" that, in response to the contemporary pop-art movement, would internationally present an image of Brazilian culture. To do this, the structure is made with the typical elements used to build the shantytown houses, such as wood, fabric, rocks, etc., placed on a sand floor, surrounded by tropical plants, parrots, and hand-written poetry. Inside one could find bags of pigments, characteristic of the *Bolides*, within spaces defined by printed cloth walls. The structure's main path leads toward the center of the structure where a television set is placed. In this way, *Tropicália* expresses the contradictions of modernity—poverty and mass communications—while avoiding any form of idealism about the Brazilian situation, highlighted on the outside by the inscription "a

Hélio Oiticica, *Tropicália*, 1967.

pureza é um mito" (purity is a myth). To transcend the simplicity of the myth of tropicalism as an externally imposed image for consumption, the work relies on its experiential character; according to Oiticica, one is to undergo "several tactile-sensorial experiences addressed to the participant who, through them, creates their imagistic meaning."[4] Ultimately, he ascribed to it the experience of being "devoured" by the piece—in specific reference to the *antropofagista* notion of consuming or cannibalizing foreign cultural ideas and production—so that its understanding was more than merely superficial perception of the work but, rather, a critical outlook on the paradoxical and hybrid conditions of Brazilian culture and its perception at the time.

Although Oiticica had created *Penetrables* prior to *Tropicália*, the projects that followed *Tropicália* become reevaluations of it and, in many cases, more architectural in quality in order to respond, according to the critic Guy Brett, to the "relationship between images—easily consumable, fixed, stereotyping—and underlying creative processes."[5] These latter processes came from the phenomenological conditions associated with the occupation and experience of the body in the environment. This is the case of *Subterranean Tropicália Projects* (1971), which are presented almost exclusively in plan and through architectural models; yet like their predecessors, they rely on the user moving through their labyrinthine forms. Likewise, the *Invençao da Cor Projects* (1977) are modifiable environmental structures that attempt to envelop the spectator with color-mediated light. The more ephemeral projects, such as *Rhodeislandia: Contact* for the University of Rhode Island, Kingston Campus (1971) or *Cosmococa* (with filmmaker Neville D'Almeida, 1973), still operate by reconfiguring space. *Cosmococa* does so by creating a series of ludic environments where the participant lies in hammocks or on cushions on the floor to become overwhelmed by a completely sensorial experience that includes, within a dark room, projections of contemporary cultural icons (e.g., Marilyn Monroe, Jimmy Hendrix, the Coca-Cola

Gego, *Reticulárea*, Museo de Bellas Artes, Caracas, 1969.

logo) covered or outlined in cocaine and accompanied by very loud contemporary music.

Although this turn toward a more experiential condition of art is analogous to what minimalist artists like Donald Judd were developing in the United States, the production of architectural environments by artists—such as Goeritz's experiments with El Eco—began to question both the character of the work of art as mere appliqué to the architectural form and the character of

the work's reception as being primarily optically based. Instead, they sought to develop work that had a more phenomenological quality.

Within this direction we can highlight the work of Venezuelan optico-kinetic artist Carlos Cruz-Diez. Beginning with investigations into perception and its changes based on chromatic and formal organization as well as on the position of the viewing subject (whether one is located on the right or left side of the paintings/constructions), Cruz-Diez began to develop work at the scale of architecture and urban interventions. These works rely on saturating the spaces with changing color (*Chromosaturations*); creating large murals of color strips that mutate into different colors along their length, such as the *Chromostructures* at the Raúl Leoni hydroelectric plant machine room (Guri, Venezuela, 1977–1986); or inserting into walls colored fins with different colors on each side, which are perceived as changing based on the viewer's location—much like El Lissitzky's *Abstract Cabinet* in Hannover (1927)—as in the *Double Physiochromy, Tribute to Don Andrés Bello* (Caracas, Venezuela, 1982).

Also part of this tradition are the *Penetrables* of Jesús Soto, which are environment-like structures that, as their name suggests, are to be penetrated by the spectator/user, who experiences them physically, sensorially, and chromatically. These structures are composed of hundreds of hanging plastic or nylon tubing pieces that react to the movement of the body as well as any external force (i.e., wind) and, in some cases, even produce sounds. Like his earlier work (such as *Cajita Villanueva*, 1955, a Plexiglas box with internal planes that are all covered with closely spaced lines), this work is activated by the movement of the users/viewers, whose perceptions change as they move around the pieces and, thus, change the parallax.

In addition to these two artists working primarily within the optical conditions of line and color, the *Reticuláreas* of the German émigré Gego (Gertrude Goldschmidt) can be seen as experiments in spatial definition. An architect by training, her *Reticulárea* for the Museo de Bellas Artes de Caracas (1969) is a complex three-dimensional rhizomatic structure that redefines the interior space of the gallery. These structures are produced using industrial materials and painstakingly handcrafted to create a series of wire grids or webs.

Although these examples oscillate between architecture, installations, and inchoate spatial practices, what is clear is that they represent an alternative within

Jesús Soto, *Penetrable*, 1967–1997.

the production of art and architecture to the appliqué
condition of plastic integration characteristic in Latin
America in the first half of the twentieth century.

FURTHER READING

Amor, et al., *Gego: Obra completa, 1955–1990.*
Brodsky, *Soto: Paris and Beyond, 1950–1970.*
Hélio Oiticica.
Ramírez, *Hélio Oiticica: The Body of Color.*
Ramírez and Olea, *Color in Space and Time: Cruz-Diez.*

1967

JESÚS TENREIRO-DEGWITZ—VENEZUELAN POSTMODERNISM

NO BUILDING CAN BE a better metaphor for Venezuelan postmodernism than the CVG (Corporación Venezolana de Guayana) headquarters designed by Jesús Tenreiro-Degwitz in 1967. The structure built in Ciudad Guayana would symbolically represent a new era of development for the Orinoco delta region. A steel mill (SIDOR) and a hydroelectric dam at Guri were the main pieces of a larger plan administered by the CVG. The program, initially for a town hall, became an administrative building for the electricity company (EDELCA) and later the headquarters of

its parent company (CVG). As if this was not enough, the government wanted it to be built quickly, so Tenreiro-Degwitz proposed using steel from the newly built Siderúrgica del Orinoco (SIDOR), the steel mill of the endeavor. No contractor, however, wanted to use the untested light profiles made by SIDOR. In the end, the director of CVG allowed Tenreiro-Degwitz's design to be built with imported U.S. steel profiles.

The building is indeed a beautiful structure in the shape of a pyramid with steel and brick panels wrapping

Jesús Tenreiro-Degwitz, Abadía Güigüe, Venezuela, 1989.

every floor and acting as sunshades. This creates a virtual envelope that becomes the public face of the building (allegedly the first to be built in this newly planned city). The panels of steel and brick continue on the inside, following a geometry resembling the U.S. artist Sol LeWitt's sculptures. An inner hollow core distributes light inside the building, while gaps between the vertical panels modulate the light from the outside.

Born in 1936, Jesús Tenreiro-Degwitz graduated in 1958 from the Universidad Central de Venezuela, where he also taught for most of his life. The CVG headquarters was his first major project. Around the same time, he also built the town hall for the city of Barquisimeto. The result of a competition, the town hall is a structure of exposed reinforced concrete inserted into the traditional fabric of a small city. If the CVG headquarters structure alluded to Mies van der Rohe, the Barquisimeto building resembles the brutalist investigations of the times. Boxy sun-shading devices protrude from external windows, and the interior is carved much like Clorindo Testa and SEPRA's Bank of London and South America of a decade earlier (see 1959 entry). Also in tune with Testa is the contrast between the reinforced concrete structure and the plastered walls and ceramic tiles of the surrounding surfaces.

Characteristic of the times, Tenreiro-Degwitz and others founded in 1979 the Instituto de Arquitectura Urbana (Institute of Urban Architecture) in Caracas. Inviting the British historian Kenneth Frampton, the Italian architect Aldo Rossi, the U.S. historian Anthony Vidler, the Argentine architect Mario Gandelsonas, and the Catalan critic Ignasi de Sola-Morales to speak in Caracas brought a cosmopolitan postmodernism to Venezuela around the same time that the Buenos Aires Biennial was doing the same in Argentina (see 1985-a entry).

Tenreiro-Degwitz's eclecticism of forms and materials would soon encounter its theoretical support within a metaphysical discourse inspired by a growing interest in phenomenology. When talking about architecture, Tenreiro-Degwitz accentuated the role of archetypes and their experiential meaning in the design process, always referring to "higher forces" or to divine inspiration. In 1989, he would materialize such thoughts in a building with a program perfectly suited for them: the Abadía Güigüe, a Benedictine abbey on a remote mountainous location of Venezuela.

For the abbey, Tenreiro-Degwitz designed a closed square courtyard at the top of a mountain ridge, with four wings spreading out as the topography dramatically slopes down. The main courtyard encloses the cloister, the heart of the complex, which is closed to the population at large. Two of the outgoing wings following the ridgeline house the church and the campanile on one side and the service core on the other. The church has a Romanesque simplicity, albeit with a sophisticated use and control of indirect light as well as the details that refer to Louis Kahn's designs (evident in Tenreiro-Degwitz's use of circular openings on square walls). The other two wings spread out perpendicular to the topographic lines and house the guest rooms and the monks' cells.

In a way, the work of Jesús Tenreiro-Degwitz is emblematic of a generation of late-modern or postmodern Latin American architects. Navigating different currents of architectural thought and feeling quite adrift, they strived for internal coherence while, at the same time, abandoning any hope of social transformation. Tenreiro-Degwitz often referred to the regular city as ugly or shameful. In response, he sought to create isolated buildings, cloisters of an ancient order disconnected from the world around them.

1968

THE OLYMPIC GAMES PROVIDE MEXICO CITY WITH OPPORTUNITIES FOR NEW FORMS OF NATIONAL REPRESENTATION

MEXICO

ON OCTOBER 12, 1968, after three years of planning, Mexican president Gustavo Díaz Ordaz inaugurated the XIX Olympic Games in Mexico City. It would be a momentous occasion. After all, it was the first time since the Games had been reestablished in 1896 that a Latin American country had been granted the privilege to host the Summer Games. It was a bittersweet moment for Mexico, however: a peaceful student demonstration ten days earlier had ended with the tragic killing of dozens (if not hundreds) of protesters in the Plaza de las Tres Culturas (Plaza of the Three Cultures) in the area of Tlatelolco, Mexico City.

The 1968 Mexican Olympic Games have been the only Olympic Games to date to take place in Latin America (although, by the time of this writing, Rio de Janeiro has been chosen and is preparing to host them in 2016, forty-eight years after Mexico). The same cannot be said for other world sports. Montevideo, Uruguay, for instance, hosted the first FIFA World Cup in 1930 at the Estadio Centenario (Centennial Stadium), named to commemorate the one hundred years of the Uruguayan Constitution. Designed by the Uruguayan architect Juan Scasso in 1929 and located in Parque Batlle, the stadium is representative of Scasso's interest in functionalism (seen, for

Opening Ceremony at the Olympic Stadium, UNAM, Mexico City, 1968.

THROUGH ARCHITECTURE; DEADLY STUDENT PROTESTS
HIGHLIGHT THE CONTESTED USE OF PUBLIC SPACE.

Félix Candela, Palacio de los Deportes, Mexico City, 1968.

example, in the expression of the reinforced concrete structural frame) but also in more classical architectural problems (such as diminishing the large mass of the stadium and seating by placing the playing field lower than ground level; this also limits the amount of wind that blows through the field). Crowning the stadium is the Torre de los Homenajes (Tower of Honors), which is placed as an axial terminus of Avenida 18 de Julio. Here, the verticality is highlighted by a series of Art Deco–inspired vertical lines and solid repeating balconies. At its base, however, two cantilevered canopies resemble airplane wings (see 1930-b entry).

Other important FIFA World Cups that took place in Latin America include Rio de Janeiro (1950) in the Estádio do Maracanã; Santiago, Chile (1962), at the Estadio Nacional;[1] Mexico City (1970 and 1986) in the Estadio Azteca; and Buenos Aires (1978) in the Estadio Monumental.

The preparation and design for the Mexican Olympics, however, was an exceptional case. At the helm of the organization was the architect Pedro Ramírez Vázquez, who had been asked by Díaz Ordaz to replace former president of Mexico Adolfo López Mateos as the head of the Olympic Game Organizing Committee. Ramírez Vázquez had been chosen because of his prominence in works intended to represent the state (such as his designs for Mexican pavilions for the 1958 Brussels, 1962 Seattle, and 1964 New York World's Fairs) as well as because of his experience managing the complexities of large projects such as the design and organization of Mexico City's Museo Nacional de Antropología (National Museum of Anthropology, 1964; see 1964-b box), which, like the exhibitions, required the collaboration of multiple experts in exhibition design, history, archaeology, etc., to make the information accessible to the layperson. The architectural design of the museum, however, would exemplify something that was desired for the Olympic Games: the dignified "display of a cultural legacy within an

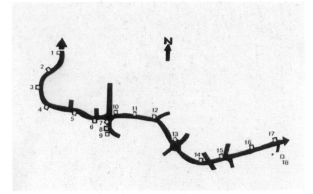

Route of Friendship, drawing by Mathias Goeritz, 1968.

architectural expression that was to be contemporary yet not alien to that legacy."[2]

The paradox of the 1968 Olympics lies in the necessity of showing Mexico's modernization while simultaneously demonstrating its deep historical roots and traditions. After all, the charge given to Ramírez Vázquez was to "give the world an image of [Mexico's] efficiency and ability [to do anything,]" to "recover the country's prestige, and to demonstrate [to the world] that we are able to host the Olympics."[3]

According to Ramírez Vázquez, the organization of the Olympics would follow the model set up in ancient times and address not only the physical (i.e., sports) but also the cultural. This allowed for a year-long series of events where all countries could promote the best cultural examples they had to offer, while, at the same time, countries with less successful athletes could shine in cultural events. In addition to this, the Olympic Identity Program team was formed to promote Mexico's modernity and tradition through the organization of all aspects of the game, the advertising, the Olympic venues, the design of the city to allow for the efficient and organized access to the events, and other logistics. This team was under the direction of Ramírez Vázquez. Architect Eduardo Terrazas (who had worked with Ramírez Vázquez in the design of the Mexican pavilions) was the head of the Department of Urban Design, and Beatrice Trueblood was the head of the Department of Publications. The result was the complete branding of the Mexican Olympics through the use of common typography, forms, and references to both contemporary and traditional art. The most notable and visible was the design of the Olympic logo itself by Terrazas and designer Lance Wyman. Based on both contemporary pop art and traditional Huichol

Indian art, the Mexico 68 logo took advantage of the concentric character of the number 68 and its formal relationship to the Olympic symbol. This design and the typography that it engendered became part of the brand identity that was applied to most subsequent designs (including printed matter, souvenirs, clothing, urban signage, etc.).

While Trueblood was in charge of publications and media, Terrazas's team was responsible for organizing the city through signage, urban furniture, logos, and sculptural pieces that oriented and welcomed the spectators and athletes. The team also organized the movement of people to the main Olympic venues, which were either new or remodeled/adapted structures for the Games built under the direction of Mexico City's Department of Public Works.

Although built in 1952 (see 1952 entry), the stadium at the Universidad Nacional Autónoma de México (UNAM; Mexican National Autonomous University) became an important venue, as it was where the inauguration of the Games took place with the symbolic lighting of the Olympic torch by Enriqueta Basilio (the first woman to ever do so) as well as where the closing ceremony was held. The stadium was also the site for the traditional track-and-field events. Retrofitted before the games to increase its seating capacity and to include new viewing, television, and filming areas, the facility also boasted expanded support spaces and changing rooms for the athletes as well as a renovated field adapted for its new needs. As part of the unifying identity with other sites, a series of repetitive parallel lines derived from the logo were painted on the ground around the whole stadium. A similar motif was painted around the Estadio Azteca as well, which, although completed in 1966, hosted soccer matches for the 1968 games.

Built expressly for the Olympics were the Palacio de los Deportes (Sports Palace; Félix Candela, Enrique Castañeda, and Antonio Peyri) and the Olympic Pool and Gymnasium (Manuel Rosen, Antonio Recamier, Javier Valverde, and Edmundo Gutiérrez Bringas), which have expressive structural solutions to the problem of long and unobstructed spans. The structure of the former, designed by Candela (see 1953-a box), is made of a dome of copper-covered hyperbolic paraboloids supported on metal arch trusses. The Pool and Gymnasium relies on steel cables resting on pillars to form a catenary-shaped roof that covers the interior space of both the pool and, past the central pillars, the gymnasium. Other structures built for the games include the Cycling Stadium (Herbert Schürmann), the Xochimilco Canal for rowing events, and the Olympic Village Housing (René Martínez, Manuel González Rul, Jaime Ceballos, et al.).

In the end, and as seen by these architectural examples, Mexico had met its obligations to express its ability to respond to contemporary problems through technology and culture. According to President Díaz Ordaz's 1968 State of the Union Address, "There was the need to solve problems that appeared for the first time in the organization of these competitions by using scientific and technological advancements." The solutions included not only the construction of new facilities that rivaled those of past Olympics but, more importantly, the development of major advances in communications that allowed for more than 600 million people worldwide to have access to the Games as "the most widespread event in the history of modern communications."[4]

Another important part of the urban and architectural organization of the city and of the cultural Olympics (and, specifically, the International Meeting of Sculptors that was held as one of the cultural events) was the Route of Friendship, organized by Mathias Goeritz (see 1953-b entry). The route, which linked the Olympic venues located in the southern area of Mexico City, was intended to showcase the work of international artists by organizing nineteen commissioned sculptures along a 17 km stretch of the Periférico highway. The sculptures, like the Olympic Games, would represent all five continents and a variety of countries. The requirements of the works were simple: they had to be monumental so as to be perceived by moving vehicles, be built out of reinforced concrete, and be individual works of art resulting from collaborative discussions. Although these were very general rules, Goeritz, in conversation with Ramírez Vázquez, suggested that the sculptures be more abstract and without any personal or historical themes in order to avoid overtly political or religious works (e.g., "The Eastern Bloc countries are going to send us their versions of Lenin or Stalin, and Latin America will send us statues of their local heroes and political leaders").[5] The formal simplicity of many of the sculptures was the result; this can be seen in the *Sundial* by Polish sculptor Grzegorz Kowalski, which consists of variations of cones, or *Spheres* by the Japanese sculptor Kioshi Takahashi. Although the works were to be perceived from

Gonzalo Fonseca, *The Tower of the Winds* (Uruguayan entry, Station 6), Mexico City, 1968.

the highway, parking was planned so that people could observe the works close up. *The Tower of the Winds* by the Uruguayan Gonzalo Fonseca, an architect by training and a disciple of Joaquín Torres-Garcia (see 1938 box), was the only inhabitable sculpture. In addition to the works along the route, Alexander Calder prepared a monumental steel sculpture, the *Red Sun*, for the exterior of the Estadio Azteca, and Mathias Goeritz prepared the geometrically shaped towers in the form of the Ursa Major constellation, *La Osa Mayor*, that were placed by the Palacio de los Deportes. For Goeritz, the ultimate goal of all of these works was to contrast the "increasingly chaotic [environment]," and by being integrated into the urban plan as a result of a new form of collaboration between artists, planners, and architects, these sculptures would be accessible to the public at large.[6]

As all of these were being planned, designed, and built in the final months of the preparations for the Olympic Games, the student protests against the authoritarian nature of the government were becoming more and more widespread. Student responses to the violent nature of the raids by the riot police—called in to stop the protests and to give an image of government control prior to the Olympic Games—included the co-opting of Olympic propaganda to show images of the riot police or doves speared by bayonets, for example, instead of what many considered to be the saccharine message of the Olympics. In the main quad at the UNAM, where many of the protest gatherings took place, a temporary mural was erected over the statue of President Miguel Alemán. Following the tradition of the Mexican muralist movement, the ephemeral mural, as it was called, used large-scale public art in the service of social protest. Other protests included marches down Insurgentes Avenue on July 30, 1968,

and in the Zócalo, Mexico City's central square, on August 28. However, as noted above, the student protests ended on October 2 when the Mexican army and a paramilitary group under orders from the president opened fire on protesters gathered at the Plaza de las Tres Culturas outside of the Tlatelolco housing development (see 1947-b box) next to the Department of Foreign Affairs.

On October 27, with the conclusion of the Olympic Games twenty-five days after the Massacre at Tlatelolco, the world spotlight on Mexico would be turned off.

FURTHER READING

Castañeda, "Beyond Tlatelolco: Design, Media, and Politics at Mexico '68."

Diseñando México 68: Una identidad olímpica.

Dubroise, ed., *The Age of Discrepancy: Art and Visual Culture in Mexico, 1968–1997.*

Morais, "La Ruta de la Amistad" in *Mathias Goeritz.*

1969-A

INVENTING NEW EDUCATIONAL PARADIGMS, ALBERTO CRUZ COVARRUBIAS AND GODOFREDO IOMMI (POETICALLY) FOUND THE CIUDAD ABIERTA IN CHILE.

CHILE

¿no fue el hallazgo ajeno
a los descubrimientos
—oh marinos
sus pájaras salvajes
el mar incierto
las gentes desnudas entre sus dioses!—
porque el don para mostrarse
equivoca la esperanza?

¿no dejó así
la primera pasión del oro
al navegante ciego
por esa claridad sin nombre
con que la tarde premia y destruye
la apariencia?[1]

GODOFREDO IOMMI, *AMEREIDA* (1967)

LIKE ULYSSES searching for Ithaca, a group of artists, philosophers, and architects began a journey in 1965 from Punta Arenas, Chile, to Santa Cruz de la Sierra, Bolivia, in search of the soul of Latin America. The act of the journey would provide the basis for what they would refer to as "the poetic founding of America." For Alberto Cruz, a Chilean architect, and Godofredo Iommi, an Argentine poet, this travel would be known as *Amereida*, the name being a combination of the words "America" and "Eneida" (from the Spanish version of Virgil's *Aeneid*). Through an epic poem, intended as a manifesto, a foundational myth was created for the Instituto de Arquitectura (Institute of Architecture), which itself had been founded within the Pontificia Universidad Católica de Valparaíso in the mid-1950s. Like much of the world, unsure of embracing rationalism after World War II, a group of visionary artists in Valparaíso were looking to poetry for the foundation of architecture.[2]

The history of the Institute of Architecture began in 1952 when Jesuits took over the Pontificia Universidad Católica de Valparaíso and opened the opportunity for a more progressive and intellectual education. As a consequence of this, Cruz was offered a position in the School of Architecture, which he accepted contingent on them also hiring Iommi. The result was the development of a faculty composed of a group of young and progressive architects, painters, poets, and engineers.[3] They shared a common desire for "removing architecture from its doctrine, buried in mathematics and formalisms, and re-centering it in the poetic word."[4] For this, they established the independent Institute of Architecture as a critical component of the new curriculum. The creation of an institute separate from the existing department provided the independence of structure that facilitated their research endeavors. The Institute of Architecture's pedagogic program was built upon reorganizing architecture around values different from functionalism or technology.

To achieve their goal of bringing poetics back to architecture, they tried to find a balance between scientific methodologies rooted in empirical observation and research and a more experimental approach based on a desire to eradicate the boundaries between art and life. In a way, they were much closer to the goals of the historic avant-garde than a more aesthetically directed educational process that left behind the fundamental ethical component of transforming life's praxis.

The commitment to poetry as a guide is most clearly evident in the beginning of each project. All of the projects at the institute begin with a poem that acts, according to Alberto Cruz, as a *"foundational act."*[5] On that note, a whole series of public events, known as *phalènes*, are performed for each new construction. These include physical exercise, spatial choreography, and poetry readings and are intended to define the initial relationships to be forged between the body, the site, and the imagined space, spiritually connected by such performances.

CL

Ciudad Abierta, Hospedería del Errante, Ritoque, Chile, 1991.

In addition to those performances, travels were an integral component of the educational mission of the school since its inception. This is clear from the journey that ten faculty members from the school took in 1965 from Punta Arenas, Chile, to Bolivia in which "numerous poetic acts [were carried out and] improvised on sites along the route . . . each poetic act initiated the construction of a physical mark, inscription, or offering on the site."[6] This *travesía*, or journey, inspired Iommi to write *Amereida* (1967). As noted above, *Amereida* operates as the institute's manifesto. Textually and visually, this poem illustrates the institute's ideas and concludes with the statement that "the road is not the road." It is interesting to note that instead of relating the field of investigation and journey to Homer's Greek *Odyssey*, Iommi connected it to the *Aeneid* and, in this way, linked the architecture of Latin America to its Latin Mediterranean roots.

From the beginning, Iommi sought to emphasize the European founding of the Continent as accidental. Likewise, *Amereida* also challenged the Eurocentrism of the mapping of the continent by invoking Joaquín Torres-García's famous 1943 inverted map of South America and his desire for an artistic creation uniquely rooted in Latin American histories, traditions, and cultures. *Amereida*, as a manifesto, calls for a more holistic understanding of the region and its traditions;

in short, it calls for a new form of pan-Americanism. For this, Iommi summons an exploration of the continent's interior, or "inner sea" (*mar interior*), as he called it, that is akin to that undertaken by the Spanish conquistadors.

Since 1984, the Travesías por América (Journeys through America) became part of the school's curriculum. Students and faculty have traveled and crisscrossed the whole continent: from the southern tip of Chile all the way north to the Amazon; from the Brazilian northeast to Easter Island on the west. Also, like the very first trip in 1965, the teams built small structures along the way. These are interventions in the landscape informed by local materials and local needs combined with their observations and investigations.

Inspired by those small constructions, Ciudad Abierta (Open City) was created in 1970, the same year that Salvador Allende was elected president. With him came a brief period of progressive reforms and higher social consciousness. As a type of experimental field laboratory, Ciudad Abierta provides students with the opportunity to broaden their education through the construction of permanent and semipermanent structures in Ritoque, a beach area 15 miles (24 km) outside of Valparaíso. Built by faculty and students

Ciudad Abierta, Capilla y Cementerio, Ritoque, Chile.

Ciudad Abierta, Hospedería de la Entrada, Ritoque, Chile.

working collaboratively, these structures include living spaces—like *hospederías* (lodges)—and public spaces that are built over extended periods of time. As these are public dwellings and open structures, anyone, especially visitors, is free to inhabit them. In this way, experimental architecture meets experimental socialism. The experimental nature of the constructions also means that construction documents are not used and, instead, their building begins with a poetic idea for the use of materials, which, as in the *travesías*, are used to create the structures. In the end, the shelters are open-ended in the sense that they are continuously worked on (sometimes remaining unfinished, in the traditional sense of that term), and they serve as the basis for collective experimentation with materials, forms, and space.

Among the first structures to be built was the Hospedería del Banquete (Feast's Lodge), a shelter designed around the dining table as the primordial architectural element. As with all other structures, the Hospedería del Banquete had its poetic founding in an open-air meal in 1971. The idea, like Pablo Neruda's *Ode to the Table,* was to build a space that could receive all people equally at the table. Another lodge, the Hospedería del Errante (Lodge of the Wanderer) took a decade to build (1981–1991).

In many of the structures, their enclosures look like a haphazard collage of pieces added by different sets of hands and minds to an irregular structure. The resultant spaces are as exciting as one can possibly imagine: the light conditions continuously change, modulated by panels, planks, and trusses that make up the shelters. Regularity and irregularity are brought face-to-face to make room for unexpected poetry.

On September 11, 1973, this all changed when the Chilean military, led by Augusto Pinochet, deposed the democratically elected government of Allende and instituted a U.S.-oriented and right-wing set of economic and social reforms. The 1970s and 1980s in Chile will always be remembered for the economic success of the

"Chicago boys," a group of Chilean economists trained at the University of Chicago who advocated market-driven capitalism, and for the executions at Estadio Nacional.

While the Catholic University of Chile in Santiago was linked to an element within the clergy that supported Pinochet, the Catholic University of Valparaíso, led by Jesuits, tried as much as possible to keep their social-oriented liberation theology alive. The Valparaíso School of Architecture, their *travesías*, and the Ciudad Abierta were, in a way, protected by this orientation and served as an alternative universe to escape the harsh realities of the Pinochet era. What remains to be discussed is how much their poetic foundation was combined with the tectonic pragmatism of the Santiago school to inform a generation of Chilean architects that came of age around the time of Pinochet's demise in the 1990s.

FURTHER READING

Pendleton-Jullian, *The Road That Is Not a Road and the Open City, Ritoque, Chile.*

Pérez de Arce. "So Far yet So Near: The Open City and the Travesías."

Pérez Oyarzún, "The Valparaíso School."

Reina-Bravo, "A Modernist Experiment: Traces of Poetry, Art, and Architecture within the Travesías and the Open City."

Torrent, "Abstraction and Tectonics in Chilean Architecture since 1950."

1969-B

PREVI: TWO OPPOSING GOVERNMENTS IN PERU BRING IN THE BEST ARCHITECTS IN THE WORLD TO ADDRESS SQUATTER SETTLEMENTS.

PERU

THE IDEA WAS SO GOOD that one might wonder why it hasn't been done more often: invite the best architects in the world to design for the poor, connect them with a selected group of local designers, arrange for the United Nations to provide technical support, and develop a finance mechanism that ensures the economical sustainability of the process. As we look deeper into that experience and understand all the complex relationships between all the agents involved (inhabitants, designers, government, United Nations, and financiers), it is clear why it didn't happen more often. Strong political will during a sustained period of time was the crucial ingredient. Lima, Peru's PREVI (Proyecto Experimental de Vivienda; Experimental Housing Project) had it all, despite evidence to the contrary. Yet, by the time the inhabitants entered the houses in 1978, the architectural media had already forgotten PREVI.

The story starts with Fernando Belaúnde Terry. Trained as an architect, Belaúnde was elected president of Peru in 1963.[1] Before becoming the leader of Acción Popular, a centrist party that proposed stitching together indigenous causes with modern social democracy, Belaúnde had founded *El Arquitecto Peruano* in 1937, the first architectural magazine in Peru (see 1947-c box). In 1965, his government invited the British architect Peter Land to advise the Banco de la Vivienda (Housing Bank) on housing and planning. Land proposed an experimental approach consisting of several pilot projects that ranged from contractor-built houses (Pilot Plan 1) to self-built ones (Pilot Plan 3). The agreement between the Peruvian government and the United Nations Development Program that would fund it was signed in September of 1968.

The very next month a military coup ousted Belaúnde's government. PREVI could have been one more well-intentioned collaboration shelved by political changes. But, unlike what was going on in most Latin American countries ruled by military dictatorships, the military junta led by Gen. Juan Velasco was further

to the left of the previous regime. Velasco's agenda (labeled Peruanismo [Peruvianism]) was dominated by the nationalization of several industries, extensive agrarian reform, and stronger government control over the economy. Contrary to the tradition of new governments discontinuing all pet projects of the previous ones, Velasco supported the ideas behind PREVI, and a competition was put together in 1969.

The competition had two stages. The first was a closed competition to which thirteen foreign architects or firms were invited.[2] The second was open only to Peruvian architects, from which another thirteen were selected.[3] The competition brief called for the design of 1,500 low-rise housing units clustered around smaller neighborhoods connected to schools and community and commercial facilities. The competition also asked the architects to consider the need for future expansion embedded in the structural and spatial concepts. The competition jury was equally composed of an international and Peruvian group of architects.[4]

The jury met in Lima in August of 1969 and awarded six prizes to the best three international projects and the best three Peruvian projects, all of which, according to the competition rules, would be built as part of PREVI Pilot Plan 1. But the outstanding quality of all the entries prompted the jury to suggest that a small number of houses from all twenty-six entries be built, maximizing the outcome of the experiment. With UN and Peruvian government approval, the architects were hired to design a few clusters of about twenty houses each (totaling five hundred units). These would fit into the master plan designed by Peter Land, with vehicular circulation at the periphery and pedestrian streets connecting the clusters with the park, school, community center, and a few commercial spaces. One wide street intended for walking, Calle Alameda, connects all major components and leads to the Pan-American Highway as well as to the bus stop on the east.

The units were built between 1972 and 1976, though a few crucial parts, such as the school and the community center, were never built. International fascination with the complex stems from the fact that it materialized different perspectives not only of housing but also, stylistically, of the multiple varieties of postmodernist architecture emerging internationally. After all, where else can we find houses designed by Correa, Kurokawa/Maki, Stirling, Candilis/Josic/Woods, and Van Eyck in the same place?

Charles Correa's house, for instance, has a series of party walls 10.5 ft. (3.2 m) apart, making it easier to expand vertically and ensuring proper light and ventilation by having setbacks on every other bay. The success of such design intentions are corroborated by the empirical evidence of a family that grew their house from 1,000 sq. ft. (93 sq. m) to 3,790 sq. ft. (352 sq. m) following the same spatial and structural logic. Aldo van Eyck, in studying existing *barriadas*, or shantytowns, devised a solution that was based on those local traditions (and, especially, on the particular group that would occupy it).[5] His solution, then, was centered on enclosing an octagonal-shaped property with a tall wall, and by unifying the units similarly, he grouped them into recognizable clusters. The housing elements within the properties, located in an elementary core, were placed so as to take advantage of prevailing winds but also designed in a way that they could be expanded later by their owners.

The value of PREVI, however, must be seen in the context of contemporary debates on housing and the city. After all, PREVI was proposed only a few years after Jane Jacobs's *Death and Life of Great American Cities* (1961), a time when most cities were still building "towers in the park" as the solution to low-income housing. While PREVI's master plan might resemble Brasília's *superquadras*, the low-rise and high-density cluster that incorporated growth and adaptation as an integral part of the design was quite radical at the time. In addition, PREVI was also designed before John Turner published his studies defending self-built informality as a solution rather than a problem, something already incorporated

1976 Aerial view of PREVI, Lima, Peru.

Charles Correa, PREVI housing, Lima, Peru, 1971.

Charles Correa, contemporary view of PREVI housing after modifications by inhabitants.

in van Eyck's solutions. Furthermore, PREVI is not public housing as understood in North America or Europe. Here, the inhabitants own their units, and the need for future expansion by owners was part of its concept since the beginning. Indeed, it is likely that the freedom inherent in the possible modification of the units (in what Le Corbusier, in a different context, would define as "the liberty allowed to the public . . . to express its own bad taste") resulted in the lack of continuous interest in PREVI by architectural publications.

In 2003, however, a team of Chilean scholars (Fernando García-Huidobro, Diego Torres Torriti, and Nicolás Tugas) knocked on the door of every house in PREVI and were allowed to document dozens of them. The resultant book, *Time Builds!* (*¡El tiempo construye!*), rescued PREVI from the oblivion it had endured for thirty-five years. Coincidentally, that same year, the Chilean architect Alejandro Aravena was taking the best of PREVI's concept of flexibility and open design and turning it into an award-winning project by building ninety-three Elemental houses at Quinta Monroy, Chile.

The PREVI idea might have been too good to be true, yet much more research is needed to evaluate its successes and shortcomings. Four decades later, though, it stands tall, telling us that it is indeed possible.

FURTHER READING

García-Huidobro, Torres Torriti, and Tugas, *Time Builds! The Experimental Housing Project (PREVI), Lima: Genesis and Outcome.*
Negrón, "Amérique Latine . . . Stop . . . Problémes et méthodes."
"PREVI/Lima: Low-cost Housing Project."
"PREVI Lima: 35 años después."

1969

FRANCISCO BULLRICH PUBLISHES ON LATIN AMERICAN ARCHITECTURE.

IN 1969, ARGENTINE ARCHITECT and scholar Francisco Bullrich published two books on Latin American architecture. Both were published in Barcelona, one by Editorial Gustavo Gili, *Arquitectura latinoamericana 1930–1970*, and the other by Editorial Blume, *Nuevos caminos en la arquitectura latinoamericana*. These two books were the first to attempt to cross-reference the diverse architecture of the region produced since Henry-Russell Hitchcock's catalogue of the Museum of Modern Art's exhibition *Architecture in Latin America since 1945* (1955).

Francisco Bullrich was born in Buenos Aires in 1929 and graduated as an architect in 1952. As a practitioner, Bullrich (with Clorindo Testa and Alicia Cazzaniga) was part of the team that designed the National Library in Buenos Aires (1961–1992) as well as the Argentine Embassy in Brasília (1970). His career as an established designer was going full force when he published *Arquitectura argentina contemporánea* in 1963. The success of the book was such that Bullrich shifted his focus to an intellectual path that would turn the young designer into one of the most respected scholars of Argentine architecture. In 1966, architectural historian Vincent Scully invited Bullrich to Yale University to teach a seminar on Latin American architecture. Its content would become the two books published in 1969. After a career of teaching, Bullrich's posts included the vice presidency of the Fondo Nacional de las Artes (National Fund for the Arts) and ambassador to Greece (1995–2000). Francisco Bullrich died in Buenos Aires in August of 2011.

Arquitectura latinoamericana 1930–1970 is organized around seven different countries: Brazil, Argentina, Uruguay, Chile, Cuba, Venezuela, and Mexico. Brazil's representation is the largest, going from the MESP building to Oscar Niemeyer's Pampulha, Pedregulho and the Museu de Arte Moderna by Affonso Reidy, the Ibirapuera pavilion by Oscar Niemeyer, Brasília, Roberto Burle Marx, and some not so canonical examples, such as houses by Joaquim Guedes and Sérgio Bernardes. Argentina is represented by Alberto Prebisch; the Austral Group, with

emphasis on Antoni Bonet, Jorge Ferrari Hardoy, and Juan Kurchan; Amancio Williams; Wladimiro Acosta; Mario Roberto Álvarez; Clorindo Testa; Claudio Caveri; and Eduardo Ellis. From Uruguay, he selected Julio Vilamajó, Mario Payseé Reyes, and Eladio Dieste. From Chile, Emilio Duhart and the CORVI group. Cuba is represented by Ricardo Porro and Fernando Salinas. From Venezuela, Carlos Raúl Villanueva and Guido Bermúdez. And from Mexico, the second-largest representation, Juan O'Gorman, José Villagrán García, Max Cetto, Félix Candela, Juan Sordo Madaleno, Teodoro González de León, Enrique del Moral, and Pedro Ramírez Vázquez. Overall, Bullrich managed to show the most celebrated Latin American architecture up to the 1960s as a catalogue of projects accompanied by a brief introduction that does not go far enough in critically addressing the architecture presented.

Nuevos caminos en la arquitectura latinoamericana was organized differently, with themes that cut across different countries. In the foreword to the 1969 North American edition (*New Directions in Latin American Architecture*), Bullrich defined his particular approach: "I chose . . . to present the architects and their works, not according to their nationality, but in relation to the problems which are now being confronted in this area of the world. Yet national features are important and should not be entirely sacrificed. Thus, wherever the opportunity arose, I referred to national development [to give a capsule image of that country's architectural characteristics]" (11). As a result, the text is much richer, as Bullrich was clearly trying to understand different Latin American architectures according to the different paths of modernization and thus he arrived at a richer contextual critique.

The book starts by trying to ground the contemporary architecture with the past through a comparison of premodern structures such as Vilamajó's early houses in Montevideo, García Núñez's Hospital Español in Buenos Aires, and Villagrán García's buildings in Mexico, among others. After discussing the classical modernism of Niemeyer in Brazil or the Austral Group in Argentina, the author addresses the urban plans for Brasília and Caracas as well as the work of Villanueva before delving into the relationship between architecture and the city, technology, and the new monumentality of buildings like Duhart's CEPAL in Chile or Nelson Bayardo's columbarium in Montevideo. A clear preoccupation with architecture as a promoter of social justice permeates the text. In the last chapter, the selection and the narrative moves further toward a defense of regionalism in the works of Joaquim Guedes in São Paulo; Rogelio Salmona in Bogotá; and Clorindo Testa, Justo Solsona, and Juan Óscar Molinos in Buenos Aires. These are, for him, members of a younger generation of architects confronting and dialoguing with the earlier ones. In this way, Bullrich anticipated by a whole decade the debates on critical regionalism in the 1980s.

FORMALIZING THE LEGACY OF THE MADÍ (MOVIMIENTO DE ARTE DE INVENCIÓN) AND UTOPIAN URBAN PROJECTS, GYULA KOSICE PROPOSES A HYDROSPATIAL CITY.

ARGENTINA • BRAZIL • MEXICO

IN 1971, THE ARGENTINE artist Gyula Kosice proposed a new form of architecture and living based on his sculptural work and on his earlier associations with the Argentine Concretist movement. His "Manifesto for a Hydrospatial Architecture and Urbanism" is a call for a new form of utopian environment no longer ruled by traditional notions of inhabitation that would use science and technology to liberate mankind from economic and social bonds and would unify the arts to create a total environment. At the core of his proposal were the polemics outlined first in *Arturo* (1944), a magazine committed to abstract art: "pure imagery, free from determinism or justification," that proposed, "Man is not bound to finish on Earth."[1] This would be developed by Kosice in the "Madí Manifesto" (1946) into a new form of architecture defined as "environment and movable forms." Also present in Madí's artistic direction—which was an affront to conventional painting and static sculpture—was a utopian vision for the work: "to invent and construct objects within absolute eternal human values . . . to construct a new classless society, which liberates energy, masters time and space in all senses, and dominates matter to the limit."[2]

The 1971 manifesto on hydrospatial architecture develops these ideas into a more specific conception of architecture and urbanism. For Kosice, contemporary architecture was obsolete and oppressive because of its functionalist vocation; this, he argued, limits

AR

BR

MX

Gyula Kosice, Hydrospatial City, 1971.

creativity and thought and is part of a broader societal exploitation of humanity. To overcome this, humans need to supplant the state—which reproduces these conditions—with a more efficient administration that uses scientific advances and imagination to develop new conditions of living. The Hydrospatial City would be a city composed of a number of pods suspended in space that utilized water—through crystallization—as their main structural support and life-giving source and fuel; the water would be split into oxygen for breathing and hydrogen for energy and fuel. The political implication of suspending the pods in space was centered on the nullification of the conditions that grant land its value and ownership of property. Art and artistic experiences would be synthesized with the built environment, thus eradicating the boundaries between art and architecture and making art accessible to all classes; life would be communal. In short, traditional architecture and environments—in a primarily nongravitational environment—would be replaced by "something calm or intense, but differentiated in every way, *as places in which to live*. Yes, within space, but occupying the space-time factor with all its attributes. And, not as an alteration in the human adventure, but as an explainable need which our condition emits."[3]

To explain his ideas, Kosice developed a series of study models made with Plexiglas, plastics, metals, and other materials that were initially collaged onto photographs of cloudy skies. These are based not only on his earlier water sculptures but also on his 1959 ideas about water as a literal and metaphoric fluid and as a constantly changing medium.[4] Each of the models presents multiple spaces whose functions deal with materializing in humans various poetical sensibilities and alternate experiences (such as places "for forgetting oblivion"; "to verify the crumbling of experience"; "for intermittent holidays"; "for the setting of sentimental, corporal, copulative, sexual and erotic coordinates in sublimated buoyancy," etc.). The designs also deal with more pragmatic concerns such as energy sources ("hydronuclear energy"), nourishment, and waste disposal ("the chemical dissolution of residues").

While Kosice's proposals are extremely radical and akin to those of the Dutch Situationist sculptor-architect Constant (Nieuwenhuys), the tradition of a social, urban, and architectural utopia in twentieth-century Latin America does not begin or end here. We can find developments for alternate social structures and environments that affect the twentieth century as far back

as the eighteenth century. One example is the proposal for Planaltina: a city located in the center of Brazil that would serve as its new capital (which would eventually be materialized with the construction of Brasília; see 1956 entry). The idea of a central capital had been brewing since 1789 and was ratified in the 1891 constitution. According to the myth of Brasília, the Italian priest Don Bosco allegedly dreamed of a just and plentiful utopian city located where Brasília would eventually be built.

In 1925, the Mexican minister of education, José Vasconcelos, similarly imagined the utopian city of Universópolis. As part of his ideas regarding the development of a new and hybrid "cosmic race," which he articulated in his 1925 book, *La raza cósmica*, Universópolis was to be a city located in the Brazilian Amazon intended to house this new race (formed from the races that constituted the American continent) and to employ all of the material and technological advances of the European and North American civilizations (see 1922 entry). These advances would be used to conquer the tropics and to tame and inhabit the Amazonian jungle and its climate. The resulting environment would reflect the location as well as the ideals of beauty that were characteristic and defining of the cosmic race:

Architecture will abandon the Gothic arch, the vault, and, in general, the roof, which answers to the need for shelter. The pyramid will again develop. Colonnades and perhaps spiral constructions will be raised in useless ostentation of beauty, because the new aesthetics will try to adapt itself to the endless curve of the spiral, which represents the freedom of desire and the triumph of Being in the conquest of infinity. The landscape, brimming with colors and rhythms, will communicate its wealth to the emotions. Reality will be like fantasy. The aesthetics of cloudiness and grays will be seen as the sickly art of the past. A refined and intense civilization will answer to the splendors of a Nature swollen with potency, habitually generous, and shining with clarity.[5]

In Universópolis, everyone would be equal. Its new culture would be founded on free will and the metaphysical and mystical qualities of the arts. From this city, according to Vasconcelos's plan, armies and planes would be dispatched intent on "educating the people for their entry into wisdom" instead of dominating them.[6]

In a similar vein of conquering the landscape and utilizing it for socially beneficial purposes is Sérgio Bernardes's *Geometrização do Brasil* (Geometricization of Brazil; late 1960s/early 1970s; see 1953-c entry). In his descriptive text, "The Paths of the First Tropical Civilization: A Continent Is Transformed into a Nation; Brazil Interconnected by Aqueducts," Bernardes outlines a project to use existing and new waterways or aqueducts (*aquavias*) throughout the country to develop the country as a whole. Sixteen interlinked aqueducts in the form of a ring would connect all of the existing riverways and allow for the redistribution of water where it was most needed. These would serve not only for the movement of water throughout the country (distributing water from areas with much water to those that suffered droughts) but also for shipping products and for hydroelectric generation. Besides these purposes, Bernardes believed that these aqueducts

Sergio Bernardes, Rio de Janeiro of the Future project, 1963–1965.

would bring all the regions of the nation closer together, integrating them and linking them, while conjoining natural resources and human efforts with the aim of putting a definite end to the problems of drought, floods, and pollution, while simultaneously finding more economic alternatives for transport and power generation. . . . [Their construction would provide] the solution for [the nation's] unemployment problem and economic crisis.[7]

In Bernardes's plan, with the establishment of this network, new urban forms dotting the totality of Brazil could develop: circular cities (*rótulas urbanas*) made up of vertical buildings surrounded by recreational and civic programs (i.e., schools, hospitals, etc.) and open green areas, all linked by waterways and high-speed monorails. In a way, his earlier 1963–1965 proposals for a Rio de Janeiro of the Future were instrumental in the development of this new urban ideal. This project for Rio de Janeiro would consist of 156 "vertical districts" containing not only housing, recreation, commerce, and civic functions but also providing land around these districts for the residents to grow crops. Each of the districts would be separated by two thirds of a

mile and would have cultural, educational, and sports complexes in between. Ultimately, the separation would provide for the "autonomy and the reorganization of social and administrative systems," spreading the decision-making processes throughout the urban fabric.[8]

In contrast to these proposals for the transformation and domestication of the landscape, metropolitan proposals of high density are also part of the utopian projects for Latin America. Francisco Mujica's Neo-American City of the Future, published in his *History of the Skyscraper* (1929–1930; see 1929-c entry), is one example of these. In it, the basic neo-American skyscraper type that he developed—based on his studies of both pre-Columbian architecture and modern skyscrapers—was placed on a base and reproduced at regular intervals. The original type, which initially had no defined use, was developed for this project into a residential skyscraper with an added base intended for commercial purposes. As a city, the proposal made reference to Harvey Wiley Corbett's 1923 studies for the subdivision of traffic that clearly separated pedestrian and vehicular traffic through pedestrian loggias and by allowing for both driving and parking within the envelope of the skyscrapers themselves (linked via

Wladimiro Acosta, City-Block (Variant A), 1927–1935.

interconnecting pedestrian bridges). The loggias would lead to large urban promenades with green spaces and urban squares, all linked by bridges. Mujica's design echoes Le Corbusier's ideas for a Contemporary City for 3 Million (1922), which Mujica addressed in his book. The similarity with Le Corbusier's city would end here; Mujica's proposal and its rendering as a seemingly endless city appear closer to Ludwig Hilberseimer's designed metropolis from his book *Groszstadtarchitektur* (The Architecture of the Metropolis; 1927).

In the vein of Le Corbusier's and Hilberseimer's ideal cities are the City Block designs that the Russian émigré Wladimiro Acosta developed for Buenos Aires between 1927 and 1935. In response to what he and others saw as the breakdown of order in the Argentine city and the lack of fresh air, sunlight, and nature in its core, Acosta developed two schemes for the capital based on the transformation of the typical and existing Buenos Aires city block. Underlying the earlier design is a series of cross-planned and T-shaped towers that are overlaid in checkerboard pattern over the city. The later design, the Integral City Block, converts these into linear blocks with buttress-like elements that contain services and work functions. These linear elements are then spaced at regular intervals from each other with gardens, public recreation areas, sports facilities, and other amenities. In both proposals, however, nature is reintroduced into the city, and housing and public spaces for work, shopping, and recreation are located within the structures. In the later one, traffic is separated from the ground, allowing for uninterrupted pedestrian movement, as proposed by the CIAM's 1933 "Athens Charter." Published in Acosta's *Vivienda y ciudad: Problemas de arquitectura contemporánea* (1937), the City Block designs were considered part of his general ideas for the reformation of architecture and the city through the introduction of sunlight and nature—conditions that he explored on a smaller scale through his Helios projects (see 1937 entry).

Amancio Williams's urban variant of his Viviendas en el Espacio (1942) is another utopian project that responds to the need to introduce light and air into the home (see 1942 box). Initially proposed as a singular apartment building for Buenos Aires, the design not only provides each unit with the needed programmatic requirements for housing but also, through its stepped form, a garden, fresh air, sunlight, and privacy. These are achieved through the sectional stepping of the units, making the roof of one be the garden of the next unit higher up. Placed together, these units would form linear urban blocks separated from each other by gardens and green spaces. Under the blocks, the ground level would contain parking, retail, and other public spaces. In the perspectives produced for the project, Williams presented a series of linear blocks that seemingly disappear into the horizon, with no other elements of the existing city in sight and as the sole alternative to the problem of housing. Socially, the project would be a "solution to the diverse housing needs for social groups with differing economic conditions."[9]

Based on the social and idealized transformation of the city, the Mexican Unión de Arquitectos Socialistas (Union of Socialist Architects)—Alberto Arai, Raúl Cacho, Enrique Guerrero, and Balbino Hernández—developed their Ciudad Obrera (Worker's City; 1938) on functionalist principles and on their *Doctrine for a Socialist Architecture*. Their project was centered on the reorganization of the northern part of Mexico City into different zones: Housing, Industry, and Farming. The Housing zone, the most architecturally developed by the group, features housing as well as a civic center, schools, collective dining halls, retail sections (for natural and manufactured products), and a bus terminal. The housing units themselves are organized according to functionalist precepts and principles of economic and minimal use of space; kitchen and dining areas, for example, are reduced in scale and presence, since their function is accounted for through the use of the collective dining halls. Formally, the apartment buildings are based on Moisei Ginzburg's Narkomfin Housing Block (Moscow, 1930), evident not only in their sparse linear appearance but also in the composition of the two-story units composed of double-height "public" zones on the entry level and living quarters on the second floor. In addition, these buildings would be raised on columns from the ground to allow for nature to pass underneath, generating a large public garden. The group even went so far as to propose the types of work, educational, and physical activities to be undertaken by its inhabitants during the week and their allotted times.[10]

As a middle ground to proposals that deal with either the transformation of the landscape or the densification of the urban metropolis is Alberto Kalach's La Ciudad Lacustre (Lake City) for Mexico City. Prepared in association with Teodoro González de León, Gustavo Lipkau, Juan Cordero, and Jose Castillo, this 1998–2002 project calls for the "return of the pre-Hispanic lacustrine city" as a solution to the environmental

and soil-related problems created by the draining of Lake Texcoco, the location of the ancient capital of Tenochtitlán and the site on which modern Mexico City presently sits.[11] By using treated residual water, accumulated rain, and collected runoff water from the surrounding mountains in the Valley of Mexico, a large parcel east of the metropolitan area as well as zones that border it would be flooded. The borders of this great lake would be filled with parks and urban amenities. In addition, small islands would be created within the lake that would serve as ecological reserves, parks, sport areas, cultural and educational centers, housing, and work. The largest of these islands would be destined for the airport as the motor force for this development and as the new gateway to this new Mexico City. The introduction of water into the basin of the Valley of Mexico would have ecological, economic, and social benefits such as the rehydration of the subsoil and aquifers, humidification of the air and development of beneficial climatic changes (such as breezes and rains that would diminish the pollution), organization and control of urban growth, and availability of open green space for the population of the city.[12]

These different proposals for the transformation of the world—physically and socially—have at their core a unique relation and reaction to the current physical, cultural, social, historic, and artistic conditions within which they would be built in Latin America. In addition, despite the many imported or foreign references the proposals made or evoked, their authors always attempted to respond both broadly and specifically to the conditions and problems within which they worked. Their urban or landscape proposals propose a seemingly endless space (either formally in scope or in influence) that suggests the universality of their aspirations: specific proposals projected for the betterment of humanity as a whole.

FURTHER READING

Amancio Williams: Obras y textos.
Arai et al., "Proyecto de la Ciudad Obrera de México."
Cavalcanti, "Sérgio Bernardes: A Modernist Adrift."
La ciudad y sus lagos.
Kosice, *La ciudad hidroespacial.*

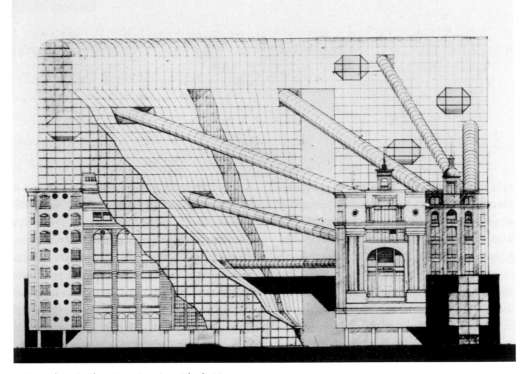

La Escuelita, Student Exercise, Avenida de Mayo

Manteola, Sánchez Gómez, Santos, Solsona, and Viñoly,
Argentina Televisora Color, Buenos Aires, 1978.

environment of La Escuelita, whose faculty, it should be noted, also maintained some relationship with and prominence within the circles of power that sought this public work from them.

As time passed, the interests of the faculty changed and the influence of outside architects and theorists (many of whom were invited to speak at the school) became more prominently reflected in the discussions, work, and assignments. One such case was Díaz's interest in populist Argentine architecture and its history, something that had begun in the TANAPO. His teaching and studio assignments became highly influenced by the ideas of collective memory and the architectural forms of the Italian architect Aldo Rossi. As a result, Rossi was invited to lecture in 1979. The lecture was controversial and made more so by critic Marina Waisman, who, in an introduction on Rossi in the magazine *Summa+*, called him and his ideas Marxist.[3] The year 1979 also coincides with Viñoly's departure from Argentina to the United States, joining César Pelli, who emigrated in 1952; Emilio Ambasz, in 1960; and Rodolfo Machado and Jorge Silvetti, in 1968.

The teaching of history also became an important reference point in La Escuelita. This was particularly the case in the investigations done on the history of modern architecture in Argentina and, especially, that of the historic Argentine avant-garde. Figures such as Antonio Vilar and Alberto Prebisch, for instance, became important because they stood for a socially committed local tradition and because they contrasted with the formal, stylistic, and functional historical interests of the UBA at the time (see 1937 box). In addition to this research, history became part of the design studios: historically related problems were given or precedents reconsidered. The "history" department of La Escuelita was formalized under the leadership of Katzenstein and Jorge Francisco Liernur (who had initially begun teaching studio there under Katzenstein). As a result, La Escuelita began developing a more organized series of exhibitions; publications (such as the periodical *Materiales* and the publication of the work of the school, *La Escuelita: 5 años de enseñanza alternativa de arquitectura en la Argentina*); and a lecture series that included the Italian architectural historian Manfredo Tafuri, Argentine cultural historian and critic Beatriz Sarlo, and others.

By the time the school closed in 1982, after the fall of the military dictatorship, the student population had reached about three hundred.

FURTHER READING

Díaz, "Apariencia y verdad: Posmodernismo y dictadura."
La Escuelita: 5 años de enseñanza alternativa de arquitectura en la Argentina.
Silvestri, "Apariencia y verdad."

1975

FILGUEIRAS LIMA, CAPELA DO CENTRO ADMINISTRATIVO DA BAHIA

JOÃO DA GAMA FILGUEIRAS LIMA was forty years old when he arrived in Salvador de Bahia in the early 1970s to build a series of administrative buildings on a new campus 10 miles (16 km) from downtown. Born in Rio de Janeiro in 1932, "Lelé" (as he is known in Brazil) had already amassed experience as a designer and builder. After graduating from the Faculdade Nacional de Arquitetura (now the Federal University of Rio de Janeiro) in 1955, he went to work for Oscar Niemeyer in the construction of Brasília. As early as 1957, Filgueiras Lima started experimenting with prefabrication for the construction of workers' housing because of the tight schedule and inexperienced workforce. His success with low-tech prefabrication brought him to another challenge: to build the University of Brasília as quickly as possible. By the early 1960s, Filgueiras Lima had been to Eastern Europe and had designed the Colina Velha Faculty Housing building (see 1953-c entry) at the University of Brasília when the military coup interrupted the university's plans. Resigning along with two hundred other faculty members in 1965, he returned to Rio de Janeiro.

In 1970, Antônio Carlos Magalhães, appointed governor of Bahia by the military government, decided to build an administrative campus for the state bureaucracy. Lúcio Costa was hired to design its master plan. Located along Paralela Avenue, which connects the city of Salvador to the airport, the Centro Administrativo da Bahia (CAB; Administrative Center of Bahia) sits on rolling hills 10 miles (16 km) north of the center of the city. Costa designed a simple loop of roads at the ridge of the hills and placed the buildings as meandering bars along this main axis and down the slope, with their service access hidden from the main entrances. Given the tight schedule and the repetitive character of the governmental buildings, Filgueiras Lima was called on to design all of them. His solution uses a reinforced concrete sectional module that articulates the subtle curves of their siting by placing the slabs as boxes transversal to the main circulation spine. The protrusion of the boxes allows them to function as sun shading devices. The whole structure is elevated by large columns that also hold elevators and stairs. Since all the buildings are located slightly below the main road, the first floor is usually level with the entrance and the spaces underneath are service spaces like garages, mechanical rooms, and delivery access. The construction of the CAB allowed Filgueiras Lima to establish his first major prefabrication plant in Bahia, an endeavor that would change the face of the city. In the 1980s and 1990s, he built city hall (a steel structure that can be disassembled), the main city bus station, and hundreds of smaller prefabricated structures such as bus stops and elevated walkways.

But the jewel of the crown of Bahia was also built at CAB: a small chapel by the entrance to the complex. Commissioned by the state government in 1975, the chapel,

João Filgueiras Lima (Lelé), Capela do Centro Administrativo da Bahia, Salvador, Brazil, 1975.

João Filgueiras Lima (Lelé), interior of Capela do Centro Administrativo da Bahia, Salvador, 1975.

Ricardo Legorreta, interior courtyard of Hotel Camino Real, Mexico City, 1968.

the Hotel Camino Real (Ixtapa, Guerrero, 1980–1981) and the City of the Arts Master Plan and School of Visual Arts (Mexico City, 1994) continue this trend. Both structures show the contrast of bright colors highlighted by natural light, use of large-scale sculptural elements, and the use of historical forms (such as the water troughs from Mexican ranches typical of Barragán, in the first, or the domes from the colonial Capilla Real in Cholula or the pyramidal-shaped spiral stairs reminiscent of pre-Columbian ruins). The formal elements of the Barraganist "kit of parts" could be seen reproduced most obviously in the Gutiérrez Cortina House (Mexico City, 1987–1988) that reuses the stair without handrails, the contrasting bright colors, and the expression of the wood rafters on the ceiling that can all be found in Barragán's own house (Mexico City, 1947–1948; see 1947-a entry). In these works, we can see how Barragán's work became representative of a protopostmodernism: historical citations without social content that announced the end of the social project of modernism and the avant-garde.

While the "hyperchromaticism" of Barragán was the most prominent style, a more North American type of postmodernism did emerge in Mexico that, as in the previous case, was equally devoid of any theoretical armature. Neither Venturi's *Complexity and Contradiction in Architecture* (1966) nor Venturi, Scott-Brown, and Izenour's *Learning from Las Vegas* (1972), which developed as historical systems through which to criticize the limits of the modern movement, became points of reference. In addition, there was no clear connection with or influence by the so-called New York school—characterized by the Institute of Architecture and Urban Studies under Peter Eisenman—or, even, with the Spanish neo-avant-garde, such as the architects and theorists who revolved around the Barcelonan magazine *Arquitecturas Bis*—a sort of response to the polemics coming from North America—which was involved in investigating the character of European architecture and theory at the time. For Mexican critics like Antonio Toca, the lack of quality work produced during the eighties was really the result of the financial situation, the trauma following the 1985 Mexico City earthquake, and a sort of uncertainty experienced by the architectural profession: "Mediocrity has been the answer to [postmodern historical references], and the very few buildings built—because postmodernism has manifested itself primarily through remodelings and decorative interventions—clearly show its theatrical

or at the populist and collective notions embedded within typologies and forms (as argued by Rossi). Thus the use of specific elements—bright colors; architectural components such as the staircase in his house; unornamented, plain, heavy, thick walls, etc.—became emblematic of a regionalist response to modernism but also a continuation of the experiments of the twentieth century. Characteristic of this tendency is the work of Ricardo Legorreta, best known as Barragán's most direct protégé. His influence can be seen in Legorreta's design for the Hotel Camino Real (Mexico City, 1968) that has the chromatic references through the use of bright pinks and yellows; the inward focus; the artistic associations (such as the large-scale entry screen by Mathias Goeritz, who collaborated extensively with Barragán); the thick, unornamented walls; and other elements that are present in many of Barragán's works. Legorreta's later works, such as

Teodoro González de León and Abraham Zabludovsky,
interior courtyard of the Colegio de México, Mexico City,
1974–1976.

Agustin Hernández, Heroico Colegio Militar, Mexico City, 1973–1976.

qualities."[1] These tendencies can be seen in Félix Sánchez's own architectural office (Mexico City, 1986). A rehabilitation of a historical building, the project's forms and details are typical of a North American postmodernism influenced by Michael Graves's early work: exposed steel structure, glass block, wood, gray-painted steel tube handrails, inset arches within square openings, among others. Other examples to be cited include the myriad of buildings designed in the Santa Fe district of Mexico City that, at the time, became one of the new centers of financial activity and information economy based on the emerging globalization. Emblematic are office buildings and shopping centers that are modeled primarily on their North American counterparts (see 1994-b entry).

The third expression of Mexican postmodernism is tied to a monumental tradition that is indebted to pre-Hispanic architecture but also to Le Corbusier's post–World War II turn to exposed and expressive reinforced concrete. As we know, the importance of and presence of Le Corbusier in Mexican architecture extends as far back as the 1920s (see 1933 entry), as does the interest in incorporating pre-Columbian forms, which were most polemically addressed in the 1929 Mexican pavilion for the Ibero-American Exhibition (see 1929-a entry) or in Alberto Arai's handball courts for UNAM (see 1952 entry). A more recent example of

the integration of both can be seen in Pedro Ramírez Vázquez's National Museum of Anthropology (see 1964-b box) where free-plan spaces, utilized for museographic purposes, surround a pre-Hispanic-inspired and -decorated central courtyard.

Following many of these tendencies is the work of Teodoro González de León. According to the North American critic Richard Ingersoll, this work can be characterized as "neo-Aztec."[2] As an architectural student, González de León was on the winning team—along with Armando Franco and Enrique Molinar—for the design of the Ciudad Universitaria competition held in 1946 (see 1952 entry). By 1947, having received a scholarship, he traveled to Paris, where he worked for Le Corbusier between 1947 and 1949 as the latter was finishing his design for the Unité d'Habitation (Marseilles, 1947–1952). Upon his return to Mexico, González de León developed work that was characterized by different formal and stylistic explorations: from glass boxes inspired by Mies van der Rohe, to designs that incorporate various Corbusian elements and forms, to apartment complexes that—like the work of Louis Kahn—utilize service towers to define interior spaces while providing a monumental appearance on the exterior. Along with Abraham Zabludovsky,

González de León developed a new architectural language that would become emblematic of a monumental postmodernism. The works from the early to mid-1970s are composed of geometrically stark and pure volumes constructed in reinforced concrete. For the Colegio de México (Mexico City, 1974–1976), the primary organizational system is a courtyard that, for González de León, references both colonial and pre-Hispanic plazas. Given the 42-foot grade change in the site, that central open space becomes subdivided into a series of platforms that allow access into the different programs and levels of the building. In addition, the design introduces a triangular geometry in plan to make the experience of moving from the large open entry portico through the courtyard more dynamic. The concrete used for the construction is hand chiseled to expose the marble aggregate, giving it, in the

words of González de León, a "warm, craft-like texture akin to that of natural stones, reflecting the fact that human hands have been at work on it."[3] Through these last elements, the work becomes less monolithic and signals a return to the importance of the handicrafts of construction. A similar organizational system and approach to handicrafts is present in J. Francisco Serrano's campus for the Universidad Iberoamericana (Mexico City, 1981–1987) that is arranged around a multilevel central courtyard. Like its predecessor, the Colegio de México, the layout of the campus also uses diagonals as a compositional method. Its stepped terraces create a dynamic spatial sense that also allows access to the surrounding structures at differing levels. And, while the structure is built with reinforced concrete, the most notable differences from the Colegio de México is the use of brick as cladding and infill throughout, giving the different zones and elements a unified and coherent reading.

Although it's easy to see how these examples—formally, materially, and spatially—could be characterized as neo-Aztec, it is truly the work of Agustín Hernández that is most emblematic of this and even of a "Hi-Tec Aztecón" (Aztec High-Tech). Hernández, by using contemporary technologies, generates forms that pre-Columbian people had built in the past. The Heroico Colegio Militar (National Military Academy; Mexico City, 1973–1976) demonstrates this clearly not only because of its overall organization around a large open plaza—reminiscent of the main plaza in Monte Alban, Oaxaca—but also because many of the buildings that surround the plaza—in addition to those that make up the whole complex—have glass curtain wall façades that angle inward to give a pyramidal profile. In other cases, the forms are monolithic constructions with continuous horizontal bands of windows that subdivide the buildings' masses. One particular structure appears to be a typical International-style building, with horizontal windows and expressive floor slabs, that has tipped over and, thus, appears pyramidal. The most emblematic is the Administration Building, which, formally, looks like an enormous pre-Hispanic mask: its mouth composed of a reinforced concrete tribune, eyes made of cantilevered and angled volumes with horizontal windows, the nose of a protruding volume with glass openings. Paradigmatic of the coming together of extreme future and past, the Military Academy's architecture—which inspired the forms of the Tyrell Corporation in a dystopian future Los Angeles

Carlos Mijares, interior of Christ Church, Mexico City, 1991–1992.

in Ridley Scott's *Blade Runner* (1982)—was used in the futuristic film *Total Recall* (1990).

The final variant of Mexican postmodernism, the work of Carlos Mijares, has had the fewest repercussions and is, perhaps, the most difficult to stylistically characterize. This work is most akin to that of the Uruguayan architect and engineer Eladio Dieste and, like it, features formal manipulation of space based on the use of brick to make primarily industrial architecture and religious buildings (see 1955 entry). In structures such as the Mortuary Chapel (Jungapeo, Michoacán, 1982–1985) or the Christ Church (Mexico City, 1991–1992), the central feature is a hyperarticulated roof plane composed of elaborate brick pendentives, in the first, and overlapping brick arches, in the second. In both cases, the spans of the brick structure allow for the simple square plan to rotate as it moves upward, creating a visual effect reminiscent of the baroque architecture of Guarino Guarini or Piranesian spatial layering. While the material and inspiration is based on local traditions of construction, the work is hardly regionalist and difficult to define as characteristically Mexican.

FURTHER READING

Ingersoll, "Mexican Architecture at the End of the Millennium."
Toca Fernández, *México: Nueva arquitectura.*

1977-A

ÉOLO MAIA, CAPELA DE SANTANA AO PÉ DO MORRO

THROUGHOUT HIS SIXTY YEARS of life and thirty-five years as an architect, Éolo Maia has witnessed a series of major transformations in Brazilian architecture. Born in Ouro Preto in 1942, the same year the Museum of Modern Art's *Brazil Builds* exhibition was being organized, Maia's architecture was hugely influenced by that generation of Brazilian modernists. His work, however, never achieved the same international exposure. Attending architecture school in Belo Horizonte, Maia struggled with modernist dogma and the turbulent times in Brazil. With a curriculum that strongly emphasized program and functionality to be materialized with a given vocabulary, the school allowed few opportunities for abstraction or experimentation. Maia's work in the early 1970s was highly influenced by Vilanova Artigas's brutalist aesthetic and Louis Kahn's playful use of cylindrical volumes and circular fenestration. This can be seen, for example, in Ouro Branco, where Maia was a member of the team that designed the city expansion adjacent to the Açominas steel plant (1977).

In Ouro Branco, Maia also designed the Verdes Mares hotel (1977–1979). The plan is a cruciform, and its organization resembles many of Kahn's buildings. In Ouro Branco, he had the chance to design a metallic enclosure around the ruins of an old church that would later be considered his *opera prima*, the Capela de Santana ao Pé do Morro (1977–1980).

The Açominas steel company owned a large property, used as a forest reserve, where the ruins of a late eighteenth-century chapel in an advanced stage of deterioration were located. Only a few adobe walls survived on top of the stone foundations. The project brief called for the stabilization of the ruins (to be covered) so that the space could be used every once in a while for religious events. Maia exposed the stone foundations on the outside and built a pebbled pavement inside. To protect the adobe walls, he designed a metal structure that hovered over the ruins. This is partially flat at the entry and becomes pitched and increases in height as it reaches the altar. Wooden trellises are used in the ceiling, and as they descend from the metal beams above, they enclose the

Éolo Maia, Capela de Santana, Ouro Branco, 1976.

Éolo Maia, interior of Capela de Santana, Ouro Branco, 1976.

space between the new roof and the old walls. Red and blue colored glass is used in some of those openings, modulating the light inside during the day. The Santana Chapel with its rusted-steel structure and colored-glass panels became famous for its elegant proportions, material experimentation, and sensitivity to the old ruins.

This spirit of experimentation and respect for the existing built environment was a new attitude, not often encountered in the Brazilian architecture of those years (see 1985-b entry). Maia's work in the 1970s also reveals an intense dedication to drawing as a design strategy that would instigate an insistent search for a local identity in response to the exhaustion of the modernist ideals.

In that regard, it is important to point out that Éolo Maia always struggled with identity, fusing together the colonial architecture of his native Ouro Preto with new materials and a contemporary sensibility. A pioneer in advocating for postmodernity in an environment that was still mired in the inertia of Brasília, Maia galvanized around him a group of architects that would lead the way toward the revision of the modernist paradigm in Brazil (see 1979 entry). His architectural activism made him a nationally known figure, an embodiment of Brazilian postmodernism.

1977-B

BRUNO STAGNO HOUSE, COSTA RICA

WHEN THE CHILEAN ARCHITECT Bruno Stagno arrived in Costa Rica in 1973 after studying architecture at the Catholic University in Santiago, Chile (1962–1967), and doing graduate studies at the École des Beaux-Arts in Paris (1969–1972), the climate shock was such that, in his words, he had to rethink everything he had learned about architecture up to that point. A native of Santiago, Chile, the architecture he had studied was one that was supposed to keep the heat inside. In Costa Rica, however, the exact opposite was needed: to ventilate as much as possible in order to allow the humidity and heat to escape.

Working at first with a late modernist vocabulary of reinforced concrete structure with brick infill, Stagno began investigating shading and ventilation devices that could be produced out of those materials by an uneducated and poorly trained workforce. His own house, designed in 1977, is an example of that. A rationalist plan organizes the ground floor in three interlocking bars: the front, housing the library and two bedrooms; the middle,

the social area; and the back, the service area. The bars are built with large concrete beams over infill masonry walls. A second and more private floor houses the master bedroom and the TV room. The structural independence allows the masonry walls to be carved out for light and ventilation up to the point where they become column-like (this is the case in the covered verandas and other transition spaces). The texture and character of the exposed concrete and brick give the house a regionalist quality, but the real adaptation lies in the generous shade and ventilation strategies of the transition spaces where the walls are dematerialized.

Adopting a discourse very much aligned with Alexander Tzonis, Liane Lefaivre, and Kenneth Frampton, Stagno described his architecture as an act of resistance against globalizing aesthetic influences in favor of climatically responsive solutions. Paradoxically, his buildings departed

Bruno Stagno, Stagno House, San José, Costa Rica, 1977.

modernism of 1960s Brazil. From both Filgueiras Lima and Vilanova Artigas (his inspiration during his school years), Maia learned to use materiality as a means of expression to counter the current dogma. Experimenting with Corten steel, vitrified ceramic tiles, and enamel surfaces (sometimes on the same building), Maia found pluralism to be the means for reconciling context with originality.

Another novelty in the pages of *Pampulha* was a spirit of experimentation and respect for the existing built environment. The country had built a lot in the previous thirty years, and by the mid-1970s, architects were calling for preservation, aware that the tabula rasa of modernism was having adverse effects on Brazil's cultural heritage. During the so-called economic miracle (1969–1973), the pressure to build fast combined with military rule resulted in the demolition of several architectural jewels from earlier times. In addition, contemporary sociological research on informal settlements was showing the damage that policies of demolition and relocation were causing. Those different influences converged into an awareness of the existing built environment in a broader sense, challenging a new generation of architects used to smaller and more contextually specific interventions. They were, after all, postmodernists, and the universal discourses of modernity were being questioned, giving way to localized solutions.

In a region very proud of its baroque eighteenth-century architecture, Éolo Maia, Sylvio de Podestá, and Jô Vasconcellos would use quotations and collages to the extreme (see 1977-a box). Shifting from program to form allowed them to expand their architectural vocabulary, embracing a kind of locally based postmodernism that would become the trademark of the so-called *pós-mineiridade*, or a postmodernism characteristic of the state of Minas Gerais. In a way, being far from São Paulo and Rio de Janeiro gave them more freedom to experiment. To work under the shadow of Niemeyer in Rio de Janeiro or Vilanova Artigas in São Paulo would have certainly limited their compositional palette. In Belo Horizonte, however, a strong regional pride and a less stratified construction industry allowed them to sell their elaborate drawings and designs to local developers. The early experiments first shown in the pages of *Pampulha* magazine would become materialized throughout the city.

Later, in the midst of the postmodern 1980s, the compositional freedom of historic quotations and formal collages allowed them to play their *mineiro* identity to the extreme. In their architecture, the translation from their collages is evident in the way they added arches and antennas to high-rise buildings and in the attentive (and many times excessive) detailing of the surfaces as they showed a combination of materials and colors. The Rainha da Sucata building (Maia and Podestá, 1984–1992), for instance, uses Corten steel, colored glass, azulejos (ceramic tiles), and an object that looks like a giant sliced orange that works as a ventilation shaft for the basement. Most of their buildings became landmarks and referential points in the city, and it is hard to know if this is due to their singularity or to some higher level of identity. In any case, the buildings establish a dialogue with their territory through direct formal quotations in ways that few other architects were able to do. Such imagery would elevate Maia and Podestá to the national scene, and thousands of Brazilian architects educated in the 1980s would attempt to emulate and draw like them.

In 1983, lacking financial support, *Pampulha* ceased operations after publishing twelve issues. By that time, Maia, Podestá, and Hardy had become nationally recognized, for they embodied spontaneity and stood for collage-based compositional strategies and a commitment to drawing that were radically new in the Brazilian scene.

At some point, reacting against the economic power of São Paulo, other Brazilian architects aligned themselves with the *mineiro* group, calling for a regional diversity, a novelty in Brazil at the time. This was happening at the same time that Kenneth Frampton's early writings on "critical regionalism" were being debated, the Buenos Aires Biennial (see 1985-a entry) was taking place, and Brazil was returning to civil government (1985). Brazil's new constitution (1988) helped propel the ideal of regionalism by placing the decision-making power at the municipal level, in a way reconnecting architecture with the international postmodern scene. Modernism could not be used as a single recipe anymore, and before the modernist aesthetic was revived in the 1990s, local diversity reigned in Brazil (see 1991 entry).

FURTHER READING

Lara, "Éolo Maia's Hybrid Architecture: The Crossroads of Information."

Santa-Cecilia, *Éolo Maia: Complexidade e contradição na arquitetura brasileira.*

1980

THE PRITZKER ARCHITECTURE PRIZE IS AWARDED TO LUIS BARRAGÁN, AND PHOTOGRAPHY IS AT THE CENTER OF THE MYTH.

MEXICO

IN 1980, LUIS BARRAGÁN became the second recipient of the Hyatt Foundation's Pritzker Architecture Prize. Established to honor lifetime architectural achievements as a sort of Nobel Prize for architecture, the prize has been awarded at the time of this writing to three architects from Latin America: Barragán, Oscar Niemeyer (1988), and Paulo Mendes da Rocha (2006). For many, the award to Barragán was something of a surprise, since his work had been, for a long time, largely unknown to many outside of Mexico. Yet, as a result of the now mythical exhibition of his work at the Museum of Modern Art (MoMA) in 1976, the prize rested to a large degree on the way Barragán's work had been photographically presented to the jury and the strong evocations its images made.

The success of MoMA's one-man show dedicated to Barragán was proof of the power of the photographs. After all, it was the first exhibition to present the work of an architect through slides.[1] Organized by the Argentine architect and curator of design of the museum, Emilio Ambasz, the exhibition ran from June 4 to September 7, 1976. More important for its dissemination was the 128-page catalogue, *The Architecture of Luis Barragán*, also by Ambasz, containing ninety-four images and some explanatory text. This book would become the de facto and only monograph on the architect's work—lacking any other formalized publications. In his acceptance speech for the Pritzker Prize, one of the few documents explaining his ideas, Barragán referenced Ambasz's book.

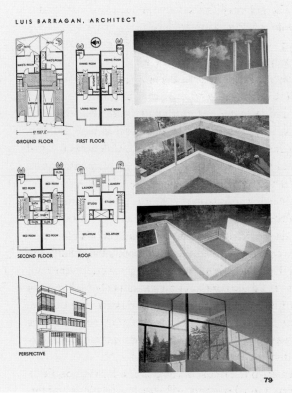

Publication of Barragán's early functionalist houses, 1937.

Ambasz referred to Barragán's work as anti-intellectual and socially uncommitted, alleging instead that Barragán preferred to deal with actions rather than with polemics.[2] Barragán himself, in his speech accepting the Pritzker Prize, further placed his work in the realm of the spiritual, magical, and poetic—characteristics autonomous from the real material conditions of its production. However, as the images reproduced in the museum's publication show, it was a work that had been carefully positioned by Barragán within contemporary strategies of marketing, advertisement, and spectacularization to transform it into a complex system of meanings based on tradition and an idealized presentation of "Mexicanness" intended to profit him.[3] What is more, the interpretation of the photographs—or, rather, the way their open-endedness can be understood by the viewer—has been central for the success of Barragán's work.

Barragán's interest in and use of photography in this way can be seen beginning in the period of his speculative functionalist architecture of the 1930s. This work provided him with the formal modernist architectural vocabulary that he would advocate and continue to develop throughout his lifetime, but also with the capital to permit him to become involved in other, larger, more speculative ventures. To capture this work, Barragán commissioned Lola Álvarez Bravo to photograph some of the houses for publication, and some were published in a 1937 special issue of *The Architectural Record* edited by Esther Born and dedicated to Mexico's modern architecture.[4] These, and unpublished images that are now part of the Barragán Foundation, show the everydayness of Barragán's house—windows, handrails, water tanks, etc.—through photographs that evoke the radical viewpoints characteristic of photos by the Soviet artist Aleksandr Rodchenko. These images, in turn, serve as instruments for a radical reconceptualization of visuality, challenging the way one sees the minutiae of the everyday and architecture itself. The photographs, in this way, transform the expectations of both by radicalizing the International style from the banality of speculative ventures into something more poetically consumable. As historian Keith Eggener argues: "These photos present fragments but provide little sense of how these might be fitted together into a whole; the floor plans published alongside the photos offer little guidance as to their interpretation . . . these photos investigate the camera's ability to manipulate architectural form."[5]

For the design, marketing, and construction of the massive Jardines del Pedregal de San Ángel residential subdivision (between 1945 and 1953; see 1947-a entry), Barragán turned to Armando Salas Portugal, who became its "official photographer," to document the site both for its design and for an active promotional campaign organized by Barragán and his associates. Salas Portugal was asked to photograph the spaces "abstractly," creating carefully framed yet fragmentary and surreal photographs. By emphasizing the character and serenity of the newly modified landscape and its architecture, these photographs became central to the marketing campaign of El Pedregal, touting the subdivision to Mexicans and foreigners alike as the "ideal place to live."

According to Eggener, by using devices of and references to marketing and fashion photography and scenography, Barragán transformed the lived reality of the site into a spectacular representation, especially since it was through these photographs that Barragán intended to preserve the ideal expression of the place. In the photographs of El Pedregal, surrealism was an important reference, both personal and logistical. Surrealism, at the time, was exalted for its marketing potential ("the basic appeals so dear to the advertiser's heart"[6]), its consciousness about tradition, and its inherent mnemonic qualities central for a project of cultural continuation and commemoration. Surely, Barragán's intention was to ultimately present a vision of Arcadia accessible to a limited sector of the population. Likewise, for a project in Majahua, Colima (1953), Salas Portugal shot a number of photographs of tree roots, driftwood, and ocean rocks to complement Barragán's few sketches. In the end, the limited accessibility of his architecture was to be the central contradiction of his work. By using references to vernacular folk traditions and forms, it was to be a popular and appealing architecture (and characteristically "Mexican"), yet by virtue of its social inaccessibility to the population at large and its limited reach, this architecture was not populist.

It should not surprise us, then, that the Museum of Modern Art's exhibition and its accompanying catalogue focused primarily on the later work of Barragán (what we have already referred to as the third phase; see 1947-a entry). Although the book contains some examples of his earlier work, these are sparsely presented both in the amount of information and the number of photographs about them. The latter, however, have a quality similar to those of the other

Luis Barragán, interior of chapel for the Capuchinas Sacramentarias del Purísimo Corazón de María with triptych by Mathias Goeritz, Tlalpan, Mexico City, 1952–1955.

projects referenced above: they are simple and incredibly evocative, yet largely uninformative of what the projects are really like.[7]

What is presented through limited text and mostly full-page photographs is the work spanning from 1945 to 1968: El Pedregal, the Barragán House, the Chapel in Tlalpan, the Torres de Satélite (with Mathias Goeritz), Las Arboledas and Los Clubes subdivisions, and the San Cristóbal stables and house. Taken mostly by

Salas Portugal, the photographs present incomplete yet evocative views of the projects. In many, it is hard to discern what functionality the space or object presented has. Although floor plans are included in the "List of Works" section, these are difficult to match with what the photographs show. And though most of the photographs are black and white, the ones in color give a sense of the rich and bright colors that would become emblematic of Barragán's color palette—which, as he would note in his Pritzker Prize speech, was associated with Mexico and its culture.

In the catalogue, the presentation of El Pedregal emphasizes primarily the rocky character of the place and the demonstration gardens built in it. For his house (Mexico, 1947), the roof terrace—which has no views into the surrounding context and which appears completely isolated—is highlighted. Also shown are the public spaces, such as the entry hall, the reception room, and the library with its cantilevered stair. For the chapel for the Capuchinas Sacramentarias del Purísimo Corazón de María (Tlalpan, Mexico, 1952–1955), the views of the interior are limited to those looking toward the altar (with a triptych designed by Mathias Goeritz), whose color, a bright ochre, is the result not only of the choice of paint hue but of the yellow stained-glass window that Goeritz designed for

Luis Barragán and Mathias Goeritz, Torres de Satélite, State of Mexico, 1957.

the space. Also shown for this project are some of the ancillary spaces surrounding the holy space (including the garden and fountain). Next are the Satélite Towers (State of Mexico, 1957), urban markers for a new residential subdivision, which were designed in association with Goeritz (see 1953-b entry). These are five triangular towers of varying heights painted in different hues of orange that harmonize with the images of the chapel (although the towers, ultimately, would be painted in different colors). The projects for the subdivisions (1958–1968) are peculiar in their focus not on the overall character of the places but on some of the individual elements that occupy them, such as plazas, fountains, water troughs with freestanding walls, and entry portals. The color palette here is made up of bright colors (electric blue and Mexican pink, for example) that contrast with the natural color of the earth and trees. The most emblematic, because of the predominance of color photographs, are the stables, pool, and house that he built for the Egerstrom family at San Cristóbal (Los Clubes, State of Mexico, 1967–1968). Here, the scale of the built walls is matched to the scale of the human on horseback. The colors are bright: Mexican pink of various hues and intensity, violet, and orange. Elements seen in the earlier projects—water troughs, reflecting pools, fountains—are prominently displayed. The house, a large part of the project, is hinted at through views of the exterior walls, but no interior photographs are shown.

The Mexican pinks, reds, yellows, etc., used in the later projects ultimately became associated with his work. Intended to serve as an index to the popular forms of Mexican architecture, festivals, clothing, and artifacts, these were, according to Barragán, based on natural elements—fruits, plants, and flowers—derived from Mexican geography and nature as well as elements that were rooted in Mediterranean traditions. Barragán claimed to use the colors in traditional and contextually specific ways: for him, when using a color, "suddenly a memory would explode in my mind about some Mexican celebration, a stand in some market, the brightness of a fruit, of a watermelon, of a small wooden horse."[8] Because of Barragán's prominence, these colors became emblematic of Mexican architecture in the 1970s and 1980s and were used by a generation of architects practicing there (see 1976 entry).

References to and use of elements from his childhood, such as the doors, water troughs, aqueducts, and fountains of his family's ranch in Guadalajara,

Luis Barragán, Egerstrom Stables, Los Clubes, State of Mexico, 1967–1968.

Jalisco, were also part of Barragán's attempt to reconstitute a historical memory. Barragán would describe his architecture and landscapes as a means to reconcile his past with the present, as a project of cultural commemoration and continuation that would only be possible through a self-consciousness about tradition. For Barragán, this operation was about countering the characteristics of modernity; as he would later state, his desire was to "find a formula so man could be calm in his home, so that he could recover from the aggressions of the city."[9] In response, he invoked silence, religiosity, serenity, and solitude in his work—elements that would become mythically associated with it.[10]

In the end, Barragán's model offers a renewed and antimodernist position centered on contemplative reception. And, while the contemplation was to occur within the spaces that he built, few were privy to those spaces. As a result, the photographic representations were imbued with the characteristics that he sought. In a way, to invoke "the silence that sings" in his fountains, or the serene quality of the work, as he did in his Pritzker speech, was akin to promoting the purely visual character of the photograph. Barragán's continuous use of spectacular images and the constant spectacularization of his work provokes in the viewer a continuous reliance and investment on something outside of the materiality of architecture for a metaphorical meaning. As a result, the location of Barragán's architecture, then, has always been in the photographs and the imaginary that they create.

FURTHER READING

Ambasz, *The Architecture of Luis Barragán*.
Carranza, "Machinating the Quotidian: Luis Barragán's *La Revolución Callada*."
Eggener, *Luis Barragán's Gardens of El Pedregal*.
Smith, *Builders in the Sun: Five Mexican Architects*.
Zanco, *Luis Barragán: The Quiet Revolution*.

1983

NIEMEYER RETURNS TO RIO DE JANEIRO TO DESIGN THE SAMBÓDROMO AND THE CIEPS: ARCHITECTURE GETS CLOSER TO POPULAR NEEDS.

BRAZIL

OSCAR NIEMEYER was back in Rio de Janeiro in 1983. To be more precise, he was back on March 15, 1983, the day Leonel Brizola and Darcy Ribeiro took office as governor and vice governor of the state of Rio de Janeiro. After a fifteen-year hiatus, Brazil's most recognized architect was again working for the current government, as he had done from 1936 to 1967 (see 1941 entry).

Interestingly enough, it was 1983 but it could have been 1963, since all the actors were the same. Leonel Brizola, the newly elected governor of Rio de Janeiro, had been governor of Rio Grande do Sul twenty years before (and brother-in-law of president João Goulart). Darcy Ribeiro, now vice governor, had served as minister of education (1962–1963) and president of the University of Brasília (1963–1964). Oscar Niemeyer was as famous in 1963 as he was in 1983. It was as if the military dictatorship had served as a twenty-one-year intermission.

In reality, many things changed during those years, and the dictatorship did not presuppose exact interruptions. Although Ribeiro was arrested right after the change of power in 1964 and Brizola fled to Uruguay days later, Niemeyer continued his routine for about a year. In 1965, he and about two hundred faculty members from the University of Brasília resigned together in protest against the new regime. At the time, Niemeyer's design for Brasília's airport was canceled, the air force commander stating that communist architects should go work in Moscow. Nevertheless, Niemeyer continued working on many projects in Brasília until 1967, including, paradoxically, the Ministry of Defense headquarters.

In 1968, with the political repression worsening, Niemeyer's office in Rio—which also served as headquarters of *Módulo* magazine—was invaded by the police, with documents confiscated and collaborators arrested. Niemeyer himself was taken into custody a few times for "depositions" but was not formally arrested nor was his professional license revoked as had

happened to many others. At that time, his friend André Malraux, the French minister of culture, arranged for French president Charles de Gaulle to issue a special license by decree allowing Niemeyer to practice architecture in France. Niemeyer formed SEPARC—Societé d'Études pour les Projets d'Architecture (Society for the Study of Architecture Projects)—whose office functioned from 1972 to 1978 at Champs-Élysées *número noventa* (no. 90). The major works from those times are the French Communist Party headquarters (Paris, 1967–1981), the Mondadori publisher's building (Milan, 1968–1975), the employment office (Bobigny, France, 1972–1976), the Cultural Center (Le Havre, France, 1972–1983), and the University of Constantine in Algeria (1969–1972).

During this time, Niemeyer continued working in Brazil and, unlike other political exiles, traveling freely back and forth (although spending most of his time in Paris). The long list of works he designed in Brazil includes a series of apartment buildings at Barra da Tijuca (1973) and the tragically unfinished project for an exhibition hall in Belo Horizonte, where sixty-nine workers died on February 4, 1971, when the roof slab collapsed.[1] The 1970s were definitely not the best decade for Niemeyer, in particular, or for Brazilian architecture, in general.

But in 1979, an amnesty law allowed all political exiles to return to Brazil. Brizola and Ribeiro came back, along with so many others. The gubernatorial elections of 1982 were a significant step toward full political normality, and the opposition won the most important states: São Paulo, Rio de Janeiro, and Minas Gerais. São Paulo and Minas would be governed by the center-right Partido do Movimento Democrático Brasileiro (PMDB; Brazilian Democratic Movement Party), while Rio de Janeiro moved further to the left with the election of Brizola and Ribeiro from the Partido Democrático Trabalhista (PDT; Democratic Labor Party). Brizola's proposal in 1982 was to implement a "brown socialism" (*socialismo moreno*), a softer version

The Sambódromo during construction, Rio de Janeiro, 1984.

of the old dogmatism of the 1960s revolutionary proposals. Twenty years later, the cracks in communist regimes had been exposed and the enthusiasm for Soviet-style planning and Cuban-style mass mobilization had faded. At the same time, there was no sympathy in Brazil for the Chicago-born and Chilean-implemented model of market-oriented reforms.

Two projects commissioned from Niemeyer in 1983 became the physical materialization of such *socialismo moreno*: the CIEPs (see below) and the Sambódromo (Sambadrome). In a way, they were the bread-and-circus of Brizola's administration. Of the two, the Sambadrome was, indeed, Niemeyer's most extravagant commission.

It is impossible to underestimate the importance

of carnival festivities in Brazil's identity, and Rio de Janeiro's parade is its most famous manifestation. The segregated parades of the 1920s (whites at Avenida Rio Branco, blacks at Praça Onze) evolved in the 1930s into a competition of samba groups (*escolas de samba*) under the leadership of Afro-Brazilian community organizations. At the same time, the elite retreated to private clubs. When Praça Onze was demolished in 1942, the parade moved to the new Avenida Presidente Vargas. By the 1960s, the parade had moved again to Rua Marques de Sapucaí, which had been provided with a scaffolding structure of bleachers and private balconies built yearly for the event. By then, Rio de Janeiro's carnival parade was a huge business that attracted hundreds of thousands of tourists to the city and was viewed by millions on television. Darcy Ribeiro had the idea to create a permanent seating

Arc at Praça da Apoteóse, Sambódromo, during construction,
Rio de Janeiro, 1984.

structure for the event in order to avoid the yearly cost
of assembling and disassembling a gigantic temporary
structure. For the other 361 days of the year, Ribeiro
proposed that a public school occupy the space under
the bleachers.

The original design for the Passarela do Samba,
popularly known as the Sambódromo, had seats on
both sides of a quarter-mile-long street, with a wider
plaza at the end. By 1983, slightly more than half of the
seating structure was built, enough to accommodate
60,000 people. For the plaza at the end, called Praça
da Apoteóse (Apotheosis Square), Niemeyer designed a
90 ft. (27 m) tall trilegged arch that became the symbol
of Rio de Janeiro's carnival parade. In 2011, the city of
Rio de Janeiro demolished an old factory nearby and
began the construction of more bleachers that will
increase the seating capacity to 80,000 spectators and
serve as the finish line for the marathon of the 2016
Olympic Games in Rio de Janeiro.

But not only was the "circus" commissioned from
Niemeyer. The "bread" of Brizola's *socialismo moreno*
included a truly revolutionary educational concept: the
Centros Integrados de Educação Pública (CIEP; Integrated Centers for Public Education). Darcy Ribeiro
was again the man behind the idea. Since the 1930s,
both public and private education in Brazil was limited

only to half days. That schedule allowed the government and schools to automatically double the number
of seats by teaching half the children in the morning
and the other half in the afternoon. Ribeiro was vocally
against this strategy and advocated building schools
in the poorest neighborhoods of Rio de Janeiro with
enough infrastructure to support six hours of classes
plus sports, cultural activities, and medical and dental
care. The CIEPs would operate from 8:00 a.m. to 5:00
p.m., and the children would get three meals per day
and a shower before going back home.

Architecturally, Niemeyer wanted to "reinvent the
school building, to design something that made no reference to old schools."[2] Despite his rhetoric, the CIEPs'
innovation resides not so much in their architecture
as in their program and their construction methods.
The generic school program was broken into three
volumes: the main classroom building, the library, and
the gym. The main building is a two- or three-story-
high rectangular volume to accommodate between six
hundred and one thousand students, depending on local demands, with a double-loaded corridor with twelve
classrooms on each floor. In addition, this structure is
raised on *pilotis* to create a covered recess area; a small
medical clinic is located on one side and the cafeteria
complex on the other, bookending the ground floor
of the main volume. The library has a hexagonal plan
and works as an independent part of the composition

that can be placed anywhere in the complex. The gym is composed of two parts, an open box 100 ft. (30 m) long, 60 ft. (18 m) wide, and 30 ft. (9 m) tall with columns along the longer sides spaced every 15 feet (4.6 m); and a smaller rectangle that encloses the locker rooms and a multifunctional hall. The two parts can be arranged differently according to specific site conditions, and the bleachers are built where they intersect, covered by the big box roof and supported by the walls of the smaller volume. A ramp occupies a central location in each building, and the bathrooms are placed at the extremities of each floor.

As noted above, the other important innovation of the CIEPs is the use of prefabricated semi-industrialized components in reinforced concrete. In order to build fast and to achieve economies of scale, Niemeyer and Ribeiro called upon João Filgueiras Lima. Filgueiras Lima (see 1953-c entry) had worked with Niemeyer in Brasília and had, since the late 1960s, become the Brazilian authority on concrete prefabrication. By 1983, Filgueiras Lima had two factories operating, one in Salvador and one in Rio de Janeiro, making prefabricated reinforced concrete building parts. For the CIEPs, he was invited to provide the technology for the concrete's formwork and to produce smaller components (window panels and furniture). Various construction companies were contracted to build the CIEPs, using the technology developed by Filgueiras Lima, and to prefabricate columns, beams, and slabs for a few schools at a time. Between 1984 and 1987 and 1991 and 1994 (the two terms Brizola served as governor of Rio de Janeiro), 406 CIEPs were built, serving 425,000 students.

By far, the CIEPs were certainly the most socially oriented project of Niemeyer's long and prolific career. Sadly, the CIEPs were abandoned and disinvested after the end of Brizola and Ribeiro's terms in office. The reasons for the failure of the CIEPs are many, and critics blame the architecture on many levels.

View of CIEP, Rio de Janeiro, 1986.

The CIEPs' spatial concept requires large sites. This means that the design cannot adapt to the hilly favelas. The cost of land forced the government to build CIEPs at the periphery of the city, which has its share of poverty but lacks the density of the downtown favelas. Architecturally problematic is the fact that to increase cross ventilation, the walls between the classrooms and the corridor stop two feet short of the ceiling, creating severe noise problems. Finally, investment in prefabricated components ended after the last building was erected in 1994, making maintenance or any kind of renovation to them very expensive. Ironically, 1982 was the year with the largest birth rate in Brazil. The demand for elementary and middle-school education (in number of seats) has slowly diminished, and, now, the challenge is centered on the quality of the education. In that context, the architectural value of the CIEPs—fast, economical construction—matters less than the environmental qualities of the space—poor by any account.

Meanwhile, the Sambadrome became one more symbolic space for Rio de Janeiro. The "circus" had more impact than the "bread," unfortunately. After those projects in Rio de Janeiro in the 1980s, Niemeyer continued working for almost every Brazilian politician. The Memorial da América Latina (Latin America Memorial) was commissioned by São Paulo's governor Orestes Quercia in 1987. The Museu de Arte Contemporânea (MAC; Contemporary Art Museum) in Niterói was commissioned by Mayor Jorge Roberto Silveira in 1989. The Curitiba Museum was commissioned by Paraná governor Jaime Lerner in 1999. The Administrative Center of Minas Gerais was commissioned by the Minas Gerais governor Aécio Neves in 2005.

Those late works never had the same level of inventiveness and elegance as Pampulha and Brasília. The military dictatorship was not just an intermission but a major disruption in Niemeyer's career. His team of contributors never achieved the level it had before the exile, because the architects that he attracted in the 1950s and 1960s became dispersed and never reunited. Without a dedicated and talented team, Niemeyer's later architecture (post-1980) appears to have been designed in a hurry, inadequately detailed, and poorly built. In Pampulha (see 1941 entry) and in many of his buildings in Brasília (see 1956 entry), Niemeyer worked available technology to its limits, pushing the materiality to achieve the sophisticated spatiality of his sketches. In his later works, the freehand sketches are translated to drawings without much concern for tectonics, which, in turn, makes the buildings seem old even before inauguration.

Niemeyer was back in business in 1983, but his business would never be the same.

FURTHER READING

Niemeyer, *Conversa de arquiteto.*
Philippou, *Oscar Niemeyer: Curves of Irreverence.*
Underwood, *Oscar Niemeyer and the Architecture of Brazil.*

1983-A

RAMÓN GUTIÉRREZ PUBLISHES *ARQUITECTURA Y URBANISMO EN IBEROAMÉRICA*.

COVERING THE 1492 ARRIVAL of the Spanish until 1980, *Arquitectura y urbanismo en Iberoamérica* by Ramón Gutiérrez is the first comprehensive study of Latin American architecture and urbanism. In it, Gutiérrez succeeded in writing Latin America's inaugural architectural and urban history from an intrinsically Latin American perspective.

Born in Buenos Aires in 1939, Gutiérrez graduated from the University of Buenos Aires in 1963. A prolific author of more than one hundred books and one of the most respected authorities on Latin American eighteenth- and nineteenth-century architecture, he would later create the Centro de Documentación de Arquitectura Latinoamericana (CEDODAL; Center for the Documentation of Latin American Architecture) in 1995. The CEDODAL library is, to this day, the best collection on Latin American architecture, with over 30,000 books and 15,000 periodicals.

Arquitectura y urbanismo en Iberoamérica is a 776-page book that devotes its first 500 pages to the four centuries that followed the conquest (Gutiérrez's main research focus), with detailed analysis of colonial architecture and an even more detailed discussion of nineteenth-century structures. Worth noting is how little space the author devotes to pre-Columbian structures, despite the complex syncretism and hybridity present in sixteenth-century Mexican and Peruvian structures. Ultimately, the Iberian and European character is emphasized to the detriment of the American past.

Despite its focus on premodern architecture, the book is a fundamental resource and reference for understanding twentieth-century productions in relation to their precedents. His chapter on the professional organization of architects during colonial times gives us an amazing insight into contemporary specificities of practice in Latin America. Carpenters, for instance, had a guild organized in Lima as early as 1549 and in Mexico in 1557. Those guilds were structured not only by trade but also by family (which normally overlapped with a certain craft) and followed the European format of masters and apprentices. The work followed a trial-and-error accumulation of knowledge, and very few masters used any drawings at all. The French model of academic training (with drawings as a core skill) was implemented first in Madrid in 1742 and shortly later in Mexico in 1781, only to be unauthorized in 1799 when Spain regained the monopoly over higher education. Although it might seem unimportant from the perspective of the history of twentieth-century architecture, this fact helps explain the insufficient development of local architectural traditions and the continuous education of Latin American architects abroad.

With regard to the twentieth century, Gutiérrez deserves credit for his interest in continuities (despite his focus on the eighteenth and nineteenth centuries) rather than ruptures characteristic of the canonical historiography of modern architecture in Latin America. Brazilians such as Lúcio Costa and Mexicans such as Juan O'Gorman carefully chose some aspects of the past (baroque in Brazil, pre-Columbian in Mexico) to support their modernist project, blatantly disregarding the nineteenth century. Gutiérrez's discussion of classical influences carrying into the 1940s in Brazil, Argentina, and Uruguay provides an important bridge between high modernism and the building traditions of previous generations. In addition, Gutiérrez's attention to local contexts and local building techniques prompted him to be among the first to recognize the importance of Ricardo Porro in Cuba, Eladio Dieste in Uruguay, and Rogelio Salmona in Colombia, giving them as much space as the paradigmatic concrete buildings of Oscar Niemeyer in Brazil and Carlos Raúl Villanueva in Venezuela.

Still not translated into English, *Arquitectura y urbanismo en Iberoamérica* remains the most comprehensive source of information on the first four centuries of Latin American architecture and urbanism.

1983-B

SEVERIANO PORTO, BALBINA ENVIRONMENTAL PROTECTION CENTER, BRAZIL

KNOWN AS THE "Architect of the Amazon," Severiano Porto worked in that region from 1965 to the late 1990s. Born in Minas Gerais, Porto graduated from the Faculdade Nacional de Arquitetura (National School of Architecture; now Federal University of Rio de Janeiro) in 1954. Working in Rio de Janeiro, Porto and his partner Mario Ribeiro probably experienced the hangover left over from a period of intense building activity that included the move of the capital to Brasília in 1960 and the intensified political polarization in the years that followed. In 1964, he accepted the invitation from the governor of the state of Amazonas to work on the renovation of the state's seat of government: the palace at Rio Negro. The project's success brought Porto the commission to design the state's legislative building, followed by schools, administrative buildings, a soccer stadium, and many other structures. Despite settling permanently in Manaus, he continued working with Ribeiro in Rio de Janeiro.

Founded in 1669 near the junction of the Solimões and the Negro Rivers that form the mighty Amazon River, Manaus was only a fortification until the end of the eighteenth century. This would change in the last decades of the nineteenth century with the sudden growth of rubber production. Manaus's Teatro Amazonas (1896) is a testament to the opulence of those times: a large opera

house with seven hundred seats that inspired the movie *Fitzcarraldo* (Werner Herzog, 1982). But after rubber trees were exported to Indonesia and Malaysia, the Amazonian production was marginalized, and Manaus's economy stagnated in the first half of the twentieth century. It was only after the 1964 military coup that an effective plan to develop the region was put in place: the creation of the Zona Franca (a zero-tax incentive for the establishment of assembly plants for electronics) and other infrastructure, transportation, and energy projects.

Severiano Porto arrived in Manaus precisely when that policy was transforming the city and when its population doubled from 170,000 in 1960 to 312,000 in 1970. Dating from his first decade in Manaus, Porto's most significant building was the soccer stadium. Designed for 45,000 spectators, the playing field was placed 33 ft. (10 m) below ground level in order to create an elegant sectional profile and to minimize the urban impact of such a large structure; this also allowed visitors to enter at street level but be at the middle of the stepping concrete rings that make up the bleachers. The stadium was inaugurated in April of 1970 with a local team playing the Brazilian national team—the very same players who, weeks later, would mesmerize the world in Mexico City. Paulo Mendes da Rocha would repeat this strategy of sinking the field in the Serra Dourada stadium (Goiás, 1975).

Starting in 1970, Porto designed the master plan and several buildings for the University of Amazonas. Here, he used a modular system of buildings connected by covered walkways to protect the users from the equatorial sun and daily rainfall. The buildings are constructed using prefabricated concrete pieces (for the living spaces) with an added metallic structure that supports the roof. The ventilation between the concrete volumes and the roof is

Severiano Porto, view of the Balbina Environmental Protection Center, Amazonas, 1983.

Severiano Porto, detail of roof structure at Balbina Environmental Protection Center, Amazonas, 1983.

maximized through the use of vents located at the ridge of the roof. The independent roof structure would become Porto's trademark element. It allowed for maximum ventilation, fundamental for the Amazonian climate, and for flexibility in the organization of the spaces below.

Porto's system would achieve its best results at the Balbina Environmental Protection Center (1983), located about 95 miles (153 km) from Manaus. The structure, designed to house a research center near the Balbina hydroelectric dam, has a meandering wooden roof structure (made, more specifically, of scrapped wood used as tiles; this technique is called *cavaco* in Portuguese). The curvilinear forms of the structure alternate in height as much as in width and connect a series of spaces below. Some of the spaces are open, such as meeting rooms, and others are fully enclosed and air conditioned, such as the laboratories. The building won several awards, including

first prize at the Buenos Aires Biennial in 1985 and *L'Architecture d'Aujourd'hui*'s main award in 1987. Today, the Balbina dam is recognized as the cause of the worst environmental damage in recent Brazilian history. Built on the shallow waters of the Uatumã River, the dam generates less energy than expected, and the 1,000-square-mile lake emits as much methane and carbon dioxide as ten coal-based plants of the same capacity. Marginalized by the energy agency that now builds similar plants with one-tenth of the inundated area, the Environmental Protection Center sits almost empty and badly maintained.

In 2001, Severiano Porto moved back to Niterói, across the bay from Rio de Janeiro. In 2010, Manaus's soccer stadium was demolished to give way to a new arena to be built for the 2014 World Cup that, ironically, has the exact same seating capacity. The same Manaus that inspired him to build such great buildings seems to have learned nothing and is slowly and surely destroying his legacy.

1985-A

IN THE MIDST OF A "NOT-SO-LOST" DECADE . . .

ARGENTINA • BRAZIL • CHILE • MEXICO

IN LOCAL ECONOMIC PARLANCE, the 1980s in Latin America was *la década perdida,* or the lost decade. The 1981 global recession was felt strongly throughout the region. Mexico's default of 1982 combined with higher interest rates in the United States pushed investments away from Latin America. Brazil's economy, after growing 6 percent per year in the 1970s, shrank 13 percent between 1981 and 1984. Argentina's economy went into a recession and similarly shrank 12 percent in the first years of the decade, while debt increased dramatically after the disastrous 1982 invasion of the Islas Malvinas, or Falkland Islands. Politically, however, the 1980s was not a completely lost decade. In January of 1980, Argentina, Brazil, Paraguay, and Chile were all under military dictatorships. By 1991, all four had returned to democratic civilian rule.

And in architecture, it was also not a lost decade at all. Much to the contrary, Latin America seems to have discovered its own architecture in the 1980s with the advent of many biennials and the Seminarios de Arquitectura Latinoamericana (SAL; Latin American Architecture Seminars).

São Paulo's Bienal de Arte Moderna, famous since the early 1950s, would create in 1975 the first "biennial" devoted exclusively to architecture—which, ironically, would take eighteen years to repeat, in 1993. The Chilean Architecture Biennial followed in 1977, and Quito's started the following year. Both survive to this day; the Chilean one, however, focuses primarily on domestic work, while the Ecuadorean one has achieved regional importance since the late 1990s. These took place before the famous Venice Architectural Biennale started its run in 1980.[1] The biennial that would galvanize a movement in Latin America was the one from Buenos Aires, started in 1985.

The Buenos Aires Biennials were organized by Jorge Glusberg, a prominent yet controversial Argentine. In 1969, his lighting fixture business led him to promote architectural events and, eventually, to the leadership of the Centro de Arte y Comunicación (CAYC; Center of Art and Communication), which was originally founded as an artist's workshop. The CAYC platform prompted Glusberg to promote higher ventures endorsing several important exhibitions of international artists in Argentina and of Latin American artists abroad. Working as promoter, curator, and merchant at the same time, Glusberg became one of the most influential figures in the Latin American art scene since the 1970s, and the Architecture Biennials were the climax of his entrepreneurial efforts. From the first (in 1985) to the third (in 1989), the Buenos Aires Biennial brought to Argentina the most celebrated international architects of the time: Mario Botta, Antoine Predock, Oriol Bohigas, Charles Correa, Léon Krier, Richard Rogers, Bruno Zevi, Arata Isozaki, and Richard Meyer, along with Latin Americans Paulo Mendes da Rocha, Enrique Browne, Abraham Zabludovsky, and Juvenal Baracco. Together, they made the Buenos Aires Biennial the best forum for debating regionalism and postmodernism with repercussions beyond the continent.

The story of the Seminarios de Arquitectura Latinoamericana is intertwined with the exhibitions of the Buenos Aires Biennial. The first SAL was organized almost informally during the first Architecture Biennial in 1985.[2] Marina Waisman from Argentina is credited with the initiative, supported by the magazine *Summa+,* the University of Buenos Aires, and the CAYC. The simple fact that Severiano Porto and Joaquim Guedes from Brazil, Rogelio Salmona from Colombia, and Enrique Browne from Chile were around the same table debating with scholars Silvia Arango (Colombia), Ruth Verde Zein (Brazil), Ramón Gutiérrez (Argentina), and William Niño (Venezuela) was absolutely unprecedented. Writing years later, Waisman remembered the moment as a foundational act when Latin American architects—usually well versed in European or North American architecture—realized *with gusto* that their neighbors also had amazing ideas.[3] Reflecting on the center-periphery relationship, Waisman pointed out that while it would be presumptuous (and quite impossible) to aspire to be the center of the world, it was still necessary to become "the center of ourselves."[4]

Indeed, the debates of the initial SALs were in one way or another responding to the idea of critical regionalism that Liane Lefaivre and Alexander Tzonis and, later, Kenneth Frampton, had articulated as early as 1983.

Frampton's proposal, based on Paul Ricoeur's critique of acculturation, was for an "architecture of resistance" that would strive to preserve local cultures from the threat of universalizing currents. For Frampton, universal trends should be combined with local needs and cultural influences to generate an architecture that can respond to both local culture and universal civilization. The core of Frampton's argument was sound, but as many in Latin America would point out, it has been misused to promote a few handpicked architects as personifying critical regionalism and elevating them to the status of cultural representatives. To historian Keith Eggener,

It is ironic that writers discussing the places where these designs appeared so often emphasized one architect's interpretation of the region over all others: Tadao Ando for Japan, Oscar Niemeyer for Brazil, Charles Correa for India and Luis Barragán for Mexico. In other words, a single correct regional style was implied, or imposed, sometimes from inside, more often from outside the region.[5]

Frampton's critical regionalism was thus intensely discussed in Latin America, generating two main responses: one from Argentine Marina Waisman, who taught in Córdoba, and the other from Chilean Cristián Fernández Cox. In the 1980s, Waisman became the leading Argentine critic, combining rigorous building analysis with a refined sensibility for the spirit of the time. Criticizing the frivolous postmodernism of Michael Graves and Hans Hollein and the theoretical

thinness of "deconstructivism," Waisman named the 1980s the "década rosa," or pink decade. All aspirations of slightly transforming the world for the better were gone in the times of Ronald Reagan and Margaret Thatcher, except in Latin America, where inequalities were still rampant. But instead of an "architecture of resistance," as proposed by Frampton, Waisman called for an "architecture of divergence." The subtle difference implied that Latin American architects could consciously choose which elements to adopt and which elements to resist, diverging from North Atlantic trends instead of opposing them.

Chilean architect Cristián Fernández Cox also responded to those debates in a series of articles in which he articulated the idea of *modernidad apropiada* (appropriated modernity). In them, Fernández Cox played with the double meaning of *apropiada* in Spanish, meaning both appropriated and proper, or correct, modernity. Denouncing centuries of an exocentric obsession (constantly looking abroad), Fernández Cox calls for an endocentric attitude and a fresh look that would reveal repressed identities and new categorizations. Those identities, now rescued, would work as a *digestor crítico*, or critical digestive process, to cannibalize foreign influences in a way that would be similar to that of early *antropofagista* theorists (see 1925 entry). Waisman's and Fernández Cox's theoretical proposals on architecture were backed by the cultural studies of the time. While the developed world engaged in the debate of postmodernity versus late modernity—characterized by David Harvey, Marshall Berman, Jürgen Habermas, and Jean-François Lyotard—the Latin Americans were more interested in understanding the specificities of their own paths of modernization.

This approach is clear in Beatriz Sarlo's *Una modernidad periférica: Buenos Aires 1920 y 1930*, published in 1988. Being prolific and versatile like no other literary critic, Sarlo was able to construct a holistic view of the development of modernism in Argentina that has the same breadth as Berman's *All That Is Solid*

Melts into Air (1981) or Carl Schorske's *Fin-de-Siècle Vienna* (1980), which inspired it. Though Jorge Luis Borges and Roberto Arlt are the focus of much of the book, the city and its urban and architectural sense—characterized by both authors as an empty city full of shadows and foreign references—is central to Sarlo's understanding. When referencing the artist Xul Solar, Sarlo touches the central nerve of the Argentine paradox: "the co-existence of defensive and residual elements together with transformative programs; traces of a creole [or local Spanish] formation in parallel with an overwhelming process of importation of goods, discourses and symbolic practices."[6] While previous studies emphasized the discontinuities of Argentine modernization, Sarlo shows that there are indeed continuities, trends, and attitudes that permeate the whole process, especially when the spatial experience of the city is considered. Xul Solar's watercolors of imagined cities in which buildings have personified features are again the perfect representation of those hybrid or mixed spaces that defined Argentinean modernization.

The idea of a peripheral modernization would be further explored by Néstor García Canclini's *Culturas híbridas: Estrategias para entrar y salir de la modernidad* (*Hybrid Cultures: Strategies for Entering and Leaving Modernity*), published in Mexico in 1990. In the now classic book, García Canclini defines the problem around the idea of Latin America's exuberant modernism in parallel to an incomplete, or deficient, modernization. In other words, the appearance of modernity exits without the existing infrastructure, means of production, and urban systems needed to produce it. Throughout the book, the author stresses the point that in the first decades of the twentieth century, Latin American traditions had not yet disappeared and modernity had not completely arrived. Since the modern did not substitute the traditional, a "multitemporal heterogeneity" resulted as the past and the present worked together as a hybrid new. So, within a generic

Latin American way of operating, the result was the development of "hybrid cultures," which are aesthetically modern but in which "high" and "low," modern and autochthonous, popular and highbrow cultures coexisted through a system of negotiations of what is kept, altered, and discarded from each. Modernism, for him, was a mask, a simulacrum conjured up by the elites and state apparatuses to impose the modern aesthetic as an ideology for consumers. According to García Canclini, the problem does not lie in Latin America not having modernized but rather in the contradictory and unequal manner in which modernization has been articulated. If the past was artificially constructed to erect a façade of modernity (thus the paradoxical entrance), the solution lies in the possible exits: emancipation, renovation, democratization, and expansion.

And so, the calls were heard by architects. Enlightened by Waisman's idea of divergence and Fernández Cox's idea of *modernidad apropiada*, Latin American scholars and practitioners embarked on a long journey of self-discovery starting in the 1980s that paved the way to a much more integrated architecture. They did not exactly become the center of themselves as Waisman had hoped for, but they certainly developed a whole new way of looking simultaneously into what was happening in the North Atlantic centers and their neighboring countries.

In architecture, the 1980s was not at all a lost decade.

FURTHER READING

Fernández Cox, "Modernidad apropiada, modernidad revisada, modernidad reencantada."
Frampton, *Modern Architecture: A Critical History.*
———, "Modern Architecture and Critical Regionalism."
García Canclini, *Hybrid Cultures: Strategies for Entering and Leaving Modernity.*
Sarlo, *Una modernidad periférica: Buenos Aires 1920 y 1930.*

LINA BO BARDI AND THE SESC POMPÉIA INAUGURATE AN INTEREST IN ADAPTING EXISTING STRUCTURES.

BRAZIL

IN 1977, AS THE BRAZILIAN "economic miracle" was going full force, Lina Bo Bardi was invited to design a sports and cultural center on the periphery of São Paulo, the SESC Pompéia. At that point, Bo Bardi had lived in São Paulo for thirty years, almost half of her life. That commission, however, surely felt like a new encounter—full of possibilities and yet a bit strange. As it happened, Bo Bardi had spent significant time in Bahia since the late 1950s, working on different museums and cultural centers. Because many of those initiatives were aborted by the military regime, she returned to São Paulo in 1968. That year, her most visible building, the MASP (Museu de Arte de São Paulo) was inaugurated (see 1957-b box). Normally, the impact of the MASP building would have brought her many other commissions, but instead she chose (or did not have that much choice) to work in theater productions for most of the following decade. After all, Lina Bo Bardi was not just any architect and those were not normal times.

When Bo Bardi first moved to São Paulo in 1946, the population was 1.6 million inhabitants. When she left to work in Bahia in 1959, the population had more than doubled to 3.4 million people. By 1970, the city had swelled to 6 million, and by the time Bo Bardi was working on the SESC Fábrica da Pompéia in 1977, the population was close to 8 million. The city had grown five times larger in those thirty years.

Lina Bo Bardi herself had also changed significantly. Living in Salvador (capital of the state of Bahia) put her in contact with more traditional forms of Brazilian culture. Its African traditions and the craftsmanship of *sertanejos* (people from the *sertão*, or northeast savannas) connected Bo Bardi with traces from colonial times that were long gone (or made oblivious) in the manufacturing-oriented São Paulo. In Salvador, Bo Bardi was in charge of a series of exhibitions of popular art that aimed to create a dialogue between vernacular and highbrow culture. On a theoretical level, she

was finally practicing what she admired in her Italian mentor Ernesto Rogers: the idea of melding cultural traditions with popular traditions. The ambience in Bahia could not have been better, given the presence of a young avant-garde that would soon conquer the cultural spotlight of the entire nation: filmmaker Glauber Rocha, composers Gilberto Gil and Caetano Veloso, and poet Waly Salomão. They loved "dona Lina," and she loved them.

Back in São Paulo, Bo Bardi found a group with similar ideas at Teatro Oficina under the leadership of Celso Martinez Corrêa. But the promising ideas of the early 1960s were, by now, an underground movement. Anything related to avant-garde or experimentation was explicitly repressed by the military.

It was under those oppressive circumstances that Bo Bardi was invited to design a new SESC facility in 1977. At that time, the whole Southern Cone was under military rule, and any political change toward democratization in Brazil would not come until a few years later (see 1979 entry). The SESC commission, however, gave Bo Bardi the first chance in twenty years to build large again.

A semipublic entity sponsored by commerce employers, the Serviço Social do Comércio (SESC; Commerce's Social Service) was created in 1946 and funded by mandatory contributions based on the payroll of retail business. In exchange, the employees and their families can use SESC sports facilities, libraries, and after-school care, as well as have access to subsidized health care and job training programs.[1]

The SESC Fábrica da Pompéia is located in a dilapidated industrial neighborhood in the inner periphery of São Paulo. When Bo Bardi received the commission, the site was a decommissioned steel barrel manufacturing facility. Her first major decision was to not demolish the old factory warehouses. Contrary to the modernist orthodoxy still in place in 1970s São Paulo, Bo Bardi understood that the country had already built

Lina Bo Bardi, SESC Pompéia, São Paulo, 1985.

too much since the 1930s. It was now time to engage those structures, make them better, turn them around, and not destroy them. The times of the tabula rasa had past. Indeed, at SESC, Bo Bardi realized that the modernist tradition of eradicating the past was something to struggle against. As a result, she decided to restore the old brick and metal truss structures to house all of the cultural facilities and to build a multistory sports facility in the only available corner of the site, an area bisected by an underground creek that once ran there. In a lecture in 1979, she defined her task as "industrial archaeology," a measure of how much she respected the existing buildings.

In the corner, Bo Bardi built two high-rise towers that are separated by the underground water system. The library, theater, and exhibition spaces were located under the old ceramic roofs of the factory warehouses. To mark the difference between the old and the new, Bo Bardi left the existing brick exposed as much as possible and introduced concrete (in blocks or cast in place) as the new material. In a space where the roof had caved in, she used a glass roof to cover the theater's foyer, again keeping with the principle of not mimicking the past or hiding the signs of time. Bo Bardi called this type of connector a *terreiro*, a term that generally translates as "backyard" but is widely used for labeling the site of Afro-Brazilian religious rites—traditionally hidden in the back, as they were prohibited into the early twentieth century. Clearly, the architect was deliberately bringing a bit of Bahia into São Paulo.

Bo Bardi's experience in Bahia also transformed her design process. At SESC, for the first time, Bo Bardi moved her office to the site in search of a more participatory design experience. Years before, in a church she built in Uberlândia, she began this practice because the site was 375 miles away and this distance made site visits infrequent. At the same time, Bo Bardi became much more interested in freehand watercolors and collages than in precise architectural drawings.

Influenced by Sérgio Ferro's *O canteiro e o desenho* (1976), a Marxist analysis of the construction process that claims that drawings are tools for controlling labor, Bo Bardi developed at SESC a rigorous but imprecise process. Details were discussed on site and sketched directly on letter-size paper with markers and colored pencils. When the project was published, Bo Bardi chose to emphasize those loose sketches over the ink-on-vellum and measured drawings that must have been produced for its construction. Since the majority of the construction workers in São Paulo were unskilled migrants from the Brazilian northeast, Bo Bardi was finding a more direct way to communicate with them while, at the same time, rescuing the popular art forms that she learned in Bahia.

In a way, the SESC was the perfect client for Bo Bardi's experimentation because it allowed her to work directly with contractors and suppliers, something unheard of in a purely governmental commission. At the same time, the project had a strong public facet. This was something that she had always craved (stating numerous times that she was not interested in designing private houses).

Besides the rehabilitation of the old industrial warehouses into cultural facilities, the SESC Pompéia also gave Bo Bardi a chance to build tall, large, and heavy structures. The program called for several sports courts and smaller halls for dance, gymnastics, and martial arts, as well as locker rooms and administrative offices for the whole complex.

The heavy tower that she built is five stories, each with a floor-to-ceiling height of 40 feet (12 m); a swimming pool on the ground floor; and four courts (named after the seasons) on each floor above. On the sides of each floor are four large irregular openings for light and ventilation that give the building its visual identity. The other tower, slender in profile, has eleven stories and houses all the other parts of the program as well as the vertical circulation, that is, the elevator and stairs for its heavier counterpart. Both structures are built out of concrete and are connected by walkways at the different levels. The visual result is expressionist in both its brutalism and in its strange simplicity, which, according to Bo Bardi, was inspired by the pragmatic roughness of Portuguese fortifications (that she experienced, again, in Bahia). The exposed concrete appears light in the thin walkways and slim tower, in contrast to the large cubic block that is perforated by gigantic openings that look like someone punched holes through the walls.

In between the towers, above the subterranean water gallery, Bo Bardi placed a wooden deck with a sequence of showers, an "urban beach" in her own words. Water was very much present from the early sketches onward. Some drawings show both towers surrounded by a water surface. Others shows a giant waterfall coming from the top of the larger tower. In the end, the water surface was moved inside one of the

Interior view of SESC Pompéia, São Paulo, 1985.

Lina Bo Bardi, detail of bridges at SESC Pompéia, São Paulo, 1985.

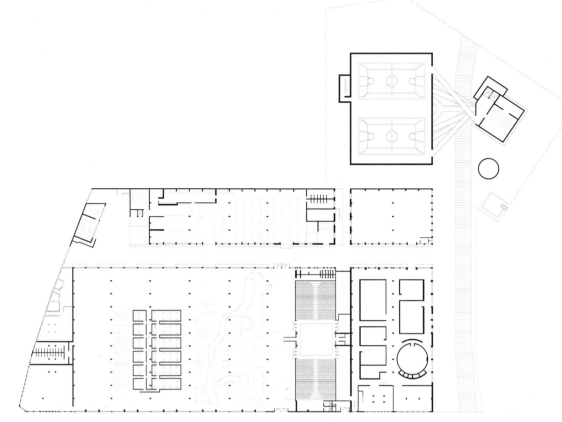

Plan of SESC Pompéia.

warehouses where an amoeba-shaped cut in the concrete floor, filled with pebbles, serves to separate the different exhibition spaces.

For the SESC Pompéia logo, also designed by Bo Bardi, an industrial chimney spews flowers instead of smoke. The architect had built an island of sensibility surrounded by the raw modern landscape of São Paulo.

FURTHER READING

Bo Bardi, *Lina por escrito: Textos escolhidos de Lina Bo Bardi, 1943–1991.*
Lina Bo Bardi.
Oliveira, "Lina Bo Bardi: Obra construida/Lina Bo Bardi: Built Work."
———, *Lina Bo Bardi: Sutis substâncias da arquitetura.*

1988

BRAZILIAN MUSEUM OF SCULPTURE

IT WOULD BE FAIR to say that the Museu Brasileiro da Escultura (MuBE; Brazilian Museum of Sculpture) built in the late 1980s is the most paradigmatic and important creation of Paulo Mendes da Rocha. It is certainly the building that brought him back to the center of attention in Brazil in the 1990s.

After designing masterpieces as early as 1958 (such as the Paulistano Gymnasium; see 1961-b entry), Mendes da Rocha was expelled in 1968 from his teaching position at the University of São Paulo by the military dictatorship and witnessed the postmodern frenzy that took over Brazil in the late 1970s (see 1979 entry). With the return of democratic government in 1985, Mendes da Rocha's building opportunities increased and resulted in iconic structures such as the Forma Show Room (São Paulo, 1987) and the Chapel of Saint Peter (Campos de Jordão, 1988). No commission, however, was as important as the MuBE.

When a generous lot (75,000 sq. ft./6,968 sq. m) became available in the middle of Jardim Europa, an affluent zone of São Paulo, the neighborhood association lobbied against commercial developments. As a result, the city donated the land with a mandate that it should be made

Paulo Mendes da Rocha, Brazilian Museum of Sculpture (MuBE), São Paulo, 1991.

Detail of MuBE water pools.

Paulo Mendes da Rocha, Brazilian Museum of Sculpture (MuBE), São Paulo, 1991.

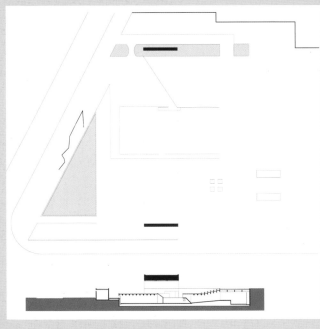

Plan and section of MuBE.

public. The response of the neighborhood association was to create a museum on it, taking advantage of the proximity to other institutions such as the Museu da Imagem e do Som (Sound and Image Museum) on the same block.

Not having a proper collection, the MuBE invited five architects to present their proposals for the site. Mendes da Rocha, at first skeptical of designing a museum without a collection, proposed to turn the site into an open garden for the city. Interestingly enough, this garden is composed of a large shading canopy and thousands of square feet of concrete pavement, with the trees and grass pushed to the periphery.

The generous canopy had been used before by the Paulista school and by Mendes da Rocha himself (see 1961-b entry). At the Brazilian pavilion at the Osaka World's Fair in 1970, Mendes da Rocha kept the canopy flat and exaggerated the undulation of the ground to create diverse spatiality.

At MuBE, he took advantage of a slight change of grade from one side of the triangular site to the other to design two major ground planes: one above, level with Avenida Europa, and one below, level with Rua Alemanha. The program of the museum is sandwiched between those two planes, as if tucked underground, except that here the "ground" is constructed of two sets of slabs, one structural and another that creates the pavement one foot above the real ground.

Topping the whole composition is an enormous slab (40 x 200 ft./12 x 61 m) hovering 7.5 ft. (2.3 m) over the ground; experientially, this means slightly above our heads. Small patches of grass and water designed by Roberto Burle Marx, in what are probably the most constrained gardens he ever designed, negotiate cuts and transitional spaces.

For Mendes da Rocha, the economy of means was the central concern. In his own words, his project was the best alternative to building nothing at all. If the Paulista school has always been about *vão livre*, wide-open internal spaces created by majestic concrete structures, at MuBE it is all about the public character of the space. The slab here does provide shade and protection but doesn't actually add to the program of the museum. Instead, it serves as a datum of the street grid (perpendicular to the main avenue) and the bourgeois houses of the neighborhood next to it.

By taking the challenge of designing a museum without a collection and responding with a public plaza that hides exhibition spaces, Mendes da Rocha realized his very best building, one in which site, tectonics, and program (or lack of it) are masterfully articulated to the advantage of them all. Twenty years after its inauguration, the MuBE has a collection, and its public character has definitely had a positive impact in a neighborhood under constant real estate pressure. Paulo Mendes da Rocha, meanwhile, collected the main honors of his profession: the Mies van der Rohe Prize in 2000 and the Pritzker Architecture Prize in 2006 (see 1980 entry).

1990

CHILEAN POSTMODERNISM IS CHALLENGED BY JOSÉ CRUZ AND GERMÁN DEL SOL.

CHILE

IN THE FINAL DECADE of the twentieth century, no other country received more attention for its architecture than Chile. Economics and politics can explain this disparity; Brazil, Mexico, and Argentina were suffering stagnant economic growth and politically turbulent regimes in the 1980s and 1990s. In the United States, President Bill Clinton won two elections with the slogan "It's the economy, stupid," and it seemed that Latin America could only follow behind his Washington Consensus. The future rise of the left at the turn of the millennium would prove that wrong, but, in the meantime, we have to admit that in the case of Chile, at least, market-oriented reforms did produce remarkable architecture.

As much as Chilean architectural excellence is a consensus, we need to look into the roots of such a phenomenon and the results it yielded. According to historian Horacio Torrent,

The most typical conditions of Chilean architecture in recent years have been dominated by several factors: a pressure to build quickly a product that expands the country's economic growth; the availability of a significant quantity of architectural projects for the market; the crisis of a welfare state; and the absence of a public entity that promotes disciplined architectural strategies.[1]

All of the variables described by Torrent came directly from President Augusto Pinochet's market-oriented reforms in the 1970s. After the military coup of September 11, 1973, Chile embarked on a radical experiment of market liberalization and a dismantling of the welfare state. As argued by historian Jorge Francisco Liernur, Chile experienced a very early globalization process as the result of Pinochet's regime, and, as could be expected, all of the good and the bad that comes with globalization affected Chile before any other Latin American country.[2]

In architecture, the move from state-commissioned programs to market-oriented developments coincides with the demise of the modern movement and the rise of postmodernism. Marina Waisman, in a lucid text published in *Arquitectura Viva* magazine in 1991, called the previous decade *"la década rosa"* not only for the favorite color of Michael Graves, Peter Eisenman, and Aldo Rossi, but mostly for the political economic reforms of U.S. president Ronald Reagan, British prime minister Margaret Thatcher, and, in Chile, Pinochet.

Chile already had a strong local modernism when Enrique Browne, Christian De Groote, and Cristián Fernández Cox rose to prominence in the 1980s. Born in 1931, De Groote graduated from Santiago's Catholic University in 1957 and proceeded to graduate school at Illinois Institute of Technology in Chicago. Back in Chile, he collaborated with Emilio Duhart at CEPAL, one of the most important commissions of the early 1960s (see 1966 entry). At Casa Vergara (Algarrobo, 1980), De Groote designed a series of porticos that are adapted to the triangular shape of the site and to the topography, something reminiscent of his many years working on industrial programs. At the house, the simplicity of the structure allows for the creation of very sensible and varying spaces with a remarkable economy of means.

Another important architect of those times in Chile is Enrique Browne Covarrubias. Born in 1942, Browne graduated from the Catholic University in 1965 and from the Massachusetts Institute of Technology in 1969.[3] Back in Chile, Browne's early work shows a strong focus on tectonic expression using brick and wood as well as his pioneering attentiveness to nature as part of the built environment. His designs for office buildings at Calle Padre Mariano (Santiago, 1974) and Calle Suecia (Santiago, 1978) propose green roofs at a time when only visionaries were doing it. A few years later, Browne built a house on Calle Paul Harris (Santiago, 1980) that used a wooden-trellis volume to be covered with vines, a design element that would recur in his work. Taking full advantage of Santiago's weather, the vine-covered box provides a lush and shaded space in the summer while allowing for the winter sun to filter thorough its deciduous vegetation. At the building for the Consorcio Nacional de Seguros (1990), Browne's mastery of foliage as a design element would be used to enhance an office building, advancing by decades the breathable façades that populate architectural magazines of the first years of the twenty-first century.

According to Liernur, this late-modern Chilean generation was not interested in the tabula rasa of modernity as the previous generation had been but, instead, in a "classic interpretation of modern traditions," an architecture of austerity, control, sensibility, and silence.[4] The fact that those four words used to describe Chilean architecture fit the Pinochet years very well is no coincidence.

What might surely be a coincidence is the fact that an alternative Chilean architecture, more truly tectonic and more attuned to the country's geography, would emerge in the early 1990s at the very same time that the Pinochet dictatorship was crumbling.

In distant Chiloé, 700 miles (1,127 km) south of Santiago, Edward Rojas developed an architecture of intense "geographic consciousness," to use a term coined by Horacio Torrent.[5] Having studied under the radical architecture program of Valparaíso (see 1969-a entry), his work would no doubt keep a distance from the market-oriented developments of Santiago. In Chiloé, Rojas had a chance to build several public structures that respond to its maritime southern conditions. A modern materialization and spatiality in wood and careful reinterpretation of the traditions of southern Chilean architecture, such as fishermen's housing, can be found in the Dalcahue fair (1978) or, a decade later, in the Chiloé Modern Art Museum (1988). At Hotel Viento Sur (1991), an Aalto-like curved form in reinforced concrete is built on a sloping site, right below a 1930s structure that was renovated to accommodate the hotel's shared spaces. The new concrete building is quite hidden in the landscape and functions as a pedestal for the old house, supporting new parking spaces on its roof.

Meanwhile in Santiago, Alvar Aalto's influence would be felt again, this time in the competition for the Chilean pavilion for the Seville Expo in 1992. Conceived to celebrate five hundred years after Columbus's famous journey, much like its past exhibition (see 1929-a entry), it was intended to support Spain's role as Latin America's motherland.

If it had been Mexico and Peru that displayed sophisticated readings of the two countries' past in 1929, this time it would be Chile that stole the limelight. A beautiful pavilion designed by José "Pepe" Cruz Ovalle and Germán del Sol housed a giant piece of an iceberg as its main exhibition. Most of the media reaction focused on the environmental provocation of refrigerating 85 tons of Antarctic ice in the middle of the Andalusian summer (not to mention the cost of hauling

Edward Rojas, Viento del Sur, Puerto Montt, 1991.

José Cruz and Germán del Sol, interior of Chilean pavilion at Seville Expo, 1992.

it back and forth), but the envelope around the iceberg deserves just as much credit for the success of the Chilean pavilion.

The result of a competition carried out in 1990, the Chilean pavilion is a rectangular box slightly curved in an S shape and oriented north–south in relation to the country's geography. Built in laminated wood and covered in copper (two prized Chilean products), the pavilion referenced Aalto's Finnish pavilion for the 1939 World's Exhibition in New York. A detached roof, also in laminated wood, lets in a soft light that floods the interior space. In the competition report, the architects wrote about carving a unified interior space from detached wood planks to allow for air circulation and for a modulated light inside.

Del Sol and Cruz were only beginning their careers when they won the competition for the pavilion in 1990. Germán del Sol was born in 1949 and started architecture school at Catholic University in Santiago in the late 1960s, transferring later to the Escola Tècnica Superior d'Arquitectura de Barcelona (ETSAB) from which he graduated in 1973. His early years working

as an architect were spent between Barcelona, Chile, California, and, finally, back in Chile in 1986. José "Pepe" Cruz Ovalle was born in 1948 and started his architectural studies at the Valparaíso school, founded by his uncle Alberto Cruz. Like del Sol, Cruz left Chile for Barcelona in 1973 and graduated from ETSAB in 1975, not returning to Chile until 1987.

In Seville, they had a unique opportunity to help redefine Chilean architecture, and they did so by combining the warmth of wood with the added value of the laminated process as well as the simplicity of the single void with the subtle curves of the longitudinal walls. This was an appropriate metaphor for a Chile that wanted to keep its modernized and globalized image while moving away from the repressive Pinochet years. The poetics of the Valparaíso school had mixed here with the tectonics of the Santiago school.

In thinking about the transformations in Chilean architecture in the 1980s and 1990s, it becomes clear that the radical globalization and market-oriented policies of Pinochet were later tempered with a Chilean seasoning. Liernur, again, connects the pavilion of del Sol and Cruz with the "NO" Campaign of 1989 that voted Pinochet out of the presidency (but not out of power completely). This new "arriving joy" (the jingle of the "NO" campaign was "*La alegría ya viene*," or "Joy is arriving") was turned into a new branding of Chilean architecture that combined the Valparaíso expressive sensibility with the Santiago rigorous tectonics. The new Chilean architecture mirrored the new Chilean man of the "NO" campaign: globalized but rooted in place; sophisticated but fond of raw materials; progressive in image but conservative in core values.

FURTHER READING

Korowin, "'Iceberg! Right Ahead!' (Re)Discovering Chile at the 1992 Universal Exposition in Seville, Spain."
Liernur, *Portales del laberinto: Arquitectura y ciudad en Chile, 1977–2009.*
Quantrill, *Chilean Modern Architecture since 1950.*

Enrique Browne, Consorcio Nacional de Seguros, Santiago, 1990.

1991

ANGELO BUCCI AND ALVARO PUNTONI WIN THE COMPETITION FOR THE BRAZILIAN PAVILION AT SEVILLE EXPO 1992,

BRAZIL

TURMOIL MIGHT BE THE BEST WORD to describe Brazil's situation in 1991. The first elected president in thirty years, Fernando Collor de Mello, was being impeached, inflation was at 20 percent a month, and local industry was hit hard by the drastic reduction of import tariffs in 1990. Meanwhile, pluralism and regionalism had become the main architectural tendencies since the mid-1980s. The end of military rule in 1985 had broken the hegemony of modernism, which, at that point, was watered down by years of authoritarian centralized planning and lack of criticism (see 1965-b and 1979 entries). It was under those turbulent conditions that the Brazilian Ministry of Foreign Relations organized a competition for the design of the Brazilian pavilion for Seville Expo 1992.

The 253 entries could not have been any more diverse. While we could still recognize in several projects the strong heritage of midcentury modernism, the majority of the submissions were mostly composed of postmodern collages and formal exercises characteristic of Italian or Spanish architecture at that time and with references closer to Michael Graves and Mario

Botta than anything else. Although we might never know what was discussed at that jury, the final result was a reaffirmation of the core principles of Brazilian late modernism and, especially, of the so-called Paulista school, as the first prize was awarded to Angelo Bucci and Alvaro Puntoni.

The selected design consisted of a simple box of exposed concrete elevated from the ground that, as a result, could be entered from three sides. Three of the façades of the rectangular shape were identical, flat and integral, having the same distance from the ground and the same height. The fourth façade acted like the back of the building and went all the way to the ground. The roof, open at times, sat two feet below the upper edge of the wall (so as not to be seen). Inside the simple volume, a ramp dominated the circulation and connected various suspended exhibition floors. The auditorium was buried and accessed through a large ramped platform that occupied a large part of

Angelo Bucci and Alvaro Puntoni, model of Brazilian pavilion project for the Seville Expo, 1992.

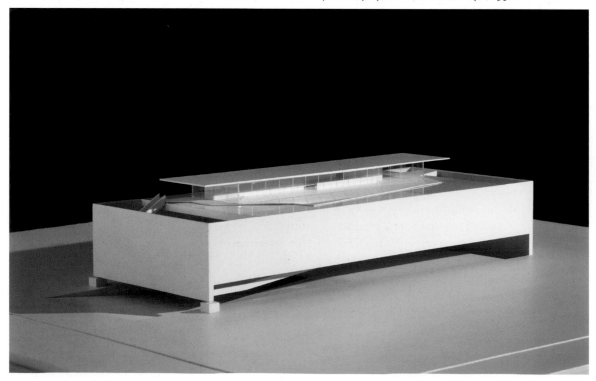

MARKING THE END OF THE POSTMODERN REIGN AND THE
BEGINNING OF NEOMODERNISM.

the ground floor and served as both foyer and extra exhibition space. The influence of Vilanova Artigas's 1961 School of Architecture building is clear (see 1961 box), given that Bucci and Puntoni had recently graduated from the School of Architecture of the University of São Paulo (FAU-USP). Their orthodox rigor surely must have looked radical for those eclectic times. Critics north and south saw it as an allegiance to times past and declared their design "anachronistic" and "outdated."

It is interesting, then, to discuss what was out of place: the concrete box inspired by Vilanova Artigas's building or the postmodern intoxication of the 1980s. The ambiguous answer lies in the significant isolation that befell Brazilian architecture after the 1960s. Once celebrated abroad as a refreshing outcast of modernism, Brazil's architecture was heavily criticized for being overtly expressive and futile. In the words of Argentine critic Jorge Francisco Liernur, "force of naturalness, impulse of youth and mystery of the myth" became respectively "childish impulses, anarchy of the jungle and overloaded sensuality."[1] At home, the tone was not much better, despite the fact that the country had built more in the 1970s than in any previous decades. At the same time, the military dictatorship had heavily repressed architecture schools for their predominantly left-wing population, and for a few years in the early 1970s there was not a single architecture magazine being printed in Brazil. The modernist project was dying from slow and steady suffocation, its transformative ideals hibernating in schools like the FAU-USP.

Elsewhere in the country the liberating winds of the late 1970s were affecting architectural discourse. The year 1979 marks the beginning of the so-called *abertura*, or opening. Taking the lead or at least establishing the debate in the 1980s, a group of architects from Minas Gerais established a new form of postmodernism for Brazil (see 1979 entry). But, as the international scene struggled to grasp "deconstructivism" and

the first computer-generated designs, the majority of Brazil's young architects identified themselves more with the new trends that seemed to be awakening local architecture from the dark spell cast by the dictatorship and the chaotic economy whose inflation reached 600 percent in 1991.

It was against this background that Bucci and Puntoni designed a pavilion celebrating a tradition that many thought was long dead. The contrast was made even more striking by the fact that all other awards were given to postmodernists from Minas Gerais: the second prize to Éolo Maia, the third prize to Joel Campolina, and a special mention to Paulo Leander's entry. Is it possible that the jury was deadlocked in a debate over which architecture best represented Mineiro postmodernism? In a way, Paulista orthodoxy and Mineiro postmodernism were both a result of a disconnection caused by twenty-one years of military dictatorship. Bucci and Puntoni's design was, then, a celebration of the Paulista school that, as we have seen, had fallen out of favor.

During the 1990s, Bucci would consolidate his position as a leading young Brazilian architect with a body of work that is marked by quality, not quantity. He began with a psychology clinic in his hometown of Orlandia (1995) and moved on to single-family houses in Ribeirão Preto (2000) and Aldeia da Serra with MMBB (2002). The overall forms are deeply connected to Mendes da Rocha's and Vilanova Artigas's designs, but are made more elegant and harmonious by Bucci. The brutalist tendency of the previous generation gave way to an attention to detail that highlights the contrast between the textures of wood and the precision of glass against the roughness of exposed concrete. Even the concrete itself has been transformed: sometimes formed with wooden planks but often cast with metal formwork, more economical, smoother, and much more precise. At the house in Ribeirão Preto, for instance, this attention to detail is elevated to the highest degree. Here Bucci embedded aluminum rails in the formwork

so that later the glass doors could run smoothly while appearing to be in direct contact with the reinforced concrete. In addition, the spatial variety created by the many different levels in this house, as in many of his subsequent projects, breaks the original rigor of the 1992 pavilion for Seville and of his earlier houses. It is fair to say in hindsight that Bucci deserves credit for awakening the seeds of Brazilian modernism after decades of hibernation.

The fact that the pavilion was never built was just one in a sequence of cancelled or drastically altered competitions that have defined Brazilian architecture in the twentieth century, such as the competition for the Ministry of Education and Public Health (MESP; see 1936 entry), the Brazilian pavilion at New York (see 1939 box), or the Hotel in Ouro Preto (see 1941 entry).

In 1992, the Brazilian Foreign Ministry once again had difficulty handling the controversy surrounding competition results. After all, a new image for the country was being articulated by the Collor de Mello presidency, and the pro-market small government agenda seemed to be in direct opposition to both the 1950s developmentalism that generated the Carioca school and the 1960s social concerns that galvanized the Paulista school. Modernism was not the image they wanted to convey, and thus the project stalled.

However, Bucci and Puntoni's winning submission sent the Brazilian architectural debate back to its own traditions—traditions that Bucci never conceived as immutable but as a fabulous palette from which many combinations could arise. In later projects (PUC-Rio library, 2006; Ubatuba House, 2009), a recognizable expressionist impulse cuts through the orthogonal rigor of the Paulista orthodoxy. Vilanova Artigas used to paraphrase August Perret on the need to make the support sing. Angelo Bucci goes beyond the classic vocabulary of the Paulista school: the singing of his concrete columns seems simple and straightforward but in reality is as dissonant as the best bossa nova. By playing with a syncopated or irregular rhythm against the structural grid, Bucci is able to break free from the constraints established by the structure and develop the best internal spatial results.

The year 1991 also marks the signature of the Treaty of Asunción establishing Mercosur, South America's common market. Not coincidentally, a new articulation between architects would arise in the final years of the twentieth century. Bucci, for instance, would become very close to Solano Benítez in Paraguay and Rafael Iglesia in Argentina. The commercial integration had an impact on architects throughout the Southern Cone on a scale never dreamed of before. Influences and cross influences only accelerated as attested by the multiple references visible in their buildings and discourses. Traces of Bucci's buildings can be seen in Iglesia's pavilions (see 2002 entry) or Benítez's tomb (see 2001 box). The strong regionalist tendencies of the 1980s had been transformed by increasing integration, a process that became fundamental to understanding contemporary architecture in Latin America.

Brazilian architecture would not be the same after those turbulent events of 1991.

FURTHER READING

"Brazilian Architect Angelo Bucci Discusses His Use of
    Space: Openings and Voids That Allow Inside and Out-
    side to Flow Together."
Futagawa, "A Dialogue with [the] Editor: Angelo Bucci
    [Interview]."
Hernández, *Beyond Modernist Masters: Contemporary Architec-
    ture in Latin America.*
Verde Zein and Junqueira Bastos, *Brasil: Arquitetura após
    1950.*
Verde Zein and Segawa, "Arquitetura em Exposição: Sevilha
    92."

1993

PABLO BEITIA, XUL SOLAR MUSEUM (PAN KLUB FOUNDATION)

THE CENTRAL PROBLEM that Pablo Tomás Beitia (with Mario González, Juan Aiello, and Raquel Adesso) faced in designing a museum to house the work of the avant-garde Argentine artist Xul Solar (see 1924 entry) had to do with remodeling an existing residential building in the center of Buenos Aires. The goal was to keep not only the exterior character of the building undisturbed but also, above the gallery, the living quarters where Xul Solar himself had lived. The second problem had to do with creating a museum that responded to the quality, character, and references within Xul Solar's works while, at the same time, designing a space that was based on his visions for a fully integrative environment. The commission, under the direction of the artist's widow, Micaela Cárdenas, required that the design be more akin to a cultural center than to a formal museum.

Beitia's solution responded to these concerns: he created an intervention that was inserted into the hollowed-out structure of the original building (whose façade was renovated and restored to its original condition) and that programmatically works more as a type of theater or workshop than as a traditional gallery space. The result is a three-dimensional labyrinthine and sectionally complex space. The experience of the space is more journey-like through the different floor plates, walkways, and mezzanines that revolve around the central zenithal-lit, theater-like space, which alludes to and materializes the architectural visions and themes that Xul Solar represented throughout many of his works (environments, for instance, constructed primarily with planes or with multiple staircases).

For Beitia, the museum is composed of smaller-scaled gallery spaces that overlap with the larger central space. The radical difference in character between the plans—which most clearly define the galleries—and the sections—where the theatrical space is most prominent—paradoxically alludes to their interconnectedness and codependence. At the end of one of the gallery accesses, a concrete spiral stair leads to Xul Solar's house, one of the four apartments of the original structure. The limited amount of natural light that penetrates into the interior is both expressive of the location of the museum within an existing building and dense urban fabric but also a response to the fragility of Xul Solar's delicate but bright-colored tempera paintings.

To heighten the distinction of the museum from the existing structure, the intervention was built with

Pablo Beitia, skylight of Xul Solar Museum, Buenos Aires, 1993.

Pablo Beitia, interior of Xul Solar Museum, Buenos Aires,
1993.

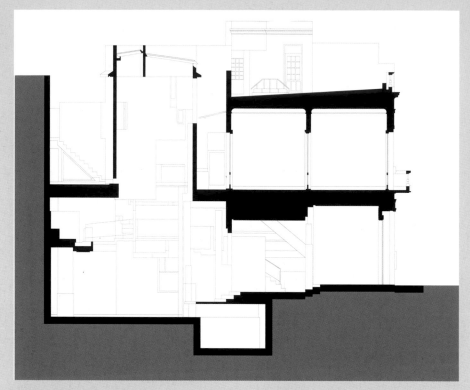

Section of Xul Solar Museum.

reinforced concrete and is structurally expressive: some-times mezzanines are supported by cables that hang from the ceiling; other times whole slabs cantilever out and appear unsupported. The labyrinthine effect of the space also serves to further exaggerate the distinction between old and new. Materially, the new reinforced concrete struc-ture is judiciously yet sporadically clad with travertine. In addition, the architectural details of the handrails, stairs, and structural connections, to name three, combine and contrast different materials (such as wood and steel against the raw concrete) that, along with the mullion-less glass, metal work, and slate and wood floors, show an indebtedness to the work of the Italian architect Carlo Scarpa.

1994-A

QUAE SERA TAMEN: ARCHITECTURE FOR THE FAVELAS

BRAZIL

IN THE REMOTE FUTURE, the twentieth century will probably not be remembered for its wars or its technological advances but for the fact that cities became home to the majority of humankind. And while a portion of this urban world became more connected than ever before, another part was absolutely excluded. The occurrence of favelas—as Brazilian slums are called—could be used to define the beginning of twentieth-century Latin American architecture. When Mayor Pereira Passos was reforming Rio de Janeiro's downtown in 1904, the favelas were already there, watching the century go by from above as if in another world (see 1903 entry). Indeed, this is exactly how a leading journalist in Rio de Janeiro described the favelas back in 1911: "I followed them and I found another world. The lighting had disappeared. We were in a rural place, in the backlands, far from the city."[1] Decades went by with very little change. In the end, dichotomies such as them versus us, darkness versus light, rural versus urban, and backlands versus city have been used and applied to Latin American cities throughout the twentieth century to define the relationship between the formal and the informal city.

The term *favela* was first used at the end of the nineteenth century when soldiers returning from the Canudos campaign started building shacks—with the War Ministry's permission—at Morro da Providência in downtown Rio de Janeiro. The nickname of their barracks in Canudos, Morro da Favela, became the name they would call this new settlement. Ever since, the term *favela* has applied to settlements built on illegally occupied land in the immediate vicinity of the formal city. What started in the first decades of the twentieth century as a desperate solution to housing needs—as workers migrated from the countryside in search of jobs in nascent industries—became the standard housing option for about one-fifth of the population of Rio de Janeiro and São Paulo; one-third of Caracas, Venezuela; and about half of Lima, Peru. One by one, people built temporary structures on any

piece of land available, only to be removed by the police in a matter of days if the land was of interest to private owners or state agencies. Consequently, informal settlements endured in areas where land was deemed unworthy of development.

By 1948, informal settlements housed 7 percent of Rio de Janeiro's population (139,000 people). This number rose to 10 percent in 1960 and 13 percent in 1970. At that point, favelas became a major problem, and the conservative governments appointed by the military dictatorship evicted 175,000 people from the southern areas of Rio de Janeiro and forcibly moved them to the western outskirts of the metropolis; these relocations are characterized by the infamous "Cidade de Deus" (City of God), whose story is captured in the 2002 movie of the same name. Nevertheless, during the "lost decade" of the 1980s, Rio de Janeiro's favelas would grow even faster. By 1990, they housed 16 percent of the city's population and 19 percent by 2000, breaking the barrier of 1 million inhabitants in six hundred different settlements.

It was against this scenario of poverty and social vulnerability that the city hosted the United Nations Conference on Environment and Development, known as the Rio Summit or the Earth Summit, in June 1992. Inside the conference, the conversation was mostly about environmental sustainability. In the streets, however, the issue of social sustainability loomed over visitors and hosts alike. The Brazilian army was deployed to control the favelas, and soldiers could be seen patrolling the boundaries between the hills (*morros*) and the asphalt, as the informal and formal city are known in Brazil.

The following year, coincidentally, the city would announce a new housing policy, based on integration, accessibility, and improved public space: the Favela-Bairro (slum to neighborhood) Project. A competition was launched in 1994 for ideas on how to intervene in midsize informal settlements. Specifically, it targeted favelas of 500 to 2,500 households housing 600,000

Cable car at Complexo do Alemão, Rio de Janeiro, 2010.

people, or 60 percent of Rio de Janeiro's informal population. The idea was that larger favelas like Rocinha or Complexo do Alemão would require more complex master plans than smaller settlements and would not yield as many results.

Thirty-two local firms submitted proposals, and fifteen were selected (one for each of the fifteen areas prioritized). The first phase of Favela-Bairro (1994–1998) had an integrated approach in which accessibility and connectivity would be addressed by building roads, public spaces, and infrastructure, including drainage improvement and sewage connections. As few families as possible were relocated from risky areas, and new housing structures were built inside each community for those displaced. In some cases, the projects developed community centers and even commercial facilities when their lack was deemed an important factor. Tenurization (issuing of property deeds or other

documents) and legalization (conforming with city laws) were supposed to follow but as of 2013 have not reached a significant number.

The implementation of the program was initially financed by the city and later by a loan from the Inter-American Development Bank. Other funding sources included the Brazilian Caixa Econômica Federal (Federal Credit Union) in 1997, the European Union, and the Brazilian federal government in 1998. In its first iteration, Favela-Bairro had a total investment of US$300 million benefiting 500,000 people in 146 settlements through the improvement of 500 miles (805 km) of roads and sidewalks, the construction of 160 miles (258 km) of new sewage connections, and 5 million sq. ft. (464,515 sq. m) of sports facilities.[2]

Those ambitious goals would not be reached

without interventions at the scale of architecture. As a matter of fact, the main difference between Favela-Bairro and previous (failed) attempts lies precisely in its architectural sensibilities. Punctual interventions replaced mass housing. The idea was to displace as few families as possible and, thus, respect the history of each area and the investment made by each family. Back in the 1970s, Brazilian urbanist Carlos Nelson Ferreira dos Santos revolutionized the thinking regarding favelas by calculating how much money was already invested in foundations, walls, and slabs at the favelas—an economic argument against demolition and relocation. Twenty years later, two architects surely helped fine-tune those policies at Rio de Janeiro's municipal government: planning secretary Luiz Paulo Conde and Sergio Magalhães, secretary of housing. Together, they stood up for design quality and created opportunities for talented architects to work for Brazil's poorest. This was something that had never happened before. Among those architects was Jorge Jáuregui. Born in Rosario, Argentina, Jáuregui moved to Rio de Janeiro in 1978 and started working for the favelas early on. When the city brought together the finances and the political will in 1994, he already had more experience than anyone else. His project for Campinho, for example, shows a developed sensibility to local materials while at the same time introduces new forms that intentionally aim to change the image of the area. According to Jáuregui, it was important to work at the level of the image (in addition to infrastructure and accessibility) in order to raise the self-esteem of the residents as well as make the whole process more sustainable and more prone to appropriation and use. Such goals were better achieved at Favela do Fubá, where Jáuregui designed a cultural center using pointed and inclined triangles as roof forms and fenestration that resembles cuts in the masonry. This striking visual identity was one reason Jáuregui was awarded the Veronica Green Prize for Urban Design by Harvard's Graduate School of Design in 2000.

Like so many other urban infrastructure projects, Favela-Bairro also suffered from political setbacks. The success of its first phase (1994–1997) catapulted Luiz Paulo Conde from planning secretary to mayor, in defiance of his "mentor" and the previous mayor, César Maia. Four years later, Maia was reelected and slowed down Favela-Bairro significantly despite the fact that he had first launched it in 1993. For Maia, one of the problems was that several of the projects begun by him during his first tenure as mayor (between 1994 and 1996) were completed and inaugurated by Conde between 1997 and 2001. As a result, a strong identity was formed between the latter and Favela-Bairro.

Following this, large-scale upgrades to informal settlements would have to wait for the second presidential

Carlos Teixeira et al., Community Center at Favela da Serra, Belo Horizonte, 2007.

term of Lula da Silva. Between 2005 and 2009, the Brazilian federal government invested US$200 billion in infrastructure all over the country, half of it on sanitation and public space improvement. The so-called Programa de Aceleração do Crescimento (PAC; Accelerated Growth Program) brought US$2 billion dollars to the city of Rio de Janeiro. This was six times more than the original Favela-Bairro budget. Although the first version did not address the housing needs of individual residents, larger interventions such as the one financed by the PAC program at Complexo do Alemão included housing for hundreds of families relocated inside the same community and a cable car line to facilitate mobility. The new version of Favela-Bairro (the name was kept the same) came with important improvements, such as mandates that construction companies hire 40 percent of their labor force from the community where work was being done, a model that was replicated in many other large cities in Brazil, such as Belo Horizonte and São Paulo. This strategy had two major impacts: it injected money into the local economy and it facilitated the dialogue (often tense) between the construction crews and the inhabitants. With the experience accumulated from years of dedication to low-income populations, Jáuregui was able to devise a low-cost small-area apartment complex that cleverly avoided the infamous problems of modernist housing complexes. The apartment buildings at Alemão are low rise (usually four stories only, no elevators), with as much direct connection between units and the street as possible. Narrow duplex units are stacked as if two sets of row houses were placed one on top of another in order to minimize circulation—always a source of conflict and costly maintenance. Open corridors and open stairways are also used and play an

important role in avoiding territorial disputes between specific groups or gangs.

Since its inception, Favela-Bairro has received its fair share of criticism. Ironically, most of it has come from the left, which questions whether urban upgrades actually improve the overall conditions that create inequality or only ameliorate the situation by treating some of its symptoms. The evaluations so far demonstrate that life has improved in the communities where upgrades were implemented. Public spaces are widely used, and accessibility has had a direct and positive impact on people's daily lives. As a result, violence has decreased and property values have risen sharply in direct correlation with the changes. Overall, it is hard to discern if life improvements are due to better infrastructure, better quality of public spaces, or the success of President Lula da Silva's income distribution policies. What we do know and celebrate is the fact that some of the best Brazilian architects are now working for the poorest. As the Brazilian rebels plotting for independence in 1789 wrote on their flag: *Quae sera tamen*, meaning, "Better late than never."

FURTHER READING

Duarte and Magalhães, "Upgrading Squatter Settlements into City Neighborhoods: The Favela-Bairro Program in Rio de Janeiro."
Fernandes, "Constructing the 'Right to the City' in Brazil."
Fiori and Brandão, "Spatial Strategies and Urban Social Policy."
Jáuregui, *Estrategias de articulación urbana: Proyecto y gestión de asentamientos periféricos en América Latina*.
Segre, "Formal-Informal Connections in the Favelas of Rio de Janeiro: The Favela-Bairro Programme."

AS A MODEL FOR INTERNATIONALIZATION, NAFTA
BECOMES EMBLEMATIC OF THE NEW CHARACTER OF
LATE-TWENTIETH-CENTURY MEXICAN ARCHITECTURE.

MEXICO

THE DEARTH OF ARCHITECTURAL production in Mexico during the 1970s and 1980s due to one of the worst economic crises the country had ever suffered (see 1976 entry) was quickly and overwhelmingly reversed in the 1990s. Starting with the neoliberal economic policies established by President Miguel de la Madrid (1982–1988) of privatization of government programs and the curtailing of social programs, the country's economy and investor confidence began to improve. President Salinas de Gortari's government (1988–1994) furthered this through a shift toward internationalization, deregulation, privatization of government assets, and an openness to the technological development of the country. These policies culminated at the end of his presidency with the signing of the North American Free Trade Agreement (NAFTA) between Mexico, Canada, and the United States in 1994. After a brief but severe economic crisis, President Ernesto Zedillo (1994–2000) was able to stabilize and begin the growth of the Mexican economy through a bailout from the U.S. government and a series of political and economic reforms and expansions to Mexico's free trade agenda. The immediate repercussions in architecture of these changes can be seen in the very development of the Santa Fe district in the western part of Mexico City by both government and private enterprise. Modeled on the popularity of the Parisian business center, La Defénse, Santa Fe aimed to become a new business center to compete with the historical center of Mexico for a new international financial clientele.

Within Santa Fe, we see a continuation of the work and concerns of the 1980s. Ricardo Legorreta built the Plaza Reforma office center (1993) with its Barragán-inspired forms and colors, use of internal courtyards, and references to traditional Mexican architecture. Immediately across the street from it is Teodoro González de León and Francisco Serrano's Hewlett-Packard Corporate Headquarters (1991–1997), which continues the hand-chiseled reinforced concrete monumental architectural line. Emblematic of the new position that Santa Fe would try to establish for itself are a series of large iconic corporate buildings such as the Arco Tower (Francisco Serrano, 1993–1996), which resembles a skyscraper version of a triumphal arch built in concrete and, according to some critics, is a homage to the Grande Arche in La Defénse (Paris, 1989) and a new emblem for the future center of economic power. Likewise, throughout the area we find repeated attempts to express a regionalist vocabulary, inspired by Kenneth Frampton's newly coined notion of "critical regionalism," such as the Centro Santa Fe—a North American–inspired shopping center that is full of Mexican architectural features and colors—the largest mall in Mexico (Juan Sordo Madaleno, 1993).

The new international and technological focus, however, did allow for the development of new forms of architecture by a group of young architects. Known as "the new moderns," and their designs as "Mex-Tec," their architecture was defined by the use of new technologies, materials, and forms that reflected a globalized vision of and audience for their architecture.

At first, their work seemed to be devoid of historical references, but the reality was that their approach to history did not negate the importance of history. Historical references within their work, in other words, were mediated by a series of social needs that made them into something more than the expression of tradition that had been faithfully and precisely copied. These architects saw history as something that could be mined, because it offered a wealth of formal, technical, or productive innovations that could be seen as operating critically. The primary relationship that the radical and innovative architects of the 1990s forged was with the historical avant-garde, particularly the Mexican one, whose legitimacy had been eroded because of its utopianism or because of its ideological or material deficiencies. In much of the architecture of the 1990s, we see a desire to reproduce the myth of the techno-scientific image of that avant-garde as a way for

MX

Mexico to represent itself as contemporary and modern (as it had done in the past).

This is clear in the work of Enrique Norten. A result of modern syncretism himself, Norten trained at the private Universidad Iberoamericana in Mexico City before studying at Cornell University in Ithaca, New York. His firm, TEN Arquitectos: Taller de Enrique Norten, was founded in 1985 and joined by Bernardo Gómez-Pimienta in 1987. Like his immediate architectural forefathers—Juan O'Gorman and the radical functionalists—Norten began his work by using the most contemporary materials—stainless steel, concrete, glass—in juxtaposition to the existing architectural forms and culture. What Norten did was to make them perform as signifiers of a new modernity to the exterior world as well as referents of a new self-identity.

The Lighting Center (Mexico City, 1988–1989) and Houses N and R (Valle de Bravo, 1989–1990) not only express traditional brick construction but also introduce industrialized materials. For the first, an etched glass panel supported by guy wires and exposed steel trusses make up the façade that faces the busy Insurgentes Street. The rear façade, on the other hand, is simple in its expression of the wiring systems—no different from what O'Gorman did in the interiors of the Diego Rivera and Frida Kahlo Studios (see 1931 box). Many of these new materials, however, were also mediated by the hand of the craftsman. The sheet-metal canopy, for example, was painstakingly perforated by hand. Finally, the project shows its indebtedness to contemporary architectural investigations by the California firm Morphosis not only through its forms and materials but also through its layered architectural rendering that echoes many of the qualities of their drawings. Houses N and R are morphological investigations of vernacular Mexican homes of brick construction and pitched tile roofs. Their interiors show a character radically different from the local architecture through the use of open, double-height spaces; the expression of steel structural elements; and the reliance on industrial materials—seen for instance in the handrail-less steel stairs.

Norten's later work illustrates an additive process of design in which forms, materials, and spaces are layered on top of one another. Paradigmatic of this are the National School of Theater at the Ciudad de las Artes (Mexico City, 1993–1994) and the TELEVISA Services Building (Mexico City, 1993–1995). Although they continue some of the earlier investigations of materials, the later work could be described as a spatial inversion of its predecessors. In it, the shift is rendered from objects in space of the earlier work (which create clearly defined spatial boundaries) to objects within space that create internalized formal and spatial relations within sometimes ambiguous boundaries. Both projects articulate this space through the creation of large semicircular or oval spaces that house both open space and programmed spaces encased in boxes clad in glass or other materials. They both appear highly technological in the way they reveal and express their steel structures and tension cables, the contrast of materials,

Enrique Norten, Lighting Center, Mexico City, 1988–1989.

Enrique Norten, National School of Theater, Mexico City, 1993–1994.

and the various programmatic elements needed. Because of their technical and technological complexities, the engineering and structural calculations were done by the English firm Ove Arup. Ultimately, these works reenact an emblematic functionalism that spectacularizes architecture's functional pieces and, through their ultramodern appearance, give the appearance of Mexico as internationally modern.

The work of Alberto Kalach is similar, as it equally negotiated the shift from more autochthonous forms and concerns to more modern ones. Like Norten, Kalach studied at the Universidad Iberoamericana before receiving his master's at Cornell University. His early work, like the House in Valle de Bravo (1994) or the Negro House (1995–1997), contrasts local materials and forms (artisanal brickwork and traditional wood rafters) with more modern open spatial sensibilities

and materials, such as reinforced concrete, glass, and steel. Also from this period is the Subway Station and Public Building (Mexico City, 1992–1994) that sits on a site affected by the 1985 earthquake. The result is a massive exposed reinforced concrete building with an inaccessible circular courtyard. The edges along the front façade allow for ground-floor circulation into the subway station, creating for the perimeter mass of that façade an appearance of semidetachment. However, it is in the details—the use of exposed steel columns and structure, the angular forms of the glass roof over the entry to the subway, the contrast of a lava rock garden at the center of the courtyard with the reinforced concrete and glass—where the building displays its character. Kalach's later work, such as the GGG House (Mexico City, 1999–2000; see 2000

box), is equally monolithic in its use of exposed reinforced concrete, yet its character is more subtle—akin to the work of Japanese architect Tadao Ando—and is emphasized through its contrast to a number of materials.

The economic situation and the emerging process of cultural globalization allowed a new generation of architects to emerge, experiment, and operate within these new prospects. So, while Barragán or neo-Aztec monumentality continued to be commissioned primarily by long-standing institutions and governmental entities, a new and diverse type of clientele actively sought these new works as an emblematic architecture to represent it. Works like Luis Vicente Flores's Centro Cultural X'Teresa (Mexico City, 1993–1994) or Isaac Broid's Centro de la Imagen (Mexico City, 1993–1994) made somewhat unprecedented but radically modern insertions of steel, glass, and concrete that contrasted with the existing historical structures in and around Mexico City's historical center. Others, like AVE (Enrique Albin, Fernando Vasconcelos, Alejandro Elizondo), experimented more freely with a wide range of historical precedents. The Saltiel House (Mexico City,

1990–1992) can be seen as a combination of standard Corbusian elements—horizontal windows and *pilotis*—around a central patio space yet is linked to the present through the presence of a large parabolic antenna on the roof of a protruding tower. Casa Roja (Valle de Bravo, 1991–1992), through the use of long horizontal masonry walls defining the landscape, is a rearticulation of the canonical Mies van der Rohe brick country house (1922). The central space of the house, however, is defined by a clay-tiled roof structure, clay-tile floors, and exposed heavy wooden rafters. Fernando Vasconcelos would continue this reconceptualization and readaptation of past forms in a more radical way. The design for the expansion of the Colegio Americano (Mexico City, 2007) references the character and rhythmic patterns of the prismatic glass International-style apartment buildings of Mario Pani and uses a variant of the Mathias Goeritz sculpture for El Eco, *La serpiente* (1953), as its structure.

However, it was the result of a diverse group of national and international publications and prizes that

Nuevo Espíritu (Fernando Vasconcelos), Colegio Americano, Mexico City, 2007.

led to the popularization, dissemination, and further commissioning of new Mexican architecture in the last decades of the twentieth century. The magazine *"a" Arquitectura* (1991–1996) became a central mechanism for presenting the work of its editorial board and close colleagues to a broader international audience. Put together by Kalach, Broid, Adriana León, Norten, Flores, and the historian Humberto Ricalde, and modeled primarily on the contemporary Spanish magazine *El Croquis*, the journal contextualized the work happening in Mexico within a broader international agenda by publishing works and writings from architects outside of Mexico. *Arquine* followed it, starting in 1997. Led by the Catalan architect Miquel Adrià, this self-described "international architecture magazine" continued the trend of presenting the high-quality work being developed in Mexico in the context of contemporary international architecture, criticism, and historiographical concerns. *Arquine* developed into a franchise that sponsors international competitions and publishes multilingual books primarily on Mexican architecture. The publication fervor at the end of the 1990s included, to name a few, Adrià's

Mexico 90s: A Contemporary Architecture (Gustavo Gili, 1996), a special number of the Italian magazine *Lotus* dedicated to Mexican architecture (1996), coverage in the Spanish journal *2G* on a new generation of Latin American architecture (1998), and issue number 2 of the North American magazine *Praxis* (2001) devoted to the same topic. This focus had its apotheosis when Enrique Norten and Bernardo Gómez Pimienta received the 1998 award of the Mies van der Rohe Prize for Latin American Architecture for their work for TELEVISA.

FURTHER READING

Adrià, *Alberto Kalach.*
———, *Mexico 90s: A Contemporary Architecture.*
Albin, *Vasconcelos, Elizondo.*
Ingersoll, *TEN Arquitectos: Enrique Norten, Bernardo Gómez-Pimienta.*
"Mexico City: Projects from the Megacity."

1997

SMILJAN RADIC, CHARCOAL BURNER'S HUT

SEVERAL CRITICS HAVE PRAISED contemporary Chilean architecture as the best in Latin America in the last years of the twentieth century. In common, they speak of a sensibility to site conditions and an attention to materiality that gets translated to a level of precision higher than in Mexico, Brazil, or Colombia. Behind that is also a conceptual intensity that elevates the architectural discourse and reaches out to contemporary art and, specifically, to installations as experimental architecture.

The work of Smiljan Radic weaves together all the elements that make Chilean contemporary architecture so celebrated. Born in Santiago, Chile, in 1965, to a family of Croatian immigrants, Smiljan Radic Clarke graduated in 1989 from the Catholic University in Chile. After his studies, Radic attended art and aesthetics classes at the Istituto Andrea Palladio and the Istituto Universitario di Architettura, both in Venice, Italy. In addition, he collaborates extensively with the Chilean sculptor Marcela Correa.

Balancing his Chilean and European roots, Radic's work is simultaneously very Chilean and extremely universal. Much like Emilio Duhart in the 1970s (see 1966 entry) and Enrique Browne in the 1980s (see 1990 entry), Radic has been widely published since the 1990s, making him a pioneer among contemporary Chilean architects despite his young age. His work combines visual appeal with intellectual rigor. This kind of work is quite common in North America and Europe, where young architects use installations and museum pieces as stepping-stones to large buildings. Radic should be praised for focusing on the intensity of installations and small structures while many of his peers jumped quickly on large commissions, at the expense of quality and rigor. At Casa Chica (Talca, 1995), Radic used rough granite slabs and recycled materials such as windows and doors to build a tiny house of 300 sq. ft. (28 sq. m). In addition to referencing the work of Le Corbusier and Alvar Aalto, it is a type of primitive hut for contemporary times with a steel structure, stones cut by prisoners, and materials salvaged from other structures. His Cooper Houses 1 and 2 (Chiloé Island, 1996–1999, and Talca, 2004–2005) and his Chilean Houses 1 and 2 (Rancagua, 2005–2006) are investigations centered on a single theme: the whiteness of Chilean houses and the material properties of copper, of which Chile is the largest world producer.

On the periphery of Santiago exist the remains of a Charcoal Burner's House and furnaces. As a point of departure to intervene at the site of the ruins, Radic looked at the traditional construction processes of charcoal-burning furnaces. At Casa del Carbonero (1997), a type of charcoal maker's hut or an addition to the charcoal maker's house, Radic's architecture is revealed in all its intensity and contradictions. The project is not an inhabitable space but an installation. For the original furnaces or "huts," a hole was dug in the ground, 10 ft. (3 m) in diameter and 4 ft. (1.2 m) deep, to be carefully filled with wood. The wood was then covered with mud and straw (for extra strength) and fired up, turning the clay into a ceramic hut.

In Radic's piece, the traditional ground excavation was turned into an aboveground sphere with wire mesh used to form the lower half. The wood sticks are carefully placed to form the sphere, and the volume is covered in mud with small holes for ventilation. Once the fire is set, the smoking giant mud ball activates the space, referencing the earlier use of the site while becoming a center point of this new public space. The platonic volume, built with traditional Chilean methods, links the local and the universal as well as old construction methods to the new world of landscape art or site constructions. Radic explains that calling the piece an "addition to the charcoal burner's hut," does not adequately explain that it is not a proper expansion of the living space but rather an amplification of its imaginary.

In another iteration, he created three more mud spheres and located them among twenty-three palm trees in a larger field called Cancha Culipran. *Cancha*, an Inca word that means "open public space," is probably the most used word of Andean origin in contemporary Spanish (used as a synonym for "field" or "court"). For Radic, architecture is a "warehouse of memories." Here and with the Charcoal Burner's Hut, he has accessed architecture's multiple layers of meaning of the forms, names, and organizing structures and has transformed them into metaphors and relationships that, for him, are as important as the materiality itself. The precision of the architecture, with sculptural inspirations that carry into his later houses, is created in a way that diffuses its significance into a variety of interpretations.

2000

COLOMBIAN RENAISSANCE: IN BOGOTÁ AND MEDELLÍN, MAYORS AND ARCHITECTS WORK TOGETHER TO CREATE BETTER CITIES.

COLOMBIA

BY THE EARLY 1990S, the mood in Colombia was quite grim. While the fall of the Berlin Wall in 1989 symbolized the end of the Cold War and a potential move beyond the strenuous struggle between extreme left and extreme right, the reality on the ground was far from optimistic. Instead of displaying a spirit of resolution and compromise, Colombia's paramilitary on the right and the Fuerzas Armadas Revolucionarias de Colombia (FARC; Revolutionary Armed Forces of Colombia) on the left were entrenched in their positions. With the state locked up by the political conflict, drug dealers were filling the power gaps and exerting control and influence over large parts of the Colombian territory. Never had Gabriel García Márquez's fictional town of Macondo seemed more real: an endless run of banal and brutal violence. Architecture was the least of

Colombia's worries but would prove to be fundamental in its turnaround.

It was in such a gloomy scene that three mayors rose to prominence as leaders whose primary banner was their independence from the old stereotypes of right and left and a strong commitment to public life and public space. Antanas Mockus and Enrique Peñalosa in Bogotá and Sergio Fajardo in Medellín brought a fresh batch of new ideas to the two major Colombian cities.

When elected in 1994, Antanas Mockus was a forty-three-year-old professor of philosophy who had no previous political experience. The son of Lithuanian immigrants, Mockus focused his administration on civic behavior campaigns. In one of them, citizens were given

Transmillennium bus system, Bogotá, 1997.

red cards (as if they were soccer referees) to show to others committing small infractions on the street, such as littering or parking on sidewalks. In another campaign, mimes would perform on the streets, validating good behavior and "punishing" bad habits by publicly (but silently) exposing it to all. Mockus also started a "day-with-no-cars" event. In a more legal framework, Mockus signed ordinances to ban gun ownership and alcohol sales after 1:00 a.m. The population responded by showing 70 percent support for Mockus's administration. Much less supported were the attempts to restrict the use of private automobiles, and as a result, a 1996 referendum on that matter failed to gather the necessary majority.

In 1997, Enrique Peñalosa, a U.S.-trained manager, was elected as mayor, and his administration changed the focus from Mockus's civic campaigns to a stronger emphasis on building public infrastructure. Aware that the public would not support restrictions on automobile usage, Peñalosa focused instead on building better public transportation. The project that would become the signature of his administration, the TransMilenio, or Transmillennium, was a system of dedicated lanes for articulated buses on main arteries, connected to feeder routes on regular streets. Inspired by Curitiba (see 1965-b entry), the Transmillennium used boarding platforms on the main arteries, with the passengers coming from feeder routes paying the fare once they get there, at the end of their first journey. Peñalosa's administration also built 185 miles (298 km) of bicycles routes and 10 million sq. ft. (929,030 sq. m) of public space. If public behavior was the signature of Mockus's administration, the quality of public space became the iconic Peñalosa achievement. He asked Bogotanos to "imagine a city full of parks, trees, bicycles, libraries, sidewalks, clean, egalitarian."[1] Such an exercise of imagination could not be achieved without good architecture, so Peñalosa took advantage of Colombia's talented pool of young architects in that regard.

Meanwhile, in 1993, the Colombian Congress promulgated Ley 80, a law enforcing a transparent process of bidding for public projects. In 1995, the federal government pushed this process even further with Decreto 2326, which states that every public building needs to be the result of a public competition and dictates how the competitions should be organized. At that point, Colombia already had an extensive tradition of architectural competitions, but the fact that they became mandatory for public buildings created a number

of new possibilities, especially for young architects who were now able to compete on more equal terms with more established firms. The impact of such legislation was an invigorated Colombian architecture.

While the capital, Bogotá, was reinventing its civic life, its transportation infrastructure, and its public spaces under Mockus and Peñalosa, in Medellín, Colombia's second-largest city, the city was aiming even higher in its turnaround based on quality architecture. The city known in the 1980s for its infamous drug cartel became the poster child for Colombia's urban renaissance. The man behind this transformation was Sergio Fajardo, a professor at the Universidad Nacional with a PhD in mathematics who founded a civic movement in Medellín in 1999 called the Grupo Compromiso Ciudadano (Citizens Commitment Group). At that point, the influence of Mockus was clear and was reinforced by their political alliance. Elected mayor of Medellín in 2003, Fajardo took the best of both Mockus and Peñalosa, combining a strong belief in architecture as a catalyst for change with creative initiatives such as community leaders signing documents pledging to maintain a new park after its inauguration. His administration also brought a participatory budgeting process (a Brazilian invention) to Colombia. These types of exchanges are becoming more and more common in Latin America. So, for instance, while Bogotá's Transmillennium was inspired by Curitiba's successes, Rio de Janeiro's most recent interventions to contain the violence in the favelas borrow from Fajardo's success in bringing the crime rate down in Medellín.

The son of a prominent local architect, Fajardo understood early on that buildings could have a significant impact on civic life, and he took full advantage of the 1993 and 1995 laws to attract the best talents to Medellín's public projects. The mayor had a powerful slogan for his proposal: "The most beautiful for the most humble."[2]

With that in mind, he set out to reorganize Medellín's finances and broaden its tax base. The extra revenue was spent mostly on public education and public spaces that are often placed together in the same project. The most iconic of those buildings is Parque Biblioteca España (2007), a library and community center built in the hilly informal neighborhood of Santo Domingo. Organized around three monolithic dark volumes enveloping the spaces, the library complex sits like "rocks" on the site, re-creating the mountain profile according to architect Giancarlo Mazzanti. While

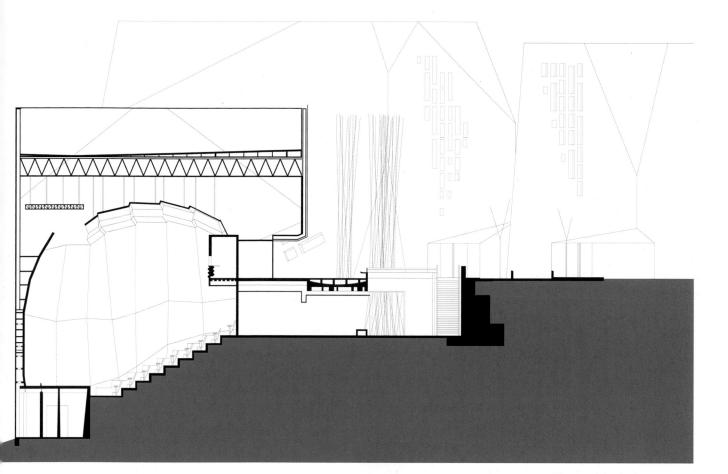

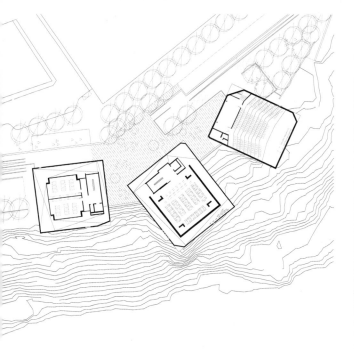

Section and plan of Biblioteca España.

Giancarlo Mazzanti, Biblioteca España, Medellín, 2007.

Felipe Mesa et al., Orquideorama, Medellín, 2006.

the library's form is closed to the point of seeming defensive (as noted by critics), its contrasting shapes of avant-garde architecture placed in the ubiquitous barrios turned the building into a symbol of Fajardo's idea of building the best architecture for the poorest inhabitants. Less visible but perhaps as important is the "park" side of the complex, which includes a series of ramps that make the library and the community around it more accessible.

Several other projects in Medellín deserving of praise have been extensively published: the intervention at Plaza de Cisneros by Juan Manuel Peláez (2005); the León de Greiff Library Park by Mazzanti (2007); the Hontanares School by Felipe Mesa and Alejandro Bernal (Plan B Arquitectos, 2006)—all of which were results of competitions called by Fajardo during his term in office. All these projects, we must note, continue the tradition of good public spaces that have been built in Medellín for decades. Spaces like Felipe Uribe's design for Parque de los Deseos (Park of Wishes; 2000), for instance, are representative of this tradition.

But the jewel in Medellín's crown is the Orquideorama (2006), designed by Mesa and Bernal (Plan B) in collaboration with Camilo and J. Paul Restrepo. To shade and support a collection of orchids in Medellín's botanical gardens, they designed a sequence of seven hexagonal-shaped roof structures that are grouped together around a centerpiece that works as a column. The roofs of the hexagons are clad with a wood trellis on the lower surface, and translucent polycarbonate above that controls light incidence and collects water to maintain the humidity level for the

orchids. The distance between ceiling (trellis) and roof (polycarbonate) also enhances ventilation. The six columns that support each central hexagon are also clad with wood trellises that rotate around them, making the whole canopy appear very dynamic. The resultant space has remarkable natural light, filtered by the trellises, and a certain degree of dematerialization achieved through the transparency and lightness of the whole structure.

In a way, Medellín's Orquideorama summarizes the qualities of contemporary Colombian architecture: an ingenuous use of simple materials brought together in a very elegant and sophisticated way to enhance public spaces that have the potential to support positive societal changes. In the process of building them with the public accountability of open competitions, they also transformed Colombia into a hub of innovative design.

FURTHER READING

Barney, "Learning from Bogotá: How Municipal Experts Transformed Public Space."

Gallanti, "Elementary School in Bogotá, Colombia. Architect: Giancarlo Mazzanti."

"Gerardo Molina School, Giancarlo Mazzanti."

Hernández, *Beyond Modernist Masters: Contemporary Architecture in Latin America.*

"Paisajes emergentes: La Piedra Horadada = The Perforated Stone."

2000

ALBERTO KALACH, GGG HOUSE, MEXICO CITY

ALBERTO KALACH ONCE SAID that "architecture is read on drawings. Verbal constructions sprung from architecture tend to be quite boring." Indeed, his GGG House (designed with Daniel Álvarez, Mexico City, 2000) can be read by looking at the drawings, yet it cannot be fully understood through them. After all, there is more to a building than its drawings, and this is certainly the case with the GGG House. For instance, how would we know from the drawings that the design of the house was inspired by the sculptures of Mexican sculptor Jorge Yapzik? The carving of spaces that defines the spatiality of the house follows a similar strategy to Yapzik's material interpenetration that highlights the voids between masses. In Kalach's design, the mass-void game is twofold: it defines both the inhabited spaces and the building's envelope, which, in turn, challenges the first by making the house resemble a three-dimensional labyrinth.

To understand the GGG House, one needs to know about its context—something that goes beyond Kalach's drawings and problematizes the assertions on drawings. Alberto Kalach himself is half of this context (see 1994-b entry). Born in 1960 in Mexico City, he studied architecture at the Universidad Iberoamericana and completed his graduate studies at Cornell University. He taught for a few years but stopped in 1997, around the time that he was designing the GGG House. Kalach does not like to lecture or aggressively pursue publications. For him, the work should speak for itself.

The other important information missing from the drawings is the house's location: nestled between an exclusive golf course, a fake (brand-new) hacienda, and a working-class apartment building. It is that very complex and challenging context that explains the centrifugal organization of the house. In Kalach's own words, "These are

Alberto Kalach, GGG House, Mexico City, 2000.

Alberto Kalach, interior view with Jorge Yapzik sculpture of GGG House, Mexico City, 2000.

the surroundings we wanted to make disappear, once you enter the site and house, the idea was to transport you to another world." And this other world was crafted like an inhabitable monolith of reinforced concrete repeatedly carved and dislocated. To increase privacy and obstruct the views of what is outside its walls, the program is organized around a patio at the wider part of a triangular lot. At the edge of the triangle, a lush garden behind walls creates its own landscape on which the social spaces open. At the entrance, a basalt lava ramp slopes gently to the garage under the house, while a reflecting pool holding one of Yapzik's sculptures seems to float by the side. The reference to Barragán's houses at El Pedregal (see 1947-a entry) is quite explicit, but Kalach, interested in alternative worlds of manipulated elements, holds the water above the wall as if to challenge gravity itself.

Reinforced concrete is the material of choice for most of Kalach's buildings, its plasticity becoming evident from the design process. According to Kalach, the house was designed using clay models, with each cut opening possibilities for other cuts. The result is that the GGG House has very few windows in the traditional sense. Instead, there are numerous cuts in the concrete surface that generate openings and precisely controlled light sources. Spaces, in turn, are connected diagonally by those openings. In addition, corridors abound in the house's centrifugal plan. The envelope, carved in the same way as the living spaces, functions as a mediator: its folds and cuts are always working to pull the spaces apart. Following the lead of Yapzik's sculptures, the voids here are much more important than the masses.

Kalach seems to thrive on complexity, and the house does not offer a single narrative or simple explanation. Walnut floors and steel details on the fenestration add to the dominating concrete walls, sometimes made rough from wooden-plank formwork and other times made smooth, as in the ceilings and bathrooms. Similar to the writings of Jorge Luis Borges, the GGG House shows a collection of materials masterly crafted to maximize their contradictions. Alberto Kalach moved on to design other remarkable structures, such as Casa Negro (Cuajimalpa, 1997), the Vasconcelos Library (Mexico City, 2006), or Casa Atalaya (Del Mar, CA, 2008). In all those projects, the careful manipulation of spaces and envelopes is reminiscent of the GGG House, a building that summarizes his path thus far.

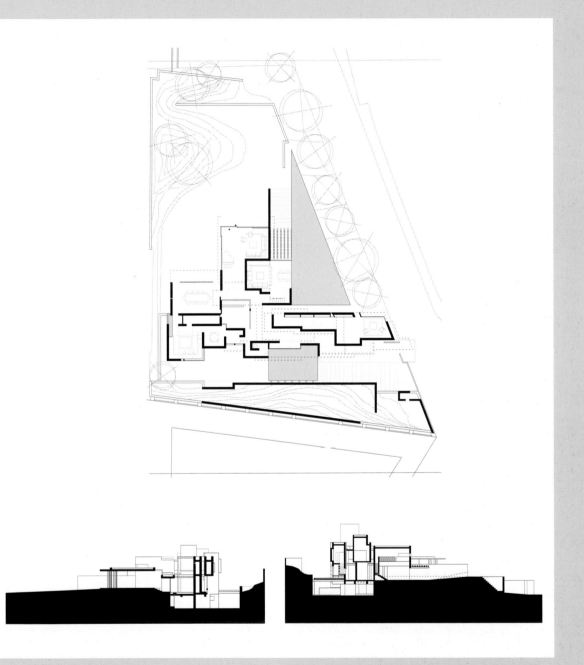

Plan and sections of GGG house.

2001

SOLANO BENÍTEZ'S TOMB FOR HIS FATHER, PARAGUAY

FOR TEN YEARS, SOLANO BENÍTEZ worked on the design and construction of a simple structure to mark his father's tomb on a family parcel in the small town of Piribebuy, Paraguay, east of Asunción. Known as "las Cuatro Vigas," it is made up of four reinforced concrete beams, as the name suggests, that come together to define a 30 x 30 ft. (9 x 9 m) square-shaped space. Each of these beams is raised off the ground and cantilevers from a single support that is located about 5 ft. (1.5 m) from each of the ends. In plan, the perpendicular placement of the supports relative to the beams, the overlapping of the beams in plan, and the openings of the square at the corners give the square a pinwheel effect reminiscent of the core of Mies van der Rohe's Brick Country House project (1922). Because of the irregular character of the site—surrounded by a small

brook that partially enters the square space—and excessive vegetation, the structure becomes a datum that registers the changes in the site, especially as the beams are no higher than a common handrail. The idea of registration is also present within the tactile and visual quality of the beams, as the concrete is imprinted with leaves of the local Amambay fern. Something magical happens, however, as one enters the square. First of all, the transition is tenuous, as the ends of the beams taper in. Because of their triangular profile in plan, the edges of the beams are hard to perceive. In addition, the concrete beams, instead of being left exposed as on the outside, are covered with mirrors. These generate a play of reflections of the vegetation and

Solano Benítez, Cuatro Vigas, Piribebuy, Paraguay, 2001.

346

everything surrounding it, making the massive structural pieces virtually disappear. Benítez describes the visual experience of entering the space as "centripetal," since, as one moves diagonally through it, the mirrors appear to reflect the context outwardly. Benítez's father's tomb is located at the center of the complex, and next to it is a place to sit and contemplate. At eye level with the beams, the reflection of the mirrors creates a mise en abyme that infinitely reflects everything within the space back onto itself. Because the experience becomes internalized to the complex, Benítez defines this experience as "centrifugal." Not unlike Alison and Peter Smithson's Patio and Pavilion at the *This Is Tomorrow* exhibition (London, 1956), Benítez uses the beams to define and enclose space in order to respond to the primal human needs of shelter and privacy within the lush Paraguayan landscape. But, more specifically, the reflective character of the beams is like the aluminum-faced plywood patio of the Smithsons' exhibition. Both enclosures with their infinite reflectivity point to the endless ubiquity of space (in the case of Benítez, of an idyllic zone of remembrance) and highlight their contents. Finally, the use of bold reinforced concrete and internal focus ties the design to the neighboring Paulista school, its form and its relationship to the landscape relates it to more contemporary site-specific artworks, and the centrality of the phenomenological experience as well as the mirrored surface recall the minimalist sculptures of Robert Morris and Robert Smithson.

Solano Benítez, Cuatro Vigas, interior, Piribebuy, Paraguay, 2001.

2002

RAFAEL IGLESIA, PAVILIONS AT PARQUE INDEPENDENCIA

Last century's model is depleted and there is nothing that remains, nothing that goes beyond the second line of the modern movement. We reached a final point. For this reason, I go backward searching for something different so that I can continue to move forward.

RAFAEL IGLESIA, *DIARIO RIO NEGRO*
(DECEMBER 2006)

IN 1992, RAFAEL IGLESIA, Gerardo Caballero, Rubén Fernández, José María D'Angelo, Gonzalo Sánchez Hermelo, and Marcelo Vilafañe founded Grupo R in Rosario, Argentina. The third-largest city in the country, Rosario is located at the banks of the Paraná River, halfway between Buenos Aires and Córdoba, the three cities forming the core of the Argentine economy. However, the neoliberal reforms of President Carlos Menem and the minister of economy Domingo Cavallo in the 1990s devastated Rosario's industrial base and increased unemployment to a record high of 22 percent by 1995 despite the fact that the Argentine economy was going full force. In that bleak scenario, Grupo R managed to transform the architectural debates in the city and soon influence the whole country despite the fact that they had no support from the university or from the city. Preaching against the "isms" of the 1980s and aligned with critical theory, Grupo R was looking for the essential qualities of architecture. Reacting against the postmodern exuberance of the Buenos Aires Biennial (see 1985-a entry), they managed to bring to Rosario the Portuguese architect Álvaro Siza, the Catalan Enric Miralles, and the Spaniard Rafael Moneo. The intensity of their debates and the quality of their architecture galvanized a contemporary Rosario school with links to Solano Benítez in Paraguay, Angelo Bucci in São Paulo, and Alejandro Aravena in Chile, among others.

From Grupo R, Rafael Iglesia is surely the densest thinker among them. Born in Rosario in 1951, Iglesia had an uncle with the same exact name who had been a successful architect in the 1950s and 1960s but from whom he says he learned nothing. Instead, his references came from the literature of Jorge Luis Borges and Roberto Arlt. A prolific writer himself, Iglesia wrote repeatedly that he had never been interested in the latest ideas or the latest materials and that, instead, he would focus his

Rafael Iglesia, bathroom pavilion, Rosario, 2003.

Rafael Iglesia, interior of the bathroom pavilion, Rosario, 2003.

experimentations on the essential. Gravity seems to be the thread that weaves through Iglesia's designs, as in the wooden stairs he built with standard 4 x 4 in. (100 x 100 mm) pieces compressed against two concrete slabs. In fact, Iglesia's tectonic focus does have a precedent in the Rosario work of architect Jorge Scrimaglio, both in how gravity is responded to by bricks and voids at Casa Lavalle (1973) and in the extreme geometric rigor of Casa Siri (1990). Iglesia's *quinchas* (barbecue pavilions) are small structures in which wood, stone, and concrete are combined in ways that stretch their inherent properties to the limit. Strategic anchoring and cantilevering become the architectural strategies that allow compression and tension to be as explicit as they can.

However, given the private character of these projects, they have had a limited impact. Iglesia's public opportunity came in 2002 when he was commissioned to build two pavilions for Parque Independencia, the largest swath of green space and sports fields in the middle of Rosario's orthogonal grid. To support its activities, he was asked to design two pavilions: one with public bathrooms and the other for birthday parties.

The bathroom pavilion sits at the entrance of the park and not, as Iglesias ironically points out, "at the very back to the right" where most bathrooms are usually located. Elevated from the ground, the pavilion is a very long rectangle defined by two reinforced concrete slabs: floor and ceiling. Concrete is also used in the inner walls (supporting the roof) that ingenuously zigzag at the inner core along the longitudinal axis, alternating toilets to the male and female restrooms while concentrating all plumbing together. That strategy also maximizes daylight by leaving all

Rafael Iglesia, party pavilion, Rosario, 2003.

external walls free of load-bearing necessities or utilities. The external envelope between the slabs is made of steel mullions with sanded glass panels. The result is the correct amount of privacy: obstructing enough from the outside but still allowing silhouettes to be perceived and, thus, making the bathrooms much safer. During the night, the bathroom pavilion glows and illuminates the entrance of the park, which also adds to the overall sense of security.

The party pavilion is even more inventive and as essential as the program permits. One continuous reinforced concrete slab at ground level folds up to create the roof of another elongated rectangle. The load of the roof slab is then carried by tree trunks displayed rhythmically at the outer perimeter of the pavilion. Iglesia had used tree trunks to support a concrete slab at a *quincha* project, and more famously and much earlier they had been used by Brazilian architect Vilanova Artigas at Casa Elza Berquó (São Paulo, 1967). But at the party pavilion, Iglesia goes one step further by slicing the trunks into three, two thinner outer caps and one thicker core piece. Placed in the building with their bark still intact, the trunks refer to

nature and the woods around the building, while the cuts accentuate the human craft involved in it. Like the Renaissance dialectic of "opera di mano versus opera di natura," Iglesia's structure mediates between the natural and the human made with a simplicity that speaks to the core of what it means to transform nature to produce architecture. With time, the trunks will lose their bark and imitate their surrounding less, showing first the redness of the wood oils and later turning gray, registering the passage of time. And as if to push the material possibilities to their limits, every partition in the party pavilion hangs from the ceiling slab. Only the trunks touch the floor slab that, in turn, rests on the ground. For Iglesia, weight is not a problem but the solution.

As we move into the twenty-first century, it is clear that the Rosario school of architecture has consistently produced some of the best contemporary works in Argentina as attested by several designs by Gerardo Caballero and Marcelo Villafañe.

PROVOCATIONS FOR A CONCLUSION: ISLANDS NO MORE

Here lies the future [of our practice]. . . . It is to interrogate the production, in imaginative and material practice, of those compound political, economic, and cultural forms by means of which human beings create community and locality and identity, especially on evanescent terrains; by means of which, in the face of material and moral constraint, they fabricate social realities and power relations and impose themselves on their lived environments; by means of which space and time are made and remade, and the boundaries of the local and the global are actualized. . . . Even the most overdetermined, most complex, most inchoate of world-historical forces . . . take shape in sociocultural processes that inhabit particular places during particular periods in particular persons. Without human agents, without specified locations and moments and actions, realities are not realized, nothing takes place, the present has no presence.

JEAN AND JOHN COMAROFF

THROUGHOUT THIS BOOK we made an effort to establish connections between ideas scattered around Latin America and people who were thinking similarly. Our commitment to write a history from a Latin American perspective (a task made even more complex because we both teach in the United States) prompted us to search deeper for those connections, often taking risks in countering a historiography that has always highlighted foreign (European and North American) relationships. Different Latin American regions, says the story, have always been islands, insulated from each other and intellectually aiming for Paris or New York. It is as if the center of gravity of architecture in Latin America were outside the region, floating somewhere in the North Atlantic. We could even use Gabriel García Márquez's *One Hundred Years of Solitude* (1967) as a metaphor, although in reality the solitude has lasted much more than a century.

But as we write this—looking for new directions in the first decade of the twenty-first century—it is a joy to perceive that Latin America is no longer isolated. In the last ten years, we had Colombian architects teaching in Brazil, Brazilians winning an important competition in Chile, Chileans building social housing in Mexico, Mexicans winning prizes in Ecuador, and so on. An unprecedented scale of integration now exists in Latin America, and we expect it to grow even more in the future.

To give some sense of closure to the century discussed here and present some possible trends to understand the contemporary moment, we need to go back a little bit to look into some key transformations that took place over the last decade of the century.

Since the 1990s, two movements have transformed the historiography (and, indeed, the practice) of architecture in Latin America. The economic integration of Mercosur prompted a renewed interest in neighboring countries while at the same time facilitating contact. A series of meetings, either academic conferences or exhibitions (the biennials would be the best example), brought Latin American architects together as never before. In addition, the easy flow of graphic information over the Internet has allowed architects to all know each other personally and follow each other's practice online in real time. Angelo Bucci, Giancarlo Mazzanti, Alejandro Aravena, and Gerardo Caballero teach abroad often and are invited to speak at several international events every year. Others are not so invested in an international career but travel no less often, showing their work and teaching in neighboring countries as well as in the United States and Europe.

When Internet sources became easily available by the end of the twentieth century, they also contributed to disseminating information faster and cheaper. Among the most successful Web portals (in qualitative and quantitative terms) are the Brazilian vitruvius .com.br and the Chilean plataformaarquitectura.cl. By expediting the publication process, the websites disseminate more information faster than their print counterparts. They also serve as a repository of information, easily searchable by anyone with an Internet connection.

Such integration (in person or virtual) paralleled an increased valorization of the region's modernist heritage (see 1991 entry). After flirting with postmodernism in the 1980s, the discourse of pluralism and regionalism mutated into a revaluation of the successes (and shortcomings) of modernism in each different country or region (see 1985-a entry). Some of the most exciting architecture of the first decade of the twenty-first century is acutely connected to local building cultures, respectfully appropriating local modernisms, and is strategically linking itself to other architectures, either near or halfway across the planet, that support its conceptual discourse.

Although it is too early for any comprehensive analysis of the architectures that have emerged in the first decade of the twenty-first century, the selections included herein serve as reference points for the establishment of possible directions or threads that might help us understand the present in reference to what happened before.

For instance, while we framed our investigation on twentieth-century modern architecture in Latin America under three main themes—art, technology, and utopia—we feel that those terms have mutated and need to be renamed for the sake of precision. The universalizing and homogenizing project of modernity has been widely scrutinized and its arbitrariness long decried. Broad discourses do not hold water anymore, and although we still have similar socioeconomic problems, the preferred solutions are much more localized in content and smaller in scale.

As a consequence, we are weary of celebrating technology as a savior and, instead, we speak highly of specific materiality for different contexts. We are no longer moved by utopias (in fact, we are quite suspicious of radical changes or proposals that suggest them), and, instead, we speak of social awareness. We do not believe in a singular definition of art anymore; instead, we value the conceptual density of certain projects that are able to translate artistic approaches into architectures that allow us to think differently and to see the world with "fresh eyes." The twenty-first-century projects discussed here are organized under those three broad topics: materiality, social awareness, and conceptual density.

Gravity has always been a fundamental component of architecture. In very basic terms, we are always trying to hold up heavy things to protect us from the elements. This challenge, literally, looms over our heads. The reference to gravity is important here because it defines an important difference between the twentieth- and the twenty-first-century approach to technology. If the twentieth century was all about defying gravity with lightness—as Oscar Niemeyer's Pampulha (see 1941 entry), Félix Candela's churches (see 1953-a box), or Eladio Dieste's brick vaults (see 1955 entry) were trying to do—the twenty-first century expresses the weight—tectonically and materially—and the effort it makes to hold up structure. Gravity, then, becomes an important issue to struggle with; the word in Spanish and Portuguese is also widely used to connote urgency, significance, and earnestness.

A prime example of that approach would be Angelo Bucci's house at Ribeirão Preto (2001). To counterbalance the bowing of a large beam from which too much weight is hanging from the edges, a water reservoir is placed in the middle of the span, immediately above the entrance. The irony here is, of course, that more weight was needed in order to avoid distortion. Since one enters the house under the volume of the water tank, its heaviness is made as expressive as possible. In other projects, Bucci has been exploring the limits of reinforced concrete by stretching overhangs and cantilevering as much as possible—such as in the House in Ubatuba (2007)—and, in this way, slightly diverging from the Paulista school that influenced him (see 1961-b and 1991 entries) to skillfully add complexity to his spaces.

Another remarkable expression of gravity as a driver for architecture is Casa Pentimento (Quito, Ecuador, 2005–2006) by José María Sáez Vaquero (in collaboration with Al Borde). A single type of concrete block, as long and hollow as a planter, is used to build all the walls of the house. Different dimensions for each of the surfaces allow the walls to achieve different degrees of privacy once the blocks are stacked in various ways. Inside the house, the blocks become shelves, window frames, or simply planters according to different needs. The wall is dematerialized by different degrees of perforation but is still load bearing. The game of stacking expresses the weights being transferred from roof slab to floor slab, while the sophistication of a diverse spatiality is accomplished by tinkering with the dimensions of the block.

In Mexico, Alberto Kalach achieves a similar effect at Casa GGG by sculpting walls and slabs, a dexterous game of variation and cuts (see 2000 box). In previous apartment buildings, Kalach exposed concrete structures both to express gravity and to reveal the systems that make a building work. Water pipes and electrical conduits (indistinguishable to the naked eye) work as railings for a stairway, and a ubiquitous pointed fence (as common in Latin American large cities as front lawns are in the suburbs of the United States) becomes an elegant metal sculpture. Kalach makes reinforced concrete seem smooth by the way he carefully treats each surface and the encounter with other materials such as wood floors or laminated glass enclosures.

On the opposite spectrum is the work of Solano Benítez in Paraguay, a master of roughness. Using mostly a very uneven artisanal brick as his main material, Benítez is able to create various types of surfaces: from the most heavy load-bearing walls to the most transparent screen-like envelopes. At the Unilever

Headquarters (Villa Elisa, Paraguay, 2000–2001), Benítez uses rows of sunscreens made out of bricks that alternate directions diagonally. The result is a surface so permeable and airy that it tricks us into thinking that the bricks are weightless (although, in reality, the very weight of each brick helps interlock the system, taking advantage of both vertical and lateral forces).

Similar elegant displays of gravity exist in the work of Daniel Bonilla in Colombia, Gerardo Caballero in Argentina, and the Arquitetos Associados in Brazil. At the Porciúncula La Milagrosa Chapel (Bogotá, 2003–2004), Bonilla used a local bright orange wood to create screens that modulate the light and bring warmth to a space that is made flexible by the sliding of the side walls. In this way, the chapel can be an intimate space for twenty people or serve as the main altar for a celebration ten times that size. The sensitivity to the place here goes beyond the siting to include the very materiality of the wood that complements the simple concrete slabs.

At Inhotim (Brumadinho, Brazil), a glittering contemporary art collection surrounded by mining terrain,

Arquitetos Associados, Galeria Miguel Rio Branco, Inhotim, Brumadinho, Brazil, 2010.

the Arquitetos Associados (Alexandre Brasil, Andre Prado, Bruno Santa Cecilia, Carlos Alberto Maciel, and Paula Zasnicoff) built several remarkable structures, such as the Burle Marx Educational Institute by Brasil and Zasnicoff (2006–2009) and the home for *Cosmococa* (2008–2010), the provocative installation designed by Hélio Oiticica and Neville de Almeida in 1973 (see 1967 entry). But it is at the Miguel Rio Branco Gallery (2008–2010) that their work resonates the most. Here, we encounter a distorted cube enveloped in Corten steel that appears to precariously hang from a cliff. Inside, the edgy photographs of Rio Branco are displayed in various manners: framed, printed, or projected on walls or on hanging pieces of white cloth. Working alongside the artist, the architects convinced the curatorial staff that the rusty steel box should have its structure exposed inside, as if the guts of the building were revealed. Since the rooms are kept in the dark, it is only when a bright photo of Rio Branco is projected for a few seconds that the structure is visible.

Structural revelations have always been the focus of architects from Rosario, Argentina. Rafael Iglesia's work (see 2002 box) can be described as a constant challenge of structural limits in which something is always cantilevered, always hanging, as if shouting at the presence of gravity. Drawing from Iglesia as much as from Jorge Scrimaglio and the Paulistas is the work of Gerardo Caballero and Maite Fernández. Their Edificio Brown (Rosario, 2005–2007) is perhaps the most successful apartment building of the last decade, an elegant combination of diverse materialities (brick, concrete, and glass) cleverly carved out of a corner block in a way that works well for both the dweller (maximizing privacy as well as views) and the city corner.

TWENTY-FIRST-CENTURY SOCIAL AWARENESS

As noted earlier, gravity can also convey urgency, necessity, significance. Throughout the book, we have addressed architectural proposals whose utopian sense served as the means to induce social change and to improve the grim realities under which many Latin Americans live. Those realities, however, slowly changed during the last century; the economies grew and political systems matured. Nevertheless, large portions of local populations still live under dire conditions. The fruits of modernization and globalization benefited some much more than others, and inequality is the most pressing issue in Latin America today.

At the same time, the idea of utopia held in the past has been abandoned, as we've become skeptical of any grand solution to the problems. Instead, we focus on the transformative power of smaller interventions and their potential for dissemination. For that reason, we now call social awareness what we called utopias before. It implies a change in scale (smaller projects) and also means that architecture no longer claims to have the power to change any given societal problem.

No single project embodies those ideas better than Alejandro Aravena's Elemental Housing (2001–). Deriving from a long list of Chilean social housing projects as well as from similar experiments such as PREVI in Peru (see 1969-b entry) and more contemporary Dutch proposals (Habraken, MVRDV, Mecanoo, etc.), Elemental tries to combine the best of the construction industry gains of scale with the best of informal processes of flexibility and affordability. The main design idea is to build smaller units (lowering costs upfront) that have within them the possibility of expansion. Each family would then expand when needed. The scheme was first built in Iquique, Chile, with ninety-three units of 320 sq. ft. (30 sq. m) each, expandable to 780 sq. ft. (73 sq. m). Since then,

Al Borde, Nueva Esperanza School, Ecuador, 2010.

Marcos Boldarini, Cantinho do Céu urbanization, São Paulo, 2011.

Aravena has also built Elemental variants in Santiago, Rantagua, and Antofagasta (Chile) as well as in Monterrey (Mexico).

In Mexico, another country with a long tradition of social housing, interesting projects have recently been built by Alberto Kalach and Derek Dellekamp. At the Perinorte Building (Mexico City, 2004), Kalach references Pedregulho by Reidy (see 1950 entry) with a curving bar that meanders for almost a half mile. By accommodating hundreds of apartments in a mid-rise (five stories), Kalach breaks the homogeneity of similar gigantic blocks and fosters a better relationship with the terrain. At Tlacolula, Oaxaca (2010), Dellekamp challenged the usual detached-house typology by setting the circulation outside under the cantilevered roof and therefore slashing several square feet off the construction costs while allowing for connections with the exterior space.

Since the mid-1990s, Colombia has produced some of the best examples of public spaces and infrastructure improvement for the poorest barrios. Giancarlo Mazzanti, whose libraries and schools have already been described (see 2000 entry), continues to produce a number of outstanding structures all over the country. In terms of social housing, it is the work of Ana

Elvira Vélez that deserves attention. Her award-winning La Playa apartment complex (Medellín, 2004) has a remarkable spatial flexibility combined with a clever circulation scheme and uses exposed plumbing in a very sensible way. Colombia's commitment to competitions as the main process for choosing public projects can be credited for giving young designers such as Felipe Mesa, Alejandro Bernal, and Camilo Restrepo the opportunity to build remarkable structures very early in their lives (see 2000 entry).

Continuing southward to Ecuador is Al Borde (Pascual Gangotena and David Barragán), who have not only managed to work for the rural poor but have also done it through an unusual participatory process. At Nueva Esperanza School (El Cabuyal, 2009), they used the same construction techniques that the community's fishermen have used for centuries—post-and-beam connections covered with thatch—but pushed the limits of its geometry.

Last but not least is the great novelty in terms of socially concerned architecture in the first decade of the twenty-first century coming from Brazil. Supported by large funds made available by the government of Lula da Silva (US$200 billion from the Programa de

Aceleração do Crescimento; PAC [Growth Acceleration Program]) and capitalizing on the experience accumulated since the mid-1990s are a number of interventions in the infamous favelas. While the bulk of the money has been spent on sewage connections (wisely) and road construction (not always wisely), many needed public spaces were also built. Experienced architects such as Jorge Jáuregui were able to change scales and design for the most populous favelas such as Complexo do Alemão in Rio de Janeiro (see 1994-a entry). Younger designers such as César Shundi at Praça do Lajeado in São Paulo (2008) and Fernando Maculan at Beco São Vicente in Belo Horizonte (2011) created surprising spaces—pergolas, soccer fields, retention walls with plazas and community areas—despite the restricted budgets and low-skilled workforce. One notch up on design quality is the work of Marcos Boldarini at Cantinho do Céu (2011), a very vulnerable community at the southern periphery of São Paulo. Working around the margins of a lake once used as a garbage dump, the Cantinho do Céu project stitches together the inhabitants and the environment through a sequence of public spaces that buffer the favela and the lake and establish a relationship between social awareness, elegant architectural details, and water filtration. This is an important example of how architecture can make a difference regarding the contemporary challenge of balancing social and environmental sustainability.

We can only hope that these successes, as localized as they now are, will disseminate throughout the region and contribute to a better-built environment for all.

TWENTY-FIRST-CENTURY CONCEPTUAL DENSITY

Architecture being the art of creating shelter and protection has always conceptually engaged the idea of gravity. In the previous century, architecture at first defied gravity with light structures and transparent envelopes (Juan O'Gorman, Amancio Williams, Oscar Niemeyer, Lina Bo Bardi), to later embrace gravity under the so-called brutalist movement (Clorindo Testa, Paolo Mendes da Rocha, Emilio Duhart, Teodoro González de León, and Abraham Zabludovsky). During

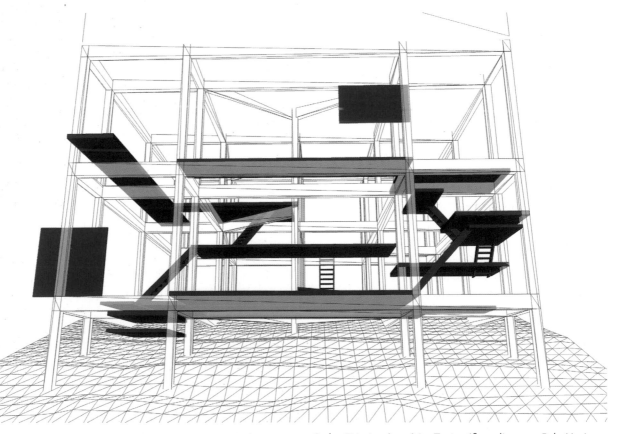

Carlos Teixeira, Amnésias Topográficas diagram, Belo Horizonte, 2001.

PROVOCATIONS FOR A CONCLUSION

the same time, architecture developed in parallel or tangentially to many artistic movements: Estridentismo, *antropofagia*, surrealism, Concretism, Neo-Concretism, and others. At the dawn of the twenty-first century, no single artistic movement takes prominence. Much to the contrary, the times are plural and diverse, but as a common denominator, we see artists engaging with the very buildings around them, be they gallery walls, historical monuments, or the city at large. Site-specific installations, as diverse as they can be from Christo to Wei Wei, dominate the scene.

Latin American architects are fully aware of such zeitgeist and respond to it with increasing conceptual density. In Brazil, Carlos Teixeira is an architect whose questions, manifested in installations of different media, are always sharp and disturbing. At *Amnesias Topográficas*, Teixeira called our attention to the waste of space caused by large structural grids built to support apartment buildings on sloped terrain. This project turned into a theater play, *Invento para Leonardo* (2001 and again in 2004), an award-winning piece that uses mediocre architecture as one of its supportive media, forging a provocative and critical look into the local building culture. More recently, *Spiral Booth* (2010) at the Victoria and Albert Museum in London and *O Outro, O Mesmo* (2010) at the São Paulo Biennial cemented Teixeira's position as a leading thinker and conceptual architect.

In Chile, Mauricio Pezo and Sofia von Ellrichshausen have built remarkable structures that also deal with important conceptual art strategies. Working with a very rigorous geometry, Pezo von Ellrichshausen's Casa Cien (Concepción, 2011), Casa Fosc (San Pedro, 2007), and Casa Poli (Coliumo Peninsula, 2005) houses are, like the early work of Sol LeWitt, variations of a cube. Here, the materials used, such

Pezo von Ellrichshausen, Casa Cien, Concepción, 2011.

Andrade and Morettin, Casa P.A., Carapicuíba, 1998.

as exposed concrete, become a surface through which to articulate perforations in unexpected places. Also in Chile are Smiljan Radic's Casa del Carbonero (see 1997-b box) and Cecilia Puga's Bahia Azul House (Los Vilos, 2002). Puga's design departs from a reinterpretation of the traditional Chilean farmhouse. The long pavilions of seriated homes commonly found in Maipo and Colchagua vineyards were sliced into three parts by Puga. Reassembled on a dry property overlooking the Pacific Ocean, one of the pieces is placed over the other two as if upside down. The raw nature of the exposed concrete used throughout the house recalls the austerity of the colonial farmhouse, here reinterpreted in a globalized Chilean version.

Wrapping up this risky assessment of early twenty-first-century architecture in Latin America, we would like to highlight three practices that could be placed in every one of the three clusters mentioned above, for their work addresses materiality and social awareness and at the same time reconceptualizes the very nature of the architectural profession: Alberto Mozó in Chile, Vinicius Andrade/Marcelo Morettin in Brazil, and Mauricio Rocha in Mexico. Mozó is the architect in the OWA (Only Wood Architecture) firm, a practice that uses laminated wood, prepared and cut with

precision in their workshop to be delivered and assembled at the site. Their BIP Building (Santiago, 2007) is a surprising structure in every way. The diagonal trellis-like laminated wood structure was assembled flat on the ground and raised by cranes. The three floors are made of identical 3 x 3 ft. (1 x 1 m) concrete blocks covered in polyethylene resin. Covered with a copper roof that folds down on the edges, the BIP Building is among the finest examples of a truly prefabricated building having minimal environmental impact during construction (minimal cuts, no waste), during the life of the building (very energy efficient), and after (almost all components can be reused).

Andrade and Morettin are also challenging the traditional architectural practice by using a variety of ready-made materials to achieve impressive effects on small and economic structures. At the Casa P.A. (Carapicuíba, 1997–1998), they designed a lightweight pavilion structure in wood that is wrapped by polycarbonate and anchored to another smaller volume of simple CMU blocks. The spatiality is straightforward and the geometry rigorous, with such attention to detail that the result is quite delicate. Now working with much larger projects, Andrade and Morettin have been able to continue their explorations in materiality and spatiality, building structures that diverge from the Paulista orthodoxy and are more in dialogue with Nordic or Chilean traditions.

Finally, the work of Mauricio Rocha operates within the parameters of art installations and interventions to radicalize architectural experience and its understanding. Works such as the Intervention in the Gallery of Contemporary Art (Mexico City, 1996), which subtracts a linear 18 in. (46 cm) circular axis through the length of an existing house/gallery, to a wooden scaffolding indebted to Vladimir Tatlin's *Monument to the Third International* (1919–1920) inside Gonzalo Fonseca's Tower of the Winds (Mexico City, 1968) allow one to perceive the material, constructive, and spatial characteristics of architecture. These experiential conditions are ultimately translated into forms that enhance the understanding and imaginary of architecture. This is most elegantly expressed in the Center for the Blind and Visually Impaired (Mexico City, 1999–2001) built for one of the poorest areas of the city. Through the inclusion of sensory cues generated by tactile material changes, reinforced concrete formwork patterns, light, fragrant vegetation, and the playful sound of water, Rocha transforms a maze of rectangular volumes into a truly poetic work that, in his words, "enables users to construct their own image of the space and their place in it."[1]

It should be clear that the first decade of the twenty-first century can be seen as one of the best ever in the region architecturally. Social awareness, conceptual density, and inventive materiality come together to create a surprisingly local yet globally connected architecture. It helps that the last decade also experienced a unique combination, for the most part, of growing economies, political stability, and center-left governments aggressively addressing old inequalities. Indeed, the celebrated qualities of architecture in Latin America at the dawn of the twenty-first century can be credited to different actors and factors, but one main thing runs through it all: its center of gravity is not outside the region anymore. Like Torres-García proposed in the 1930s (see 1938 box), the Travesías searched for in the 1960s (see 1969-a entry), and the Seminarios de Arquitectura Latinoamericana argued in the 1980s (see 1985 entry), the center of gravity can now be found in Latin America: somewhere between Quito, Medellín, Brasília, Rosario, Tijuana, and Asunción.

Mauricio Rocha, Center for the Blind and Visually Impaired, Mexico City, 1999–2001.

NOTES

(NOTES TOWARD AN) INTRODUCTION

1. Paz, *Labyrinth of Solitude*, 166.
2. Tafuri, "The Historical Project," 3.
3. Deleuze and Guattari, *Kafka*, 18.
4. Foucault, "Nietzsche, Genealogy, History," 88.

1903

1. In November of 1807, King João VI of Portugal, fleeing Napoleon, moved his entire court to Rio de Janeiro. The Brazilian city became the capital of the newly minted United Kingdom of Portugal, Brazil, and the Algarves. After João VI returned to Portugal, his son Pedro was installed as governor of Brazil and eventually declared its independence in 1822. João VI's grandson, Pedro II, governed until 1889 when a rising elite of professionals joined the military to take power and institute the First Brazilian Republic.

1904

1. The tax was implemented, but the funds were spent otherwise.
2. Only twenty years earlier, Brazil had an emperor whose family name, Orléans e Bragança, spoke to his Portuguese and French royalty roots. The proclamation of the Republic in 1889 and the exile of Emperor Pedro II (to Paris) did little to change this influence, as the Brazilian elite continued speaking French and looking to Paris for the latest trends until the beginning of World War II.
3. Liernur, *Trazas de futuro*, 92.
4. To this day, when a building in Buenos Aires is behind schedule, people refer to it as being "as delayed as the Congress."

1906

1. Hitchcock, *Architecture*, 416.
2. *Cambridge Encyclopedia*, 145.
3. Liernur, *Arquitectura en la Argentina del siglo XX*, 123–124.
4. F. Ramírez, *Crónica de las artes plásticas*, 22.

1914

1. Founded in 1909, this group was composed of young intellectuals opposed to Porfirio Díaz's dictatorship and philosophical outlook.
2. Emblematic of the possible loss of works from the past were H. Ravell's photographs of what he termed a "vanishing Mexico," which he published in *Harper's* magazine in December of 1916. In the brief introduction, it was noted that these were works that presented "a Mexico that is slowly vanishing" as an effect of the "stress and upheaval of revolution." Ravell, "Vanishing Mexico," 97–104.
3. Acevedo, see "Apariencias arquitectónicas" in *Disertaciones de un arquitecto*, 37. Also "[Nations] are the ones who really give monuments their character" (50).
4. Ibid., 90–91.
5. Ibid., 51.
6. Ibid., 53.
7. Mariscal, *La patria y la arquitectura nacional*, 7–9.
8. Ibid., 10.
9. Ibid., 11.
10. The monumental legacy of colonial architecture was something that the Boston-based American architectural historian Sylvester Baxter was also deeply interested in for the United States. He believed that the availability of resources and building materials, the political tranquility, and the dominance of ideas led to the monumental character of this architecture. Baxter's interest in this quality revealed his frustration with American architecture (with the exception of that of H. H. Richardson) and his search for a monumental language for American architecture. See Baxter, *Spanish-Colonial Architecture in Mexico*, 1–24. This would translate into Bertram G. Goodhue's designs for the 1915 Panama-California Exposition in San Diego created in the Spanish-colonial style, as well as into other architectural explorations by those architects close to Baxter. Goodhue, it should be pointed out, was not only Baxter's traveling companion in Mexico but was also responsible for the illustrations for Baxter's book.
11. This position continues to be reproduced as attested by the 2002 Guggenheim Museum exhibition *Brazil: Body and Soul*.
12. See "Martín Noel" in *Diccionario de arquitectura en la Argentina*, 4:197.

1922

The source for the epigraph is Vasconcelos, *The Cosmic Race/La raza cósmica*, 39–40.

1. Vasconcelos, "Indología: Una interpretación de la cultura iberoamericana (1926)," in *Obras completas*, 2:1231–1232.

2. A replica of the statue of Cuauhtémoc (originally by Miguel Noreña, 1887) was also sent to Rio de Janeiro as part of Mexico's cultural interchange with Brazil. The statue can still be found there at Praça Cuauhtémoqua.

3. Benjamin, "The Work of Art in the Age of Mechanical Reproduction," in *Illuminations*, 240.

4. *Manifesto of the Union of Mexican Workers, Technicians, Painters and Sculptors*, reprinted in Ades, *Art in Latin America*, 324.

5. After Vasconcelos's departure as education minister, Rivera's murals became more socialist in nature and showed not only the injustices perpetrated by the bourgeoisie and its differences with the working class but also, more explicitly, scenes depicting a future class struggle and continuing revolution.

6. This was later renamed the "Court of Labor" because of the iconography present in Rivera's murals.

7. Vasconcelos, *The Cosmic Race/La raza cósmica*, 39–40.

8. Vasconcelos, "El desastre," 44, 113.

1924

1. Girondo, "Cuidado con la arquitectura," 3.

2. The name Martín Fierro referred to José Hernández's 1872–1879 epic poem about a gaucho and the traditional way of life in late-nineteenth-century rural Argentina. Hernández's text can also be understood as a critique of the emerging modernization of the country under President Sarmiento.

3. Prebisch, "El XIVo Salón Nacional de Bellas Artes," 6.

4. See Novick, "La ciudad como arquitectura."

5. Girondo, "Cuidado con la arquitectura," 3.

6. Vautier and Prebisch, "Un proyecto de Museo de Bellas Artes," 3.

7. See, for instance: Prebisch and Vautier, "Fantasía y cálculo," *Martín Fierro* 20 (August 5, 1925); "Hacia un nuevo estilo," *Martín Fierro* 21 (August 28, 1925); "Arte decorativo y arte falso," *Martín Fierro* 23 (September 25, 1925); "El 'standard,' base del estilo arquitectónico," *Martín Fierro* 25 (November 14, 1925); "Como decíamos ayer," *Martín Fierro* 27–28 (May 10, 1926); "La arquitectura y el mueble," *Martín Fierro* 30–31 (July 8, 1926); "¿Arte decorativo?," *Martín Fierro* 33 (September 3, 1926).

8. The cover of the journal is characterized by an arrow pointing downward.

9. Siqueiros, "En el orden burgués reinante," n.p.; emphasis in original.

10. *Horizonte* 8 (November 1926) and Martí Casanovas, "Pastelería y arquitectura," *¡30-30! Organo de los Pintores de México*, no. 3 (September and October 1928), 8–9.

11. Qouted in Perrone, *Seven Faces*, 48.

12. A. Campos, Pignatari, and H. Campos, "Pilot Plan for Concrete Poetry," 72.

13. Haroldo de Campos, "Contexto de uma vanguarda," quoted in González and Treece, *The Gathering of Voices*, 242.

14. Décio Pignatari, "Construir e expressar," quoted in González and Treece, *The Gathering of Voices*, 242.

15. Haber, "Pintura y arquitectura," 3.

1925

1. García Canclini, *Hybrid Cultures*, 7.

2. Warchavchik, "On Modern Architecture," 620–621.

3. It is important to note that Warchavchik's place in the traditional historiography of Brazilian modernism (as articulated by Lúcio Costa [see 1930 and 1936 entries; 1943 box]) was limited to his activities before 1931. Recent scholarship by José Lira has challenged this partial view with a broader and more detailed analysis of his work.

4. "Manifesto Antropófago," reprinted in Ades, *Art in Latin America*, 312.

1928

1. Barrett, *Pan American Union*, 99.

2. González, *Designing Pan-America*, 118.

1929-A

1. *Seville: Spanish American Exposition, 1929–1930*; our emphasis.

2. Schávelzon, "El Pabellón Xochicalco," 165–171. The pavilion, despite representing Mexico, was created by the French in the last year of French intervention in Mexico.

3. The combination of different pre-Hispanic styles as well as their modern adaptation by the designers resulted in a flurry of controversy and debates. There were objections not only to the combination of styles, functions, and traditions from different regions and historical times within the pavilion but also to their combination with more modern, European forms.

1929-B

1. Le Corbusier, *Precisions*, 244.
2. Ibid., 201.
3. Ibid., 238.
4. Ibid., 241.
5. Ibid., 245.

1929-C

1. Tafuri, "The New Babylon," 186–187.
2. Born, *The New Architecture in Mexico*, 2.
3. The project by Dupré is a stepped terrace building in cruciform plan (1929); Henri Sauvage's pyramidal projects include the Giant Hotel (1927), Metropolis Building (1928), and two pyramidal blocks for the Rosenthal competition for Porte Maillot (1929); Adolf Loos's interest in these forms can be seen in the Grand Hotel Babylon in Nice (1923) and a sketch design for a town hall in Mexico (1923).
4. This design and its source of influence were first published in "Alfred Bossom Develops a New Skyscraper," 34.
5. Mujica's first appearance in relation to this is his student project for an archaeological museum for Mexico City presented at the First Pan-American Congress of Architects held in Montevideo, Uruguay, in 1920.
6. Mujica, *History of the Skyscraper*, 14–17.
7. Ibid., 14–17 and Plate I.
8. Ibid., 36.
9. Ibid., 15.
10. Ibid., 35–36.
11. Mujica published many of these designs in *History of the Skyscraper*.
12. Although Mujica included the earlier "Thirty-Four-Story Skyscraper" project in the *History of the Skyscraper*, it was clear from his description of it that its design operated under an outdated paradigm: "A plan sketched only for demonstrative purposes, to show the similarity between the second classic type of skyscraper ('small temple' type) and the native pyramids of America" and "This project does not reflect [the author's] opinion concerning the solution of the skyscraper problem. He sketched it during his first visit to the city of New York with the sole object of demonstrating that it was possible to express on American lines what was being constructed in those days." Mujica, *History of the Skyscraper*, 60 and Plate XLI.
13. Ibid., 72.
14. Weiss, *El rascacielos*, 32.
15. Guido, *Catedrales y rascacielos*, 37.
16. Ibid., 39; Weiss, *El rascacielos*, 36.
17. Guido, *Catedrales y rascacielos*, 39.

1930-A

1. *O Globo* (Rio de Janeiro, December 29, 1930), reprinted in Costa, *Lúcio Costa: Registro de uma vivência*, 68.
2. The other juror, Eliel Saarinen, on the other hand, chose not to make any public appearance.
3. Costa, "Muita construção, alguma arquitetura e um milagre," *Correio da Manhã* (Rio de Janeiro, June 15, 1951), reprinted in Costa, *Lúcio Costa: Registro de uma vivência*, 21.
4. Costa, "Autobiografia," *Jornal do Brasil*, February 27, 1982.
5. Niemeyer, *Conversa de arquiteto*, 31; our translation.

1930-B

1. The author of the quote, quite unexpectedly, is Karol Wojtyla, aka Pope John Paul II.
2. To this day, the Uruguayan national soccer team is called "La Celeste Olímpica" after winning the gold medal in both the 1924 and 1928 Olympic Games.
3. Curtis, *Modern Architecture since 1900*, 491.

1933

1. Bassols, "La educación pública en 1932," 125.
2. Aguilar M. and Mesa, "Preámbulo: Dentro del gobierno," 115.
3. O'Gorman, "Conferencia en la Sociedad de Arquitectos Mexicanos," in *Pláticas sobre arquitectura*, 17–34.
4. O'Gorman, "Conferencia en la Sociedad de Arquitectos Mexicanos," 23.
5. O'Gorman's radical commitment to the logic of function and the principal tenets of his radical functionalism echoed the functionalist theories of Hannes Meyer. The similarity in the theories and positions of both architects was exceptional. For example, for Meyer, all industrial products were "the product of a formula: function multiplied by economics. They are not works of art. Art is composition, purpose is function. . . . Building is a technical not an aesthetic process, artistic composition does not rhyme with the function of a house matched to its purpose." Meyer, "The New World, 1926," 93. See also Meyer, "Building, 1928," 95–99.
6. O'Gorman, "Conferencia en la Sociedad de Arquitectos Mexicanos," 24–25.
7. This was precisely what Henry-Russell Hitchcock and Philip Johnson argued about functionalism in 1932: "One may therefore refuse to admit that intentionally functionalist building is quite without a potential aesthetic element. . . . European functionalists follow, rather than go against, the principles of the general contemporary style." For them, American functionalists precisely

understood the "international style" of that production and, therefore, utilized design as a "commodity like ornament." In the end, the transformation of functionalism was reflected in its stylized use: "While the functionalists continue to deny that the aesthetic element in architecture is important, more and more buildings are produced in which these principles are wisely and effectively followed without sacrifice of functional buildings." Hitchcock and Philip Johnson, "Functionalism," 50–54.

8. O'Gorman, "Conferencia en la Sociedad de Arquitectos Mexicanos," 29–30.

1936

1. From 1889 to 1930, the Brazilian government followed the model of the United States in which the states had a high degree of independence in taxation, expenditure, and legislation. The Vargas coup in 1930 would drastically change that. A much higher share of power (and resources) would become controlled by the federal ministries in the capital, Rio de Janeiro (see 1930-a entry).

2. Marajoara is the name of a tribe in the delta of the Amazon River whose ceramics are decorated with geometric patterns. Inspired by them, the "Marajoara style" was popular in the 1920s and 1930s in Brazil as a way to forge a link with the Indians that first inhabited the land.

3. The same argument, ironically, was used by Costa in 1935 to oppose the hiring of Marcello Piacentini, the favorite designer of the group of senior faculty, to design the University of Rio de Janeiro campus. Piacentini came and stayed in Brazil only eleven days before returning to Italy to work on the project while the Brazilians debated its feasibility at home.

4. Niemeyer was one hundred and four years old and still practicing when he passed away on December 5, 2012.

5. The ABI Building (1936–1938) by the Roberto brothers has fixed vertical concrete panels as *brise-soleil*, and Luiz Nunes used fixed horizontal panels at the Usina Higienizadora do Leite in Recife (1934). In 1936, Nunes would design the Olinda Water Tower using a void ceramic block (*cobogó*), a Pernambuco invention patented by a local manufacturer, to control shade and light while allowing for ventilation. The use of *cobogó* would become a trademark of Brazilian modern architecture.

6. Le Corbusier's sketches drawn in the mid-1940s from photographs of the complete building have been widely reproduced by many as "later studies," as if he had drawn them immediately upon his return to France. Costa's denunciation of their falsity as design process studies was widely known in Brazil, although Costa himself never publicly denounced these in any of his many publications.

1937

1. In a recent book about Gregori Warchavchik, Brazilian scholar José Lira states that he found no document attesting that Acosta and Warchavchik had much contact despite both being Jews from Odessa who attended the same school in Italy and emigrated to South America a few years later. See Lira, *Warchavchik: Fraturas da vanguarda*.

2. Acosta, *Vivienda y ciudad*, 11.

3. Upon his arrival, Acosta associated himself with architect Alberto Prebisch.

4. Acosta, *Vivienda y ciudad*, 26.

5. Ibid., 20.

6. Ibid., 10.

7. Ibid.

8. Acosta, *Vivienda y clima*.

9. This responds to the local vernacular typology of the "casa chorizo," the Argentine variant of the railroad apartment plan.

10. Acosta, *Vivienda y ciudad*, 161.

1938

1. Vidler, "'Architecture-to-Be,'" 61.

2. Matta Echaurren, "Sensitive Mathematics—Architecture of Time," 216–218.

3. Katzenstein, Natanson, Schvartzman, *Antonio Bonet*, 11.

4. These can be seen, for instance, in Charles and Ray Eames and Eero Saarinen's investigations with bentwood furniture at the same time.

5. Liernur and Pschepiurca, *La red austral*, 269.

6. O'Gorman would later self-criticize the library murals as illegible and unintelligible.

1939

1. The Italian government estimates that there are 25 million Italian descendants in Brazil, 20 million in Argentina, and 18 million in the United States.

2. The United States did receive more immigrants than any other country in the Americas: almost half of the 60 million that left Europe between 1815 and 1930. After receiving as many as 8 million immigrants between 1900 and 1910, the United States lowered its immigration numbers to 2.7 million in the 1920s and to only 443,000 between 1931 and 1940. Such drastic reduction was the result of the 1921 National Origins Formula, a quota system that essentially gave preference to immigrants from Northern and Western Europe, severely limiting the numbers from Eastern and Southern Europe, and declared all

potential immigrants from Asia to be unworthy of entry into the United States.

1941

1. Lara, "One Step Back, Two Steps Forward."

2. There is plenty of controversy over who advised Kubitschek to hire Niemeyer: some say it was Gustavo Capanema, minister of education; others say it was Rodrigo Melo Franco, director of the National Preservation Office (IPHAN); some even say that it was the result of a chance encounter between the mayors of Belo Horizonte and Ouro Preto.

3. The last building, which was never built, was to be a hotel located on an island on the lake.

4. Frampton, *Modern Architecture*, 255.

1943-A

1. Goodwin, *Brazil Builds*, 25.

2. French scholar Yves Bruand, an archivist and paleographer, wrote a dissertation on the history of architecture in Brazil (1977) that would later become the 1981 book, *Arquitetura contemporânea no Brèsil* (Contemporary Architecture of Brazil). Bruand's historical narrative absolutely coincided with the intellectual construction that Lúcio Costa had framed in the 1940s: that progressive rationalism prevailed over the plethora of styles that existed until the reformation of the ENBA in 1931 and Le Corbusier's visit in 1936, which, in the end, found its highest expression in the works of Oscar Niemeyer. Departing from Costa's basic thesis, however, Bruand did an exhaustive archival work and compiled hundreds of architects and their buildings in five hundred pages.

3. Goodwin, *Brazil Builds*, 96.

4. Ibid., 94–95.

1943-B

1. Rovira, *José Luis Sert*, 126.

2. Rovira cites what the architects described in their presentations as the "life of the typical family of Cidade dos Motores." See Rovira, *José Luis Sert*, 126–127.

3. This type of wall will reappear in the design of a church with an open patio for Puerto Ordaz. This church not only referenced architectural developments of churches during the Spanish colonization—through the creation of an open atrium—but also sought to incorporate decorative motifs representing the Passion of Christ in the wall intended to be the bell tower. See Octavio L. Borgatello, "1951: Church and Civic Centre of Puerto Ordaz," in Rovira, *Sert, 1928–1979*, 140.

4. In addition to these three cities, TPA worked on the master plan of Lima, Peru (1947), and Cali, Colombia (1950). See Rubert de Ventós, "Cities in Latin America."

5. Mumford, "CIAM and Latin America," 66.

6. *LC BOG: Le Corbusier en Bogotá, 1947–1951*, n.p.

7. Le Corbusier, "Town Planning: The Theory of the 7 V," 109–110.

8. Rovira, *José Luis Sert*, 177.

9. This also coincides with the dissolution of the TPA in March 1959.

10. Roberto Segre, *La Habana de Sert: CIAM, ron y cha cha cha*, quoted in Rovira, *José Luis Sert*, 181.

1944

1. It should be noted, however, that historians, such as Kenneth Frampton, have shown that the effects of Semper's "primitive hut" are not limited to the tropics but that, in fact, the example served in a broader redefinition of modern architecture.

2. Lefaivre and Tzonis, "Tropical Regionalism," 15–16.

3. "Building types developed in the temperate zones were carefully restudied in their relationship to the function of heat economy." Quoted in Hines, *Richard Neutra and the Search for Modern Architecture*, 194. Original from "Puerto Rico," *Architectural Forum* 82 (March 1945): 121.

4. Neutra, *Architecture of Social Concern*, 40.

5. Neutra had met Warchavchik in 1945 when he was sent to Brazil by the U.S. Department of State as part of the Good Neighbor Policy.

6. Hitchcock, *Latin American Architecture since 1945*, 57. The other, earlier follower of Wright in Puerto Rico was, of course, Antonin Nechodoma (see 1915 box).

7. "Klumb of Puerto Rico," 87.

8. Vivoni Farage, "Henry Klumb and the Poetic Exuberance in Architecture," 32.

9. Quoted in Leatherbarrow, "Henry Klumb's Works at Work," 145.

10. These observations on the relationship of the Princeton Drawings and Klumb's articulation of light are the result of discussions with Klumb scholar Marisa Oliver. See "Henry Klumb" in Tafel, *Frank Lloyd Wright: Recollections*, 100–102.

1947-A

1. Barragán, "Official Address," 206.

2. It should be noted that Barragán's interest in gardens begins with his admiration of Bac's work at the Decorative Arts Exposition. We can see it materialized in his integration of motifs that recall the Alhambra or Generalife in his early houses in Guadalajara as well as in his design (with his brother) of a public park in Guadalajara, the Parque Revolución (1936).

3. Poniatowska, "Luis Barragán," 24; from an interview conducted in December 1976.

4. Rivera, "Requisitos para la organización de El Pedregal."

5. "La psicología del patio," *Espacios* 8, n.p.

6. Pallares, "El Pedregal de San Ángel," n.p.

1947-B

1. Hitchcock, "Architecture of Bureaucracy," 4.

2. Wright, *USA: Modern Architectures in History*, 156.

3. A careful analysis of the chronology of several of the buildings analyzed here—many designed before the Lever House and the Seagrams Building—challenges the traditional narrative that insists that Latin America was at the receiving end of architectural production.

4. On the project for Havana, see Lambert, "Mies Immersion," 474–487. On the Mexican building, see "Mies Builds in Mexico," *Architectural Forum* (January 1962), 94; and Lizárraga Sánchez, "Bacardí Breezer," 104–107.

5. Smithson and Smithson, *Without Rhetoric*, 27.

6. Bullrich, "Technology and Architecture," in *New Directions in Latin American Architecture*, 54.

7. Hitchcock, *Latin American Architecture since 1945*, 191.

8. Ibid.

1950

1. Bonduki, "Habitação social," 91–112.

2. At the turn of the millennium, the 23 de Enero housing neighborhood (apartment complex and informal houses at ground level) would continue to write Venezuelan history as a major locus of support for Hugo Chávez's Bolivarian Revolution. As we write these lines, weeks after the death of Chávez, his body lies embalmed and exposed under a glass casket right there, at the Cuartel de la Montaña, a military facility turned into a "Museum of the Revolution" by Chávez himself.

1952

1. C. R. Villanueva, "Synthesis of the Arts (1954)," 168.

2. Lazo, "La Ciudad Universitaria en realización," n.p.

3. Lazo, "Universo y universidad (1951)" in *Pensamiento y destino de la Ciudad Universitaria de México*, 19. See also Lazo, "Presencia, misión y destino de la Ciudad Universitaria de México (1950)" in ibid., 34.

4. C. R. Villanueva, "Synthesis of the Arts (1954)," 168.

5. Damaz, *Art in Latin American Architecture*, 142.

1953-A

1. "Cariocas" is the term used to designate those people from Rio de Janeiro; "Paulistas" are those from São Paulo. These two important Brazilian cities battle for prominence in the national scene.

2. Instead, in the Public Works office, they downplayed their relationship to avoid the charge of nepotism.

1953-B

1. Goeritz, "Manifiesto de la arquitectura emocional" (1953), 260.

2. Nelken, "En torno a la integración de la pintura," n.p.

3. Carlos Mérida, quoted in Paltridge, "En la polémica de la integración plástica," 131.

4. Goeritz, "Manifiesto de la arquitectura emocional," 260.

5. Mathias Goeritz, quoted in Ricalde, "La repercusión del Eco de Mathias Goeritz," 50.

6. Goeritz, "Manifiesto de la arquitectura emocional," 261.

7. Mathias Goeritz, quoted in Ricalde, "La repercusión del Eco de Mathias Goeritz," 50.

8. Goeritz, "Manifiesto de la arquitectura emocional," 260.

9. Ibid., 260.

10. Brenner, "Summer in Mexico," 67.

11. Luis Barragán, quoted in Ambasz, *The Architecture of Luis Barragán*, 8.

1953-C

1. Bill, "Report on Brazil," 238–239.

2. Costa, *Lúcio Costa: Registro de uma vivência*, 201.

3. Rogers, "Report on Brazil."

4. Guimarães, "Editorial," *Arquitetura & Engenharia*.

5. Niemeyer, "Statement," 628.

6. Cavalcanti, *Sérgio Bernardes: Herói*, 115.

1955

1. Pedreschi, *Eladio Dieste*, 21.

2. Liberation theology was mostly developed in Latin America in the 1950s and 1960s as a reaction to the poverty caused by social injustice. The term was coined in 1971 by the Peruvian priest Gustavo Gutiérrez, who wrote one of the movement's most famous books, *A Theology of Liberation*. Other noted exponents are Leonardo Boff of Brazil, Jon Sobrino of El Salvador, and Juan Luis Segundo of Uruguay, whom Dieste met personally.

3. Antonio Dieste, quoted in Anderson, *Eladio Dieste: Innovation in Structural Art*, 29.

1956

1. Valerie Fraser in *Building a New World* and Richard Williams in *Brazil* suggest that Brasília's fate in twentieth-century historiography was decided right there.

2. Costa, *Plano Piloto de Brasília*, 175.

3. Ibid., 164.

4. Niemeyer, "Statement," 628.

5. Niemeyer, "Form and Function in Architecture (1960)," 311.

6. Ibid., 313.

7. James Holston's most acute critique of this emerges when his anthropological lens is directed toward the periphery. See *The Modernist City: An Anthropological Critique of Brasília*. Like Joaquim Pedro de Andrade in his 1967 film, *Brasília, Contradições de uma Cidade* (Brasília: Contradictions of a City), Holston deserves credit for including the unplanned periphery as an integral part of the city's operation. For him and others, it is there that Brasília's paradoxes of a split-faced society emerge—those who can live in the city and those who live outside it but must come in to support it—in what is referred to as "Brazil's exuberant and perverse modernity."

8. The most sophisticated analyses were undertaken by David Underwood (1994) and Styliane Philippou (2008) in English; Danilo Macedo (2008) and Carlos Eduardo Comas and Marcos Leite Almeida (2010) in Portuguese.

1959

1. In contesting the sole authorship that has been attributed to Testa for this building, architectural historian Jorge Francisco Liernur shows how it is linked to existing traditions and precedents—local and international—that ground it within the context of Argentine production as well as of broader contemporary architectural investigations. Liernur, "Polysemy: Rereading the Readings of BLAS."

2. "Banco de Londres," in González Montaner, *Vanguardias argentinas: Obras y movimientos en el siglo XX*, 78.

3. Banham, "'The New Brutalism,'" 172.

4. Smithson and Smithson, "The New Brutalism," 241.

5. Liernur, "Polysemy: Rereading the Readings of BLAS," 26.

1961-A

1. Cavalcanti, *When Brazil was Modern: A Guide to Architecture, 1928–1960*, 250.

2. Rodríguez, *The Havana Guide: Modern Architecture, 1925–1965*, xxxiii.

3. Porro, "An Architectural Autobiography of Ricardo Porro," 62–63.

4. "Cluster of Bubbles: School of Plastic Arts in Suburban Havana," 82.

1961-B

1. Vilanova Artigas, "Aos formandos da FAU-USP de 1955."

2. Zein, "Brazilian Architecture, Modern Tradition, Contemporary Culture," 169–179. Zein is also correct to point out that by the time Banham wrote his classic book in 1966, "brutalismo paulista" was more than a decade old.

3. *Bandeirantes* is the name given to seventeenth-century Paulistas who mounted expeditions into the Brazilian hinterland in search of slaves (native Brazilians) and precious metals.

1965-A

1. Venancio Filho, "Paisagismo, pintura e natureza," 153.

1965-B

1. Lerner would be popularly elected mayor in 1989 and governor of the state of Paraná in 1995 (reelected in 1999). Another IPPUC director, Cassio Taniguchi, would also be elected mayor of Curitiba in 1997, reelected in 2001.

2. See, particularly, Clara Irazábal, *City Making and Urban Governance in the Americas: Curitiba and Portland*; and Steven Moore, *Alternative Routes to the Sustainable City: Austin, Curitiba, and Frankfurt*.

1966

1. Cardoso and Faletto, *Dependencia y desarrollo en América Latina*.

2. Pérez de Arce, "Material Circumstances," 46.

3. Emilio Duhart, quoted in Montealegre Klenner, *Emilio Duhart, arquitecto*, 85.

4. "Santiago Caracol," 158–159.

1967

1. Ferreira Gullar, *Vanguarda e subdesenvolvimento* (1969), 330.

2. Ibid.

3. Ferreira Gullar, "Neo-Concrete Manifesto," 336.

4. Oiticica, "Tropicália," 124.

5. Brett, "Experimental Exercise of Liberty," 230.

1968

1. Eleven years later, following the coup d'état of September 11, 1973, that ousted Salvador Allende's democratically elected government, the stadium was used as a concentration and torture camp by Augusto Pinochet's military junta.

2. Ramírez Vázquez, *The National Museum of Anthropology: Mexico*, 15.

3. Ramírez Vázquez and Trueblood, *Pedro Ramírez Vázquez en la arquitectura*, 144; "What We Can Do: Pedro Ramírez Vázquez in Interview with Tania Ragasol," 212.

4. Díaz Ordaz, *V Informe de Gobierno (1968)*, 356.

5. "What We Can Do: Pedro Ramírez Vázquez in Interview with Tania Ragasol," 220.

6. Goeritz, "The Route of Friendship: Sculpture," 402.

1969-A

1. was not the founding alien
    to the discoveries
    —oh, seamen
    their wild birds
    the uncertain sea
    the naked people among their gods!—
    because the gift to be displayed
    causes hope to be mistaken?

    did not
    the first passion of gold
    leave the sailor blind
    to that unnamed clarity
    with which the afternoon rewards and destroys
    appearance?
    (Translation by Luis E. Carranza)

2. Around the same time, the Texas Rangers were working on parallel ideas in Austin, Texas.

3. Among the new faculty was Claudio Girola, an Argentine Concretist sculptor who had been a part of the renowned Asociación Arte Concreto-Invención.

4. Pendleton-Jullian, "Autopoetic Architecture," 267.

5. Rispa, *Valparaiso School: Open City Group*, 14; emphasis ours.

6. Pendleton-Jullian, "Autopoetic Architecture," 274.

1969-B

1. Fernando Belaúnde Terry graduated from the University of Texas School of Architecture in 1935. After working in Mexico for two years, he returned to Peru and founded the magazine *El Arquitecto Peruano* that same

year. Teaching since 1943, Belaúnde became dean of the Civil Engineering and Architecture Department and later was elected to the Peruvian Congress (1944–1948). Having served twice as Peruvian president (1963–1968 and 1980–1985), Belaúnde is, to our knowledge, the first trained architect ever to be elected to such a high national post in the world. (Ecuador elected Sixto Duran in 1992.)

2. James Stirling (UK); Knud Svenssons (Denmark); Esquerra, Samper, Sáenz, Urdaneta (Colombia); Atelier 5 (Swizerland); Toivo Korhonen (Finland); Charles Correa (India); Kikutake, Maki, Kurokawa (Japan); Iñiguez de Onzoño, Vásquez de Castro (Spain); Hansen, Hatloy (Poland); Aldo van Eyck (Netherlands); Candilis, Josic, Woods (France); and Christopher Alexander (USA).

3. Miguel Alvariño; Ernesto Paredes; Miró-Quesada, Williams, Núñez; Gunther, Seminario; Morales, Montagne; Juan Reiser; Eduardo Orrego; Vier, Zanelli; Vella, Bentín, Quiñones, Takahashi; Mazzarri, Llanos; Cooper, García-Bryce, Graña, Nicolini; Chaparro, Ramírez, Smirnoff, Wyszkowsky; Crousse, Páez, Pérez-León.

4. José Antonio Coderch (Spain), Halldor Gunnlogsson (Denmark), Peter Land (UN) Ernest Weissmann (UN) Carl Koch (US/UIA), Manuel Valega (Peru), Ricardo Malachowski (Peru), Eduardo Barclay (Peru), and the consultants Darío González (Peru) and Álvaro Ortega (UN).

5. Strauven, *Aldo van Eyck: The Shape of Relativity*, 545–546.

1971

1. Kosice, "Abstract Art," 492.

2. Kosice, "Madí Manifesto," reproduced in Ades, *Art in Latin America: The Modern Era, 1820–1980*, 330.

3. Kosice, *La ciudad hidroespacial*, n.p.

4. Kosice, "The Architecture of Water in Sculpture," 520.

5. Vasconcelos, *The Cosmic Race/La raza cósmica*, 24.

6. Ibid., 25. For Vasconcelos, the opposite of Universópolis was "Anglotown," which he defined as a metropolis. Oswald Spengler had used this term to define the material, architectural expression of a civilization at its peak and, therefore, on its way into decline. From "Anglotown," colonizing troops were to be dispatched to conquer the world and to eliminate the rival races.

7. Bernardes, "The Paths of the First Tropical Civilization," 254.

8. Calvacanti, "Sérgio Bernardes: A Modernist Adrift," 243.

9. *Amancio Williams: Obras y textos*, 16.

10. Arai, et al., "Proyecto de la Ciudad Obrera de México." This project was presented in the 1938 International Congress on Planning and Housing that was celebrated in Mexico City. Congreso Internacional de

Planificación y de la Habitación, *Proyecto de la Ciudad Obrera en México, D.F., Doctrina Socialista de la Arquitectura, por la Unión de Arquitectos Socialistas*, Vol. 7 (Mexico City, 1938).

11. Adrià, *Alberto Kalach*, 160.

12. Kalach, "Vuelta a la ciudad lacustre."

1974

1. Solsona, *Entrevistas: Apuntes para una autobiografía*, 100–101.

2. Silvestri, "Apariencia y verdad," 46.

3. Waisman, "Editorial: Racionalismo a Tres Voces: Ungers-Rossi-Krier," 127.

1976

1. Toca, *México: Nueva arquitectura*, 11.

2. Ingersoll, "Mexican Architecture at the End of the Millennium," 36.

3. Gónzalez de León, "Two Constants in My Architecture," 133.

1979

1. Segawa, *Arquiteturas no Brasil, 1900–1990.*

1980

1. "Press Release: The Architecture of Luis Barragán," The Museum of Modern Art, June 4, 1976, 3. http://www.moma.org/docs/press_archives/5393/releases/MOMA_1976_0053_42.pdf.

2. Ambasz, *The Architecture of Luis Barragán*, 107–108.

3. Studies such as Keith L. Eggener's *Luis Barragán's Gardens of El Pedregal* (2001) show that Barragán's work is astutely commercial and part of a reactionary architectural tradition intent on rejecting the social changes enacted by the Mexican Revolution and by modernity.

4. Born, *The New Architecture in Mexico.*

5. Eggener, "Barragán's 'Photographic Architecture,'" 183.

6. Eggener, *Luis Barragán's Gardens of El Pedregal*, 82.

7. Ambasz, see "List of Works" in *The Architecture of Luis Barragán*, 111–123.

8. Poniatowska, "Luis Barragán," 29. Based on an interview conducted in December 1976.

9. Ibid., 24.

10. Barragán, "Official Address, 1980 Pritzker Architecture Prize."

1983

1. The Exhibition Hall at Gameleira in Belo Horizonte was an elegant rectangular building of 150 x 840 ft. (46 x 256 m) supported by two gigantic beams that stretched the longitudinal distance with only five pyramidal supports each. The state governor was Israel Pinheiro, who had managed the construction of Brasília. In a hurry to inaugurate the building before the end of the governor's term (March 15, 1971), the head engineer authorized the removal of scaffolding earlier than prudence would recommend. One-fourth of the complex's roof collapsed after a 150-foot-long beam (46 m) that supported it gave way at lunchtime, killing sixty-nine workers who were eating together. The great structural engineer Joaquim Cardozo, who had worked with Niemeyer since Pampulha, subsequently became severely depressed and died a few years later. None of Niemeyer's many monographs mentions the project. For more information on it, see Vladimir Carvalho's documentary *Conterrâneos Velhos de Guerra* (1991) or the PhD dissertation by Antonio Libério de Borba (Unicamp: Faculdade de Educação, 2007).

2. Niemeyer, *Conversa de arquiteto*, 38.

1985-A

1. Vittorio Gregotti had organized architectural exhibitions paralleling Venice's art *biennales* since 1975, but the independent format of Venice's Biennale di Architectura started with the famous Strada Novissima of 1980.

2. Subsequent Seminarios de Arquitectura Latinoamericana were held in Buenos Aires, Argentina (1985 and 1986); Manizales, Colombia (1987); Tlaxcala, Mexico (1989); Santiago, Chile (1991); Caracas, Venezuela (1993); São Paulo, Brazil (1995); Lima, Peru (1999); San Juan, Puerto Rico (2001); Montevideo, Uruguay (2003); Oaxtepec, Mexico (2005); Concepción/Chiloé, Chile (2007); Panama City, Panama (2009); and Campinas, Brazil (2011).

3. Waisman, "Primer Seminario de Arquitectura Latinoamericana: Un auspicioso comienzo," 8.

4. Waisman, "Un proyecto de modernidad," 92.

5. Eggener, "Placing Resistance," 230.

6. Sarlo, *Una modernidad periférica*, 28.

1985-B

1. In 2010, the SESC had 5 million registered members throughout Brazil, and the São Paulo chapter alone had a yearly budget of US$750 million.

1990

1. Torrent, "Abstraction and Tectonics in Chilean Architecture since 1950," 91.
2. Liernur, "Portales del laberinto," 4.
3. While many of the best Chilean architects came to the United States for graduate school, Argentine architects preferred to go to Europe. Brazilian architects of the same generation rarely pursued foreign degrees.
4. Liernur, "Portales del laberinto," 12.
5. Torrent, "Abstraction and Tectonics in Chilean Architecture since 1950," 101.

1991

1. Liernur, "Un nuovo mundo per lo spirito nuovo," 107–109.

1994-A

1. Rio, *Vida vertiginosa*, 53.

2. It has been difficult to find precise quantitative data on Favela-Bairro, with different authors using very different numbers. The sums here presented were taken from Luiz Paulo Conde and Sergio Magalhães, *Favela-Bairro: Uma outra história da cidade do Rio de Janeiro*, 147–155.

2000

1. Montezuma, "Facing the Environmental Challenge," 1–10.
2. Mazzanti, "A Conversation between Sergio Fajardo and Giancarlo Mazzanti," 34–41.

CONCLUSION

1. *Mauricio Rocha: Taller de Arquitectura*, 246.

BIBLIOGRAPHY

Abrahams, Tim. "Interview: Jaime Lerner." *Blueprint* 286 (January 2010).

Abreu, Mauricio de Almeida. *Evolução urbana do Rio de Janeiro*. Rio de Janeiro: Iplanrio, 1997.

Acevedo, Jesús T. *Disertaciones de un arquitecto*. Mexico City: INBA, 1967.

Acosta, Wladimiro. *Vivienda y ciudad: Problemas de arquitectura contemporánea*. Buenos Aires: Anaconda, 1937.

———. *Vivienda y clima*. Buenos Aires: Nueva Visión, 1976.

Ades, Dawn. *Art in Latin America: The Modern Era, 1820–1980*. New Haven: Yale University Press, 1989.

Adrià, Miquel. *Abraham Zabludovsky y la vivienda*. Mexico City: Arquine Ediciones, 2000.

———. *Alberto Kalach*. Barcelona: Editorial Gustavo Gili, 2004.

———. *Mario Pani: La construcción de la modernidad*. Mexico City: Editorial Gustavo Gili, 2005.

———. *Mexico 90s: A Contemporary Architecture*. Mexico City: Gustavo Gili, 1996.

———, ed. *Teodoro González de León: Obra completa = Complete Works*. Mexico City: Arquine + RM, 2004.

Aguilar M., Alonso, and Manuel Mesa. "Preámbulo: Dentro del gobierno." In *Narciso Bassols: Obras*. Mexico City: Fondo de Cultura Económica, 1964.

Alberto Prebisch: Una vanguardia con tradición. Buenos Aires: Fundación CEDODAL, 1999.

Albin, Vasconcelos, Elizondo. Mexico City: Gustavo Gili, 1995.

"Alfred Bossom Develops a New Skyscraper: The Building Is Based upon Ruins of Architecture Nearly Two Thousand Years Old Discovered in Guatemala." *Arts and Decoration* 22 (April 1925).

Almandoz, Arturo. "From Urban to Regional Planning in Latin America, 1920–50." *Planning Perspectives* 25, no. 1 (2010).

Amábilis, Manuel. *La arquitectura precolombina de México*. Mexico City: Editorial Orion, 1956. Originally published 1928.

———. *El pabellón de México en la Exposición Ibero-Americana de Sevilla*. Mexico City: Talleres Gráficos de la Nación, 1929.

Amancio Williams: Obras y textos. Buenos Aires: Donn, 2008.

Amaral, Aracy, ed. *Arquitectura neocolonial: América Latina, Caribe, Estados Unidos*. Mexico City: Fondo de Cultura Económica, 1994.

———. *Artes plásticas na Semana de 22*. 5th ed. Rio de Janeiro: Editora 34, 1998.

Ambasz, Emilio. *The Architecture of Luis Barragán*. New York: Museum of Modern Art, 1976.

Amor, Mónica, et al. *Gego: Obra completa (1955–1990)*. Caracas: Fundación Cisneros, 2003.

Amorim, Luiz Manuel do Eirado. "Modernismo recifense: Uma escola de arquitetura, três paradigmas e alguns paradoxos." *Arquitextos* (São Paulo) 01.012 (May 2001). http://www.vitruvius.com.br/revistas/read/arquitextos/01.012/889.

Anda Alanís, Enrique Xavier de. *La arquitectura de la Revolución Mexicana: Corrientes y estilos de la década de los veinte*. Mexico City: Universidad Nacional Autónoma de México, 1990.

Anderson, Stanford, ed. *Eladio Dieste: Innovation in Structural Art*. New York: Princeton Architectural Press, 2005.

Andrade, Oswald de. "Manifesto Antropófago (1928)". Reprinted in *Art in Latin America: The Modern Era, 1920–1980*, ed. Dawn Ades. New Haven: Yale University Press, 1989.

Andreoli, Elisabetta, and Adrian Forty, eds. *Brazil's Modern Architecture*. London: Phaidon, 2004.

Anelli, Renato, Abílio Guerra, and Nelson Kon. *Rino Levi: Arquitetura e cidade*. São Paulo: Romano Guerra, 2001.

Arai, Alberto T., et al. "Proyecto de la Ciudad Obrera de México." *Arquitectura y Decoración*, no. 11 (September 1938): 202–216.

Arana, Mariano, and Lorenzo Garabelli. *Arquitectura renovadora en Montevideo, 1915–1940*. Montevideo: FCU, 1991.

Arango, Jorge, and Carlos Martínez, eds. *Arquitectura en Colombia*. Bogotá: Talleres Litografía Colombia, 1951.

Arango, Silvia. *Historia de la arquitectura en Colombia*. Bogotá: Centro Editorial and Facultad de Artes, Universidad Nacional de Colombia, 1989.

Arantes, Otilia. *O Lugar da Arquitetura Depois dos Modernos*. São Paulo: Edusp, 1995.

Arenós, Xavier, ed. *A.B.C.: Casa de Estudios para Artistas, Canòdrom*. Barcelona: Associació per a la Cultura i l'Art Contemporani, 2010.

Arquivo Brasília. Edited by Lina Kim and Michael Wesely. São Paulo: Cosac Naify, 2010.

Arredondo Zambrano, Celia Ester. "Modernity in Mexico: The Case of the Ciudad Universitaria." In *Modernity and the Architecture of Mexico*, ed. Edward R. Burian, 91–106. Austin: University of Texas Press, 1997.

Ballent, Anahí. *Las huellas de la política: Vivienda, ciudad, peronismo en Buenos Aires, 1943–1955*. Bernal, Argentina: Universidad Nacional de Quilmes, 2005.

Banham, Reyner. *Age of Masters: A Personal View of Modern Architecture*. London: Architectural Press, 1962.

———. "'The New Brutalism' (excerpts)." In *The Independent Group: Postwar Britain and the Aesthetics of Plenty*, ed. David Robbins. Cambridge: MIT Press, 1990. Originally published in *The Architectural Review* (December 1955).

Barragán, Luis. "Official Address, 1980 Pritzker Architecture Prize." In *Barragán: The Complete Works*, ed. Raúl Rispa, 205–209. Revised edition. New York: Princeton Architectural Press, 2003.

Barrett, John. *The Pan American Union: Peace, Friendship, Commerce (1911)*. Whitefish, MT: Kessinger Publishing, 2010.

Bassols, Narciso. "La educación pública en 1932." In *Narciso Bassols: Obras*. Mexico City: Fondo de Cultura Económica, 1964.

Bastos, Maria Alice Junqueira. *Pós-Brasília: Rumos da arquitetura brasileira*. São Paulo: Perspectiva/Fapesp, 2003.

Bastos, Maria Alice Junqueira, and Ruth Verde Zein. *Brasil: Arquiteturas após 1950*. São Paulo: Perspectiva, 2010.

Baxter, Sylvester. *Spanish-Colonial Architecture in Mexico*. Vol. 1. Boston: J. B. Millet, 1901.

Bayeau, Gloria Maria. "O debate da arquitetura moderna brasileira nos anos 50." PhD diss., FAU-USP, São Paulo, 1991.

Benjamin, Walter. *Illuminations*. New York: Schocken Books, 1968.

Benton, Tim. *The Rhetoric of Modernism: Le Corbusier as a Lecturer*. Boston: Birkhäuser, 2009.

Berman, Marshall. *All That Is Solid Melts into Air: The Experience of Modernity*. New York: Simon & Schuster, 1982.

Bernardes, Sergio. "The Paths of the First Tropical Civilization: A Continent Is Transformed into a Nation; Brazil Interconnected by Aqueducts." Reprinted in *Drifts and Derivations: Experiences, Journeys and Morphologies*, ed. Manuel Borja-Villel, Flavio De Carvalho, and Lisette Lagnado. Madrid: Museo Nacional Centro de Arte Reina Sofía, 2010. Exhibition catalog.

Berney, Rachel. "Learning from Bogotá: How Municipal Experts Transformed Public Space." *Journal of Urban Design* 15, no. 4 (2010).

Bernstein, Fred A. "50-Year Watch: United Nations Headquarters." *Oculus* 65, no. 3 (2003).

Bill, Max. "Report on Brazil." *The Architectural Review* 116, no. 694 (August 1954): 238–239.

Bo Bardi, Lina. *Lina por escrito: Textos escolhidos de Lina Bo Bardi, 1943–1991*. São Paulo: Cosac Naify, 2009.

Bonduki, Nabil Georges. "Habitação social na vanguarda do movimento moderno no Brasil." In *Textos fundamentais sobre história da arquitetura moderna brasileira*, Vol. 2, ed. Abílio Guerra. São Paulo: Romano Guerra, 2010.

———. *Origens da habitação social no Brasil*. São Paulo: Estação Liberdade, 1998.

Borchers, Juan. *Institución arquitectónica*. Santiago: Editorial Andres Bello, 1968.

Borges, Jorge Luis. "On Exactitude in Science." In *Collected Fictions*, ed. Andrew Hurley. New York: Penguin Books, 1998.

Born, Esther. *The New Architecture in Mexico*. New York: Architectural Record and William Morrow, 1937.

Bossom, Alfred. *Building to the Skies: The Romance of the Skyscraper*. New York: Studio Publications, 1934.

Braga, Milton. *O Concurso de Brasília*. São Paulo: Cosac Naify, 2010.

Braun, Clara, and Julio Cacciatore, eds. *Arquitectos europeos y Buenos Aires, 1860–1940*. Buenos Aires: Fundación TIAU, 1996.

"Brazilian Architect Angelo Bucci Discusses His Use of Space: Openings and Voids That Allow Inside and Outside to Flow Together." *GA Houses* 114 (January 2010).

Brenner, Anita. "Summer in Mexico." *Art News* (June 1954).

Brett, Guy. "The Experimental Exercise of Liberty." In *Hélio Oiticica*. Rotterdam: The Center, 1992.

Brodsky, Estrellita B., ed. *Soto: Paris and Beyond, 1950–1970*. New York: Grey Art Gallery, 2012.

Bruand, Yves. *Arquitetura contemporânea no Brasil*. São Paulo: Perspectiva, 1981.

Bruna, Paulo. "Restauro e ampliação no edifício da Cepal em Santiago do Chile: Uma intervenção controvertida." *Projetos* (São Paulo) 11.125 (May 2011). http://www.vitruvius.com.br/revistas/read/projetos/11.125/3863.

Bullrich, Francisco. *New Directions in Latin American Architecture*. New York: George Braziller, 1969.

Buzio de Torres, Cecilia. "The School of the South: The Asociación de Arte Constructivo, 1934–1942." In *El Taller Torres-García: The School of the South and Its Legacy*, ed. Mari Carmen Ramírez, 7–24. Austin: University of Texas Press, 1992.

Caldeira, Teresa P. R. *City of Walls: Crime, Segregation, and Citizenship in São Paulo*. Berkeley: University of California Press, 2000.

The Cambridge Encyclopedia of Latin America and the Caribbean. 2nd ed. New York: Cambridge University Press, 1992.

Campbell, Tim. "Smart Cities: Curitiba." *Urban Land* 66, no. 4 (April 2007).

Campos, Augusto de, Décio Pignatari, and Haroldo de Campos. "Pilot Plan for Concrete Poetry" (1958). Reprinted in *Concrete Poetry: A World View*, ed. Mary Ellen Solt. Bloomington: Indiana University Press, 1970.

Canales, Fernanda, and Alejandro Hernández Gálvez, eds. *100x100: Arquitectos del siglo XX en México*. Mexico City: Arquine Ediciones, 2011.

Cardoso, Fernando Henrique, and Enzo Faletto. *Dependencia y desarrollo en América Latina: Ensayo de interpretación sociológica*. Buenos Aires: Siglo Veintiuno Editores, 1977.

Carlos Mérida: Su obra en el multifamiliar Juárez: Nacimiento, muerte y resurrección. Mexico City: INBA, 1988.

Carranza, Luis E. *Architecture as Revolution: Episodes in the History of Modern Mexico*. Austin: University of Texas Press, 2010.

———. "Horror Vitreo: Ciudad Universitaria and the New Humanism." *Praxis* 2 (2001).

———. "Machinating the Quotidian: Luis Barragán's *La Revolución Callada*." *AULA* 4 (September 2004).

———. "Mathias Goeritz: Architecture, Monochrome, and Revolution." *Journal of Decorative and Propaganda Arts: Mexico Theme Issue* 26 (May 2010).

———. "Transgressing Function: Excess and Pleasure in the Work of Wladimiro Acosta." *Journal of Romance Studies* 2, no. 2 (2002).

Carvalho, Flávio de. "A Curious Thesis—The City of the Naked Man (1930)." In *Flávio de Carvalho*. São Paulo: Museu de Arte Moderno, 2010.

Carvalho Ferraz, Marcelo. *Vilanova Artigas*. São Paulo: Instituto Lina Bo e P. M. Bardi, 1997.

Castañeda, Luis. "Beyond Tlatelolco: Design, Media, and Politics at Mexico '68." *Grey Room* 40 (Summer 2010).

———. "Pre-Columbian Skins, Developmentalist Souls: The Architect as Politician." In *Latin American Modern Architectures: Ambiguous Territories*, ed. Patricio del Real and Helen Gyger. New York: Routledge, 2012.

Castillo, Jose. "Smiljan Radic Interview." *BOMB* 106 (Winter 2009).

Cavalcanti, Lauro. *As preocupações do belo: Arquitetura moderna brasileira anos 1930/40*. Rio de Janeiro: Taurus Editora, 1995.

———. "Sérgio Bernardes: A Modernist Adrift." In *Drifts and Derivations: Experiences, Journeys, and Morphologies*, ed. Manuel Borja-Villel, Flavio De Carvalho, and Lisette Lagnado. Madrid: Museo Nacional Centro de Arte Reina Sofía, 2010.

———. *Sérgio Bernardes: Herói de uma tragédia moderna*. Rio de Janeiro: Relume Dumará, 2004.

———. *When Brazil Was Modern: A Guide to Architecture, 1928–1960*. New York: Princeton Architectural Press, 2003.

Cavalcanti, Lauro, and Marta Caldeira. "The Role of Modernists in the Establishment of Brazilian Cultural Heritage." *Future Anterior* 6, no. 2 (2009): 14–31.

Cavalcanti, Lauro, and Farès El-Dahdah. *Roberto Burle Marx: A permanência do instável—100 Anos*. Rio de Janeiro: Rocco, 2009.

Cavalcanti, Lauro, Farès El-Dahdah, and Francis Ramber. *Roberto Burle Marx: The Modernity of Landscape*. Barcelona: Actar, 2011.

Cetto, Max. *Modern Architecture in Mexico*. New York: Praeger, 1961.

Chaloub, Sidney. *Cidade febril: Cortiços e epidemias na corte imperial*. São Paulo: Companhia das Letras, 1996.

The Christopher Columbus Memorial Lighthouse Competition: Second Stage. N.p.: Pan-American Union, 1930.

La ciudad y sus lagos. Mexico City: Clío, 1998.

"Cluster of Bubbles: School of Plastic Arts in Suburban Havana." *Architectural Forum* 124 (January 1966).

Coffey, Mary K. *How a Revolutionary Art Became Official Culture: Murals, Museums, and the Mexican State*. Durham: Duke University Press, 2012.

Cohen, Jean-Louis. "The Future of the Modern." *Architecture* 89, no. 12 (December 2000).

Comas, Carlos Eduardo Dias. "Centro de recreación SESC-Pompeya, São Paulo, Brazil." *Escala* 30, no. 173 (1996).

———. "Pampulha y la arquitectura moderna brasileña." *Summa+*, no. 81 (August 2006).

Comas, Carlos Eduardo Dias, and Marcos Leite Almeida. "Brasília cinquentenária: A paixão de uma monumentalidade nova." *Arquitextos* (São Paulo) (April 2010). http://www.vitruvius.com.br/revistas/read/arquitextos/10.119/3362.

Comas, Carlos Eduardo Dias, Anna Paula Moura Canez, and Glênio Vianna Bohrer. *Arquiteturas cisplatinas: Roman Fresnedo Siri e Eladio Dieste em Porto Alegre*. Porto Alegre: UniRitter, 2004.

"El Concurso del Faro de Colón: Un reencuentro con el monumento olvidado de la arquitectura panamericana/ The Columbus Lighthouse Competition: Revisiting Pan-American Architecture's Forgotten Memorial." *ARQ* 67 (2007).

Conde, Luiz Paulo, Júlio Roberto Katinsky, and Miquel Alves Pereira, eds. *Arquitetura brasileira após Brasília: Depoimentos*. Vol. 3. Rio de Janeiro: IAB-RJ, 1978.

Conde, Luiz Paulo, and Sergio Magalhães. *Favela-Bairro: Uma outra história da cidade do Rio de Janeiro*. Rio de Janeiro: Viver Cidades, 2004.

Conduru, Roberto. "Razão em forma: Affonso Eduardo Reidy e o espaço arquitetônico moderno." *Risco: Revista de Pesquisa em Arquitetura e Urbanismo*, no. 2 (2005). http://www.revistasusp.sibi.usp.br/scielo.php?script=sci_arttext&pid=S1984-45062005000100003&lng=pt&nrm=iso.

Costa, Jurandir Freire. *Ordem médica e norma familiar*. Rio de Janeiro: Edições Graal, 1989.

Costa, Lúcio. *Lúcio Costa: Registro de uma vivência*. São Paulo: Empresa das Artes, 1995.

———. *Plano Piloto de Brasília*. In Braga, *O Concurso de Brasília*. São Paulo: Cosac Naify, 2010.

Crease, David. "Progress in Brasilia." *The Architectural Review* 131, no. 782 (April 1962).

Crisp-Ellert, JoAnn. "Henry Klumb in Puerto Rico: Architecture at the Service of Society." *AIA Journal* 62, no. 1 (July 1974).

Cuadra, Manuel, with Alfonso Corona Martínez. *Clorindo Testa, Architect*. Rotterdam: NAi Publishers, 2000.

Cuadra, Manuel, and Wilfred Wang, eds. *O'Neil Ford Monograph 4: Banco de Londres y América del Sud— SEPRA and Clorindo Testa*. Austin: Center for American Architecture and Design, 2012.

Curtis, William J. R. *Modern Architecture since 1900*. London: Phaidon, 1982.

Da Costa Meyer, Esther. "After the Flood: Lina Bo Bardi's Glass House." *Harvard Design Magazine*, no. 16 (Winter/Spring 2002).

Dal Co, Francesco, and Tomaso Trombetti. "Statica, Struttura, Natura: Oscar Niemeyer e Roberto Burle Marx." *Casabella* 73, no. 777 (May 2009).

Damaz, Paul. *Art in Latin American Architecture*. New York: Reinhold, 1963.

Daniele Calabi: Architetture e progetti, 1932–1964. Venice: Marsilio, 1992.

Davis, Howard. *The Culture of Building*. New York: Oxford University Press, 2000.

Davis, Mike. *Planet of Slums*. London: Verso, 2006.

del Cueto Ruiz-Funes, Juan Ignacio. "Cien años de Félix Candela: Vuelos impensados." *Revista de la Universidad de México*, no. 69 (November 2009): 82–90. http://www.revistadelauniversidad.unam.mx/6909/cueto/69cueto.html.

Deleuze, Gilles, and Félix Guattari. *Kafka: Toward a Minor Literature*. Minneapolis: University of Minnesota Press, 1986.

Del Rio, Vicente. "Introduction: Historical Background." In *Contemporary Urbanism in Brazil: Beyond Brasília*, ed. Vicente Del Rio and William Siembieda. Gainesville: University Press of Florida, 2009.

———. "Urban Design and Conflicting City Images of Brazil: Rio de Janeiro and Curitiba." *Cities* 9, no. 4 (November 1992).

Del Rio, Vicente, and William Siembieda, eds. *Contemporary Urbanism in Brazil: Beyond Brasília*. Gainesville: University Press of Florida, 2009.

Díaz, Tony. "Apariencia y verdad: Posmodernismo y dictadura." *Block* 5 (December 2000).

Dieste, Eladio. *Eladio Dieste: La estructura cerámica*. Bogotá: Escala, 1987.

———. *La invención inevitable*. Montevideo: Cachimba del Piojo, 2009.

Diez, Fernando. "La cueva y la nave." *Summa+*, no. 65 (April–May 2004).

Diseñando México 68: Una identidad olímpica. Mexico City: Museo de Arte Moderno, 2008.

Dixon, John Morris. "64-Year Watch: The Design of the Iconic United Nations Headquarters Called for an Unprecedented International Collaborative Effort Initiated in 1947." *Oculus* 72, no. 4 (January 2010): 41.

Duarte, Cristiane R., and Fernanda Magalhães. "Upgrading Squatter Settlements into City Neighborhoods: The Favela-Bairro Program in Rio de Janeiro." In *Contemporary Urbanism in Brazil: Beyond Brasília*, ed. Vicente Del Rio and William Siembieda. Gainesville: University Press of Florida, 2009.

Dubroise, Olivier, ed. *The Age of Discrepancy: Art and Visual Culture in Mexico, 1968–1997*. Mexico City: UNAM, 2007.

"Dwelling House Series." *Architecture and Building* (May 1918).

Eggener, Keith L. "Barragán's 'Photographic Architecture': Image, Advertising and Memory." In *Luis Barragán: The Quiet Revolution*, ed. Federica Zanco. Milan: Skira Editore, 2001.

———. *Luis Barragán's Gardens of El Pedregal*. New York: Princeton Architectural Press, 2001.

———. "Placing Resistance: A Critique of Critical Regionalism." *Journal of Architectural Education* 55, no. 4 (May 2002).

Eladio Dieste, 1917–2000. Seville: Consejería de Obras Públicas y Transportes; Montevideo: Dirección General de Arquitectura y Vivienda, 1998.

El-Dahdah, Farès. "Brasília, um objetivo certa vez adiado," *Arquitextos* (São Paulo) 10, no. 119.02 (April 2010). http://www.vitruvius.com.br/revistas/read/arquitextos/10.119/3363.

———, ed. *CASE: Lucio Costa, Brasília's Superquadra*. New York: Prestel, 2005.

———. *Oscar 102/Brasilia 50: Eight Cases in Brazil's Architectural Modernity*. Houston: Rice University, 2010.

La Escuelita: 5 años de enseñanza alternativa de arquitectura en la Argentina. Buenos Aires: Espacio Editora, 1981.

Evenson, Norma. *Two Brazilian Capitals: Architecture and Urbanism in Rio de Janeiro and Brasilia*. New Haven and London: Yale University Press, 1973.

"Expresión de principios de la 'Agrupación Espacio.'" http://www.arqandina.com/espacio/espacio01.html.

Faber, Colin. *Candela: The Shell Builder*. New York: Reinhold, 1963.

Fernandes, Edésio. "Constructing the 'Right to the City' in Brazil." *Social & Legal Studies* 16, no. 2 (June 2007).

Fernández, José Antonio. *Architecture in Puerto Rico*. New York: Architectural Book, 1965.

Fernández Cox, Cristián. "Modernidad apropiada,

modernidad revisada, modernidad reencantada." *Summa+* 289 (1991).

Ferraz, Geraldo. "Roberto Burle Marx y sus jardines." *Arquitectura Mexico* 13, no. 58 (June 1957).

Ferreira Gullar (José Ribamar). "Neo-Concrete Manifesto." In *Art in Latin America: The Modern Era, 1820–1980*, ed. Dawn Ades. New Haven: Yale University Press, 1989.

Ficher, Sylvia. "Brasília, Ciudad Nueva: Cincuenta años de la fundación de la capital brasileña." *Arquitectura Viva*, no. 128 (2009): 68–70.

Figuerola, Valentina. "Razão, sensibilidade e maestria." *AU—Arquitetura & Urbanismo* (São Paulo), no. 175 (October 2008).

Fiori, Jorge, and Zeca Brandão. "Spatial Strategies and Urban Social Policy." In *Rethinking the Informal City: Critical Perspectives from Latin America*, ed. Felipe Hernández, Peter Kellett, and Lea K. Allen. Oxford and New York: Berghahn Books, 2010.

Foucault, Michel. "Nietzsche, Genealogy, History." In *The Foucault Reader*, ed. Paul Rabinow. New York: Pantheon Books, 1984.

Frampton, Kenneth. "Le Corbusier and Oscar Niemeyer—Influence and Counterinfluence, 1929–1965." In *Latin American Architecture 1929–1960: Contemporary Reflections*, by Carlos Brillembourg, 34–49. New York: Monacelli Press, 2004.

———. *Modern Architecture: A Critical History*. New York: Oxford University Press, 1980.

———. "Modern Architecture and Critical Regionalism." *Transactions* 3 (1983).

Fraser, Valerie. *Building the New World: Studies in the Modern Architecture of Latin America, 1930–1960*. London: Verso, 2000.

———. "Cannibalizing Le Corbusier: The MES Gardens of Roberto Burle Marx." *Journal of the Society of Architectural Historians* 59, no. 2 (June 2000).

Futagawa, Yoshio. "A Dialogue with [the] Editor: Angelo Bucci [Interview]." *GA Houses* 106 (August 2008).

Gaite, Arnoldo. *Wladimiro Acosta*. Buenos Aires: Nobuko, 2007.

Gallanti, Fabrizio. "Elementary School in Bogotá, Colombia. Architect: Giancarlo Mazzanti." *Abitare* 490 (March 2009).

Garay Arellano, Graciela de. *Modernidad habitada: Multifamiliar Miguel Alemán, ciudad de México, 1949–1999*. Mexico City: Instituto de Investigaciones Dr. José María Luis Mora, 2004.

García Canclini, Néstor. *Hybrid Cultures: Strategies for Entering and Leaving Modernity*. Minneapolis: University of Minnesota Press, 1995.

García-Huidobro, Fernando, Diego Torres Torriti, and Nicolás Tugas. *Time Builds! The Experimental Housing Project (PREVI), Lima: Genesis and Outcome*. Barcelona: Gustavo Gili, 2008.

Garnier, Tony. *Une cité industrielle: Étude pour la construction des villes*. New York: Princeton Architectural Press, 1989. Originally published 1917.

"Gerardo Molina School, Giancarlo Mazzanti." *Space* 496 (March 2009).

Ghirardo, Diane. *Architecture after Modernism*. London: Thames and Hudson, 1996.

Giedion, Sigfried. "Burle Marx et le jardin contemporain." *L'Architecture d'Aujourd'hui* 23 (August 1952).

———. "Roberto Burle Marx und das Problem der Gartengestaltung." *Werk* 40 (August 1953).

———. *Space, Time, and Architecture: The Growth of a New Tradition*. Cambridge: Harvard University Press, 1962.

Giorgi, Manolo De. "Roberto Burle Marx: Giardini del Moderno." *Domus*, no. 705 (May 1989).

Girondo, Oliverio. "Cuidado con la arquitectura." *Martín Fierro* 24 (October 17, 1925).

Goeritz, Mathias. "Manifiesto de la arquitectura emocional" (1953). Reprinted in Kassner, *Mathias Goeritz: Una biografía, 1915–1990*. Mexico City: INBA, 1998.

———. "The Route of Friendship: Sculpture." *Leonardo* 3, no. 4 (October 1970): 397–407.

González, Mike, and David H. Treece. *The Gathering of Voices: The Twentieth-Century Poetry of Latin America*. New York: Verso, 1992.

González, Robert Alexander. *Designing Pan-America: U.S. Architectural Visions for the Western Hemisphere*. Austin: University of Texas Press, 2011.

González de Canales, Francisco. "The Mask House: Juan O'Gorman, House in the Pedregal de San Angel, Mexico, 1948–56." In *Experiments with Life Itself*. Barcelona: Actar, 2012.

González de León, Teodoro. "Two Constants in My Architecture." In *Teodoro González de León: Collected Works*, ed. Miquel Adrià. Mexico City: Arquine + RM, 2004.

González Montaner, Berto, ed. *Vanguardias argentinas: Obras y movimientos en el siglo XX*. Buenos Aires: Arte Gráfico—AGEA, 2005.

Goodwin, Philip L. *Brazil Builds: Architecture New and Old, 1652–1942*. New York: Museum of Modern Art, 1943.

Gorelik, Adrián, and Jorge Francisco Liernur. *La sombra de la vanguardia: Hannes Meyer en México, 1938–1949*. Buenos Aires: Proyecto Editorial, 1992.

Goulart Reis Filho, Nestor. *Quadro da arquitetura no Brasil*. São Paulo: Perspectiva, 1997.

———. *Racionalismo e proto-modernismo na obra de Victor Dubugras*. São Paulo: FBSP, 1997.

Guerra, Abílio, ed. *Affonso Eduardo Reidy*. São Paulo: Instituto Lina Bo e P. M. Bardi, 2000.

———, org. *Textos fundamentais sobre história da arquitetura moderna brasileira*. 2 vols. São Paulo: Romano Guerra, 2010.

Guido, Ángel. *Catedrales y rascacielos*. Buenos Aires:

Colegio Libre de Estudios Superiores de Buenos Aires, 1936.

———. *Fusión hispano-indígena en la arquitectura colonial.* Rosario, Argentina: Editorial "La Casa del Libro," 1925.

Guillén, Mauro F. "Modernism without Modernity: The Rise of Modernist Architecture in Mexico, Brazil, and Argentina, 1890–1940." *Latin American Research Review* 39, no. 2 (January 2004).

Guimarães, Eduardo. "Editorial." *Arquitetura & Engenharia* 23 (September/October 1952).

Gutiérrez, Ramón. *Arquitectura y urbanismo en Iberoamérica.* Madrid: Ediciones Cátedra, 1983.

———. "Sense and Sensuality: Engineer and Architect Eladio Dieste Infuses the Tradition of Brick Building with Modernist Logic." *Architecture* 88, no. 8 (1999): 57–59.

Haber, Abraham. "Pintura y Arquitectura." *Perceptismo: Teórico y Polémico* 2 (August 1951).

Hamerman, Conrad. "Roberto Burle Marx: The Last Interview." Brazil Theme Issue: *The Journal of Decorative and Propaganda Arts* 21 (1995): 156–179.

"Helicoide de la Roca Tarpeya: Centro comercial y Exposición de Industrias." *Integral* 5 (1956).

Hélio Oiticica. Rotterdam: The Center, 1992.

Henry, F. "Competition for the Construction of a Monumental Lighthouse to the Memory of Christopher Columbus." *Architecture* (Societé Centrale des Architectes, France) 45 (1932).

Heredia, Juan Manuel. "The Work of Max Cetto: Restorations of Topography and Disciplinarity in Twentieth-Century Modern Architecture." PhD diss., University of Pennsylvania, 2008.

Herkenhoff, Paulo. "The Hand and the Glove." In *Inverted Utopias: Avant-Garde Art in Latin America*, ed. Mari Carmen Ramírez and Héctor Olea. Houston: Museum of Fine Arts; New Haven: Yale University Press, 2004.

Hernández, Felipe. *Beyond Modernist Masters: Contemporary Architecture in Latin America.* Basel: Birkhauser, 2010.

Hernández, Felipe, Peter Kellett, and Lea K. Allen, eds. *Rethinking the Informal City: Critical Perspectives from Latin America.* Oxford: Berghahn Books, 2009.

Hernández, Felipe, Mark Millington, and Iain Borden, eds. *Transculturation: Cities, Spaces and Architectures in Latin America.* Amsterdam: Rodopi, 2005.

Hill, Jonathan. *Occupying Architecture: Between the Architect and the User.* London: Routledge, 1998.

Hines, Thomas S. *Richard Neutra and the Search for Modern Architecture.* Berkeley: University of California Press, 1982.

Hitchcock, Henry-Russell. *Architecture: Nineteenth and Twentieth Centuries.* New Haven: Yale University Press, 1989.

———. "The Architecture of Bureaucracy and the Architecture of Genius." *Architectural Record* 101 (January 1947): 3–6.

———. *Latin American Architecture since 1945.* New York: Museum of Modern Art, 1955.

Hitchcock, Henry-Russell, and Philip Johnson. "Functionalism." In *The International Style*, 50–54. New York: W. W. Norton, 1966. Originally published 1932.

Hoidn, Barbara, and Kevin Alter, eds. *The O'Neil Ford Duograph Series*, Volume 2: *Brazil—House in Rio Bonito, House in Santa Teresa.* Austin: University of Texas at Austin Center for American Architecture and Design; Tübingen: Ernst Wasmuth Verlag, 2009.

Holanda, Armando de. *Roteiro para construir no Nordeste: Arquitetura como lugar ameno nos trópicos ensolarados.* Recife: MDU/UFPE, 1976.

Holanda, Frederico de. *Brasília: Cidade moderna, cidade eterna.* Brasília: Faculdade de Arquitetura e Urbanismo, Universidade de Brasília, 2010.

———. "Brasilia: The Daily Invention of the City." *Ekistics* 56, no. 334–335 (January–April 1989): 75–83.

———. *O espaço de exceção.* Brasília: Editora Universidade de Brasília, 2002.

Holston, James. *The Modernist City: An Anthropological Critique of Brasília.* Chicago: University of Chicago Press, 1989.

Howard, Ebenezer. *Garden Cities of Tomorrow.* Cambridge: MIT Press, 1965. Originally published 1898.

Hugo, Victor. "This Will Kill That." In *Notre-Dame of Paris*, trans. John Sturrock. New York: Penguin Books, 1978. Originally published 1831.

Iglesia, Rafael. "Pabellones Parque Independencia, Rosario, Argentina." *ARQ* (Santiago), no. 59 (2005).

Ingersoll, Richard. "Mexican Architecture at the End of the Millennium." *Lotus* 91 (1996).

———. *TEN Arquitectos: Enrique Norten, Bernardo Gómez-Pimienta.* New York: Monacelli Press, 1998.

Irace, Fulvio. "Caracas Villa Planchart." *Abitare* 253 (April 1987).

———. "Corrispondenze: La Villa Planchart di Gio Ponti a Caracas." *Lotus International* 60 (1989).

———. "Documenti di architettura: Uruguay: Una chiesa di Eladio Dieste, 1959/Architectural Portfolio: Uruguay: A Church by Eladio Dieste, 1959." *Abitare*, no. 296 (May 1991).

Irazábal, Clara. *City Making and Urban Governance in the Americas: Curitiba and Portland.* London: Ashgate, 2005.

Irigoyen, Adriana. "Frank Lloyd Wright in Brazil." *Journal of Architecture* 5, no. 2 (2000).

Jáuregui, Jorge Mario. *Estrategias de articulación urbana: Proyecto y gestión de asentamientos periféricos en América Latina.* Buenos Aires: Facultad de Arquitectura, Universidad de Buenos Aires, 2003.

João Vilanova Artigas. 2G: International Architecture Review 54 (2010).

Julián García Núñez: Caminos de ida y vuelta. Buenos Aires: CEDODAL, 2005.

"Julio Vilamajó: Guía de obras." *Elarqa: Arquitectura y Diseño* 1–2 (December 1991): 1–19.

Kalach, Alberto. "Vuelta a la ciudad lacustre." In *La ciudad y sus lagos*, ed. Antonieta Cruz. Mexico City: Clío, 1998.

Kassner, Lily. *Mathias Goeritz: Una biografía, 1915–1990*. Mexico City: INBA, 1998.

Katzenstein, Ernesto. "Argentine Architecture of the Thirties." Argentine Theme Issue: *Journal of Decorative and Propaganda Arts* 18 (1992).

Katzenstein, Ernesto, Gustavo Natanson, and Hugo Schvartzman. *Antonio Bonet: Arquitectura y urbanismo en el Río de la Plata y España*. Buenos Aires: Espacio Editora, 1985.

Klich, Lynda. "Estridentópolis: Achieving a Post-Revolutionary Utopia in Jalapa." *Journal of Decorative and Propaganda Arts: Mexico Theme Issue* 26 (May 2010): 102–127.

Klumb, Henry. *Klumb: Una arquitectura de impronta social/An Architecture of Social Concern*. Edited by Enrique Vivoni Farange. San Juan: La Editorial Universidad de Puerto Rico, 2007.

"Klumb of Puerto Rico." *Architectural Forum* 101 (July 1954).

Korowin, Erika. "'Iceberg! Right Ahead!' (Re)Discovering Chile at the 1992 Universal Exposition in Seville, Spain." *Studies in Latin American Popular Culture* 28, no. 1 (2010).

Kosice, Gyula. "Abstract Art." In *Inverted Utopias: Avant-Garde Art in Latin America*, ed. Mari Carmen Ramírez and Héctor Olea, 492. Houston: Museum of Fine Arts; New Haven: Yale University Press, 2004.

———. "The Architecture of Water in Sculpture." In *Inverted Utopias: Avant-Garde Art in Latin America*, ed. Mari Carmen Ramírez and Héctor Olea, 520. Houston: Museum of Fine Arts; New Haven: Yale University Press, 2004.

———. *La ciudad hidroespacial*. Buenos Aires: Ediciones Anzilotti, 1972.

———. "Madí Manifesto." Buenos Aires, 1946. http://www.kosice.com.ar/eng/manifiesto-madi.php.

Kroll, Lucien. "Creative Curitiba." *The Architectural Review* 205, no. 1227 (May 1999).

Lambert, Phyllis. "Mies Immersion." In *Mies in America*, ed. Phyllis Lambert, 474–487. New York: Whitney Museum of American Art, 2001.

"La psicología del patio." *Espacios: Revista Integral de Arquitectura y Artes Plásticas* 8 (December 1951).

Lara, Fernando. "Brazilian Popular Modernism: Analyzing the Dissemination of Architectural Vocabulary." *Journal of Architectural and Planning Research* 23, no. 2 (Summer 2006): 91–112.

———. "Éolo Maia's Hybrid Architecture: The Crossroads of Information." *AXIS Journal of the Caribbean School of Architecture*, no. 10 (2010): 12–21.

———. "Incomplete Utopias: Imbedded Inequalities in Brazilian Modern Architecture." *Architectural Review Quarterly* 15, no. 2 (August 2011).

———. "Modernism Made Vernacular: The Brazilian Case." *Journal of Architectural Education* 63, no. 1 (Fall 2009): 41–50.

———. "One Step Back, Two Steps Forward: The Maneuvering of Brazilian Avant-Garde." *Journal of Architectural Education* 55, no. 4 (May 2002): 211–219.

———. *The Rise of Popular Modernist Architecture in Brazil*. Gainesville: University Press of Florida, 2008.

Larrañaga, Enrique. "Toward the Visibility of the Invisible: Notes on Caracas, Modernity, and the University City of Caracas by Carlos Raúl Villanueva." In *Cruelty and Utopia: Cities and Landscapes of Latin America*, ed. Jean-François Lejeune. New York: Princeton Architectural Press, 2005.

Lazo, Carlos. "La Ciudad Universitaria en realización." *Espacios: Revista Integral de Arquitectura y Artes Plásticas* 7 (June 1951).

———. *Pensamiento y destino de la Ciudad Universitaria de México*. Mexico City: Miguel Ángel Porrúa, 1983.

Lazo, Pablo. "Dislocating Modernity: Two Projects by Hannes Meyer in Mexico." *AA Files* 47 (Summer 2002): 57–63.

LC BOG: Le Corbusier en Bogotá, 1947–1951. Bogotá: Universidad de Los Andes, Facultad de Arquitectura y Diseño, 2010.

Leatherbarrow, David. "Henry Klumb's Works at Work." In *Klumb: An Architecture of Social Concern*, ed. Enrique Vivoni Farage. San Juan: University of Puerto Rico Press, 2006.

Le Corbusier. *Precisions: On the Present State of Architecture and City Planning: With an American Prologue, a Brazilian Corollary Followed by the Temperature of Paris and the Atmosphere of Moscow*. Translated by Edith Schreiber Aujame. Cambridge: MIT Press, 1991.

———. *Toward an Architecture*. Los Angeles: Getty Publications, 2007. Originally published as *Vers une architecture*, 1923.

———. "Town Planning. The Theory of the 7 V." In *Le Corbusier 1946–1952*. Zurich: Editions Girsberger, 1953.

Lemos, Carlos A. C. *Arquitetura brasileira*. São Paulo: Edições Melhoramentos, 1979.

Leonídio, Otavio. *Carradas de Razões: Lucio Costa e a arquitetura moderna brasileira*. Rio de Janeiro: Edições Loyola, 2007.

Liernur, Jorge Francisco. *Arquitectura en la Argentina del siglo XX: La construcción de la modernidad*. Buenos Aires: Fondo Nacional de las Artes, 2001.

———. "Polysemy: Rereading the Readings of BLAS." In O'Neil Ford Monograph 4: *Banco de Londres y América del Sud—SEPRA and Clorindo Testa*, ed. Manuel Cuadra and Wilfred Wang. Austin: Center for American Architecture and Design, 2012.

———, ed. *Portales del laberinto: Arquitectura y ciudad en Chile, 1977–2009*. Santiago: Universidad Andrés Bello, 2009.

———. "Portales del laberinto: Comentarios sobre la arquitectura en Chile, 1977–2007." In *Portales del laberinto: Arquitectura y ciudad en Chile, 1977–2009*, ed. Jorge Francisco Liernur. Santiago: Universidad Andrés Bello, 2009.

———. "Rafael Iglesia en Rosario: Una obra abierta." *Arquine: Revista Internacional de Arquitectura* 21 (October 2002).

———. "'The South American Way': El 'Milagro' Brasileño, los Estados Unidos y la Segunda Guerra Mundial (1939–1943)." *Block* 4 (December 1999).

———. *Trazas de futuro: Episodios de la cultura arquitectónica de la modernidad de América Latina*. Santa Fe, Argentina: Universidad del Litoral, 2008.

———. "The Tree in the Box: Abstraction and Nature in the Virrey del Pino Apartments." *Assemblage* 40 (1999): 26–35.

———. "Un nuovo mundo per lo spirito nuovo: Le scoperte dell'America Latina da parte della cultura architettonica del XX Secolo." *Zodiac* 8 (1993): 107–109.

Liernur, Jorge Francisco, and Fernando Aliata, eds. *Diccionario de arquitectura en la Argentina*. Vols. 1–4. Buenos Aires: Diario de Arquitectura de Clarín, 2004.

Liernur, Jorge Francisco, and Pablo Pschepiurca. *La red austral: Obras y proyectos de Le Corbusier y sus discípulos en la Argentina (1924–1965)*. Bernal, Argentina: Universidad Nacional de Quilmes, 2008.

Lima, João da Gama Filgueiras. *Jornal do arquiteto*. Brasília: Fundação Athos Bulcão, 2006.

Lima, Zeuler. "The Faces of Janus: Modernism and Hybridisation in the Architecture of Lina Bo Bardi." *The Journal of Architecture* 11, no. 2 (2007): 257–267.

Lina Bo Bardi. São Paulo: Instituto Lina Bo e P. M. Bardi, 1994.

Lira, José. *Warchavchik: Fraturas da vanguarda*. São Paulo: Cosac Naify, 2011.

List Arzubide, Germán. *El movimiento estridentista*. Jalapa, Veracruz, Mexico: Ediciones de Horizonte, 1927.

Lizárraga Sánchez, Salvador. "Bacardí Breezer." *AA Files* 62 (2011): 104–107.

Loomis, John A. *Revolution of Forms: Cuba's Forgotten Art Schools*. New York: Princeton Architectural Press, 1999.

Loos, Adolf. "Ornament and Crime (1908)." In *Programs and Manifestoes of 20th Century Architecture*, ed. Ulrich Conrads. Cambridge: MIT Press, 1970.

Lowenstein, Oliver. "Visionary Architecture—Alive and Well in Amereida." *Fourth Door Review* 5 (2001).

Luchini, Aurelio. *Julio Vilamajó: Su arquitectura*. Montevideo: Universidad de la República, 1970.

Macedo, Joseli. "City Profile: Curitiba." *Cities* 21, no. 6 (December 2004).

———. "Urban Land Policy and New Tenure Paradigms: Legitimacy vs. Legality in Brazilian Cities." *Land Use Policy* 25 (2008).

Mariani, Riccardo. "Utilizzare l'Architettura Minore: San Paolo (Brasile), da una fabbrica." *Abitare*, no. 220 (December 1983).

Mariscal, Federico E. *La patria y la arquitectura nacional: Resúmenes de las conferencias dadas en la casa de la Universidad Popular Mexicana*. Mexico City: Imprenta Stephan y Torres, 1915.

Marques, Sonia, and Guilah Naslavsky. "Eu vi o modernismo nascer . . . foi no Recife." *Arquitextos* (São Paulo) 11.131, (April 2011). http://www.vitruvius.com.br /revistas/read/arquitextos/11.131/3826.

Marvel, Thomas S. *Antonin Nechodoma, Architect 1877– 1928: The Prairie School in the Caribbean*. Gainesville: University of Florida Press, 1994.

Matoso Macedo, Danilo. *Da matéria à invenção: As obras de Oscar Niemeyer em Minas Gerais, 1938–1955*. Brasília: Câmara dos Deputados, 2008.

Matta Echaurren, Roberto. "Sensitive Mathematics— Architecture of Time." Reprinted in *Drifts and Derivations: Experiences, Journeys, and Morphologies*. Madrid: Museo Nacional Centro de Arte Reina Sofía, 2010.

Mauricio Cravotto, 1893–1962. Montevideo: Editorial Dos Puntos, 1995.

Mauricio Rocha: Taller de Arquitectura. Mexico City: Arquine, 2011.

Mazza Dourado, Guilherme. "Roberto Burle Marx et le Paysagisme du XXe siécle." *Cahiers de la Recherche Architecturale et Urbaine*, nos. 18–19 (May 2006).

Mazzanti, Giancarlo. "A Conversation between Sergio Fajardo and Giancarlo Mazzanti." *BOMB Magazine* 110 (Winter 2010).

McCoy, Esther. "The New University City of Mexico." *Arts and Architecture* 69, no. 8 (August 1952).

Méndez-Vigatá, Antonio E. "Politics and Architectural Language: Post-Revolutionary Regimes in Mexico and Their Influence on Mexican Public Architecture, 1920–1952." In *Modernity and the Architecture of Mexico*, ed. Edward R. Burian, 61–90. Austin: University of Texas Press, 1997.

Meurs, Paul. "De Braziliaanse Identiteit en het Moderne: het Werk van Lina Bo Bardi." *Architect* 25, no. 5 (May 1994).

"Mexico City: Projects from the Megacity." *Praxis* 2 (2001).

Meyer, Hannes. "Building, 1928." In *Hannes Meyer: Buildings, Projects and Writings*, by Claude Schnaidt, 95–99. New York: Architectural Book Publishing, 1965.

———. "The New World, 1926." In *Hannes Meyer: Buildings, Projects and Writings*, by Claude Schnaidt. New York: Architectural Book Publishing, 1965.

"Mies Builds in Mexico." *Architectural Forum* 116 (January 1962).

Milheiro, Ana Vaz, Ana Luiza Nobre, and Guilherme Wisnik. *Coletivo*. São Paulo: Cosac Naify, 2006.

Mindlin, Henrique E. *Modern Architecture in Brazil*. Rio de Janeiro: Colibris, 1956.

Mitchell, Brian R. *International Historical Statistics: The Americas 1750–1988*. Basingstoke, England: Macmillan, 1993.

Moholy-Nagy, Sibyl. "Brasilia: Majestic Concept or Autocratic Monument?" *Progressive Architecture*, no. 40 (October 1959).

———. *Carlos Raúl Villanueva and the Architecture of Venezuela*. New York: Frederick A. Praeger, 1964.

———. "Mexican Critique." *Progressive Architecture* (November 1953).

Molina y Vedia, Juan. "Lo moderno y lo nacional en nuestra arquitectura: Wladimiro Acosta." *Summa+* 215–216 (1985).

Montaner, Josep María. *Después del Movimiento Moderno: Arquitectura de la segunda mitad del siglo XX*. Barcelona: GG, 1993.

———. *La modernidad superada*. Barcelona: GG, 1997.

Montealegre Klenner, Alberto. *Emilio Duhart, arquitecto*. Santiago: Ediciones ARQ Pontificia Universidad Católica de Chile, 1994.

Montezuma, Ricardo. "Facing The Environmental Challenge: The Transformation of Bogota, Colombia, 1995–2000: Investing in Citizenship and Urban Mobility." *Global Urban Development* 1, no. 1 (May 2005). http://www.globalurban.org/Issue1PIMag05/Montezuma%20article.htm.

Moore, Steven. *Alternative Routes to the Sustainable City: Austin, Curitiba, and Frankfurt*. Lanham, MD: Lexington Books, 2007.

Morais, Federico. *Mathias Goeritz*. Mexico City: UNAM, 1982.

Mujica, Francisco. *History of the Skyscraper*. Paris, 1929/New York: Archaeology and Architecture Press, 1930. Reprinted in 1977 by Da Capo Press, New York.

Mumford, Eric. "CIAM and Latin America." In *Sert: Arquitecto en Nueva York*, ed. Xavier Costa and Guido Hartray. Barcelona: Museu d'Art Contemporani de Barcelona, 1997.

Mumford, Eric, and Hashim Sarkis, eds. *Josep Lluís Sert: The Architect of Urban Design, 1953–1969*. New Haven: Yale University Press, 2008.

Nechodoma, Antonin. "Concerning Architecture in Puerto Rico." *Western Architect* (December 1927).

Negrón, Marco. "Amérique Latine . . . Stop . . . Problémes et méthodes." *L'Architecture d'Aujourd'hui* 173 (1974).

Nelken, Margarita. "En torno a la integración de la pintura a la función general de las artes plásticas." *Espacios: Revista Integral de Arquitectura y Artes Plásticas* 7 (June 1951).

Neruda, Pablo. *Memorial de Isla Negra*. Buenos Aires: Editorial Losada, 1964.

Neumann, Dietrich. "Gustavino System in Context: History and Dissemination of a Revolutionary Vaulting Method." *APT Bulletin* 30, no. 4 (1999).

Neutra, Richard. *An Architecture of Social Concern in Regions of Mild Climate*. São Paulo: Gerth Todtmann, 1948.

Niemeyer, Oscar. *Conversa de arquiteto*. Rio de Janeiro: Editora UFRJ, 1993.

———. "Form and Function in Architecture (1960)." In *Architecture Culture, 1943–1968: A Documentary Anthology*, ed. Joan Ockman. New York: Rizzoli, 1993.

———. "Statement." In *Brasil 1920–1950: De la antropofagia a Brasília*, ed. Jorge Schwartz. Valencia, Spain: IVAM, 2000. Originally published in *Modulo* 9 (February 1958).

1950: El espíritu moderno. Caracas: Fundación Corp Group, Centro Cultural, 1998.

Nobre, Ana Luiza. *Carmen Portinho: O moderno em construção*. Rio de Janeiro: Relume-Dumara, 1999.

Noel, Martín S. *Fundamentos para una estética nacional: Contribución a la historia de la arquitectura hispano-americana*. Buenos Aires: Talleres Rodríguez Giles, 1926.

Noelle Merles, Louise. "The Architecture and Urbanism of Mario Pani: Creativity and Compromise." In *Modernity and the Architecture of Mexico*, ed. Edward R. Burian, 177–190. Austin: University of Texas Press, 1997.

Novick, Alicia. "La ciudad como arquitectura: La *Cité* Azucarera de 1924." In Prebisch, *Una vanguardia con tradición*. Buenos Aires: Fundación CEDODAL, 1999.

O'Gorman, Juan. "Conferencia en la Sociedad de Arquitectos Mexicanos." In *Pláticas sobre arquitectura*, 17–34. Mexico City: INBA, 2001. Originally published 1934.

———. *Juan O'Gorman: Autobiografía, antología, juicios críticos y documentación exhaustiva sobre su obra*. Edited by Antonio Luna Arroyo. Mexico City: Cuadernos Populares de Pintura Mexicana Moderna, 1973.

Oiticica, Hélio. "Tropicália." In *Hélio Oiticica*. Rotterdam: The Center, 1992.

Oles, James. "In Pursuit of Salamone." *Cabinet* 34 (Summer 2009): 21–28.

Oliveira, Olívia Fernandes de. "Lina Bo Bardi, des dessins comme des rècits." *L'Architecture d'Aujourd'hui* 371 (July–August 2007): 70–77.

———, ed. "Lina Bo Bardi: Obra construida/Lina Bo Bardi: Built Work." *2G: Revista Internacional de Arquitectura* 23–24 (2002).

———. *Lina Bo Bardi: Sutis substâncias da arquitetura.*

São Paulo: Romano Guerra; Barcelona: Gustavo Gili, 2006.

"Paisajes emergentes: La Piedra Horadada = The Perforated Stone." *Arquine: Revista Internacional de Arquitectura* 50 (Winter 2009).

Pallares, Alfonso. "El Pedregal de San Ángel se incorpora a la ciudad." *Espacios: Revista Integral de Arquitectura y Artes Plásticas* 4 (June 1949).

Paltridge, Blair. "En la polémica de la integración plástica." In *Homenaje nacional a Carlos Mérida: Americanismo y abstracción*. Mexico City: Museo de Monterrey, 1992.

"The Pan-American Union Monument Competition." *Western Architect* 37 (1928).

Pani, Alberto J. *La higiene en México*. Mexico City: Imprenta de J. Ballesca, 1916.

Paz, Octavio. *The Labyrinth of Solitude*. New York: Grove Press, 1985.

Pedreschi, Remo. *Eladio Dieste: The Engineer's Contribution to Contemporary Architecture*. London: Thomas Telford, 2000.

Pendleton-Jullian, Ann M. "Autopoetic Architecture: The Open City, Ritoque, Chile." In *Architecturally Speaking: Practices of Art, Architecture, and the Everyday*, ed. Alan Read. London and New York: Routledge, 2000.

———. *The Road That Is Not a Road and the Open City, Ritoque, Chile*. Cambridge: MIT Press, 1996.

Pereira, Juliano Aparecido. *Lina Bo Bardi: Bahia, 1958–1964*. Uberlândia, Brazil: EDUFU, 2008.

Pereira, Sonia Gomes. "A reforma urbana de Pereira Passos e a construção de uma identidade carioca." PhD diss., Escola de Comunicação da Universidade Federal do Rio de Janeiro, 1998.

Pérez de Arce, Rodrigo. "Material Circumstances: The Project and Its Construction." In *Chilean Modern Architecture since 1950*, ed. Malcolm Quantrill. College Station: Texas A&M Press, 2010.

———. "So Far yet So Near: The Open City and the Travesías." In *Valparaíso School: Open City Group*, ed. Raúl Rispa Montreal and Kingston: McGill-Queen's University Press, 2003.

Pérez-Méndez, Alfonso, and Alejandro Aptilon. *Las casas del Pedregal, 1947–1968*. Barcelona: Editorial Gustavo Gili, 2007.

Pérez Oyarzún, Fernando. "Le Corbusier: Studies for South American Cities." *AULA* 2 (2001).

———. *Le Corbusier y Sudamérica: Viajes y proyectos*. Santiago: Ediciones Arq, 1991.

———. "The Valparaíso School." In Rispa, *Valparaíso School: Open City Group*. Montreal and Kingston: McGill-Queen's University Press, 2003. Published in Spanish as *Escuela de Valparaíso: Grupo Ciudad Abierta*. Sevilla: Tanais Ediciones, 2003.

Perrone, Charles A. *Seven Faces: Brazilian Poetry since Modernism*. Durham, NC: Duke University Press, 1996.

Pessoa, José, Eduardo Vasconcellos, Elisabete Reis, and Maria Lobo, eds. *Moderno e Nacional*. Niterói, Brazil: EAU/UFF, 2006.

Petrina, Alberto. "Severiano Porto: Arquitectura e identidad regional." *Summa+*, no. 210 (March 1985): 26–31. Interview.

Philippou, Styliane. *Oscar Niemeyer: Curves of Irreverence*. New Haven: Yale University Press, 2008.

Piñón, Helio. *Mario Roberto Álvarez*. Barcelona: Edicions UPC, 2002.

Ponce de León, Mónica. "Villa Planchart—Gio Ponti: Snapshots from Caracas." *Harvard Design Magazine* (Summer 1998).

Poniatowska, Elena. "Luis Barragán." In *Todo México*, Vol. 1. Mexico City: Editorial Diana, 1990.

Porro, Ricardo. "An Architectural Autobiography of Ricardo Porro." *A + U: Architecture and Urbanism* 94, no. 3 (March 1994).

Prebisch, Alberto. "El XIVo Salón Nacional de Bellas Artes." *Martín Fierro* 1, no. 10–11 (September–October 1924).

"PREVI/Lima: Low-cost Housing Project." *Architectural Design* 40 (April 1970).

"PREVI Lima: 35 años después." *ARQ (Santiago)* 59 (March 2005): 72–76.

Pschepiurca, Pablo. "BKF: Annuncio di una Modernita." *Casabella* 711 (2003).

Quantrill, Malcolm, ed. *Chilean Modern Architecture since 1950*. College Station: Texas A&M Press, 2010.

Quezado Deckker, Zilah. *Brazil Built: The Architecture of the Modern Movement in Brazil*. London: Taylor and Francis, 2001.

Radic Clarke, Smiljan. "Extension for the Charcoal Burner's Hut." *A + U: Architecture and Urbanism* 10, no. 361 (October 2000).

Rama, Ángel. *La ciudad letrada*. Hanover, NH: Ediciones del Norte, 1984.

Ramírez, Fausto. *Crónica de las artes plásticas en los años de López Velarde, 1914–1921*. Mexico City: UNAM, 1990.

Ramírez, Mari Carmen. *Hélio Oiticica: The Body of Color*. London: Tate Publishing, 2007.

Ramírez, Mari Carmen, and Héctor Olea, eds. *Color in Space and Time: Cruz-Diez*. New Haven: Yale University Press, 2011.

———. *Inverted Utopias: Avant-Garde Art in Latin America*. Houston: Museum of Fine Arts; New Haven: Yale University Press, 2004.

Ramírez Vázquez, Pedro. "The Architecture of the Museum." In Ramírez Vázquez, *National Museum of Anthropology, Mexico: Art, Architecture, Archaeology, Ethnography*. New York: Harry N. Abrams, 1968.

———. *National Museum of Anthropology, Mexico: Art, Architecture, Archaeology, Ethnography*. New York: Harry N. Abrams, 1968.

Ramírez Vázquez, Pedro, and Beatrice Trueblood. *Ramírez Vázquez en la arquitectura*. Mexico City, Editorial Diana, 1989.

Ramos, Jorge. "Salamone en la Pampa—Una estética del Justismo." In *Francisco Salamone en la provincia de Buenos Aires: Reconocimiento patrimonial de sus obras*, ed. Alejandro Novacovsky, et al. Mar del Plata, Argentina: Universidad Nacional de Mar del Plata, 2001.

Ravell, H. "Vanishing Mexico." *Harper's* 134, no. 799 (December 1916): 97–104.

Reina-Bravo, Doris. "A Modernist Experiment: Traces of Poetry, Art, and Architecture within the Travesías and the Open City." *Arquitextos* (São Paulo) 12.136 (September) 2011. http://vitruvius.es/revistas/read/arquitextos/12.136/4000.

Revilla, Manuel G. *El arte en México en la época antigua y durante el gobierno virreinal (1893)*. Whitefish, MT: Kessinger Publishing, 2010.

Ribbeck, Eckhart. "City of All Shades: Redevelopment Projects in Rio de Janeiro." *Topos: The International Review of Landscape Architecture and Urban Design*, no. 64 (2008).

Ribeiro, Luiz Cesar de Queiroz, and Robert Pechman, eds. *Cidade, povo e nação: Gênese do urbanismo moderno*. Rio de Janeiro: Civilizacão Brasileira, 1996.

Ricalde, Humberto G. "La repercusión del Eco de Mathias Goeritz." *Arquine* 4 (Summer 1998).

Rio, João do. *Vida vertiginosa*. Rio de Janeiro: H. Garnier, 1911.

Rispa, Raúl. *Luis Barragán: The Complete Works*. New York: Princeton Architectural Press, 2003.

———, ed. *Valparaíso School: Open City Group*. Montreal and Kingston: McGill-Queen's University Press, 2003. Published in Spanish as *Escuela de Valparaíso: Grupo Ciudad Abierta*. Sevilla: Tanais Ediciones, 2003.

Rivera, Diego. "Requisitos para la organización de El Pedregal." Reprinted in *Luis Barragán's Gardens of El Pedregal* by Keith L. Eggener. New York: Princeton Architectural Press, 2001.

Rizza, Giulio G. *Roberto Burle Marx: Il giardino del Novecento*. Florence, Italy: Cantini, 1992.

Rodrigues, Antonio Edmilson Martins. *João do Rio: A cidade e o poeta—O olhar de flâneur na Belle Époque tropical*. Rio de Janeiro: FGV, 2000.

Rodríguez, Eduardo Luis. *The Havana Guide: Modern Architecture, 1925–1965*. New York: Princeton Architectural Press, 2000.

Rodríguez Prampolini, Ida. *Juan O'Gorman: Arquitecto y pintor* Mexico City: UNAM, 1982.

Rodríguez Prampolini, Ida, and Ferruccio Asta, eds. *Los ecos de Mathias Goeritz: Ensayos y testimonios*. Mexico City: INBA, 1997.

Rogers, Ernesto. "Report on Brazil." *The Architectural Review* 116, no. 694 (August 1954).

Rovira, Josep M. *José Luis Sert*. Milan: Electa Arcitecture, 2003.

———, ed. *Sert, 1928–1979: Half a Century of Architecture*. Barcelona: Fundació Joan Miró, 2005.

Rubert de Ventós, Maria. "Cities in Latin America: The Work of Town Planning Associates, 1943–1956." In *Sert: Arquitector en Nueva York*, ed. Xavier Costa and Guido Hartray. Barcelona: Museu d'Art Contemporani de Barcelona, 1997.

Said, Edward. *Culture and Imperialism*. New York: Alfred A. Knopf, 1993.

Sánchez-Albornoz, Nicolás. *The Population of Latin America: A History*. Berkeley: University of California Press, 1974.

Santa-Cecilia, Bruno. *Éolo Maia: Complexidade e contradição na arquitetura brasileira*. Belo Horizonte: Editora UFMG, 2006.

"Santiago Caracol." *Progressive Architecture* 47 (December 1966): 158–159.

Sarlo, Beatriz. *Una modernidad periférica: Buenos Aires 1920 y 1930*. Buenos Aires: Ediciones Nueva Visión, 1988.

Schávelzon, Daniel. "El Pabellón Xochicalco en la Exposición International de París de 1867." In *La polémica del arte nacional en México, 1850–1910*, ed. Daniel Schávelzon. Mexico City: Fondo de Cultura Económica, 1988.

Schorske, Carl E. *Fin-de-Siècle Vienna: Politics and Culture*. New York: Knopf, 1980.

Schwartz, Jorge, ed. *Brasil 1920–1950: De la antropofagia a Brasília*. Valencia, Spain: IVAM, 2000.

Secretaría de Educación Pública. *Edificios construidos por la Secretaría de Educación Pública en los años de 1921 a 1924*. Mexico: N.p., 1924.

Segawa, Hugo. *Arquiteturas no Brasil, 1900–1990*. São Paulo: Edusp, 1998.

———. "The Essentials of Brazilian Modernism." *Design Book Review* 32–33 (1994).

———. "Le Belle Americhe = America the Beautiful." *Spazio e Societá* 19, no. 80 (October–December 1997).

———. "Severiano Porto: La sfida dell'Amazzonia = Severiano Porto the Amazonian Challenge." *Spazio e Societá* 16, no. 61 (January 1993).

Segre, Roberto, ed. *América Latina en su arquitectura*. Mexico City: Siglo XXI and UNESCO, 1975.

———. "Formal-Informal Connections in the Favelas of Rio de Janeiro: The Favela-Bairro Programme." In *Rethinking the Informal Cities: Critical Perspectives from Latin America*, ed. Felipe Hernández, Peter Kellet, and Lea Allen. Oxford and New York: Berghahn Books, 2010.

———. *La Habana de Sert: CIAM, ron y cha cha cha*. Typescript. N.d.

Serapião, Fernando, and Otávio Leonídio. *Monolito Nº 1: Angelo Bucci*. São Paulo: Monolito Editora, 2011.

Seville: Spanish American Exposition, 1929–1930. Seville, Spain: Official Committee of the Spanish-American Exposition, 1929. Brochure.

Silvestri, Graciela. "Apariencia y verdad: Reflexiones sobre obras, testimonios y documentos de arquitectura producidos durante la dictadura militar en la Argentina." *Block* 5 (December 2000).

———. "Julio Vilamajó: L'ornamento che custodische il piacere." *Casabella* 66, no. 697 (February 2002).

Silvetti, Jorge, ed. *Amancio Williams.* New York: Rizzoli, 1987.

Siqueiros, David Alfaro. "En el orden burgués reinante, hay que buscar la causa de la decadencia arquitectónica contemporánea." *El Machete* (May 1924).

Smith, Clive Bamford. *Builders in the Sun: Five Mexican Architects.* New York: Architectural Book Publishing, 1967.

Smithson, Alison, and Peter Smithson. "The New Brutalism." In *Architecture Culture 1943-1968: A Documentary Anthology,* ed. Joan Ockman. New York: Rizzoli, 1993.

———. *Without Rhetoric: An Architectural Aesthetic, 1955–1972.* Cambridge: MIT Press, 1973.

Soilleux, G. A. "The Planning of the United Nations Headquarters." *Architect and Building News* 107 (1948).

Solsona, Justo. *Entrevistas: Apuntes para una autobiografía.* Buenos Aires: Ediciones Infinito, 1998.

Solt, Mary Ellen, ed. *Concrete Poetry: A World View.* Bloomington: Indiana University Press, 1970.

Soto: Paris and Beyond, 1950–1970. Edited by Estrellita Brodsky. New York: Grey Art Gallery, 2012.

Strauven, Francis. *Aldo van Eyck: The Shape of Relativity.* Amsterdam: Architectura & Natura Press, 1998.

Tafel, Edgar. *Frank Lloyd Wright: Recollections by Those Who Knew Him.* Mineola, NY: Dover Publications, 1993.

Tafuri, Manfredo. "The Historical Project." In *The Sphere and the Labyrinth: Avant-Gardes and Architecture from Piranesi to the 1970s.* Cambridge: MIT Press, 1987.

———. "The International Panorama in the Fifties and Sixties." In *Modern Architecture* by Manfredo Tafuri and Francesco Dal Co, 339–356. New York: H. N. Abrams, 1979.

———. "The New Babylon: The 'Yellow Giants' and the Myth of Americanism." In *The Sphere and the Labyrinth: Avant-Gardes and Architecture from Piranesi to the 1970s.* Cambridge: MIT Press, 1987.

Tattara, Martino. "Brasilia's Superquadra: Prototypical Design and the Project of the City." *Architectural Design* 81, no. 1 (January–February 2011).

———. "(Re)Writing the City: An Assessment of Brasilia's Legacy." *Hunch: The Berlage Institute Report,* no. 12 (2009).

Teatro Oficina = Oficina Theater: São Paulo, Brasil, 1980–1984. Lisbon: Editorial Blau; São Paulo: Instituto Lina Bo e P. M. Bardi, 1999.

Teixeira, Carlos M. *Em Obras: História do Vazio em Belo Horizonte.* São Paulo: Cosac e Naify, 1999.

———. "La vraie nature de Brasília = The True Nature of Brasilia." *L'Architecture d'Aujourd'hui,* no. 359 (July–August 2005).

Téllez, Germán. *Rogelio Salmona: Obra Completa, 1959–2005.* Bogotá: Escala, 2006.

TEN Arquitectos: Enrique Norten, Bernardo Gómez Pimienta. New York: Monacelli Press, 1998.

Tenorio-Trillo, Mauricio. *Mexico at the World's Fairs: Crafting a Modern Nation.* Berkeley: University of California Press, 1996.

Thrall, Ashley P., Maria E. Moreyra, and David P. Billington. "Church of Our Lady of the Miraculous Medal." In *Félix Candela: Engineer, Builder, Structural Artist,* by Maria E. Moreyra Garlock and David P. Billington. New Haven: Yale University Press, 2008.

Toca Fernández, Antonio. "Juan Segura: The Origins of Modern Architecture in Mexico." In *Modernity and the Architecture of Mexico,* ed. Edward R. Burian, 163–176. Austin: University of Texas Press, 1997.

———. *México: Nueva arquitectura.* Barcelona: Gustavo Gili, 1991.

Torrent, Horacio. "Abstraction and Tectonics in Chilean Architecture since 1950." In *Chilean Modern Architecture since 1950,* ed. Malcolm Quantrill. College Station: Texas A&M Press, 2010.

Torres-García, Joaquín. *La tradición del hombre abstracto.* In *Art in Latin America,* ed. Dawn Ades. New Haven: Yale University Press, 1989.

Tzonis, Alexander, and Liane Lefaivre. "Tropical Regionalism in an Age of Globalization." *Aula* 3 (2002): 6–17.

Tzonis, Alexander, Liane Lefaivre, and Bruno Stagno, eds. *Tropical Architecture: Critical Regionalism in the Age of Globalization.* New York: Wiley Academic, 2001.

Underwood, David. "Interview with Max Abramovitz" (March 23, 1991). In *Oscar Niemeyer and the Architecture of Brazil.* New York: Rizzoli, 1994.

———. *Oscar Niemeyer and the Architecture of Brazil.* New York: Rizzoli, 1994.

"United Nations Building, Santiago, Chile." *Architectural Design* 37 (January 1967).

Vaccarino, Rossana, ed. *Roberto Burle Marx: Landscapes Reflected.* Princeton, NJ: Princeton Architectural Press with the Harvard University Graduate School of Design, 2000.

Valporto Leal, Ledy. "Técnica e arte a serviço da cura." *AU—Arquitetura e Urbanismo* (São Paulo), no. 175 (October 2008): 48–57.

Vargas Salguero, Ramón. "La arquitectura de la Revolución Mexicana: Un enfoque social." In *México, 75 años de revolución: Educación, cultura y comunicación,* Vol. 2, section 4. Mexico City: Fondo de Cultura Económica and INEHRM, 1988.

———. *Búsqueda de una arquitectura moderna nacional.* Manuscript.

———. "Las reivindicaciones históricas en el funcionalismo socialista." In *Apuntes para la historia y crítica de la arquitectura mexicana del siglo XX: 1900–1980,* Vol. 1. Mexico City: SEP and INBA, 1982.

Vasconcelos, José. *The Cosmic Race/La raza cósmica.* Translated by Didier T. Jaén. Baltimore: Johns Hopkins University Press, 1997. Originally published 1925.

———. "El desastre." In *Memorias,* Vol. 2. Mexico City: Fondo de Cultura Económica, 1993. Originally published 1938.

———. *Obras completas,* Vol. 2. Mexico City: Libreros Mexicanos Unidos, 1958.

Vasconcelos, Sylvio de. "Belo Horizonte—A Metropole de 50 Anos." *Arquitetura e Engenharia* (1947).

Vautier, Ernesto, and Alberto Prebisch. "Un proyecto de Museo de Bellas Artes." *Martín Fierro,* no. 37 (January 20, 1927).

Veikos, Cathrine. "To Enter the Work: Ambient Art." *Journal of Architectural Education* 59, no. 4 (May 2006).

Venâncio Filho, Paulo. "Paisagismo, pintura e natureza." In *Roberto Burle Marx 100 Anos: A Permanência do Instável,* ed. Lauro Cavalcanti and Farès El-Dahdah. Rio de Janeiro: Rocco, 2009.

Venturi, Robert. *Complexity and Contradiction in Architecture.* New York: The Museum of Modern Art, 1966.

Venturi, Robert, Denise Scott-Brown, and Steven Izenour. *Learning from Las Vegas.* Cambridge: MIT Press, 1972.

Vera, Paloma. "Después del sueño moderno: Lina Bo Bardi y la enseñanza de la arquitectura." *Arquine,* no. 52 (Summer 2010).

Verde Zein, Ruth, and M. A. Junqueira Bastos. *Brasil: Arquitetura após 1950.* São Paulo: Perspectiva, 2011.

Verde Zein, Ruth, and Hugo Segawa. "Arquitetura em Exposição: Sevilha 92." *Projeto* 138 (February 1991).

Vicente, Henry, ed. *Arquitecturas desplazadas: Arquitecturas del exilio español.* Madrid: Ministerio de Vivienda de España, 2007.

Vidler, Anthony. "'Architecture-to-Be': Notes on Architecture in the Work of Matta and Gordon Matta-Clark." In *Transmission: The Art of Matta and Gordon Matta-Clark.* San Diego: San Diego Museum of Art, 2006.

Vilanova Artigas. São Paulo: Instituto Lina Bo e P. M. Bardi; Fundação Vilanova Artigas, 1997.

Vilanova Artigas, João Batista. "Aos formandos da FAU-USP de 1955." In *Caminhos da arquitetura.* São Paulo: Editora Cosac Naify, 2004.

———. "College of Architecture and Urbanism—São Paulo University—FAU-USP." In *Vilanova Artigas.* São Paulo: Instituto Lina Bo e P. M. Bardi, 1997.

Villagrán García, José. *José Villagrán.* Mexico City: INBA, 1986.

Villanueva, Carlos Raul. "Synthesis of the Arts (1954)." Reproduced in *Carlos Raul Villanueva and the Architecture of Venezuela,* by Sybil Moholy-Nagy. New York: Frederick A. Praeger, 1964.

Villanueva, Paulina, and Maciá Pintó. *Carlos Raúl Villanueva.* New York: Princeton Architectural Press, 2000.

Vivanco, Sandra. "Lina Bo Bardi: The Chameleon of Brazilian Modern Architecture." *AULA* 1 (Spring 1999).

Vivoni Farage, Enrique. "Henry Klumb and the Poetic Exuberance in Architecture." In *Klumb: An Architecture of Social Concern,* ed. Enrique Vivoni Farage. San Juan: La Editorial Universidad de Puerto Rico, 2006.

Waisman, Marina. "Editorial: Racionalismo a tres voces: Ungers-Rossi-Krier." *Revista Summarios* 4, no. 22 (1978).

———. "Primer Seminario de Arquitectura Latinoamericana: Un auspicioso comienzo." In *Arquitectura Latinoamericana: Pensamiento y propuesta.* Mexico City: UAM-Xochimilco, 1991.

———. "Un proyecto de modernidad." In *Modernidad y postmodernidad en América Latina,* ed. Cristián Fernández Cox. Bogotá: ESCALA, 1991.

———. "La unidad recuperada: Eladio Dieste, Formas y técnicas." *Arquitectura Viva,* no. 18 (May–June 1991).

Waldheim, C. "Landscape as Monument: J. L. Gleave and the Columbus Lighthouse Competition." *Archivos De Arquitectura Antillana* 3, no. 7 (1998).

Warchavchik, Gregori. "On Modern Architecture" (1925). In *Brasil 1920–1950: De la antropofagia a Brasília,* ed. Jorge Schwartz, 620–621. Valencia, Spain: IVAM, 2000.

Weiner, Gunter. *Arquitetura popular brasileira.* São Paulo: Martins Fontes, 2005.

Weiss, Joaquín. *El rascacielos: Su génesis, evolución y significación en la arquitectura contemporánea.* La Habana: Tipos-Molina, 1934.

Werthmann, Christian. "Making History: Rio de Janeiro—the Favela Bairro Program and More." *Harvard Design Magazine,* no. 28 (Spring–Summer 2008).

"What We Can Do: Pedro Ramírez Vázquez in Interview with Tania Ragassol." In *Diseñando México 68: Una identidad olímpica.* Mexico: Museo de Arte Moderno, 2008.

Wilheim, Jorge, and Jane Richards. "Jorge Wilheim: Desiring Global Change, from an interview by Jane Richards." *Architectural Design* 67, no. 1–2 (January–February 1997).

Willcox, Walter F., ed. *International Migrations.* 2 vols. New York: National Bureau of Economic Research, 1929–1931.

Williams, Richard. "Brasília after Brasília." *Progress and Planning* 64, no. 4 (2007).

———. *Brazil: Modern Architectures in History.* London: Reaktion Books, 2009.

Wisnik, Guilherme. "Faculty of Architecture and Planning, University of São Paulo (FAU-USP), São Paulo." *2G: Vilanova Artigas*, no. 54 (2010).

Wolff, Ilze. "Lesson in 'Spatialising' Heritage: The Conservation Work of Lina Bo Bardi." *Architecture South Africa: Journal of the South African Institute of Architects* (March-April 2007).

The Works of Affonso Eduardo Reidy. New York City: Frederick A. Praeger, 1960.

Wright, Frank Lloyd. "The Art and Craft of the Machine (1901)." In *Frank Lloyd Wright: Essential Texts*, ed. Robert Twombly. New York: W. W. Norton, 2009.

———. *Studies and Executed Buildings by Frank Lloyd Wright*. New York: Rizzoli, 1986. Originally published as *Ausgeführte Bauten und Entwürfe*, 1910.

Wright, Gwendolyn. *USA: Modern Architectures in History*. London: Reaktion Books, 2008.

Xavier, Alberto, ed. *Arquitetura moderna brasileira: Depoimento de uma geração*. São Paulo: Pini, 1987.

Xavier, Alberto, and Ana Luiza Nobre. *Arquitetura moderna no Rio de Janeiro*. Rio de Janeiro: Rioarte, 1991.

Zalduendo, Ines. "Buenos Aires: La Ciudad Frente al Río."
Paper delivered at the SAH 63rd Annual Meeting, Chicago, IL, 2010.

Zanco, Federica. "Inward Outward: Barragán in Transition." *Journal of Decorative and Propaganda Arts: Mexico Theme Issue* 26 (May 2010): 180–205.

———, ed. *Luis Barragán: The Quiet Revolution*. Milan: Skira, 2001.

Zein, Ruth Verde. "A arquitetura da escola paulista brutalista, 1953–1973." PhD diss., Propar—UFRGS, 2005.

———. "Brazilian Architecture, Modern Tradition, Contemporary Culture." In *Non West Modernist Past*, ed. William Lim, 169–179. Singapore: World Scientific Publishing, 2012.

———. "Habitat, Lina Bo Bardi y la crítica de arquitectura no alineada." *Summa+*, no. 101 (June 2009).

———. *Lugar da crítica: Ensaios oportunos de arquitetura*. São Paulo: ProEditores/Ritter dos Reis, 2001.

Zevi, Bruno. "Inchiesta su Brasília." *L'architettura cronache e storia*, no. 51 (January 1960).

Zúñiga, Olivia. *Mathias Goeritz*. Translated by Sonia Levy-Spira. Mexico City: Editorial Intercontinental, 1963.

ILLUSTRATION CREDITS

p. 83	Photo by Luis E. Carranza.
p. 84	Drawing by Catherine Varnas.
p. 85	Courtesy of James Oles.
p. 86	Photo by Luis E. Carranza.
p. 87	Photo by Luis E. Carranza.
p. 87	Drawing by Caitlin Osepchuk.
p. 88	From Acosta, *Vivienda y ciudad*.
p. 90	From Acosta, *Vivienda y ciudad*.
p. 91	Nettie Lee Benson Latin American Collection, University of Texas at Austin.
p. 91	From Acosta, *Vivienda y ciudad*.
p. 92	Photo by Luis E. Carranza.
p. 92	Photo by Alison Carranza.
p. 93	Photo by Luis E. Carranza.
p. 94	© 2014 Artists Rights Society (ARS), New York/ADAGP, Paris
p. 95	Photo by Luis E. Carranza.
p. 97	By permission of the Cetto family.
p. 98	Photo by Esther McCoy. Esther McCoy Papers, Archives of American Art, The Smithsonian Institute.
p. 99	Photo by Luis E. Carranza.
p. 102	© Bauhaus Dessau Foundation (I1948 D). Courtesy of Bauhaus Dessau Foundation/Picture Department.
p. 103	By permission of Donatella Calabi.
p. 104	By permission of the Cetto family.
p. 105	Courtesy of The New York Public Library. New York World's Fair 1939–1940 records, Manuscripts and Archives Division, The New York Public Library, Astor, Lenox, and Tilden Foundations.
p. 105	Courtesy of The New York Public Library. New York World's Fair 1939–1940 records, Manuscripts and Archives Division, The New York Public Library, Astor, Lenox, and Tilden Foundations.
p. 106	Courtesy of The New York Public Library. Milstein Division of United States History, Local History and Genealogy, The New York Public Library, Astor, Lenox, and Tilden Foundations.
p. 106	Drawing by Caitlin Osepchuk.
p. 108	Photo by Fernando Lara.
p. 109	Photo by Fernando Lara.
p. 110	Drawing by Caitlin Osepchuk.
p. 110	Photo by Fernando Lara.
p. 111	Photo by Luis E. Carranza.
p. 111	Drawing by Caitlin Osepchuk.
p. 113	Drawing by Catherine Varnas.
p. 113	Photo by Walter Salcedo.
p. 116	© The Museum of Modern Art/Licensed by SCALA/Art Resource, NY.
p. 116	© The Museum of Modern Art/Licensed by SCALA/Art Resource, NY.
p. 118	Courtesy of the Frances Loeb Library, Harvard Graduate School of Design.
p. 120	Courtesy of the Frances Loeb Library, Harvard Graduate School of Design.
p. 121	Courtesy of the Frances Loeb Library, Harvard Graduate School of Design.
p. 124	Archivo de Arquitectura y Construcción Universidad de Puerto Rico (AACUPR). Reprinted with permission.
p. 125	Photo by J. Alex Langley. Archivo de Arquitectura y Construcción Universidad de Puerto Rico (AACUPR). Reprinted with permission.
p. 126	Photo by J. Alex Langley. Archivo de Arquitectura y Construcción Universidad de Puerto Rico (AACUPR). Reprinted with permission.
p. 127	Drawing by Catherine Varnas.
p. 128	Photo by Jose Oliver.
p. 128	Photo by Luis E. Carranza.
p. 129	Drawing by Caitlin Osepchuk.
p. 130	Courtesy of the Arxiu Històric del Collegi d'Arquitectes de Catalunya.
p. 131	Drawing by Amy Freedberg.
p. 132	Photo by Marcel Gautherot, by permission of Instituto Moreira Sales.
p. 133	Photo by Kristine Stiphany. Courtesy of School of Architecture Visual Resources Collection, University of Texas at Austin.
p. 135	Photo by Armando Salas Portugal. Courtesy of the Barragán Foundation. © 2014 Barragán Foundation, Switzerland/Artists Rights Society (ARS), New York/© 2014 Artists Rights Society (ARS), New York/ProLitteris, Zurich.
p. 136	Photo by Luis E. Carranza.
p. 137	Photo by Armando Salas Portugal. Courtesy of the Barragán Foundation. © 2014 Barragán Foundation, Switzerland/Artists Rights Society (ARS), New York/© 2014 Artists Rights Society (ARS), New York/ProLitteris, Zurich.
p. 138	Photo by Armando Salas Portugal. Courtesy of the Barragán Foundation. © 2014 Barragán Foundation, Switzerland/Artists Rights Society (ARS), New York/© 2014 Artists Rights Society (ARS), New York/ProLitteris, Zurich.
p. 141	Photo by Luis E. Carranza.

p. 142	From *L'Architecture d'Aujourd'hui*, October 1956.	p. 181	Photo by Kristine Stiphany. Courtesy of School of Architecture Visual Resources Collection, University of Texas at Austin.
p. 143	From *L'Architecture d'Aujourd'hui*, October 1956.		
p. 144	By permission of UN Photo Library.	p. 182	Photo by Leonardo Finotti.
p. 144	By permission of Farès el-Dahdah/Rosalyn Lu.	p. 183	Photo by Leonardo Finotti.
p. 145	By permission of UN Photo Library.	p. 184	Photo by Luis E. Carranza.
p. 148	Courtesy of Fundación ICA, A.C.	p. 185	Photo by Luis E. Carranza.
p. 148	Photo by Susleriel.	p. 185	Photo by Luis E. Carranza.
p. 151	Courtesy of the Frances Loeb Library, Harvard Graduate School of Design.	p. 186	Photo by Luis E. Carranza.
		p. 187	Drawing by Caitlin Osepchuk.
p. 152	Courtesy of the Frances Loeb Library, Harvard Graduate School of Design.	p. 187	Photo by Luis E. Carranza.
		p. 188	Photo by Luis E. Carranza.
p. 152	Courtesy of the Frances Loeb Library, Harvard Graduate School of Design.	p. 189	Drawing by Amy Freedberg.
		p. 189	Photo by Luis E. Carranza.
p. 153	Courtesy of Archivo Fundación Villanueva.	p. 191	Photo by Ken Dineen.
p. 154	Photo by Paolo Gasparini. Courtesy of Archivo Fundación Villanueva.	p. 192	Photo by Ken Dineen.
		p. 192	Photo by Ken Dineen.
p. 155	Courtesy of Archivo Fundación Villanueva.	p. 193	Photo by Jorge Villota.
p. 155	Photo by Paolo Gasparini. Courtesy of Archivo Fundación Villanueva.	p. 194	Photo by Jorge Villota.
		p. 195	Archives Jorge Villota.
p. 156	Photo by Nelson Kon.	p. 197	Photo by Miguel Braceli.
p. 157	Photo by Luis E. Carranza.	p. 198	Photo by Miguel Braceli.
p. 158	Drawing by Caitlin Osepchuk.	p. 199	Photo by Ana María León.
p. 158	Photo by Paolo Gasparini. Courtesy of Archivo Fundación Villanueva.	p. 200	By permission of Casa de Lúcio Costa.
		p. 201	Photo by Ana María León.
p. 160	By permission of Instituto Bardi.	p. 202	Photo by Marcel Gautherot, Instituto Moreira Sales.
p. 161	Drawing by Amy Freedberg.		
p. 161	By permission of Instituto Bardi.	p. 203	Photo by Marcel Gautherot, Instituto Moreira Sales.
p. 164	Courtesy of Fundación ICA, A.C.		
p. 164	Photo by Luis E. Carranza.	p. 204	Drawing by Caitlin Osepchuk.
p. 165	Drawing by Amy Freedberg.	p. 204	Photo by Nelson Kon.
p. 165	Photo by Luis E. Carranza.	p. 206	© The Museum of Modern Art/Licensed by SCALA/Art Resource, NY/ARS/© 2014 Artists Rights Society (ARS), New York/VG Bild-Kunst, Bonn
p. 167	Courtesy of Archivo Fundación Villanueva.		
p. 167	Courtesy of Archivo Fundación Villanueva.		
p. 168	Photo by Jorge Villota.		
p. 168	Courtesy of Archivo Fundación Villanueva.		
p. 170	Photo by Luis E. Carranza.	p. 207	Photo by Balthasar Korab.
p. 171	Photo by Luis E. Carranza.	p. 207	Photo by Balthasar Korab.
p. 171	Drawing by Amy Freedberg.	p. 208	Drawing by Caitlin Osepchuk.
p. 172	Photo by Leonardo Finotti.	p. 209	Photo by Nelson Kon.
p. 173	Photo by Leonardo Finotti.	p. 209	Photo by Kristine Stiphany. Courtesy of School of Architecture Visual Resources Collection, University of Texas at Austin.
p. 174	Drawing by Caitlin Osepchuk.		
p. 174	Courtesy of School of Architecture Visual Resources Collection, University of Texas at Austin.		
		p. 210	Photo by Arq. Facundo Savid.
p. 177	Photo by Luis E. Carranza.	p. 212	Photo by Larry Speck. Courtesy of School of Architecture Visual Resources Collection, University of Texas at Austin.
p. 178	Photo by Armando Salas Portugal. © 2014 Artists Rights Society (ARS), New York/ProLitteris, Zurich		
		p. 213	Photo by Luis E. Carranza.
p. 179	Courtesy of Ing. Daniel Goeritz Rodríguez.	p. 214	Photo by Luis E. Carranza.
p. 179	Courtesy of Ing. Daniel Goeritz Rodríguez.	p. 215	Photo by Luis E. Carranza.

p. 216   Photo by Ana María León.

p. 217   Drawing by Caitlin Osepchuk.

p. 220   Escritório Paulo Mendes da Rocha.

p. 220   Escritório Paulo Mendes da Rocha.

p. 221   Photo by Kristine Stiphany. Courtesy of School of Architecture Visual Resources Collection, University of Texas at Austin.

p. 222   Photo by Fernando Lara.

p. 223   Photo by Luis E. Carranza.

p. 224   Photo by Luis E. Carranza.

p. 224   Drawings by Caitlin Osepchuk.

p. 225   Drawings by Caitlin Osepchuk.

p. 226   Photo by Fernando Lara.

p. 227   Arquivo Luis Amorim.

p. 227   Arquivo Luis Amorim.

p. 228   Arquivo Luis Amorim.

p. 229   Photo by Luis E. Carranza.

p. 230   Photo by Luis E. Carranza.

p. 231   Photo by Arq. Andrés Téllez Tavera.

p. 232   Photo by Arq. Andrés Téllez Tavera.

p. 232   Drawing by Caitlin Osepchuk.

p. 234   Photo by Marcel Gautherot, Instituto Moreira Sales.

p. 235   Photo by Kristine Stiphany. Courtesy of School of Architecture Visual Resources Collection, University of Texas at Austin.

p. 237   Prefeitura de Curitiba, photo by Cesar Brustolin.

p. 238   Drawing by Fernando Lara and Caitlin Osepchuk.

p. 239   Prefeitura de Curitiba, photo by Maurilio Cheli.

p. 240   Fondo Documental Juan Borchers F. Archivo de Originales SLGM. FADEU. Pontificia Universidad Católica de Chile.

p. 240   Drawings by Caitlin Osepchuk.

p. 241   Fondo Documental Juan Borchers F. Archivo de Originales SLGM. FADEU. Pontificia Universidad Católica de Chile.

p. 243   Drawing by Caitlin Osepchuk.

p. 244   Courtesy of CEPAL Sección de Información Pública y Servicios Web.

p. 245   Photo by Fernando Lara.

p. 247   Photo by Paolo Gasparini. © Fundación Gego. Todos los derechos reservados. Prohibida su reproducción total o parcial.

p. 248   By permission of Projeto Hélio Oiticica.

p. 249   Photo by Denise Dea.

p. 250   Photo by Jorge Villota.

p. 252   Photo by Francisco Uribe. Published with permission from the United States Olympic Committee and the International Olympic Committee.

p. 253   Photo by Mauricio Alfaro Moreno.

p. 254   Courtesy of Ing. Daniel Goeritz Rodríguez.

p. 255   Courtesy of Patronato Ruta de la Amistad.

p. 258   Photo by Doris Reina Bravo.

p. 259   Photo by Doris Reina Bravo.

p. 260   Photo by Doris Reina Bravo.

p. 263   Courtesy of Peter Land.

p. 264   Ministerio de Vivienda del Perú. Courtesy of Diego Torres Torriti, Fernando García-Huidobro, and Nicolás Tugas.

p. 264   Photo courtesy of Diego Torres Torriti, Fernando García-Huidobro, and Nicolás Tugas.

p. 267   Courtesy of Gyula Kosice.

p. 269   Courtesy of Acervo Sergio Bernardes.

p. 270   From Acosta, *Vivienda y ciudad*.

p. 272   Photo by José Yee.

p. 273   Photo by José Yee.

p. 274   Photo by Álvaro Arrese. Courtesy of Sandro Borghini.

p. 276   Project by Jorge Grin. Courtesy of Sandro Borghini.

p. 276   Courtesy of Carlos Sallaberry and M/SG/S/S/S/ Arquitectos.

p. 278   Photo by Rodrigo Baeta.

p. 279   Photo by Rodrigo Baeta.

p. 282   Photo by Luis E. Carranza.

p. 283   Photo by Mauricio Alfaro Moreno.

p. 284   Photo by Luis E. Carranza.

p. 285   Photo by Mauricio Alfaro Moreno.

p. 287   Photo by Bruno Santa Cecilia.

p. 288   Photo by Bruno Santa Cecilia.

p. 289   Courtesy of Bruno Stagno and Jimena Ugarte de Stagno.

p. 291   Courtesy of Sylvio de Podestá.

p. 292   Photo by Fernando Lara.

p. 293   Drawing by Caitlin Osepchuk.

p. 295   From *Architectural Record*, courtesy of the Barragán Foundation, Switzerland.

p. 297   Photo by Armando Salas Portugal. Courtesy of the Barragán Foundation. © 2014 Barragán Foundation, Switzerland/Artists Rights Society (ARS), New York/© 2014 Artists Rights Society (ARS), New York/ProLitteris, Zurich

p. 298   Photo by Armando Salas Portugal. Courtesy of the Barragán Foundation. © 2014 Barragán Foundation, Switzerland/Artists Rights Society (ARS), New York/© 2014 Artists Rights Society (ARS), New York/ProLitteris, Zurich

p. 299   Photo by Armando Salas Portugal. Courtesy of

the Barragán Foundation. © 2014 Barragán
Foundation, Switzerland/Artists Rights Society
(ARS), New York/© 2014 Artists Rights Society
(ARS), New York/ProLitteris, Zurich

p. 301   Arquivo Público do Estado do Rio de Janeiro.
p. 302   Arquivo Público do Estado do Rio de Janeiro.
p. 303   Photo by Kristine Stiphany. Courtesy of School
of Architecture Visual Resources Collection,
University of Texas at Austin.
p. 306   Photo by Gonzalo Núñez Melgar.
p. 307   Photo by Gonzalo Núñez Melgar.
p. 312   Photo by Fernando Lara.
p. 313   Photo by Kristine Stiphany. Courtesy of School
of Architecture Visual Resources Collection,
University of Texas at Austin.
p. 313   Photo by Fernando Lara.
p. 314   Drawing by Caitlin Osepchuk.
p. 315   Photo by Nelson Kon.
p. 315   Photo by Fernando Lara.
p. 316   Photo by Kristine Stiphany. Courtesy of School
of Architecture Visual Resources Collection,
University of Texas at Austin.
p. 316   Drawing by Caitlin Osepchuk.
p. 319   Courtesy of Enrique Browne.
p. 320   Courtesy of Edward Rojas.
p. 321   Courtesy of Germán del Sol.
p. 322   Photo by Nelson Kon.
p. 324   Photo by Nelson Kon.
p. 326   Photo by Luis E. Carranza.
p. 327   Photo by Luis E. Carranza.
p. 328   Drawing by Caitlin Osepchuk.
p. 330   Photo by Sophia Monahon, Courtesy of School
of Architecture Visual Resources Collection,
University of Texas at Austin.
p. 331   Photo by Fernando Lara.

p. 334   Photo by Laura Cohen. Courtesy of Enrique
Norten and TEN Arquitectos.
p. 335   Photo by Timothy Hursley. Courtesy of Enrique
Norten and TEN Arquitectos.
p. 336   Courtesy of Fernando Vasconcelos.
p. 337   Courtesy of Fernando Vasconcelos.
p. 339   Photo by José Carlos García. Courtesy of School
of Architecture Visual Resources Collection,
University of Texas at Austin.
p. 341   Drawings by Caitlin Osepchuk.
p. 341   Photo by José Carlos García. Courtesy of School
of Architecture Visual Resources Collection,
University of Texas at Austin.
p. 342   Photo by José Carlos García. Courtesy of School
of Architecture Visual Resources Collection,
University of Texas at Austin.
p. 343   Courtesy of Adriana León and Taller Arquitectura X.
p. 344   Courtesy of Adriana León and Taller Arquitectura X.
p. 345   Drawings by Amy Freedberg.
p. 346   Photo by Leonardo Finotti.
p. 347   Photo by Leonardo Finotti.
p. 348   Photo by Walter Salcedo.
p. 349   Photo by Gustavo Frittegotto.
p. 350   Photo by Walter Salcedo.
p. 353   Photo by Fernando Lara.
p. 354   Courtesy of Al Borde.
p. 355   Photo by Daniel Ducci.
p. 356   Courtesy of Carlos Teixeira.
p. 357   Courtesy of Pezo von Ellrichshausen.
p. 358   Photo by Nelson Kon.
p. 359   Photo by Luis Gordoa. Courtesy of Mauricio Rocha and Taller de Arquitectura.

function, 119–120, 122; "Four Functions," 119, 121
Atlantis, theories of, 49–50, 56
Augé, Marc, 3
Aula Magna, Universidad Central, Caracas, 166–168, *168*, 169
Austral Group, 129, 265; "Voluntad y Acción" (Will and Action, 1939), 96
avant-garde, 4, 25, 30–39, 49, 61, 64, 66, 69, 73, 77, 93, 99, 117, 159, 172, 213, 246, 257, 274, 277, 282, 311, 326, 333, 342; in Brazil, 34–37; in Mexico, 38–39
Azevedo, Arthur, 10
Azevedo, Francisco Ramos, 13

Bac, Ferdinand, 134
Bacardí Building, Mexico City, 206–207, *206, 207*
Bacardí Rum Headquarters Building project (1956), 206, 215
Banco de Londres y América del Sud, Buenos Aires, 211–213, *212, 213*, 251
Bandeira, Manuel, 77, 227
Banham, Reyner, 112, 212, 219
Bardi, Pietro Maria, 104, 160, 208
baroque, influence of, on Brazilian architecture, 19–20, 107, 108, 112, 115–117, 222, 361(1914), 365(1943a)
Barragán, David, 355
Barragán, Luis, 97, 101, 103, 117, 134–139, 176–179, 281–282, 295–299, 309, 333, 336, 344; antimodernism of, 299; Convent of the Capuchin Nuns, Tlalpan, 178–179, 297, 298; Demonstration Gardens for El Pedregal, Mexico City, *138*, 139; Duplex in the Colonia Hipódromo, Mexico City, 134; early work of, 365(1947a); Egerstrom Stables, Los Clubes, *290*, 298; Four Painters' Studios, Mexico City, 134; functionalism of, 134–136; Jardines del Pedregal de San Ángel, Mexico City, 134–139, *135*, 296, 297, 298; Luis Barragán House, Mexico City, 136, *136*; marketing of El Pedregal, 136–137, 139, 369(1980); and Mathias Goeritz, Torres de Satélite, Mexico City, 178, 179, 298, *298*; and Max Cetto, Demonstration Houses, Mexico City, 137, 139; Orozco and De Garibi Houses, Guadalajara, 134, 139; Prie-to López House, Mexico City, 139; Pritzker Architecture Prize (1980), 134, 179, 281, 295, 299; use of color by, 298–290; use of

photography by, 139, 296–299
Basilio, Enriqueta, 254
Bassols, Narciso, 74
Bassov, Nikolai G., 144
Batlle Planas, Juan, 187
Bauform, 61, 62
Bayardo, Nelson: Columbarium, Montevideo, 99, 213, 223–224, *223, 224*, 266
Beistegui, Carlos de, 51
Beitia, Pablo Tomás: Xul Solar Museum, Buenos Aires, 326–328, *326, 327, 328*
Belaguer, Joaquín, 46
Belaúnde Terry, Fernando, 149, 150, 262, 368(1969b)
Belém, Brazil, 183
Belo Horizonte, 13, 63, 82, 116, 157, 181, 183, 239, 287, 291, 292–293, 294, 300, 365(1941), 369(1983); favelas, 332, 356; Pampulha, 108–112, 160
Bénard, Émile: Legislative Palace, Mexico City, 13, 19
Benítez, Solano, 346–348; Tomb for his Father, Paraguay, 325, 346–347, *346, 347*; Unilever Headquarters, Paraguay, 353
Berlingieri House, Punta Ballena, 129, 190
Berman, Marshall, 205, 309
Bermejo, Jesús, 240
Bermúdez, Guido, 265
Bermúdez, Guillermo, 225
Bernadelli, Rodolfo and Henrique, 10
Bernardes, Sérgio, 180–183, 265, 271; Brazilian Pavilion, Brussels, 182; Casa Lota de Macedo Soares, Petrópolis, 181, *182*; Convention Center, Brasília, 182; *Geometrização do Brasil* project (Geometricization of Brazil, 1960s–1970s), 268–269; Laboratório de Investigações Cenceituais (Laboratory for Conceptual Investigations), 182–183; Pavilion for the Companhia Siderúrgica Nacional, São Paulo, 182; Rio de Janeiro of the Future project (1963–1965), *269*, 269; São Cristóvão Fair, Rio de Janeiro, 182
Betón brut, 210, 211, 219, 223, 241, 273
Bidinost, O., J. Chute, J. M. Gassó, M. Lapacó, and M. Meyer: Manuel Belgrano School, University of Córdoba, 211
Biennials: Buenos Aires, 251, 294, 307, 308, 348; Chile, 308; São Paulo, 131, 175, 180, 246, 308, 357
Bilac, Olavo, 10

Bill, Max: critique of Brazilian architecture, 180–181; "Report on Brazil" (1954), 180–181
Biocleta, 182
BKF Chair (Bonet, Kurchan, and Ferrari Hardoy), 96, 101, 151
Boari, Adamo: Palace of Fine Arts, Mexico City, 13, 14; Post Office Building, Mexico City, 13
Bo Bardi, Lina, 104, 245, 356; Casa de Vidrio, São Paulo, 160–161, *160, 161*; Museu de Arte de São Paulo (São Paulo Museum of Art, MASP), São Paulo, 160, 208–209, *208, 209*, 219, 311; SESC Pompéia, São Paulo, 311–314, *312, 313, 314*
Boff, Leonardo, 366(1955)
Bogotá, Colombia, 3, 9, 119, 141, 143, 225–226, 239, 242, 266, 339–342, 353; master plan for, 121–122
boîte à miracles, 210, 212, 240
Boldarini, Marcos: Cantinho do Céu, São Paulo, 355, 356
Bolívar, Simón, 42
Bonet, Antoni, 94–98, 100–103, 151–152, 211, 265; Berlingieri House, Punta Ballena, 129, 190; emigration of, to Argentina, 101; with Horacio Vera Barros and Abel López Chas, Suipacha and Paraguay Artists Ateliers, Buenos Aires, 95, 96, 101; Hostería Solana del Mar, Punta Ballena, 101, 129–130, *129, 130*; Punta Ballena master plan, 129, 152
Bongestabs, Domingos, 239
Bonilla, Daniel: Porciúncula La Milagrosa Chapel, Bogotá, 353
Borchers, Juan: *Institución Arquitectónica* (1968), 240; with Isidro Suárez and Jesús Bermejo, Cooperativa Eléctrica, Chillán, 240–241, *240, 241*
Borges, Jorge Luis, 4, 30, 310, 345, 348
Borges, Max, 215; Nautical Club, Havana, 216; Tropicana Club, Havana, 216
Borges, Norah, 30
Borghini, Sandro, 274
Born, Esther: *The New Architecture of Mexico* (1937), 55, *295*, 296
Bornhorst, Dirk, 195
Borsoi, Acácio Gil, 227; Cajueiro Seco, Recife, 228, *228*; Melo Mota Residence, Recife, 228; Queiroz Galvão Residence, Recife, 228
bossa nova, 182, 325
Botta, Mario, 292, 308, 322

Brasil, Alexandre, and Paula Zasnicoff: Burle Marx Educational Institute, Ihnotim, Brumadinho, 354

Brasília, Brazil, 9, 33, 63, 112, 132, 141, 181–183, 199–205, 235, 237, 242, 245, 263, 265, 266, 278, 288, 293, 300, 303, 304, 306, 359; Alvorada Palace, 194, 202–204, *202*; competition for design, 201–202; critique of, 205, 367(1956); early ideas of new capital, 199–200, 268; Monumental Axis, 201–202; National Congress, *199*, 203; role of Juselino Kubitschek, 199–201; Superquadras, 202, 204–205, *204*, 263; Three-Powers Plaza, 202, 203; transfer from Rio de Janeiro to new capital, 199, 219

Brazil Builds. See Museum of Modern Art

Brazilianness, 34, 35

Brazilian Pavilion: Brussels (1958), 182; New York (1939), 105–107, 112, 115, 144, 324; Osaka (1970), 316; Seville (1992), 322–323

Breuer, Marcel, 100

brick, use of, 170–171, 190–192, 226, 286, 353

brise-soleil, 80, 88, 103, 106, 108, 125, 128, 142, 143, 166, 186, 188, 189, 211, 241, 292, 364(1936)

Brizola, Leonel, 300–303

Broid, Isaac, 336, 337; Centro de la Imagen, Mexico City, 336

Browne Covarrubias, Enrique, 308, 321, 338; Consorcio Nacional de Seguros, Santiago, 319, *321*; early work of, 318–319

Bruand, Yves: *Arquitetura contemporânea no Brasil* (1981), 82, 365(1943a)

Brumadinho, Brazil, 353–354

Brunfaut, Gaston, 144

brutalism, 174, 212, 220, 228, 244, 251, 272, 287, 323, 356

Bucci, Angelo, 322–325, 348, 351; and Alvaro Puntoni, Brazilian Pavilion project (1992), 322–323, 324; House, Aldeia da Serra, 323, *324*; House, Ribeirão Preto, 323–324, 352; House, Ubatuba, 352; later projects of, 324–325

Buenos Aires, Argentina, 3, 13, 14, 20, 30, 31, 32, 53, 54, 55, 56, 67, 84, 88, 89, 90, 91, 92, 96, 100, 101, 129, 151–152, *152*, 186, 188, 242, 251, 253, 265, 266, 270, 274, 294, 307, 308, 309–310, 326, 348, 361(1904), 369(1985a);

Avenida de Mayo, 12, 28, 275, *276*; Bajo Belgrano, 151; Casa Rosada, 10, 12; plan for, 51–52, *52*, 151, *151*, 189, 211; Plaza San Martín, 83; Retiro Station, 83; Teatro Colón, 10, 16

Bullrich, Francisco, 129, 142, 266; *Arquitectura latinoamericana 1930–1970* (1969), 265; with Clorindo Testa and Alicia Cazzaniga, National Library, Buenos Aires, 265; *Nuevos caminos en la arquitectura latinoamericana* (New Directions in Latin American Architecture, 1969), 265–266

Burle Marx, Roberto, 37, 62–63, 107, 215, 265, 317, 354; Copacabana Beach designs, Rio de Janeiro, 236; early gardens of, 228, 233; garden for Brazilian Pavilion, Brussels, 182; gardens in Brasília, 204; interest of, in native plants, 233, 235; Kronsforth House, Teresópolis, 233–234; murals for Pedregulho Housing Development, 131, 235; Pampulha landscape designs, 109–111, 235; Parque do Flamengo, Rio de Janeiro, 175, 233–236, *234*, *235*; Praça Casa Forte, Recife, 233; Praça Euclides da Cunha, Recife, 233; Roof Terrace garden at MESP, Rio de Janeiro, 81, *81*, 234; riverbed gardens for CEPAL project, 244

Bustamante, José Alberto, 134, 137

Bustillo, Alejando: Villa Ocampo, Buenos Aires, 32, *32*

Butterfly Chair. *See* BKF Chair

Caballero, Gerardo, 348, 350, 351, 353; and Maite Fernández, Edificio Brown, Rosario, 354

Cacho, Raúl, 271; science building, UNAM, Mexico City, 165

Calabi, Daniele, 100–104; emigration of, to Brazil, 101, 103; Medici Pavilion, São Paulo, 103; Villa Daniele Calabi, São Paulo, 103, *103*; Villa on Avenida Paulista, São Paulo, 101

Calder, Alexander, 158, 255; *Flying Saucers* (1953), Aula Magna, Universidad Central de Venezuela, 168, *168*

Cali, Colombia, 226

California Building, São Paulo, 180, *181*

Campolina, Joel, 323

Campuzano, Carlos, 229

Candela, Félix, 100–103, 122, 194, 229, 265, 352; Church of Our Lady of the Miraculous Medal, Mexico City, 184–185, *184–185*, *185*; Cosmic Rays

Pavilion, UNAM, Mexico City, 184; development of hyperbolic paraboloids by, 101; emigration of, to Mexico, 100–101; with Enrique Castañeda and Antonio Peyri, Palacio de los Deportes, Mexico City, 253, *254*, *255*; with Pedro Ramírez Vázquez, Mercado de Coyoacán, 101, 228

Cap Ducal, Viña del Mar, 59–60, *60*

Capela da Pampulha, Pampulha, 108–110, *108*, *109*

Capilla Real, Cholula, 165, 282

Capitolio, Havana, 13

Caracas, Venezuela, 27, 141–142, 154–156, 158, 162–163, 166–169, 176, 193–194, 195–196, 197, 248, 251, 266, 329, 369(1985a); Avenida Bolivar, 142; growth of, in twentieth century, 153

Caracas Art Museum project (1955), 193, 203

Caribbean hut, as per Gottfried Semper, 123, 128, 365(1944)

Caribe Hilton, San Juan, 127–128, *128*

Carioca/s, defined, 8, 366(1953a)

Carioca school, 8, 107, 172–175, 218, 219, 324

Carrillo Puerto, Felipe, 50

Carvalho, Flávio de, 44–45, 82; Alameda Lorena Housing, São Paulo, 69; "City of the Naked Man" (1930), 69–70; Columbus Lighthouse Competition project (1928), *44*, 45, 69; de Carvalho House, Valinhos, 69; Palace for the Governor of São Paulo project (1927), 69, *69*

Casa del Dr. J. B., Buenos Aires, 89–90, *90*

Casa de Vidrio, São Paulo, 160–161, *160*, *161*

Casa do Baile, Pampulha, *111*, 112, 180

Casa en Belgrano, Buenos Aires, *88*

Casa en La Falda, Córdoba, 90, *91*

Casa Lota de Macedo Soares, Petrópolis, 181, *182*

Casa sobre el Arroyo, Mar del Plata, 113–114

Casino, Pampulha, 110–112, *110*

Castillo, Jose, 271

Catalan vaulting system, 96, 129, 214

Cataño, Puerto Rico, 125, 127

Cecil O'Gorman House, Mexico City, 71, *71*

cemetery portal, Laprida, 85, *85*

Centro Administrativo da Bahia, Salvador, 183

Vila Madalena church, São Paulo, 219
Guerrero, Enrique, 271
Guerrero, Xavier, 25
Guido, Ángel, 55; and Alejandro Bustillo, Monument to the Flag, Rosario, 17; *Catedrales y rascacielos* (Cathedrals and Skysrapers, 1936), 58; *Fusión hispano-indígena en la arquitectura colonial* (1925), 20
Guilbert, Albert, 10, 11
Guimarães, Eduardo, 181
Guimard, Hector, 16
Gutiérrez, Gustavo, 366(1955)
Gutiérrez, Ramón, 308; *Arquitectura y Urbanismo en Iberoamérica* (1983), 305
Gutiérrez Bringas, Edmundo, 254
Gutiérrez Cortina, Bosco, Gutiérrez Cortina House, Mexico City, 282

Haber, Abraham, "Pintura y arquitectura" (Painting and Architecture, 1951), 33
Habermas, Jürgen, 309
Hardy, Álvaro, 292, 294
Harrison, Wallace K., 144–146, 242
Harvey, David, 309
Haussmann, Baron Georges-Eugène, 7
Havana, Cuba, 15, 47, 121–122, 206, 214–217; master plan for, *121, 122*
Hejduk, John, 293
Helicoide, Caracas, 195–196
Helios system, 88–90
Hernández, Agustín, 213, 284–285; Heroico Colegio Militar, Mexico City, *284, 285*–286
Hernández, Balbino, 271
Herzog, Werner: *Fitzcarraldo* (1982), 306
Hilberseimer, Ludwig: *Groszstadtarchitectur* (1927), 90, 91, 270
Hilversum, Holland, 68
Hispaniola, 45
historic preservation, Brazil, 238–239, 294, 311–314. *See also* Instituto do Patrimônio Histórico e Artístico Nacional; Serviço do Patrimônio Histórico e Artístico Nacional
historiography, modern architecture in Latin America, 265–266, 305; in Brazil, 61–62
Hitchcock, Henry-Russell, 14, 117, 124, 127, 140, 242, 265, 363–364(1933); *Latin American Architecture since 1945* (1955), 143

Hoffmann, Josef, 15
Holford, Sir William, 201
Hood, Raymond, 43, 45
Horizonte, 33
Horkheimer, Max, 210
Horta, Victor, 16
Horta Barbosa, Luiz Hildebrando, 201
Hospital Español, Buenos Aires, 14–15, *15*
Hostería Solana del Mar, Punta Ballena, 101, 129–130, *129, 130*
House at Rua Itápolis, São Paulo, 36–37
housing, public, in Latin America, 153–157, 262–264
Howard, Ebenezer, *Garden Cities of Tomorrow* (1902), 70
Huidobro, Vicente, 39
hyperbolic paraboloids, 101, 185, 193, 194, 211, 254

Iate Clube, Pampulha, 112
Ibarapuera pavilions, São Paulo, 203
Ibero-American Exposition (1929), Seville, 43, 47–49, 60, 68, 284
Ibirapuera Park, São Paulo, 107, 182, 203, 218, 265
Iglesia, Rafael, 325, 348–350, 354; Bathroom Pavilion at Parque Independencia, Rosario, *348,* 349–350, *349*; Party Pavilion at Parque Independencia, Rosario, 350, *350*
Iglesia de Cristo Obrero, Altántida, 170–171, *170, 171,* 190, 192
immigration, to Latin America, 14, 364–365(1939); early visitors to Latin America, 100
informal settlements, Latin America, 8, 183, 246, 263, 329–332; favelas, *9,* 35, 132, 133, 235, 304, 340; villa miseria, 274
Inspección General de Monumentos Artísticos, Mexico, 18
Institute of Architecture and Urban Studies, New York, 282
Instituto de Arquitectura Tropical (Institute for Tropical Architecture), 290
Instituto de Arquitectura Urbana (Institute of Urban Architecture), 251
Instituto de Higiene y Granja Sanitaria (Higiene Institute and Vaccine Farm), Mexico City, 40
Instituto do Patrimônio Histórico e Artístico Nacional (National Conservation Institute, IPHAN), 63, 77, 115–116, 228
Integral, 196

International Congress of Planning and Housing (1938), Mexico, 102
International Exhibition of Modern Industrial and Decorative Arts (1925), Paris, 17
International Exposition (1867), Paris, 48
International Exposition (1889), Paris, 48
International Exposition (1922), Rio de Janeiro, 25
International Exposition (1929), Barcelona, 47
International style, 3, 102, 107, 124, 127, 140, 163, 165, 285, 296, 363–364(1933); new International style, 140, 143, 336
Internet, impact of, on architecture, 351–352
Iommi, Enio, 187; *Continual Forms* (1953), 189
Iommi, Godofredo, 256–258
IPHAN. *See* Instituto do Patrimônio Histórico e Artistico Nacional
Itaipu Dam, Paraguay/Brazil, 173
Italian Fascist architecture, influence of, in Latin America, 84–85
Itamaraty Palace, Brasília, 202, 203–204, *203*

Jacobs, Jane: *Death and Life of Great American Cities* (1961), 263
Jameson, Fredric, 281
Jardines del Pedregal de San Ángel, Mexico City, 134–139, *135,* 296
Jáuregui, Jorge Mario, 331–332, 356
Jaussely, Léon, 67
Jéquier, Emile, Museo Nacional de Bellas Artes, Santiago, 11
JK (Juscelino Kubitschek) Complex, Belo Horizonte, 157, *157*
João VI of Portugal, 61, 361(1903)
Johnson, Philip, 117, 242, 363–364(1933)
Johnson, William Templeton, 47
Joselevich, Alfredo, 143
Juan O'Gorman House, Mexico City, 97–98, *98*
Judd, Donald, 248

Kahlo, Frida, 18, 37, 71–74, 98, 334
Kahlo, Guillermo, 18
Kahn, Ely Jacques, 55
Kahn, Louis, 124, 228, 275, 292; influence of, 251, 284, 287
Kalach, Alberto, 337; GGG House, Mexico City, 335, 343–345, *343, 344,*

Luis Barragán House, Mexico City, 136, *136*, 282

Lula da Silva, Luiz Inácio, 291, 332, 355

Lyotard, Jean-François, 309

Maas, Marcolino, 127

Macapá, Brazil, 183

Macedo Soares, Lota de, 175, 181–182, 235

Maculan, Fernando: Beco São Vicente, Belo Horizonte, 356

Madí (Movimiento de Arte de Invención), 267–268

Magalhães, Antônio Carlos, 278

Magalhães, José de, 13

Magalhães, Sergio, 331

Maia, César, 331

Maia, Éolo, 291–294, 323; Capela de Santana, Ouro Branco, 287, 287–288, *288*; Edifício Barca do Sol, Belo Horizonte, *292*; Verdes Mares Hotel, Ouro Branco, 287; and Sylvio de Podestá, Rainha da Sucata, Belo Horizonte, *293*, 294

Maipú Votive Temple, Maipú, 60

Malfatti, Anita: *A boba* (1915–1916), 34

Mallet-Stevens, Robert, 85

Manaure, Mateo, 166, 168–169

Manifesto of the Union of Mexican Workers, Technicians, Painters and Sculptors, 25

Manizales, Colombia, 226, 369

Manteola, Sánchez Gómez, Santos, Solsona, and Viñoly, Argentina Televisora Color, Buenos Aires, 275, *276*

Maples Arce, Manuel, 39

Marajoara Indians, 45, 77, 364

Mariano Filho, José, 61–62

Mariátegui, José Carlos, 149

Marinetti, Filippo Tommaso, 36, 100

Mariscal, Federico, 17–20, 23–24; *La Patria y la arquitectura nacional* (1915), 19

Markelius, Sven, 144

Martínez, Carlos, and Jorge Arango: *Arquitectura en Colombia* (1951), 159

Martinez Corrêa, Celso, 311

Martínez Gutiérrez, Juan: Pavilion of Chile, Seville, 48, 60; School of Law, Santiago, 60; Votive Temple, Maipú, 60

Martínez Sanabria, Fernando, 225

Martín Fierro, 30–31, 100, 362(1924)

Massilia, 51, 53

mass production, 74, 147–148

materiality, twenty-first century, 352–354

Matta Echaurren, Roberto (MATTA): *Architectural Study* (1936), 95; "Sensitive Mathematics–Architecture of Time" (1938), 94–96, *94*; *Wet Sheets* (1936), 94–95

Mauritsstad, Brazil, 227

Max Cetto House, Mexico City, 97, *97*

May, Ernst, 96, 139

Maya architecture, 48–50

Mayagüez, Puerto Rico, 125

Mayakovsky, Vladimir, 100

Mazzanti, Giancarlo, 351, 355; León de Greiff Library Park, Medellín, 342; Parque Biblioteca España, Medellín, 340–342, *341*

Meano, Víctor (Vittorio), 10; and Cayetano Moretti, Legislative Palace, Montevideo, 13; Congreso Nacional, Buenos Aires, 12–13, *12*

Medellín, Colombia, 121, 339, 359; informal settlements, 340–342, 355

Meireles, Cecília, 77

Mejorada del Campo, Spain, 192

Mello Barreto, Henrique Lahmeyer de, 235

Melnikov, Konstantin, 134; Columbus Lighthouse Competition project (1928), 43, *43*

Melo, Heitor de, 61

Melo Franco, Rodrigo, 77

Memória, Arquimedes, 61–62, 77

Mendelsohn, Erich, 59

Mendes da Rocha, Paulo, 218–220, 245, 295, 306, 308, 323, 356; Brazilian Pavilion, Osaka, 316; Museu Brasileiro da Escultura (Brazilian Museum of Sculpture, MUBE), São Paulo, 315–317; Paulistano Stadium, São Paulo, 219, *220*

Méndez Rivas, Federico, 24; Secretaría de Educación Pública, Mexico City, 23–27, *23*, *26*

Menotti del Picchia, Paulo, 34

Mercado de Coyoacán, Mexico City, 101, 229

Mercosur (Mercado Común del Sur), 3, 325, 351

Mérida, Carlos, 176; *Los Adoratorios* (1964), 230; *Caperucita Roja* (1923), 25; murals for Multifamiliar Benito Juárez, 27, 147

Mesa, Felipe, and Alejandro Bernal (Plan B): Hontanares School, Medellín, 342; Orquideorama, Medellín, 342, *342*

Mexican Pavilion: in Paris (1867), 48,

362(1929a); in Rio de Janeiro (1922), 25; in Seville (1929), 48–50, *48*, *49*, 284

Mexican Revolution, 1, 17–18, 23–24, 32, 39, 48, 49–50, 73, 75, 102, 134, 281

Mexico. *See* Mexico City; Yucatán

Mexico City, 13, 19–20, 23, 25–27, 40–41, 55–56, 71, 73–74, 97–98, 102, 104, 116, 134, 136–138, 141–143, 147–148, 157, 162–165, 176–179, 184–185, 206–207, 229–230, 242, 244, 252–256, 271, 282–286, 297, 306, 334–337, 343–345, 355, 358–359, 363(1929c), 368(1971); Escuela Nacional Preparatoria, 24; Fine Arts Academy, 17; growth in twentieth century, 153; Plaza de las Tres Culturas, 148, 252, 256; Route of Friendship, 179, *254*, 255–256; Santa Fe District, 333–334; Tlatelolco, 252, 256

"Mex-Tec," 333

Meyer, Hannes, 73, 100–104; association of, with Taller de Gráfica Popular, 102; Centro Deportivo Cultural Suizo project (1940), 102; emigration of, to Mexico, 101–102, 104; Manzana de Corpus Christi project (1946–1947), 102, *102*

Mies van der Rohe, Ludwig, 11, 12, 101, 104, 130, 139–142, 204, 317, 336–337; Bacardí Rum Headquarters Building project (1956), Havana, 141, 206, *206*, 215; Bacardí Building, Mexico City, 141, 206–207, *207*; Brick Country House project (1922), 346; Crown Hall, Chicago, 206; Farnsworth House, Plano, IL, 161; influence of, 130, 140–141, 142, 149, 161, 182, 215–216, 229, 251, 284, 336; New National Gallery, Berlin, 206; Seagrams Building, New York, 140; Tugendhat House, Brno, 180

Mies van der Rohe Award for Latin American Architecture, 317, 337

Mijares, Carlos, 285–286; Christ Church, Mexico City, *285*, 286

Mijares, Rafael, 229

Milan, Carlos, 220

Milman, Boruch, 201

Minas Gerais, Brazil, 7, 61, 63, 203, 227, 291, 294, 300, 304, 306, 323

Mindlin, Henrique, 101, 103, 201; *Modern Architecture in Brazil* (1956), 82

mineiro, 294, 323

Ministério da Educação e Saúde Pública (Ministry of Education and Public

University of Brasilia, 63; United Nations design, *144*, 145–146, *145*; work of, during exile, 300
Nietzsche, Friedrich, 4
Niterói, Brazil, 54, 304, 307
Noel, Martín: Escuela San Marón, Buenos Aires, 20, *20*; Museo Fernández Blanco, Buenos Aires, 20; Pavilion of Argentina, Seville, 47
Noigandres, 33
Norten, Enrique, 334–337; Houses N and R, Valle de Bravo, 334; Lighting Center, Mexico City, 334, *334*; National School of Theater, Mexico City, 334–335, *335*; TELEVISA Services Building, Mexico City, 334–335
North American Free Trade Agreement (NAFTA), 281, 333
Nuestra Señora del Carmen Church, Cataño, 127
Nunes, Luis, 80, 82, 227–228, 233, 364; Escola de Anormais, Recife, 215; Milk Processing Plant, Recife, 228, 364(1936); Water Tower, Olinda, 215, 228, 364(1936)

Obelisk, Buenos Aires, 92, *93*
Oberpauer Building, Santiago, 59, *60*
Obregón, Álvaro, 24
Obregón Santacilia, Carlos, 19–20, 45, 73; and Carlos Tarditti, Mexican Pavilion (1922), Rio de Janeiro, 25; Centro Educativo Benito Juárez, Mexico City, 19, *20*, 25
Ocampo, Victoria, 31–32, 51, 100; Villa Ocampo, Mar del Plata, 31, *32*
Oficina del Plano Regulador de Bogotá (Office of the Regulating Plan of Bogotá, OPRB), 121
O'Gorman, Juan, 41, 150, 163–165, 177, 265, 305, 334, 356; Cecil O'Gorman House, Mexico City, 71, *71*; Diego Rivera and Frida Kahlo house and studio, Mexico City, 37, 71–72, *71*, *72*, 74; with Gustavo Saavedra and Juan Martínez de Velasco, library, UNAM, Mexico City, 97–98, 163–164, *165*, 364(1938); Juan O'Gorman House, El Pedregal, Mexico City, 97–98, *98*, 195; *Pláticas sobre arquitectura* (1933), 73–76; Public Elementary School, Mexico City, *74–75*; and realistic or organic architecture, 97–98; rejection of functionalism by, 97–98; Tres Guerras Technical School, Mexico City, 73; views of, on functionalist

architecture, 75–76, 364(1938); work of, for Secretaría de Educación Pública, 74, *74–75*
Oiticica, Hélio, 246–249; early artistic work of, 246; *Invençao da Cor Projects* (1977), 247; with Neville D'Almeida, *Cosmococa* (1973), 247–248, 354; *Rhodeislandia: Contact* (1971), 247; *Subterranean Tropicália Projects* (1971), 247; *Tropicália* (1967), 246–247, *247*
Oliveira Passos, Francisco de, 10–12; and Albert Guilbert, Theatro Municipal, Rio de Janeiro, 8, *11*
Olympic Games, 64, 302; Mexico City (1968), 148, 179, 229, 252–256
Ópera de Arame, Curitiba, 239
O Pirralho, 34
Orozco, José Clemente, 24–25, 139; influence of, on Luis Barragán, 134, 137
Orquideorama, Medellín, Colombia, 342
Ortiz Monasterio, Manuel, 75; La Nacional, Mexico City, 55
Otero, Alejandro, 166; Polychrome for El Paraíso, Caracas, 155; Polychrome for School of Architecture, Universidad Central, Caracas, 169
Otero, Raúl, with Eugenio Rayneri Piedra: Capitolio, Havana, 13
Ottalagano, Alberto, 274
Ouro Preto, 82, 107, 228, 287–288, 293, 365(1941); Ouro Preto Hotel, 108, 112, 175, 324
Ove Arup, 335
Ozenfant, Amédée, 72

Palace for the Governor of São Paulo project (1927), 69, *69*
Palace of Fine Arts, Mexico City, 13, *14*
Palacio Barolo, Buenos Aires, 14, 17, 28–29, *28*, 55
Palacio de los Deportes, Mexico City, *253*, 254, *255*
Palacio Salvo, Montevideo, 17, 28–29, *28*, 29, *52*, *53*
Palanti, Giancarlo, 104, 201
Palanti, Mario, 31, 64; Palacio Barolo, Buenos Aires, 14, 17, 28–29, *28*, 55; Palacio Salvo, Montevideo, 17, 28–29, *28*, 29, *52*, *53*
Palau de la Generalitat, Barcelona, 99
Pampulha, 291–294, *291*
Pampulha (Belo Horizonte, Brazil), 63, 82, 107, 108–112, 116–117, 160, 180, 235, 265, 291–294, 304, 352, 369(1983)

Panama-California Exposition (1915), San Diego, 361(1904)
Pan American Congress of Architects, 56, 69; first meeting of, in Montevideo (1920), 64, 363(1929c); meeting of, in Lima, Peru (1947), 149
Pan-American highway, 262
Pan-Americanism, 42, 45–46, 258
Pan-American Union, 42, 45
Pani, Alberto: *La higiene en México* (Hygene in Mexico, 1916), 41
Pani, Mario, 27, 142–143, 163–164, 336; Edificio Reforma 76, Mexico City, *141*, 142; with Enrique del Moral, Rectoría building, UNAM, Mexico City, 163, *164*; Multifamiliar Miguel Alemán, Mexico City, 147, 153–154, 157; Multifamiliar Nonoalco-Tlatelolco, Mexico City, 147–148; with Salvador Ortega, Multifamiliar Benito Juárez, Mexico City, 147, *148*
Papadaki, Stamo, 201
Pape, Lygia, 246
Paraíba, Brazil, 61
Parque Batlle, Montevideo, 64, 252
Parque de María Luisa, Seville, 47
Parque do Flamengo, Rio de Janeiro, 9, 233–236, *234*, *235*
Passarela do Samba. *See* Sambódromo
Paulista, 61, 103, 172, 175, 221–222, 316–317, 322–325, 347, 352, 354, 358, 366(1953); architecture, 223, 228, 323; brutalism, 219, 220, 367(1961); school, defined, 218–220, 221, 317
Paulistano Stadium, São Paulo, 219, 220, 315
Payseé Reyes, Mario, 265
Paz, Octavio, 1
PDF (Revista de Engenharia da Prefeitura do Distrito Federal), 172
Pedregulho Housing Development, Rio de Janeiro, 131–132, *131*, *132*, 133, *133*, 154, 157, 173, 175, 228, 235
Peláez, Juan Manuel, Plaza de Cisneros, Medellín, 342
Peñafiel, Antonio, 48
Peñalosa, Enrique, 339–340
Penteado, Fabio, 220
Peralta Ramos, Federico, 211
perceptism, 33
Perceptismo: Teórico y Polémico, 33
Pereira Passos, Francisco, 7–9, 10, 329
Pérez de Arce, Rodrigo, 232, 244
Pérez Jiménez, Marcos, 155–156, 162–163
Peruanismo, defined, 262
Petrópolis, Brazil, 181–182

Ribeiro, Darcy, 183, 300, 301, 302, 303
Ribeiro, Maurício Andrés, 292
Ricalde, Humberto, 337
Rio de Janeiro, 9, 13, 17, 25, 45, 52, 53, 61, 62, 63, 69, 78, 81, 82, 100, 107, 108, 116, 117, 119, 154, 160, 172, 183, 195, 199, 218, 219, 227, 228, 239, 252, 253, 269, 278, 294, 300, 302, 303, 304, 306, 307, 329–330, 331, 332, 364(1936), 364(1936), 366(1953a); Aterro do Flamengo, 9; Botafogo, 7–8; Catacumbas Hills, 131–132; Cidade de Deus, 329; Copacabana, 8, 235–236; Cristo Redentor, 17; Favelas, 329–332, 355–356; Flamengo, 7–8, 174–175, 233–236; Gávea, 54, 131, 132, 173; Gloria, 7, 8, 174, 236; growth of, in twentieth century, 153; Guanabara Bay, 8, 51, 77, 131, 174, 175; history of, as capital, 361(1903); Leme Hill, 233; Mangueira Favela, 246; Morro de Santo Antônio, 9; Morro do Castelo, 8, 9, 10; Parque do Flamengo, 9, 233–236, 234, 235; Pão de Açúcar (Sugarloaf Mountain), 54, 175; plan for (1875), 7; Praça Cuauhtémoqua, 362(1922); Praça Onze, 301; Rodrigo de Freitas Lagoon, 132; São Cristóvão district, Rio de Janeiro, 131
Rio Grande do Sul, Brazil, 61, 300
Rio Negro, Brazil, 306
Río Piedras, Puerto Rico, 125
Rivera, Diego, 37, 49, 71, 72, 74, 137, 362(1922), 362(1922); La Creación (1922), 24; influence of, on El Pedregal development, 134, 136; work of, for Secretaría de Educación Pública, 25–26
Roberto, MMM (Maurício, Milton, and Marcelo brothers), 201; ABI Building, Rio de Janeiro, 80, 364(1936); Santos Dumont Airport, Rio de Janeiro, 234, 235
Robertson, Sir Howard, 144
Roca, Miguel Ángel: Plaza de Armas, Cordoba, 275; Plaza Italia, Cordoba, 275
Roca Tarpeya, Caracas, 195
Rocha, Glauber, 311
Rocha, Mauricio: Center for the Blind and Visually Impaired, Mexico City, 358, 359, 359; early projects, 358–359
Rodchenko, Aleksandr, 296
Rogers, Ernesto Nathan, 180, 311
Rogers, Richard, 212, 308

Rojas, Edward: Hotel Viento Sur, Puerto Montt, 319, 319
Rolland, Modesto: stadium, Jalapa, 33
Romañach, Mario, 122; José Noval Cueto House, Havana, 215–216
Romero, Jorge, Dick Bornhorst, and Pedro Neuberger: Helicoide, Caracas, 195–196, 195
Ron Bacardí y Compañía, 141, 206–207, 215
Rosario, Argentina, 17, 331, 348–350, 354, 359
Rosen, Manuel, Antonio Recamier, Javier Valverde, and Edmundo Gutiérrez Bringas: Olympic pool and gymnasium, Mexico City, 254–255
Rossi, Aldo, 251, 277, 281, 282, 318
Rossi, Francisco, 211
Route of Friendship, Mexico City, 179, 254, 255–256
Rowe, Colin, 293
Rozo, Rómulo, 48
Rudofsky, Bernard, 104, 196
Ruiz, Macedonio Oscar, 186

Saarinen, Eero, 364(1938)
Saarinen, Eliel, 43, 62, 363(1930a)
Sáez Vaquero, José María, with Al Borde: Casa Pentimento, Quito, 352–353
Said, Edward, 100
Saint-Exupéry, Antoine de, 51
Salamone, Francisco, 17; cemetery portals, 84–85, 85; Rauch town hall, 84, 84
Salão Nacional de Belas Artes, 62–63, 227
Salas Portugal, Armando, 139; photographs, 296–298, 297, 298, 299
Salgado, Plínio, 35
Salinas, Fernando, 265
Salmona, Rogelio, 121, 194, 266, 305, 308; with Fernando Mártinez Sanabria and Guillermo Bermudez: Casa Cajial Bogotá, 225; with Fernando Mártinez Sanabria and Guillermo Bermudez: Casa Latorre, Bogotá, 225; Torres del Parque, Bogotá, 225–226, 225, 226
Salomão, Waly, 311
Salvador de Bahia, Brazil, 8, 117, 183, 227, 239, 278–279, 303, 311
Sambódromo, 300–304
Sánchez, Felix: Sánchez Arquitectos office, Mexico City, 284
Sánchez, Gregorio, 55, 83

Sánchez, Lagos, and de la Torre: Edificio Kavanagh, Buenos Aires, 55, 83
Sánchez Elía, Santiago, 211
Sánchez Hermelo, Gonzalo, 348
San Jose, Costa Rica, 289–290
San Juan, Puerto Rico, 21–22, 124, 127–128, 369(1985a)
San Martín de Porres Church, Cataño, 125, 126, 127, 127
San Martín, José de, 42
San Pedro Church, Durazno, 191–192
Santa Lucia Building, Santiago, 59, 59
Sant'Elia, Antonio, 36, 39, 70
Santiago, Chile, 11, 59, 231, 242–245, 253, 261, 288, 318–319, 320, 338, 355, 369(1985a)
São Cristóvão Fair, 182
São Luís, Brazil, 183
São Paulo, Brazil, 3, 7, 10, 13, 16, 34–37, 51–54, 61, 63, 69, 82, 101–104, 107, 117, 130, 143, 156–157, 160–161, 174–175, 180–182, 203, 213, 218–220, 221–222, 223, 227, 233–234, 237, 239, 245, 246, 266, 291, 293–294, 300, 304, 308, 311–314, 315–316, 323, 329, 348, 350; Avenida Nove de Julho, 208; Avenida Paulista, 208, 209; Avenida Presidente Vargas, 9, 301; favelas in, 332, 356; growth of, in twentieth century, 153, 218
Sarlo, Beatriz: Una modernidad periférica (1988), 309–310
Sasaki, Hideo: garden design for Presidential Palace, Havana, 122
Satélite Towers, Mexico City, 178–179, 297–298
Sauvage, Henri, 55, 363(1929c)
Scarpa, Carlo, 328
Scasso, Juan: Estadio Centenario, Montevideo, 64, 252–253
School of Architecture, Belo Horizonte, 291
School of Architecture, Catholic University, Chile, 231, 261, 320
School of Architecture, Mackenzie University, 63, 218
School of Architecture, Pontificia Catholic University, Valparaíso, 257, 261, 320; new curriculum, 257–258
School of Architecture, UNAM, Mexico City, 163
School of Architecture, University of Buenos Aires, 274–275
School of Architecture, University of São Paulo (FAU-USP), 63, 218; building, 213, 219–220, 221–222, 221, 222,

El Árbol para Vivir, Lecherías, 194; Club Táchira, Caracas, 193–194; Iglesia del Divino Rendentor de la Concordia, San Cristobal, 194; Venezuelan Pavilion, Hannover, 194

von Ellrichshausen, Sofia, 357

Warchavchik, Gregori, 34, 62, 82, 88, 124, 218, 233, 234, 362(1925), 363(1937), 365(1944); "Acerca da arquitetura moderna" (About Modern Architecture, 1925), 35–36; House at Rua Itápolis, São Paulo, 36–37; Warchavchik House at Rua Santa Cruz, São Paulo, 36–37, 36, 37

water, centrality of in design, 268–269, 271

Weiss, Joaquín, 55; El Rascacielos . . . (The Skyscraper, 1934), 58

White, Stanford, 10

Wiener, Paul Lester, 118

Wiley Corbett, Harvey, 269

Wilheim, Jorge: Curitiba master plan (1965), 237–238

Williams, Amancio, 112–114, 188, 245, 265, 356; Casa sobre el Arroyo, Mar del Plata, 113–114; Suspended Office Building project (1946), 55; Viviendas en el Espacio project (1942), 270–271

World Cup (soccer), 60, 64, 182, 252–253

World's Columbian Exposition (Chicago, 1893), 21, 48

World's Exhibition (New York, 1939), 105, 320

Wright, Frank Lloyd, 62, 97, 113, 114, 123, 216, 365(1944); Dana House, Springfield, 22; Fallingwater, Bear Run, 113–114, 161, 180; Gordon Strong Planetarium and Automobile Objective project (1924–1925), 195; influence of, 21–22, 68, 70, 98, 124, 127, 149, 161, 195, 218, 221; as judge for Columbus Lighthouse Competition, 195; Raúl Bailleres House project (1952), 195; Solomon R. Guggenheim Museum, New York, 195, 221; support of Lúcio Costa by, 45, 62, 82; Ullman House project, 21; Wasmuth Portfolio (1910), 124

Wyman, Lance, 254

Xitle Volcano, 134

Yapzik, Jorge, 343, 344, 344

Ydígoras Fuentes, Miguel, 272

Ydígoras Laparra, Miguel, 272

Yeang, Ken, 290

Yucatán, Mexico, 3, 48, 49, 50

Zabludovsky, Abraham, 142, 213, 273, 284, 308, 356

zócalo, 164, 243, 256

Zum Felde, Alberto, 47